HARVARD STUDIES
IN BUSINESS HISTORY

HARVARD STUDIES IN BUSINESS HISTORY
V

EDITED BY N. S. B. GRAS

STRAUS PROFESSOR OF BUSINESS HISTORY

GRADUATE SCHOOL OF BUSINESS ADMINISTRATION

GEORGE F. BAKER FOUNDATION

HARVARD UNIVERSITY

LONDON: GEOFFREY CUMBERLEGE

OXFORD UNIVERSITY PRESS

Francis Wayland Ayer, Founder

THE HISTORY OF
AN ADVERTISING AGENCY

N. W. Ayer & Son at Work
1869–1949

RALPH M. HOWER, D.C.S.

PROFESSOR OF BUSINESS ADMINISTRATION
GRADUATE SCHOOL OF BUSINESS ADMINISTRATION
GEORGE F. BAKER FOUNDATION
HARVARD UNIVERSITY

Revised Edition

CAMBRIDGE, MASSACHUSETTS

HARVARD UNIVERSITY PRESS
1949

TO MY WIFE

CONTENTS

PART I

GENERAL HISTORY OF N. W. AYER & SON, INC.

PART II

ANALYSIS OF PARTICULAR ASPECTS OF AYER DEVELOPMENT

ILLUSTRATIONS

TABLES

CHRONOLOGY

1817. Jan. 21. Nathan Wheeler Ayer born, Preston, Conn.

1841. Volney B. Palmer started the first American advertising agency, Philadelphia.

1848. Feb. 4. Francis Wayland Ayer born, Lee, Mass.

1865. George P. Rowell began the space-wholesaling phase of agency development, Boston.

1868. F. W. Ayer began to solicit advertising for the *National Baptist*, Philadelphia.

1869. April 1. F. W. Ayer founded the advertising agency which bears his father's name.

1873. Feb. 7. Death of N. W. Ayer.

1873. Oct. 1. George O. Wallace, an employee, admitted to partnership.

1875. June. Printing department added to the agency organization.

1876. Jan. Ayer instituted the first advertising contract charging a commission on the *net* cost of the space.

1877. Oct. Ayer purchased Coe, Wetherill & Co., successors to Volney B. Palmer, the first American advertising agent.

1878. Jan. 1. Henry Nelson McKinney admitted to partnership.

1879. First formal market survey made by agency as a basis for advertising.

1880. First issue of *American Newspaper Annual* (now *N. W. Ayer & Son's Directory of Newspapers and Periodicals*).

1882. Ayer concessions in religious newspapers separated from agency and formed into the Religious Press Association.

1886. Firm adopted motto, "Keeping Everlastingly At It Brings Success."

1886. First stenographer hired.

1887. Dec. Death of George O. Wallace.

1888. Ayer established the Keystone Type Foundry to manufacture printer's type.

1892. Ayer employed a full-time copy-writer: the start of the first agency copy department.

1896. Ayer service extended to include magazine as well as newspaper advertising.

1896. Decision against handling any advertising of alcoholic beverages.

1896. Management of the firm began to emerge as a separate function.

1898. Jan. Albert G. Bradford and Jarvis A. Wood admitted to partnership.

1898. First artist hired.

1898. Service expanded to include outdoor advertising.

1900. June. Saturday half-holidays instituted for Ayer employees during summer months.

1900. Reorganization of departments to improve efficiency.

1903. Branch office opened in New York City.

1905. Decision against advertising patent medicines.

1905. Branch office opened in Boston.

1906. Summer camp established for employees at Meredith, N. Y.

1907. April. Saturday half-holidays given to employees throughout the year.

1908. Separate staff created to plan advertising campaigns.

1909. Rowell's *American Newspaper Directory* purchased and combined with the Ayer *Annual*.

1910. Branch office opened in Chicago.

1911. Branch office opened in Cleveland.

1911. Wilfred W. Fry admitted to partnership.

1912. Sept. Reorganization of departments to improve efficiency.

1916. Wilfred W. Fry appointed general manager of N. W. Ayer & Son.

1917. Keystone Type Foundry sold.

1917. Group insurance provided for all Ayer employees.

1918. Jan. 1. William M. Armistead admitted to partnership.

1918. April. Death of Henry Nelson McKinney.

1919. Fiftieth Anniversary Celebration and presentation of a gold loving cup by American publishers as a tribute to the agency.

1919. Jan. Ayer commission raised from 15 to $16\frac{2}{3}$ per cent.

1920. Jan. Adam Kessler, Jr., and James M. Mathes admitted to partnership.

1921.   May. Death of Albert G. Bradford.

1922.   Ayer pioneered in the handling of broadcast advertising.

1923.   Mar. Death of Francis Wayland Ayer.

1923.   George H. Thornley admitted to partnership.

1924.   San Francisco branch opened; Cleveland branch closed.

1925.   Death of Jarvis A. Wood.

1928.   Saturday holidays instituted for Ayer employees in summer
months.

1929.   Jan. Firm occupied the new Ayer building.

1929.   May. Incorporation of N. W. Ayer & Son.

1929.   Nov. N. W. Ayer & Son, Ltd., opened in London, England.

1929.   Nov. Branch office opened in Detroit.

1931.   Annual Exhibitions of Newspaper Typography instituted by the
firm, in conjunction with the competition for the F. Wayland
Ayer Cup for Excellence in Newspaper Typography.

1932.   Branch offices opened in Buenos Aires and São Paulo.

1932.   Five-day week inaugurated for Ayer staff.

1933.   James M. Mathes resigned from N. W. Ayer & Son.

1933.   The Ayer agency assisted with the opening of the NRA campaign and contributed the Blue Eagle.

1934.   William M. Armistead and Adam Kessler, Jr., retire.

1934.   N. W. Ayer & Son, Ltd., of Canada established in Montreal.

1936.   July. Death of Wilfred W. Fry.

1936.   Aug.–Dec. Fight for the control of the Ayer agency, terminating
in the presidency of H. A. Batten and withdrawal of George
H. Thornley.

1937.   N. W. Ayer & Son, Ltd., of Canada opened a branch in Toronto.

1938.   Rearrangement of departments in Philadelphia.

1938–1942.   Suspension of dividend payments.

1941.   Beginning of recovery period, after changes in organization and
management.

1941.   First handling of television programs.

1941.   Establishment of bonus plan for outstanding contribution.

1941–1942.   Closing of branches in Canada and South America.

1942.   May. Establishment of Motion-Picture Bureau.

1944.   Establishment of Creative-Production Board.

1944. Sale of Ayer Building to Yale University.

1944. May–June. Formulation of written policies.

1947. December. Closing of branch office in London, England.

1949. February. Abandonment of the net-cost-plus-commission plan of compensation.

EDITOR'S INTRODUCTION

ALTHOUGH PRIOR to the publication of the first edition, N. W. Ayer & Son was somewhat less than enthusiastic about this study, in 1947, long after the first edition had been exhausted, the company called for a new edition. I have come to believe that the writing of a business history is like the painting of a portrait. At first the subject does not like the result. The family is not quite satisfied. Only the acceptance by friends or by the public turns the tide to approval.

In this second, up-to-date edition Professor Hower has somewhat revised his opinion of the Fry administration and has also developed a generous acceptance of the company's new administrative policy. This change does not mean that the author has become less critical but that his own studies have indicated that the present management has developed new strength. Possibly, however, he has been influenced somewhat by the fact that his information concerning the Ayer company for the most recent period has come chiefly from personal interviews and personal contacts rather than from cold and detailed records. Only the future can determine how wise the company has become and how judiciously the author has appraised its policies, unless, to be sure, other factors should enter the picture. Here we are confronted with the inherently difficult problem of evaluating more or less current events.

N. S. B. GRAS

2 November 1948

EDITOR'S INTRODUCTION TO THE FIRST EDITION

IN CONCENTRATING attention on the typical business men of an era, we can easily forget the agents whom they have employed as adjuncts to their business. In the days of mercantile capitalism there were such agents as supercargoes, resident factors, brokers, and so on. In the régime of industrial capitalism, beginning about 1800, the number and kinds of agents increased greatly, largely to meet the needs of industrial specialization in a world of growing complexity. There were, for instance, commission agents, credit-rating agents, commercial lawyers, public accountants, and advertising agents. Such agents were characterized by their independence of any single firm or client and dependence upon a whole group of clients, more or less homogeneous. They were strongly imbued with the confidential nature of their work. They received a fee for their services — a fee which approximated uniformity. Some of them had a public aspect and a social responsibility that might grow into a professional point of view.

Many of these agents performed advisory services for their clients and in this capacity acted as business auxiliaries. The advertising agent came to give advice on the subject of merchandising, marketing, and public relations. To be sure, some of this advisory work has been taken over by specialized auxiliaries, such as marketing counselors and public relations counselors; and some of it has been delegated to special departments within the organizations of larger clients.

As financial capitalism has gradually come to dominate a section of big business, it might be expected to influence the advertising agency. I do not mean that Wall Street has set up its own special advertising agencies, though certain investment bankers may already have developed preferences. The large business units, sponsored by financial capitalists, *tend* to build up their own advertising departments. On the other hand, some advertising agencies have shown a slight tendency to reach out to control smaller clients so as to ensure themselves of business, particularly in time of depressed trade. After having gone some slight distance in this direction, the advertising agency which is the subject of this history has abandoned the practice.

A reader of this book may learn for the first time how many functions an advertising agency performs. He will be impressed with the difficulty of evaluating these functions not only in an accounting way but also from the social point of view. He will be impressed with the tremendous educational value of advertising and also with the waste that is sometimes involved. At times he will have to admit that the only justification for some advertising is that, in furthering the goods of one firm against those of another, advertising is simply playing the game of private business capitalism. In other words, the cost of some advertising is the price we pay for private business capitalism, and this system seems to be worth the price we pay for it.

In this history of N. W. Ayer & Son we see illustrated one of the ways in which private enterprise works. It grows from small beginnings to large accomplishments. It plans and replans. It yields to pressures and makes adjustments. Its success comes to depend upon a synthesis of the ideal and the useful, of the right and the profitable. Such is the creative work of the business man. The reward has been the satisfaction of meeting the challenges of administration combined with personal profit. The success of the Ayer agency in substituting honesty, rationality, and service for the selfish trading of advantages is notable in the history of American business. All who are interested in the increasingly popular subject of *social service* will find a mine of material in this history.

The great reality in business is the group of men who make up a single firm. In this book we find a rich array of facts concerning the hard work and planning that have gone into the creation and maintenance of one business unit. In such histories as this we shall find the stuff out of which a new history will be built. Today we ignorantly worship or condemn; tomorrow we may be justified in forming an opinion. In these pages we learn, step by step, how policy has arisen out of practice. We see the flowering of a professional attitude by the roadside of hard struggle. The cynic will learn that ethical principles have been closely related to religious precepts.

The history of an individual business firm may be written from the outside: a student may read the records of such a firm in the Baker Library or elsewhere. On the other hand, someone inside a firm may use the records under his own roof in the compilation of a history. Two different kinds of histories are likely to eventuate, each with its own strength and weakness. The present history is of a third type: it was written by an outsider from inside materials. As a member of a faculty of Harvard University, Dr. Hower has been an independent researcher. As a scholar looking for truth, he has been diligent in examining records, talking with employees and clients, and weighing the evidence garnered.

Coöperating with business in such an enterprise as this has provided high adventure. It has required courage, understanding, and judgment. The goal is truth, information, and candor. The results of the present effort are obviously good beyond all reasonable expectations. The results of other efforts over a long period may be watched by those interested.

The present history took its start in two circumstances. First, Wilfred W. Fry, when president of N. W. Ayer & Son, wished to obtain a volume that would stand as a memorial to the founder of the agency, who was his father-in-law and a man greatly admired. Second, upon learning this, my colleague Professor Georges Doriot proposed that, instead of a personal biography, he should have a history of the firm prepared, since the firm itself was F. W. Ayer's chief lifework. This arrangement fitted in with the desire of the Harvard Graduate School of Business Administration to increase knowledge and interest in the history of American business. The work in question was to be impartial and yet appreciative. By explicit agreement, any facts might be given to the public, provided they were not so presented as to impair the firm's relations with its clients. All the pertinent records were to be made available — fortunately, the editor's first visit to the firm was just in time to postpone the impending destruction of the oldest surviving account books. The resulting manuscript was to be submitted to the sponsor for criticisms and suggestions. When the history was first

(1935) submitted, Fry opposed publication, partly because the text raised insoluble questions of business policy and also, I feel, partly because the exposition was more critical and less personal than was expected. The illness and death of Fry prevented negotiation that would, I am sure, have ironed out all difficulties, for Fry was as honest as he was true. When the project was again taken up, with the painstaking aid of President H. A. Batten, we could still recall that it was Fry's financial support that had made possible the years of research and the final publication. In this book, Fry's life of service to others may continue in another form — assistance to students of business history.

The criticisms of opinion and corrections of fact that the firm has provided since Fry's death have been used by Dr. Hower for what they were worth — and they have proved to be invaluable. Sometimes I have agreed with one side and sometimes with the other. I have been impressed with the difficulty of arriving at the truth of situations even when the records are available and the participants are anxious to be helpful. Even the actors in the events have given conflicting testimony. At least we have avoided the writing of a business history which is on the one hand blindly favorable to business, as in so many memorial volumes, and on the other hand so savagely hostile, as when based on *ex parte* government reports, muckraking journalistic efforts, and communistic diatribes.

Many a firm has only itself to blame for popular misinterpretations of its actions and motives; held back by an antiquated notion that business, being private, should be secretive, many a business has suffered in popular esteem. The fear of disclosure of unfortunate events, often not justified, has shut the gates of business to scholars. Candor would open these gates and there disclose both good and evil, blended in about the same grayish hue that is reflected by life in general.

The present book is but one item in the Harvard Studies in Business History. It is indeed the fifth work and the seventh volume in the series. There has been no specific plan behind the selection of the subjects dealt with — John Jacob Astor, Jay Cooke, the Jacksons and the Lees, and the Massachusetts-First National

Bank of Boston. We have been guided by what is available, feasible, and important.

In the treatment of the subjects dealt with in the series there is one outstanding criterion that is decisive: we must have records that make the study worth while. Business history, written from outside material, is but the false shadow of reality.

The first three works in the series deal with persons whose lives were closed, with firms whose service had ended. In the fourth and in the present work, the firm is alive — proud of its past, interested in its present, and ambitious for its future. In such instances we may and we must secure facts and generalizations from persons now alive; moreover, we have the valued opportunity of securing criticism from those who know well the organization of which they are a part. In this way many a silly story is seen to be false, even though it has long floated through the halls of scholars. In studies of existing firms which are owned by single entrepreneurs or by partners — which is essentially the case of N. W. Ayer & Son up to date, we may expect to fall somewhat short of full information on the financial side. To be sure, this is likely to be more a matter of complete details than of broad essentials. Perhaps we must expect, no matter how we may regret, that such private matters will remain private both in business and outside. If no more serious limitations ever arise, there can be no great cause for lamentation.

Some day there will be enough material available, in the form of sizable monographs, to make possible a general business history of the United States and of other countries. It was perhaps to be expected that America would play a part in unfolding the contributions and shortcomings of business because of its preoccupation with production, distribution, and private finance. Business comes near to being America's only attainment esteemed, studied, and imitated abroad. I should agree that this may prove to be a contribution to the world of vital importance to human society.

N. S. B. Gras

April 18, 1939

AUTHOR'S PREFACE

I HAVE UNDERTAKEN the preparation of a revised edition of the history of N. W. Ayer & Son primarily in order to bring the story up to date while meeting the demand for additional copies of the book. This undertaking, in turn, has given me an opportunity to modify certain judgments in the original edition about developments within the Ayer organization, particularly for the period since 1929. The modifications made, so far as I can determine, arise from two factors: First, the passage of a decade and the course of events inside the firm since 1939 have placed in sharper perspective the earlier history of the Ayer agency. Secondly, my own thinking about business administration has undergone a significant development during the intervening years.

This second factor may need further explanation. Like many other people, I went through some profound experiences after Pearl Harbor. The most impressive for me consisted of three years of gruelling administrative work with the United States Army in the European Theater of Operations. Before that experience my knowledge of administration had been gained largely as a student and observer. During the war, in sharp contrast, I was an active participant in groups charged with heavy administrative responsibilities, under conditions which, to say the least, were trying. From that participation I acquired a good deal of firsthand knowledge and understanding about the administrative process in general. The fact that I was often involved in bad, rather than good, administration made the experience no less educational. My perception of the complexities of the administrator's task deepened, and my judgment of the relative importance of the various elements involved undoubtedly improved. Keenly aware of our woeful lack of knowledge and skill in the area of administration, impressed as never before with the need for progress in this field, and fascinated by its boundless opportunities, I resolved on my return to civilian life to abandon Clio in favor of administration. By happy coincidence this change in my own interests was matched by a corresponding development within the Harvard Business School, likewise arising out of war experiences. As a result, since January, 1946, I have specialized in the study and teaching of administration, particularly in those aspects having to do with human relations in management.

The material in Chapters VII and VIII undoubtedly reflects my altered views as to the phases of management which are of primary importance. I have been less interested than formerly in the mechanisms of the Ayer organization and management and much more in the underlying motivations and attitudes which influence the behavior of the Ayer staff.

Some comment may be advisable about the source material on which I have based my account of developments in N. W. Ayer & Son since 1939. Having limited time at my disposal for the revision, I have relied mainly on interviews with people in the Ayer organization. This fact has prevented me from going into as much detail as might be desirable, but it has not, I feel sure, prevented me from getting close to the essential truth. Human memory is fallible, of course, but the developments concerned are virtually contemporary, and in any event the significant aspects of recent Ayer history are more matters of spirit than of tangible fact. Hence they are less likely to be recorded in the written documents produced in the course of everyday business, except as subtle reflections. I have not relied exclusively upon interviews with top management but have talked with people at every level of the organizational hierarchy. I have paid particular heed to the views expressed by men who returned to the firm after war service and by those who have joined the staff since 1945 after experiences with other firms. In a wide variety of ways the people interviewed have all indicated general agreement on the most significant developments within N. W. Ayer & Son since 1937, namely that the philosophy of Ayer management has gone through a significant evolution and that the spirit of the entire organization has made a fundamental advance. I have tried to set forth in Chapters VII and VIII the developments which impressed them and me as being of primary importance. As before, the Ayer management gave me free access to the firm's records, and I have made use of documentary material whenever I felt the need to do so.

Had time permitted, I should have preferred to appraise the general developments in the agency business and in the advertising industry as a whole since 1939, so as to include such material as background for the events within the Ayer firm. Again, however, limitations of time and also of space prevented me from going far in this direction. I have reason to believe that advertisers and agencies alike have become increasingly aware of their wider responsibilities and that some of the more progressive firms have made improvements of the kind which are seen in N. W. Ayer & Son.

I am indebted to many people within the Ayer organization for help in digging out facts and interpreting them. Professor N. S. B. Gras has read the revised manuscript and made many useful suggestions. I am also indebted to Mrs. Elsie Hight Bishop who has again performed the difficult task of editing the entire revised manuscript, read the proof, and prepared the index. No reader can ever possibly appreciate how much this book owes to her long experience and her patience and skill in dealing with authors.

RALPH M. HOWER

27 December 1948

AUTHOR'S PREFACE TO THE FIRST EDITION

IN WRITING this book I have tried to keep in mind the interests of both the layman and the special student. Part I is a chronological account which sets forth and explains, within fairly brief compass, the history of the Ayer firm. Part II assumes a knowledge of Part I and proceeds to a detailed analysis of various aspects of the business; it is organized by topics and contains a great deal of factual information, documented and rather fully discussed. To a large extent Part II is intended to be a source of reference, and it is my hope that the scholar who is trying "to find out what really happened" in the history of (for example) advertising procedure, business management, or accounting technique will see there a great many useful facts of the sort that have seldom hitherto been recorded.

Throughout the preparation of the manuscript and the lengthy research which preceded it, I have scrupulously endeavored to preserve an impartial point of view: to apprehend the facts and not distort them. It was not the purpose of this book either to attack or to defend the advertising agency as an institution. If it had been, my task would have been simpler; for most of us write more easily and effectively when we are hot in praise or blame. My sole object has been to trace the history of one of the country's leading business firms; not merely to compile annals, but rather to unearth and present a series of connected historical developments and help the reader to interpret them; not to repeat the old wives' tales of advertising, but to consider every piece of evidence critically and relate it to the general business and social context.

I have not rearranged events for dramatic effect, for drama is not my concern. And I have avoided the so-called romance of business because it usually means dragging in by the heels sensational material which has little or nothing to do with business save chronological coincidence. During the entire process of research and composition I have tried to keep attention focused sharply upon policy, management, and economic functions — the three fundamental aspects of a firm's development.

It is impossible for a historian to avoid judging the value of actions: that is his proper duty as an expert. The judgments that he makes are not the opinions of a partisan, but the conclusions of a judge who has sifted the evidence and whose very impartiality obliges him to pronounce some actions bad and others good. Of course, no author ever succeeds in being entirely objective. We are all inevitably influenced by biases of one sort or another, conscious and unconscious. All the historian can do is to take such distorting influences into account, as far as possible, in the process of formulating his judgments. In order to make an exact appraisal of the history of N. W. Ayer & Son, the reader really should know all about the author. That is obviously impossible, but I can at least state briefly the circumstances in which the actual work on this book was done.

First of all, I was assigned to the task not because I was an expert in advertising but because I was trained in economics and history and had specialized in the history of business. Since I knew nothing at all about the Ayer agency and very little about the agency business, my initial attitude toward them was wholly neutral: the opinions about both which I have expressed in this book were reached only as the result of extensive research. I question whether my attitude at the outset toward contemporary advertising itself was strictly objective. Perhaps it is impossible for anyone to achieve that. I regarded advertising as an inevitable accompaniment of a free competitive economic system, and I recognized its value to individual firms, but I was (and still am) dubious about some of its social consequences. Advertising as such, however, is not the subject of my inquiry, although closely related to it. The point that I want to make quite explicit is that I was not and am not a champion of the advertising industry or any part of it. My interest throughout has been that of a student trying to learn all he can about an important influence in modern history.

Most of the research was done in Philadelphia between June,

1932, and September, 1933. The Ayer firm provided me with comfortable working quarters within the agency, brought literally truck-loads of records to me for examination, patiently answered all my questions, and left me to work in my own way. Circumstances which I have explained in the text made the management unwilling to open recent financial records for my inspection, and confidential data supplied by clients to the agency had, of course, to be withheld; but all other extant records of the firm were made freely available, and I feel confident that I saw every surviving document of real importance to the firm's history. Not many firms dare permit such an intimate inspection by an outsider, and I am sincerely grateful for the honor and trust which the Ayer management reposed in me.

I was in daily contact with members of the agency staff, from the janitor's assistant to the president. All of them contributed to my knowledge and understanding, though some of them were not conscious of doing so. In the course of time I made many valued friendships among officers and employees. An author always becomes enamored of his subject, and fifteen months of close association with the Ayer staff, plus the friendships formed, gave me a feeling of attachment to the Ayer firm. I realize that this circumstance may have colored my narrative slightly, but, by way of compensation, it opened sources of information which would otherwise have been closed, even unknown — information which was essential to my grasp of events in the firm's history.

In addition to the records examined and many conversations with officers and employees at the Ayer headquarters in Philadelphia, I made many visits to the New York office, interviewed publishers and publishers' representatives in New York, Philadelphia, and Boston, talked to former employees, and discussed the Ayer firm with a number of clients and rival agents. After a trial effort I decided not to pursue further the interviewing of clients and rivals. It was expensive in money, energy, and time, and it yielded little beyond rather general expressions of opinion which were difficult to evaluate. Accordingly I came to place my principal reliance upon the correspondence files and other records which showed the day-to-day duties, problems, and decisions of the firm.

But the few competitors and clients that I did see gave me a point of view which was useful, and I am grateful to them for their courtesy and time.

Strictly speaking, no business firm can be considered by itself. From the day of its inception it wages a ceaseless battle against competitors, and we fall short of full understanding unless we know what the rival concerns have been doing. I have used as much relevant information about other agencies as I could readily obtain, but, until we have many firm histories as a basis for comparison, we must be content with treatment which is somewhat short of the ideal.

A few words are necessary about the criticisms and suggestions made by members of the Ayer firm after I had completed the first draft of the manuscript in 1935. There were surprisingly few important differences of opinion between us. For the most part, it was a matter of changing a word here or a phrase there to avoid giving an impression which I did not intend, or to forestall misinterpretation. All points of difference were freely discussed, and those in which I could not agree to the validity of the criticism were referred to Professor Gras as the final arbiter. This process prevented a number of errors of fact or interpretation, and the history has definitely benefited from it. I am exceedingly grateful to President Batten for his patience in going over the entire manuscript with me and for his fair-mindedness and tolerance.

So many persons have helped me in the writing of this history that it is difficult to make proper acknowledgment. Professor N. S. B. Gras has been a wise counselor and valued friend every step of the way, and I shall always be grateful for his generous guidance. I am also indebted for suggestions and advice to other colleagues on the Faculty of the Harvard Graduate School of Business Administration, especially Professors Melvin T. Copeland, Georges F. Doriot, and Neil H. Borden, and Dr. Henrietta M. Larson, Assistant Professor of Business History.

It is impossible to cite all the members of the Ayer organization who have been exceedingly helpful to me, but I owe a special debt of gratitude to Wilfred W. Fry, the late president, Mr. Adam Kessler, Jr., formerly treasurer of the corporation, Mr. George

H. Thornley, until 1936 a vice-president and director of the firm, and to Mr. Harry A. Batten, the present head of the agency.

Miss Janice Tarlin and Miss Dorothy Nassau assisted with the laborious and often dusty task of research in Philadelphia, and Miss Tarlin spent another year in Boston helping me to prepare the manuscript. Mr. John L. Ward gave me indispensable technical assistance in working out the accounting developments in Ayer history. Miss Dorothy Moody, Miss Frances Carpenter, and Mrs. Elsie Hight Bishop have given invaluable aid in getting the copy ready for the printer and seeing it through the press, and Mrs. Bishop prepared the index. It is impossible to mention individually many other friends in Boston, New York, and Philadelphia who helped with encouragement and suggestions. Finally, I am deeply indebted to my wife, who not only cheerfully endured the move to Philadelphia and back again and gave me unusual moral and culinary support but also performed some expert editing in Part I.

RALPH M. HOWER

April 21, 1939

PART I

GENERAL HISTORY OF
N. W. AYER & SON, INC.

CHAPTER I

ORIGIN OF THE ADVERTISING AGENCY AND DEVELOPMENT TO 1869

ALTHOUGH advertising is the most familiar facet of modern business, there is a good deal of ignorance and confusion about it, even among its practitioners. Still less is generally known about the advertising industry itself — a vast and complicated industry with ramifications throughout almost the entire world.

An essential element in that industry is the advertising agency. A large portion of the public has learned about the agency's existence mainly through a number of popular detective stories and motion pictures in which advertising agencies formed the background for murder and romance. Recently, moreover, a best-selling novel, *The Hucksters* (subsequently made into a motion picture), has given the American people some lively glimpses within the industry, although the total impression conveyed is highly misleading and woefully incomplete. A great deal of serious material has been published about advertising; hardly anything has appeared in book form about the advertising agency.[1]

SUBJECT AND PURPOSE OF THIS BOOK

This study is primarily concerned with the history of N. W. Ayer & Son, Incorporated, an advertising agency which was founded in Philadelphia eighty years ago. Tracing the firm's development will take us behind the scenes of the advertising industry and should throw additional light upon the tortuous road along which products of the factory now move on their way to the ultimate consumer.

Distribution of merchandise involves not only the physical movement of goods from producer to consumer but also the diffusion of information about them. Unknown wares find no buyers.

And, since a wide distance in time and space lies between producer and consumer in our highly specialized society, distribution must be accompanied with such information on a large scale. In short, it must be accompanied with advertising.

To handle goods, numerous middlemen — wholesalers, retailers, dealers, and carriers of all kinds — have come into existence. As the physical distribution has grown in volume and ramification, advertising too has increased both in volume and in technical complexity. And, with the development of its many new branches, advertising has had to develop a host of specialists, including middlemen of its own. The leader among these, the advertising agent, is the one who brings the divergent activities of the advertising industry into synthesis. Originally a one-man business, the agency has long since become an institution composed of many people and devoted to many related activities. This agency may be regarded as a special kind of workshop which helps to create and execute advertising campaigns. Producing goods and services of the greatest importance to the ordinary citizen, the agency works not for him but for a large number of other business enterprises.

In terms of the convenient dollar sign the present scope of the agency business in the United States is indicated by the $600,000,-000 volume which, according to conservative estimates, agencies handled in 1930,[2] before the crash of '29 had greatly reduced advertising appropriations. In 1935, before much business recovery had been felt, agency billings totaled only slightly less than half a billion dollars.[3] In 1947 total agency volume probably exceeded one billion dollars.[4] The real importance of the advertising agency, however, is not to be judged by the volume of business it handles, its complexity, or the scope of its activities, but rather by the important rôle which it plays in modern life.

From the initial mapping-out of a nation-wide sales campaign to the painstaking selection of the words and pictures that make up a finished advertisement, from the first vague germ of a selling idea to the actual details of multifarious business transactions, the advertising agency works hand in hand with its clients. It employs market experts, statisticians, writers, illustrators, clerks, accountants, printers, photographers, radio artists, dietitians, engineers, engravers, and many others — an extraordinary army of specialists. Moreover, it deals constantly with over 1,500 radio and television broadcasting stations, hundreds of billboard owners, and more than 18,400 newspapers and periodicals (1947 figures) in the United States alone, to say nothing of those published in foreign countries. Thus, from a single organization a manufacturer or distributor is able to obtain services which he could otherwise secure only by contracting with thousands of separate firms.[5]

N. W. Ayer & Son, Incorporated, of Philadelphia, is one of the oldest advertising agencies in America, boasting a history of continuous development from 1869 to the present day. By purchased heritage, it is a direct descendant of the first advertising agency to be founded in this country. The annals of this firm provide an excellent subject for the student of business history: the growth of a modern business enterprise from a small beginning to a position of unquestioned prominence, and from a service so simple that a single man could handle it to a far-flung organization of highly complex functions. In addition, the firm has a record of consistent leadership in improving advertising technique and advancing standards of agency service. While it is in no sense here held up as a model, the Ayer agency has achieved a remarkably high position in terms of ethical principles as well as of business success.

Of even greater interest than the mere record of this individual company, however, is the light which a study of its development throws upon little-known aspects of the history of advertising. Modern American business is so bewildering in its size and complexity that an understanding of any one phase of it is often better sought through study of a typical example than through an attempt to analyze the subject as a whole. This is particularly true in the field of advertising, where the methods used and the results obtained have varied to such an extraordinary degree that useful generalizations about it are almost beyond possibility of achievement. If they are to be made at all, they must depend upon the study of many cases; and, while advertising itself has formed the subject of many serious inquiries, the advertising agency has hitherto received little attention. The Ayer firm, as one of the largest agencies in the world and one whose history covers the main period of the agency's development, may well claim to represent this branch of the advertising industry.

The story of N. W. Ayer & Son has many threads. To make the task of following them easier, the first part of this book will consist of a historical sketch, tracing the general development of the company from its start to the present time. When this framework has been established, it will be easier to handle the detailed analysis of various aspects of the business which forms Part II. Before describing the firm's founding, however, it will be helpful to consider the historical background, with particular reference to the forces which brought the advertising agent into existence and molded his early development.

BACKGROUND OF MODERN ADVERTISING

The advertising agent is essentially a product of modern conditions following the Industrial Revolution and did not make his appearance until the nineteenth century. But the field of his operations was not new. Advertising itself is as old as history. From Greek and Roman times through the Middle Ages, however, it did not develop beyond the primitive stage of the display of wares and the use of pictorial signboards and public criers. With few exceptions, its function was simply to identify places, tradesmen, and craftsmen, and to inform the populace where certain goods and services were for sale. The persuasive message which is characteristic of modern advertising was almost completely absent. Even the calls of the public criers — these alone contained what is now known as "selling appeal" — became stereotyped, and in their traditional form served merely as reminders that wine, fish, or bread was for sale.[6]

The explanation of this simplicity is not far to seek. There is inevitably a close relationship between the nature of advertising and the state of trade development, mechanical technique, and general culture. Production in medieval times was undertaken largely to meet existing demand; and, since it took most of the available energy and material to supply ordinary daily needs, competition among producers was not intense. There was, in consequence, little need for advertising. So long as trade and industry remained predominantly local, advertising was likely to be of little value except in large towns, in which people could not be familiar with all the tradesmen and to which many strangers came to trade. And, of course, since the common man was unable to read, the only practicable advertising media were pictorial devices and word-of-mouth announcements.

With the invention of printing and the spread of literacy, the printed advertisement appeared and effected a great revolution in the art of advertising. No longer need the advertiser restrict himself to mere identification. Through the printed handbill, the poster, the pamphlet, and the newspaper, he could distribute advertising that would explain, describe, argue, persuade, and lure. He could make advertising into a powerful instrument for the aggressive selling of goods and services.

Circumstances eventually made such an instrument not only an advantage but a necessity to the business man. As the Industrial Revolution gained momentum, production began to overtake demand and the factory to supplant home industry. The consumer was confronted with a choice of many sources of supply and also with a great variety of goods to choose from — not all of which he considered necessities. At the same time, population rapidly increased in both Europe and America, with a larger proportion living in towns, so that the simple neighborly relation between producer and consumer vanished forever.

In these circumstances a merchant had not only to inform possible customers what commodities he offered; he had to use persuasion as well to encourage them to buy this product rather than that, and to buy from him rather than from his rival down the street. It is not surprising to find that as early as 1725 the newspaper was firmly established as the primary medium for advertising by local concerns in the American colonies as well as in Europe;[7] or that by the 1780's such notable manufacturers as Josiah Wedgwood were resorting to advertising in order to stimulate dull business.[8]

First Appearance of the Advertising Agent

Until the nineteenth century there was no advertising agent either in Europe or in America. Anyone who wished to advertise

dealt directly with the newspaper. So long as advertising was confined to small districts, so long as it originated with local advertisers and was intended for local readers, neither shopkeeper nor
newspaper editor felt the need for outside assistance. Nor was
there much opportunity for a middleman to force his way between
them. To the editor a newspaper was primarily a political party
organ; and advertisements, while as welcome as any other form
of manna if they appeared without solicitation, were a matter of
minor concern. So long as advertising technique was crude and
advertisements did not have to compete with one another or with
many other attractions in order to win attention, the business
man required no special skill to prepare an advertisement or see
to its publication. All the details could be handled personally by
the editor and the advertiser. The time required for this was of
little importance, and, since the amount of money involved was
never large, the savings which might be made by greater efficiency
were probably not worth considering.

By 1800, however, difficulties and complexities were beginning
to grow up around the simple, direct relation between merchant
and newspaper. The expansion of markets which was then in
progress entailed sales promotion over wider areas, and advertisers were reaching out beyond the local districts. This expansion
might mean, for example, that an advertiser located in Boston
had to make arrangements with newspapers in Gloucester, Con-
cord, Plymouth, and even as far afield as Springfield, Hartford,
and New London. He had to bargain about the amount to be paid
for the advertising; he had to give directions for the printing of
his announcements (not an easy matter for those unfamiliar with
printers' jargon even in its early and unsophisticated days); he
had to see that the advertising was inserted properly so that he
got what he was charged for; and, finally, he had to send money
in payment. In short, he had to manage for himself (or neglect)
many of the tiresome details which have since become a part of
the service performed by an agency like N. W. Ayer & Son.

The newspaper publisher, too, was beginning to have his difficulties. It was clear by 1800 that no paper could long pay its
expenses with the money received from the subscribers alone. As
the Paris *Journal des Débats* confessed on abandoning (1799) its

policy of refusing to print advertisements, *"Il faut bien vivre."* [9]
And, in America, when the Massachusetts legislature placed a tax
upon newspaper advertisements (1786–88), the *Massachusetts
Spy* of Worcester was forced to suspend publication, and some of
the other papers resorted to subterfuge in order to evade the tax.[10]
The income derived from advertising was absolutely essential to
the newspapers' existence. As publishers began to realize this,
they found it advisable, first, to facilitate the placing of advertisements by shopkeepers and manufacturers, and, later, to solicit
business among those who might have occasion to advertise in
newspapers.

About 1800, therefore, the new complexities of business had
created a need for a specializing middleman. He would take as
his province the purchase and sale of advertising space, leaving
both advertiser and publisher free to devote full attention to their
principal work. It was to meet this need for a redistribution of
functions that the advertising agent came into existence.

The development traced above is an example of that type of
evolution which has for centuries modified the course of business.
As existing functions grow and ramify, a new function emerges,
or an unimportant operation develops until it comes to require
some person's undivided attention; and this new or expanded activity is taken over by an independent specialist.

The work of the advertising specialist was to assist in the buying and selling of a commodity, namely, newspaper space. In
other fields similar needs and forces have given rise to commission agents, brokers, and dealers who handle agricultural products; insurance underwriters, brokers, and agents; selling agencies in the textile industry; the various financial middlemen —
bankers, underwriters of securities, investment counselors, bill
brokers, and the like; and the vast army of specialists who assist
in the intricate process of moving commodities from producer to
consumer. Some of them buy and sell tangible goods; others buy
and sell services; but this difference does not affect the value of
their work. They win a place in our economic structure through
their ability to perform a service more cheaply or more effectively
than the non-specialized business man can do it.[11]

The exact line of evolution which leads to the modern advertising agent is not altogether clear, for at first we find the work which eventually became his being handled as a side line by men in several different callings. As early as 1786 English newspapers were appointing shopkeepers to collect and forward advertisements.[12] The eighteenth-century American postmaster frequently accepted advertisements and forwarded them to newspapers; he probably received a commission for his services.[13] It is evident that stationers and booksellers acted in the same way, for the early nineteenth-century directories for London and New York show that many of these were also "newspaper agents," "newsmen," and "news agents," and there is reason to believe that they forwarded advertisements, as well as subscriptions, to newspaper publishers.[14]

The newspapers themselves, however, supplied the first advertising agents who attained any prominence in the United States. By the 1830's editors in large cities were finding it advisable to send out employees from time to time among the local merchants and manufacturers to solicit orders for advertising. Some of these employees soon perceived that they could solicit orders for several publications as readily as for one and that they could make a great deal more money by doing this on a commission basis than by working for a single paper. Such an arrangement had the additional advantage that it enabled the advertiser to buy space in a number of papers while dealing with only one person, thus saving time and trouble. That the number of publications might be important is apparent from the fact that the number of newspapers in the United States increased from about seventy-five in 1790 to over three hundred and sixty in 1820, one thousand in 1830, and fourteen hundred in 1840.[15]

The two earliest advertising agents of whom we have definite record, Volney B. Palmer, of Philadelphia, and John Hooper, of New York, started their advertising careers by canvassing orders for newspapers. We shall see later that the founder of N. W. Ayer & Son followed the same path. Palmer is of especial interest because he was, according to his own claim and long-accepted tradition among advertising men, the first agent in this country, and also because N. W. Ayer & Son eventually took over what was left of his original business.[16]

Volney B. Palmer (1799–1864) is said to have started his agency in Philadelphia in 1841.[17] At any rate, as early as 1844 he styled himself "Agent for Country Newspapers." [18] While several English advertising agencies had been founded before that time, there is no evidence to indicate that Palmer had any knowledge of them, and in making his start he may well have been influenced by American experience alone.[19] His father had been publisher of the Mount Holly, New Jersey, *Mirror,* and Palmer apparently began his business career by soliciting advertisements for his father's paper. For some years, too, Palmer was connected with the *Miner's Journal* of Pottsville, Pennsylvania, and it is said that, when he was assigned to Philadelphia to obtain subscriptions and advertising for the *Miner's Journal,* he succeeded so well that he decided to establish an independent agency.[20]

For several years Palmer conducted his advertising agency in conjunction with a real-estate, wood, and coal office.[21] Possibly the advertising business alone was not large enough to support him at the outset. American business had been severely depressed since the panic of 1837, and men were ready to try any sort of combination which seemed likely to yield profits. Advertising soon crowded out the other activities, however; and Palmer's stout, pompous figure, brass buttons, and gold-headed walking-stick became a familiar sight to publishers and merchants, not only in Philadelphia but in other cities as well. In 1845 he established a branch in Boston; about the same time he opened another in New York; and for a short time he maintained a third in Baltimore.[22] Meanwhile, in 1842, another agency had been opened in New York by John Hooper, an honest, slow, and unpretentious man who had previously solicited advertisements for the New York *Tribune.* Little is known about Hooper's business.[23]

Although it is often said that the advertising agent began as a space-broker, this is clearly disproved by Palmer's methods, which are a matter of record. On behalf of newspapers throughout the country, he solicited orders for advertising, forwarded the copy, and collected payment. One point is worthy of special note: Palmer stated explicitly that the publishers — usually they were editors and printers combined — were his principals and that, as their agent, he was authorized to make contracts with persons who wished to advertise in their papers. (The reader should not take the terms agent and agency, used in this book, as having their strict legal connotation. Palmer was apparently an agent in the legal sense. Whether or not the succeeding agents have been the same depends upon the particular arrangements they made with their customers. The economic meaning of the terms, while not precise, should be clear from the context.) It is true that Palmer pointed out the trouble and expense which he could save the advertiser. He also kept a large file of newspapers for inspection, assisted advertisers in selecting the particular papers to be used, and offered to help them with the writing of their advertisements. He made it plain, however, that he was working for the newspapers and stated that, if an advertiser dealt through his agency, the rates charged would be the same as those charged by the publishers.[24]

Palmer frequently described himself as "newspaper agent" rather than as advertising agent. For his services he deducted a portion of the money paid by advertisers, usually 25 per cent, and the publishers quickly adopted this plan of compensation in dealing with other agents. Since many publishers named Palmer as their official agent, and since Palmer's competitors closely imitated his methods, the fact that the advertising agent was originally the agent of the newspaper (i.e., resembling the special representative of today rather than the modern agent) can hardly be questioned.[25]

This point must be stressed because much confusion later developed (and to some extent still exists) about the advertising agent's position and obligations. The reason for this confusion seems to be that Palmer's immediate successors became independent dealers in space, while they retained the title of agent and continued to claim a commission from publishers on the advertising which they forwarded for publication. We shall see that N. W. Ayer & Son took the lead in trying to clarify the relationships. Later on, in the detailed discussion of the relations between the agency, advertisers, and media-owners, more will be said on this subject.

Early Changes in the Advertising Agency

The business of the advertising agent passed through four stages of development before N. W. Ayer & Son was founded: (1) *newspaper agency*, (2) *space-jobbing*, (3) *space-wholesaling*, and (4) *advertising concession agency*. These stages overlapped, and there were traces of all of them in the Ayer agency during the early years of its existence. We may avoid confusion later by considering them now in some detail.

The first or *newspaper agency* stage was the one inaugurated by V. B. Palmer, in which the agent represented the newspaper publisher. It lasted from 1841 to some time in the 1850's, and a vestige of it survives today in the so-called commission which publishers allow to advertising agencies.

In the second or *space-jobbing* stage the agent became an independent middleman. Instead of working for publishers for a commission, he became a jobber working for his own profit, who sold space to advertisers and then bought space from newspapers to fill his orders. Thus he bought and sold space on his own account, but piecemeal only, according to orders actually received. This new phase of the agency's development was not a sudden growth. It came about gradually, as a result of the lively competition which Palmer's success had attracted. In the 1850's newspaper publishers, going on the theory that the more numerous their agents the more space they would sell, were usually willing to deal with anyone who wished to imitate and rival Palmer. Before long, New York, Philadelphia, and Boston each had a number of advertising agents clamoring for business, and each agent claimed authority to represent every paper of any importance in the country. The advertiser found all these agents vying with each other for his business, and, since he could buy space in essentially the same papers from any of them, he quickly learned to seek the one who offered it at the lowest prices. Indeed, there was hardly any other basis for selection.[26]

This state of affairs inevitably confused the relations and obligations of all parties concerned and encouraged the agent to butter his bread on both sides. To get business away from his competitors, an agent might offer space to advertisers at low prices, either by sacrificing a part of the commission which the publisher allowed him or by reducing the publisher's gross rate. In practice the agent kept the percentage of his commission intact. During the transition period he could do this because, as the authorized representative of the publisher, he was able to establish rates for space at what seemed to him a suitable figure, and his prices were understood to be binding upon the publisher. For a time many publishers permitted this demoralizing practice because (like most American business men until after the Civil War) they had never held to their stated prices. They tended to regard advertising revenue as so much extra income, and they preferred to accept almost any price for space rather than risk letting it go unused.[27] In such circumstances it was inevitable that their rates, rather than the agent's commission, should bear the brunt of the price-cutting.

Owing to the abuses which naturally followed, publishers were sometimes compelled, for self-protection, to repudiate the rates established by advertising agents. Whenever this happened, the agent lost part or the whole of his commission from the publisher because he had already agreed upon a price with the advertiser and could not raise it. To guard against such contingencies the agent began to create a margin against loss by offering to each paper a lower gross price than the one which he set in contracting with advertisers. He hoped, not without reason, that enough publishers would accept the low figure to offset those who would repudiate his cuts in rates, thus enabling him to come out with his usual reward. In short, he began to deal in space. In this way, as a contemporary agent expressed it, "The principle of getting from the Advertiser all that he could be induced to pay, and offering to the Publisher as little as he would consent to accept, became established."[28] In other words, the agent represented neither publisher nor advertiser but drove a sharp bargain with both. He had now ceased to be an agent in the proper sense of the term, and had become a space-jobber.

In this space-jobbing stage, however, the agent clung to his title of agent and to what he called his commission from the publishers (now really a discount), in spite of the fact that he was no longer an authorized representative of the newspapers. Publishers

Volney B. Palmer

NATHAN WHEELER AYER AND FRANCIS WAYLAND AYER

seemed to feel that they should continue the commission because the business which came to them from the agents involved less work and less credit risk than that which came directly from advertisers. They believed, moreover, that the agent, in promoting the general cause of advertising for his own profit, advanced their interests and that the commission allowed gave him additional encouragement to push the sale of their advertising space.[29]

This arrangement has been continued by the publishers and most agencies down to the present time, although it is a survival which changing conditions have, in the opinion of many independent observers, made irrational and uneconomical in certain respects. It explains, without excusing, the paradox which confronts many an advertiser: he employs an advertising agent to plan his advertising, supervise its execution, and guard his interests throughout; yet it is the publisher who provides the so-called commission by which the agent gains his pay; while the advertiser, at least in theory, has no voice in determining the amount of that payment.

In 1865 the third stage, a logical development of the second, was ushered in by George P. Rowell of Boston, who was soon to become the country's leading agent. This was the *space-wholesaling* phase in which the agent, anticipating the needs of advertisers, bought space in large quantities and resold it to them, as they wanted it, in smaller lots.

As advertising solicitor for the Boston *Post*, Rowell had discovered a chance for profits which early agents had apparently overlooked. The usual charge for a "square" (about one inch in a newspaper column) in country weeklies was one dollar for the first insertion and fifty cents for each of several subsequent insertions. Most publishers, however, were so glad to receive a large order for advertising that they would sell a whole column for a year for $100 or even less, and allow the agency a commission on this amount as well. Thus if Rowell could resell the space to advertisers at the comparatively low price of one dollar per square per month, he could make a handsome profit.[30]

Rowell made several noteworthy changes in the business. His predecessors, in ceasing to be true agents and becoming independent middlemen, had made themselves into space-jobbers who assumed a certain degree of risk. Buying space only when they already held orders from advertisers, they staked their knowledge of the market and their bargaining power against the inferior knowledge and power of the publisher on the one hand and the advertiser on the other. But they were speculators only to a limited extent, for they did not buy space in anticipation of the advertiser's needs.

Rowell, however, speculated in a larger and more useful way. By purchasing large quantities of space in advance of actual orders, he took over some of the risk that the publishers had previously borne; and, while retaining a good profit for himself, he rendered a service to advertisers by parceling out the space to them at prices substantially lower than they could obtain elsewhere. He was, in short, a capitalistic middleman, like those who had intervened between producer and consumer in other lines of commerce — particularly in the handling of staple commodities — at a much earlier date.[31] Rowell also introduced another financial change by agreeing to pay cash to any publisher who would allow an additional discount of 5 per cent. Country publishers are traditionally short of cash, and, since the prevailing commercial practice was to take three to six months' credit as a matter of course, Rowell's offer was particularly welcome.[32]

Rowell's plan of buying space at wholesale and selling it at retail succeeded immediately. By concluding arrangements with a large number of papers he was able to announce to the advertising world such tempting offers as "One inch of space a month in one hundred papers for one hundred dollars." Other agents promptly imitated his scheme and turned the competition in this new direction.

The fourth stage began about 1867, when the idea of wholesaling space was carried one step further to what I have termed the *advertising concession agency*. Carlton & Smith (subsequently the J. Walter Thompson Company) and other agents began to contract annually with the publications they represented, to pay a lump sum and take over most of the risk and management of the *entire* advertising space in the papers. They thus acquired, so to speak, the advertising concession in a publication. This arrangement revived the original close connection between the advertising agent and the publisher, but the so-called agent in fact continued to be an independent middleman, buying and selling space in the hope of obtaining a profit. When Rowell was asked in 1866, "Whom does the agent represent?" he replied frankly that he represented himself.[33]

Thus arose both the practice of wholesaling space and the "list" system which dominated the agency business for many years. To have a special list of papers was the favorite plan among agencies when the Ayer agency began. Each agent owned space in a group of papers, and for advertising in this group — his list — he made a special price. Such a list, of course, would not be suitable for the advertising of all kinds of products, but the agent tried to convince the advertisers of its value, and, owing to the prevailing ignorance about effective sales promotion, he usually succeeded. To meet the demand for advertising in given geographical areas, agents usually made up a number of lists, one for New England, one for the Middle States, and so on.[34]

It was impossible for agents, however, to fit all advertisers into this bed of Procrustes, no matter how profitable for themselves. Different products went to different geographical areas, and some of them obviously could not be advertised so effectively in religious weeklies (for example) as in ordinary newspapers. Those advertisers, moreover, who had definite ideas about the media to be used insisted on the inclusion of papers not on an agent's list. To meet contingencies of this kind, every agent was obliged to send orders to many papers in which he owned no space. He demanded and received a commission from the publishers on such orders. If he could obtain the desired space only through another agent, he placed the order through that agent and received a commission from him rather than from the publisher. In other words, while an advertising agent operated primarily as an independent jobber or wholesaler of space, he continued to act as a broker in many transactions. And as a broker he received a commission on these transactions from the person on whose behalf he sold space. For these particular services the commission was a suitable remuneration. This arrangement undoubtedly helped to keep alive the idea that the advertising agent was an agent in the true sense of the word and was entitled to a commission on all transactions regardless of the part he played in them.

The agency business as it existed in 1869 was a confusing combination of all these arrangements. So, also, was the business conducted by N. W. Ayer & Son during the firm's early years. Contemporaries criticized the position of agents generally because it led to the abuses mentioned, but their shafts were aimed at evils which are inherent in most competitive commercial enterprises. Less obvious and usually overlooked by the critics was another bad feature of the arrangement, which was not the result of competition but came rather from the fact that the advertising industry quickly outgrew the machinery set up to carry it on. As a consequence the agent was forced into an attempt to serve two masters: he had to sell space for the publisher and, at the same time, to act as an expert and impartial counselor to the advertiser.

It was this duality of function which for years constituted the real evil of the agency business. Not one of the trading arrangements described above, taken by itself, can be challenged as unfair or unethical. The possibility of serious mischief appeared only when all were combined in the operation of one enterprise. Such a situation positively invited conflicts between the interests of the publisher, the agent, and the advertiser; and the continued use of the ambiguous terms "agent" and "commission" tended to conceal these conflicts.

In practice, no harm resulted unless the advertiser allowed the agent to influence him in the choice of advertising media. In that case the agent tended to recommend his own space, regardless of its merits. Both publisher and advertiser, unfortunately, encouraged the agent to act as a counselor in the use of advertising. At least, their separate interests thrust this rôle upon him. For, in order to sell the publisher's space, the agent had to show the merchant how to advertise, just as the early automobile salesman had to give driving lessons; and prospective advertisers, in turn, wanted all the help that the agent was willing to give, because without advice they were only too likely to waste money on misdirected and ill-conceived advertising efforts. And yet the interests of advertiser and publisher did not always lie in the same direction; good advice for the advertiser was bad advice from the point of view of the publisher whose paper was left off the list of media to be used. Obviously the agent could not satisfy both. It was to remove this conflict, as will appear later, that N. W. Ayer & Son adopted a different plan of operation.

Such were the origins of the advertising agency. Apart from the interest which attaches to the inception of a spectacular modern phenomenon, it is evident from this sketch that the agency played a vital part in the development of American business. Its rôle from 1841 to 1869 may be summarized as follows: The advertising agency came into existence because the ignorance of both publisher and advertiser, together with their genuine economic need for assistance, presented an opportunity for profit. The agent facilitated the purchase and sale of space. He made it easy for the publisher of the Podunk *Clarion* to fill his advertising columns with profitable advertisements from distant cities and for the merchant and manufacturer of Metropolis to advertise his wares in out-of-the-way markets. In a larger sense, however, the agency's chief service in this early period was to promote the general use of advertising, and thus to aid in discovering cheaper and more effective ways of marketing goods.[35]

CHAPTER II

FOUNDING OF N. W. AYER & SON, 1869–1876

IN 1868 Francis Wayland Ayer entered the advertising world. Although a mere youth of twenty and without any business experience, he was soon to outdistance all the established advertising agents. He had a clear head and high ideals, and within twelve years he had revolutionized the agency business by applying to it clear thinking and idealism. Unlike many of his rivals, he looked beyond immediate profits. In essence his policy was to give honest service and through it to win steady customers, rather than to seek individual orders by means of the shabby lures which many agents were using. The agency he founded was N. W. Ayer & Son, named after his father and first partner, Nathan Wheeler Ayer.

BOYHOOD OF FRANCIS WAYLAND AYER

Both father and son were New Englanders by inheritance as well as by birth. They were direct descendants of John Ayer, who came to the Massachusetts Bay Colony from Norwich, England, in 1637 and helped to found both Newbury and Haverhill, Massachusetts. One branch of the family settled in Connecticut before the end of the seventeenth century; and there, in the village of Preston, Nathan Wheeler Ayer was born on January 21, 1817.

Of N. W. Ayer's life only a few facts are known. He was graduated from Brown University in 1840 and for several years practiced law in western Massachusetts.[1] Circumstances, however, soon induced him to become a schoolmaster. He taught at various places, including North Adams and Pittsfield, Massachusetts, and Lansingburg and Penn Yan, New York; and finally, in 1867, he purchased what was known at the time as a "female seminary" in Philadelphia.[2] He was not, in the popular sense of the term, a successful man. In a land where public schools were numerous and few families could afford the expense of private schooling, it is hardly surprising that he did not prosper financially. Moreover, especially in his later years, he suffered almost continuously from ill health. Had it not been for the business genius of his son, N. W. Ayer's name would long ago have passed into oblivion.

Francis Wayland Ayer, the only son of N. W. Ayer to reach maturity, was born on February 4, 1848, at Lee, Massachusetts. He was named after Dr. Francis Wayland who, in his father's undergraduate days, had presided over Brown University.[3] As revealed by the fragmentary information which survives, his youth was that of the traditional self-made business man of nineteenth-century America: a humble but eminently respectable home; hard work at an early age, combined with strong religious principles and intelligence, and courage derived from aggressive self-confidence; frugal living and thrift. Our age has come to think of this upbringing as Victorian, outworn, and faintly ridiculous. But, beneath the cynicism and disillusionment of our modern attitude, there is still entrenched a belief in character as the basis of success, whether in advertising, industry, or finance.

At an early age, Wayland Ayer developed strong religious tendencies and a serious outlook on life. His whole environment must have been one of sober piety, for his ancestry was Puritan, his father and stepmother[4] were devout members of the Baptist Church, and his favorite uncle was a Baptist minister. Many a youth has rebelled against such a background, has plunged to the opposite extreme; and it says much for young Ayer that his character was distinguished from the first by the traits that were to prove his strength in later life.

The earnestness of his disposition was supplemented and to some extent balanced by spirited energy and determination. Indeed, though undersized and weakly as a child, he occasionally caused his parents some anxiety by his wilfulness and boyish mischief, innocent as it really was.[5]

The stern sobriety which was his all through life was intensified by the family's constant struggle during his childhood to obtain a decent living. Both parents taught school, and Wayland, even at the age of nine, had to turn out at six-thirty in the morning to build the schoolroom fires.

His early experience left its indelible mark on Wayland Ayer. The simple rural life, the constant need for thrift, the importance of individual effort — these influences were plainly evident in the man he came to be. But it is to his father that a large share of the credit must be given. N. W. Ayer could do little for his son in a material way, but he gave freely from the resources of a cultivated mind. All the formal schooling that the boy received before starting out for himself was from his father;[6] and the excellent quality of that schooling is amply proved by the self-reliance, integrity, and clear thinking which marked his entire career.

When he was fourteen years old, Wayland Ayer was offered the position of master of a small country school near Dundee, New York. The Civil War was in its second year, and the grown men were needed at the front; otherwise the proposal could hardly have been made to so young a boy. One aspect of the position which must have seemed especially difficult was the fact that he would have to discipline pupils of his own age or even older, some of whom were likely to be unruly.

Formidable as the job must have seemed, it could not fail to interest young Ayer. It would provide the beginning of a worthy career in the profession to which his father and mother belonged. He would be paid twenty dollars per month, and he would be fed and lodged by the families of his pupils. The latter provision meant, as he knew, constant moving from one family to another, frequently indifferent food, and, at times, sour looks from parents who resented the extra mouth to feed. But he could overlook these discomforts, since he might in time be able to save enough from his salary to pay for a college education like his father's. That was the object of his most earnest desire, and he decided to accept the offer. The expected problem of discipline soon arose. Ayer told about it later:[7]

I have never forgotten the first time I punished a boy in that school. He provoked me to the limit. He got an extension of the limit, and then he got a licking. I went home thoroughly ashamed of myself, and I got up in the morning feeling that I owed that boy an apology. I went to him and made it. I told him that he deserved the punishment I gave him the day before and deserved more than he got, and that if he ever did the like again he would get more than he had got, but that he would never get it again while I was angry. My punishing him was "letting off steam," I was thoroughly angry at him, and I was ashamed of it. I told him that thereafter I intended to control myself before attempting to control him. I never had to punish anybody in that school again.

This incident plainly reveals the searching self-criticism to which his Puritan nature impelled young Ayer; at the same time it exemplifies one of the prime factors of his later success: his indomitable will, tempered by self-control and an understanding of others. With such equipment the boy was rapidly making his way in the world. His physical constitution, which had been a delicate one, soon became vigorous; and, more important, his success in handling pupils led to early promotion.

Before the end of the first year of teaching the youthful schoolmaster was requested to see the village doctor of Dundee, who was on the school board. The doctor went directly to the point:

The County School Commissioner says you have the best school in the county, and that you have no trouble with discipline. We want to engage you to come and take charge of the village public school here. I think it is only fair to warn you, however, that the last teacher didn't finish his term, and that the one before him was thrown through a window by the husky pupils and never came back. But the Commissioner is sure you could handle them. Would you like to tackle the job?

Wayland Ayer had just turned fifteen, weighed only 75 pounds, and had only a few months of teaching experience behind him. The offer, though flattering, was not one to be accepted hastily, and he went home to discuss it with his father. His father encouraged him to try it. Without further hesitation Ayer took charge of the village school, and applied the methods of discipline which he had just learned.

The new group of pupils gave him no trouble at all. In fact, he succeeded in making the lessons so interesting that the pupils voluntarily lengthened the school day in order to study more subjects, and the enrollment grew rapidly from 11 to 70. It was not

long before the private academy in the village, which had previously profited by the poor reputation of the district school, had
to close its doors.[8]

Other promotions followed the first, until Wayland Ayer was
in charge of the boys' hall of a coeducational school and had five
years of successful teaching to his credit. It was a good record
for a lad of nineteen; but he had higher ambitions, and the cher-
ished dream of a college education was almost within his grasp.

F. W. AYER'S ENTRANCE INTO BUSINESS

In the fall of 1867 young Ayer was matriculated in the University of Rochester, but his career there lasted only one year.
Apparently college life was more expensive than he had anticipated, for his savings were soon gone. The only person from
whom he could expect help was his father. But, far from being
able to help his son, N. W. Ayer was himself in difficulties: the
girls' school in Philadelphia was not prospering, and his health
was getting steadily worse.

To a loyal son only one course was possible. Wayland decided
to rejoin the family and do what he could for them. Accordingly,
June, 1868, found him trudging the streets of Philadelphia in
search of work.[9] Like many another newcomer, he found Philadelphia cool to strangers. Like many another youth, he searched
day after day without finding a job. Nobody seemed to want a
country boy whose only experience was schoolteaching. Eventually he obtained a part-time teaching position which helped to
support him while he continued to look for a satisfactory opening. Other teaching opportunities arose, but young Ayer declined
them. By this time he had decided — possibly because of his
father's inability to make a satisfactory livelihood as a schoolmaster — that he would not return to the schoolroom. Like his
pioneering forefathers he gave up limited certainties for unlimited
possibilities.

Meanwhile a classmate of his father's, a Dr. Boyd, editor of
the *National Baptist* (a weekly religious newspaper which was
then published in Philadelphia),[10] was taking an interest in the
young man; and, on learning that he had refused an attractive
teaching position, Boyd sent for him. "I hear you declined an of-

fer of $700 a year and all found," he said. "Why didn't you take it?"

Ayer explained that he had made up his mind to become a business man. The editor walked over to a window and pointed to the buildings along the street below him. "All these houses should advertise," he declared, "and they should advertise in our paper. There's 25 per cent commission in it for you. Why don't you take up this line of work?"

After sleeping on the suggestion, F. W. Ayer accepted Boyd's offer and started to solicit advertisements for the *National Baptist*. Thus, in the summer of 1868, began the connection with advertising which was severed only by his death in 1923.[11]

In this incident we catch a glimpse of the newspaper publishing business when advertising was regarded as a casual by-product of relatively small importance. Of greater interest is the light which it throws upon the beginning of a successful career. Here, as in so many cases, fortuitous circumstance was the deciding factor. Up to that time Ayer had known nothing about advertising. According to his own statement he had never even heard of an advertising agent. All that he wanted was a suitable opportunity to make money. Given the opportunity, however, Ayer quickly saw the potential value of advertising and resolved to take advantage of it.

For one entire week Ayer canvassed the business firms of Philadelphia without obtaining a single advertisement for his paper. Disheartened but still determined, he resumed his efforts on the following Monday, and before the day closed he had obtained his first order for advertising. It amounted to $200 and entitled him to a commission of $50.

Tʜᴇ Fᴏᴜɴᴅɪɴɢ ᴏғ N. W. Aʏᴇʀ & Sᴏɴ

In less than a year Ayer had earned $1,200 in commissions, and his employers had offered him $2,000 a year for his services. He promptly refused it. Having acquired a firsthand view of advertising during his brief business experience, Ayer had concluded that the advertising agency offered the best future for his talents. At the same time, to gratify his innate Yankee passion for independence, he had resolved to establish his own business. Accord-

ingly, on April 1, 1869, after persuading his father to join him at
the close of the school year, F. W. Ayer started his own advertising agency in Philadelphia.[12]

In this event there was a neat reciprocity. The first advertising agency, as we have seen, was born in the bustle of Philadelphia's commercial activity. Transferred to New England when
Palmer opened a branch office in Boston, it had acquired new
functions. And it was but just recompense, perhaps, that in Philadelphia a New Englander — Yankee to the bone — should develop the agency into its present form and its present orientation
in the business structure.

There is no doubt about the courage which the venture required. F. W. Ayer was barely twenty-one and had had less than
a year's experience in the business world. His father, now in
chronic ill health, could contribute to the new enterprise little
energy, limited business ability, and no money whatever. The
only capital available for the undertaking consisted of $250 which
F. W. Ayer had saved during his work for the *National Baptist*.[13]

From many points of view the year 1869 was not a propitious
time for a new business venture. The South was in the midst of
the agony and confusion of Reconstruction; and even the North,
only partially recovered from the economic and social disruption
of the Civil War, had experienced a deceptive flush of postwar
activity which was beginning to fade. Prices were drifting downward, and the disputes about greenbacks and the resumption of
specie payments injected additional uncertainty into the many
problems of the business man.

At the same time, perplexing economic and social changes of
the greatest magnitude were in progress throughout the land. Under the impact of science, invention, and enlarged opportunity,
revolutions were taking place in agriculture and industry, commerce and finance, transportation and communication — indeed,
in every phase of human activity. Over the western world and
especially in the United States a heightened spirit of enterprise
had arisen, and new energies were advancing. Towns were growing into cities, small firms into large corporations, general workers into specialists, all at an unprecedented rate. The surge of
population westward and the growing flood of immigrants from

Europe were visible evidence of one phase of the growth of the nation.

Rapid expansion, feverish activity, ceaseless change, alarming complexity in every walk of life — how in all this confusion could an inexperienced youth chart a course of action? To a timid man the prospect must have seemed utterly bewildering. But to a man of courage and enterprise the very enlargement of economic life meant opportunity. In the economic organization that was growing up in America after the Civil War, the rôle of advertising was to become a more vital one. There was to be almost unlimited opportunity, as well as profits commensurate with the risks and efforts involved.

The truth is, of course, that no man could see all the grim complexities of the situation as we look back upon them today. F. W. Ayer could see only the immediate task or opportunity before him and pursue there his own advantage to the best of his ability and resources. It may well be that he faintly glimpsed the new products seeking markets, the new markets wanting goods, and the growing need to bridge the ever-widening gap between producer and consumer. The only thing really clear to him in 1869, however, was a chance to make profit. As he himself later admitted, he "was simply anxious to get business, place it and get money for it, doing this in such a way that the advertisers would rather I should have it again than anyone else, and the publishers rather it should come from me than from anyone else." [14] If the future seemed uncertain or confused to him, he gave no sign of hesitation. Ayer had the courage of youth, boundless confidence in himself, and an abiding faith in the benevolence of God.

To his new business Wayland Ayer gave the name which it bears today — N. W. Ayer & Son. Undoubtedly this was meant to be a sincere and lasting tribute to his father. I suspect, however, that the youthful founder of the firm was not unmindful of other qualities in the name. N. W. Ayer & Son sounds bigger and more impressive than F. W. Ayer. For years Wayland Ayer was conscious of his youthful appearance and feared that it might count against him in his relations with other men. [15] In the name he chose for the firm, in the partnership itself, there was a suggestion of experience and stability which would go far to offset this possible handicap. Whatever the explanation of the firm name, it is important to observe that the son alone was the founder of the Ayer agency. The share which N. W. Ayer held in it was given to him by his ambitious and dutiful son, and it soon proved to be a highly profitable gift.

The new firm, as befitted its slender resources, began in a very modest way. It was located at 530 Arch Street, where young Ayer had rented part of a third-story room adjoining the publication office of the *National Baptist*.[16]

How much we should like to know about those early years! — the routine of everyday business, the special problems and difficulties that arose, the first methods of solicitation, the various products advertised, the day-by-day hopes and fears of the young founder, and the main changes which took place. Unfortunately the complete answers can never be forthcoming. The men who did the work are gone; of the thousands of letters they received and wrote only a handful remain; and from the anecdotes and recollections which have come down we can glean only a limited amount of dependable information. To the present-day researcher's dismay, tons of records were long ago destroyed for lack of storage space.

There is no original material of any kind for the first year of the firm's history; and for most of the period before 1900 the chief reliable source is a collection of some fifty ledgers — great, heavy volumes with crumbling leather covers, filled with millions of accounting entries. But the perpetual handicap of the historian blocks our path to understanding them; important records are missing. Entries in ledgers are made from journals and other records of original entry which briefly explain the transactions concerned, and the journals covering this period of Ayer history have long since disappeared, save for a single section covering the months from April to December, 1878. For the most part, therefore, much-needed explanations are missing, and the real meaning of many of the facts contained in the ledgers is hidden from us. Even the most skilled accountant has difficulty in extracting any useful knowledge from the bald terms "To Sundries" or "By Sundries." Still, the ledgers contain hard facts and dates beyond dispute as a framework for the rest of the available data, and when the entries are illuminated by outside information they become invaluable.

It is fortunate that someone, early in the history of N. W. Ayer & Son, conceived the idea of putting into scrapbooks newspaper clippings, an occasional letter, firm advertisements, examples of advertisements inserted for customers, and various odd bits of material relating to the business and, occasionally, to its competitors. By fitting together the pieces of information to be gleaned from the dusty ledgers, the tattered scrapbooks, and the somewhat battered stories and traditions which have been handed down, with facts gathered from a few outside sources, it is possible to construct something like an adequate history of the early years of N. W. Ayer & Son.

According to an advertisement printed in 1877, the Ayer agency entered on its career with a list of eleven religious newspapers, to which it expected to confine its efforts.[17] One of them was undoubtedly the *National Baptist,* and the others were probably the *Episcopalian,* the *Lutheran Observer,* the *Presbyterian,* the *Catholic Standard,* the *Reformed Church Messenger,* the *Christian Instructor,* the *Methodist Home Journal,* the *Episcopal Register,* the *Christian Recorder,* and the *Friends Review.*[18]

Such a list was much more appropriate for an advertising agent of the period than might appear to a modern reader. The already strong religious predilections of the nineteenth century had been stimulated, after the Civil War, by the lyceum, the Chautauqua, the cause of temperance, the preaching of Henry Ward Beecher and Phillips Brooks, and the sensational evangelism of Moody and Sankey. All these whetted the public appetite for religious publications of a popular nature. Suitable periodicals accordingly appeared in large numbers; and their existence, like that of the secular newspapers, ultimately depended upon advertising.[19]

The religious weekly, indeed, was a favorite advertising medium of the latter half of the nineteenth century. In many homes it provided the principal reading material; it occupied the place now monopolized by the popular magazine and was read from cover to cover in the absence of livelier printed attractions. The advertiser, moreover, could assume that such a paper went mainly into the homes of hardworking, substantial citizens, who spent no

money on frivolity or drink, and therefore could afford to buy
comforts and luxuries. In spite of the obvious fertility of this
field, however, agents had generally neglected the Philadelphia
religious papers until F. W. Ayer began to exploit them.[20]

AGENCY WORK AND ITS REWARDS, 1869–1878

The work of the Ayer agency was, in simple terms, soliciting
advertisements from advertisers and placing them in the publications with which it had business dealings. Outwardly, then, Ayer's
work as agent differed from his previous work as solicitor only
in that he represented eleven papers instead of one. There were
other differences, however, which are important from the point
of view of economic functions and more complicated to describe.
As representative of the *National Baptist* Ayer had done nothing
but solicit advertisements, an employee with but a single function
to perform. The reproduction of the advertisements, the billing,
the collecting, and the bookkeeping had been primarily the affair of the *National Baptist* and its advertisers. When Ayer set
himself up as an agent, on the other hand, he became directly responsible for seeing that the advertisements were properly reproduced in the newspapers, keeping accounts with advertisers, billing them, collecting the money, and paying the publishers. Like
other agents, too, he saved the individual merchant the trouble
and expense of dealing with a number of papers and, at the same
time, reduced the number of firms with which the publisher had
to do business.

The reader might well ask what Ayer gained by the change.
One answer, of course, is that he could get more business for several papers than for one alone and thereby could increase the
income which he derived from commissions. But that is only a
partial explanation. There was, in addition, that independence so
dear to the heart of a Yankee, and there were large profits to be
gained from shrewd buying and selling.

It is interesting to recall in passing that Ayer, like Palmer,
Hooper, and Rowell before him, became a business agent only
after serving his apprenticeship as a specialized employee. To
the question where do middlemen come from and why, this fact
suggests an answer.

Ayer, at the outset, operated an agency which was essentially like those of Rowell, Pettengill, and other contemporary agents.[21] That is to say, Ayer, like his competitors, sought to make a wholesaling and speculative profit in addition to the commission which publishers usually allowed to agents.

In its early years, N. W. Ayer & Son neatly epitomized the preceding history of the advertising agency. A detailed examination of the sources of this firm's revenue will disclose the four principal types of activity described in Chapter I, and show how their combination put the so-called agent in an exceedingly anomalous position. The importance and order of appearance of the four types in the Ayer agency do not correspond to their historical sequence; this does not aid one's grasp of the situation, but it is worthy of note.

The first type of income was derived from Ayer's original arrangement with the eleven religious weeklies. It arose out of the activities carried on in the advertising concession or fourth stage of agency evolution. Ayer was more than an agent for these papers: he had bought, for a lump sum, their entire advertising space. He thus acquired, so to speak, their advertising concessions and was in substance the manager of eleven advertising departments. Indeed, printed cards and billheads exist in which F. W. Ayer (and later various employees of the Ayer firm) is referred to as advertising manager of the paper concerned.[22]

In addition to his work as manager of advertising concessions, Ayer actually assumed financial risks: he speculated in space. Because they preferred a fixed moderate income to an uncertain one, the owners of many publications were willing to sell their entire advertising space to an agent who would handle all the details of selling, billing, and collecting for advertising, together with the credit risks and other uncertainties involved. Ayer was willing to work on this basis, granted advantageous terms, because the potential profits were considerably greater than those accruing from commissions alone. In such cases he was principal rather than agent, and he expected to make an entrepreneurial profit, the reward for organizing, directing, and assuming the risks involved.

An example will show how this worked out. Ayer bought from

a publisher the exclusive use of his advertising columns for one year, paying (say) $3,600 for the right. The exact amount of space at his disposal was apparently not fixed, but there may have been an upper limit. He then established for the paper space rates which he estimated would yield $3,600 plus the usual agency "commission," or a total of about $4,800 for the year. He hoped to obtain more than this amount, however, in order that he might have a return for the extra work and risk involved. The $1,200 would be the reward for his services as "agent," while any sales over the $4,800, less the small clerical expense involved, were entrepreneurial profit.

Thus, the firm account with the *National Baptist* for 1871 shows that Ayer paid $6,400 for the use of the advertising columns of this religious weekly. On each occasion when some of this space was sold, the cost of the space (according to the rates established by Ayer on the basis of the anticipated volume) was credited in this ledger against the $6,400. The difference between that cost and the price received from the advertiser was immediately recorded in the Profit and Loss account. This difference represented the agency "commission" (though it was really a wholesaler's or jobber's profit, since in these transactions Ayer was a principal rather than an agent); and it varied according to the price which was obtained from the advertiser to whom the space was sold. Sometimes it was virtually nothing; in other cases it ran as high as 70 per cent of the gross price; on most transactions it seems to have ranged between 20 and 30 per cent.

At the end of 1871, after taking this profit on each transaction, the firm had a favorable balance of $1,758.98 in the *National Baptist* account for the year. That is, the sums credited as the calculated cost against the $6,400 originally paid exceeded by $1,758.98 the amount actually paid for the space.[23] This was Ayer's speculative and entrepreneurial profit.

Sometimes the firm was not so fortunate. In 1878, for example, the *National Baptist* account showed a small entrepreneurial loss at the end of both six-month periods.[24] Such a loss would result when the agency was unable to sell the amount of space upon which the costs and rates were calculated for the period or had to sell some of it below cost in order to avoid a greater loss.

The fact that profits were calculated both on the individual space transactions and on the space in the publication as a whole indicates, beyond much doubt, that Ayer recognized a difference between the profits arising from the ordinary work of the agency and those arising out of the extra managerial and financial burdens which he assumed as advertising manager for a paper.

Another type of revenue came from the firm's activities in wholesaling space, as distinct from managing a space concession. Ayer anticipated the needs of customers and bought space from a number of publishers in bulk lots which, though they represented only a fraction of the space available in the publications concerned, were still large enough to enable him to get the substantial price advantages. The space was then resold to advertisers on the best terms obtainable.[25] This practice conforms to that of the third or space-wholesaling stage described in Chapter I.

Like the arrangement first described, this one also enabled the publisher to sell his space (in part) to the agency for a fixed sum of money known in advance. By thus sacrificing part of his potential revenue the publisher shifted to the agency a part of the risk of his advertising department. Here, again, Ayer hoped to obtain extra profits to compensate him for the speculative risk and financial outlay involved. His reward was the difference between the cost of the space and the total sum realized from its sale to various advertisers — a wholesaler's profit.

A third type of income was derived from the slightly different activity of space-jobbing. The agency frequently obtained orders for advertising in papers in which it owned no space and with which it had no agreement about rates. Of course, the agency knew the published or "card" rates fixed by the publisher. It likewise had fairly good knowledge of the deviations from those rates which could be obtained by skillful bargaining. In this situation the usual practice was as follows. Ayer, on the basis of his knowledge and experience, calculated how much the space would probably cost him. He then quoted to the advertiser a price as much above this estimated cost as the competitive situation allowed. If his bid won the order, he then sent "advertising proposals" to the publishers, stating that he was prepared to send them an order for advertising if they could accept the rate he offered to pay (usually a figure well under the card rates). Sometimes this first tender was accepted; sometimes there was further bargaining. In any event, Ayer's remuneration on such contracts was the difference between the price obtained from the advertiser and the actual cost of the space after the bargaining had been completed.[26]

Transactions of this third kind belong to the second or space-jobbing stage of agency development and differ in no way from those described by Rowell in the quotation earlier cited.[27] Ayer got as much as possible from the advertiser and then paid as little as possible to the publisher. Here, again, he was acting as principal rather than agent. These transactions, however, differed from the first two types in that there was no buying in advance of customers' needs, no wholesaling. The agency both bought and sold piecemeal, according to the orders it received. It made a contract with the advertiser before buying the space; in other words, it sold short. And, while the proposals generally quoted a price "less the usual agency commission," the agency's remuneration was neither this "commission" nor a profit derived from buying in large quantities, but rather a profit from speculation. It is worth noting, too, that this speculation was not based on any anticipated fall in prices but simply on the agency's superior bargaining power and knowledge of the market for space.

There was still a fourth type of income, arising out of the original work of the advertising agency. The list of papers which an advertiser wanted to use frequently contained publications the advertising space of which was controlled by some agent other than Ayer. A few publishers, moreover, held firmly to their card rates. In both cases the Ayer agency received for the sale of space (or the purchase of it, if you look at the situation from the point of view of the advertiser) a commission fixed by the owner of the space. In such instances alone could the Ayer agency be considered an agency in the true sense of the word — a firm working for others on a commission basis.

It must be noted that the transactions of N. W. Ayer & Son seldom fell neatly into any of these categories. A single order for advertising sometimes involved all four types of space transactions. The agency's compensation for such an order was a blend of managerial, entrepreneurial, wholesaler's, and speculator's profits, return on investments in space, and agency commission. The same was undoubtedly true of other agencies.

In these circumstances it is hardly possible to define the agency's position as a middleman at this time. The functions of Ayer's agency, like its income, show clearly that it occupied a confused and anomalous position between advertiser and publisher. It bought and sold space for itself and others. It persuaded merchants and manufacturers to use advertising and helped them to place it. It saved the advertiser clerical work by placing his advertisements and paying for them. It saved the publisher work by soliciting business, looking after the clerical details, and collecting the bills. It also aided the publishers by advancing money and by assuming credit and financial risks.

Here is a tangle of functions and relationships, in which conflicts of interest and confusion of responsibility were bound to occur. The agent had to reconcile the interests of the publishers (who allowed him commissions) and the advertisers (who ultimately footed the bills and had to be kept satisfied), as well as look out for his own profit. While there were good economic and historical reasons for this complicated situation, it clearly needed to be reformed and clarified.

The first seven years of N. W. Ayer & Son's history provide little indication of far vision, clear-cut policy, or inspired innovation. They show, rather, a young enterprise scrambling to success by whatever path seemed, at a given moment, to provide the best foothold.

The Character behind the Business

At the outset F. W. Ayer alone handled the entire work of the agency. During the day he canvassed for business among Philadelphia merchants. Early in the morning and in the evenings, when there was no chance of getting orders, he wrote up the accounts, conducted all the correspondence, and did the necessary janitor work. There were long hours of trudging around Philadelphia's business district, long hours with pen and paper, infinite detail — a hard job from every point of view. When N. W. Ayer's school closed toward the end of June, the youthful agent received as much assistance as his father's broken health would permit, but this relief was probably more than offset by the expanding volume of business. Since his family lived across the river in Camden and his day was usually too full to permit commuting, Wayland rented a room near his office. There he would turn in to sleep for the few hours which he could snatch from his work.[28]

Every Saturday, however, he crossed to Camden, in order to spend the week end at home and to attend the North Baptist Church of which he was to be an active and valued member. A story has survived which well indicates the kind of men that Wayland and his father were. In 1869 the two were considering which of the Baptist churches in Camden they should attend. At that time the North Baptist Church of Camden was deep in debt, a small church in difficulty. "We'll go there," said N. W. Ayer to his son, "they need us." In the same year the father was made a trustee of the church, and the son became superintendent of the Sunday School, a position which he held for more than fifty years.[29]

Overworked though he was, Ayer always managed to find time for his religious activities. If business compelled him to be away on a Sunday, he left clear and concise instructions for the conduct of services in his absence. Indeed, he carried over into his church work some of his business efficiency, just as he carried over into his business activities some of his piety and religious fervor. The only letter book of his to survive gives a glimpse of the man's personal character in this respect, and is so revealing that I feel justified in quoting an excerpt:[30]

The main department of the [Sunday] school has nearly doubled in numbers since I have been connected with it and although I feel sometimes that the labor is too great and the expense too much for me, still I have not yet been able to break away from it. I tried to last month, but they clung to me so that I had to yield and go on. With all our increase there was only *one* conversion from the school during the year. I can but think that I have a talent to direct the affairs of the school and to conduct its exercises in such a way as to make them interesting and attractive, but I feel that I lack in vital piety, strength as a Christian and power in prayer, and while I try to thank the Lord for the material prosperity He has seen fit to bestow upon us, still the thought "only one conversion" recurs to me continually to make me feel that I am not the man He would see in that position.

Proud before men, humble before God, determined to succeed in everything to which he put his hand — this was the essence of Wayland Ayer's character, and it was as true of him at twenty-three as at any time in his life. Being a business man, he could not help thinking of his church work in terms of quantitative results. Like so many business men of his time, too, Ayer instinctively kept a reckoning with God, and always sought to keep the balance on the right side of the ledger. During the whole of his fifty years as superintendent of the North Baptist Sunday School, he devoted to that work the same careful thought and tireless energy that he put into his business, with corresponding success. In trying to understand Ayer the business man, we must never lose sight of Ayer the churchman. We godless moderns may smile derisively, but their religious faith gave men like Wayland Ayer a strength which most of us would gladly have.

EXPANSION OF ACTIVITIES

The young firm quickly took root and flourished. Before the end of its first year, N. W. Ayer & Son extended operations to include the representation of other papers besides the eleven religious weeklies. The expansion arose out of the needs of customers, according to F. W. Ayer's own account:[31]

One of these men [customers of N. W. Ayer & Son] said to me one day, "I wish I could do more business with you but I do not think it pays me to advertise in the religious papers. If you could give me something like this I would do business with you." He handed me a list of 200 papers in which he was using one inch four weeks for $150. I told him I would take it.

Although I had no idea what this order would cost me, I wanted to make the acquaintance of publishers to learn how business was done. I thought I would have to pay for my experience and the quicker I did it the better. So I wrote these 200 publishers, asking them their price for an inch a month. I received a quick reply from nearly all of them. The highest rate was $12, for which I would get 75 cents, and the lowest one was "whatever you think it is worth. We would like to begin business with you."

I had my choice from whatever I thought it was worth to $12, and I was in for a loss of several hundred dollars on that first order for general newspaper business. But one of the publishers mentioned that they took that advertisement the last time from an advertising firm in Philadelphia. Another said that the advertisement came to them from an advertising firm in New York.

That night I took the Owl train for New York. The sleeper was an ordinary seat in the passenger coach. The train left at midnight and got in at 4 A.M. I had some little time for breakfast before I could see anybody. Then I went to 75 Fulton Street, to call on a firm called Cooley and Dauchy.

Having introduced myself, I asked if they had a list of 200 papers which they offered for $150 an inch a month. They said that they had a list of 1,100 papers of which the 200 comprised one section. I asked whether I could place my advertisement through them and found they would be glad to have it and would give me a commission.

Thus I learned how the business was done and made a little on the transaction.

Other large orders followed, some of which were handled through Cooley & Dauchy and other agents, while the rest were placed directly with the publishers. This enlarged the volume of business, and it soon added to the inside work of the Ayer firm. There were more customers on the books, more publishers to negotiate with, and the stream of accounting entries swelled to a raging flood. The growth of business — said to have been $15,000 for the first year[32] — soon taxed the partners' time and office space to the limit, and in 1870 Ayer moved his business to larger and better-situated quarters on the second floor at 719 Sansom Street. At the same time he hired his first employee, George O. Wallace, who was later to become a partner in the business.[33] Wallace's primary task was to look after the voluminous details of the firm's bookkeeping — a part of its activities which F. W. Ayer heartily disliked.[34] But with only three men available, one of whom was frequently ill and another constantly out of the office in search of business, only a limited amount of specialization was possible.

Another year, and the Ayer agency had more than doubled its

volume and greatly enlarged its scope. The number of customers increased, the amounts they spent through the agency grew larger, and the publications with which the agency dealt increased rapidly in number. The firm had added to the original 11 religious weeklies, until by the end of 1871 it dealt directly with 324 publications — religious, secular, daily, and weekly. Although the publications were concentrated largely in Pennsylvania, New York,

Counting-Room, N. W. Ayer & Son, 1876
733 Sansom Street

and New Jersey, they were also found in the District of Columbia and 27 of the 37 States then in the Union. Through other agents, N. W. Ayer & Son also placed advertising in many additional papers.[35]

Checks were slight and temporary. Late in the fall of 1871, the combined effects of the Chicago fire and an epidemic of small-pox in Philadelphia brought a pause.[36] But by the beginning of 1872 the growing volume of business compelled another move, this time only a short distance away to 733 Sansom Street,[37] and by August it was necessary to hire a second employee.[38] Clearly the boyish ex-schoolmaster was getting on in the world!

The year 1873 was a busy one for the Ayer agency. In spite of the economic troubles of the country, which led to the failure of Jay Cooke and the ensuing period of depression, the volume of the agency's work continued to expand. Indeed, the total business for the year was over $79,000 — nearly double that of 1872, and Ayer had to add four employees to his staff to cope with the increased work.[39] During the course of 1873 the agency's quarters again became inadequate. This time they were expanded to include the entire second floor of the building at 733 Sansom Street, and at least one newspaper editor thought that they were unsurpassed "in elegance and convenience by any other agency in the country." [40]

The year, however, was not without its sorrow. N. W. Ayer, Wayland's father, whose health had grown steadily worse during the preceding winter, died on February 7, 1873. In terms of actual work his part in the founding of the agency had been small. Wayland, however, had been devoted to him, had relied constantly upon him for advice and encouragement, and from the personal letters that he wrote in the months following his bereavement it is clear that he felt the loss of a business counselor no less than that of a father.[41]

The passing of N. W. Ayer raised one of the first questions of policy to be settled. His half of the business was left to his wife. Should the agency be continued with Mrs. N. W. Ayer as a silent partner? The son decided against this and purchased his father's interest. He reasoned that absentee ownership might put pressure upon the firm to consider immediate profit before service to customers and eventually wreck the business. To guard against this possible outcome, he determined that the owners of N. W. Ayer & Son should always be active in its management. This policy has been strictly adhered to down to the present time (1949).[42]

A second policy was determined a few months later. The expanding volume of business and the resultant increase in the number of employees made it difficult for Ayer to give his personal attention to all aspects of the business, especially since he was frequently out of the office in quest of orders. To provide responsible and interested assistance in management, he decided that he should take in George O. Wallace, his first employee, as a partner. He believed, however, that the business should expand from its own earnings rather than from outside capital. He therefore established the policy (likewise continued down to the time of the firm's incorporation) that the incoming partner should not contribute any money to the enterprise, but should pay for his share out of his part of the subsequent earnings of the business. On this basis Wallace was given a one-fourth interest in the firm, and the new partnership was announced on October 1, 1873.[43]

Financial stringency, general hard times, savage competition — nothing interfered with the progress of N. W. Ayer & Son. By 1876 — the year of the Philadelphia Centennial Exhibition — the annual volume had risen to more than $132,000, the staff numbered 20 employees, and the agency claimed that it was prepared to insert advertising in any newspaper published in the United States or Canada.[44]

With all this expansion of volume and activities, the Ayer agency again quickly outgrew its office quarters. It had employees working on three floors of the building at 733 Sansom Street, and larger accommodations were clearly needed. Hearing that the publishers of the Philadelphia *Times* were preparing to put up a new building at the corner of Eighth and Chestnut streets, Ayer immediately made arrangements to occupy all the second and a part of the third floor and had the rooms designed especially for the agency's use. Consequently, in December, 1876, the firm moved into the building which it was to occupy for the next quarter of a century.[45]

In October, 1877, N. W. Ayer & Son took over the advertising agency of Coe, Wetherill & Co., of Philadelphia.[46] This gave Ayer basis for the claim, by right of succession, to ownership of the oldest agency in the country, for Coe, Wetherill & Co. were successors to Joy, Coe & Co., who had bought out Palmer's business.[47] Thus the age of the firm can be traced back to 1841, the founding date of Volney B. Palmer's agency.

Ayer did not, however, take over his competitor for any sentimental reason of date or priority. For some years prior to 1877, Coe, Wetherill & Co. had prospered, but competition, hard times, and the death of Wetherill had combined to put the firm on the verge of bankruptcy.[48] Among its obligations was a fairly large one to N. W. Ayer & Son for advertising which it had placed in Ayer lists. To recover as much of this as possible Ayer arranged to take over the unexpired orders and space contracts on the Coe, Wetherill books.[49] His move cannot, therefore, be regarded as an attempt to curb competition or to expand by taking over another firm. He had already shown his ability to expand without resorting to either of those dangerous expedients, and he was far too much of a Yankee to do things without practical reasons.

While these important developments were taking place, Ayer had also increased the scope of activity within the agency. Following the example of Rowell, Dauchy, and other older agents, he had, as early as 1872, started to supplement his revenue by selling type and ink to publishers in exchange for advertising space in their publications.[50] By this means it was possible to make two profits — one on the space he sold to his customers, and the other on the printers' material which went to the publishers in payment for that space.[51]

In 1874 Ayer again followed the lead of older agencies by putting out *Ayer & Son's Manual for Advertisers,* an annual publication, which contained the various lists of papers for which the agency sought business, together with information about rates and circulation. It also included advertisements for many of the newspapers with which the agency dealt. Using the plan devised by Rowell for his *Directory,* Ayer handled this advertising on an exchange basis. For the cost of the advertisements the publishers credited N. W. Ayer & Son with space in their own papers against any orders that the agency might send them; and accounts were settled by suitable bookkeeping entries when advertisers paid Ayer for inserting advertisements in the publications concerned.[52]

In 1876 the Ayer agency started another publication of a similar character, *The Advertiser's Guide.* This was a quarterly magazine "filled with interesting and instructive reading matter" (mostly short articles on business, odd bits of news, jokes, et cetera, reprinted from various newspapers and magazines), together with material urging the advantages of advertising. It, too, contained the Ayer lists and advertisements for publications, but since it purported to be a magazine of general interest, a subscription price of 50 cents per year was charged — except to those who advertised through the Ayer agency to the amount of five dollars.[53]

Publications like the Ayer *Manual* and *Guide* were a regular part of the agent's stock-in-trade at the time and yielded substantial profits to their owners. They were obviously of limited intrinsic merit and came to be regarded by the publishers of newspapers and magazines as a kind of racket. The publishers felt, often rightly, that they were obliged to insert advertisements in these agency publications in order to maintain the agent's goodwill. A more serious objection can be raised which also applied to the trade in printers' supplies: the fact that the resulting credit on the publishers' books for advertising or printers' supplies undoubtedly gave every agent a temptation to place advertising in particular papers, quite apart from their merits as advertising media, in order to collect the amount due him. There is, however, no evidence that the Ayer agency yielded to the temptation. This matter, in any case, must be considered in the light of contemporary standards; and, in view of the general prevalence of such practices, N. W. Ayer & Son certainly cannot be singled out for criticism.[54]

A further addition to the Ayer agency — one in the direction of economic integration — was made in 1875, when a printing department was installed as a part of the business. Most agencies at the time (and this is true also today) had their work done by independent printers, and this practice had been followed by N. W. Ayer & Son for some years. In 1872 Ayer had tried having his own printing shop, but he abandoned the idea early in the following year, possibly because his volume at the time was insufficient to make the scheme practical. Since 1875, however, the Ayer printing department has been in continuous existence,[55] and the agency itself has set up the advertisements which it places. This is done not only to show the advertiser in advance how his advertisement will look in print, but also to save time, trouble, and mistakes in sending instructions to publishers. It also has helped to bring about improved quality of typography. Even more important in recent years is the fact that the agency can handle the most confidential work (and there is frequent need for this) with complete privacy.

The establishment of the Ayer printing department was therefore of considerable significance, for it meant that the Ayer agency was beginning to have a direct influence upon the final appearance of the advertisements which passed through its hands. This influence was to grow until N. W. Ayer & Son took over the entire work of producing advertising ideas and copy. It also paved the way for the close, confidential relation between agency and client which subsequently emerged.

CHARACTER OF ADVERTISING FIRST HANDLED BY AYER

An examination of the advertisements sent out by N. W. Ayer & Son in the 1870's provides a background against which we can see the marked progress made by the firm in later years. A substantial part of the total business consisted of small, local announcements which a modern agency would consider too trivial to handle — legal notices, boys wanted, dogs lost, offers of board and lodging, secondhand furniture for sale, and the like. In addition to this picayune work, the Ayer agency handled a great deal of business which today it would reject instantly on grounds of character.[56]

The backbone of the typical advertising agency's business in the nineteenth century was patent medicine, and the Ayer firm was no exception to this rule. It advertised sure cures for cancer, for consumption, for fits, for stuttering. It advertised "Compound Oxygen," which cured almost every human ailment; Kennedy's Ivory Tooth Cement, which made "Everyone his own dentist!"; and "Dr. Case's Liver Remedy and Blood Purifier," which would supplant the doctor entirely. Other aids to good living included liver and stomach pads, worm destroyers, cough remedies, antibilious bitters, and cures for gout, rheumatism, deafness, ague, neuralgia, and rupture. "Rock & Rye," for example, was a "Sure Cure for Lung Diseases. $4 per Gal." (a price, incidentally, which closely matches that of Pennsylvania country-distilled corn whiskey in the days of Prohibition). Most ingenious of all, perhaps, was the Pino-Palmine mattress which introduced "into every home, wherever situated, the VERY AROMA WHICH MEDICATES AND TONES THE FLORIDA AIR" and expelled rheumatic and neuralgic pains from the body.

Today such advertisements are at once amusing and shocking. In judging them, however, one must bear in mind the circumstances of the time. The universal human desire for panaceas was as strong in the 1870's as it is today, and there were undoubtedly many persons in the country who would have sought some other basis for a faith cure had patent medicines not been available. I mention this, not to excuse misleading advertisements, but because it is a relevant fact which must not be forgotten.

Bearing in mind the state of the medical profession at the time, we are not surprised that Americans were easily tempted to self-medication. As late as 1870 the head of the Harvard Medical School declared that written examinations could not be given because most of the students could not write well enough.[57] In addition to their deficiencies of talent and training, the doctors were too few to serve the whole nation. A large portion of the population, moreover, lived miles from the nearest physician, good or bad. And many Americans, sickly as a result of faulty diet and bad living conditions, could not have paid for proper medical attention had it been available. This situation provided a golden opportunity for the quack, and he made the most of it. There were also patent medicine manufacturers who were sincere in believing that their product was really good. The result in either case was a great variety of fantastic concoctions, some of them without any physiological effect, others definitely harmful, and perhaps the majority composed largely of alcohol, designed to lull pain by intoxication or satisfy the cravings of "teetotalers."

No one, at that time, attempted to check such enterprises. Laissez-faire, expressed or implied, was the watchword. It would never have occurred to the business man of the day — even a sincerely religious one — to introduce into his business activities a social point of view. Nor did it occur to an agent that he was in any way concerned with the merits of the things advertised, any more than a railroad was concerned with the commodities it carried, or a bank with the source of the money deposited. His

job was simply to buy and sell space. Had he wondered about
their merits, there would have been no means available for a
reliable test.

There were other products besides patent medicines advertised
by the Ayer agency in the 1870's which it would hastily refuse
today — "Lefevre Diamonds — the only perfect facsimile of real
diamonds in the world," mammarial balm, Allen's Anti-Fat pills,
"Ten Dollar Revolvers for $2.50," "Incino" which was guaran-
teed to grow whiskers on the smoothest face in a few weeks,
"Psychomancy — How either sex may fascinate and gain the love
and affection of any person they choose, instantly." Such advertisements, too, must be laid at the door of general public indifference and the lack of a sense of responsibility among business men.

One must remember that the Ayer agency's record in this
respect was no worse, possibly it was even a little better, than
that of competing firms. Ayer undertook this advertising as a
matter of course, because the other agencies did and because
most publications — even the religious weeklies — were glad to
accept it.[58] But there is clear evidence to show that, when he
became convinced that such advertising was wrong, he stopped
handling it.

In happy contrast to the products just described stands a long
list of commodities that have proved their worth and today still
proclaim their merits to an appreciative audience. Famous names
appeared among the Ayer clientèle from the beginning: John
Wanamaker, whose fame was starting to spread far beyond
Philadelphia, was one of Ayer's first customers; Jay Cooke & Co.
in 1871 entrusted some of its financial advertising to the Ayer
agency; and Montgomery Ward & Co., born of the decade's
Granger movement,[59] advertised its mail-order business in the
Ayer religious lists. Equally familiar names included Whitman's
chocolates, Ferry seeds, Pond's Extract, Burnett's flavoring ex-
tracts, Lewis' Perfumed Lye, Blackwell's Durham smoking tobacco ("see that it bears the trade-mark of the Bull"), Lippin-
cott's books, Singer sewing machines, Mason & Hamlin organs,
and Bradstreet's reports.

More interesting even than these are advertisements which
show current trends of American life — most notably, new de-

velopments in agriculture, education, and general living conditions. Seeds and nursery stocks, for example, were widely advertised by Ayer, along with agricultural implements and machinery — hay forks and knives, self-acting cow-milkers, chilled-steel plows, horsepower threshers and separators, grist mills, and tools of all kinds.

Another important part of the business was the advertising of educational institutions — schools, seminaries, academies, "female institutes," colleges, and universities — running the whole gamut from correspondence schools in telegraphy to Harvard College. Owing to his early association with teaching, Ayer had resolved to do his part toward the spread of education. To this end he made a special point, apparently from the very beginning, of encouraging schools and colleges to advertise, and granted them special credit terms so that struggling institutions might pay him when they received their tuition fees — the results of their advertising — in the late autumn rather than at the time of publication in the spring and summer when they were usually short of cash. This policy has been continued down to the present.

Ayer likewise did a large business in advertising books and publications — the religious weeklies, *Godey's Lady's Book, Littell's Living Age, The Saturday Evening Post* (even before Curtis's ownership), and a wide assortment of books like *Free Masonry Exposed, Errors of the Roman Catholic Church, Strong Drink — the Curse and the Cure, The Great Trial of Benj. Hunter for the Cold Blooded Murder of John M. Armstrong, Stanley in Africa, How To Be Your Own Lawyer, Manners That Win* ("a new book on society and the rules that govern it"), dictionaries, Bible concordances, and tracts of all kinds.

During this same decade N. W. Ayer & Son placed the advertising for many commodities that have come to be considered typically American — metal screens against flies and mosquitoes, improved stoves and gaslight mantles, lamps, washing-machines, portable bathtubs, knitting-machines, churns, butter-workers, refrigerators, steam engines, and water turbines — a wide miscellany of manufactured goods.

There is no way of appraising accurately the economic services performed by the Ayer agency at this time, but their existence cannot be denied. Even small factories depend upon wide market areas; to reach these markets through the medium of traveling salesmen would have been far too expensive, in many cases utterly impossible. Advertising — with all its faults — was indispensable, and the advertising agency was the most efficient method of getting advertisements before the people.

PUBLICATIONS USED BY AYER

The publications in which this advertising was placed provide similar points of interest, historical and reminiscent. Some of them are still familiar names: the Boston *Evening Transcript*, the New York *Herald*, the Chicago *Tribune*, the Philadelphia *Inquirer*, the Baltimore *Sun*, *Harper's Weekly*, and the Springfield *Republican*, to mention only a few. The great bulk of the advertising, however, went into religious and local papers, now in the limbo of crumbling yellow paper which recalls modern America in its lusty and undiscriminating youth. Most of their names are now of little interest or significance. Over and over again the titles *Journal*, *Times*, *Chronicle*, *Gazette*, *Ledger*, *Post*, *Advertiser*, and *Telegraph* appeared, as they do today. Every religious denomination had its *Banner* or *Standard*, its *Herald* or *Advocate*, its *Review* or *Recorder*, its *Instructor* or *Messenger;* and some sects managed to have them all!

But among the hundreds of publications were names with a bolder character and an arresting appeal, reflecting the era of individualistic journalism and numerous public causes to which some of them belonged — the Nashville *Banner of Peace*, for example, or the Cape May *Ocean Wave*, the Belvidere (N. J.) *Apollo*, The Austin *Texas Ploughboy*, the Dayton *Herald of Gospel Liberty*, the West Chester (Pa.) *Jeffersonian*, the Bellefonte (Pa.) *Democratic Watchmen*, the Phoenixville (Pa.) *Independent Phoenix*, the San Francisco *Golden Era*, the Boston *Pilot*, the Worcester *Spy*, and the Pottsville (Pa.) *Emerald Vindicator*. Among the publications, too, were foreign language papers, such as the *Wahrheits Freund* of Cincinnati, *Der Sendbote* of Cleveland, the *Neue West* of Philadelphia, and *L'Aurore* of Montreal.[60]

Of the hundreds of papers with which N. W. Ayer & Son dealt in those days, all but a handful have gone down before the over-

whelming tide of national and metropolitan interests, the economies of mass production, and the general standardization of journalism. A few of them were good, but most were appallingly bad.
They did, however, reach the common people; and they played
a part in spreading information and culture (of a kind) in this
country, a part which is easily overlooked. Advertising was their
main support; and, in so far as it made them possible, advertising
has shared indirectly as well as directly in the molding of the
American mind.

CHAPTER III

BEGINNING OF THE OPEN CONTRACT, 1875–1880

THE YEAR 1875 was a crucial one for N. W. Ayer & Son and, indeed, for all the advertising agents in America, though they did not then realize the fact. The advertising agency was, by this time, established as a definite and important part of the economic machinery of the age. N. W. Ayer & Son, beginning modestly, had prospered mightily, as had other agencies of the day. But it had gone about as far as initiative, activity, and youthful enthusiasm could take it. Only by adopting a clear-cut, progressive policy could the firm forge further ahead. The time had come for drastic stocktaking and the establishment of the entire advertising industry on a firmer basis.

NEED FOR A GENERAL REFORM OF THE AGENCY BUSINESS

In 1875 N. W. Ayer & Son was still making a net profit of nearly 15 per cent on the volume handled, and this, considering the poor business conditions that followed the panic of 1873, might be regarded as a triumph for Ayer. Yet the rate of net earnings had been declining steadily since 1871, until in 1875 the dollar profits barely rose above the previous year's figure, in spite of a volume increase of 20 per cent.[1] This trend must have aroused grave doubts as to the continuance of profits and focused Ayer's attention not only on the operations of his individual firm but also on the general position of the agent. A shrewd observer could see that agents were in serious danger of alienating both parties upon whom their existence depended, namely, the publisher and the advertiser.

About this time publishers were beginning to wonder — and with considerable justification — how the typical agency could properly represent their interests. Nearly every agent had purchased large amounts of space in a few papers which he was bound, in the interests of his own investment, to urge upon advertisers. Even though this source of bias was removed, the agent would still be far from a satisfactory representative. He could hardly devote himself to the best interest of any individual paper when he was selling space in hundreds of papers, many of which competed with one another for advertising. And because of the variation in the size of the "commission" allowed, the agent was naturally suspected of favoring the publications which granted the higher rates. The temptation existed beyond any dispute; and, in the absence of any accepted professional standards, probably few agents thought of resisting it. For these reasons some of the more thoughtful publishers were beginning to feel that their interests could be properly advanced only if an agent confined his efforts to one or at most to a very few papers.[2]

In addition, the agents (Ayer included) further alienated publishers by their wrangling for special rates and favors. From this it might appear that the agent was operating in the advertiser's interests; actually, he was merely operating as best he could in spite of the advertiser. Each agent sought lower rates solely in order to underbid his rivals, and advertisers naturally encouraged such competition by demanding bids from many agents on every contemplated order for advertising. Thus the advertiser bore down on the agent; and, if the agent could not force the publisher to yield in turn, he suffered a "squeeze" which sometimes ruined him. Many publishers realized that an agent who had won an order for space in particular papers had to pay the price they demanded or break his contract. Wise agents accordingly tried, though without much success, to keep their commitments secret.[3] There was, of course, a limit to the concessions which a publisher could make without ruining himself, and sufficient resentment and criticism existed to indicate that the agent frequently tried to overstep this limit.[4] Here, too, it was obvious that the interests of agents and publishers were in conflict, in spite of the commission or discount which the publishers allowed to agents.

Relations of agents with advertisers were likewise in jeopardy. From Palmer's time onward, the agent had encouraged adver-

tisers to look to him for information and advice about the
thousands of papers which might be used for advertising. But
advertisers, like publishers, had discovered that he was not always
to be trusted — certain publications yielded him larger profits
than others and this special inducement tended to warp his
judgment.

It was almost inevitable that an agent should favor those
publications in which he had bought space wholesale or, if he
owned no space, those papers which allowed him the largest "commission." Sometimes he tried to persuade the advertiser to use
one paper rather than another simply in order to make a larger
profit. At other times more was at stake: in order to get the
advertiser's business the agent had made his bid so low that his
problem was to avoid an actual loss. Suppose, for example, that
the agent had made a successful but very low bid on an order
calling for the use of a hundred specified papers. He would then
try, on one pretext or another, to induce his customer to make
two or three substitutions in the list, and would see to it that the
substituted papers yielded him enough revenue to convert the
whole transaction into a profitable one. As Ayer himself later
described the situation, when an advertiser asked for bids on an
order, the first aim of his competitors "was to get our papers off
and theirs on, and ours was, if we came first, to keep ours on, or if
we came later, to get theirs off and ours on, by making a proper
substitution to the [alleged] advantage of the advertiser!" [5]

Some agents, needless to say, resorted to trickery rather than
persuasion in making substitutions. And there were other practices which the advertiser had to guard against. An agent could
make a handsome profit simply by giving nine lines of space
where ten were due, or nine insertions of an advertisement when
ten had been promised. Unless the advertiser checked the published advertisements carefully — a large task by itself — he was
in constant danger of being cheated by the agent or the publisher.
There is no evidence that the Ayer agency was ever guilty of anything worse than trying to persuade an advertiser to use papers
on its own lists rather than those on the lists of other agents.
Agents as a class, however, came to be regarded with distrust, and

N. W. Ayer & Son was tainted with the general odium even when its practices were beyond reproach.[6]

Questionable practices among advertising agencies arose, to some extent, out of the moral obtuseness which characterized so much of American business after the Civil War. Graft, corruption, and sharp dealings were widespread. The Crédit Mobilier episode was only one outstanding example of scandals which took place in every part of the country on a smaller scale. It is clear, moreover, that such evils were not confined to situations in which the paths of private enterprise crossed those of politics. They existed in business dealings which had nothing to do with government officials.[7]

On the whole, however, the trouble in the advertising business seems largely to have been the outcome of the agent's equivocal position. Both publisher and advertiser were aware that he was really an independent middleman seeking his own interests rather than theirs, and yet each entrusted him with work which could properly be handled only by a deputed and responsible agent. Why they did so is not altogether clear. It may have been because of the force of strongly entrenched tradition, or because they found difficulty in otherwise obtaining the brokerage services he continued to render. It may be that the advertiser, like the publisher, felt that he was really paying the commission and therefore ought to receive honest agency service. Or the agent himself may have been responsible; he undoubtedly clung to his misleading title and encouraged both publisher and advertiser to look upon him as one working on their behalf.

But no one person or group can really be blamed for the clash of interests which developed. A number of forces were at work, and it is probably correct to say that the situation arose spontaneously out of the callow adolescence of advertising, as its practitioners blindly fumbled to organize the young industry. The agent had started out as a specialist in selling space in a restricted number of papers. He was a special advocate for their use; and, so long as he restricted himself to special pleading, no valid criticism of his efforts could be made. Unfortunately he could not stop at that point. The economic interests of both publisher and advertiser, to say nothing of his own profits, compelled him to give advice to business men about advertising. On the one hand, the publisher leaned heavily upon the agent because advertising paid a large part of his expenses and all his profits. On the other hand, the business man depended upon the agent because he himself did not know how to use advertising. In order to sell space for the publisher, therefore, the agent had to show merchants and manufacturers how to advertise profitably. Yet those two aspects of the agent's work were not in harmony, for the space-seller must urge the merits of the papers which he represents, while the teacher and adviser must urge only the means which, regardless of their ownership, promise to yield the results wanted. The two activities overlap, of course, but they often conflict; and when both were thrust upon the agent, he was in a difficult position.

We must not judge too harshly in this matter. There are still middlemen in business who try to serve two conflicting interests, as the 1929–38 disclosures about banking and security-selling activities abundantly proved. And there is also a good deal of confusion about the interests and obligations of (say) a real-estate or insurance broker who is sought out by the buyer but receives his commission from the seller. Possibly the advertising agency business of the 1860's and 1870's was worse because, since advertising is intangible and the results have always been difficult to trace, the inexperienced business man could hardly be a competent judge of the value of the advertising space which he purchased. This circumstance undoubtedly encouraged sharp practice among agents. Whatever the reason, as matters stood, the position of the agent was steadily being undermined.

ORIGIN OF THE AYER CONTRACT, 1875–1876

F. W. Ayer seems to have given the confused and unsound situation of the advertising agent no particular thought until, shortly after the death of his father, an event took place which sharply challenged him. An older man for whom he had great respect called one day (the date is not known, but it was probably 1874 or early 1875) and asked for a private interview. He said that he had come to respect young Ayer for his own personal qualities.

He regretted, however, that he could have no respect for the business in which Ayer was engaged.

"What is an advertising agent?" this friend demanded. "Nothing but a drummer, and he never will be anything else!" He went on to say that he could introduce Ayer to a firm of recognized standing in which Ayer would have a chance to establish himself.

That interview hurt. Ayer often said later that he felt as if a knife had been thrust into him. There were things about his business that were not ideal, he knew; but his heart was in it, and the thought that it was not respectable in the eyes of others came to him as a sudden and unpleasant shock. Ayer kept his composure, however, thanked his friend for his interest, and requested time to consider the matter. He was afraid even to ask what the proposed connection might be lest the knowledge influence his judgment.

On the following day Ayer went to report his decision. "The proposition you made does not appeal to me," he said. "I have put my hand to this plow, and by the help of the Lord I am going to finish the furrow. Before I have finished, if we both live, you are coming to me some day and say that you respect me for my business as well as for myself." As Ayer himself later avowed:[8]

That was really for me the beginning of this business. I said to myself, "I will not be an order taker any longer. I will not take orders for these lists of magazines and lists of newspapers and get my commission out of them and be satisfied just to make money. I will have a business, I will mean something to somebody every time I take any business, and I will have clients rather than people who just give me orders."

The young advertising agent had made up his mind that somehow he was going to reform his business. What was to be done was not clear in his mind, but with an unshakable faith in the future and in his own ability, Ayer made the resolution.[9]

Meanwhile an older agent, George P. Rowell, had also started to think about the agency business. He seems to have been seriously concerned about the constant danger of being "squeezed" between advertiser and publisher. After considering the whole matter at length, he concluded that the advertising agent should represent the advertiser *as well as the newspaper,* and in January,

1875, he announced a new policy for his agency. "One thing we clearly perceived . . . ," his statement ran, "that advertising agencies succeeded best when studying the interests of advertisers not newspapers. . . . We have fully decided to announce as a rule for our future guidance (but which we have followed pretty closely for the past three years) that we will not hereafter be a party to any competition for advertising contracts."

PRIVATE OFFICE, N. W. AYER & SON, 1876
733 SANSOM STREET

Rowell's plan, thus introduced to the public, was in brief to take the advertiser into his confidence. There was to be no competing with other agencies for an order: Rowell expected the advertiser to rely on him to get the lowest rates. He was to share with his customer all his information about newspapers — their circulation, reputation, and space rates. In the matter of clerical details, too, he was to aid the advertiser: bargaining with the publishers, placing the advertisements, checking the insertions, and paying the bills. Final decision as to the space and publications to be used, however, was to be left to the advertiser himself. Rowell, in short, was to exchange his function of selling space for one of helping the advertiser to buy space. For this service, however, he was to continue to receive the commission which the publishers allowed.[10]

On the whole, Rowell's plan represented a distinct advance over the prevailing practice among agents. To Ayer, following as it did closely on the recent insult to his choice of a career, it was a challenge; and within a year he had worked out an arrangement undeniably superior to Rowell's. He recognized the validity of Rowell's contention that the agent should cultivate the interests of the advertiser rather than those of the publisher. One feature of the scheme, however, seemed to him to be definitely wrong: Rowell expected to continue to get his remuneration out of the commission allowed by the publishers. How, Ayer wondered, could an agent effectively serve two masters? How could he honestly serve one master while receiving a reward from the other?

As Ayer saw it, Rowell's plan meant in practice that the advertiser hired a confidential employee whose salary was indefinite and unknown to him — whose salary was, in fact, determined by a third party. And that third party, to make matters worse, was selling the very commodity which the confidential employee was buying for the advertiser! Rowell had designed a plan, in short, which was meant to curb competition among agents, but he had done nothing to eliminate the worst evil of the agency situation: the agent's judgment was still bound to be prejudiced in favor of the publisher who allowed the highest commission.

Ayer immediately set to work devising a new basis of operations. He determined to make a sharp break with the existing agency tradition and practice. He would put an end to the prevailing confusion and misunderstanding, to the biased advice, and to the downright trickery which unquestionably existed in the agency business. An agent worthy of the name must represent the interests of someone other than himself. Ayer decided to represent the advertiser. But, unlike Rowell, he would establish the relationship on a clear-cut, logical foundation. The advertiser should know exactly what Ayer — his agent — paid for space after all commissions, rebates, and special price concessions had been deducted from the card rates. He should, moreover, know exactly what Ayer received for his services. To remove any possible cause of misunderstanding it would be arranged that the advertiser should pay a commission to Ayer for the work that Ayer performed in his behalf. In this way responsibility would be clearly fixed, and the compensation would be determined exclusively by Ayer and the advertiser who hired him.

Two provisions were necessary to make the plan fair to the agent. First, competition with other agents should be eliminated by an agreement covering a definite period of time. In this way there would be an end to the disputes which arose every time the advertiser wanted to do some advertising, and the agency would be able to gain a little perspective on the advertiser's interests and its own. The merits of the agency might then be judged, not by the few cents' difference between its bid and the bids of rival agents before the advertising appeared, but rather by the results which it obtained; and these results would be likely to improve from year to year as the agency accumulated experience in handling the advertiser's particular problems. Secondly, the compensation agreed upon should be sufficient to permit Ayer to cover expenses and make a reasonable profit.

To prevent "squeezes" and enable Ayer to bargain with publishers to the best advantage, the plan would have to provide for an "open" contract. That is to say, the specifications for a campaign would be left flexible, open to change, in order to permit the dropping from the list of any paper which held out for too high a price. This feature would also enable the advertiser to alter his plans as market situations changed. In short, as in Rowell's plan, the advertiser would make all final decisions, receive all the benefit of Ayer's knowledge of the publications, their rates, and their bargaining positions, and Ayer would become a space-buyer rather than a space-seller. But, unlike Rowell, Ayer would take his pay from the men for whom he worked.

First Ayer Open Contract, 1875–1876

Having worked out these revolutionary ideas fairly well in his own mind, Ayer decided to discuss them with an advertiser. An opportunity soon arose, apparently late in 1875.[11] For two years the Ayer agency had been placing the advertising of Dingee & Conard, a firm of rose-growers in West Grove, Pa. Previously this firm had done its advertising through Rowell, but Ayer had succeeded in underbidding him. The third year's business was just opening and the list was about to be submitted for competitive bids. Meeting Conard on the street one day, Ayer seized the chance. "Mr. Conard," he began, "I suppose if we are underbid twenty-five cents, the other fellow will get the business, will he not?"

"Yes," replied Conard, "don't you think he ought to?"

"I don't know any reason why he shouldn't, and I couldn't complain if he did," was the reply. "However, I would regret it greatly."

Conard said he would regret it too. "Our relations have been very pleasant and I should be very sorry to have somebody else get the business, but I don't know of any other way than to go right ahead on this basis because we must have the most that the money will buy."

"Well," Ayer resumed, "may I say, Mr. Conard, that that is not the way to get it? You have put us in a position in which we have to protect ourselves. We want the lowest rate for our protection; the other agent wants the lowest rate for his protection. We do make a profit on your business but we do it in spite of you. You put us in competition with you, working to get the most money out of you we can. Then after we have got the business we put ourselves in competition with the publisher in order to get the most out of him. If we can, we send this business out for six insertions and get him to give seven; or charge you for 25 lines and get him to take it for 24. That is our profit. You are such a close dealer that about the only way we can make any profit is by cutting corners like that."

"How would you want to do it?" asked Conard.

"I think we ought to be your advertising department," Ayer replied. "I think you ought to come to us for advice in the preparation of your list. We ought to tell you something about the papers to be put on — and you ought to give us a better reason than ours if any paper is not put on. Our judgment as to the choice ought to be worth a good deal to you, and the difference of a few dollars in the price of it would not affect the condition particularly."

Conard objected that his firm had to be protected from an overcharge.

"Well, let's see how far we can agree," suggested Ayer. "Would you be willing to agree that we ought to make a profit?"

"Yes," said Conard, "I would."

"Would you be willing to agree how much profit we should make?"

"I don't know," was the reply, "I might, but I don't know whether you would or not."

Then Ayer countered, "As to what you think would be a proper profit for us to make — a gross profit on the handling of your business — could we agree on that basis?"

To this proposal Conard consented. Before the close of the interview it was agreed that the Ayer agency should, as an experiment, place the Dingee & Conard advertising for a year at the lowest prices that could be obtained from the publishers, and that for this service it should receive a commission of $12\frac{1}{2}$ per cent of the actual cost of the space.[12]

Thus, late in 1875, the Ayer open-contract-plus-commission plan was initiated, and in January, 1876, the first orders for space on this new basis were sent out to publishers. This first contract was, however, only the embryo of the ultimate Ayer plan; its rounding-out was a matter of long development following the slow realization of the larger implications and possibilities of the basic idea. Several problems, indeed, arose immediately. In the first place, the cost of handling advertising had not been carefully analyzed, and it was not certain that the $12\frac{1}{2}$ per cent commission would cover all the agency expenses involved and still allow a reasonable net profit. By way of further experiment, other advertisers were persuaded to make similar contracts at different rates — one at 8 per cent, one at 10 per cent, one at one-ninth of the cost (11.1 per cent), and at least one other at $12\frac{1}{2}$ per cent.[13] In view of the fact that Ayer's expenses had to be paid out of them, these rates were remarkably low, for in 1875 Ayer's *net* profit after all expenses was 14.9 per cent for the business as a whole.

Ayer's experiment with rates of commission was apparently not a very scientific one. There is no evidence to indicate that the firm made any precise calculation of the cost of handling the advertising for different customers. Indeed, with the bookkeeping methods which the Ayer agency used anything like a precise reckoning of costs per customer would have been impossible to obtain. Ayer must have judged the experiment by personal observation and rough estimates. Within a year the firm decided that any business handled at less than 10 per cent was unprofitable, and in July, 1878, at least one new contract was made at 15 per cent. For sentimental reasons the Dingee & Conard advertising, a comparatively small account in later years, was long kept on a basis of 12½ per cent, but shortly after 1878 the rate for all other customers who agreed to the arrangement was stabilized at 15 per cent.[14]

In addition to fixing the rate of commission to be charged, there were other aspects of the new plan to be worked out. Should it be applied to all customers? Should N. W. Ayer & Son, as Rowell proposed doing, refuse to bid in competition? If this issue ever arose, Ayer decided to continue bidding against other agents whenever he had to, for until after 1900 a considerable portion of his business was taken upon the competitive basis.[15] This seems to have been true also of Rowell's agency, in spite of Rowell's original announcement to the contrary.[16]

The position apparently was that the agency needed every dollar's worth of business that it could get on an acceptable basis, and, if the advertiser chose to refuse the logical plan which was offered to him, that was his concern and his loss. One must bear in mind that N. W. Ayer & Son, even with an obviously superior basis for relations with customers, had still to compete with other agencies for business. To some advertisers the open contract made a convincing appeal. From other firms only the lowest bid on an estimate would receive consideration, and Ayer had either to bid in competition for their business or give up all hope of getting it.

It is obvious that the open-contract plan could not be put into general use until the prevailing suspicion of agencies was overcome, for the advertiser had to trust Ayer to charge the true net costs and give him the benefit of all discounts and inside prices.

Some advertisers, having had unfortunate experience with other agencies, were chary about placing so much confidence in N. W. Ayer & Son, in spite of the fact that its owner was a prominent churchman.

The Ayer agency, on the other hand, hesitated to trust some of its customers with its confidential information about rates. Like its competitors, N. W. Ayer & Son had special rates with many publications, from which it gained a decided advantage for itself and its customers. To a large extent the continuation of those special rates depended upon the strict maintenance of secrecy. The moment another agent learned about them, he, too, would demand them from the publishers concerned, and the Ayer advantage would be lost. Since the open-contract plan involves the disclosure of net prices to the customer, it has always been a part of the Ayer contract that the advertiser should keep all rates strictly confidential. In the early days of the plan, therefore, the agency could not offer to do business on this basis unless it was reasonably certain that the advertiser could be trusted to keep this part of the agreement.[17]

Years later, in looking back upon that first agreement with Dingee & Conard, Ayer said that the adoption of the scheme put an end to ready-made advertising and began, for the first time, made-to-measure advertising — campaigns designed to fit a particular customer's needs.[18] This was true, but it came later as a long-time result rather than as the immediate consequence of the plan. From all the contemporary evidence it is clear that Ayer's first idea was to put his own business on a sound and honest basis. The immediate result of the adoption of his plan was to give N. W. Ayer & Son a strong selling point in soliciting business from advertisers and to place emphasis upon winning steady customers rather than upon individual orders.

In putting his business on a clear-cut, honest basis, however, Ayer inevitably opened new lines of agency development. Until 1876 the agent had been a middleman dealing in a commodity. Henceforth he was to deal in service and to grow into an expert on advertising, offering professional services which included many things besides the expert purchasing of space.

It was not that a whole new philosophy of the agent's functions was suddenly born. Rather the Ayer plan called for a new point of view which inevitably led the agency in a new direction. Buying space at the lowest net cost for the advertiser meant buying for him wisely — in terms of ultimate profits rather than first costs. This, in turn, led to a consideration of the advertiser's particular needs — the product he had to sell, its market, and the means of communicating with the people who might buy it.

It requires no very deep analysis to see that Ayer now stood to gain most in the long run by making his customer's sales (and therefore his appropriation for advertising) grow soundly, profitably, and continuously. Consequently Ayer's chief concern was to make advertising produce favorable results for his customers. He had a real inducement to offer to his customers any service that would make their advertising more effective. The door to the service agency was open.

Beginning of a Lifelong Friendship

The open contract was one of the main foundation stones of F. W. Ayer's success. But, while Ayer devised the plan, its amplification and ultimate triumph owed much to the efforts of Henry Nelson McKinney, who was admitted to partnership on January 1, 1878. Like Wallace before him, McKinney brought no new capital into the business. His contribution was rare sales ability, unlimited faith in the power of advertising, and a great enthusiasm for the open-contract plan — a contribution so great that many observers used to attribute to him the success of N. W. Ayer & Son. This high estimate, as will appear later, was an exaggeration; but, beyond all question, McKinney's importance in the Ayer agency was second only to that of F. W. Ayer himself.

In their work for the firm the two men supplemented one another to such a remarkable extent that it is almost impossible to arrive at a fair estimate of their separate contributions. In their careers, also, a striking parallel exists. In childhood both had experienced a strongly religious environment, brief and irregular schooling, and the need to face the world early in life — a need met by both men with self-confidence, idealism, and faith. The background of the two men is worthy of note because it goes far to explain their unusual energy and their achievements. Like the other leaders of their time, Ayer and McKinney were strong because they were sure of themselves and their work. Forced to shift for themselves in youth, they quickly acquired resourcefulness, self-reliance, and faith in the idea that God's world held ample scope for their abilities. Their environment combined with these qualities to foster ambition. Their religious training sanctioned the determined individual effort and thrift which necessity thrust upon them. And, for all the difficulties which confronted business during the long period 1873 to 1897, their business world clung to the philosophy of individualism, prized material progress, and assumed that its foundations were sound and its opportunities unlimited. Full of assurance, in harmony with the times, and confident of Divine approval, Ayer and McKinney were spared the doubts and fears which sap our strength today.

Because McKinney played so large a part in the history of N. W. Ayer & Son, we must turn aside for a few paragraphs in order to trace his youth. The son of an American missionary, McKinney was born in Natal, British South Africa, on December 8, 1849.[19] Owing to the circumstances of his boyhood his education was entirely in the hands of his mother. The life of a missionary in Natal at that time, of course, involved severe physical hardships, and his mother died when he was but twelve. Shortly thereafter his father, broken in health, abandoned his calling and returned to the United States.

For a short time the family lived in Binghamton, N. Y., where young McKinney had his first and only term in a public school. This was followed by a term in Professor Eastman's Business College at Poughkeepsie — an institution which a contemporary described as "one of the marvels of the times and having more students than the Universities of Oxford and Cambridge, England, combined!"[20] To his everlasting regret, this was all the formal schooling that McKinney ever received. His father remarried, and, in an effort to regain his health, took up truck-gardening at Vineland, N. J.

The boy accompanied the family. Not for long, however; truck-gardening was not to his taste, and his relations with his stepmother were not happy. He was ambitious to get on in the world, he liked to meet people, and he had a decided talent for winning

HENRY NELSON McKINNEY

THE TIMES BUILDING, PHILADELPHIA, 1876

their confidence and friendship. In April, 1866, he decided to leave home and seek a career in Philadelphia.

When he stepped off the Market Street Ferry, Henry McKinney had nothing in the world except the clothes on his back and fifty cents in his pocket — a boy of sixteen with no experience, no job, and not even one acquaintance in the city. In an era of self-made men these circumstances were regarded as a favorable start. Before the end of the day he had obtained work as bookkeeper for the Presbyterian Board of Publication. After a short time he was promoted to selling books for the organization, a task well suited to his abilities and one which helped to prepare him as an advertising man.

One day, after he had served in this capacity about three years, McKinney overheard one of the principals of the Board decline a proposal to publish a book of the type which found greater vogue a half century ago than now, namely, a treatise hostile to a religious group. He personally was unusually tolerant of faiths other than his own, but here was an opportunity to start in business for himself. Having accumulated some savings, he immediately offered to undertake the publication. His proposal was promptly accepted, with the result that, at the age of nineteen, he suddenly found himself launched in the book-publishing business.

During the six years which followed, McKinney was the principal member of three different publishing houses in succession, and not one of the three was a financial success. He could sell with the best of men, but it was simply not in him to give a business concern the close managerial supervision which assures profits — a fact to be remembered in estimating McKinney's contribution to N. W. Ayer & Son. When his partner disappeared with all the available cash, the last of these ventures came to an end and left McKinney penniless.

Since the nation was still suffering from the crash of 1873, McKinney's chances of soon finding a good position were distinctly poor. However, one opening did present itself. For several years he had been advertising his books through N. W. Ayer & Son; and, since the agency was the principal creditor, he made Ayer the assignee to wind up the affairs of his company. When this had been accomplished, Ayer, partly as a personal favor, gave McKinney a job as clerk and bookkeeper in his agency at $15 a week (December, 1875).[21]

Not long after the new connection had been formed, Ayer summoned McKinney for a conference. He explained that he wanted to avoid any possible misunderstanding of the situation. He fully realized that McKinney had previously held better positions than the present one and that, naturally, he wanted to get ahead. Ayer wanted to have it definitely understood, however, that there was no prospect of McKinney's being taken into the firm as a partner. His services were satisfactory and Ayer liked him; but, since Wallace had already been made a partner, there would not be room for another. In the circumstances McKinney could do nothing but accept Ayer's statement without comment.[22] Within two years' time, however, he had been taken into the firm and was rapidly surpassing Wallace in importance! Ayer was a determined man, but he could change his mind when there was reason for doing so.

Once McKinney had been hired, it was not long before he showed his real abilities. From time to time, when opportunities for business arose, it happened that he was the only suitable employee available to do the soliciting, and Ayer soon learned that when McKinney went after an order he got it. Moreover, Ayer began to realize that his partner, George O. Wallace, was by nature fundamentally unsuited for soliciting business on the open-contract plan. Wallace belonged to the old school of advertising agents: price was everything to him — not one price, but any price that would get the business. To him the open-contract plan was merely the impractical dream of a pious schoolmaster. Try as he would, Ayer could not make Wallace see that there was anything in the agency business besides the getting and placing of orders for advertising. McKinney, on the other hand, grasped the merits of the open-contract plan at once. It appealed to his sense of honesty, it challenged his imagination, and it gave ample scope for his selling ability.

Appreciating the position, Ayer reversed the work of the two men. McKinney was put in charge of getting business, Wallace in charge of placing it with the publishers. It was a simple solution, an obvious change perhaps, but business history is full of instances in which equally simple and obvious remedies have been overlooked, with disastrous consequences.

Shortcomings of the Ayer Plan as Originally Applied

Ayer had a sound basic idea and also a man especially fitted to promote it. He still had much to do, however, in pruning away rotten branches left by the old system before his own business arrangements would be completely adapted to the new policy. If he realized the full extent of the changes to be made, he must have decided to move slowly, for there was no sudden shift in method or policy.

Ayer had not yet severed old-time connections with the publisher, in spite of his decision to represent the advertiser. He still controlled the space of a number of religious weeklies; he was still saddled with a number of lists based on special purchase arrangements; he still had credit on various publishers' books in return for printing supplies which he had sold them, and for advertising which they had run in his *Manual* and *Guide*. He still had, in short, special interests, special inducements to urge the use of particular publications — financial interests which made difficult any effort to arrive at an impartial choice of advertising media.

The new plan of business contained one defect which survives to the present day and exists in all agencies: the idea of basing the charge for services on the cost of space used. This brings about an undeniable motive for urging customers to spend more on space in newspapers and periodicals than sound judgment might warrant. We shall see later that N. W. Ayer & Son has seldom, if ever, yielded to this temptation; since, however, it has been the basis of much criticism of advertising agencies, it must receive mention here. The larger the advertiser's total expenditure, of course, the larger the revenue for the agency. There is also a temptation to urge the use of the most expensive publications. Ordinarily it costs the agency no more to deal with a publication whose rates are high than one whose rates are low, and therefore an order to an expensive paper is more lucrative than to a cheaper one. Although they do not necessarily influence actual practice, these points should be borne in mind in appraising methods of agency compensation.

Clearly recorded instances are found in the Ayer experience of warning customers against excessive and profitless advertising. The temptation to urge overspending is offset, at least in part, by the long-run interests of the agency. Excessive expenditures on advertising or the use of unduly expensive publications are bound to eat into the advertiser's profits. If an agency goes very far in this direction, the advertiser is likely to see what is wrong and sever relations. It must be admitted, of course, that it is ordinarily impossible to trace the results of advertising with close accuracy. This fact prevents anyone from judging the merits of borderline cases and certainly would facilitate a certain amount of abuse by agents.

To be sure, this kind of danger exists throughout the business world. Every person who benefits from increased volume of business is subject to similar temptation, and the buyer must always be on his guard against it. It is likely, too, that the business man is better able to appraise wisely the amount he should spend on advertising than the particular way in which he should spend it. To devise any scheme for the agency less open to criticism has proved an exceedingly difficult problem and one which has not yet been solved. In any case, at the time the Ayer plan was worked out, the agency was only beginning to have an influence upon the advertiser's appropriation for sales promotion; accordingly, this aspect of the Ayer plan was not of great importance.

Ayer's failure to cut loose entirely from space-selling was a more serious matter and must, I think, be attributed to the experimental character of the new plan. Cautious in every business move, Ayer could not emphasize the open-contract idea or put it into full force until he was reasonably sure that he could make it succeed. In 1877 his agency was continuing to say to the public, "Our profits are not derived from the advertiser, but from the newspaper publishers to whom we become responsible for all orders sent, and by whom we are credited a percentage on each." [23] And it is clear, too, that the agency did less than half its volume on the open-contract basis in 1878.[24]

EFFECT OF THE AYER PLAN UPON THE ADVERTISING INDUSTRY

When these criticisms have been recorded, however, the fact remains that Ayer's open-contract system, even in its groping start, was a signal contribution to American business. Years of experience were slowly to eliminate the major inconsistencies, as its full implications became manifest. Given the existing circumstances, its theory was sound and businesslike. It brought about an immediate and radical improvement over existing relations between agency and advertiser; and it had a widespread effect upon the entire advertising industry.

Once the news of the Ayer plan had spread, a clear light was thrown upon the anomalies and tangles of conflicting interests and functions which characterized the agent's position in general. Other agents might scoff, but the merits of Ayer's stand were too obvious to be obscured by ridicule or argument. As a result, the structure of the advertising business as a whole began to crystallize into a more definite and logical structure. The realization gradually spread that advertising agents would be obliged to take sides. Many of them followed Ayer's example by going definitely over to the side of the advertiser. They were then known as "general agents" or "advertising agents" and their primary function was to *buy* space. Not many of them accepted the net-cost-plus-commission plan, but all recognized the necessity of looking after the advertiser's interests in buying space and in the effective use of that space.

The agents who did not make this move went in the opposite direction and became, in fact as well as in theory, the agents of the publisher, restricting their business to only a few publications. Henceforth they were known as "publishers' representatives" or "special agents." They received a commission from publishers, as before, and their function was to promote the sale of space in the publications they represented.[25]

These changes took place slowly, as we shall see; once the new plan had been instituted, however, they were inevitable. There could be no middle ground. After the 1880's, to buy or to sell became unavoidable alternatives. The day when one firm could do both was rapidly fading. It may seem strange that the agencies which abandoned the original function of representing the publishers were the ones to retain the original name of advertising agent, while those who resumed the original function took the new name, special representative. The new terminology, however, was more accurate. Henceforth the general advertising agent's work was to advance the general cause of advertising, to seek possible users of space, and to assist them with experienced judgment in the purchase and use of that space. The special representative's job was to plead the cause of particular publications in competition with other advertising media. He could not, from the very nature of his position, promote the general use of advertising. He could only argue that the papers which he represented, if advertising was to be done, were the best for the purpose.[26]

Thus there came to be two middlemen between advertiser and publisher instead of one. Only a few decades before, there had been none at all. The rapid multiplication of middlemen and specialists in this way may be alarming to contemplate, but, given the competitive economic system and the complexities of modern industry and commerce, there can be little question about the value of the services rendered. This new alignment created one new problem which long disturbed the advertising world and still is not wholly a dead issue: What should be the attitude of the publishers toward the general agent, now that they had their own special representatives to whom they granted a commission? Many publishers felt that they no longer received direct benefits from the general agent. Some of them indeed refused to continue the discount or "commission" which they had allowed him in the past, and their representatives frequently sought business from advertisers in direct competition with him.[27]

Eventually the publishers adopted the normal practice of having the special representative seek business from the general agent, allowing commissions to both. This solution, however, was not reached until the 1890's, and we shall have to defer further consideration of it to a later chapter.

It would be an exaggeration to claim that Ayer alone brought about this development in the industry; his plan was admittedly the product of more than one mind, and it is possible that the movement had already begun in a general way. His bold step,

however, cut right through the prevailing confusion and forced
a new alignment. His particular contribution was to recognize the
superiority of the new basis over the existing one, and to create an
effective business organization to put it into practice. Ayer was
not so much an advertising technician as he was a business man
— an entrepreneur — one who organizes the factors of production
and determines the major policies governing operations. In the
adoption of the open-contract plan, and the selection of McKinney to promote it, lay his great contribution to American business.

CHAPTER IV

GROWTH OF AYER SERVICE, 1879–1920

BETWEEN 1880 and 1923, when F. W. Ayer died, N. W. Ayer & Son took on the formal organization and main characteristics of the great modern institution which it is today. Many innovations were made — some accidentally, some of set purpose; none dramatically or unconditionally. The development of N. W. Ayer & Son was not a mere problem on paper to be solved with words and figures. The firm was a living organism contesting with other like organisms for survival; and, for the most part, its new efforts were tentative, experimental, and necessarily hedged about with compromise. In the course of this chapter we shall observe how, when time had proved their merits, many new ideas were wholeheartedly adopted and surpassed their precursors in importance.

FIRST MARKET SURVEY MADE BY AYER, 1879

One of the most valuable services performed by an advertising agency today is that of analyzing the market for its customers. This is, indeed, the cornerstone of the intelligent planning of an advertising campaign. The preceding chapter shows how the open-contract arrangement opened the way for additional service. But the first realization of its possibilities came in 1879 and arose from the suggestion of a prospective client.

For several years prior to 1880 N. W. Ayer & Son had been trying to obtain the advertising contract of the Nichols-Shepard Company of Battle Creek, manufacturers of threshing machines. For two successive years, on arriving at Battle Creek, the Ayer representative found that George P. Rowell & Company had already carried off the order. In the following year, 1879, McKinney determined to get a chance to compete for the next order and went to Battle Creek early in the season before the Nichols-Shepard Company had begun to plan their advertising for 1880.

They agreed, however, to consider a bid from N. W. Ayer & Son along with bids from Rowell and other agents. McKinney therefore asked for the list of papers in which the Nichols-Shepard advertisements were to run. "Make up your own list," was the reply. "We want to advertise wherever we can sell threshing machines."

McKinney was taken aback, "Well, where do you sell threshing machines?"

"That's for you to find out."

"But," protested McKinney, "how are you going to compare our list with Rowell's if the papers are not the same?"

"Suppose you leave that to us," the Nichols-Shepard representative answered. "We will use our own judgment when it comes to that. But we would like to have you prepare your own list, and we are asking Rowell to do the same."

Perplexed but full of determination, McKinney returned to Philadelphia and reported the interview. Since the business was well worth having, his partners agreed that the agency should try to compete against Rowell on the basis proposed, and they hastily put the entire agency staff to work. They sought help from the government in Washington. At that time, unfortunately, the desired crop statistics were not available. The government bureau concerned with agricultural affairs (the Department of Agriculture had not yet been created) suggested that State officials, in some parts of the country at least, might be able to supply useful data.

The firm immediately sent telegrams to the appropriate officials of every State in the Union and to those publishers who seemed likely to have firsthand information about agricultural conditions. For three days and three nights the Ayer staff worked frantically; some of the men paused only for short naps in the offices of the agency, and every employee worked long overtime. As the information came in, they arranged it, as far as possible, to show the production of wheat, oats, rye, and other threshable grains throughout the country by States and by counties. At the same time they assembled and analyzed the available data on the circulation and rates of the newspapers which they thought the farmers were most likely to read in each of the districts. By the end of the third day they had completed a crude but fairly adequate market survey by States and counties, together with a detailed plan for advertising in the various areas. The data were gathered into a large, heavy volume which McKinney took back to Michigan on the next train.

The manager of the Nichols-Shepard Company could not conceal his surprise. "We have been trying for years to get this information," he said, "but without any success. How much will you sell it for?"

"It is not for sale," McKinney replied. "We are not in the book business. We are in the advertising business. If you are not our customer, it is not for sale at any price. If you are our customer, it is yours for the asking." There was no resisting this constructive kind of salesmanship, and the Nichols-Shepard advertising for 1880, amounting to $18,000, was immediately telegraphed to Philadelphia.[1]

DEVELOPMENT OF AYER SERVICE IN THE FIELD OF MARKETING, TO 1920

This survey for the Nichols-Shepard Company marked the beginning of a new phase in advertising practice. Indeed, it was apparently a pioneer effort of its kind in the history of marketing generally. It is the first recorded example, so far as I have been able to discover, of an advertising campaign based upon a special survey of the market for a given commodity; that is, upon a formal study undertaken to learn where to find the possible buyers of a particular product and how to reach them through the use of newspaper advertisements.

Before this time, manufacturers and their advertising agents had been content to fire shotguns into the dark, hoping that some of the pellets would hit a prospective buyer. The analysis which Ayer made was an attempt to cut out waste by turning lights on the targets before pulling the trigger. It formed the basis for *planned* advertising, and stood in marked contrast with the haphazard efforts of earlier years.

Thus, late in 1879, N. W. Ayer & Son began to give attention to the wider aspects of advertising and to provide services which were not directly linked with space-buying, but which were of vital importance to the success of an advertising campaign. It was only a beginning, to be sure. Unlike the open contract, this innovation was not deliberately instituted, but arose out of an attempt to capture one particular order. The firm was no more conscious of its significance for the future than the man who crosses a field is aware that the ground he treads for the first time is eventually to become a beaten path. For many years, help of the kind given to the Nichols-Shepard Company was not regarded as a part of the agency's regular work; it was given only occasionally when some special need arose. The primary work of N. W. Ayer & Son continued to be buying newspaper space for its customers.

COUNTING-ROOM, N. W. AYER & SON, 1878
TIMES BUILDING, EIGHTH AND CHESTNUT STREETS

There were forces, however, both inside the agency and out, which drove N. W. Ayer & Son in the direction of further sales assistance to the advertiser and eventually to undertake the new economic function which we now call marketing research and counsel. It must be remembered that until about 1900 N. W. Ayer & Son had to fight not only against its many rivals in the agency field but also against the indifference or ignorance of its potential customers, many of whom were difficult to convince that a program of aggressive advertising would increase their sales and profits. Those in the agency who solicited business therefore ap-

pealed to advertisers by giving informal assistance with marketing problems. Here McKinney was a source of strength to the
firm, for he instinctively saw advertising, not as a separate entity,
but rather as a part of a larger scheme of selling into which it
must be fitted. Moreover, he had a remarkable knack of sizing up
the peculiarities of the market for a given product, and of making
this, rather than a blind desire to sell, the basis of advertising
efforts. The Nichols-Shepard survey proved that Ayer did not
have to snatch business from his rivals by prying a few cents off
publishers' rates, so long as he could give extra value in the form
of additional service to the advertiser.

In the Ayer agency, moreover, the attitude was growing that
it was desirable, for the sake of the agency's own profits, to give
greater consideration to the pecuniary advantage of the advertiser himself. Advertising is a management tool which pays only
when it is handled with knowledge and skill. A number of advertising agents, hot in pursuit of quick profits, encouraged their
customers to advertise lavishly and blindly. Ayer, however, had
learned not to be so shortsighted. He and McKinney realized
that this policy ruined advertisers, in addition to discrediting advertising and frightening off other customers, and thus destroyed
the agency's source of income. The two men decided that they
must nurse small advertisers into prosperous growth. The tendency is unmistakable: gradually and inevitably N. W. Ayer &
Son was taking over the functions of studying the actual and possible markets for the commodities sold by its customers and of
devising advertising plans for tapping those markets.

By 1900 the preparation of advertising plans had become a
part of the regular service offered by N. W. Ayer & Son to its
clients. The plans were typically based upon a rough appraisal
of the client's marketing problem made by McKinney and other
Ayer executives. The emphasis was upon a judicious selection of
media, but selling appeals and art work were considered and field
investigations were occasionally made in order to gather data relating to the campaigns. The field surveys were usually confined
to a few inquiries among dealers; the analysis of the selling problem and the resulting plan were necessarily crude, but they repre-

sented a substantial advance in marketing technique and agency service.

This work was at first done by the Ayer solicitors with help from other members of the agency staff. By 1908, however, the volume of work had become so great that the firm appointed several men in the Business-Getting Department to devote full time to it; this was probably the first time that any agency assigned men to the specific task of planning.[2] The sole duties of this department were to study publications in relation to given products and to prepare plans for reaching potential buyers through various forms of advertising. By modern standards its approach was limited and crude, but the direction in which the agency was expanding was clear and significant. The Plans Department was rightly felt to be the fruit of the long evolutionary process which had brought N. W. Ayer & Son to a commanding position. It thus furnishes an excellent example of the way in which a new path, entered on accidentally and almost unwillingly, may prove to be a highroad to success.

Preparation of Advertising Copy by the Ayer Agency, to 1900

Meanwhile, between 1880 and 1895, the advertising agency was undertaking a second new service or function, that of preparing copy for its customers; and again N. W. Ayer & Son was certainly among the first in the field, if not indeed the foremost. Advertising was now produced in such volume that the simple printed announcement of former days no longer sufficed to attract the reader's attention, but was lost in a welter of similar notices. In order to be distinctive the message had to have a striking appearance. In other words, the advertisements themselves were beginning to compete with each other for public notice, just as the men who used them were competing with one another for business. For a time it was enough to use larger space and heavier type in order to make an advertisement of the ordinary kind stand out from the mass; but the realization slowly dawned that something more than a simple announcement or notice was required to sell goods, and the persuasive advertisement began to appear. As the general technique of preparing advertisements improved, moreover, it became progressively more difficult to devise copy which would outshine the general run of advertisements. Accordingly, the work called for a kind of literary skill which most business men did not possess.

Advertisers who could afford to pay for expertly written messages engaged the services of free-lance writers, men with literary or journalistic experience. John Wanamaker, for example, hired John E. Powers, who by 1880 was well known as a writer of effective advertisements.[3] And many a hardworking journalist followed the example of Henry J. Raymond, founder of the New York *Times,* who in his younger days wrote patent-medicine advertisements on the side.[4] Most advertisers, however, felt that they could not afford this extra expense and tended to depend on the advertising agency for help.

Like Palmer and other early agents, Ayer and McKinney had on occasion helped advertisers in writing their copy. Usually they did nothing more literary than polish up an occasional phrase or rewrite the message to fill a smaller space. As early as 1880, N. W. Ayer & Son sent out the following announcement to business men:[5]

The Composition, Illustration and Display of Newspaper Advertisements has so long been a study with us that we have become admittedly expert in preparing the best possible effects.

Having at command the services of an Artist, a Wood Engraver, and a number of Printers who have been for years engaged almost exclusively in this work under our direction, we possess entirely unequaled facilities for serving those who desire to entrust their business to our care.

No one, however, had regarded the actual writing of advertisements as the proper work or responsibility of the agent. But competition again advanced the industry by forcing agencies to give extra service; moreover, the agents began to realize that the ineffectiveness of a poorly written advertisement was sure to react against themselves.

A scant four years after the appearance of the advertisement given above, N. W. Ayer & Son gave convincing proof that it could meet the new demand for versatility. In 1884, the manufacturers of Police Plug Tobacco having placed an appropriation at its disposal, the agency planned and executed every phase of an advertising campaign; this included a careful selection of papers, a planned sequence of advertising messages, and a contest with prizes going to those who collected the largest number of tobacco tags within a given time. "CHEW POLICE," in large distinctive type, confronted every newspaper reader in the Philadelphia area. In praising N. W. Ayer & Son for its part in the campaign, the Philadelphia *Evening News* described it as "one of the best advertising schemes ever known to business." [6]

The agency did not undertake the work of preparing copy with any idea of finding new worlds to conquer. Ayer, like his competitors, was opposed to the innovation when it first thrust itself upon him. He felt that the advertiser must know his business better than any outsider could possibly know it, and that he was therefore better qualified to write his own advertisements.[7] Competition was keen, however, and in order to get business the Ayer solicitors were obliged to spend a good deal of time in thinking up advertising ideas and making copy suggestions. In 1888, Ayer took on his staff Jarvis A. Wood, a young man with a gift of ready words, who immediately began to devote much of his time to writing advertisements for Ayer customers.[8]

Other agencies were moving in the same direction. The National Advertising Company advertised in 1887, as Ayer had done earlier, that it stood ready "to prepare copy and furnish designs," [9] and Rowell offered similar services in 1891.[10] By that time the preparation of advertising copy was becoming a fairly well-recognized part of an agency's work, and early in 1892 Ayer hired a man to devote his entire attention to it. N. W. Ayer & Son thus was among the first agencies to offer the new service and, from all the available evidence, it was the very first to have a full-time copywriter on its staff.[11]

It soon became apparent that this somewhat grudging capitulation was only the thin edge of the wedge. As more and more advertising appeared, increased distinction was demanded from the writers. In addition, new forms of advertising — magazine and outdoor — appeared, making possible a more plentiful use of color and illustration. Technical advances in the printing and engraving trades also complicated the preparation of copy, and augmented the need for specialists in this field. It was no longer enough for a copyman to write cleverly; he had to have a good knowledge of art work and its reproduction by mechanical processes. Copy preparation, which began as a sort of poor relation, a mere adjunct of the Business-Getting Department, now became one of the most important activities of N. W. Ayer & Son. In June, 1900, this change was formally recognized by the establishment of a separate Copy Department.[12]

EXTENSION OF AYER SERVICE TO NEW MEDIA, 1880–1900

During the time that N. W. Ayer & Son was widening its service to include market counsel and copy preparation, it was extending the scope of its activities to advertising media which it had not previously used. Up to 1890 the firm had specialized in newspaper advertising; indeed, Ayer advertisements dated as late as 1892 made a special point of the fact that the agency handled nothing else and refused to undertake the placing of painted or poster advertisements.[13] The Ayer firm had, in point of fact, placed small amounts of advertising in magazines from its first year, but it had never urged magazines upon advertisers, and it had regarded their increasing use as a temporary fad.[14]

Magazines, notwithstanding, continued to advance by great strides. Between 1880 and 1890 their number increased 93 per cent, while their average circulation increased 50 per cent.[15] Here was an important new means of reaching the public, an advertising medium considerably less ephemeral than the newspaper, in short, an opportunity which the observant advertiser could not fail to note. Moreover, the enterprising J. Walter Thompson agency had early begun to specialize in magazine work and dinned its virtues into the ears of business men.[16] By the middle 'nineties, the growth of such periodicals as *McClure's, Munsey's,* and the *Cosmopolitan* could no longer be ignored; and in 1896 N. W. Ayer & Son announced that it would handle magazine as well as newspaper advertising.

Ayer's decision to extend his business in magazine advertising may have been determined less by the growing importance of the medium than by Thompson's announcement in 1895 that he intended to handle newspaper advertising.[17] Ayer probably regarded this move as an invasion of his own field which could be met only by a spirited counterattack. Within the Ayer agency there was some doubt of the possibility of translating his decision into practice, for the field was practically monopolized by Thompson. But by dint of making special price offers to advertisers and handling a good deal of magazine advertising at actual cost or very little above, the Ayer agency succeeded in establishing a footing in this new field of enterprise.[18] Despite this innovation, however, the firm continued to be known for many years primarily for its work in the newspaper field.

The Ayer agency likewise altered its position with regard to outdoor advertising. Before 1895 advertising by means of posters and signs had been generally frowned upon; it had been regarded as an unsightly and undignified method of sales promotion used only by manufacturers of patent medicines, who took no heed of such nice considerations. In the course of the 1890's, however, some of its worst features were eliminated, and several of the most respectable advertisers began to recognize its value as a selling device. It was especially useful in reaching people who never read newspapers or magazines, notably the immigrants who were arriving in swarms from Europe. But the medium presented special problems which discouraged agents from handling it. The owners of billboard and sign space were scattered all over the country, unorganized and often unbusinesslike. The difficulty was to make sure that signs and posters which the agency paid for were actually put up, and to see that they were kept before the public for the allotted time.

In the late 'nineties, however, the billposters and distributors began to organize their service on a more reliable basis; and in 1898, to comply with the wishes of an important client who wanted to use outdoor signs, N. W. Ayer & Son agreed to try placing advertisements in this (to the agency) new medium. In the following year the firm announced the creation of a new department to place outdoor advertising, and stated that it would thenceforth handle this medium as a part of its regular business.[19]

SPACE-BUYING ACTIVITIES, 1880–1900

Although the Ayer agency was thus adding new departments to its business, it was not neglecting its primary work of space-buying. It emphasized the value of its knowledge about newspaper rates and circulations and its experience and impartial judgment in the selection of newspapers for advertising. "We have no 'lists' or specialties to push upon the advertiser," the agency's advertisements asserted in 1882 and subsequent years. "Our constant aim is to maintain such relations with the publishers of all newspapers that we can at all times give an unprejudiced opinion as to the value of different mediums for any given line of enterprise." [20]

The claim to impartiality was doubtless sincerely meant. For a number of years, however, N. W. Ayer & Son, like its competitors, continued to act as a space wholesaler and hence remained subject to a certain temptation to use some newspapers in preference to others. Until about 1900 it bought space in various publications in advance of its needs whenever it could get a cheaper rate by purchasing in large quantities. Such purchases were protected by an agreement that the space thus acquired was "good until used"; that is to say, the agency did not have to use it within any definite time in order to avoid loss.[21] There remained, however, a natural desire to liquidate such investments as quickly as possible.

It must be remembered, too, that Ayer still owned the advertising concessions of a number of religious weekly newspapers, and was therefore interested in seeing that their advertising columns were well filled. Indeed, for many years rival agents asserted that N. W. Ayer & Son favored such papers unduly.[22] Certainly the temptation existed; and whether or not these accusations were well founded, they were none the less embarrassing.

In addition to its direct purchasing activities, N. W. Ayer & Son acquired a great deal of space in exchange for inserting publishers' advertisements in its own publications, *Ayer & Son's Manual for Advertisers* and *The Advertiser's Guide,* by a process which has been described in Chapter II.[23] Ayer carried this plan still further in his *American Newspaper Annual* (now famous as

N. W. Ayer & Son's Directory of Newspapers and Periodicals),
which appeared for the first time in 1880. This publication contained:[24]

a list of all newspapers and periodicals published in the United States
and Dominion of Canada, arranged alphabetically by towns in states
grouped in geographical sections, giving the counties in which the places
are situated, with the population of each according to the United States
and Canadian census, the political majority of each state and county in
the United States at the last presidential election, and in connection
with the papers, the year of establishment, time of issue, politics, denomination, or general character, publisher's price for the ten lines
one month, etc.

It has often been said by officers of the Ayer agency that the
Annual was instituted as a result of the agency's success in making the Nichols-Shepard survey. There is, however, a more plausible explanation. To an increasing extent the agency had to have
expert knowledge about newspapers and their circulations, which
it could use in advising its customers. But the expense of compil-
ing a really adequate collection of this kind of data was too great
to be borne by the agency out of its ordinary revenue. Ayer met
this problem by selling such information to the public in his
American Newspaper Annual. His main source of revenue from
the *Annual,* however, was not derived from the sale of copies but
rather from the advertising which the *Annual* contained. His
practice here followed that devised by George P. Rowell when he
published his *American Newspaper Directory:* Ayer persuaded
publishers to advertise their papers in his *Annual* in exchange for
space in their papers and then sold to his customers the space thus
acquired. From 10 to 15 per cent of the total pages in the *Annual*
were devoted to advertising during the period from 1880 to 1914.
Through the publication of its *Annual,* therefore, N. W. Ayer &
Son came to own space in a large number of publications, a fact
which further tended to impair the impartiality of its judgment
about media.[25] Considering the total volume of Ayer business,
the value of this space must have been relatively small, but it may
have been enough to influence somewhat the selection of certain
country newspapers.

A third way in which Ayer acquired space resulted from the flourishing business which he had developed in handling type, ink, and other printers' materials. This practice had been developed in the late 1860's by another agency, Cooley & Dauchy, which had acquired an interest in a type foundry. These men found that they could sell more type to publishers than the publishers could pay for in cash, and quickly hit upon the idea of exchanging type for newspaper space. The arrangement enabled them to make a handsome profit on both the space and the printers' supplies; and other agencies, being able to buy printers' supplies at wholesale prices, promptly copied the idea by establishing printers' warehouse departments.[26] Shortly after its foundation, N. W. Ayer & Son followed suit.[27]

Many of its orders for space specified that the publishers were to accept in payment printers' materials instead of cash. "We offer printing material," such proposals ran, "because the small profit we make on it enables us to secure insertion in many papers which the limited price in our order would prevent our using, were we to pay cash only." [28] Probably the "small profit" to Ayer was worth having; the New England Type Foundry Company, for example, allowed N. W. Ayer & Son discounts ranging from 25 to 40 per cent on type.[29] Apparently the trade needed no great urging, for many publishers, on their own initiative, ordered printing materials from the Ayer agency to be paid for in future advertising from the agency.[30]

These transactions in printers' supplies were clearly more than a negligible side line. The employees in the Ayer agency who handled this business formed one of its largest departments for some years.[31] Furthermore, in 1884, Ayer went so far as to acquire a printers' supply house to facilitate the purchase of materials; and, in 1888, when the typefounders of the country stopped giving discounts to independent dealers and set up their own selling organizations, Ayer established his own concern, the Keystone Type Foundry, in order to continue these exchange dealings with publishers.[32] Such arrangements provided convenient credits for publishers and made possible business transactions which could not have taken place on a cash basis. They did not, however, promote strict impartiality in the agency's judgment of advertising media.

Changes in Organization Arising out of the Open Contract

That Ayer eventually recognized the conflict of interests in his agency, and was sensitive to criticism of it, is clear from the changes in organization which he made from time to time. These began with the management of the religious papers, which seem to have aroused the most comment among his early rivals. In 1880 he placed these advertising concessions in the hands of an independent manager with a separate office; and in December, 1882, he formed a separate corporation, the Religious Press Association, to take them over. Thenceforth the only connection between the religious weeklies and N. W. Ayer & Son was the fact that F. W. Ayer personally owned the controlling interest in both; and the agency thereafter asserted that it received no special concessions but dealt with these papers on exactly the same terms as any other agency.[33]

A more sweeping reform took place some time before 1884, when Ayer established the Forwarding Department (at a later date considered by the agency to have been the first of its kind) to take over the purchase of space and the sending of advertisements to the papers. As Ayer himself expressed it, "This was to separate those who made promises to the advertisers from those who performed the promises made." In other words, the employees who helped the customers to select advertising media were separated from those who had to do with the acquisition of space, in order that choice of papers might not be influenced by the knowledge of the firm's space commitments.[34] And in the 1890's, if not earlier, strict rules were made to prevent those who made up lists of papers for customers from having any access to the firm's ledgers. The object of this was to prevent such employees from finding out for themselves what space the agency owned.[35]

The *American Newspaper Annual* was dealt with along similar lines. By 1900 it had become substantially what it is today — a standard guide to newspapers and magazines in the United States and Canada. In 1909 the Ayer firm purchased the name and good-will (about all that remained) of Rowell's *Directory* and combined it with the *Annual*.[36] To the annoyance of many publishers, N. W. Ayer & Son continued to solicit advertising for the *Annual and Directory,* as it was rechristened, in exchange for newspaper space. So many agents had sought extra profits through this device in the past that publishers had come to regard any newspaper directory which was produced by an agency as a kind of racket. They felt that they gained little from advertising in such publications, and some of the more suspicious of them believed that the circulation figures were padded in favor of papers which accepted the proffered exchange.[37]

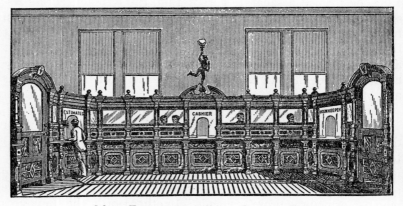

MAIN ENTRANCE TO AYER OFFICE, 1878
TIMES BUILDING

In the 1914 edition the Ayer firm finally excluded all advertising from its directory. This change in policy wiped out several thousand dollars of annual profit, but it eliminated a source of irritation to publishers.[38] It also removed grounds for criticism from the point of view of clients. No longer could anyone charge that N. W. Ayer & Son placed advertising in certain small papers solely in order to use up space acquired through the *Annual and Directory.*

Today *N. W. Ayer & Son's Directory of Newspapers and Periodicals* is an important standard book of reference — an enormous tome of nearly fourteen hundred pages which contains "a guide to publications printed in the United States and its Possessions, the Dominions of Canada and Newfoundland, Bermuda and Cuba, descriptions of the states, cities and towns in which they are published; classified lists; 70 maps." [39]

The matter of space acquired through trading in printers' supplies also received attention. But, for reasons which are not altogether clear, Ayer was slow to dissociate this part of his business from his advertising activities. Perhaps he felt that he had segregated it enough in 1880 when he created a separate Merchandise Department to handle the sale of printers' supplies [40] and had taken steps to prevent the solicitors from knowing about the space owned by the agency. As we have seen, Ayer established his own Keystone Type Foundry in 1888, after the incorporation of which (1906) the agency continued to hold the controlling interest. [41] Until 1907 N. W. Ayer & Son frankly urged publishers to patronize its subsidiary, [42] and until 1917 it continued to make credit transfers on its own books and those of the type foundry in settlement of accounts with publishers. [43]

By 1917 the capitalization of the Keystone Type Foundry had grown from the original $10,000 to $1,500,000, and the concern not only had large manufacturing establishments in Chester and Philadelphia but also branch houses in New York, Boston, Chicago, Detroit, Kansas City, Atlanta, and San Francisco. Then, having built up a large business despite the American Type Foundry Company's domination of the market, Ayer and his associates decided to sell the properties; the steel plant and products were sold to the Hamilton Manufacturing Company, and the type and printers' supply business to the American Type Foundry Company. The transaction involved in part the exchange of more than half a million dollars of Keystone common and preferred stock at par for bonds of the American Type Foundry, leaving N. W. Ayer & Son with a substantial investment in the type business but no direct control. [44]

Long before the sale, however, the connection between the Ayer agency and the Keystone Type Foundry had ceased to mean much. With the exception of the Accounting Department, the agency staff had not known which publications were indebted to the Foundry, and their purchase of space had not been subject to this particular source of bias. Most of the Ayer clients probably knew nothing of the connection between the two enterprises, and there is no record of any criticism from them. Publishers, however, were inclined to feel that the arrangement placed them under an obligation to buy type from the Keystone Type Foundry in order to keep in the good graces of the advertising agency. It has been impossible to discover any evidence whatever to justify this feeling; but the sale of the type foundry in 1917 removed all possible cause for suspicion, and marked the final step in divorcing the agency from all proprietary interests which might possibly color its judgment of advertising media.

Thus it was that Ayer simplified as well as expanded the activities of his agency. Repeating the general pattern of nineteenth-century business, he split off from the newspaper publishing business and specialized narrowly in the sale of space for publishers; later he diversified by adding the management of space concessions, the publication of his *Manual, Guide,* and *Newspaper Annual,* and by engaging in the manufacture and sale of printers' supplies. Then, as his main field developed, he discarded the side lines. This division and recombination of activities is a never-ending process in the history of business.

To some observers it may seem that the adjustment of N. W. Ayer & Son to the open-contract policy was too slow and full of compromise, and that Ayer should at once have ruthlessly cut off those branches of his business which might obscure the interests of his customers. We must remember, however, that N. W. Ayer & Son was caught between the demands of its customers and the practices of its competitors — practices hardened by nearly forty years of agency development. Advertisers expected the agency to give them impartial advice; but, at the same time, the continuing instability of publishers' rates led them to demand price concessions. Ayer's competitors, moreover, used every known device to lower prices in their efforts to get business;[45] and Ayer felt that he had to resort to some of the same devices, even though he recognized that the arrangements were not ideal. Lastly, the issues which are perfectly clear as we look back seventy years must have seemed confused indeed to men who were in the midst of change. Naturally he was reluctant to cut off appendages which were, for a time at least, highly profitable when they did not, in his own judgment, interfere with the proper handling of clients' business.

Development of Ayer Policy

Every successful business enterprise eventually acquires some sort of business policy which determines its objectives and, in a general way, the principles and methods to be followed in their attainment. This policy is supposed to be highly rational; but in most firms it is a blend of reasoning, empirical knowledge, tradition, and prejudice — a composite pattern of action which defies close analysis.

The period from 1880 to 1910 witnessed the gradual evolution of certain managerial practices and attitudes which we might well label Ayer policy. The application of the open contract to all business involving a substantial amount of professional advice was a basic ingredient. Another was the firm's insistence upon professional integrity and its right to discriminate among prospective customers, a policy arising directly out of the open contract. From about 1880 onwards the Ayer agency refused advertising when, in its opinion, the advertising was not likely to bring about the desired results. And, as early as 1887, employees of the firm could cite "instances when they had, with the approval of the firm, declined advertising proposals amounting to many thousands of dollars because they were not of a character to do credit to the agency or because the results would be disappointing to the advertiser." [46]

Ayer was beginning to regard himself not as a mere dealer in space but as a counselor with professional standards to maintain; and in 1886 and later years the Ayer agency made announcements like the following:[47]

When you want a lawyer, do you ask all the attorneys you know to make a "bid" and then employ the cheapest? Do you not rather look for the attorney whose skill, knowledge of the law, and personal character ensure a thorough and honest effort in your interest? Level headed business men seek the best legal talent — in their judgment the best is the cheapest.

Why doesn't the same principle apply to newspaper advertising? . . .
Isn't it cheaper for you — better and cheaper, too — to employ the
advertising agent whose personal character is sufficient guaranty that the
advertising will be well done, and that you will not be overcharged,
whose admitted skill ensures a telling advertisement, and whose knowledge of Newspapers and Newspaper Advertising, enables him to select
such papers as will best serve you?

An Ayer circular of 1887 enunciated the firm's "creed" as
follows:[48]

We do not wish any advertising which cannot reasonably be expected
to pay the advertiser.

We do not wish any advertiser to deal with us unless it is to *his interest
to do so.*

We always say just what we believe, even though we have to advise a
man not to spend any money in newspaper advertising.

We aim to give as conscientious consideration to little as to larger
matters. Small orders entrusted to us receive just as careful attention
as the largest ones get.

We thoroughly believe in newspaper advertising, and that there is more
value in it than most people think. We therefore contend that the
subject deserves an intelligent and unprejudiced consideration, to
which should be applied as good business sense as any other matter of
business commands.

We are not anxious for any order with which there does not come the
reasonable expectation, *first,* that the advertising will pay our customer; and *again,* that we can so handle the business as to convince
him that his interests will be best served by entrusting to us all his
future advertising orders.

The ideals and the general policy thus expressed received additional strength from the close association between Ayer and
Cyrus H. K. Curtis, which dated from the time when Curtis began
to promote his *Ladies' Home Journal* in 1888. Curtis advertised
his magazine through N. W. Ayer & Son; and Ayer, in the course
of his business, placed a good many advertisements in the *Ladies'
Home Journal,* whose advertising Curtis was determined, at least
after 1890, should be "kept as clean and safe as its literary
material."[49]

Whether he was moved by his association with Curtis, the growing agitation for temperance, or his own personal convictions cannot be determined, but Ayer decided in the 1890's to give up advertising alcoholic liquors. This part of N. W. Ayer & Son's business had, in fact, never been of any great consequence. Although the firm had handled small amounts of whiskey advertising, a careful examination of the ledgers shows that N. W. Ayer & Son advertised no wines or spirits after 1899, and at no time had it handled any considerable amount of beer advertising.[50] Both Ayer and McKinney had always disliked advertising of this type, and, according to the statements of employees, they had refused a number of large contracts for liquor advertising which were voluntarily offered to them.[51] In 1896, at any rate, Ayer directed his staff to omit breweries from their list of prospective customers,[52] and three years later the two or three small beer and whiskey accounts which the firm had been handling came to an end. The agency continued to advertise medicinal port for a few years, but in 1903 even this was dropped.[53] Henceforth N. W. Ayer & Son was a dry agency.

Ayer's policy of rejecting the advertising of alcoholic liquors involved a sacrifice and is especially noteworthy because it was applied in the face of adverse business conditions. The country as a whole was suffering from the long, severe depression of the 1890's; the agency itself, moreover, earned lean profits from 1894 to 1898 and barely met expenses in 1896, the year that the decision to drop beer advertising was finally made.[54] It would be difficult to find a more striking illustration of a side of Ayer's character which determined his course of action throughout his life, namely, his steadfast adherence to any principle he considered right, even at the expense of friendship or profit.

Ayer likewise came to view with disfavor the advertising of so-called patent or proprietary medicines. This change in attitude is particularly interesting because patent-medicine advertising contributed one-fourth of N. W. Ayer & Son's total volume during the first decade of the firm's existence.[55] Indeed, the patent-medicine business was the mainstay of every agency of importance at the time. Some agencies had gone beyond the mere advertising of nostrums; they had become part owners of the

companies which produced them. The Rowell agency, Lord &
Thomas, of Chicago, and Pettengill & Company, of Boston, had
done this deliberately, while others (Ayer included) had acquired
an interest in exchange for unpaid advertising bills. The financial
connection, in fact, was a useful device employed by many agencies to obtain and hold customers.[56]

Until the late 'nineties the amount of money spent on patent-
medicine advertising through N. W. Ayer & Son continued to
increase considerably, but the business from other sources increased even more rapidly. By 1900 the advertising of foodstuffs
had risen to first place in volume, and in the following year a large
number of commodity groups surpassed patent medicines in importance to the Ayer agency.[57] Indeed, at the turn of the century
the patent-medicine advertising placed by Ayer showed an actual
decline.

This decline came as a result not of the mere loss of business,
but rather of Ayer's growing distaste for the outrageous claims
made by patent-medicine vendors. In the late 1890's, again in the
face of difficult business conditions, the firm dropped one of its
largest accounts, a nostrum called "Paine's Celery Compound,"
on which $400,000 had been spent in a single year.[58] And in 1900
it also parted company with another large enterprise, "Dr. Williams' Pink Pills for Pale People," with the result that its total
volume of patent-medicine advertising dropped from over $216,-
000 in 1900 to $66,000 in 1901.[59] This kind of business, as Ayer
expressed it, "had finally reached the point at which it became
necessary to make or fake miracles to secure commensurate results . . . we thought ourselves better off without it." [60]

It is evident, however, that Ayer was not yet ready to close the
doors to all patent medicines, for letters were sent out in 1902
soliciting business from the owners of proprietary preparations,[61]
and the firm continued to handle the advertising of several patent
medicines of doubtful merit. Instead of drawing the line on all
business of this kind, Ayer evidently chose to feel his way by
weeding out one or two accounts at a time. It soon became clear,
however, that all patent-medicine accounts would have to go.

An aroused public opinion, following the onset of the muckraking era, apparently determined the final step. In 1904 and

1905 the *Ladies' Home Journal* published a number of articles exposing patent-medicine frauds. In the following year *Collier's Weekly* likewise took up the cudgels against patent medicines. From that time onward everyone concerned with the best interests of advertising became conscious of the social aspects of the industry, and some real reforms were made.[62] In 1903 the Ayer agency had placed advertising copy which asserted that Dr. Davis' Compound Syrup was a "sure cure for consumption," and as late as 1905 it sent out advertisements containing the following statement: "Rapid recovery follows relief by Dr. Davis' Compound Syrup Wild Cherry and Tar in all cases of Consumption, Coughs, Asthma, Influenza, Bronchitis, Croup, Whooping Cough, Palpitation of the Heart." [63] Since none of the advertising placed by the agency after 1905 contained any such extravagant claims, one may fairly conclude that the campaigns by the *Ladies' Home Journal* and *Collier's Weekly* were the determining factors in the agency's decision to refuse all patent-medicine advertising.[64]

To offset the loss of business resulting from this policy of selection, N. W. Ayer & Son made a determined effort to gain the advertising of staple commodities. Withdrawal in one direction called for advance in another. The total volume handled by N. W. Ayer & Son in the 1880's had been made up largely of the business of dozens of small customers and hundreds of separate orders for advertising, among which the advertising of retail stores, seeds and nursery stock, and schools and colleges bulked large. Thanks especially to McKinney's efforts, however, the agency was developing a number of large accounts, some of which have become famous: Hires' root beer, Montgomery Ward's mail-order business, J. I. Case threshing machines, Procter & Gamble soaps, Henry Timken's machinery, and Burpee seeds.[65] As early as 1891 Ayer was handling large amounts of advertising for the N. K. Fairbanks Company (makers of Fairy Soap, Cottolene, Gold Dust Washing Powder, etc.), Mellin's Baby Food, various brands of flour and textiles, and several lines of clothing.[66] In 1898 the Ayer firm began to advertise Mica Axle Grease for Standard Oil and before long was handling the advertising of at least eleven Standard Oil subsidiaries, including the Glucose Sugar Refining Company.[67]

Perhaps the triumph of McKinney's career came at this time when he won for N. W. Ayer & Son the advertising business of the newly formed National Biscuit Company. In January, 1899, the Ayer agency launched the first series of advertisements in a campaign which was probably the largest conducted in this country up to that time and also was one of the first to feature a staple food, ready for consumption, and sold in individual packages. It involved the creation of an air-tight package, a distinctive brand name and trade-mark, and a coördinated plan for reaching the public through newspapers, magazines, streetcar advertisements, posters, and painted signs.

To serve this new account every talent of the Ayer agency was brought to bear on the campaign, every department and resource called into action. Here N. W. Ayer & Son set a precedent in the field by placing at the disposal of an advertiser the expanding facilities of the modern advertising agency. And here, as never before, an advertising agency amply proved its ability to plan and execute advertising as an integral part of a general selling campaign. The Ayer agency and the National Biscuit Company worked in such close coöperation that one cannot say which made the greater contribution. This much is beyond question: N. W. Ayer & Son, largely through McKinney, gave counsel at every step, helped to coördinate the advertising with the efforts of the company's own salesforce and its retailers, and contributed the name around which the campaign centered. Almost overnight the words "Uneeda Biscuit" became celebrated, and a flood of orders swamped the bakeries of the National Biscuit Company.[68] The open cracker barrel of the good old days was doomed. Small wonder, after this success, that N. W. Ayer & Son began to speak of its customers as "clients." Flushed with success, neither the agency nor the National Biscuit Company realized the extent to which it was helping to remold our daily life.

It was evident by 1900 that profits from advertising lay fully as much in pushing the sale of particular brands of an established staple commodity as in presenting new articles to the public. Advertising as an aid to technical progress was being overshadowed by advertising as a competitive weapon and as a correlative of mass production. N. W. Ayer & Son was becoming aware that its chief problem was not so much to persuade the public to buy soda crackers (for example) as to induce them to buy the Uneeda brand of soda crackers rather than some other kind.

In 1900, therefore, the Ayer firm launched a special advertising campaign on its own behalf, urging business men not to assume that a staple commodity could be sold widely without advertising.[69] The succeeding years brought it the business of the American Tobacco Company, H. J. Heinz (food), Simmons Hardware Company (Keen Kutter tools), Cluett Peabody (collars and shirts), the American Sugar Refining Company, and the International Silver Company, the International Correspondence Schools, the Cadillac Company (automobiles), and Steinway & Sons (pianos).

Efforts, however, did not stop with everyday commodities. After the great insurance exposure of 1905 (the Armstrong investigation), N. W. Ayer & Son undertook a campaign to restore public confidence in the chastened New York Mutual Life Insurance Company. This effort is worthy of note in that it shows a new and important extension of advertising. Advertising was ceasing to be merely an adjunct of selling and was starting to be a device for communication. We shall see later how its informational function has come to be used also to *discourage* sales — thereby putting an end to the concept of advertising as merely a selling tool. Three years later the agency was hired to make known to the public the activities of the American Telephone and Telegraph Company and the Western Union Telegraph Company by means of "institutional" advertising campaigns.[70] Here the objective was not so much to sell goods and services as to develop a public opinion favorable to the company. Advertising had now passed out of the patent-medicine stage of its history; beyond question, it was established as a communications device worthy of the most respectable business enterprises, and it formed an almost indispensable weapon in the growing battle for public patronage.

Evidence of Successful Growth

Such, in brief, was the functional and professional growth of N. W. Ayer & Son during its middle period. An examination of its accounts shows a parallel growth in financial strength and in the organization of the enterprise.

As a result of hard work, careful management, and improvement of its advertising techniques, the Ayer agency advanced steadily in volume and profits during the period from 1880 to the end of the century. In 1880 its total volume was $366,962.97 and its profits were $21,465.55; by 1899 the volume had risen to $2,030,523.73, and the profits to $58,382.74.[71] One should note in passing that, for reasons which are not altogether clear, the profits increased more slowly than the volume. N. W. Ayer & Son claimed, as early as 1882, to surpass all other agents in size, boldly published the total of its volume for 1884 ($917,639),[72] and in 1891, in an advertisement on the cover page of *Printers' Ink* which Rowell himself owned, challenged Rowell's claim to supremacy.[73] Less than three years later *Printers' Ink* published editorially the following estimate:[74]

> The advertising agency of N. W. Ayer & Son, of Philadelphia, is unquestionably the largest and probably the best equipped of any in the United States. It has more and larger patrons than any other, and taking one thing with another, it is questionable whether they are not entitled to the credit of securing for their patrons better service than can be counted on from any other.

Coming from Rowell, an important competitor, this opinion is entitled to respect.

The Ayer organization was forced to expand to handle this growing volume of business. The pay roll increased steadily from 40 persons in 1880 to 110 in 1890 and more than 160 in 1900. Some of these additional employees brought time-saving skills: the firm began to use typewriters as a labor-saving device before 1886, and in 1886 it hired its first shorthand stenographer.[75]

It was in 1886, too, that the Ayer motto, "Keeping Everlastingly At It Brings Success," appeared in print for the first time.[76] This phrase was meant to encourage business men to advertise continuously. From the recollections of Ayer employees, however, one soon comes to the conclusion that it accurately described the labors of the agency itself. The prescribed working day was from 8 A.M. to 6 P.M., but overtime was usual in the Ayer firm as in

American business generally. Even the women, who appeared on the Ayer staff after 1876, frequently worked two or three hours in the evening, and the bookkeepers often worked long into the night in their efforts to record the thousands of daily transactions.[77]

To some extent the overwork resulted from the fact that the Ayer organization was growing rapidly and without definite plan. At first there was much duplication, little specialization, and no scheduling of work, with the result that the staff was frequently overwhelmed with rush orders. By 1890 necessity had forced most of the operations into specialized departments. But, owing to the lack of detailed supervision and coördination between departments, there was confusion and delay in the handling of business.

Ayer himself tried to provide the required central direction, but of course there was a limit to the amount of detail which he personally could handle. His agency had reached the stage which every growing business passes through, in which the old system had been outgrown and the new system had not yet been completely worked out. For the next fifteen years or more the problem which thrust itself upon the firm, and particularly upon F. W. Ayer, was to organize the various departments and weld them into a unified, smoothly running machine, in which each part was made to work in harmony with the others.[78]

The Ayer partners bore their full share of this labor and worked without regard for health or the amenities of private life. George O. Wallace died in December, 1887, when only thirty-seven years of age, and it is said that overwork contributed to his early decease.[79] McKinney worked without respite, traveled constantly in search of new business, and devoted every spare moment to the creation of new advertising ideas, with the result that his health after 1900 was seriously affected.[80]

Shouldering the entire burden of organization and management, Ayer, too, worked like a man of iron. Of course, his generation took pleasure in work and scarcely knew the meaning of recreation. Until late in life, he was usually the first to appear at the office in the mornings, and often he was the last to leave. Outside interests, moreover, came to demand a share of Ayer's attention and energy. Becoming a director of the Merchants National Bank of Philadelphia in 1888, he was elected to its presidency in 1895, and he contributed a great deal to its growth and success.[81] In the early 1890's an additional burden was thrust upon him when several firms, among them the Brown Chemical Company (manufacturers of Brown's Iron Bitters) and the Saratoga Spring Water Company, got into financial difficulties while owing large amounts of money to his agency for advertising. Ayer promptly took a hand in their management and succeeded in bringing them back to a profitable basis. For weeks on end, his only relaxation from business was the daily ferry trip across the Delaware to his home in Camden and his church activities on Sunday.[82]

Even before the addition of these burdens, Ayer had overtaxed his strength, and his physician had prescribed more rest and outdoor life. This prescription took him back to the scenes and pleasures of his youth. In 1886 he purchased a farm in the quiet hills of Meredith, New York, which he had often visited as a boy, and there he began to indulge his enthusiasm for fine horses. By 1890 his natural inclination for rural hobbies had led to a substantial investment in blooded Jersey cattle, an interest which McKinney shared. Within a short time Ayer's irrepressible business instincts rose to the surface. The hobby was put upon a paying basis and the firm of Ayer & McKinney, owners of Meridale breeding and dairy farms, rapidly attained importance for milk products as well as blue-ribbon cows.[83]

In January, 1898, a step was taken that reduced the burden upon Ayer and McKinney, and promoted a more equable distribution of managerial duties. Two employees of the firm, Jarvis A. Wood and Albert G. Bradford, were advanced to partnership.[84]

Wood had started to work for N. W. Ayer & Son in 1888 as assistant to F. W. Ayer. Genial, friendly, and gifted with a ready flow of words, he was expected to follow McKinney as the agency's leading business-getter and producer of advertising ideas. His talents, however, lay in other directions. For a number of years he supervised the preparation of copy; his associates believe that he was the first man to head an agency copy department. Later he was made manager of the large staff of employees and placed in charge of the general routine work of the Philadelphia organization. In that capacity his tact, his fatherly manner, and his complete loyalty enabled Wood to serve the agency well.[85]

Bradford was of a different type. Like Ayer he was a New Englander, with a flair for figures and a talent for financial management. He had come to the agency in 1884 as a bookkeeper, and had succeeded Wallace as head of the space-buying department. Shrewd, imperturbable, possessed of a simple manner and unfailing courtesy, he managed somehow to get low space rates from publishers without losing their goodwill toward the firm or himself. To many a publisher today the memory of A. G. Bradford is a pleasant one; some of them recall occasions when, in financial straits, they hurried to him to ask for an advance of cash, and not in vain. After gaining a reputation as one of the foremost space-buyers in the country, he later relieved Ayer by taking over the duties of treasurer of the firm. Bradford's success with the publishers, together with his sound financial judgment, hard work, and active devotion, was of great importance to N. W. Ayer & Son up to the time of his death in 1921.[86]

In addition to lightening the burden upon the two senior partners, the admission of Bradford and Wood represented an attempt to provide for a continuity of management. It is significant that these two had not been brought in from the outside. Both had been employed in the agency for more than ten years and knew every phase of its work. Like Wallace and McKinney, neither of them contributed any new capital to the business; each paid for his share out of earnings received after admission to partnership. Their promotion, like every promotion to top management in N. W. Ayer & Son before or since, was based not on financial interest but on their ability, promise, and experience within the firm, a fact which has given Ayer employees an incentive to put forth their best efforts.

After the admission of the new partners, the responsibilities of the business were divided as follows: McKinney was in charge, as before, of the business-getting activities; Bradford handled the buying of space and other dealings with publishers; and Ayer, with Wood as his assistant, exercised a close supervision over operations as a whole. In the following year (1899) Ayer caused some far-reaching changes to be made in the organization. Following a practice which was then becoming popular in business circles, he brought in an "efficiency engineer" to study the business. As a result of the engineer's recommendations the clerical work was simplified; in the interest of specialization existing departments were divided and subdivided; and a new department was created to coördinate the various divisions and supervise the execution of routine work.[87]

The mounting volume of business compelled N. W. Ayer & Son to seek new accommodations. As early as 1895 the agency was outgrowing its offices in the old Times Building, even after overflowing into the Times Annex, and it had advertised for larger quarters.[88] It did not move at once, however, possibly because of the poor profits during the ensuing three years and because general business conditions, after showing promise of expansion in the fall of 1895, fell back into deep depression in 1896. But in 1902, with the annual volume running regularly over two million dollars, further delay was impossible, and N. W. Ayer & Son took over much larger quarters in the Mariner and Merchant Building at Third and Chestnut Streets.[89]

This corner, owned by the Girard Estate, was one of Philadelphia's most historic spots. The site of the First United States Bank, it had passed into the hands of Stephen Girard. There he had helped to finance the War of 1812; there E. W. Clark had helped to finance the Mexican War; and there Jay Cooke had helped to finance the War between the States. It was a corner with advertising associations, too, for many a Philadelphia newspaper had been published there, including Benjamin Franklin's *Saturday Evening Post;* and it was, accordingly, an appropriate site for N. W. Ayer & Son to occupy during the next twenty-seven years of its history.[90]

Besides the move in Philadelphia, N. W. Ayer & Son began to open branch offices in other parts of the country — New York in 1903, Boston in 1905, Chicago in 1910, and Cleveland in 1911.[91] It established these branches both in its own interest and in the interest of its clients. As the firm worked to increase its volume it had to go farther afield to find customers; and, while Ayer had traveling representatives, it was difficult to direct their work from Philadelphia. As early as 1896 the Ayer solicitors had complained that the lack of branch representation handicapped

MARINE AND MERCHANT BUILDING, 1903
THIRD AND CHESTNUT STREETS

their efforts.[92] Moreover, now that the firm was taking such an important part in the marketing of goods, it was essential to maintain closer relations with clients and to find some means of keeping constantly in touch with them. Both the agency and its clients were continually being confronted with questions of advertising plans, marketing tactics, copy preparation, and general selling policy which could best be dealt with in personal conferences. The branch offices provided the necessary decentralization of service contacts, while the execution of the principal agency functions — the preparation of advertising plans and copy, the purchase of space, and routine services — remained the work of the

Philadelphia organization. Neither then nor since has the firm believed in having branch offices which were in effect self-contained agencies. Where service to clients made it necessary, specialists were occasionally assigned to branches — to provide, for example, emergency copy; but the main creative effort has always been concentrated in the home office.

CHAPTER V

F. W. AYER: THE LAST PHASE, 1906–1923

THERE are two severe tests which every growing business must pass if it is to endure. One comes when the enterprise outgrows the personal supervision of the man who created it, compelling him to change the method of management. The second comes when the founder ceases to take an active part in running the business, thereby placing the burden of management in new hands. These tests may come together or separately, but each has its own special problems, and the transition from old to new control often ends in failure. N. W. Ayer & Son had to face both of these tests between 1906 and 1923. Although the forces involved are intangible and difficult to describe satisfactorily, this period of Ayer history is of the utmost significance.

NEW MANAGEMENT FOR OLD

The decade from 1906 to 1916 was a trying one for N. W. Ayer & Son. In spite of the apparent vigor indicated by the establishment of branch offices, the irresistible forward drive of the early years seemed, to some observers at least, to be giving way to a stolid jog trot. The Ayer agency had originally distinguished itself by keeping one step ahead of its competitors in the services offered to its clients; or, failing that, by adopting and improving on its competitors' ideas. But by 1906 the industry as a whole had reached the point where little spectacular innovation was possible, and there was not much to distinguish one good agency from another. Statistics bore out the impression of stagnation. Thus, while the annual volume of the Ayer firm was tripled between 1900 and 1909, most of the gain had been made between 1900 and 1903.[1] N. W. Ayer & Son still held a commanding place in the advertising industry, but it seemed to be complacent; to outside observers it appeared to have settled into a rut, had reached its peak and, unable to advance farther, must inevitably suffer a decline.[2]

Fortunately the founder of the business saw the danger signals. Ayer realized that the reorganization of 1900 had left one major problem unsolved: the business was now so big that he could no longer give all departments his close personal supervision. Some means had to be found to supply the rank and file with energetic drive and control from the top of the organization. Ayer may not have fully understood at first that no one person could handle the job singlehanded and that a new system of management was required. He did recognize, however, that he himself could no longer cope with the work. It had grown tremendously, he was no longer a young man, and his other interests — banking, church and Y.M.C.A. work, and the livestock and dairy business — required much of his attention. He would have to delegate part of his work to a subordinate. But to whom?

None of Ayer's partners could supply the kind of leadership which was needed to pull the firm out of its lethargy. McKinney was in poor health, and even had he been in the best of condition he could not have accomplished the reform which was needed, for he had no great amount of administrative ability. Although unexcelled in his own particular branch of activity — the creation of advertising ideas and the solicitation of business for the firm — he was not good at organizing men, and he was fully aware of his own shortcomings. He had not indeed been able to organize even the Business-Getting Department on a satisfactory basis, although that was the branch of the agency which most concerned him. Nor were the two younger partners, though able in their own special fields, any better qualified to meet this issue. Their experience had been too narrow to qualify them for the handling of general business problems. They had learned to execute orders, not to originate commands.

Was F. W. Ayer to see his agency go the way of the agencies of Palmer, Rowell, Pettengill, and many others which had not survived their founders? This situation was probably the great crisis of F. W. Ayer's life, although its seriousness was not fully apparent until later. Ayer rose to the occasion. He studied the

situation until he had defined the problem, and, having decided
that the only possible solution was to bring into the organization
a man who could take over most of the managerial work which
he himself had previously handled, he went forward without any
hesitation. From outside he obtained a man whose training and
ability seemed to fit him for the position of general manager of
the agency. There was, however, no marked improvement.

Still convinced that his course was the right one, Ayer brought
in another manager, a man of forceful personality with flashy,
aggressive qualities which N. W. Ayer & Son had not previously
known. The new manager took determined action at once. He
gave the whole firm a thorough shaking, dropped some of the
staff, and brought in new men. In September, 1912, he undertook
a complete reorganization designed to attain further specialization and coördination and, above all, to allocate responsibility
more definitely.[3]

From one point of view the results were eminently satisfactory.
Wide-awake and eager, N. W. Ayer & Son was now prepared to
handle a large volume of business with skill and dispatch. In this
process of revitalization, however, something of the basic Ayer
spirit had been lost. The new manager clearly understood the
need for imaginative leadership, but he neglected some of the
close attention to detail which is so important in advertising. Under his leadership there appeared a carelessness about the interests of clients which was utterly alien to the true Ayer tradition.

The events which then ensued have never been recorded, and
it is difficult for an outsider to find out exactly what happened.
Those within the agency who went through the experience prefer
not to talk about it, and regard it as an episode which should be
forgotten. Indeed, they *have* forgotten most of the details. To the
historian, however, the matter is of the greatest importance, since
it involves the kind of difficulty which comes at some time or
other to most businesses of long standing and continued growth,
but which is not usually recorded. I have, therefore, pieced together the story told here from interviews with people inside
N. W. Ayer & Son and from a number of outsiders who had dealings with the Ayer agency at the time.

Those in the Ayer agency who opposed the new turn of affairs found that protest was useless. In order to allow the new manager the widest scope for action Ayer had given him full authority to run the business, and the other partners were powerless to interfere except by appealing to Ayer himself. The employees of the agency, moreover, were made to feel fear — fear of dismissal for putting devotion to the best interests of the firm above allegiance to the executive in charge. The manager, they felt, was too much inclined to replace the old staff, having their established loyalties, with new men who would look to him as their personal leader, while Ayer standards of performance were being neglected. This view may well have exaggerated the real facts, but there can be no doubt about the effect upon the morale of a large proportion of the staff.

Thus the solution of one problem had created another. Months went by and Ayer took no action. His apparent indifference puzzled observers and bewildered his loyal employees. He had never been greatly influenced by sentiment alone, but he shared the paternalistic attitude of his contemporaries in business. He constantly referred to his employees as "members of the Ayer family," looked upon them as fellow workers who shared his ideals, and in return for their loyalty gave them genuine affection. One can well imagine the anguish that he must have felt as he saw the old spirit of the firm threatened by the new manager whom he himself had introduced.

Having given the manager full authority, Ayer was determined to avoid interference as long as possible, although the new administration was not altogether to his liking. As some of his employees expressed it, "He always gave a man plenty of rope to hang himself with." Ayer probably felt that the objectionable features of the new management were too intangible to be made a basis for definite action. He saw, too, that definite improvements had been achieved in some directions. Whatever his decision may have been, he waited for the manager himself to bring matters to a head. The occasion came in 1916 when the manager, after a prosperous year, sought admission to partnership. Quite apart from other considerations, Ayer felt that this was an impertinence. An interest in the firm was, in his opinion, an honor to be conferred, not a position that a man could ask for. He indignantly refused the request. The manager immediately resigned, and in his place was appointed one of the junior partners, Wilfred W. Fry.

Fry had been a schoolmate and close friend of H. N. McKinney's son, William Ayer McKinney. Through this friendship he had come to know the Ayer family, and in 1904 he had married Ayer's oldest daughter, Anna Gilman Ayer.[4] For several years after this, Fry followed his chosen career as a Y.M.C.A. worker. In 1909, however, he yielded to the invitation of his father-in-law and became an employee of N. W. Ayer & Son. Two years later, the firm admitted him to partnership.

Fry's position was never an easy one. To many people he was simply F. W. Ayer's son-in-law, and any promotion that he won was looked upon as a result of favoritism. But the truth is that, in bringing his son-in-law into the business, Ayer intended to give him nothing more than the opportunity he had given to many a promising young man. With the candor and cold rationality which were characteristic of the man, he gave Fry to understand that he must prove his worth and earn every advancement which was given to him. There is reason to believe that Ayer meant exactly what he said. He had put his blood into the agency; it was his life's work; and its success was always his first consideration. He had long resolved that its control should go to none but the man who proved his competence in handling it. Fry had shown himself to be earnest, hardworking, and conservative. By the time the general manager resigned, Ayer felt that his son-in-law had demonstrated sufficient promise to warrant appointing him to the place.

N. W. Ayer & Son during and after World War I

The period of World War I and its immediate aftermath was to provide an acid test of the new régime, as to both its versatility and its financial soundness. On both counts the Ayer firm showed its enduring strength.

After the first rude shock of 1914, American business began to expand rapidly, and by 1916 the Ayer agency's volume had increased substantially over that of 1913. With the entrance of the United States into the World War, advertising became an in-

strument of direct social action, used to arouse patriotic sentiment, sell government bonds, conserve food supplies, and promote many other war enterprises. N. W. Ayer & Son assisted in
preparing and placing advertisements in the first three Liberty
Loan drives, and contributed to the cause its commissions on the
advertising which it placed for the second and third of these campaigns. Both the firm and its employees subscribed liberally to
the loans, and, of course, participated in other war-work activities. Forty-nine members of the Ayer staff (averaging 329 employees in 1918) entered government service.[5] The founder of
N. W. Ayer & Son insisted on doing his bit too:[6]

> I was naturally too old for service in the Army, but I asked my Firm
> to release me for service that would be helpful and I entered with all the
> energy that I possessed into the endeavors of the Y.M.C.A. to supply
> needed funds and men for overseas service. It was a patriotic service at
> first, but I had the opportunity to see how my associates were going to
> conduct this business when I was no longer here to have a hand in its
> direction.

As far as the agency's regular activities were concerned, the
chief effects of the World War were strikes and paper shortages
in the publishing industries, and the restriction by the government of the production of many clients who were engaged in non-
essential industries and consequently had to curtail their advertising appropriations. Agency expenses rose sharply, along with
the general level of prices, and N. W. Ayer & Son was compelled
to announce that, beginning on January 1, 1919, its commission
would be increased from 15 per cent to 16⅔ per cent on the net
cost of space.[7] In obtaining this increase Ayer anticipated action
by his rivals, for between 1919 and 1921 the American Association of Advertising Agencies sought and obtained from most publishers a uniform commission of 15 per cent off the gross or card
space rates. Before 1919, most publishers had allowed only 13 per
cent.[8] As a result of the new rates an advertiser could save a
small amount of money by dealing with Ayer. Agencies generally
bought $100,000 worth of space for $85,000 (gross price less 15
per cent). Most of them charged their clients $100,000 and kept

the difference. Ayer charged the net price plus 16⅔ per cent ($85,000 plus $14,166.67), making the price to the client $99,-166.67.

The succeeding years brought nerve-racking mutability of fortune. By 1919 a great advertising boom was in full swing. This resulted partly from the desire of manufacturers to spend large amounts of money on advertising rather than give it to the federal government in the form of excess profits taxes, partly from the resumption of peace-time commerce, and to a large extent from the growing competition which marked the postwar period. The prosperity arising out of war-time profits had increased real wages and raised the general standard of living in the country. As soon as peace had been declared, there was a frantic rush to capture the expanded market which resulted. Aided by this boom, the volume of N. W. Ayer & Son's business leaped from $6,528,000 in 1918 to $13,734,000 in 1919, and profits passed the half-million mark for the first time in the agency's history.[9] As might be expected, the economic difficulties of 1920–21 checked this sudden advance and brought the total business for 1922 down to $10,882,000, but in 1923 another period of rapid growth began.[10]

GOLDEN ANNIVERSARY OF N. W. AYER & SON

The year 1919 marked the fiftieth anniversary of the founding of N. W. Ayer & Son. On April 4, 1919, the firm celebrated the occasion with a banquet at the Hotel Bellevue-Stratford, Philadelphia, attended by more than eight hundred guests and members of the Ayer staff. A more notable and sincere tribute has seldom been paid to a commercial institution and the man responsible for it.

In a congratulatory address ex-President William Howard Taft paid a sincere compliment to his friend and host:

We are honoring a man who has made advertising a science, who has made it useful, and who has robbed it of many of its evil tendencies, and who has a right to be proud of the record he has made. . . . we owe a debt of gratitude to Mr. Ayer, for having rendered a form of publicity so useful and elevating, which might have been vicious and deplorable.

Other guests at the banquet — clients of N. W. Ayer & Son and publishers with whom the agency had long dealt — praised the firm out of their firsthand experience; and, in the course of the ceremonies, the agency was presented with a large gold loving cup which bore the names of 210 of the nation's leading publishers, together with the following inscription:

In recognition of the splendid service rendered the cause of advertising by N. W. Ayer & Son, Philadelphia, the publishers of the United States present this token of their appreciation and regard, on this, their golden anniversary, and felicitate them on the effectiveness of their slogan — Keeping Everlastingly At It Brings Success.

This presentation is unique in American advertising agency history.[11]

In his speech of welcome, however, Ayer indicated that he was not one to rest on his laurels. He reviewed briefly the history of his own business and the changes which had taken place in advertising since 1869. But he went on to show that in spite of success and the passage of years he was looking to the future rather than to the past, for he outlined developments for advertising which, after thirty years, are only beginning to be realized:

In the early days, and for many years, no one thought of advertising except to promote the interests of the merchant or manufacturer. In these later years there has, however, come what seems almost marvellous recognition of advertising as a social force. We have learned that advertising can do much more and bigger things than merely sell goods. Today advertising educates people regarding political situations, industrial crises, social development. Can you conceive a more remarkable demonstration than has been the war use of advertising to sell Liberty Loans, to create favorable opinion toward America, to develop our own morale, to undermine the morale of our enemies?

These more recent uses of advertising clearly point the way toward the field of its greater future usefulness in the extension of goodwill advertising for private commercial business, as well as for the more efficient service of the community at large and the country as a whole.

The Passing of Three Ayer Leaders

Between 1918 and 1923 N. W. Ayer & Son lost the three men who had provided its chief leadership during the middle period of its history. Without some estimate of their personal worth, this record of the firm's development would be far from complete. Carlyle today is unfashionable, and the theory that history is a collection of biographies has given way to the concept that history is the resultant of deep economic and social forces in which individual men are simply the puppets of fate and history tends to become a vast collection of statistics. As we learn more about the personal influence of Adolf Hitler upon world events it becomes clear that a single man can, within a given cultural environment, extend a tremendous influence upon the course of history. And the desperate search for leadership in the miserable chaos following the end of hostilities in World War II is further evidence that individual men help to shape human destiny. Certainly in viewing an enterprise which began as a one-man show, quickly passed its rivals, weathered the economic storms of 1873, 1893, 1896, 1907, 1920–21, and 1929–33, and constantly raised its essential standards in the teeth of the gales, one cannot escape the conviction that the men behind it have had much to do with the character and success of the firm.

Henry Nelson McKinney died on April 28, 1918. It is hardly possible to overestimate his importance to the business during the forty-three years of his association with it. His work in promoting the open contract and in securing desirable accounts has already been dealt with; indeed, he was connected with nearly every important event chronicled thus far, and his achievements won him a high reputation in the general field of advertising.

His contribution to the success of the firm lay in three directions. In the first place, he was a salesman par excellence. More than any other person, he was directly responsible for the growth of the business handled by N. W. Ayer & Son. His rare personal magnetism won friends for him wherever he went, and enabled him to obtain a hearing from hard-boiled business men who refused to listen to other advertising salesmen. His outstanding ability as a salesman was coupled with an unrivaled talent for working out new and clever ideas for promoting his clients' products. He not only sold N. W. Ayer & Son to advertisers, but he also showed advertisers how to sell their goods, and thought out copy ideas, trade names, and slogans with which to catch the public fancy. Thirdly, in working with clients he discovered from time to time new services by which the Ayer agency might make advertising more effective and thus add to its own prestige and profit. He was largely instrumental in the agency's assumption of the work of making advertising and marketing plans and of preparing copy for clients. He was a craftsman in advertising in the full sense of the term.

But it was more than McKinney's business abilities which endeared him to his associates. Everyone he met fell under the spell of his personal charm and ready sympathy. He numbered among his close friends many of the leading business men of the country, but he remained simple and unpretentious to the end. His long and intimate association with F. W. Ayer went far beyond a mere business partnership. There was an unusually strong bond of friendship and understanding between the two, and they shared the activities which each prized most highly — their business, their church and charity work, and the cattle-breeding and dairy business. One catches a glimpse of the bond between them in the following excerpt from one of McKinney's letters, written while he was trying to repair his broken health:[12]

Many times this summer I have wished I could have several of our old fashioned chats. I miss those old times more than I can tell.

In the months I have been away I've had time to think, and the most satisfactory part of all the years we have been together is not the business or its success but the old time friendship and association. What the future has in store for me in the way of business is very doubtful but nothing can disturb the sweetness or permanency of the long-lasting love.

Many were the tributes paid to McKinney's character by the business men who knew him. Typical among them was the statement of Earl D. Babst, chairman of the American Sugar Refining Company: "He gave power and spirit to everything he touched. His successes are everywhere. His name and the influence of his character will live as traditions in many of the foremost industrial organizations of the country." [13]

In May, 1921, came the death of another senior partner, Albert G. Bradford. His contribution had not been spectacular, but it was nonetheless valuable to the agency. In his unassuming way he had shown himself to be capable, diligent, and intensely loyal. Like his associates he had worked up from the bottom rung by dint of hard work and ability; like them he was an active church worker and a respected man in his community. Whereas McKinney's friends were chiefly among advertisers, Bradford's were among the publishers with whom he had dealt; and, like McKinney, he had also won a position of love and respect among his fellow workers in the agency. His place as treasurer was taken by Adam Kessler, Jr., who had risen from the ranks to partnership (1920), and who was the first native Philadelphian to become a member of the firm.[14]

Francis Wayland Ayer, founder of N. W. Ayer & Son, died on March 5, 1923, at the age of seventy-five. Although he did not die in harness, the circumstances show him true to his own sterling character to the very end. For some weeks before his death he had been suffering from a cold, and he had gone to his beloved hills at Meredith, New York, "to freeze it out," as he said. Undaunted by the snow and cold of winter in the western Catskills, he had taken part in the Sunday services of the village church as usual; and he had driven out, a few days later, to inquire about a member of the Bible school who had been absent. It was a typical example of Ayer's energetic personal interest in everything which concerned him. Unfortunately the exposure to severe weather was too much for him, and his cold developed into a fatal attack of pneumonia.

Francis Wayland Ayer, the Man

To any reader of this history the predominance of Ayer, both in his own firm and in the industry of which that firm was a part, is obvious and undeniable. That very predominance arouses interest in the man's character and activities. But it is exceedingly difficult for one who did not know Ayer to give an adequate estimate of his personal character and achievements. A man of dignity and restraint, he was not one to bare his soul to the world. He seldom made public speeches, he wrote no books and only a few articles,[15] and the mere handful of his letters which we have — apart from revealing a quick, direct, and businesslike mind — throw little light upon his fundamental thinking. And, since few of his own words remain to explain the man and his philosophy of life, we are compelled to base our estimate almost wholly upon his deeds and the opinions of the men who knew him in his daily round of work.

Moreover, Ayer was a typical product of the nineteenth century, a type of business leader which the present generation does not understand. Men like Jay Cooke, John Wanamaker, E. H. Harriman, F. W. Ayer, and John D. Rockefeller were active in the affairs of their churches and there is every reason to believe that they were all sincere in their strong religious ideals. Yet, because there seems to be a conflict between their religious tenets and the effects of their business activities, writers of the postwar period are prone to regard them as hypocrites.

It is easy to forget the spirit of the times in which such men lived. Few men of the nineteenth century gave thought to the business implications of Christian ideals. Religion with them was a personal thing; business belonged to a different sphere of activity, one which had few established ethical standards. At the same time there can be no doubt about their zeal to better others as well as themselves. In their business life, Ayer and others of his time were dominated by the economic and social ideas then prevailing — the theory that lively competition was good for society, the early nineteenth-century Liberal doctrine that the individual furthered the best interests of society when he sought his own best interests, and the popular conception of the implications of the survival of the fittest arising out of Darwin's theory of evolution — which seemed to lend countenance to every device for getting ahead in the business world.

These men of the nineteenth century had blind spots; they seldom gave careful heed to the human side of their business activities or to the social consequences of their enterprises — at any rate, not to the particular problems about which we are especially sensitive today. It is easy now to say that they were selfish and anti-social, but such criticism is as unjust as it is unintelligent. These men cannot be judged by standards which did not exist in their time. All that the modern observer can do is to fit them into their background, and Ayer's generation gave little heed to social considerations because other matters were more urgent at the time.

The qualities which particularly stood out in Ayer's character and life were clear thinking, determination, and good, old-fashioned rectitude. These qualities were lightly attributed to so many people in the nineteenth century that we have come to look upon them as either meaningless or commonplace, but they are, in fact, uncommon and exceedingly valuable; and Ayer's success in business and in life was built on them.

Ayer succeeded in everything that he undertook, because he knew precisely what he wanted to do. He was a man of strong emotions, but his feelings never clouded his vision nor weakened his grasp of reality. It was contrary to his nature to drift aimlessly. "We must have a purpose," he told his staff. "We must have a plan to carry out that purpose. And we must have men to make that plan effective." [16]

Because he knew what he wanted, Ayer gave up teaching and went into business. Although advertising commanded little respect at the time, he quickly discerned his opportunity in it and started an advertising agency. He saw through the evils and confusion which marked the early agency business, and he devised his open-contract plan to eliminate them. And, because he caught a glimpse of the larger possibilities of advertising and took a long view of the interests of his own agency, he adopted business policies calculated to remove his firm from the common run of advertising agencies. Referring once to his position in the Merchants National Bank (later merged with the First National of Philadelphia), Ayer said:[17]

I thought that my election to the presidency of that bank . . . was a recognition by my townspeople that I had their respect in my business, and I had the determination that in so far as I had anything to do with it, or N. W. Ayer & Son had anything to do with it, this [advertising] should be just as honorable a business as the banking business.

In advertising, in church and Y.M.C.A. work, in banking, in the cattle-breeding and dairy business — in everything he undertook, Ayer sought out the facts and steered his course by them. But this concern with facts did not prevent him from taking a large view; unlike many men he could see reality without cynicism, without losing ideals. Throughout his life Ayer was intensely practical in all that he did, but he remained to the end an idealist in the realm of hope. Dr. John R. Mott, who knew Ayer well, has often told how his vision went beyond his business and matters of the moment:[18]

As I recall his planning, he was not regulating his plans and activities by the passing changes of the hour, but by the abiding requirements of the age . . . ; he was building not simply for today, or even for tomorrow, but for the long future.

Another friend found this characteristic symbolized in a familiar habit:[19]

At Meredith, Mr. Ayer often took his friends to the hill where the water tower stands and to the lookout on the hill above the village. His reason for doing so was that thence one could see so very far over the rolling hills and valleys of "God's country" [as Ayer often called it]. It was like him to love that kind of a prospect.

Ayer's instinctive desire to see a situation or problem as a whole and to bore to the heart of it before coming to any decision made him a cautious man. He never drifted, but, where other men rushed blindly into action, Ayer patiently waited until he could discover a definite goal and a means of reaching it. One of the fundamental rules of business is to define a problem or issue before trying to meet it. Indeed, this definition is usually the greater part of the difficulty; once the issue is sharply defined, the solutions usually suggest themselves. Such procedure seems quite simple and obvious, yet Ayer was one of the few American business men who has really applied the rule.[20] Once Ayer had come to a decision or settled on a course of action, he drove straight to his goal with abundant energy and resource. One incident, taken from his cattle business, well illustrates his decisive way of handling things. In 1921, after going over the records of his herd, Ayer decided that it needed some new blood. Summoning Mr. Dutton, his farm superintendent, he asked which was the best bull on the Isle of Jersey.

"Dairylike Majesty," Mr. Dutton replied after a moment's consideration.

"Buy him and ten of his daughters," was the brief command which Ayer immediately gave. Ayer had studied the records of the native breeds, he knew the able judgment of his superintendent, he knew what his own herd needed. Within a year he had what he wanted, and the outstanding record of the Meridale Herd after 1922 proved how well he had reasoned.[21]

In every field of action Ayer's determination was unshakable. He allowed nothing to stop him — difficulties, opposition, enemies, costs, not even close friendship. He sought no conflict, but he never hesitated to fight for what he wanted. He had an iron will, tireless energy, and a tenacity which nothing could wear out. To many men this strength of will seemed to be sheer obstinacy, but Ayer never pursued a course without good reason, and his tenacity was not blind. When he saw that McKinney had qualities that the agency needed, Ayer changed his decision not to have another partner and took McKinney into the firm; and, when he understood the forces which were throwing upon the agency the expensive burden of copy preparation, he withdrew his opposition to the new function.

Perhaps the incident which best reveals Ayer's judicious flexibility is, again, one relating to his cattle and dairy business. When Ayer and McKinney took up the raising of thoroughbred Jersey cattle as a hobby, they resolved to build up one of the best herds in the country. At the same time, in order to provide a satisfactory market outlet for the milk produced by their cows, they organized among the farmers of Delaware County, N. Y., a chain of milk stations, set up a creamery and a powdered milk factory, and soon established a profitable market for the dairy products of the region. By 1899 this creamery business had grown until there was a serious conflict between it and the breeding business.

One or the other interest had to be dropped. Recognizing this and the fact that, when they established a system for marketing the milk and butter of the region, they had incurred a responsibility to the neighboring farmers, Ayer and McKinney decided to sacrifice their own hobby. In 1900, accordingly, they auctioned off 184 registered cattle, nearly all the animals they owned. In Jersey cattle circles, men said that the famous Meridale Herd was at an end, but this was not true. The sacrifice was only a temporary one made to save both hobby and business. As soon as the creamery business was sufficiently well established, the two partners resumed their activities in breeding Jerseys and built the herd to a position of unquestioned leadership.[22] Ayer was the active manager of the project, and he was plainly the one who preserved both interests by a temporary shift of policy in favor of one. His administration of his agency shows similar examples of his ability to adapt his plans to changing circumstances. He was a strong-minded man, but he was never blindly stubborn.

Ayer's firm adherence to decision and principle won him much respect but few friends in the business world. He was always courteous, even in the heat of conflict, but he possessed little tact or diplomacy. William Howard Taft said of him, "When he wants a thing he gets it; and he doesn't mince matters about getting it, either." [23]

People who did not know him well misunderstood his blunt manner. He was never effusive, and it was simply not in him to cajole or dissemble. Sure of himself, sure of his path, Ayer was stiff-necked almost to a fault. He would condone errors of judgment in others, but he could not tolerate a deliberate departure from what he regarded as right principle. Once when a friend and neighbor failed to pay a pledge made to a charitable enterprise in which Ayer was interested, Ayer did not hesitate to bring court action to compel payment. In later years he mellowed and showed in his business dealings the warm heart and sympathy which had always marked his private life; but his poorly developed sense of humor, the shyness which he hid beneath his brusque manner, and his stern righteousness combined to make Ayer a comparatively lonely man.

Ayer realized his limitation, as Cyrus H. K. Curtis testified:[24]

I remember one time in the old Merchants Bank that he surprised us by saying that he would not stand for renomination as its president. We were surprised and asked him why. He said, "Well, you know Mr. Law has come up here, and it was expected that he would succeed me. I think he is perfectly able to do that. The bank needs a man who can mix with people, and Mr. Law is popular — he goes to bankers' conventions and he meets people and make friends easily. And you know I can't do that — I can't do that so well."

One thinks of an advertising man as being easy going, friendly to all, effervescent, and rather witty; and it is a remarkable paradox that the head of one of the world's largest advertising agencies should have been so cold and reserved to all except his family and close friends. The truth is, as I have already pointed out, that Ayer was not primarily an advertising man. He had none of the qualities of the conventional salesman or promoter. His disposition and abilities were those of the entrepreneur; his work, in every field that he entered, was to plan, to organize, and to manage.

Ayer never undertook anything unless he thought it worthy of his best efforts, and his best efforts invariably yielded fruit. Besides making N. W. Ayer & Son one of the largest and most successful agencies in the world, he developed the Religious Press Association and the Keystone Type Foundry into large and prosperous businesses, played a leading part in the growth of the Merchants National Bank and later the First National Bank of Philadelphia, and nursed back to solvency at least three smaller business enterprises which got into financial difficulties while indebted to N. W. Ayer & Son. At the time of Ayer's death the Meridale dairy and creamery business had a volume of well over a million dollars per year; and the cattle hobby had grown to the point where Ayer owned the second largest herd of thoroughbred Jerseys in the world, second to none in quality and importance. It had, in fact, become a business enterprise concerned not only with breeding fine cattle but also with importing stock from Jersey on a large scale and holding auction sales of international fame.[25]

Ayer devoted the same determination, energy, and ability to

religious activities. In addition to his work in the North Baptist
Church of Camden, he served for twenty-five years as president
of the New Jersey Baptist Convention, and one term as president
of the national church organization, the Northern Baptist Convention. He was chairman of the National Committee of North
Baptist Laymen which raised six million dollars for missionary
and other denominational activities, and he was a leading spirit
in the Baptist New World Movement.

Ayer also devoted much of his time and strength to the youth
of the nation. He was president of the Camden Y.M.C.A. from
1899 until his death; he had directed the raising of money for the
Camden building and for a retirement fund for the workers of the
national organization; he had long served as chairman of the New
Jersey State Executive Committee and as a member of the International Committee of the Y.M.C.A.; and to this work, as to his
other charitable interests, Ayer had made large, very large, contributions of money.

Nor did he neglect the field of education. Throughout his life
Ayer maintained the interest in teaching which had played such
an important part in his youth. It will be remembered that he
had taken a special interest in the advertising of schools and colleges and had always granted special credit terms, so that struggling institutions might pay him when they received their tuition
fees — the results of their advertising — rather than at the time
their advertising was published, when they were usually short of
cash. The interest, however, went further than mere financial assistance. At the time of his death Ayer had given seven years of
active service as a trustee of Colgate University, and fifteen on
the Board of Corporations of Peddie Institute; and he was, at
the same time, president of the New York Baptist Union for Min-
isterial Education (holding corporation for Rochester Theological Seminary).

Unlike many business men who lend their names and influence
to religious and educational organizations while taking no active
part in the work, Ayer gave to all such interests the same close
attention and hard work that he devoted to his principal business
enterprises. Even on his deathbed he insisted on discussing some
correspondence relating to Y.M.C.A. work along with business

matters. With Ayer any undertaking which merited his attention at all was worthy of his best.[26]

Everything that Ayer touched became successful; in every undertaking — business, education, church work, philanthropy, cattle raising — he rose to a position of leadership. What was the secret of his achievements? What force or motives drove him to the top? In his business interest he undoubtedly worked for profit, but desire for gain obviously had nothing to do with his prominence in other lines of endeavor. And it is clear that even in business Ayer was not primarily interested in the acquisition of wealth for its own sake. To him profits were evidence that a business enterprise was performing useful work in an efficient manner, an indication that it was a success. Money itself was no incentive in his life, nor were the things money could buy — luxury, pleasure, social distinction, or great influence. He made no lavish expenditures in fine homes, estates, or art collections, he joined no expensive clubs, he had no social ambitions whatever. These things did not interest him. He was a Yankee, a man of simple tastes and one who took the teachings of Christ seriously, and he disliked ostentation. The only expensive tastes he had were his fine cattle which he made pay for themselves (there were no elaborate barns and trappings at Meridale), and fine horses which he could use around his farm. Much of his wealth he gave to religious and educational projects; the rest he re-invested in the businesses which earned it.

Ayer's chief pleasure was hard work and the satisfaction of accomplishment. He was never idle; for him the first principle of living was to be usefully active, and the nearest thing to recreation in his life was looking after his cattle and horses. Since he was never satisfied, he never stopped; and the most remarkable thing, perhaps, is that so practical a man should choose intangible service rather than material accomplishment as his goal. He left no great railroad or industrial plant behind him. In business as in other fields his work was to serve others, and his strong sense of honesty and duty compelled him to do his best for them.

Ayer accomplished much because he was a good judge of men and because he had an unusual talent for getting them to work effectively. His real genius, however, lay in his ability to build organizations which would survive him. He institutionalized his business, religious, and educational activities so that they would outlast him, for to him it was continuous accomplishment in these fields, not his own activity, that mattered. In the men he chose, in the organizations he built, the spirit of F. Wayland Ayer lives on.[27]

CHAPTER VI

YEARS OF GREAT PLENTY, 1923–1930

THE DEATH of F. Wayland Ayer marked the end of a period in the history of N. W. Ayer & Son. For a period of fifty-four years he had controlled the work and the policies of the agency. For fifty-four years, thanks to his efforts, the agency had enjoyed steady growth, substantial prosperity, and marked progress. What was to happen, now that the original guiding hand and driving force were gone? This question was asked in advertising circles — by publishers who remembered Ayer's unblemished record of fair dealing and full payment, by competitors who had been only too keenly alive to Ayer's successful rivalry, and by many advertisers to whom Ayer's name was synonymous with successful advertising. There were even some within the firm itself who were a little doubtful about the future.[1]

All these misgivings rapidly disappeared as the new Ayer management proved its ability to cope with the situation. In truth, that management was not new; it had gradually learned its work and taken over control of the agency before the senior partners had fully relinquished their grasp on the reins. Thus, there was no break in policy or any loss of pace after Ayer's death. The old policies continued, the old standards of service rose even higher, and the growth of the firm continued. Indeed, as we look back over the entire history of N. W. Ayer & Son, the years between Ayer's death and the time when the depression hit the agency stand out as a period of almost phenomenal prosperity. The problems which emerged were not those of transition in management but rather those of rapid expansion.

NEW BLOOD IN THE PARTNERSHIP

Even before the old partners passed on, young men had been brought into the partnership to provide continuity of management as well as to give suitable recognition to service and ability. The first addition (after the admission of Wilfred Fry in 1911) was William M. Armistead, a Southerner who had had considerable newspaper and advertising experience in Tennessee and Georgia before he joined the Ayer staff in 1909. His promotion to partnership, January 1, 1918, only a few months before the death of H. N. McKinney, was especially opportune, for Armistead brought to the management qualities remarkably like those which had made McKinney so valuable. His personal charm, combined with shrewd selling ability and an instinctive grasp of advertising fundamentals, made him one of the most effective solicitors the Ayer firm has had. Many advertising accounts stand to his credit, but his greatest *coup* was undoubtedly winning the R. J. Reynolds Company business which N. W. Ayer & Son handled from the launching of the first Camel cigarette advertising in 1913 until the account was transferred to another agency in 1931. Ultimately Armistead was placed in charge of the general servicing of all Ayer accounts.[2]

In 1920 two others were admitted to partnership: Adam Kessler, Jr., and James M. Mathes. Kessler had entered the agency's employ in 1901 and was the person chiefly responsible for the development of the Ayer Plans Department. After Bradford's death he was given charge of the firm's financial affairs, and eventually he became Wilfred Fry's most trusted adviser in matters of policy. Mathes had begun his Ayer experience in 1911 when he was fresh out of Dartmouth College. His greatest interest and ability lay in the direction of selling and business promotion, and it was for this reason that he was placed in charge of the agency's New York office.[3]

Three years later, George H. Thornley was admitted to partnership. He had come to the agency in 1907, at the age of nineteen, and had won promotion because of his achievements in selling the agency's services. His first major task after becoming a partner was to establish and organize a branch office on the Pacific Coast. Subsequently he opened a branch in Detroit and later headed all the agency's business-getting activities.[4]

By the time of Ayer's death, therefore, the firm had five young partners every one of whom possessed at least a dozen years of experience in N. W. Ayer & Son. Fry had come up the adminis-

WILFRED W. FRY

THE AYER BUILDING

trative side, Kessler in planning (during its formative stage) and
subsequently in administration, while Armistead, Mathes, and
Thornley had risen to prominence in business-getting activities.
Armistead alone was an all-around advertising man of the McKinney type, although each of the partners was intimately familiar
with all aspects of agency work. It is worth noting that none of
them could be regarded as a specialist in space-buying and that,
after the death of Jarvis Wood in 1925, there was no member
of the firm whose specialty had been the preparation of copy.
Space-buying, as already indicated, had lost much of its original
strategic importance in the agency business, particularly as the
Planning Department came to work out the actual selection of
publications; hence space-buying, while in no sense reduced to
routine work, called more for experience, technical knowledge, and
tact than for executive talent of the kind which leads to general
administrative positions. Copy preparation, on the other hand,
had grown steadily in importance, although the men who were
most skillful in handling it seldom had shown much capacity for
administration.

With the highly creative aspects of agency work (preparation
of plans, copy, and art work) rising to prominence, a far-sighted
management might have felt the desirability of giving them more
explicit personal representation in the firm: that is, to have the
partnership represent specialized agency functions as well as ownership and general management. The Ayer firm, however, followed the pattern established in the past and usually observed by
agencies generally at the time — that of giving the most lucrative
and influencial positions to the men who owned the capital or
brought in the business which provided the profits. It was a perfectly natural development, and no one could deny that the partners were highly competent men. We shall see later, however, that
the next decade called for a change in the pattern at the top.

ADVERTISING IN THE PERIOD 1923–1929

American industry and commerce, swollen by the abnormal
demands of the period 1914–19, strove to keep up a huge volume
of activity by stimulating peace-time consumption in every conceivable manner. In addition to staple goods in huge quantities,
there was a growing stream of motor cars, electrical appliances,

and other new products of the factory to be disposed of — products once regarded as luxuries but rapidly becoming an indispensable part of everyday life. And there were whole new industries — chemical, radio, electric refrigeration, rayon, and the like — seeking buyers among the public.

As never before in history, the consumer was faced with more goods than he knew what to do with. As never before, national prosperity was dependent upon a large and rapidly moving flow of goods to the consumer. The great productive forces which were unleashed during the two preceding centuries had been creating a situation which was relatively novel in human history, in which the supply of material goods was rapidly overtaking the existing demand. Out of this relatively new situation arose complicated economic problems which were apparent before the end of the nineteenth century, but which reached a crisis in the period 1920–30. Early in the 'twenties there were signs that the flow of goods was being checked — not at its source as had so often occurred in centuries past but at the outlet — through the consumer's failure to absorb all the commodities which were thrust upon him.

A superman might have observed this danger and set about to remove it by correcting the faulty distribution of goods among the whole mass of people. But there were no supermen then; there are none now. All that the individual business man could do was to seek profits by discovering ways of increasing consumption; and the only means at his disposal were to increase selling efforts and to facilitate the purchase of goods. What happened in the ensuing years is too familiar to need retelling here. It is only necessary to recall that in his frantic efforts to move his wares the merchant or manufacturer used advertising in huge amounts in order to tell the public what he had to sell. More important still, he also attempted — by logical persuasion, by appeals to vanity, fear, and other emotions, and by various subtle means — to mold consumer taste and create new wants so as to sell more and more of the goods which threatened to accumulate.

We know now what came of these efforts, and we are inclined to jeer. Yet it is not clear what other efforts, in a competitive society like ours, the business man should have made to meet the situation. As an individual he was powerless to take any great steps toward a fundamental remedy. He might have used more intelligence about expanding production and more ingenuity in developing new merchandise. Advertising has come in for severe criticism, some of it well justified; but many of the critics have related it too intimately with the mad speculation, the blind folly, and the downright deception and dishonesty of the so-called New Era. There is, in fact, no necessary connection; and, if both the friends and the enemies of advertising would modify their extreme views, we should see more clearly that advertising has a legitimate place in modern society.

Sooner or later we shall have to recognize that material progress — increased production, wider variety of goods, new commodities, greater physical comfort, and the like — must be accompanied by continual efforts to educate and persuade people to adapt themselves to new products. If we want that kind of progress, we shall have to learn to use it and be willing to alter some of our ways of life. This would still be true if we were to adopt a communistic or socialistic form of society. New products must be announced and described to the public, their uses and advantages must be explained; and, if their price is to be within general reach, a demand must be created for them quickly so as to make quantity production feasible.

Western civilization has a tradition of thrift and frugality, born of an age of scarcity. This tradition — long fostered by our teachers, bankers, and economists — has at some points been pushed too far; and advertising has been one of the few corrective forces which urge the purchase and use of goods rather than the piling-up of funds. Advertising is one of those "senseless agencies" which, in the words of a modern philosopher, "coöperate in the work of driving mankind from its old anchorage." [5]

It is basically this educational work, as President Coolidge pointed out, that advertising performs in modern economic life: [6]

It makes new thoughts, new desires, and new actions. . . . It is the most potent influence in adopting [adapting?] and changing the habits and modes of life, affecting what we eat, what we wear, and the work and play of the whole nation.

President Coolidge's remarks were widely publicized. A less complacent people might have been alarmed at this powerful influence which was developing in their midst, might have taken steps to ensure the wisest use of advertising. Above all, they might have recognized that advertising, at its best, is education with a strong bias which, in the public interest, needs a strong corrective. And we were too frequently getting advertising at its worst. A few observers did sound a warning; but their words fell on deaf ears, and this phase of education was allowed to remain entirely at the mercy of private enterprise. The business man, left to solve his problem in his own way, chose high-pressure salesmanship, extensive advertising, and elaborate credit arrangements — palliatives rather than cures. But even if he had correctly diagnosed the economic pains, the individual business man could have offered little except palliatives. We blame him for selfishness and stupidity. Yet, even with the advantage of the increased knowledge and perspective which we gained during the depression, we are not yet agreed on the exact nature of the trouble or the proper cure. The entire nation, rather than the business man alone, was at fault.

However history may ultimately judge the "New Era," certain facts are clear. As a result of the tremendous efforts to sell goods, the volume of advertising in newspapers and magazines alone in the United States rose from $528,300,000 in 1919 to $1,120,240,000 in 1929.[7] Other forms of advertising showed a like increase; and at least one new medium, radio broadcasting, made a considerable addition to the total before the end of the decade.

N. W. Ayer & Son participated in this striking growth. The firm's annual volume, reduced by the depression of 1920–21 from the peak of the postwar boom, recovered in 1924, doubled by the end of 1926, and by 1930 was over $38,000,000, nearly three times the highest figure ever reached during Ayer's life. And, as we shall see in a later chapter, the firm's profits rose with the same startling rapidity. The vigor of the new generation of Ayer management is reflected in the fact that the firm's volume rose more rapidly than the general increase in advertising expenditures.[8]

It was worth noting, too, that the Ayer volume in this recent period was made up largely of goods and services of proved merit — Kellogg cereals, Old Town canoes, P. H. Hanes underwear, Steinway pianos, Camel cigarettes, Sani-flush cleaning powder, Atlantic gasoline, Hills Bros. coffee, Cannon towels, Ferry seeds, International Correspondence Schools, American Telephone and Telegraph Company, and, after 1927, Ford motor cars, to mention only a few. Thus, for the most part, N. W. Ayer & Son advertised American business at its best and generally refused to advertise goods of questionable value to the consumer.

The Ayer agency likewise refrained from using certain offensive types of appeal which have appeared in so much advertising in recent years. It consistently refused to buy testimonials from anyone — film star, society matron, or hero of the hour; and it refused to stoop to such devices as emphasis upon halitosis or perspiration odors, in order to frighten people into buying. The Ayer management took this stand not only because it regarded these practices as unworthy of its name and reputation but also because they bring advertising into disrepute. It believed (and still does) that such methods tend to destroy the consumer's faith in advertising and ultimately will decrease the effectiveness of all advertising dollars, including those devoted to the objectionable methods just mentioned. Such practices look to immediate profits and ignore the long-run results. The effect of sensational selling appeals, like that of drugs, wears off with constant use; so that sales can be maintained only by resort to greater doses of sensationalism until the limits of exaggeration and indecency are reached. Witness the outrageous advertisements, during the depression, of some of the most popular cigarettes, soaps, cosmetics, disinfectants (so-called), and toilet papers.

To anyone who examines objectively the campaigns prepared by the Ayer agency during this period, it will be apparent that N. W. Ayer & Son avoided most of the abuses of advertising. It chose the more difficult course of trying to advertise the products of its clients on the basis of appeals which, though often emotional in character, conformed to high standards of decency and truth. Such a policy lays the firm open to charges of excessive conservatism, complacency, stiff-necked righteousness, and ignorance of modern methods, and rival agents have seldom hesitated to seize the opportunity. But the policy is a conscious one, and the agency has adhered to it even when doing so meant loss of profits. Whatever one may say, it is clear that the Ayer management has conscientiously tried to give first consideration to the long-run interests of its clients and of advertising as an institution. This policy has been a basic factor in the strength and progress of the House of Ayer.

THE AYER BUILDING

The growth of the Ayer business following World War I necessitated adjustments within the agency organization. In addition to changes within the Philadelphia headquarters which will be described later in detail,[9] there were several changes in the branch offices. In 1924 the Cleveland office (established in 1911) was closed and its work divided between the Philadelphia and Chicago offices. At the same time the firm opened a branch office in San Francisco, thus making the scope of its organization nation-wide.[10] It is interesting to note that N. W. Ayer & Son, like most of the large advertising agencies, has not felt the need to establish branches in the southern States, despite the development of southern industry and commerce since 1900.

As in the prewar period the primary purpose of the Ayer branches was to solicit new business and to maintain close service contacts with clients. The details of planning campaigns, preparing copy, and placing advertisements remained largely in the hands of the staff in Philadelphia. (Eventually the principal branches were equipped to give emergency copy service.) The continued growth of the firm's volume and organization necessitated additional space at headquarters, and the problem of housing the firm properly again began to rise.

As early as 1920 the Philadelphia staff had outgrown the building at Third and Chestnut streets, and the firm purchased additional space in adjoining properties.[11] The depression of 1920–21 led to a postponement of any building project, but the steady growth of business between 1924 and 1926 made new quarters imperative. After further consideration of the problem of location, the firm abandoned its original plans and purchased a site on the west side of Washington Square (originally laid out as a park by William Penn), with Independence Square and the historic old Pennsylvania State House diagonally across from the front, the Robert Morris house adjoining in the rear, and other landmarks of the Revolutionary period in the neighborhood. This environment, interesting as it was, confronted the Ayer management with the problem of erecting a building which would symbolize the progressive and modern spirit of advertising, while avoiding a clash with the earlier architecture of the surrounding section of Philadelphia.

The result of the partners' wishes and the architect's design was a simple, dignified shaft of Indiana limestone, thirteen stories high, reflecting in a restrained manner the influence of the *art moderne* which was just beginning to spread in the United States. The decorative motifs throughout are modernistic and symbolize fundamentals of the advertising business.[12]

In addition to the many offices of the agency, carefully arranged to provide satisfactory working conditions and interdepartmental communication, the building provided three galleries for exhibiting art, photography, and other material connected with advertising; the large Printing Department of the agency; and, on the thirteenth floor, a cafeteria and rest, recreation, and assembly rooms. On the roof, provision was made for games and sunbathing.

Ground was broken for the building on October 12, 1927; on February 4, 1928 — the eightieth anniversary of F. Wayland Ayer's birth — the cornerstone was laid. In the cornerstone members of the Ayer firm placed, among various objects, a brief history of the business, biographies of the partners, photographs, lists of employees and clients, proofs of advertisements, copies of current Philadelphia newspapers and periodicals, a copy of the *American Newspaper Annual and Directory* for 1928, and F. W. Ayer's Bible. On January 1, 1929, the agency staff left the quarters at Third and Chestnut, which it had occupied for 27 years, and took possession of the new building. Formal dedication and opening ceremonies were held on April 1, 1929, the sixtieth anniversary of the founding of N. W. Ayer & Son.[13] To members of the Ayer organization and to many others the Ayer building is not only a monument to F. W. Ayer but is also a symbol of the strength, stability, and dignity of the advertising business as conducted by N. W. Ayer & Son.

PIONEER WORK IN RADIO ADVERTISING

Long before it acquired its new quarters N. W. Ayer & Son had started work on a new medium of advertising, that of radio broadcasting. When the wireless transmission of sound advanced out of the buzz of dots and dashes to the stage in which vocal and instrumental sounds could be sent through the air, radio rushed into the American home. N. W. Ayer & Son was quick to recognize the new opportunity and made a notable pioneering effort, largely as the result of its connection with two clients, the American Telephone and Telegraph Company and the National Carbon Company. The Telephone Company had opened a broadcasting station, WEAF, in the summer of 1922, and was interested in having its station facilities used. The National Carbon Company, which was manufacturing batteries for receiving sets, desired to promote programs of general interest as a means of encouraging the use of radios and so enlarging its own market. The original policy of broadcasting stations did not permit any direct advertising to be broadcast, but the mention of the sponsor's name at the beginning and end of a program had a goodwill value which N. W. Ayer & Son soon began to exploit.

N. W. Ayer & Son was the first advertising agency to arrange a broadcast program, and it was also the first agency to study broadcasting seriously. Early in the autumn of 1922 it completed arrangements for a radio talk by a representative of the Shur-on Optical Company over KDKA of Pittsburgh (the first general broadcasting station in the United States), and a little later in the same year it arranged another one for E. R. Squibb & Sons, over WEAF of New York. In May, June, and July of 1923 the Ayer agency assisted with occasional programs for other clients over WEAF and, in September, over stations in Philadelphia (WDAR) and Minneapolis (WLAG).[14]

These early broadcasts were merely publicity talks, quite unlike the advertising program of later years. More important, by far, was the inauguration of the National Carbon Company's program, the "Eveready Hour," on December 4, 1923. This was the first regular series of broadcast entertainment and music to be sponsored by an advertiser in this country or elsewhere;[15] and N. W. Ayer & Son recommended and originated the program.

The difficulties which the Ayer agency had to contend with in the early years of broadcasting cannot be fully appreciated by the layman. Radio was still a novelty, receiving sets were few, and the listeners were interested less in the programs themselves than in the technical achievements of radio and in the experience of hearing sounds transmitted over a long distance without the use of wires. In the first Eveready announcement, however, it was stated that radio would grow as an integral part of daily life only as the quality of the programs improved. With the coöperation of the National Carbon Company and officials of WEAF, the Ayer agency arranged a series of weekly programs embodying minstrel shows, dramatic sketches, educational lectures, instrumental, orchestral and vocal music, and variety entertainment of many kinds.[16]

The work of an agency in arranging programs for broadcasting is highly complicated and extremely important. Let the reader consider for a moment the need for building up interesting and effective programs day after day, of giving continuity and individuality to a series of broadcasts, and of assembling competent talent for a wide variety of rôles. The routine details alone are stupendous — making contracts with many stations, arranging for the use of copyrighted material, conducting rehearsals, paying bills, and the like. Consider, too, the incalculable influence of the radio upon the general public and the responsibility which — though it is not often recognized — rests upon the people who direct the use of this important medium of communication and culture.

In these later days, when we have become satiated by the wide choice which the radio offers and when twisting the dial sometimes provides an alternation between boredom and downright annoyance, we tend to overlook the excellence of radio entertainment as a whole. We forget, too, the difficulties faced by the industry and the great advance since 1923 in the technique of planning and broadcasting programs over the air. Radio offered an entirely new medium of artistic expression. Like the cinema, it possessed a number of advantages over the ordinary theatre or music hall, such as its freedom from space limitations; but it depended upon sound alone for the transmission of ideas and images and upon entertainment as a carrier for advertising messages. Clearly its proper use depended upon the application of experience and imagination in a direction which, for advertising agencies, was absolutely new.

In general the history of radio broadcasting from 1923 to the present day has been the evolution of a technique for working in the medium of sound. The broadcasting companies themselves, particularly the national chains, have been a major factor in advancing the medium, but substantial assistance has also come from other sources. In this evolution the Eveready Hour programs, extending over six years, played an important part. Through its work with these and other broadcasts, N. W. Ayer & Son has made a definite contribution to the exploitation of radio as an advertising medium and (since American broadcasting has been supported almost wholly by advertising revenue) to radio's development as an instrument of entertainment and education.

In 1924 the public development of chain broadcasting began, and here, again, N. W. Ayer & Son and the two clients mentioned above played important parts. The first radio programs in this country were broadcast from the station of origin alone, and this fact seriously limited their value to advertisers. There were no networks or chains of stations like those of today to carry the programs to all parts of the country. In 1924, thanks to circumstances in which advertising played an important part, the development of such networks began.[17]

One factor in this change was the desire of advertisers for a wider circle of listeners. The Eveready programs, for example, initially reached only the territory covered by WEAF — little more than a local area. Dealers of the National Carbon Company elsewhere, of course, desired radio publicity in their markets and felt that the New York area was being favored unduly. The company recognized both the justice of the dealer feeling and its own pecuniary interest in contributing to the growth of a radio public and stimulating the market for batteries in other parts of the country. To some extent it met the need by sending out groups of artists to give broadcasts over stations throughout the United States. This was not altogether satisfactory. It was far too costly for the sponsors, and the quality of the programs could not be maintained.

The American Telephone and Telegraph Company, meanwhile, was faced with related problems. It wanted to obtain a wider audience for station WEAF, and it also was directly interested in making good programs available to other communities. Through the Western Electric Company it was engaged in the manufacture and sale of broadcasting equipment. Many stations had been established without any well-defined purpose and without consideration of the many operating problems involved. Their owners had reckoned with the cost of installation and maintenance, but not many of them had considered the difficulty and expense of providing suitable programs day after day. Amateur and inexpensive talent sufficed only for a short time, and became less satisfactory as the public gained in discriminating taste. Advertising brought in some revenue, but all the advertisers in the country could hardly bear the tremendous cost of supplying good programs for all the individual stations. Some means had to be found for providing a large number of stations with a steady stream of varied and interesting material without much expense to the station owners, or else the radio industry would grow stagnant.

The solution was fairly obvious: link several stations together. One good program could then be broadcast from ten stations at a small fraction of the cost of ten separate programs of mediocre quality. This would satisfy the demand of the sponsors for wider distribution without material increase in cost; it would enable local station owners to offer better programs and sell their unused time; and it would promote the expansion of the industry, thus giving an outlet for the radio equipment which the Telephone Company, through its subsidiary, produced. And, if the chain programs were sent over long-distance telephone wires to the local stations, the Telephone Company would receive further benefit. The difficulty was that telephone facilities, designed for conveying the human voice, could not properly transmit the high and low tones of music until a great deal of scientific research and improvement had been made.

The technical achievement of chain broadcasting is a story in itself. In working out the commercial problems involved the Telephone Company obtained assistance from its advertising agency, N. W. Ayer & Son. It is impossible to say how much credit for the final results should be attributed to the Ayer firm, but its insistence upon the urgent need of transmitting the advertising programs over several stations at once undoubtedly hastened the commercial development of multiple-station broadcasting. The first sponsored broadcast to be presented to the public over a network was the Eveready Hour on February 22, 1924, produced by N. W. Ayer & Son for the National Carbon Company.[18]

The application of radio to national advertising spread slowly until after 1926 when the first great national network (N.B.C.) was formed. For very good reasons everyone connected with advertising was doubtful about using the new medium for sales promotion. Almost from the start restriction had been imposed against any direct advertising in broadcast programs, and this meant, in effect, that radio could do little for sponsors beyond the creation of goodwill and publicity.[19] Even when, about 1927, the broadcasting stations began to relax their rules against direct advertising, no one had more than a vague idea of the limits of radio's utility in relation to the older advertising media. Did it supplant them or merely supplement them? If the latter, was it suitable for all types of products or not? And what were its relative advantages and disadvantages when compared with other media? Many such questions arose about radio, and after another decade of experience we still lack satisfactory answers to some of them.

Certainly radio was no special boon to the agencies. It forced them into the entertainment business, a field in which they had no experience and one which contains many severe headaches. It compelled them to extend operations into a medium in which rates and selling arrangements were bound, for some years, to be unstable, in which the number of persons reached would long be a matter of wild guesses, in which the results of a campaign (so long as efforts were confined to goodwill objectives) would be intangible indeed.

In using periodicals, agencies had supplied the advertisements, while the editors had provided the editorial content (entertainment and educational material). In using radio, agencies had not only to alter their advertising message to conform to the medium of sound (in contrast with a visual one) but also to prepare the "editorial content" of the programs which were to bear that message. Moreover (and this is still a bitter pill to swallow!), the editorial content had to predominate in quantity and the advertising message be small and unobtrusive. Additional difficulties arose from the fact that agencies had to buy time rather than space — time which could not be expanded as pages are added to a newspaper or magazine when additional advertising is to be inserted. Time which varied widely in advertising value at different hours of the day and different days of the week. Time, too, which confronted agencies with the problem of exclusiveness: a large number of advertisements can be printed in the same issue of a periodical and the reader can see them all if he wants to; but only a single program can be broadcast from a given station at a given time, and, if a listener tunes in to that program, the others which are being broadcast at the same hour are irrevocably lost to him.[20]

In short the advent of radio gave the agencies much trouble and expense, without any considerable amount of gain in revenue to offset the new burden. For the testimony of agency executives and of statistics of advertising in the various media is that, to a large extent, the expenditures on radio advertising represent money and effort diverted from periodical and other printed forms of advertising rather than any substantial addition to the total amount of advertising.[21] Even so, the advantages which radio offered made its use in advertising practically inescapable.

All this is clear now, but it was not readily apparent in 1928 and 1929 when the volume of broadcast advertising really began to reach impressive figures. Some agencies at that time chose to regard radio as practically superseding all other forms of advertising, and they urged it upon advertisers with little discrimination. Certain other agencies took the view that radio was an unproved medium which they, for the time at least, were not going to handle. N. W. Ayer & Son took the middle road and used broadcast advertising with caution, judging its merits as impartially as possible in comparison with other advertising media, and recommending it only when it promised to yield tangible results in a client's general selling campaign. Many an over-enthusiastic advertiser, to whom the glamour of radio made a strong appeal, was advised by the Ayer agency not to sponsor broadcasts because the prospects of satisfactory results were too poor.[22]

The Ayer agency believed, too, that radio advertising was particularly open to abuse which might alienate public opinion. It therefore adopted the policy that it would maintain direct control over the arrangement and production of all programs for which it was responsible, instead of leaving program production to the stations. Gradually it developed a staff of workers especially trained and experienced in this work; and in 1928, when the possibilities of radio advertising were clearly established, this staff was separated from the firm's other publicity work and organized as an independent department. Its duties were to assemble information about all phases of broadcast advertising, build up programs, hire talent, direct production, and handle the leasing of station time and all other details connected with broadcast programs.[23]

N. W. Ayer & Son claims a number of "radio firsts" for this period. Documentary proof of anything connected with the radio industry as a whole is difficult to obtain for the years preceding 1930,[24] but available evidence supports the claims made, and they are indicative of the firm's leadership in broadcasting: 1922, the first commercial broadcast arranged by an agency; 1923, the first continuous series of commercial programs; 1924, the first commercial network program and the first "continuity" or drama-type program designed especially for broadcasting; 1925, the first commercial adaptation of a full-length play for radio; 1926, the first commercial adaptation of a full-length novel (*Show Boat*) and the introduction of Eddie Cantor, George Gershwin, and The Revelers Quartette to radio audiences; 1927, the first orchestra using special scores for radio (Nathaniel Shilkret's); 1930, the first big "variety show" program.[25]

THE INCORPORATION OF THE AYER PARTNERSHIP

In May, 1929, came a fundamental alteration in the legal organization of N. W. Ayer & Son. Abandoning the partnership form which had endured for the first sixty years of its life, the firm became a corporation under the laws of the State of Delaware. The purpose of this step was, as stated in the public announcement, "to afford more members of the Ayer organization opportunity to participate in the business through stock ownership than was feasible in the past under the partnership form." [26]

It had long been a matter of pride with F. W. Ayer that he was personally responsible for all the obligations of his business, and on many occasions he had said that as long as he lived the firm would remain a partnership. Individualist that he was, he preferred to keep both ownership and control safe from any dilution. By the time of his death, however, the partnership form of organization was beginning to present difficulties. The staff had steadily increased in number; and there were junior executives who, as a matter of good management, should receive a share of the profits they helped to make. The firm had instituted a plan for distributing bonuses out of profits; but, while this device gave the staff members an interest in operating results, it did not give them the actual stake in the business which they desired and which, for the best interests of the firm, they should have had. Admitting more men to partnership would have complicated the problems of control and legal liability too much. The only workable solution was to incorporate the enterprise.

At the time of incorporation the five partners entered into a trust agreement, the purpose of which was to enable Fry to retain control of the business while effecting a broader distribution of its ownership among key officers and employees.[27] Since this agreement later became the basis of litigation, certain details require mention here. The ex-partners deposited with five voting trustees (the five men themselves) a majority of the stock issued (Fry deposited 234,000 shares and the other four 39,000 each) and received trust certificates in exchange. It was agreed that, if any depositor should die or leave the firm, the other depositors would have the right to purchase his interest and divide it accord ing to the will of the "majority in interest." This term was defined as "a majority in interest according to the number of shares deposited" under the agreement.

The incorporation was not intended to bring additional capital into the company. Indeed, instead of creating shares of stock to be sold for cash by the corporation, the firm allotted all the issue to the five partners according to the amount of their previous interest (60 per cent to Fry and 10 per cent to each of the other four). The partners themselves were then asked, in effect, to sell a portion of their holdings to other members of the organization. Stock ownership, moreover, was restricted to members who had at least two years of continuous service to their credit. It is still true today, therefore, that every dollar invested in N. W. Ayer & Son, apart from the original $250 capital, has been earned in the business itself.[28]

EXTENSION OF AYER SERVICE TO FOREIGN COUNTRIES

Shortly after its incorporation, N. W. Ayer & Son opened a branch office in Detroit and extended the sphere of its activities to include certain foreign fields. On November 1, 1929, the agency opened a fully equipped branch agency in London;[29] in 1930 it established representatives in South America;[30] and, as we shall see in the next chapter, it eventually not only enlarged its Latin American organization to provide full agency service but also established branches in Canada.

This expansion abroad was a decidedly new venture for N. W. Ayer & Son, and it represents a field of activity which was abandoned in the period from 1940 to 1947. Nevertheless it deserves consideration here — if for no other reason simply because it now appears to have been a mistake.

The Ayer firm had occasionally received small orders from European firms which wished to advertise their goods in American markets, but until the World War it gave little thought to the marketing of American goods abroad. American concerns which wished to advertise overseas had either resorted to foreign agents or hired one of the few New York agencies which specialized in export advertising. The Ayer attitude in earlier years was expressed when a client asked about advertising for American exports in 1919:[31]

> We must frankly say that we do not know anything about the export business. . . . Owing to the complexities of the situation, we have not seen fit to enter this field, and we are not in a position to advise our client intelligently about it.

When the matter was again brought up in 1924, the firm was still not interested; it had no knowledge about foreign marketing conditions and did not feel justified in making any efforts abroad.[32] By 1926, however, the interests of its clients were beginning to force the Ayer agency to consider venturing into the foreign field. Both the Victor Talking Machine Company and the R. J. Reynolds Tobacco Company, for example, were advertising in Latin American countries; and, while their advertisements were placed by specialists in export advertising, they expected Ayer to produce the copy used abroad. This compelled the agency to tackle the problem of preparing copy in foreign languages and adapted to foreign points of view. In 1927, moreover, the firm undertook, at the request of the California Prune Growers' Association, a market survey in a number of European countries. While this investigation was going on, it decided to examine the entire question of export advertising. With many clients established in foreign markets, the possibility of extending Ayer services overseas had to be faced. It was particularly advisable to provide facilities in England where several of the firm's clients were already entrenched.[33]

The immediate occasion for extending activities abroad was the desire to give additional service to the Ford Motor Company. Ford had become an Ayer client in 1927, and the agency had done a distinguished piece of work in advertising the new Model A which first appeared in public in December, 1927. The Ford Company had factories and a selling organization in Great Britain; and, being dissatisfied with its English advertising, it urged Ayer to undertake the work. Ayer executives studied the situation during 1928 and decided that, if the firm went abroad at all, it should arrange to give complete agency service on a permanent basis. It would be essential to maintain a complete, essentially self-sufficient staff in England; and, while this would be costly, some of the expense might be absorbed if other American advertising accounts could be handled at the same time. Eventually it might even be possible to obtain some English clients, although among English firms there was a definite feeling against the use of foreign agencies.

It was evident that American-made advertising and selling methods could not be successfully transplanted to England, and a study was made of British advertising organization and technique as a basis for branch operations. The firm decided to have a British staff under an American manager who had proved himself in the parent organization. Thus was established the policy which the Ayer firm applied when it set up other foreign branches, namely, to recruit the main staff from the country in which the office is located. The task of organizing N. W. Ayer & Son, Ltd., was assigned to Douglas Meldrum (who remained in charge until 1939). Until all phases of operation were well in hand, he was assisted by three other men from the Philadelphia staff.[34]

The Ford Motor Company also desired to have its advertising in Latin American countries improved and unified. It had been spending large sums of money on advertising there, but the selection of media, preparation of copy, and placing had been left to local dealers, with the result that much effort was wasted on many small, unrelated, poorly conceived, and badly executed campaigns. In spite of the cloudy economic outlook of late 1929, N. W. Ayer & Son agreed to extend its service to South America, and early in 1930 it set about forming the required organization. In this, as in all moves of major importance, N. W. Ayer & Son moved cautiously, sought information from all possible sources upon every phase of export advertising, and gave no hint of its ultimate plans.[35]

In some respects at least, the establishment of service in South America was not so important as that in England; but the South American venture illustrates more sharply the difficulties which are typically encountered when an agency extends operations to a foreign country. For this reason, as well as the fact that a considerable amount of evidence is available on the episode, it seems wise to treat the initial effort in some detail.

Going into South America, of course, raised many problems of language, diplomacy, and racial temperament. To assist in handling them, the Ayer firm engaged a man who had devoted much of his life to commercial and diplomatic work in Latin American countries, Boaz W. Long, formerly Chief of the Latin American Division, Department of State, and one-time United States Minister to Cuba.

After Long and a representative of the Ford Motor Company had spent five months in conferring with Ford agents and making a general survey in Mexico and Central and South America, the agency attacked the problem of providing adequate agency facilities. The economic and political difficulties which had developed in Latin America during the course of 1930 made it obvious that this part of the Ayer organization held no immediate prospect of self-support; but, while the agency executives endeavored to keep the losses as low as possible, there was no thought of skimping service. As one member of the staff put it:[36]

. . . after the Ford Motor Company were absolutely satisfied that they were getting the maximum service and we also were satisfied that our organization was up to the Ayer standard, then the possibility of new clients would be considered. No energy, however, would be dissipated in seeking or serving new clients until the first objective, as mentioned above, had been reached.

N. W. Ayer & Son made its beginning in a small way without fanfare. During 1931 it opened small offices in Buenos Aires and São Paulo in order to provide emergency service and personal representation in the field. At the same time, the management arranged to handle routine copy preparation and other details in the Philadelphia headquarters and, as far as possible, to place the advertising through the firms in this country that represent South American publications. Since only the largest newspapers and periodicals have such representatives in the United States, the agency was obliged to deal directly with a great many publishers in South America. Eventually both offices were made completely self-contained, so that each planned, wrote, and placed the advertising that it handled.

The difficulties which N. W. Ayer & Son encountered in South America resemble in many ways the conditions which were common in the early days of advertising in the United States. Reliable information about the circulation and advertising value of the various publications was sadly lacking. Space rates and agency discounts were subject to bargaining and special favors. Market information and statistics were exceedingly difficult to obtain at any cost. Among the local agencies, moreover, there was widespread and ruthless cutting of rates which made the Ayer one-price policy seem quixotic and unduly expensive to advertisers.

To problems arising out of the relatively new and unstabilized condition of the advertising industry in South America were added all the complications of working in unfamiliar surroundings. The Ayer organization encountered a certain amount of nationalistic hostility, not only among rival agencies, but also among publishers and business men. There were endless language difficulties, for copy written in correct Portuguese and Castilian Spanish had to be modified to conform to local usages and variations. And there were problems of illustration to be solved in order to avoid any outlandish or incongruous note in the finished advertisements — to show, for example, cars with right-hand drives in Argentina, and to use correct South American scenes for backgrounds. To meet these difficulties and to avoid undue emphasis upon the advertising methods and techniques used in the United States, N. W. Ayer & Son employed Latin Americans with advertising experience, both in Philadelphia and in the South American offices.

Until the branches were made self-contained and independent of Philadelphia, there were also problems to be solved in maintaining satisfactory communication between Philadelphia and the South American representatives — in scheduling orders and copy to arrive on time despite the vagaries of international mail service, in adapting newspaper mats and illustration plates to fit the unstandardized papers of South America, and in getting material transported and passed through customs without too much delay and expense. And, shortly after the Ayer organization had got under way, all sorts of regulations and difficulties arising out of the depression were encountered in connection with the monetary exchanges.

To complicate matters still further, the Ayer staff had the delicate task of providing the improvements and continuity which the Ford Motor Company wanted without antagonizing the local agents who had previously controlled the advertising. In other words, it had to work not only with Ford officials in Detroit but also with a great many different Ford dealers of widely varying experience, nationality, and points of view. Most of the dealers, believing that a foreign agency could not prepare their advertising or bargain with publishers so well as a local agency could, were inclined to resent the intrusion.

To find a way through the tangled labyrinth of personal connections, political machinations, national and racial prejudices, unfamiliar business practices and customs, and yet to keep all parties reasonably contented, was a task which demanded the utmost tact and business ability of a rare order. But by dint of patience, hard work, and a willingness to learn, N. W. Ayer & Son achieved success. After the Ford advertising was well in hand, it sought and obtained business from other firms operating in South America. If the opinion of important South American press representatives is a reliable guide, Ayer advertising was effective, the firm's integrity impressed publishers, Ayer policies with regard to space rates and charges to clients helped to introduce order into the rather chaotic condition of South American advertising, and N. W. Ayer & Son established a general reputation for stability and sound business practice.[37]

THE PLENTEOUS YEARS COME TO AN END

At the very time it was expanding its organization abroad, the Ayer agency was confronted with a declining market at home. Advertising suffered, as every phase of business did, from the crash of 1929. During 1930 the volume of advertising for the United States as a whole dropped more than 20 per cent from the 1929 figures.[38] At first, however, N. W. Ayer & Son rose against this ebbing tide: thanks partly to foreign business and a marked increase in radio advertising, the firm's volume for 1930 rose slightly above that of the preceding year to the highest mark in its entire history, a mark not to be surpassed until the 1940's.

Men talked bravely in 1930 about recovery being just around the corner, and for a while it may have looked as if N. W. Ayer & Son might escape the general decline. But we know now that the corner was a mirage and that lean years were really on the horizon. We shall see that the Ayer agency felt the depression after 1930 and felt it severely. Between 1923 and 1930, however, it had prospered mightily. It had attained the status of a corporation, it had reached out beyond the American borders, and it had made great strides forward in advertising techniques. In all respects it had been a credit to its founder and to the man who succeeded him at the helm.

CHAPTER VII

THE LEAN YEARS, 1931-1936

FOR N. W. AYER & SON, as for many other American business institutions, the six years after 1930 constituted a long and severe trial. The biblical succession of seven lean years after seven years of plenty worked out almost exactly for the firm. Volume shrank alarmingly in 1931, profits dropped almost out of sight, and the competitive struggle against rivals tested the Ayer organization and its policies as never before. When, in 1933, the external business situation began to improve, a series of untoward events started inside the agency which could certainly have wrecked a weaker firm. In the preceding period (1923–30) the Ayer agency had had to adapt itself to new leadership and greatly increased business, but it did so when the times, being relatively prosperous, were favorable. Between 1931 and 1936 it again had to adapt itself to new leadership and decreased business, and to do so in times which the word "adverse" scarcely begins to describe. It may well be that this period from 1931 to 1936 will ultimately stand out as the most critical one in Ayer history, and surviving it appear the greatest single achievement of the firm's management.[1]

A DEPRESSION HITS THE ADVERTISING INDUSTRY

After 1930 all branches of the advertising industry were hard hit by the depressed economic situation. Many firms curtailed their advertising expenditures sharply, while others stopped their general advertising altogether. The use of all periodical advertising declined rapidly during 1931 and 1932. In 1933 even radio, which had enjoyed a substantial gain during the preceding three years, joined the downward slide.[2] Of the firms which continued to advertise in this trying period, a great many stressed bargain prices rather than quality and resorted to sensational advertising tactics in a desperate attempt to capture sales. It was a natural reaction and in some respects a wise one, but, before recovery set in, American advertising had reached some new lows in objectionable practice.

The frantic scramble for business added new burdens to the advertising agencies' complicated task. For, although clients were advertising in smaller volume, they needed and demanded more aid than ever before in handling their distribution problems. Chain and department stores intensified marketing difficulties not only by slashing the prices of nationally advertised goods but also by vigorously promoting their own privately branded merchandise. And a new headache for national advertisers appeared in the form of the supermarket, which began by reducing equipment and service to the very minimum and was able to reduce prices still more, thus aggravating a thoroughly demoralized price situation.[3]

The urgent need for rigid economy, plus a natural desire to exploit every available means of stimulating sales, ultimately led to more efficient advertising techniques, but the first result was a nation-wide rash of cheap and nasty copy. Expensive art work yielded place to cheaper (though often effective) photographic illustrations. The tabloid or display type of layout almost crowded out other copy arrangements, and the comic-strip technique was adopted with a vengeance.[4] The use of testimonials of all kinds increased,[5] while premiums were recklessly offered and prize contests swept the country as swiftly as the craze for jig-saw puzzles. The shrieking headlines, gross exaggeration, and downright deceit which appeared had no parallel except the patent-medicine advertising of the nineteenth century, while the use of pseudo-scientific arguments and appeals to emotion and appetite surpassed all previous efforts and violated previously accepted standards of decency.[6]

The desperate tactics employed by many advertisers at this time were in part the cause and in part the result of strenuous competition among agencies for the dwindling volume of business. In their desire to reduce every possible expense, advertisers frequently demanded concessions from agencies in the form of lower rates, secret rebates, or special services to be given without compensation. One firm even made the announcement (later retracted) that it was going to handle its own advertising and demanded from media owners the discount ordinarily given to agents. Advertisers were obviously in a position to make demands which both agencies and media owners, fearing further loss of business, would hesitate to refuse.

It was evident, too, that advertisers were not the only ones who initiated breaches in established practice. Certain agencies were volunteering concessions of one sort or another in an effort to retain existing clients or to lure new ones away from other agencies. Similarly, agents frequently proposed "a new copy approach" if the advertiser failed to demand it, and the approach suggested was often the extreme type to which reference has just been made. The situation was aggravated, of course, by agency men who were led by circumstances to set up new agencies and stood in desperate need of clients.

It is impossible to determine the relative extent of unethical practice which goes on in any industry at any time. Concrete evidence is seldom obtainable, and judgment in such matters is largely a matter of personal opinion. There is good reason, nevertheless, for believing that unethical conduct increased substantially in advertising between 1929 and 1933.[7] Certainly this view was held by many men who occupied important positions in the industry. There was unquestionably an increase in the turnover of advertising accounts,[8] and agencies felt that they were subject to expensive and unreasonable demands. Those who, like N. W. Ayer & Son, refused to lower their rates or copy standards lost some accounts to less scrupulous rivals.[9]

All agencies, ethical or otherwise, strove to keep old accounts and get new ones. Despite all efforts, some of them went into bankruptcy and others sought salvation in mergers.[10] All of them had to retrench on the one hand and improve service on the other. Thus it was no accident that substantial gains were made after 1930 in the application of scientific methods to the analysis of markets and advertising results, as is evident from the notable progress of the Gallup and Starch surveys among newspaper and magazine readers, the Crossley, Hooper, and other analyses of radio listening habits, the Traffic Audit Bureau studies of outdoor advertising coverage, and various developments in testing advertising copy. There was also considerable improvement in the styling of products and design of packages.[11] In advertising, as in other branches of business, business depression seems to provide a necessary purge, one which involves hardship and suffering but ultimately results in the elimination of weak firms and economic waste and the development of improved techniques.

In many ways the tide turned toward improvement in the second half of 1933. The volume of newspaper advertising began to rise in July, followed by radio and magazine advertising in October. There was also a gradual but definite improvement in the copy which appeared, while competitive tactics generally moved to a somewhat higher plane as business conditions improved. Not all was smooth sailing, however, for advertisers had revived with increased spirit the old argument about the traditional commission plan of agency compensation. More serious still was the fact that, for the first time in advertising history, those concerned went beyond heated debate to dig up facts about actual practice. Although there was disagreement as to interpretation, both sides produced evidence indicating that a considerable number of agents and clients were operating with arrangements which did not conform to the traditional system. Some of these might be regarded as undermining it — possibly an indication of a coming fundamental shift.[12]

Perhaps the development which did most to perplex advertising men was a profound change in public attitude toward advertising in particular and private enterprise as a whole. A tendency in this direction was discernible before 1929, one manifestation being the popular reception of two books, *The Tragedy of Waste*,[13] and *Your Money's Worth*.[14] But the crash and subsequent events brought rapidly to the fore something like a revolution in public thinking which, as we all know, touched every aspect of economic, political, and social life. Advertising was an obvious field for attack.

One indication of the new attitude was an unprecedented public skepticism about advertising. *Ballyhoo* and other satirical magazines, which were devoted wholly to the ridicule of advertising, found an appreciative audience, while both stage and screen presented successful burlesques of the industry. *Consumers' Research*, a confidential service for testing commercial products and services, experienced a rapid growth and exerted an influence quite out of proportion to the size of the organization. Books like *100,000,000 Guinea Pigs*[15] and *Skin Deep*[16] not only attacked advertising but also dared to name products and cite evidence of the deceit involved in their promotion, and they were widely read. The consumer, moreover, found a sympathetic government in Washington. Various pieces of legislation were prepared on his behalf, culminating in 1938 with the passage of the Wheeler-Lea amendment giving the Federal Trade Commission regulatory control over all advertising, and the new Federal Food, Drug, and Cosmetic Act (Copeland Bill) which greatly extended the power of the Department of Agriculture to safeguard the public against harmful or fraudulent products.[17] That a widespread change in public attitude was taking place is reflected in the fact that more magazine articles on consumers and their problems were published during twelve months in 1933–34 than in the twenty-year period from 1900 to 1920.[18]

Reputable advertisers and agencies had little to fear from intelligent government regulation and the proper education of consumers. In fact, they stood to gain from the restraining effect of such a movement upon less scrupulous rivals. For several years, however, the enthusiasm on the consumer's behalf threatened to go much too far. Confused thinking was rife because many people, including a large proportion of advertising men themselves, identify advertising with high-pressure selling. It is, of course, simply one means of communication, and whether it is good or bad depends upon how it is used. Not many people condemn axes because one is occasionally used to commit murder or mayhem, but the public is less discriminating in the realm of advertising. Those who make the sharpest attacks on private enterprise and advertising do not hesitate to advertise and indeed are compelled to do so if they are to be heard. The confusion about advertising, plus widespread doubts as to what could and could not be stated in advertisements or on packages, made advertisers hesitate to advertise and greatly accentuated the problem of preparing copy for publication.

The attacks on advertising and private enterprise frightened both agencies and their clients, but, to some extent, the experience proved to be a blessing in disguise. Counsel on public relations, long regarded as a more or less superfluous activity carried on in the interests of vain executives, became an essential service which promised to help business regain public confidence. Not all of the resulting institutional advertising and publicity material was wisely conceived or well executed, but it gave agencies additional work to do and carried them still further away beyond the original function of buying space.

On the whole, this period was a perplexing one for the entire advertising industry. Faced with acute operating difficulties because of the total business situation, subjected to public ridicule and to sharp attacks by reformers, harassed by bitter competition within the industry and by rapid change in business generally, and threatened with legislative action of a drastic nature, every phase of advertising was forced to undergo readjustment. It emerged considerably deflated, both in the eyes of the consuming public and in the opinion of the firms that used it. And yet it emerged a more effective and essential mechanism than ever in our social and economic life.

Within the Ayer organization the period 1931–36 was marked by numerous changes and adjustments, many of them occasioned by the dizzy succession of economic and political developments going on outside. Painful as they must have seemed at the time, the various adjustments, together with the strength of the organization today, constitute evidence of the remarkable adaptability and vigor of N. W. Ayer & Son.

In spite of the deepening world-wide depression, the firm decided to go ahead with its extension into foreign fields. During 1932 the services of its Latin American organization were formally advertised, and late in the same year the agency announced that it was prepared to handle general export advertising for American firms.[19] On March 19, 1934, it opened an office in Montreal, Canada, completely equipped to handle all phases of agency work, and three years later it established a branch in Toronto.[20] Like the entry into England and South America, the extension of service into Canada was primarily for the benefit of the Ford

Motor Company. International conditions prevented any world-wide development of Ayer business, apart from a few advertisements placed in Far Eastern papers during 1933, but the offices in England, Canada, and South America made satisfactory progress so long as Ayer retained the Ford account.

Meanwhile, in 1932 the Ayer agency resumed operations in the field of outdoor advertising, a medium which it had given up in 1915 because the owners of outdoor plants at that time were trying to eliminate advertising agents. When changes in the structure of the industry again made it possible for agencies to handle the medium on satisfactory terms, N. W. Ayer & Son promptly acquired membership in the Outdoor Advertising Association of America, Inc.[21] In 1932 the Ayer agency also assigned men to familiarize themselves with motion pictures as a medium for sales promotion. While this field was still of relatively minor importance, N. W. Ayer & Son assisted with the production and distribution of industrial motion pictures for a number of clients and systematically kept informed on the latest developments affecting the medium.[22]

The firm also made substantial advances in handling broadcast advertising. Until 1930 all agencies tended to look for attractive programs and then to seek advertisers who would take a fling at broadcasting. After 1930 much of the original glamour and mystery of radio had vanished, and men had to take a more realistic approach. The Ayer firm rapidly developed the view that an agency must start with the client's sales problems, determine whether radio can help, and then devise a program which will achieve specific ends in terms of sales. The complete reversal of the method is significant.

In spite of the general demoralization of advertising at the bottom of the depression, the Ayer firm held firmly to its high standards and integrity. In the face of bitter competition from other agencies it steadfastly refused to reduce its commission or make any special concessions in order to gain new business or retain existing accounts. It turned a deaf ear to the demands of some of its clients for vulgar or sensational copy appeals. In fact, the management actively opposed this tendency, and Harry Batten, then head of the Ayer Copy Department, was encouraged to wage a campaign against copy developments which the firm regarded as detrimental to the long-term interests of advertising.[23]

In many ways the most significant development in Ayer service during this period was an increased emphasis upon research work — in market analysis, copy testing, and field work. One notable example was an extensive survey launched by the Ayer organization in 1931 to determine the coverage and influence of more than 450 radio stations. At that time information of this kind was not available and even the "Coöperative Analysis of Broadcasting" had only been started. Unwilling to rely on any one set of facts in making its appraisal of station values, the Ayer firm made one of its own, despite the expense involved.[24]

The Ayer management, like other firms, naturally had to retrench in order to prevent the sharp decline in volume from causing serious financial loss between 1931 and 1934. In 1931 President Fry renounced his entire salary, and other Ayer executives took substantial reductions. The management reduced its budget wherever possible, tightened its check upon expenditures, and began to charge customers for a number of advertising services which it formerly had given as a part of the work covered by its 16⅔ per cent commission. It also suspended dividend payments (1931–33), and scrutinized credit with great care in order to protect its cash position.

So far as possible, the firm tried to maintain its general staff of employees. Although vacancies were not filled, there were no wholesale discharges, and there were no wage cuts until 1932. Early in 1933 the decline in the volume of work made it essential either to reduce the size of the staff materially or to operate only part time. Being reluctant to add to the general unemployment and also anxious to avoid losing able and experienced employees, the management chose to spread the existing work. All staff members were required to take one day off per week without pay, and the absences were divided over the week in order to maintain continuous operation. Similar steps were taken by other agencies, though some were rather ruthless in reducing their pay rolls.[25]

The equality of treatment which Fry insisted upon, in making pay cuts and spreading work, was well meant, but it damaged the morale he intended to protect. There was a considerable proportion of dead wood in the organization, and the members who were making recognized contributions naturally resented being treated in exactly the same way as the incompetents. We shall see later that Fry's successor as president inherited serious personnel problems.

The passage of the National Industrial Recovery Act in June, 1933, was followed by a request to N. W. Ayer & Son to use its resources in aiding economic recovery through explaining the NRA to the public. This was a logical request. It called for the type of service which the firm had given during World War I and for which F. W. Ayer had predicted a vast future; the firm was among the leaders in its field, and several Ayer executives had close friends among men who went into the Roosevelt administration. Nevertheless, although it appreciated the proffered honor, the Ayer management felt obliged for two reasons to refrain from undertaking the work on a contractual basis: the success of the campaign would ultimately depend upon the active coöperation of newspaper publishers, and the agency believed that requests to publishers for gratuitous assistance in publicity work would come with better grace from the government itself than from a commercial agency which was receiving compensation for its efforts. The Ayer management, moreover, could not favor a connection which might involve it in partisan political entanglements.

On the other hand, N. W. Ayer & Son was eager to promote the recovery program in every possible way, and it had no intention of shirking its public duties. It freely gave its best counsel on the steps to be taken by the government, and it temporarily released a part of its staff for service in Washington. Members of the Ayer organization assisted in preparing publicity and advertising material explaining the plans and procedure of the National Recovery Administration; and, when the designs submitted by various artists for an NRA emblem proved unacceptable, the Ayer art director, Charles T. Coiner, hastily supplied the famous Blue Eagle.[26] It was soon evident that the whole project was becoming a political football, and, since the Ayer firm had really given its assistance as a temporary measure while the NRA developed its own staff of workers, the agency was shortly able to withdraw, but not until it had rendered genuine public service.[27]

The repeal of the national Prohibition Amendment in 1933 brought up for reconsideration the Ayer policy on liquor advertising. There was considerable financial inducement for the agency to withdraw its old opposition, for large appropriations for advertising were in prospect. Moreover, public opinion about alcoholic beverages had changed, and the Ayer scruples about advertising such things might well be reconsidered. In view of its reduced volume the Ayer management could not afford to dismiss lightly the opportunity for new business. Nor could it postpone making the decision, for at least one large brewery had requested N. W. Ayer & Son to handle its advertising, and an important client, Canada Dry Ginger Ale, Inc., had decided to sell alcoholic beverages as soon as repeal became effective. Hence, for the agency to adhere to its dry policy of pre-prohibition days involved not only rejecting new business but also giving up one of its existing accounts. On the other hand, some of the officers felt that a change in policy would probably alienate certain other clients.

In July, 1933, the Ayer management decided to continue its established policy and gave notice of its decision to terminate its advertising contract with Canada Dry.[28] In a statement later made public, Fry indicated that the firm had based its action upon business as well as moral grounds. "The return of liquor," he said, "will divert an important share of America's mass purchasing power from essential commodities." After pointing out that the increased government revenues arising out of repeal would come from those people who could least afford the taxes, he mentioned other considerations:[29]

Many decades ago my firm adopted the policy of not advertising alcohol. The reason for this is simply that, as an advertising agency, we must identify ourselves so closely with the affairs of our clients that we are in effect, a part of their businesses. In the case of a client who manufactures or distributes alcoholic beverages, this would create for us an impossible situation, since we would then be in the position of making alcohol attractive to the youth of this country. Furthermore, we do not wish to classify our other clients with the liquor business.

To a critical observer, these reasons are not altogether convincing. It is true that the liquor business would divert some of the nation's purchasing power. But automobiles, soft drinks, musical instruments, cosmetics, and other luxury goods advertised by Ayer have exactly the same effect. If the Ayer management desired to advertise only essential commodities, where would it draw the line? And if it is true, as the second argument suggests, that the firm really wished to avoid "making alcohol attractive to the youth of this country," one is compelled to ask why, during prohibition, it frequently prepared advertisements which emphasized the mixing qualities of ginger ale and even contained recipes for cocktails; and why, after the restatement of its dry policy, the agency made similar appeals in its advertising for other clients.[30] In practice, the liquor business is so closely bound up with many others that it is impossible to separate it sharply from them, and any attempt to do so must inevitably result in inconsistency or compromise. The Ayer management was fully cognizant of this and more.

In the final analysis, the dry policy of N. W. Ayer & Son in 1933 was based upon an understandable mixture of moral and practical considerations. Fry, like F. W. Ayer before him, disapproved of the use of intoxicants, and a number of important Ayer clients held the same view. There is much to admire in his willingness to sacrifice profits in the interests of a policy, and this in a time of severe depression. There were, however, additional considerations which the management stresses today. The amount of money for agencies which is available in the liquor business has generally been overrated. It is notorious, moreover, that the liquor industry is shot through and through with many irregular trade practices which greatly complicate the work of sales promotion. The present Ayer management feels that, now as in the past, it can afford to refuse liquor accounts on a straight business basis.

CHANGES IN THE OWNERSHIP AND MANAGEMENT OF N. W. AYER & SON, 1930–1936

The Ayer firm had faced depression a number of times in its history, but never before had it been obliged to do so while adjusting itself to important changes within its own organization. Moreover, there had never before been a serious rift among the owners of the business. In 1933, however, a period of stress be-

gan among the principal stockholders which was not to end until
two disagreements had become public and the ownership of the
business had substantially changed. It is essential to note, before
examining these events, that the final outcome left the firm in the
hands of men who started their employment under F. W. Ayer
himself and who were firmly resolved to carry on Ayer traditions
and policies.

The first break occurred in March, 1933, when two vice-presidents of N. W. Ayer & Son resigned and took with them a number of employees and several advertising accounts. The leader in
this step was James M. Mathes, who had been made a partner of
the Ayer firm in 1920. Two factors were the occasion for the
resignation. Mathes had long been an officer of the Canada Dry
Ginger Ale Company, which for ten years had been an important
Ayer client. When, with the approach of the repeal of the Prohibition Amendment, Canada Dry decided to handle alcoholic beverages, friction arose because Wilfred Fry was unwilling to accept
that type of advertising. Secondly, Fry objected to the amount of
time that Mathes devoted to stock promotions which had nothing
to do with the work of the agency.[31] The break involved more
than a disturbance in top management and the loss of several accounts: Mathes had excelled in getting new business, and within
Ayer management he had been the principal advocate of radio
advertising; his departure left a gap which was not easy to fill.
He was succeeded as head of the New York office by Gerold M.
Lauck, who had been made a resident partner in 1925 and elected
to the Ayer board of directors in 1931. Mr. Lauck's subsequent
success with the position has amply proved the wisdom of the
choice.

This episode was simply another one of the very frequent ways
in which new agencies come into being. Every agency, from Volney B. Palmer's time down to the present day, has been subject
to a splitting-off process by which a part of its staff and business
separates to form a rival firm. Of course this type of parturition
happens in all lines of business, but it is especially prevalent
among advertising agencies because the agency business requires
little initial capital and depends so much upon individual talents
and personal contacts. Once an enterprising employee has become

familiar with the routine work, accumulated some savings, demonstrated his ability to create effective advertising ideas and copy, and become friendly with one or two advertisers, he is in a position to start an agency. And when he thinks he can do better on his own than as an employee, he frequently makes the attempt. It is a gambler's choice, but the stakes are high if he wins. Probably most existing agencies were born in this way.[32]

Like other agencies, N. W. Ayer & Son had suffered from this amoeba-like division on a number of previous occasions. For example, in 1919 several of its employees left to form the agency of Snodgrass & Gayness, Inc.;[33] and in 1923 another group left to form Young & Rubicam, now one of the largest agencies in the United States. Both the Mathes agency and Young & Rubicam have since produced offshoots, and the Ayer firm, like the Lord & Thomas agency (now Foote-Cone-Belding) and a number of other long-established houses, can be said to have produced at least two generations of offspring.[34]

Late in 1934 the Ayer firm lost two more of its former partners when William M. Armistead and Adam Kessler, Jr., retired because of ill health. Since both men had long played important rôles in the Philadelphia organization and had been close personal friends of Fry, their withdrawal was keenly felt. After their departure, the most influential men remaining in the firm were President Fry and Vice-president George H. Thornley (who had been partners until 1929), and Messrs. H. A. Batten, Clarence L. Jordan, and Gerold M. Lauck. While the latter three had not been members of the old partnership, they had all had long experience in the business. Batten had started his career in the Ayer organization in 1911 as a printer's devil and had worked up to the headship of the Copy Department. Jordan had begun with the firm in 1915, and, having assisted Armistead in supervising general service, he was placed in charge of that branch of the management upon Armistead's retirement. Lauck had joined the Ayer staff in 1919 and had been made head of the New York office in 1933. Upon the incorporation of the firm in 1929, Batten, Jordan, and Lauck had been made vice-presidents along with Thornley, and they had also been members of the Board of Directors since 1931.

President Fry was ill during much of 1934 and 1935, and in this period his associates were obliged to assume an increased share of the burden of managing the firm. In April, 1936, when it became known that he was dying of cancer, the other members of the board of directors — Batten, Jordan, Lauck, and Thornley — felt the need of an arrangement which would permit them, as a group, to carry on the management of the firm. They presented the matter to Fry in the hospital, and with his approval they set up a management committee consisting of the four men, under Batten's chairmanship.

The death of Wilfred Fry on July 27, 1936, was a severe blow to the Ayer organization. It brought to the surface a long-smoldering disagreement among the top executives, and it deprived the staff of the man who was the embodiment of the original Ayer tradition. Fry's death, much more than that of F. W. Ayer, marked the end of an era in the firm's development. Viewed in perspective, a change in leadership had to come if the firm was to survive, but his death meant nonetheless a period of adaptation which was inevitably difficult.

Fry had never been an advertising man in a technical way, and there are those who assert that he was not a business man in the usual sense of the term. He was an idealist, a man of simple honesty, integrity, and personal generosity, and it is always difficult to appraise the ultimate contribution of such a man. Fry had firmly endeavored to carry out the principles and ideals laid down by his father-in-law. The difficulty was that times were changing and some of the things he stood for were out of date or fast becoming so. He continued the paternalism of F. W. Ayer when paternalism was ceasing to be acceptable in business. He was solemnly dignified when such a trait was viewed by the younger generation as stuffy and outmoded. A peace-loving man, he often tried to avoid or postpone disagreements or solve them by compromises which sometimes left basic questions unanswered, when the situation demanded a frank facing of issues and clear-cut solutions which might give pain but disposed of problems once for all. Like many a deeply religious man, he failed to understand that it takes hard work and penetrating analysis to solve business and social problems, that patience and goodwill are not enough.

It is hardly too much to say that he was a naïve man faced with a situation of extreme complexity and that he tended unconsciously to insulate himself against it.

We must judge the man as fairly as we can against the background in which he lived. The interval from the time Fry took over the business until his death was a period of unprecedented change, and successful adaptation to it called for extraordinary capacity and insight. Fry tried to do what F. W. Ayer expected him to do — uphold the policies by which Ayer had made the firm great. But those policies (like most) demanded firmness in their application. Fry lacked the capacity to apply the policies in a new and complex situation with the necessary strength and resourcefulness. His qualities were those of a whole generation of men; his shortcomings were those of a troubled era which is not yet past. It is clear from events within the Ayer organization during the next ten years that the firm needed a younger man at the helm, a man who knew the technical side of advertising intimately and at the same time possessed administrative skills of a new order.[35] We shall see that it got such a man as a result of events following Fry's death.

If Fry's performance fell short of the ideal, it was nonetheless valuable. The younger, more ambitious members of the organization might feel frustrated and misunderstood, but the older members loved Fry and so did many others outside the firm. His contribution to the business was a sincere idealism, even higher perhaps than that of his father-in-law. It consisted of an unpretentious, honest integrity, an innate, rather oversimplified, sense of fairness to others, a desire to have organization above reproach, and a generous conception of the responsibilities to which he was heir. With it went dignity, steady courage, and a sure stability much needed in the dark days of 1932 and early 1933.

Everyone who met Fry felt at once his kindly sympathy and great personal charm. One of his clients wrote of him:[36]

His great honesty and integrity, his unfailing courtesy, his kindness and consideration for those about him were apparent to everyone. His business standards and ideals were reflected in every aspect of his work and in the work of his organization.

Perhaps the best brief summary of his life was expressed in an editorial of the New York *Times*:[37]

Altogether he was a public spirited citizen of the highest type as well as a successfully diligent man in business. One of his prime interests was in perfecting the use of the printed word. His own life was a "fair edition" and of great worth.

With Fry's death the question of the future control of the agency at once arose, to be decided by the disposal of the large block of the firm's stock which he had owned. The four men principally concerned in the management could not agree on the manner in which it should be divided, and a fight for control ensued which received a considerable amount of publicity.[38] The issues involved are complicated, a number of facts are in dispute, and feelings are still so strong that it is difficult to appraise the merits of the case. It seems wise, however, to give a brief account of the affair here, since it illustrates the kind of situation which sometimes arises in business, especially when men attempt to provide for future control by means of legal devices. What follows is a series of statements of facts and events arranged in chronological order, so that the reader may judge for himself:[39]

It is apparent that friction had developed between Lauck and Thornley prior to the summer of 1934, and in August of that year matters reached the point where Lauck tried to resign from the firm. To retain his services President Fry is alleged (by Lauck and Batten) to have promised Lauck that he would arrange to let Batten, Jordan, and Lauck purchase enough stock to equalize their holdings with that of Thornley. Fry is also said to have assured Lauck that Thornley would not succeed him in control of the business. Thornley states that if any such promises were made, he was not informed of them.

It is clear that Batten, Jordan, and Lauck each purchased 30,000 shares of Ayer stock in August, 1934, and that the salaries of the four directors were equalized thereafter.

When Armistead and Kessler retired in November, 1934, there was a written agreement among the remaining depositors under the voting trust agreement of 1929, waiving their option under the agreement and consenting to the purchase of the stock by the Corporation, with the understanding "that the aforesaid voting trust certificates shall remain

HARRY A. BATTEN

INTERIOR VIEW OF THE AYER BUILDING

subject to the Voting Trust Agreement when acquired by the said Company." (This had also been done in 1933 when Mathes resigned.) As a result, the Corporation owned 117,000 shares deposited under the trust agreement.

On April 6, 1936, President Fry, who was in the hospital, authorized Kessler to hold an election of additional voting trustees. A meeting was immediately held and the trust agreement was amended, making it possible to elect trustees who were not employees of the Corporation or depositors under the agreement. This amendment was approved not only by Fry as depositor of 234,000 shares and Thornley as depositor of 39,000 shares but also by the Board of Directors of the Corporation for the 117,000 shares which the firm held under the trust agreement. The trustees who were then elected were: Fry, Thornley, Kessler (formerly a vice-president of the Corporation and an executor of the Fry estate), H. Eugene Wheeler (secretary and treasurer of the Corporation), and Frank L. Swigert (then head of the Ayer Media-Contract Department).

Just before Fry's death on July 27, 1936, the holdings of Ayer stock and trust certificates were:

Wilfred W. Fry	335,995	shares	of which	234,000	were	deposited.
N. W. Ayer & Son Inc.	221,180	"	"	"	117,000	"	"
George H. Thornley	71,356	"	"	"	39,000	"	"
Other employees	51,078	"	"	"	none	"	"
Gerold M. Lauck	34,696	"	"	"	"	"	"
Clarence L. Jordan	32,250	"	"	"	500	"	"
Harry A. Batten	31,000	"	"	"	500	"	"
Total	777,555	"	"	"	391,000	"	"

Upon Fry's death his shares immediately became subject, under the trust agreement, to an option which had to be exercised within 60 days by the holder of the majority in interest of the deposited shares. Kessler, as co-executor with Mrs. Fry of her husband's estate, requested Batten, Jordan, Lauck, and Thornley to meet with him to consider a request from Mrs. Fry regarding the disposal of certain shares of Ayer stock in connection with several bequests which Fry had made.

The meeting was held on August 19, 1936, although Lauck was unable to attend. Batten raised the question of procedure as to the disposition, under the agreement, of all the Fry holdings, since Kessler had been instrumental in arranging the trust agreement in the first place and was believed to have a better understanding of its provisions than the other officers of the Corporation. It was suggested that Batten, Jordan, and Lauck purchase additional shares of stock to equalize their holdings with Thornley's, the balance of the Fry stock to be purchased by the Corporation. Thornley was understood by the other men present to assent to this proposal, but he subsequently denied giving his approval, and the subsequent court testimony on the point is not conclusive, except that he did not express disapproval of the suggestion to equalize ownership.

On August 25, 1936, Thornley notified Mrs. Fry that he understood that he alone had the right to purchase the 234,000 shares of trusteed stock left by her husband and that he wished to exercise the right.

On September 4, 1936, the matter was again brought before the management committee, presumably to conclude the arrangements outlined on August 19. Thornley, however, presented a written statement to the effect that he had consulted legal counsel, that he had been advised that the trust agreement gave him the sole right to buy the shares, and that he proposed to purchase the entire lot. Faced with a conflict, both as to interpretation and as to desires, the committee adjourned without taking any action.

Thornley contended that the firm needed a leader whose dominating position could not be challenged. He felt that he should have control of the Corporation since he was the largest individual shareholder, was the only member of the original partnership then active in the business, and, unlike Batten, Jordan, and Lauck, was a trustee under the agreement of 1929. The opposing directors contended that the holdings should be equalized to make the capital interests of all four correspond to their respective positions in the business as indicated by the equality of their salaries and the similarity of their responsibilities.

On September 18, 1936, Batten and Jordan called a special meeting of the board of directors, to be held on September 22, in order to act upon the option to purchase the Fry stock which they believed to accrue to the Corporation by virtue of its ownership of 117,000 shares which had been deposited under the trust agreement with the consent of all the other depositors.

Thornley did not attend the meeting of September 22, but presented a letter protesting the holding of the meeting and asserting that its purposes were illegal. The other directors (Batten, Jordan, and Lauck) unanimously approved a resolution requesting the trustees to allocate 117,878 of the shares in dispute to the Corporation and the remainder to themselves so as to give each a total holding equivalent to Thornley's. They also voted to submit their resolution to a special meeting of the stockholders for ratification and called the meeting for October 7, 1936.

The secretary of the Corporation was authorized to present the directors' resolution to a special meeting of the voting trustees which had been called for the same day, September 22. All the existing trustees (Kessler, Swigert, Thornley, and Wheeler) attended. Thornley presented a statement in which he claimed the exclusive right to purchase all the 234,000 shares subject to the voting trust. Wheeler then presented the resolution of the board of directors. It was approved by the majority present, and Thornley's offer to purchase was rejected. The allocation was then transmitted to the executors of the Fry estate before the expiration of the 60-day time limit.

On October 6, 1936, Thornley's attorneys served a bill of complaint against N. W. Ayer & Son, Inc.; Mrs. Anna Ayer Fry and Adam Kessler, Jr., executors under Wilfred Fry's will; Adam Kessler, Jr., Frank L. Swigert, and H. Eugene Wheeler, trustees under the voting trust agreement; and Harry A. Batten, Clarence L. Jordan, and Gerold M. Lauck.

On October 7, 1936, the special meeting of stockholders was held to consider the action of the board of directors with regard to the stock. Thornley did not attend this meeting but sent a letter which was read, stating his desire to purchase the entire block. When the vote was taken on the ratification of the directors' allocation (200 stockholders were eligible to vote), 138 voted in person and 41 by proxy in favor of the resolution, 20 were not present in person or by proxy, and 1 voted against it. In this tally the ballots cast for the stock subject to the voting trust agreement were counted as one ballot.

On October 15, 1936, there was a regular meeting of the board of directors, attended by Batten, Jordan, Lauck, and Thornley. Francis H. Scheetz, of Evans, Bayard & Frick, counsel for the Corporation, also attended. Thornley requested permission to have his personal counsel present, but this request was refused by vote of the majority of directors, and Thornley then withdrew.

At this meeting the board elected as director William M. Armistead (a member of the old Ayer partnership and a former voting trustee, vice-president, and director of the Corporation) in order to fill the vacancy caused by Fry's death. Batten tendered his resignation as vice-president and was elected president of the Corporation to succeed Fry. The management committee was dissolved, and the board voted to remove Thornley as an officer and employee of the Corporation (this did not affect Thornley's position as a director).

On October 19, 1936, Thornley started legal action to compel the parties concerned to sell him the 234,000 shares of Ayer stock.

The legal points advanced by both sides are many and complicated, but the main contentions are fairly clear. Thornley based his suit on the well-known fact that a corporation cannot directly or indirectly vote its own stock, contending that in consequence the Ayer corporation had no right to vote, by means of the voting trust agreement, on the question of allocating shares of stock. It would follow from this view that Thornley held the majority in interest in the voting trust and could decide the allocation.

The defendants argued that it was not a case involving internal management of the company but rather one of property rights and hence the Corporation was not voting in the sense referred to, but was exercising the right which it clearly had "to purchase, hold, sell and transfer the shares of its own capital stock." In other words, while the Corporation could not vote the trusteed shares in deciding questions of management, it could (because of owning them) participate in the option to purchase the Fry stock or to determine the allocation of that stock among the depositors.

The defendants also contended that their interpretation was supported by the written agreement made when the Corporation was allowed to purchase the 117,000 shares of trusteed stock and also by the amendment to the trust agreement, both of which were approved by Thornley himself. They argued alternatively that, if their interpretation was incorrect, the entire arrangement was illegal and hence the executors of the Fry estate would be free to sell the stock to whom they pleased.

The suit came up for trial on December 10, 1936. After one day of testimony, plaintiff's attorneys discontinued the suit. The Corporation then purchased Thornley's entire stock holdings for cash, the price being determined by the formula contained in the trust agreement made in 1929 (seven times the average annual earnings for the preceding three years).

At a meeting of the board of directors, on December 16, 1936, Kessler was elected a director of the Corporation.

It is impossible for a layman to make a competent analysis of the legal aspects of the case. Several points seem clear. First, since December, 1936, Harry A. Batten has been the unquestioned leader of N. W. Ayer & Son, and the cleavage in management, which had existed for some years, has disappeared. Secondly, the result evidently conforms to the majority view of the men who made the original trust agreement, as evidenced by the action of Armistead and Kessler. Thirdly, the firm remained in the hands of experienced men who had won positions of re-

CLARENCE L. JORDAN

GEROLD M. LAUCK

sponsibility long before Fry's death — men who had, in fact, joined the agency while F. W. Ayer was still active in the management. Lastly, if the trust agreement had never been made, the outcome would have been much the same, since the combined shares of Batten, Jordan, and Lauck exceeded those held by Thornley. Indeed, if the agreement had never been made, the dispute probably would not have taken place.

The whole episode suggests the futility of thinking legalistically about an agency organization. The principal assets of an advertising agency are its people and the intangible but all-important sentiments which bind them together into fruitful collaboration. No trust agreement can hold unwilling workers together, and no court order could have preserved the Ayer organization unless it had the enthusiastic support of the rank and file of the agency personnel. It is clear from the attitude of the vast majority of the Ayer staff during the contest for control and afterwards that Batten, Jordan, and Lauck held the loyalty of the organization and that Thornley did not. With the right kind of behavior on the part of the chief executive an organization will continue without any trust agreements or legal device to maintain control. Without such behavior legal measures are futile, and in the Ayer case they nearly wrecked the firm. Only an organization with strong internal cohesion could have survived.

CHAPTER VIII

KEEPING EVERLASTINGLY AT IT . . .

AT THE BEGINNING of 1937 the outlook for N. W. Ayer & Son was uncertain, to say the least. The internal shock of a change in leadership had been aggravated by the fight for control; and organizational morale, damaged by the depression, sank lower still. Fry's death and Thornley's withdrawal created a financial problem of considerable magnitude, for in both instances the firm had to buy large holdings of stock. Inevitably, too, the news of the fight for control spread in business circles and caused some harm: a firm which has gone through a period of marked internal dissension is usually dubiously regarded, and hence the new management faced obvious difficulties in retaining its old clients and getting new business.

In the mythology of American business a decisive, hard-driving man takes over a situation of this kind and within a few weeks has the business running smoothly toward new heights of achievement. Of course in reality it does not happen that way, and nearly five years were to pass before N. W. Ayer & Son was clearly on the road to recovery. Within ten years it was forging ahead with a professional competence, vigor, and high morale unsurpassed in the entire history of the firm.[1]

NEW LEADERSHIP

At this critical juncture in its history the Ayer agency received precisely the kind of leadership required for its survival. That leadership, in the person of Harry A. Batten (then aged 39), differed from anything that the organization had experienced before. Unlike F. W. Ayer and Fry, Batten possessed detailed, firsthand knowledge of every phase of advertising. At the age of fourteen he had started to work for the agency as a printer's devil. In the quarter-century between 1911 and 1936 he had worked in the printing, engraving, planning, and copy divisions of the business and had been head of the Copy Department for seven years before becoming president. In addition, he had had considerable experience in soliciting new business and in servicing accounts; he had been a director since 1931. Thus he knew intimately the technical operations of the agency business. Moreover, unlike McKinney, whose strength lay in great creative ability, Batten possessed administrative skills of a high order; these will become evident as the story since 1936 unfolds. And like Ayer and Fry, Batten had developed important civic and business interests outside the agency which helped him to view the agency's work in larger perspective.[2]

Of major importance, too, is the fact that in developing broadly and rising to top management Batten had retained close contact with the rest of the people in the organization. He understood the problems and attitudes of the lower ranks. That he had received only common schooling and had risen the hard way helped with this, as did his service in the Navy in World War I. Batten "belonged" to the working force in the agency in a way that Ayer and Fry had never done. Basic factors in the recovery of the firm have been his understanding of the people under him and the respect and confidence that he had earned.

But there was more to the new leadership than the technical knowledge and broad understanding of one man. Closely associated with Batten were Clarence L. Jordan and Gerold M. Lauck, both of whom had had long experience in the business and wholeheartedly shared Batten's aspirations for N. W. Ayer & Son. Jordan had started to work in the firm in 1915 after graduating from Georgia Institute of Technology. He had had a distinguished career as an officer in the French and American armies in World War I but apart from that interlude had been a member of the Ayer staff continuously, first in copywriting and later in servicing accounts. Lauck had come to the firm in 1919 after eight years of business experience in sales and advertising. He brought with him a mind alert not only to the techniques of modern business but to those of art and literature. His strong personal interest in good painting and writing was reflected in the creative work of the agency. Largely through his influence such well-known artists as Salvador Dali, André Derain, Raoul Dufy, Marie Lawrencin, Pablo Picasso, Pierre Roy, and Ignacio Zulaogo were induced to enter the field of advertising illustration and design. A sound and aggressive merchandiser, he nevertheless was insistent upon the importance of good taste in advertising.

The three men belonged to the same age group, had long been close friends, and shared deep interest in the technical quality of advertising. The fact that they stood together in the fight for control of the agency was simply one manifestation of the common philosophy of business and advertising which they jointly held. After 1936 there was no division in the top management of the Ayer agency. It was more closely united and had a greater sense of purpose in a way than at any time since F. W. Ayer's death.

Perhaps even more important than the unity at the top was a fundamental change in emphasis and interests represented there. To a considerable extent under Fry's administration, top management had focused attention upon dollar volume and profits. It was not done explicitly, and everyone in top management would have sincerely denied it had the point been raised, but the general pattern of behavior pointed unmistakably in that direction. In the old partnership (after McKinney's death) Armistead alone had been an advertising man in the technical sense of the term, and apart from him the creative departments of the business had no representation in the firm at all. By the promotions made, by the things they talked and worried about, by the attention paid to agency representatives who solicited new business and handled relations with clients, Fry and his immediate associates unwittingly indicated that they were primarily interested in developing agency billings and that plans, research, copy, and art work were incidental to getting and placing business. It was a "natural" attitude and not peculiar to the Ayer firm. That was, as we have seen, the way in which the agency business had grown up. But such an attitude made the creative staff feel that they were mere hirelings. Inevitably they resented it.

The admission of Batten, Jordan, and Lauck to the Board of

Directors in 1931 had given the creative side more representation at the top, but the three younger men were a minority and were too new in top management to exert strong influence. The depression, too, inevitably made everyone anxious about volume of business, and thus until 1936 the creative and professional branches of the business remained in a subordinate rôle. The result was that the people concerned with these aspects of advertising farther down the managerial ladder had felt a sense of frustration and lack of understanding on the part of Fry, Mathes, Thornley, and even Kessler.

Since the beginning of Batten's régime the members of the organization have felt that the technical departments of the business have real representation in top management, that professional advertising abilities are fully recognized, and that the emphasis of the whole organization is on quality performance. We shall see shortly some other reasons why they feel that way, but the fact that the men who believed most in the importance of high-quality technical production had risen to the very top made a profound difference to the rest of the organization. The ultimate effect on morale and consequently upon the achievements of the staff can hardly be overestimated.

PROBLEMS OF RECONSTRUCTION

The problems which confronted the new management were many and varied, but for the most part action upon them had to take place over a period of time. In an organization as old and closely knit as Ayer, no single step would be effective in restoring strength. Any drastic move would shock it dangerously. Batten understood that it would take many actions at various levels, initiated gradually, to effect the process of reconstruction. There was need to restore morale and improve the quality of personnel. It seemed clear that a certain amount of reorganization of departments and clarification of responsibilities had to be worked out and that the underlying philosophy of the business required restudy and refinement. Somehow it was necessary to achieve a transition from a family affair to an efficient business team, bringing the whole organization up to date and at the same time preserving the very real values for which the Ayer agency had long been noted. The situation called for a long-range program carefully administered.

The immediate problem was financial. The firm had paid Thornley outright the sum of $552,000. Settling with the Fry estate called for different treatment, for the value of Fry's shares at the time exceeded $2,600,000. The new management could have financed this sum through bank loans had it been desirable. Batten felt, however, that the firm should not be subjected to this financial burden at a time when all available funds were needed for the expansion of certain departments, the launching of new projects, and for giving proper recognition to new and promising talents within the firm. He therefore arranged for the Ayer corporation to purchase the Fry shares by means of notes, under a contract which required the agency to make only small annual payments on the principal sum, while allowing it to pay off larger amounts when it so desired. This arrangement gave the agency a long financial breathing spell in which to strengthen its position.

At the very outset Batten began to focus attention upon improvement of the quality and morale of the Ayer personnel. He recognized that the depression and the internal strife had impaired the spirit of the working force. He also was aware that, owing to previous personnel policies, there were opportunities for grading up the quality of the staff. The firm had, to be sure, always attracted able people but it had not always been able to retain them. In general the Ayer agency had paid going rates but not much more. Employees, typically, had not received increases unless they pressed for them, and there had been a tendency, as indicated above, for the lion's share of the rewards to go to a small group of top men who had least to do with the actual creative production of the business. Both Ayer and Fry had felt that, since the firm offered pleasant working conditions and security, there was less need to offer extra financial inducements. Seniority had played a large part in advancement. As a result, ambitious people of outstanding ability frequently left for more lucrative opportunities, and the firm tended to accumulate rather more than its share of competent and loyal, but uninspired, workers. Moreover, because the Ayer management had always "taken

care of" its employees even after they had outlived their usefulness, in some instances men who had risen to high positions and
corresponding salaries in the lush 1920's had slackened their
efforts and were coasting. The over-all result was that the organization was cluttered with dead wood and employees of only
average performance. The more capable members of the staff
felt themselves hampered in turning out top-notch work and lacking in adequate recognition.[3]

The Ayer business was sufficiently profitable during 1937 to
permit the new management to start corrective measures. It made
a review of the performance and remuneration of the staff, particularly the members engaged in creative work. It gave increases
in pay immediately where they were merited. As fast as circumstances permitted, it made changes in assignments and advanced
employees of promise. There were no large-scale dismissals, but
the process of natural attrition, through retirements and turnover,
was watched carefully and used as a means of grading up the staff.
The management indicated clearly by actions, as well as words, its
new policy regarding personnel: rewards were to be for current
performance — not for past achievements; nor would employees
have to wait years for recognition and be content to take part of it
in the form of old-age security; management itself would push
advances in position and pay, for those who deserved them.

Underlying all this was a concept of management which differed
sharply from that previously held in the firm. Batten, Jordan, and
Lauck did not look upon themselves as principal owners of a
property which, by the fact of ownership, entitled them to large
profits. To them the agency was an organization of which they
were an integral part; they were the leaders of a team engaged
primarily in creative work. To them the agency's only real assets
were its staff: cash reserves, buildings, and other tangible possessions counted for little if the agency did not possess professional
talent to serve its clients well. Profits were necessary and desired,
to be sure; but the new management felt that ample financial
returns would come if the entire organization did its job with
wholehearted enthusiasm and trained skill. And they felt entitled
to rewards only in so far as they were important members of the
team. Their basic conception was that employees are not hirelings,

but rather that they are people capable of great achievement if properly led and made to feel that they are a part of the organization. This trend of thought led the new management to emphasize the development of people and teamwork. The process would take time and effort, but it would yield both profits and satisfactions to all.

The process of improving personnel did not stop with pruning dead wood and making judicious promotions and transfers. In 1938 the Ayer agency began to canvass college graduating classes for promising talent, something that it had not done before. Equally important, it shortened and enriched the period of apprenticeship for new employees, which formerly had consisted of an overly long period in clerical routines in the Business Department. It began to devise ways of explicitly training people in the fundamentals of advertising and Ayer policies, rather than to depend almost entirely on the slow process of absorption upon which the firm had previously relied. By this means promising employees could be advanced more rapidly.

At the same time that the firm was working on the improvement of its personnel, it began the process of improving the organizational structure. One of the first steps in this direction was to rejuvenate the department charged with planning campaigns. In the past its function had been the analysis of the product and its market, with heavy emphasis upon the selection of media for reaching that market. This arrangement harked back to the days when knowledge of media had been a part of an agency's secret stock in trade. The management took the view that greater emphasis in planning should be given to the analysis of business conditions, the state of the particular industry concerned, the client's position in that industry, and the marketing strategy by which the position of the client could be improved. Selection of media came after this planning and was a matter for media experts to handle after the broader analysis and plans had been completed. The firm appointed a new head of the Plans-Merchandising Department, by means of which a young, able, and aggressive employee was given recognition and the department itself revitalized. Steps were taken to transfer the selection of advertising media (except for radio and outdoor advertising) to the Media Department, which previously had been responsible only for the actual purchase of space.

The flow of paper work through the agency by which transactions with clients and media were controlled was reviewed. In the past a good deal of the clerical work connected with the production of advertising copy and art work had been handled in the Copy Department, thus duplicating much of the work of the Business Department. As a result of this study the detail and traffic bureaus were transferred to the Business Department, which was rechristened Business-Production and given a new head. This saved personnel and improved operations. A similar study was made of the handling of bookkeeping transactions and the analysis of accounts, as a result of which personnel was shifted, operations which had been scattered through the agency were combined, and management was able to obtain a more accurate and cogent picture of the financial results of operations.

Scrutiny soon turned to two major departments in which operations had not been satisfactory, namely, radio and publicity. In part the difficulty lay in the personnel, and in part in the way these departments were organized in relation to the agency as a whole. In the past the Radio Department had operated in New York City almost as a private subdivision of the agency's New York branch. Ayer management felt that the activities of the Radio Department should be brought into closer and more effective integration with the other activities of the agency. To this end the planning section of the Radio Department was moved to Philadelphia. This step proved unsatisfactory because of the high degree of concentration of the radio industry in New York City and (as regards program production) in Hollywood. Consequently the Radio Department was reorganized in New York City, with facilities for program production both in Hollywood and in New York, but with a careful integration of all radio operations with the over-all operations of the agency — principally through Plans Department, Media Department, and Accounting.

Like the Radio Department, the Publicity Department needed to be brought up to date and integrated more closely with other agency activities. As originally conceived, its function had been to develop and distribute news stories and photographs concerning clients. During the period after 1930, however, public relations activities in American business had assumed new importance and had gone well beyond mere publicity work. The new Ayer management recognized the need for a broad conception of public relations in its own activities on behalf of clients. Between 1937 and 1939 the firm revamped the old Publicity Department into Public Relations, acquired new personnel, developed a broader view of public relations as an integral part of advertising counsel, and moved the department to New York to give it direct contact with news services and radio networks. Other changes in internal organization took place as new possibilities became apparent.

The most important phase of the agency's organizational developments, however, lay not so much in the structural rearrangements (although they simplified and streamlined operations) as in the spirit behind them. Authority previously had been largely concentrated at the top, with the result that final decisions sometimes were made there on matters which could have been better handled at lower levels by people who had a firsthand grasp of the problems concerned. Departmental lines had been blurred, and departmental heads frequently had found their subordinates working on odd jobs for partners or vice-presidents. Batten rapidly gave his department heads full authority and responsibility for their respective areas. As fast as they could adapt themselves, all executives were encouraged to decide issues at the working level and to present their own views on matters of policy which could be concluded only at the top. The new management provided leadership, but it fostered participation in management by the rest of the organization. In describing the change one enthusiastic executive related to the author the following episode:[4]

> One day I came up with a new idea which I thought would help our operations. I went to Mr. Batten, described it, and told him it would cost $10,000. He asked a few questions about it and then said, "If you think it is the right thing to do, go ahead. It's your department and I want you to run it." I went back exhilarated. In the old days we had to argue hard to get a man a five-dollar raise. After I thought the project over I decided against it and didn't spend the money, *but I could have!* It's hard to describe how much that did for me.

As that kind of attitude spread down through the organization, members of the organization gained a new sense of importance and responsibility and began to develop a new interest in their work.

Attention then turned to the question of research in advertising. The Ayer agency had long been interested in research; indeed in 1879 it had planned and executed the first formal research project in the history of advertising, a study of farm markets and media for the Nichols-Shepard Company. During the Roaring Twenties, however, research — and particularly copy readership research — had been used by many agencies primarily as a means of impressing clients. The true function of research, to disclose the truth whether palatable or unpalatable, had been too often obscured and lost sight of — with a consequent loss of prestige to advertising research in general. This unhealthy trend was for the most part reversed by the strains and pressures of the depression, and by 1939 the Ayer management felt that research techniques had developed to the point where they could be used as tools for continuing studies. In the belief that such studies ought properly to be centralized, a separate organization, called the Ayer Foundation for Consumer Research, was set up. The announced scope of its activities included consumer attitudes and reactions, the qualitative analysis of copy and media, promotion techniques, and trends in buying habits.[5]

After several years of operating experience and a change in the directorship of the Foundation, the management decided to decentralize its research activities among the operating departments. It had concluded that research studies were more practical and useful when closely related to current departmental operations. It felt, too, that by putting such activities within the specialized departments, it would facilitate the task of keeping personnel constantly in touch with the latest developments in their respective fields. Thus, research in advertising media became the responsibility of the Media Department; economic development, market trends, and industrial developments became the province of the Plans-Merchandising Department; and so on. At the same time the firm made full use of recognized independent research services such as the Starch Readership Surveys; Advertising

Research Foundation; C. E. Hooper, Inc.; Opinion Research Corporation; Pulse of New York; Schwerin Research Corporation; Nielsen Radio Index; Audience Research Inc.; and others. This reliance upon outside agencies did not mean any slackening of effort or interest in research. Rather it was a means of gathering basic data economically. The Ayer organization itself recognized and accepted responsibility for interpreting the assembled information and applying it to current work.

It would be pleasant to record that the various measures taken in the first two years of the new régime brought an immediate improvement in the Ayer volume and profits. The truth is, however, that the firm's total business sagged slightly in 1937, dropped in 1938 and 1939, recovered a bit in 1940, and then dropped sharply again in 1941; whereas U. S. advertising volume as a whole rose steadily in 1939 after a check in 1938 and continued rising until checked again in 1942. (See Table 1.) It was not until 1942 that N. W. Ayer & Son began an unmistakable and continuous recovery of business volume.

In part this pattern was the result of external circumstances. The business recession in 1937 and 1938 affected most branches of American industry and trade. Competing agencies, too, were quick to take every possible advantage of the internal Ayer situation. In advertising circles rumors were rife that the House of Ayer was torn by dissension and on the verge of falling apart. Some Ayer clients held steadfast, others hesitated, and a few decided to give their business to agencies which, outwardly at least, seemed to be stronger. The Ayer firm had all it could do to hang on to most of its accounts and at the same time prepare itself for the future.

To a considerable extent, then, the decline in Ayer volume in this period was the result of the firm's internal situation and a shift in policy with regard to new business. It was several years before Batten's efforts to revitalize the staff could bear fruit. Much of the growth of national advertising after 1935 was the result of a great increase in radio advertising. Although the Ayer firm had pioneered in this medium, its Radio Department had not kept pace with new developments — to a considerable extent because Fry had personally disliked radio advertising. Batten, Jordan, and Lauck were well aware of the importance of radio as an advertising medium but they also were determined that radio should be considered objectively as advertising in its proper relation to other media. Despite the temptation to strive for volume of billing in radio, they decided against building the agency's position through special emphasis on broadcasting, as was then common among competing agencies. Fluctuations in the Ayer radio volume alone account for a large part of the changes in the firm's total volume. (See Table 1.)

The figures in Table 1 show dramatically what was happening to the Ayer firm during the period of the fight for control and the reconstruction years. Dollar figures for these years are still confidential, but the indices tell the story when one compares the Ayer performance with the indices representing the best available estimates of national advertising volume. (Figures derived from Professor Borden's estimates have been included as an independent check on the *Printers' Ink* index and also to cover the two years before 1935 for which no other good index is available.) By 1941 the total Ayer volume, having declined when national advertising was steadily increasing, stood at about half what it would have been if the agency had kept pace with the industry. Then, with the new leadership beginning to have its effect, the story changes. Between 1941 and 1947 the total Ayer volume increased 244 per cent, while the national advertising volume advanced 212 per cent. During the same years Ayer radio volume rose 262 per cent, while national radio volume increased 182 per cent, despite the fact that the Ayer radio volume did not start to recover until 1942.

These figures, while not conclusive proof of the excellence of the new Ayer management, are strongly indicative. From 1941 onwards, Ayer volume has grown faster than that of the advertising industry as a whole. Of course the fluctuations of any single agency depend to a considerable extent upon losing or obtaining a few big accounts, but maintaining volume is one of the tests of an agency organization. This objective evidence, then, confirms the recovery within the Ayer firm to which members of the staff

TABLE 1

INDICES OF AYER AND NATIONAL ADVERTISING VOLUME
1933–1947
(Average of 1935–39 = 100 for all indices)

Year	Total Advertising			Radio Advertising		
		Printers' Ink			*Printers' Ink*	
	Ayer Billings[a]	General Index[b]	Borden Estimates[c]	Ayer Billings[d]	Radio Index[e]	Borden Estimates[f]
1933.......	73.4	..	68.5	30.2	..	46.0
1934.......	85.5	..	81.8	61.7	..	61.0
1935.......	103.3	83	85.7	104.5	69	69.8
1936.......	112.3	99	102.6	118.5	89	86.3
1937.......	109.6	110	111.2	120.1	107	105.8
1938.......	90.6	101	96.9	85.2	112	111.4
1939.......	84.0	107	103.5	71.7	123	126.5
1940.......	88.8	118	114.2	88.6	144	147.9
1941.......	67.0	127	122.8	62.6	162	169.0
1942.......	71.6	122	120.9	49.5	179	182.0
1943.......	84.1	153	149.0	58.9	213	214.6
1944.......	105.7	180	...	96.0	265	...
1945.......	110.5	198	...	118.8	289	...
1946.......	138.8	229	...	138.1	299	...
1947.......	163.5	269	...	159.0	296	...
1948.......	165.1	290	...	161.2	309	...

[a] This column shows total Ayer billings for all advertising each year in terms of the average of the agency's billings for the years 1935 to 1939, inclusive.

[b] The *Printers' Ink* index of general advertising activity is based on estimates of total expenditures in the principal advertising media in terms of the 1935–39 average. No figures are available in this series for the years before 1935. *Printers' Ink*, vol. 226, no. 11 (Mar. 18, 1949), pp. 65–67.

[c] This index has been calculated from the estimates made by Neil H. Borden of expenditures for advertising in newspapers, general magazines, radio, and farm journals for the period 1933–43, using the average of the figures for 1935–39 as a base. See Neil H. Borden, Malcolm D. Taylor, Howard T. Hovde, *Revenues and Expenses of Newspaper Publishers in 1941* (Division of Research, Harvard Graduate School of Business Administration, 1946), p. 29.

[d] This index is based on the Ayer billings for radio time, production and talent costs, and related items, including television for 1940 and subsequent years.

[e] These figures are taken from the *Printers' Ink* index of radio advertising; the series starts with 1935.

[f] This index has been calculated from the estimates made by Neil H. Borden of expenditures by national advertisers on network and national non-network broadcasts for the years 1933–43. See printed source indicated in note c above.

themselves have testified. The record is impressive. If it can be maintained through a period of economic recession, the new régime will indeed have proved its mettle.

Meanwhile the Ayer management, although fully cognizant of the need to maintain dollar volume, was working toward a new policy with regard to getting new accounts. The firm had long chosen clients with considerable care as to the products they sold. It now began to feel that even more important was the character of the client's business and the quality of its management; in short, clients should be selected with regard to the possible effect of their business upon the agency itself. Not the least of the considerations involved was that of size. Big accounts are generally considered desirable; they are also dangerous. Once an agency is staffed to handle them, it must be able to replace a lost one quickly or rapidly shrink its organization. Either alternative is so difficult that an agency is tempted to go to extreme lengths in order to retain a large account — a course which results invariably in harm to both parties. In addition, some clients, large or small, insist upon forcing their own views about advertising upon the agency which handles their business, even when the agency knows and protests that the ideas are unsound. The new Ayer management felt that the firm should not take a new account unless it was certain that it could work agreeably with the client's management and that the professional status of the agency could be preserved. As a result, even though the Ayer agency was having its difficulties, it exercised more discrimination than ever before in the accounts it would handle and it turned down a number of opportunities to get business which Batten and his associates felt would ultimately prove unsatisfactory. The Ayer management suspended dividends between 1938 and 1942 to conserve its financial position and make more money available for deserving employees; and it worked resolutely at rebuilding the organization and its clientèle on stronger lines.

Difficulties and policy formulation reached a climax in 1940 when the Ayer agency lost a large account, which it had handled for more than ten years. To Batten and his associates the handling and loss of this one account provided a dramatic demonstration of the dangers which threaten any agency which is unduly dependent upon one advertiser. At times the advertising expenditures for the client concerned had accounted for more than 20 per cent of the total Ayer billings. While this was a far smaller ratio than that existing in some agencies, where one account sometimes represents as much as 90 per cent of the agency's income, the consequences of losing such a large account were uncomfortably clear to the entire Ayer staff. Fear of its loss had weighed heavily upon the entire organization. With the odds against holding any account indefinitely, people worried about a blow that seemed certain to fall sometime and might well come when the agency was not prepared to sustain it. Such a preoccupation always impairs the quality of managerial and creative thought — not only in behalf of the account in question, but all the other accounts in the house. It hampers objective thinking in the client's interest and makes difficult for management the task of providing a calm yet stimulating working atmosphere for the organization as a whole.

In its efforts to satisfy the management of the account in question, the agency had frequently made compromises that it felt were against the long-run interests of the client. In 1940 came a demand of a kind familiar to all agencies and one to which many have acceded: an executive of the company concerned asked the Ayer firm to put a man on its pay roll. The man knew nothing about advertising, and indeed there was no expectation that he would even appear; the agency was simply to pay him! Batten and his associates felt that the time had come to draw the line. With full knowledge that it meant the severing of the relationship, they refused the request point-blank and immediately lost the account.[6]

Ayer executives now regard that episode as a turning point. "It was then," they say, "that we resolved never again to be in a position of being afraid. The loss of the business hurt, of course, but we all felt as if a terrible weight had been lifted. We determined then that we would never again knowingly take an account which would keep us lying awake nights. And we decided to work out a policy of balanced accounts so that we would not only have our business diversified geographically and by industries, but also spread as to size. Once we got a new large account we would immediately devote extraordinary efforts to win enough smaller accounts to offset it. We could in this way assure our professional independence and provide reasonable security for our business and our personnel. We had been moving toward such a policy, but that one blow forced us to clarify our thinking and reconsider our fundamental philosophy of operation."

In the process of thinking anew about agency-client relationships, Ayer executives also began to ask themselves penetrating questions about the nature and usefulness of advertising in the changing world which business would have to face. They concluded that advertising would be, as it always has been, a means of producing profit; that this would be the primary function of advertising. But they tried to think through some implications which had received too little attention.

Batten and his associates were attentive to the broadening range of problems which were confronting American business generally in its dealings with the public. During World War II they were to see advertising used constructively to *discourage* demand and to solve difficult and dangerous business problems. The clear and inescapable authority with which an advertiser could inform the public on a wide range of subjects not obviously related to immediate selling eventually led Ayer to a broader concept of advertising which to the agency had (and still has) far-reaching implications: "Advertising is a specialized technique for mass communication. It exists for two reasons — because it is fast, and because it costs less than any other method."

Believing that management would inevitably be forced to meet the public on more fronts than the sales counter, Batten and his associates identified advertising not simply as a selling device but rather as a basic tool of *all* management, useful as it always had been in the direct promotion of sales, and additionally useful whenever management had anything which it needed to say to the public, on any subject.[7]

The Ayer management itself was impressed with two implications of its definition. First, advertising as a communications device has a much bigger and broader function than advertising solely as a sales tool. This, they believed, meant larger scope for new accounts and planning service for clients. Secondly, advertising as a tool of management meant that the agency should strengthen its contacts with top management in client organizations, in order to be sure that it was dealing with the problems of the firm as a whole and not simply those of its sales department. Ayer management had seen these concepts dimly for years, but after their explicit articulation the firm began to develop specific policies and to take them into account.

WORLD WAR II

The outbreak of the second world war complicated life for N. W. Ayer & Son, as for other concerns, and tested the mettle of its new management.

One of the first problems raised was what to do about advertising "war babies." The rearmament program had begun to bring prosperity to certain firms as early as 1939, and that prosperity spread in the succeeding years as industrial activities expanded in support of the war effort. As in World War I, the advertising appropriations of existing advertisers frequently increased and new enterprises sought to establish their names by various forms of publicity. The tax situation, of course, encouraged increased expenditures for advertising: within broad limits it cost individual companies very little to advertise inasmuch as the money so devoted would otherwise contribute to excess profits and go to the government in the form of taxes. This influence was plainly reflected in indices of advertising activity in 1940 and 1941. Pearl Harbor brought uncertainty and a decline for 1942, but in 1943 began a sharp rise which showed no signs of slackening until late 1947 and brought advertising volume in the United States far beyond the peak reached in 1929.

N. W. Ayer & Son could easily have capitalized upon this growth by taking on new war clients, many of whom offered their advertising accounts to the agency. The Ayer management declined to accept them. Batten and his associates knew that they would have difficulty in maintaining a staff sufficiently large and capable to handle existing accounts and that new business would seriously aggravate personnel and managerial problems. They realized, too, that with the termination of the war most of the war business would vanish, thereby greatly complicating the period of postwar adjustments. The Ayer management decided it would take no new accounts at this time unless they showed real promise as postwar clients. Thus the Boeing Aircraft Company was the only war client the Ayer agency undertook to serve, and since V-J Day the Boeing business has justified the agency's faith in its postwar potentialities.

Inevitably many Ayer clients expanded their advertising expenditures, but others were adversely affected and sharply reduced their advertising. Ayer executives have estimated that for every dollar of business resulting from the war, the firm lost at least three dollars in accounts which shrank because of the war situation. Thus the increase in Ayer business after 1941 came mainly as a result of securing such new accounts as De Beers (diamonds) and the Electric Light and Power Companies, together with the winning of established advertisers like Plymouth (automobiles) and the Chrysler Corporation and parts of National Dairy and General Electric advertising.

There was one important exception to the Ayer policy of refusing war business. In 1940 the agency competed with other agencies and won the contract to advertise for recruits for the United States Army. This exception was made mainly because Batten and his associates were personally concerned about the war outlook and because Jordan, long active in the Army Ordnance Association, knew from military contacts how urgently the Army needed to win recruits. The Ayer firm was convinced that it could help and determined to do so even if the Army business proved to be unprofitable.

The story of Ayer activities on behalf of the Army is too long to be told in detail here. Suffice it to say that between July, 1940, and December, 1942 (when volunteer enlistments ceased) the agency's campaigns helped the Army to fill every quota it set — for the Ground Force, Air Force cadets, Amphibious Force personnel, paratroopers, special categories of mechanics and electricians, and eighteen- and nineteen-year-olds for foreign service — more than 1,500,000 volunteers in all.

One aspect of the Army advertising deserves special comment. An agency must pay publishers and suppliers within 10 days after receiving bills, in order to earn the usual 2 per cent discount. On the other hand, the Government does not pay its bills until they have been fully substantiated and audited, a process usually requiring from 30 days to more than two months. Had the agency waited for payments from the Government before paying media owners and suppliers, it would have failed to earn the discount, and thousands of publishers throughout the country, waiting for their money, would have viewed Army advertising as an unwelcome financial burden. In accordance with its long-established policy of regarding N. W. Ayer & Son as the principal in such transactions, the Ayer management paid all accounts within 10 days and itself bore the financial burden of waiting for final payment from the Government. Often it had as much as two million dollars of cash tied up in this manner. It was able to do this because of Batten's insistence upon maintaining a strong cash position. Because it was unwilling to profit from the transaction, however, the Ayer agency credited the Government with the usual 2 per cent discount for cash, even though payments were long delayed. Not many agencies have been in a position to assume such a financial burden. Indeed the Services have, for this reason, found it difficult to get more than a few large agencies interested in competing for the recruiting campaigns.

CHANGES WITHIN THE ORGANIZATION SINCE 1940

The war, of course, made inroads in the Ayer staff. The total number of employees who left for the various services totaled 103, more than 10 per cent of the agency's working force. This was less serious than it might have been because nearly every department was discovering, as a result of improved organization and methods of operation, that it could accomplish more work with fewer people. But some replacements were inevitable, and the agency made increasing use of women to meet the need for personnel. For years women had been employed in considerable numbers at N. W. Ayer & Son, not only for routine clerical and stenographic duties, but in order to provide the feminine point of view as copywriters, planners, and consultants in the preparation of campaigns for products of which women themselves are the principal purchasers and for products on the purchase of which women's opinions have a great deal of influence. Now, because of the war, the firm experimented in using women even more widely in executive and semi-executive positions, particularly in the Business-Production and Media Departments. It found them eminently satisfactory. For N. W. Ayer & Son there has long been an honored place for women in agency work, and since 1936 the scope of that place has increased noticeably.

During the war years the Ayer agency closed out its foreign branches — those in Canada in 1941 and those in South America during 1942. Closing of the London office did not take place until 1947, because the Ayer management did not want to quit under Nazi fire, and wished subsequently to give clients there a chance to find a satisfactory replacement agency before terminating Ayer service in England. Of major importance in the decision to close the foreign offices was Batten's view that it was fundamentally unsound for N. W. Ayer & Son to try to operate in foreign countries so long as it had not exhausted opportunities in the United States. Foreign branches necessarily involve time and attention on the part of top management. Batten felt that top executives should concentrate on their domestic problems and not have to make trips abroad or even to think about foreign business. Further, foreign offices as distant as Europe or South America involve self-contained operations — a complete agency staff working for the most part independently of the home organization. This conflicts with the Ayer policy of having all operations controlled from Philadelphia so that the staff there can give to all accounts the benefit of all the best talent and experience the firm has been able to assemble. The London office had continued to make a profit through the war and afterwards, but Batten felt nonetheless that the Ayer organization should concentrate its energies and resources upon the American market.

The major change in organization was the establishment of the Creative Production Board in 1944. This Board consists of the heads of the Plans-Merchandising, Copy, Art, Radio, Media, and Public Relations Departments, the executive home-office supervisor of services, the account representative, and the branch office manager concerned with the account to be discussed. It meets once a week and conducts a systematic review of accounts. (Each account is thus reviewed at least once a year and certain accounts more frequently, depending upon circumstances.) Each review covers every area of agency work (actual or potential) on the account — plans, media, copy, art, radio, public relations, and so on — critically and incisively. The object is to integrate all phases of agency service on the account and to appraise both the work done in the agency and its effectiveness in relation to the needs of the client.

The significance of the Creative Production Board can hardly be overemphasized, for it has solved a problem of long standing in the agency business — that of bringing to bear upon every account the full force of the combined skill, experience, and resources of the house. That problem existed for Ayer and for other agencies doing a national business through branches because of the geographical distances involved; and, also, because of a certain human tendency on the part of those in closest daily contact with an account to avoid what they sometimes regard as outside interference, and to try to "run their own show." Yet no matter how intimately an individual or a small group may be acquainted with the intricacies of an account, it is obvious that they cannot supply the variety of skills and experience which is at the command of the whole organization; nor can they provide the necessary objectivity of view.

The difficulty of this general agency problem was enhanced for Ayer because of the Ayer policy of providing centralized production for nation-wide service. Like other large agencies, Ayer services its national accounts through branch offices; but whereas other agencies seek to provide these services largely through small production staffs maintained in each branch, Ayer has concentrated all its planning and virtually all its creative production activities in Philadelphia where the agency maintains the best combination of talent and experience that it can obtain. Yet there is always a need to make sure that the account is not getting into a rut; that the basic plan, once evolved, is kept in step with the client's needs; and that the various productive departments are working according to plan and in conformance with the best standards of the agency.

Other large agencies have attempted to solve this problem through the setting up of "Plans Boards," roughly analogous to the Creative Production Board at Ayer. These attempts have been only partially successful for one of two reasons, and sometimes both: (a) usually no machinery exists to ensure that all accounts shall come before the Board periodically for review (in at least one large agency such reviews take place, if ever, only at the request of the account representative); and, (b) the findings of the Board, once made, are arbitrary and binding. In the first instance, where Plans Board review is purely optional, the agency tends to break up into a number of little agencies under one name, each with its small world of accounts and its limited resources of experience and advertising skills. In the second, where all findings are final and mandatory, the opinions of the dominating member or members of the Board tend to color the production of the entire agency, and expert professional opinion frequently is overruled.

Prior to 1944 Ayer had attempted to cope with this vexing problem through a "Service Committee" composed of anyone whose presence seemed desirable at the moment. This committee was loosely organized, did not conform to a set schedule of meetings, and included so many people that it was too difficult to assemble and too unwieldy for proper criticism and thorough analysis.

The success of the new Creative Production Board has stemmed largely from a set of wisely contrived policies, plus the superb leadership of its chairman, a man of long service with the firm, who had brought new life to the Plans-Merchandising Department after 1936 and assumed responsibility for the Board in 1946. The meetings are strictly private, thus facilitating frank discussion. The Board maintains a detailed set of minutes, but issues no instructions and requires no reports back as to action taken on any points discussed in its meetings. Instead, it assumes that each operating executive is fully aware of his responsibilities and is competent to deal with any situation brought to light during discussions. Thus the Board does not interfere with established lines of authority: the operating executives are responsible to the President, not to the Board. While the Board may review and report on any phase of service (including the question of whether lack of understanding has been detected between the client and agency representatives), the firm depends for appropriate action upon its regularly constituted departmental executives. By this means, a standard of performance for the productive work of the entire agency is established — a standard based not upon individual judgment but upon the combined judgment of the ablest and most experienced people in the organization, i.e., the principals and department heads. At the same time ample scope is left for the free exercise of original thinking on client problems within the framework of the policy approved.

The Creative Production Board may look like increased centralization, which is often dangerous. In practice it has not had that result. It has been accompanied by a definite increase of responsibility for the individual departments; and the Board acts both as a means of helping the various specialists to keep in step on a specific program and also as a means by which top management keeps in touch with actual operations. There is, of course, increased committee work for department heads who are already heavily loaded. But the alternative is inefficiency at best, chaos at worst. One result is that department heads are compelled to delegate responsibility for many details, and this in turn helps to develop the next level of management — a consequence which strengthens the organization and improves opportunities for growth and advancement for the employees.

Besides contributing directly to better service to clients, the Board has yielded important by-products for the staff itself. Board meetings have made departmental executives examine problems of service from the over-all agency point of view, rather than from the viewpoint of their own specialties. Each specialist, through its discussions, has gained a better understanding of the contribution of other departments and of their relation to his own work. As a result he has obtained greater perspective on the account and a clear conception of his own responsibilities toward it. The organization as a whole has gained through better balance and integration among the operations of all its departments. Thus the Board has not only benefited clients through the constructive analysis of operations, but it has also been a powerful influence in welding the various Ayer departments together and in developing well-rounded, responsible executives. One should note that Board operations press final decisions upon executives at the operating level while helping them to see the problems in perspective, and so a high-level decision (as under the old régime) is not permitted to overrule professional opinion. This process illustrates one of the ways in which Ayer executives have been learning, under Batten, that they are integral members of the agency management and not mere hirelings. No other single factor has contributed more to the development of unity, understanding, and close coöperation throughout the organization.[8]

By 1942 the Ayer Radio Department had passed through the rejuvenation process mentioned above and was beginning to move ahead with great strides. It was again wholly located in New York where it had started, but it was now firmly integrated with agency operations in Philadelphia, principally through the Plans Department and the Creative Production Board. It was no longer operating as it had done in earlier years, mainly as an adjunct of the New York office. That it was alive to new developments is evident from the fact that it began to work with television in 1940 before commercial television had been authorized, and began to handle the broadcasting of football games in Philadelphia by television for the Atlantic Refining Company in 1941 when the Federal Communications Commission first permitted commercial sponsorship of television programs. This was the first agency operation in the new medium of television. Wartime restrictions prevented any real development of television, but Ayer handled the Atlantic Refining Company football telecasts throughout the war, and it continued the study of every phase of commercial television so as to participate fully in the development of this new advertising medium. In 1946, when television began to emerge from wartime restrictions, Ayer rapidly began to expand its operations and in the next two years was producing telecasts for Atlantic, Goodyear Tire & Rubber Company, Waltham Watch Company, A. T. & T., United Air Lines, the U. S. Army and U. S. Air Force Recruiting Service, and other clients. At the same time, recognizing that Hollywood's show atmosphere tends to warp business judgment in men working there, the Ayer management arranged for a regular and frequent exchange of top personnel between New York and Hollywood.

One other phase of the Radio Department development deserves mention here. Ayer had begun to produce commercial films, both motion pictures and slide films, for clients as early as 1928. These were employed for sales work, industrial education, and public information. Because the production of such films is so closely related to the production of radio programs (both put the agency into the show business), that activity has been allied informally with the Radio Department. The systematic and progressive development of this field in the Ayer agency really dates from May, 1942, when the Motion Picture Bureau was organized within the Radio Department on a formal, explicit basis to work with the production and distribution of commercial films for Ayer clients. Since that time the agency has made good progress with the medium of motion pictures, which are important not only as a communications device when projected before audiences in the normal way, but also promise much for the future in connection with television.

FINANCIAL DEVELOPMENTS

During this period the Ayer management executed several financial transactions which have long-run significance. As stated above, Batten had long felt that an agency's most important asset is its staff. Accordingly, he viewed with disfavor the fact that N. W. Ayer & Son had invested over two million dollars in constructing its own building and also, as a result of transactions before 1930, still owned several blocks of semi-speculative stocks. Believing in the importance of having strong liquid reserves in case of trouble, he took steps to sell the securities as soon as the market situation seemed propitious. He also arranged (in 1944) to sell the Ayer Building to Yale University, at the same time taking a twenty-year lease on the premises. The Federal tax laws, of course, facilitated this transaction, for the loss incurred on the real-estate transaction could be spread over three years of war operations and hence materially reduced the corporation profit taxes which had to be paid on general business operations. More important, however, it strengthened the firm's financial position and put management's attention wholly on agency business where it belonged. (Incidentally, the Coast Guard had taken over the use of the top floor and the roof deck of the building in 1942 for defense purposes.)

One might criticize the sale of the building as unsound in that it meant exchanging a tangible asset for dollars of fluctuating value. The Ayer view is, however, that ownership of real estate is neither essential nor advantageous to the agency business, and that its assets will be more productive used in advertising than if invested in real estate. Shifts in site values, and specifically those which have occurred in Philadelphia, lend support to that view. It is conceivable, and even probable, that by 1960 Washington Square will not be a good location for the agency; hence the Ayer management believes it should not concern itself with property risks but rather should concentrate its attention and its capital in the field of advertising.

By 1941, in spite of the decrease in billings, Ayer earnings had begun to improve, and the new management announced a profit-sharing plan for selected employees who show outstanding ability. It set aside a bonus fund annually based on the agency's net earnings, the sum to be distributed being determined as follows:

On company earnings up to $100,000.................. 20%
If over $100,000 and less than $200,000............... 25 "
If over $200,000 and less than $300,000............... 30 "
If over $300,000 and less than $400,000............... 35 "
If over $400,000................................... 40 "

The Ayer management, through department heads and bureau chiefs, selects for bonus awards a limited number of men and women of exceptional performance for the year. The bonus has no necessary relationship to salary received, and the list of recipients varies from year to year. The management believes that the plan has been an important factor in its success, because it offers immediate rewards to employees for current performance and yet does not build up overhead, inasmuch as the bonus fund varies with the fortunes of the business. It is again characteristic of the new régime that the three top executives, Batten, Jordan, and Lauck, draw comparatively modest salaries and do not award bonuses to themselves.

Although the profit-sharing plan reaches only a selected group of employees, there is a bonus for every member of the staff when times are good. In 1946 each Ayer employee received as bonus an extra two weeks' pay up to a maximum of $200; at the end of 1947 each employee received an extra four weeks' pay up to a maximum of $400. The fact that all employees received a bonus of some sort may have checked any possible dissatisfaction arising as a result of the special bonuses. At any rate, no discontent on this score was expressed to the writer. It is of course difficult to appraise the long-run contributions of employees as distinct from current performance. Further, any system of bonuses, in the final analysis, depends upon the personal judgment — and prejudices — of management. Hence management may make mistakes in awarding bonuses and so create friction. No system of compensation, however, can eliminate this difficulty, and the only safeguard possible is to broaden the basis of evaluation by consulting a number of persons who are in a position to judge the employees' performance. Certainly the Ayer management today is more alert to this problem than it was before 1936 and the executive group which is regarded as "top management" is larger and more representative of the staff as a whole than it was under Ayer or Fry. So long as it preserves this relationship and its present concern for the advancement of deserving employees, the bonus plan is likely to work well.

Payments to Ayer stockholders, likewise, increased after dividends were resumed in the last quarter of 1942 as follows:

1943	$1.25
1944	1.25
1945	1.25
1946	1.75
1947	2.50
1948	2.50

There has been a noticeable shift in Ayer stock ownership since 1936. The firm's policy has always been to have ownership restricted to people who are actively engaged in the business, and the corporation has invariably purchased the shares of any employee who left the firm (at a price formula established at the time of incorporation). A number of employees who had purchased Ayer stock in 1929 were unhappy about the drop in earnings and consequent decrease in the value of their shares (early in the depression it declined from the original $15.00 per share to $3.61). Knowing this, the company offered in 1941 to buy back any shares they wished to sell at the stipulated price-earnings ratio, which was $16.02 per share at the time. About half the stockholders, glad to get back more than they had originally paid, took advantage of the offer. It is interesting to note that those who held on had the satisfaction of seeing the share value rise to $32.00 by the end of 1947. The present management does not believe that it is advantageous to the average employee to own stock in the company. Current policy at Ayer is to limit stock ownership to those who are making major contributions to the growth of the business.

With an eye to the future control of the business, Batten and his associates began to look for men within the organization whose character and ability marked them as possible leaders for the firm — the next generation of management that it would develop. By 1945 the management had decided upon several, and it allotted to each of them a block of stock at half the current price, to be paid for out of dividends subsequently earned. Remembering how he had felt in 1934 when he had had to sign a promissory note for a large sum to pay for shares allotted to him, Batten was unwilling to make the arrangement a burden to the men selected. Accordingly, he provided that the Corporation would hold the stock in their names until the dividends paid for it. By this device the new régime is providing for succession from within the ranks. At the same time it has given tangible recognition to outstanding men. Here is one more reason for the new zeal within the organization and one more piece of evidence that Batten and his immediate associates regard themselves as the management of an institution, rather than the owners of a piece of property. Fry had held 60 per cent of the stock outstanding. Today no one person owns more than 21 per cent, and the management is prepared to pass even more ownership and authority to younger men as fast as they can handle it.

Maturing Policy

The prosperity of N. W. Ayer & Son during the past seven years is, of course, related to general prosperity in the United

States. It would be a mistake, however, to interpret the developments within the agency as mere reflections of the external environment. There is, for example, a vast difference between the Ayer atmosphere in 1929 and today: the staff today is smaller numerically and yet it is turning out substantially more work than in 1929 with less effort, and its technical quality is higher. The firm has prospered because of steps taken between 1936 and 1941 in the face of adversity. It has consciously developed a staff of young, able, and enthusiastic men and women who are working well together. They feel that it is their show and that there is full scope for all their energy and talent and ample recognition for their achievements. They have responded to the new leadership.

But the success of the firm is the result of something more than the technical excellence and enthusiasm of the staff. In a very real sense the House of Ayer is prospering because of the basic business policies evolved during the history of the firm. And those policies have come into sharp focus since 1940 — partly because of events like the loss of the large account referred to above, page 181, and partly because of Batten's feeling that the whole organization required something more than rather vague good intentions as a guide. He believed that the firm needed a well-defined, explicit statement of objectives and principles to enable everyone to work according to a uniform pattern. To this end he and several other officers of the firm prepared a preliminary draft of a policy memorandum, covering nearly 200 typewritten pages, as a basis for discussion. It was a preliminary draft because Batten understood that others would be able to make improvements in it and also because he knew the staff would not fully understand it until they had considered it at length and digested its contents. He arranged for a two-day conference, held in Atlantic City in May, 1944, to be attended by every member of the Ayer staff holding an executive position. There they read and discussed the document section by section. Afterwards Batten distributed a copy to each executive, ninety-two in all, and asked for comments and suggestions for incorporation in the finished statement.

Out of this process has been emerging a carefully drawn policy statement which is not yet in final form. Indeed it will never be in "final" form, because the Ayer management regards its policies as continuously evolving and subject to improvement. At the same time it wants any change to come as a result of conscious deliberation, rather than as unwitting variations in operations which become policy as a result of repetition. There is, of course, no necessary relation between avowed policies and the daily execution of business, but Ayer policy and execution have corresponded to an unusual degree. What follows is an attempt to state briefly the basic principles which now govern the operations of N. W. Ayer & Son.

Ayer policy starts with the fundamental premise, originally conceived by F. W. Ayer, that the agency works exclusively for the advertiser and that it must "spend the advertiser's money as if it were your own." As initially interpreted this meant getting the lowest price from media and making sure that the client received what he paid for. It still means that, but Ayer management sees broader implications. Because the agency must serve the long-run interests of the client, it must scrutinize current projects to make sure they fit the ultimate objectives. Thus it must give business counsel in the fullest sense and not simply prepare advertising campaigns. Since it interprets advertising broadly as a communications device, the agency must cover the whole range of media — newspapers, magazines, radio, television, commercial films, posters, direct-mailing pieces, and news releases — and it must think in terms of what the client's business should ultimately be, what the client should say generally, and how he should say it, rather than simply in terms of selling products or services. And because it views advertising as a tool of management, the agency staff must confer at least periodically with top management and not confine its contacts to sales or marketing personnel in the client organization. Only by this means can it be sure that it fully understands the client's objectives and is working in harmony with them; if it cannot do this, it cannot serve the client's interests or its own and must withdraw.

All this is substantially the position that N. W. Ayer & Son reached before 1930, but during the past ten years the position has been more sharply defined and better understood throughout the organization. Further, Ayer management has perceived certain implications for the internal operation of the agency that the previous administration had not fully understood. First, if the agency is to work effectively for the long-run growth and stability of the client, its own organization and operations must provide for growth and stability. Hence it is not to be regarded as the property of a few men, but rather as an enduring institution; management must work continually at the task of developing a succession of qualified people capable of handling the various positions of responsibility. Growth is to come, not from striving for bigness, but as a consequence of a superior over-all performance. To keep that performance high, the agency must through continuous research keep in touch with progress in the field of marketing, advertising, and general business development; and it must so relate research to current operations that members of the staff keep abreast of changes and advances in their specialties. To make sure that its service is always up to standard and the various phases properly integrated, the agency must not only concentrate all creative work in Philadelphia (with the exception of those creative functions that are necessarily carried on elsewhere, such as the operations of the Radio, Television, and Public Relations Departments in New York), but must develop systematic coördination and review of operations on such accounts through the Creative Production Board.

But there is more to effective operations than stability and technical excellence, important as they are. If the agency is to provide advertising counsel of the highest order, it must preserve its independence and professional integrity. To that end it must be financially strong and have a balanced clientèle, so that it can resist pressure from a client who seeks to compromise its principles and so that it can withstand the loss of any account it is serving. In the interests of its own future and the client's ultimate welfare, it must avoid methods which would tend to destroy the consumer's faith in advertising. To preserve professional integrity it must also restrict its clientèle to accounts which its staff can serve with pride and self-respect; and it must have, or be able to develop, working relations with the client's organization which assure good understanding and coöperation. Again, if the agency is to have stability and integrity in dealing with clients, it must provide reasonable security for its own employees, develop the professional competence and integrity of its creative staff, provide its employees with work which they can regard as respectable and useful, and show by its daily conduct that Ayer management itself respects the ability and contribution of that staff. In the past the agency had provided security of an elementary sort, but the old top management had sometimes shown little regard for the professional opinions of its most capable employees and so had blocked their best technical contributions. Batten, on the other hand, has stated the new emphasis clearly:[9]

> No business can be better than the people in it. We believe in getting and keeping the best and most gifted people we can find.
> We believe also that, once having got them, we must do everything possible to develop them to the fullest extent of their potentialities. . . .
> Whenever possible, from such developed and productive personalities brought up within the business, key positions should be filled. This offers a powerful incentive to individual growth, and an equally powerful incentive to organizational growth through the added experience and loyalty of the management.

Since 1936 Batten and his associates have shown by their actions that such statements of policy are not empty words. The staff, in turn, has shown that it understands and accepts with enthusiasm the concepts of operation that have emerged, and it has responded fully to the challenges and opportunities implied.

All these basic policies have implications at the operating level which are being worked out in detailed principles and procedures. Such subordinate policies are presented under appropriate topical headings in Part II of this volume.

What does the history of N. W. Ayer & Son since 1936 mean when reviewed critically? In the writer's considered judgment it means that the firm has survived the most difficult period in its history and has come through with flying colors. Its volume has increased tremendously, and that increase has been achieved profitably without sacrifice of principle. Its performance has improved in quality in every department of the business. Its organizational structure is more effective. It has graded up and integrated the personnel of its entire staff, so that it is not only of top-notch quality in technical competence, but is also working with enthusiasm and organizational teamwork unsurpassed in the firm's history. Its financial position is beyond question. It has developed a set of definitive policies and a professional point of view which promise strength, stability, and integrity for the organization itself and service for its clients, which few other agencies can equal and none can surpass. A real test will come when hard times again hit the advertising industry, but it is unlikely that any future depression will present more difficult problems than those of the period of readjustment since 1936.

The present strength of the Ayer firm has come mainly from strong and wise leadership. But, in contrast to earlier days, that strength is not concentrated at the top. One of the best features of the present management has been its willingness and ability to draw out the capabilities of subordinates and so to develop power in depth throughout the organization. In short, the firm has emerged from the status of a family business into that of a strong institution governed by mature organizational policies rather than by personal prejudices and tastes. The iron paternalism of F. Wayland Ayer and the somewhat vague idealism of Wilfred W. Fry have disappeared. Idealism in abundance is still there, but it is an idealism which is both democratic and practical. Gone, too, is the smug complacency which marked the organization in the 1920's and the cynicism and discontent manifested by the staff during the early 1930's. Today the atmosphere of N. W. Ayer & Son is charged with personal enthusiasm, professional pride, mutual respect and confidence, and a strong sense of common purpose.

*   *   *   *

So, in outline, runs the history of an individual advertising agency. Like others in the industry, the Ayer firm arose directly out of the needs of publishers and advertisers, and indirectly out of the general public's need for guidance in a vast market place. It has changed and expanded operations with the change and growth of business activities everywhere. And, while no serious observer could pretend that it is perfectly adapted to its work —

human institutions seldom are — N. W. Ayer & Son has been part and parcel of the commercial life of the United States and has successfully adjusted to the changes involved.

Starting while the advertising agency was still in the formative state of development, N. W. Ayer & Son has won financial success and a position of leadership in the field. Able management and a loyal staff have developed an effective organization which has been tested and strengthened by both good times and adversity. The result is an enduring institution with a proud record of achievement in serving American business.

PART II
ANALYSIS OF PARTICULAR ASPECTS OF AYER DEVELOPMENT

Note: In Part II a great deal of detail and exposition has been included for the benefit of students and specialists in advertising.

The general reader may find the material too detailed for him in many places and should, therefore, skip without qualm those sections which do not interest him.

CHAPTER IX

THE AGENCY'S CLIENTS

ALL THE efforts of an advertising agency, all its resources, all its manifold activities are bent toward serving firms which advertise. Like other business organizations it has something to sell, and that something is service. The advertisers are its customers, or — to use the term which agents employ to indicate the professional nature of their work — its clients. Without them it is nothing; less, even, than a shop without buyers, for it has no goods on its shelves except experience, ideas, and ability. The agency's purpose, its sole economic justification, is to employ the various techniques of advertising in behalf of clients whenever an informed state of public opinion will benefit them and to do that job more effectively or more cheaply than they themselves can do it. N. W. Ayer & Son works only for others; it progresses only by serving them well; and its relations with its clients are its very life stream.

THOSE WHO HAVE ADVERTISED THROUGH N. W. AYER & SON

Who are these advertisers upon whom the agency depends? Simply to name all who have used N. W. Ayer & Son at one time or another would require a fair-sized book; and the list would include a surprisingly large proportion of the well-known business enterprises of the country. The Ayer agency has advertised nearly everything under the sun, ranging from elaborately printed and scented personal visiting cards of the 1870's and 1880's to Caterpillar tractors and Blue Bell work clothes, from Philadelphia boarding houses to the United Air Lines, from Ferry seeds to Steinway grand pianos, Felt and Tarrant Comptometers, and Hawaiian pineapple products.

Throughout its existence N. W. Ayer & Son has advertised so many schools and colleges that it has long had a large separate department to handle this work (even such conservative and well-known institutions as Harvard University resort to advertising). It has also publicized other non-commercial enterprises, such as the Liberty Bond campaigns, various projects of the Young Men's Christian Association, and U. S. Army recruiting drives. The vast bulk of the agency's work, however, has come from commercial and industrial firms of one kind or another. Some of them have sought the agency's help in bringing before consumers a new product, as the Noiseless Typewriter Company did. A few, like the American Telephone and Telegraph Company, have advertised not to sell goods but to explain to the public their organization and services. The majority of them come to the agency for assistance in highly competitive selling; in urging, for example, the merits of Cannon towels, Atlantic gasoline, or Kellogg cereal breakfast foods against those of rival brands.[1]

During the past thirty-five years the Ayer agency has drawn clients from a new group of advertisers engaged in selling competition of another kind: trade associations, which want to advance the interests of a whole industry in its struggle for a share of the nation's business. In 1907–08, for example, the Alaskan Packers' Association — one of the first trade associations to use advertising — employed N. W. Ayer & Son to promote the sale of Alaskan red salmon; in 1909 the Association of American Portland Cement Manufacturers explained through Ayer advertisements the use and advantages of portland cement; and the agency has since prepared association advertising for rice, Spanish green olives, Brazilian coffee, glass containers, western pine lumber, structural steel, and many other commodities, as well as for the electrical industry.

The character of the Ayer clientèle has changed noticeably over the years. From 1869 to 1875 the agency's business was derived mainly from concerns located in the Philadelphia area. By 1900 N. W. Ayer & Son was acting as advertising agency for enterprises in all parts of the United States. And in 1933 it numbered among its customers firms as far afield as Europe, Asia, and South America.[2] Between 1940 and 1947 all foreign branches were again closed out, the Ayer management having decided, as indicated in Chapter VIII, that it would concentrate all attention in domestic business. A change of another kind is also apparent. In the 'seventies and 'eighties those who advertised through the Ayer firm were largely retailers and others who sold directly to the public. By 1890 most of these had ceased to use the Ayer agency, and its principal work was the advertising of manufacturers who sold through dealers and retailers but preferred to get control over their ultimate market.

Some clients, notably industrial firms like the Wyandotte Chemicals Corporation and the American Rolling Mills Company, advertise mainly to other business enterprises. Some want to reach that relatively limited portion of the public which can afford such expensive commodities as Steinway pianos and De Beers diamonds. Certain other clients, among them the Atlantic Refining Company and subsidiaries of the National Dairy Products Corporation, have to direct their advertising to markets limited by geographical rather than income factors. Still others, like the Kellogg and Plymouth companies, want to appeal to customers of all classes in all parts of the country.

The amounts spent on advertising by these clients — the size of their accounts as advertising men put it — have varied widely. Before 1880 the range was from single orders of fifty or seventy-five cents to a few thousand dollars annually. By 1900 most of the very small accounts had dropped out; and, while many of those remaining were still under a thousand dollars per year, some of them ran into the hundreds of thousands. In 1903 the agency still had a large number of small accounts, more than six hundred under $100 and nine hundred running less than $1,000.[3] The absence of complete records makes it impossible to present an exact analysis for earlier years, but Table 2 shows the continued growth in size of accounts since 1921.

It is noteworthy that, in spite of a marked increase in the total dollar volume during the ten years between 1921 and 1930, the number of individual accounts dropped steadily. This decrease took place in the accounts running less than $100,000 per year. Meanwhile those of $100,000 or more per year actually increased in number. The data from which this table was derived also disclose the striking fact that, by 1930, 90 per cent of the Ayer volume came from accounts amounting to $100,000 or more.

Since 1930 further changes in the size of Ayer accounts have taken place. The total number of accounts decreased and the proportion of large accounts increased, so that the great bulk of Ayer business comes from less than a hundred accounts. The firm

TABLE 2

Size of Ayer Accounts, 1921, 1925, and 1930

Dollar Volume	Number of Clients		
	1921	1925	1930
1,000,000 or over.	1	3	7
500,000 to 999,999.	1	5	5
400,000 to 499,999.	2	1	1
300,000 to 399,999.	3	2	8
200,000 to 299,999.	3	9	8
100,000 to 199,999.	11	15	16
75,000 to 99,999.	12	11	10
50,000 to 74,999.	11	14	16
40,000 to 49,999.	10	12	6
30,000 to 39,999.	11	10	8
20,000 to 29,999.	13	21	20
Less than 20,000.	227	164	121
Total number of accounts.	305	267	226

Source: Records supplied by the treasurer of N. W. Ayer & Son.

is still interested in small accounts which have growth potentialities, but it scrutinizes small accounts more carefully now than in former years, since it is less interested in volume for its own sake.

Changes in the Commodities Advertised by Ayer

These changes in the nature of the clientèle are paralleled by significant changes in the products advertised. In an effort to show the shift in a factual way, I have tried to analyze the expenditures made through N. W. Ayer & Son at selected periods in its history. The lack of records prevents showing figures for the first few years of the agency's existence; but the character of the business as reflected by the data for the two years 1877 and 1878 is apparent from Table 3. Patent medicines easily take the lead, with books and printed tracts occupying an important place. This is interesting in view of the fact that books and patent medicines were among the first commodities to be produced in quantity and likewise the first to be advertised in newspapers.[4] This suggests a relationship between large-scale production and advertising which is borne out by the other items on the list. The man who produced wares in quantity had to seek buyers over a wide area, and he used advertising as an economical means of enlarging his market.

One cannot assume that the Ayer statistics give a true cross section of advertising in general. It frequently happens that an agency, for one reason or another, handles no advertising for (let us say) cigarettes or typewriters when these commodities are being widely advertised. Thus, after World War I the automobile industry was one of the leading advertisers, but until 1927 it contributed a comparatively small part of the Ayer volume. One cannot therefore conclude that farm implements, because they contributed only .6 per cent of the Ayer total in 1877 and 1878, were not being widely promoted by advertising. The agency may have a great deal more or a great deal less than its proportionate share of the advertising of any particular commodity at any one time. The make-up of its volume varies, just as the diet of a man changes, with season, individual preference, and chance.

In general, however, the Ayer statistics are bound to reflect the character of advertising as a whole. It is no accident that the amount spent on food was small in 1877–78. It would be smaller if we eliminated the sums devoted to advertising retail grocery stores rather than the various goods they sold. The explanation is obvious: manufactured foods were confined mostly to staples like flour, sugar, tea, and coffee. The American family was fed from the home kitchen rather than from the factory. It leaned heavily on the general store, of course, but the groceries it bought came to the store in bulk quantities in bags and barrels rather than in small, handy packages. And if these bags and barrels bore the manufacturer's brand or trade-mark, the housewife paid little attention. For quality she depended mostly upon her own shrewd knowledge and the local storekeeper's reputation.

Other features of the list are interesting. Dry goods and clothing stand high, but most of the advertising was for piece goods

TABLE 3

AMOUNTS SPENT ON VARIOUS COMMODITY GROUPS, 1877–1878

Group	Amount		Percentage of Total[a]
Patent medicines and treatment.....		$68,484	21.6
Printed matter: Books, tracts, etc....	$32,466		10.2
Greeting cards, chromos..........	24,653		7.7
Newspapers and periodicals.......	9,320	66,439	2.9 20.8
Jewelry and silverware.............	——	27,424	—— 8.6
Dry goods and clothing.............		23,901	7.5
Seeds and nursery stock............		21,333	6.7
Machinery:			
Industrial machines, hardware, and			
building materials..............	$15,663		4.9
Sewing machines.................	3,641		1.1
Farm implements................	1,763	21,067	.6 6.6
Schools and colleges...............	——	13,719	—— 4.3
Tobacco products..................		13,479	4.3
Pianos and musical instruments.....		11,343	3.6
Groceries.........................		10,217	3.2
Household furnishings..............		7,721	2.4
Hotels and restaurants.............		6,445	2.0
Patents and war pensions procured...		5,556	1.8
Agents wanted....................		3,819	1.2
Houses and real estate.............		3,706	1.2
Toilet goods......................		3,007	.9
Railroads and transportation........		2,313	.7
Insurance........................		1,759	.6
Puzzles, tricks, and novelties........		1,639	.5
Firm notices......................		1,454	.5
Office equipment..................		839	.3
Printing and supplies..............		786	.2
Livestock........................		560	.2
Legal notices.....................		138	.04
		$317,148	99.74

[a] These computations are based on the expenditures which can be traced definitely to the advertising of commodities listed. Many items cannot be identified, but nearly every expenditure of any consequence has been traced. The total volume of business handled by N. W. Ayer & Son in 1877 was $195,791.75, of which $131,629 or 67.2% was related to advertising specified products and included in the study. The total volume of 1878 was $228,642.83, of which $185,519 or 81.1% was identified and included above. For the two years, 74.7% of the total was identified.

SOURCE: Calculated from Ledgers 3, 4, and 5. For added details of analysis, see Appendix

and trimmings. Only a small amount of ready-made clothing was advertised, partly because a great deal of wearing apparel was still made in the home — a modern relic of primitive economy. The jewelry and silverware were mostly cheap, plated stuff; the tobacco was almost all snuff and cut plug; the musical instruments were old-fashioned organs, mandolins, and guitars; and the novelties were ventriloquists' whistles, magic lanterns, artificial flowers, and curios. Toilet goods and cosmetics had not assumed their modern prominence in America. Such aids to female elegance had little place in a society which was essentially rural in character. In any case, respectable women at that time were chary about using them.

The list clearly reveals the state of advertising in the 'seventies — the large place occupied by patent medicines and knick-knacks of little value, the reliance of the consuming public and most manufacturers upon the local merchant who had little occasion to use an advertising agency, and the general absence of what modern business parlance refers to as branded staple merchandise. In short, a typical agency was getting most of its revenue during 1877–78 from commodities which are of little or no importance to it today, and it was placing hardly any advertising for those which now contribute the greater part of its volume. In spite of objectionable features, advertising has made obvious progress since those early years.

By 1900 and 1901 the list of products advertised had altered greatly, as Table 4 shows. The rise of the National Biscuit Company and other food manufacturers, together with their development of aggressive marketing programs, explains the position of food at the head of the list. The advertising of the Standard Oil subsidiaries brought fuels and lubricants to second place. Books and tracts had dropped in importance to the agency, and those fancy postcards and lurid chromolithographs which were so dear to Americans of the previous generation had almost disappeared.

Schools and colleges had increased in importance to the agency, and they were supplemented by a comparatively new form of education, correspondence courses, the existence of which suggests some shortcomings in the public educational opportunities of the time. The Ayer agency still handled patent medicines in considerable volume, but between 1878 and 1900 the amount had decreased in comparison with the rest of the business; and, as we have noted earlier, the patent-medicine advertising was shortly to drop out altogether.

The records for 1900–01 show that N. W. Ayer & Son was placing a considerable amount of advertising for ready-made clothing: the factory was fast winning in this battle with household industry. They also reflect to some extent the greatly increased importance of mechanical products; and, although the automobile was still in its infancy, N. W. Ayer & Son was already advertising it.

The amount devoted to confectionery and soft drinks reveals the American sweet tooth as already well formed. And in the item for drugs and toilet goods (mainly soaps, face creams, and lotions) we may see the beginnings of one of the largest fields of advertising today. The building industry, too, was beginning to attain some of its later importance as an advertiser. The item for public utilities is small in contrast; gas, electric, and telephone companies were still mainly local enterprises with little occasion to use an advertising agency in developing their markets or goodwill.

It is apparent from the data for 1900–01 that advertising had become well established by the turn of the century as an indispensable adjunct of large-scale enterprise. It is evident, too, that the clientèle of N. W. Ayer & Son changed as technical and evolutionary advances took place in American business.

Now consider the Ayer business in 1930 as revealed in Table 5. Perhaps the most striking feature is the size of the individual items, for the first eight groups were in millions of dollars. One can see, too, that important shifts had continued to take place in the Ayer clientèle, shifts which reflect to some extent changes in the emphasis of American advertising. At the top was the automobile industry (including tires and accessories) which provided a quarter of the entire Ayer volume. In the course of its rise this juggernaut had wiped out the carriage and wagon advertising, which had formed more than 2 per cent of the Ayer business in 1900–01. Tobacco, an important advertiser ever since the beginning of the agency, had risen to second place; in contrast with

TABLE 4

Amounts Spent on Various Commodity Groups, 1900–1901

Group	Amount		Percentage of Total	
Foods................................		$595,769		17.69
Fuel and lubricants...............		341,404		10.14
Education:				
Schools and colleges.............	$190,516		5.66	
Correspondence schools..........	110,797	301,313	3.29	8.95
Printed material:				
Newspapers and periodicals......	$222,542		6.61	
Books and tracts...............	61,101		1.81	
Cards and chromos.............	2,652	286,295	.08	8.50
Patent medicines.................		282,375	——	8.39
Dry goods and clothing:				
Ready-to-wear.................	$154,587		4.59	
General........................	78,438		2.33	
Textiles.......................	20,768	253,793	.62	7.54
Tobacco products.................		240,794	——	7.15
Mechanical equipment:				
Farm implements...............	$139,541		4.14	
General........................	46,978		1.40	
Household appliances...........	36,269		1.08	
Automobiles...................	6,094	228,882	.18	6.80
Seeds and nursery stock...........		148,438	——	4.40
Confectionery and soft drinks......		147,119		4.37
Drugs and toilet goods............		106,617		3.17
Construction industry:				
Paints and hardware............	$47,850		1.42	
Plumbing and heating...........	41,032		1.22	
Building material and fences.....	16,299	105,181	.48	3.12
Carriages and wagons.............		80,481	——	2.39
Jewelry and silverware............		75,091		2.23
Pianos and musical instruments....		34,578		1.03
Metals...........................		22,642		.67
Public utilities, communication and transportation.................		20,837		.62
Household furnishings.............		12,936		.38
Travel...........................		12,272		.36
Banking.........................		10,037		.30
Office equipment.................		8,025		.24
Agents wanted...................		4,584		.14
Livestock and poultry.............		4,341		.13
Miscellaneous....................		21,579		.64
Unidentified.....................		21,420		.64
		$3,366,803		100.00

Source: Calculated from accounts in Personal Ledgers 25, 30, 35, and 40. See Appendɪᴀ or further details.

TABLE 5

AMOUNTS SPENT ON VARIOUS COMMODITY GROUPS, 1930

Group	Amount		Percentage of Total	
Automobiles, tires, and accessories...		$9,686,704	25.45	
Tobacco products.................		6,818,463	17.91	
Food and food drinks..............		5,969,735	15.68	
Drugs and toilet goods.............		2,410,493	6.33	
Chemicals.......................		1,679,186	4.41	
Confectionery and soft drinks.......		1,640,486	4.31	
Transportation and communication..		1,361,982	3.58	
Dry goods and clothing............		1,178,754	3.10	
Construction industry:				
Plumbing and heating...........	$577,653		1.52	
Building materials...............	367,804		.96	
Paints and hardware.............	204,458	1,149,915	.54	3.02
Education:				
Schools, colleges, and camps......	$574,477		1.51	
Correspondence schools..........	451,098	1,025,575	1.18	2.69
Gasoline, oil, and fuel.............		745,604		1.96
Agriculture:				
Stock foods and tonics...........	$328,558		.86	
Seeds and nursery stock..........	248,624		.65	
Farm implements and machinery..	72,115		.19	
Livestock......................	30,342	679,639	.08	1.79
Household supplies................		638,502		1.68
Office equipment and supplies.......		597,443		1.57
Jewelry and silverware.............		531,845		1.40
Machinery.......................		352,098		.92
Musical instruments...............		341,581		.90
Printed material:				
Newspapers and periodicals.......	$286,121		.75	
Books and maps................	21,272	307,393	.06	.81
Household furnishings.............		223,464		.59
Insurance and financial............		221,435		.58
Shoes, trunks, and leather goods....		89,848		.24
Sporting goods...................		85,272		.22
Miscellaneous....................		333,197		.88
		$38,068,614		100.00
Associations[a]...................		$ 1,468,734		3.86

[a] Expenditures by trade and manufacturers' associations have been included in the above analysis and are recapitulated here to show the extent of such advertising.

SOURCE: Data supplied by the treasurer of N. W. Ayer & Son, Inc. See Appendix for further details.

earlier times, most of its advertising was devoted to the sale of cigarettes. Patent medicines had dropped entirely out of the picture, and in their stead were drugs and toilet goods — with heavy emphasis upon tooth paste, aspirin, perfumes, and cosmetics.

The advertising of educational institutions, although the dollar volume had increased threefold since 1900, was dwarfed by the greater growth of commercial advertising in the agency. The publishing business, too, had ceased to occupy a position of importance. On the other hand, chemicals, gasoline, transportation and communication (mainly telephone advertising), and office equipment stand high enough to indicate the essential part they play in modern life.

The amount of advertising devoted to trade and industrial associations indicates the part that N. W. Ayer & Son has been playing in the competition between industries mentioned a few paragraphs earlier.

Since the business now consists of a relatively small number of large accounts, a similar analysis of commodity groups advertised by the Ayer agency since World War II would not reveal any significant changes except those resulting from the gain or loss of a large individual account. No detailed analysis is possible at this time because certain clients can be identified simply by the commodity classification. As a result such an analysis would reveal confidential information.

When one contemplates these data thoughtfully in terms of their economic and social significance, some interesting — even disturbing — questions are bound to emerge. Some observers wonder whether it is wise for society collectively to spend so much on the advertisement (for example) of motor cars, which to a large extent advertise themselves, on food and tobacco products, which satisfy wants that need no stimulation. One answer is that individual industries compete for the consumer's dollar — automobiles vs. houses, meat vs. bread and other cereal products, tobacco vs. candy, and so on. And even when such commodities as a whole need little promotion (which is rarely true today), competition between individual units within a given industry is keen, and large sums of money must be spent in selling brand A in the face of rival efforts to gain patronage for brand B. It is clear that individual firms find it advantageous — even necessary — to advertise, but there is room for argument about the social consequences. Has the automobile, for instance, attained such a preponderant place in our economy (partly through advertising) that it jeopardizes the whole economic and social structure? [5] For the present, however, let us turn from such doubts and go on to consider other aspects of agency-client relations.

How the Agency Obtains Clients

The advertiser's relations with N. W. Ayer & Son usually begin when an Ayer representative approaches him to solicit business. It is true, of course, that throughout the history of the Ayer agency various business concerns have come to it voluntarily for help with their advertising. They have heard of the agency from publishers or from other advertisers, or they have seen advertisements which the firm itself has used to establish its own name in the commercial world, and they come because they have encountered problems which they think advertising might solve and they want the firm's expert assistance.

But the great majority of the firms that have become Ayer clients have been persuaded to do so through the initiative of the Ayer agency. Although agency work, at least in some respects, is now professional in character, still the advertising industry has not yet reached the stage in which agencies can wait for business to come to them without urging. Like its rivals, therefore, N. W. Ayer has a solicitation or Business Development Department charged with obtaining clients whose advertising will provide work for the rest of the staff.

The work of the Business Development Department has always been to promote the use of advertising and to urge advertisers to employ the Ayer agency. Solicitation of business was, of course, essential in the early years of the firm, for then almost the entire work of the agency was to obtain orders for advertising. F. W. Ayer himself devoted most of the ordinary working hours to canvassing prospective customers; he could make his spare time early in the morning and late at night suffice for the actual execution of the orders. Long after McKinney had come into the firm and the partners had enjoyed the benefit of a large staff of assistants, it was still true that the agency's work centered in the Business-Getting Department, as it was then called. Indeed, the activities which now occupy most of the Ayer organization — the analysis of markets, planning of advertising campaigns, preparation of copy, and placing of advertisements — were, in the earlier years, merely adjuncts of the solicitation work.

This emphasis upon getting orders rather than upon executing them seems to be inverted and illogical at first glance — like a doctor working harder to get patients than to cure them. To understand it we must recall the immature stage of development of advertising and the advertising agency business before 1890. Both were old in years, but both were only in the early stage of their evolution. Advertising was not widely accepted as a necessary part of competitive effort, and the agencies were only beginning to emerge from their space-selling days. In order to get business, they had to explain the whole purpose and method of advertising and convince conservative merchants and manufacturers that printed messages to the public would increase their sales and profits. In short, the agent had to take the initiative or go hungry; and it was primarily for his aggressive work in inducing the skeptical merchant to use advertising at all that he received a "commission" or trade discount from publishers on the space sold.

In its early years, then, N. W. Ayer & Son obtained customers by persuading business men to advertise and by quoting rates for space low enough to capture orders. Other agents operated in the same way. And, since there were many of them contesting for business from firms which were hesitant about advertising, there was a buyer's market for advertising, as there was in American business generally between 1873 and 1896. Agents cut rates ruthlessly in order to tempt reluctant business men, as well as to get orders away from rival agents.

It was to avoid this unhealthy situation that F. W. Ayer, as shown earlier, devised his open-contract plan. But the shift from selling space for publishers to buying space for advertisers did not enable Ayer to dispense with active solicitation. He still had to convince possible customers of the soundness of his scheme; and he had, moreover, to continue selling the idea of advertising: to induce more people to advertise, and to persuade those who were already advertising to extend their efforts as far as good judgment could possibly warrant. Only by incessant efforts to promote the use of advertising could Ayer make his own business grow.

Ayer was sufficiently far-sighted to know that this work of teaching and persuasion would have to produce tangible results or his agency would have but a short life. If his customers could not advertise effectively, it behooved him to give them help. Thus, while Ayer did not diminish his selling efforts, he altered the emphasis from the economical purchase of space to constructive promotional work, explaining to business men how advertising would help their sales, showing them where and how to advertise, and helping them even to the extent of mapping out a definite course of action, writing their copy, and obtaining illustrations for them. To offer suggestions for advertising campaigns gradually became a part of the Ayer solicitation. N. W. Ayer & Son enlarged the volume of its business by laying down for prospective clients the foundation of successful advertising and, at the same time, by winning customers away from less enterprising rivals through the offer of extra services.

These are the circumstances which led the Ayer firm — no one knows exactly when — to adopt as one of its watchwords the phrase, "Make advertising pay the advertiser." The idea expressed in it seems obvious, even superfluous; yet it proclaimed an emphasis which was far from common in the agency business before the 'nineties.[6] Nor was the slogan an empty one uttered merely for effect. Ayer meant it with all his heart, and in H. N. McKinney he had a partner who could translate the ideal into reality.

McKinney was more than a salesman for the agency, as I have already pointed out; he had a talent for what business men sometimes call creative advertising. He spent much of his time and energy in developing new advertisers: discovering unadvertised products of merit for which advertising might enlarge the market. He was particularly good at this because he possessed a rare knack of seizing upon a feature or use of a product and dramatizing it in a way which impressed the public. He coined names and phrases which appealed to people and stuck with them when they were shopping. And he combined with his talent for advertising ideas a marked ability to formulate an advertising plan suited to the product, so that the advertisements would reach the people who were most likely to buy it.

Thus N. W. Ayer & Son won customers because it offered them practical suggestions and plans. Instead of making vague and sweeping assertions about the power of advertising, the firm pointed out both its advantages and its limitations. Instead of airily recommending the indiscriminate use of newspapers, the firm selected papers designed to reach consumers without too much waste. Both Ayer and McKinney often took occasion to remind prospective clients that advertising was not all-powerful. It could not, they held, create a profitable market for goods which were useless, or poorly made, or more highly priced than similar articles offered by other manufacturers; nor could it sell goods if a sales organization failed to get them into dealers' hands. Advertising has long been regarded by the Ayer firm as a supplement to other means of selling, not a substitute for them.

Because advertising failures are bound to reflect upon the agency which makes the arrangements, N. W. Ayer & Son adopted, sometime before 1890, the policy of refusing to accept as clients business concerns whose advertising did not show reasonable promise of bringing satisfactory returns to the advertiser. Of course the agency sometimes made errors in judgment, but all the evidence points to the fact that the Ayer management made a sincere effort to adhere to the policy.

This attitude of frankness and caution, contrasting sharply with the extravagant claims made by some of the rival agencies, won the confidence and business of advertisers. The extent to which Ayer preserved an attitude of circumspection is well indicated by the following excerpt from correspondence with a prospective customer:[7]

Philadelphia, Pa.,
August 5, 1897.

We doubt the advisability of your addressing . . . [any Ayer clients] concerning our house or our methods of business until we have had a conference in which both you and we can decide whether or not it would seem to mutual advantage that we should attempt to serve you. In other words, from our point of view, the first thing to be decided is are both you and we agreed that you have something which it will pay to advertise; next, are we agreed that there is reasonable prospect of our being able to make advertising pay you; further, would a business association be personally pleasant; and finally, is our business reputation and your commercial standing such that we could expect to deal together satisfactorily. In our judgment, this is the way in which the matter should be considered, and if you agree in this view of it, we will be pleased to have one of our representatives call upon you.

In the early 'nineties N. W. Ayer & Son, as a part of its efforts to win new clients, went so far as to make an offer to prospective advertisers "to prepare copy and submit proof of your advertisement, suggest papers for your use, and submit estimates on any selection desired." [8] As a natural development from its policy of caution, however, the firm later refused to prepare complete plans and copy for advertising before it had had an opportunity to study the prospective client's market and his selling problems.

As indicated in Chapter VIII, N. W. Ayer & Son has, during the past ten years, become more selective than ever before in the choice of clients. It seeks balance, not only as to industry and geographical location, but also as to size of account. It is determined to avoid having any one account provide more than 10 per cent of its total volume. Thus, when it obtains a client whose business will exceed this proportion, the management promptly devotes extra effort to getting other accounts to offset it and restore the balance. By this means it is achieving greater financial stability, greater professional independence, and greater peace of mind for its employees. Again, because it stresses its function in providing advertising counsel to clients, it is more careful than ever before to determine whether or not it can work harmoniously with a prospective client; that is, whether the management of the business concerned is likely to be frank, coöperative, and open-minded in dealing with the agency and give serious consideration to the recommendations which the agency staff makes. The staff, of course, accepts the need on its part to work closely with the client and to give serious consideration to his views. If, however, the prospect is that relations will be subject to friction or suspicion, the agency will not take the account. It can do its best work for the client only if there is a reasonable expectation of developing mutual confidence and an enduring relationship.

The Problem of Speculative Presentations

The submission of advertising material designed for the prospective client's business in advance of a definite contract is known among agencies today as a speculative presentation, since the agency which does it gambles on the chance of obtaining business to compensate for the expense involved. The practice hardly existed before 1890, for until that date agencies had little to do with the actual preparation of plans and copy. Agents, however, soon began to make speculative presentations, not only because business men liked to see what they were buying but also because the sight of finished advertisements helped to sway merchants who hesitated to advertise.

So long as advertisements were small and simple and advertising plans crude and based on experience alone, speculative presentations were of no great importance. With developments in illustration and advertising technique, however, and with the growing scale of campaigns and the application of scientific method to marketing, the presentations necessarily became more elaborate, and the practice of making them became open to serious objection.

In the first place, agencies had to prepare advertising campaigns without a proper knowledge of the facts upon which they should be based. Until an agency has been engaged by a client, it has no chance of obtaining the requisite information about sales, dealer organization, or other confidential data concerning the business to be advertised. What physician would submit for the approval of a prospective patient an outline of treatment which he would prescribe, without any diagnosis or assurance of having the case to treat? Further, the competing agencies were involved in a heavy expense: only one presentation could win; the rest were of no use in making other solicitations and were therefore a total loss. A third result was that the advertiser tended to base his choice of an agency upon the attractive features of a single stunt or campaign. In doing so, he neglected the other important services which an agency must provide if the advertising

is to be successful; and, at the same time, he overlooked the fact
that a business needs a steady flow of effective advertising. One
swallow does not make a summer, and one striking presentation
is no true sample of an agency's regular work.

As soon as it realized the evils of speculative plans and copy,
N. W. Ayer & Son stopped making them. The date of this change
is not known, but it took place before 1905. Speaking to a gathering of the Ayer staff in that year, McKinney voiced the opinion
of the firm:[9]

Plan and copy in advance is always the cry. Every advertiser wants
it, and every advertiser gets it from every other agency than our own.
Why won't we furnish copy and plan in advance? We do not wish the
merits of Ayer & Son [to be] decided by a look at a few advertisements;
and as for making a plan in advance, I do not know enough to make
a plan until I know somewhat of the business to be advertised. . . .
I have never seen anyone who could make an intelligent plan for an
advertiser without a study of his business. The fact that all other agents
will give a plan makes the distinction between them and us all the
stronger.

It is certain that McKinney employed no speculative material
to get his largest accounts. Indeed, he made a merit of his refusal
to do so, as the following incident illustrates.[10]

In 1904 the Simmons Hardware Company had decided to
undertake an advertising campaign in order to promote the sale
of Keen Kutter tools and cutlery. It had requested bids from a
number of prominent agencies, among them N. W. Ayer & Son.
McKinney was in Florida nursing ill health at the time, and,
when he came north, only two days remained of the time allotted
for receiving bids. He found that a dozen agencies were hotly
contesting for the contract and had submitted over five hundred
copy designs. Undismayed by this apparent handicap, he went to
W. D. Simmons, president of the company, and said that he had
no bid to submit. To make one, he explained, meant drawing up a
selling plan which would be worthless unless it was based upon
facts about the Simmons Company and its markets. In his opinion it was obviously impossible to gather, in a few days, infor-

mation which the Simmons Company had been forty years in acquiring. "Without such information," he declared, "it would be presumptuous for our agency to attempt to advise you in regard to your advertising problems."

McKinney's argument effectively undermined the elaborate plans which had been submitted. In awarding the advertising to N. W. Ayer & Son, Simmons remarked to McKinney, "I think I would rather entrust my advertising to you than to any of your rivals, as I feel certain that it will be taken care of in a business-like manner."

The Simmons Company wanted to start advertising at once, but Ayer officials refused to place a single line until they had studied the entire Simmons selling problem, from product to consumers. The success of the Keen Kutter campaign which they subsequently launched testified to the correctness of the Ayer methods.

The situation which McKinney met in 1904 has frequently arisen since. The Ayer representatives regularly call upon firms which are advertising through other agencies, not to urge the discharge of the rival agency, but rather to keep the advertisers reminded of the existence of N. W. Ayer & Son and to tell them about its many services, so that they will consider using it when they decide to make a change. The advertiser sometimes suggests that, if the agency will present a sufficiently attractive plan, complete with effective copy and illustrations, it will be given his contract.

Some agencies will comply with the suggestion to provide copy in advance, in spite of the fact that the American Association of Advertising Agencies (formed in 1917) has decreed the submission of speculative plans and copy to be an unethical practice. So far as I have been able to discover, however, the Ayer reply has invariably been a refusal, accompanied by a convincing explanation which often turns the negative answer into a positive selling point, indicating that when N. W. Ayer & Son handles advertising, it does so on a solid foundation of facts uncovered by a careful and comprehensive investigation. Such a study cannot be conducted until the client relationship comes into existence.

CONSTRUCTIVE SOLICITATION

N. W. Ayer & Son's refusal to make speculative presentations does not mean, however, that the agency fails to solicit new accounts aggressively, nor that it does not devote a great deal of time and money to its efforts to get additional business. Instead of offering a definite campaign to the prospective client, the Business Development Department explains how the Ayer agency operates, describes its manifold resources and the wide variety of talent and experience represented on its staff, and urges the value of the many services which it performs as a part of its regular work. These statements are supported by examples of advertising done for Ayer clients in the past, together with reference to the long and successful history of N. W. Ayer & Son, and the citation of numerous instances in which the firm's work has brought outstanding results.

In recent years the Ayer solicitation has usually embodied some sort of survey of the prospective advertiser's industry and a discussion of the general problems which confront it. This survey is to show the firm's general approach to advertising, to indicate its understanding of various aspects of its client's business, and to suggest ways in which advertising might help.

McKinney and his assistants often made such analyses in an unstudied and informal way; but, limited as they were by the absence of useful statistical data and marketing information, their efforts were important because of their promise of more scientific procedure rather than for their intrinsic value. Several letters, written in 1902, survive to reveal some attempts of this kind, addressed to firms in the textile and heavy steel industries. In the light of present knowledge they seem crude and almost futile, but they apparently marked a distinct advance in agency practice. In contrast with them, a solicitation addressed to the Pacific Borax Company in 1911 reflects great progress in method. It was obviously prepared by specialists in the Ayer Plans Bureau; and, while it contained no analysis, it presented suggestions for a careful marketing study which reveals a firm grasp of the marketing concepts and principles which were evolving in this country.

The solicitations since 1920 indicate still further progress.

They draw freely upon the increasing body of information made available by governmental and commercial surveys, and they plainly reflect preparation by men familiar with marketing and merchandising problems which were not even perceived in 1911. Thanks to the general advance in the theory and practice of business, to the specialization of work within the agency itself, and to the application of more scientific method to business-getting efforts, the Ayer solicitations have gradually become elaborate undertakings, based on detailed industrial studies which can hardly fail to be of interest and value to the business men who receive them. Indeed, the material which now accompanies an Ayer solicitation embodies so many suggestions and recommendations that, apart from the absence of specially prepared copy and detailed schedules, it is sometimes hardly distinguishable from a speculative presentation. Its purpose, however, is utterly different: speculative presentations are essentially completed jobs. The Ayer solicitation is only a good starting point.

The persistence of the Business Development Department is in harmony with the agency's motto. The firm thinks nothing of soliciting an advertiser for four or five years. Thus, in 1922 the agency finally landed one account which it had begun to solicit in 1911. In another instance the Ayer representatives tried for eight years before they were able to get even an interview with the owners of a business, and five more years elapsed before they won the account!

Self-Advertisement by N. W. Ayer & Son

No exposition of the Ayer methods of obtaining clients would be complete without a brief description of the advertisements which the agency has issued on its own behalf. Throughout its history, N. W. Ayer & Son has depended primarily upon the personal efforts of partners and representatives in seeking new business; but in 1870, if not earlier, the firm began to supplement this work by the use of various forms of self-advertisement.[11]

Between 1870 and 1890 the agency confined its own advertising largely to circular leaflets, letters, and printed souvenirs of various kinds. In January, 1890, however, it added a series of advertisements in *Printers' Ink,* a trade magazine then in the second year of its existence. Every week during 1890 and nearly every one in 1891 an Ayer advertisement appeared on the front cover, with the result that people sometimes sent their subscriptions for the magazine to Ayer rather than to his rival, George P. Rowell, who owned the publication.[12] *Printers' Ink* was read then, as now, by business men who were interested in advertising, either as advertisers or as makers of advertising for others. It therefore provided a useful medium for presenting N. W. Ayer & Son to prospective customers. In 1892, when Rowell increased the price of the front page to what Ayer regarded as an exorbitant rate, Ayer transferred his magazine advertising to the *Century,* *Harper's,* and *McClure's,* and occasionally added campaigns in selected newspapers. Despite their appearance in magazines, the advertisements of the firm, through 1895, stressed newspaper advertising. Between 1900 and 1909 the firm inserted its advertisements from time to time in such publications as *Profitable Advertising* and *The Bill Poster.* Then, late in 1909, it again purchased space on the cover page of *Printers' Ink* where its advertisements have regularly appeared ever since.

Of course, the firm's main object is to reach advertising and sales managers and general business executives, and it has consequently had little occasion to address messages to the general public; but between 1919 and 1932 the firm inserted full-page advertisements at regular intervals in the *Saturday Evening Post* and the *Literary Digest* — consumer publications with nationwide circulation. Previous Ayer advertisements had featured Ayer services and facilities, but this new series was devoted to the philosophy of advertising. The hope was that it would increase public understanding of advertising and enhance its value as a business tool. The series attracted a great deal of interest at the time, and the Ayer management believes that the investment (over one and one-half million dollars during the thirteen years) was a profitable one.[13] For several years after 1930 Ayer advertisements appeared in *Fortune.* In 1945 the agency began a new series of advertisements in *United States News* and *Newsweek* devoted to business management and its functions. It defined management, profits, financial statements, the need for surplus, the sources of management personnel, and so on. In 1947–48 a

The PIONEER and the VISION

THE greatness of our country's commercial development stands as a tribute to the creative genius of its industrial pioneers. From out the daring of their vision grew railroad systems, the telegraph and the telephone, the mastery of electricity, and commercial institutions which are now the world's standards.

During the days when many of our mightiest industries were in their infancy, some fifty years ago, an advertising organization was brought to birth in the city of Philadelphia. From a beginning based on a vision backed by determination, from a local effort with a national outlook, this institution has grown until its activities encompass the country; this is the summary of the record of the house of N. W. Ayer & Son.

With that genius of vision to see the fullness of opportunity within the accomplishment of its many and varied clients, this organization has maintained the leadership of its pioneer days.

Hardly can there be a public service story or an advertising problem taken from the course of American commerce that does not pay tribute to the efforts of this institution.

Fifty years of constructive endeavor with thousands of commodities, has built a complete organization. The smallest mechanical detail and the most involved advertising problem have each at its command the trained service of experience. From the beginnings of business through all the stages of development, this agency has been councilor, creator and active operator.

Here the new enterprise finds a strength of experience to back its inexperience; the great industry finds a breadth of service capable of carrying the most varied and most exacting burdens. Constant contact with many clients maintains lines of information which keep the newest and the best of commercial methods in continuous circulation. This service is at the disposal of the makers of any worthy commodity.

N . W . A Y E R & S O N

ADVERTISING HEADQUARTERS
PHILADELPHIA

NEW YORK   BOSTON   CLEVELAND   CHICAGO

HOUSE ADVERTISEMENT, 1919

ADVERTISING

POWER, MAGIC, WIZARDRY, ENCHANTMENT—to the amateur no word seems strong enough to describe the undeniable accomplishments of advertising. But from a professional view-point, advertising merits somewhat more sober terms. As a matter of fact the making of successful advertising is a difficult business, requiring both skill and experience.

It is true that advertising will speed up sales and secure a larger volume in a shorter time for a manufacturer with foresight, courage and financial resources to carry definite business policies to completion. . . . But no amount of advertising will sell a product that cannot be sold without advertising.

It is certain that advertising can and does create valuable good-will for a brand or a trade-mark. Witness the actual money value of any well-advertised name. . . . But it is equally certain that back of that name, there must be fair dealing and full value for the price asked. Advertising an unworthy product simply means that a larger number of people will presently discover its disadvantages.

Advertising pays its way, often many times over. It will permit lower prices through increased volume. It can reduce selling costs. It can lessen the time in which a product moves from factory to consumer. . . . But advertising that does not consider the problems of the jobber, the retailer and the salesman often loses more than it gains. Advertising must contain the principles of sound merchandising to be successful.

Advertising points out the merits of a product and impresses the buyer with its desirability. . . . But advertising cannot create a single point of superiority in a product, nor add a single virtue to its manufacturer.

Advertising is accepted as a necessary part of modern business promotion. It has won a place for itself in virtually every industry. Rightly directed and prepared, advertising has proved that it can return a profit to the advertiser. But advertising always should be considered as a business enterprise, and not as a magic formula for unearned success. . . . N. W. AYER & SON, Inc., Washington Square, Philadelphia. New York, Boston, Chicago, San Francisco, Detroit, London, Buenos Aires, São Paulo, Toronto, Montreal.

HOUSE ADVERTISEMENT, 1930

similar series was appearing in *Time*. It attracted widespread attention and helped to convey to business executives the firm's interest in the broader aspects of management.

From 1870 to 1880 the Ayer self-advertisements were hardly more than lists of papers and announcements about the advantageous prices at which the agency could sell space in them. During the next decade they continued to mention the savings which an advertiser could obtain by dealing with Ayer; but the lists disappeared, and there was a greater emphasis upon the value of advertising, the large size and wide experience of N. W. Ayer & Son, the difference between its methods and those of other agencies, and its primary interest in getting results for its customers. The general attitude of the Ayer management at this time appears to be summed up in one of its advertisements in *Printers' Ink* in 1890:

It is often a cause of comment that we decline to enter the general scramble for business, and some of our competitors declare it's because we are so "high-toned" that we don't do business as others do; but the fact is, it has paid us to consider our customers' interests . . . and our establishment has been run that way so long it isn't fitted to run in any other way.

During the 'nineties the Ayer advertisements began to emphasize the service rather than the space-buying facilities of the agency — the importance of wise planning, good copy, and honest attention to small details. Thus the firm described its work in 1896 as follows:[14]

N. W. Ayer & Son, Newspaper Advertising Agents, counsel advertisers, furnish plans and suggestions, select mediums, buy necessary space, prepare advertisements, register service [i.e., see that the advertisements appear in the publications as ordered], and attend to all other details in Newspaper Advertising.

Widen the scope to include magazine, outdoor, radio, and television advertising, and you have in this statement a fairly complete summary of the work of an advertising agency today.

Between 1900 and 1910 the advertisements placed stress upon

WHAT IS MANAGEMENT?

Management is as old as the hills. There is nothing complicated about it at all. It is a natural function of human society.

A man and a woman marry, set up housekeeping, and raise a family. Both are managers.

They manage as they buy a home, educate the children, plant a garden, pick out a car, a refrigerator, a piano. A hundred decisions a day around the house are management decisions.

Management occurs at all levels in government, charity, education, lodge. It is the plumber with his helper, the elevator starter, the superintendent of schools, the master of the grange.

But, in America, management probably has had its most scientific application in *business*.

Business management, even before World War I, helped build up a volume of production surpassing that of any other nation. In World War II, the results were even more spectacular. *America outproduced all other countries combined.*

By 1941, the value of an hour of work in terms of the staple necessities of life, bread and butter, had so been raised that an American could buy *from 2 to 8 times as much* as a man in Europe. This didn't just happen.

.   .   .

Neither the men and women in industry nor the money in industry can be effective without good management. Nothing else is so important to the workers' welfare, the investors' welfare or the public welfare.

N. W. AYER & SON, Inc.

Philadelphia, New York, Chicago, Detroit, San Francisco
Hollywood, Boston, Honolulu

copy and trade-mark ideas, and upon the agency's value as counselor. One of them pointed to the change in emphasis: "Twenty-five years ago it was hard to convince a man that advertising could be made to pay. Today the hardest thing we have to do, at times, is to make a prospective advertiser understand advertising limitations and successfully insist upon getting at the matter right." [15] And, while it was urging the importance of properly planned campaigns, the Ayer firm took occasion to criticize some of the methods employed by its rivals:[16]

> We do not know enough to solve your advertising problems and we won't even attempt it unless after going into the matter quite fully you elect to tie up with us, stick by us, and help us with the job.
> Other agencies of lesser age, fewer workers, and scantier experience will readily draw pictures, write copy, prepare plans, and tell you without any considerable amount of difficulty just how to make two dollars grow where one grew before.
> We are anxious to talk with business men who do not believe in fairies.

In the years since 1910 the Ayer advertising has covered all phases of agency work. It has, however, placed an increasing amount of emphasis upon its work in analyzing markets, solving merchandising problems, and correlating advertising campaigns with all the sales efforts from factory to consumer. In the *Printers' Ink* advertisements, especially, the firm has told, week after week, the story of its success with different clients. And, while carefully avoiding any violations of confidence, it has gradually abandoned the anonymity and vague generalization which marked allusions to its everyday work in the earlier years, naming the clients, outlining the problems encountered, and explaining in a general way the methods used by the agency in getting results for them.

To supplement these magazine advertisements which keep its name and services before business men, the Ayer agency has sent out to prospective clients printed pieces showing notable examples of its copy and art work. It has, in addition, prepared a number of interesting public exhibits, arranged to illustrate various aspects of advertising. Some of these exhibits, featuring the art and photography used by N. W. Ayer & Son, have been accessible only to people in Philadelphia. During 1931, however, the agency prepared an elaborate one dealing with the art of writing; and this exhibit, under the title "The Written Word," was shown in a number of cities throughout the country. In 1932 the firm prepared another elaborate exhibit illustrating the major changes in fashion in the United States during the period from 1880 to 1932, picturing some of the influences which have brought about those changes, stressing the importance of styling in all phases of modern industry, and pointing out, by way of conclusion, the part played by the modern advertising agency in interpreting fashion trends to industry and to consumers. This exhibit, like its predecessor, was subsequently shown outside Philadelphia.

The business-getting efforts of N. W. Ayer & Son, to summarize, reflect the transition of the agency's work during the course of seventy years from space-selling to teaching business firms how to use advertising properly as an integral part of their work.

CHAPTER X

BASIS OF AYER RELATIONS WITH CLIENTS

THE RELATIONS between agency and client, while determined in many respects by trade custom, are based specifically upon the agreement reached during the solicitation. In the course of N. W. Ayer & Son's history the nature of such agreements has materially changed. Since the kind of service performed by the agency depends upon the agreement, an explanation of its development must precede any analysis of the firm's work for clients.

As the reader will recall from Chapter III, N. W. Ayer & Son long conducted most of its business on the "open-contract-plus-commission plan." For many years, however, the firm regularly used two other arrangements: (1) the "competitive" or "order" basis, which still survives in modified form; and (2) one which was known as the "open-contract-without-commission plan," which disappeared shortly after 1900.

COMPETITIVE OR ORDER BASIS, 1869–1900

The order or competitive basis, which was used by N. W. Ayer & Son during its early years, was a direct survival of the old space-selling period in which Ayer founded his agency. An advertiser, occasionally with the assistance of an agent, prepared an order for space in a chosen list of papers, to run during a prescribed period of time. Nothing was left to the agent's discretion: the size of the advertisement, number of insertions, and choice of papers were all settled in advance. The advertiser then asked one or more agents to bid on this specific order, which later came to be known as a "closed" order because it was definite and not ordinarily subject to change after the bid had been accepted.

In theory, the agent would bid the sum of the prices charged by each of the papers on the list, according to its "gross" or "card" rates and take as his compensation the difference between the gross and net prices.[1] As we have seen, however, both rates yielded to pressure, and competition led agents to cut below the gross rates. Each one usually submitted a bid calculated to be just under those of competitors, and his compensation was the difference between the amount of the winning bid and the actual cost of the space to him. Thus, the order basis was ordinarily a competitive basis.

After Ayer had instituted his open-contract plan (1876), the amount of order or competitive business which his agency handled quickly declined. According to an advertisement sent out by the firm in 1885, nearly three-fourths of the Ayer volume during 1884 had been handled on the open-contract plan, and the proportion of order or competitive business to the total volume became still smaller in the years which followed. The Ayer agency continued to accept a part of its business on the order basis after 1876 because some advertisers stubbornly refused to consider using an agency on any other terms and because the Ayer management hoped eventually to convert them to the open-contract plan.[2]

Between 1900 and 1905, when publishers' rates became stabilized and the leading agencies began to regard the cutting of gross rates as unethical, the competitive feature of the Ayer order business disappeared entirely. Since that time such advertising has been termed "fixed-price" advertising, owing to the fact that N. W. Ayer & Son charges for it the price set by the publishers. The fixed-price or order-basis advertising which N. W. Ayer & Son places has declined to 5 per cent of the agency's total volume, as is at once apparent from the figures in Table 6.

The advertiser who used the agency on the order or competitive basis was an occasional customer, not a regular client. His relation with N. W. Ayer & Son endured only from the time he accepted its bid until he paid the bill. He might place one order with Ayer and, at the same time, another with George P. Rowell or some other rival agent; he might give all his orders to Ayer over a long period, or he might change frequently from one

TABLE 6

Advertising Handled on the Fixed-Price or Order Basis at
Selected Periods

Year	Amount	Percentage of Total Ayer Volume
1870...............	All (exact total not known)	100
1884...............	Over 25% of total	Over 25
1900...............	$ 354,673.94	25.7
1910...............	1,131,177.28	20.7
1920...............	1,197,892.01	8.7
1940...............	a	4.5
1945...............	a	5.0

ᵃ Recent figures on dollar volume are not available for publication.
    Source: For 1870, data from Ledger 1; for 1884, advertisement of N. W. Ayer & Son, 1885;
for later years, General Ledgers 1, 2, and 3, and summary records supplied by the treasurer of
N. W. Ayer & Son.

agency to another. The Ayer firm had to bid against rivals on
each order of advertising that he wanted to place.

Open-Contract-without-Commission Basis

In addition to the order basis, Ayer offered (after 1876) his
open-contract-plus-commission plan and another which he called
"open-contract-without-commission." Since the first of these has
already been described, we can pass on to a consideration of the
second. Like the contract with commission, the open-contract-
without-commission arrangement was an agreement by which an
advertiser was to place through N. W. Ayer & Son all the newspaper advertising that he required during a year or more; in return for this promise Ayer pledged the best resources of his firm
in the selection of media and purchase of space. Hence the contract without commission differed from the order basis in two important respects: (1) it provided for a contractual relationship
continuing over a long period of time and involving a number of
orders, instead of a contract for a single order at the completion
of which relations terminated; (2) it left the amount and kind of

space open, to be settled upon from time to time jointly by the advertiser and the agency according to changing circumstances, instead of having these details fixed before the conclusion of the agreement.

In contrast with the advertiser who required agents to bid for individual orders, the advertiser who accepted the open-contract arrangement became a regular client of the Ayer agency, depending exclusively upon it for placing advertisements and receiving useful advice as well. He gave the agency a temporary monopoly of his advertising business in return for extra service. In the first instance, the agency sold space, one order at a time; in the other, it contracted to buy whatever space the advertiser decided to use and to give him continuous assistance in advertising matters.

As in the order basis, compensation by the open-contract-without-commission plan lay in the margin between the cost of the space used and the price obtained from the advertiser. But that price, instead of being determined by a bid, was set by the agency according to a provision in the client's contract that N. W. Ayer & Son was "to secure the best terms possible . . . and charge to our account at prices which will allow you [N. W. Ayer & Son] a satisfactory profit. These charges, however, are not in any case to exceed publishers' rates." [3]

It is apparent that the contract-without-commission plan, unlike the order basis, established a continuing fiduciary business relationship. This is also true of the open-contract-plus-commission plan. In fact, the two contract plans were alike except in the terms of the agency's compensation. The contract-plus-commission plan provided for a specified percentage of the net cost, while the contract-without-commission plan allowed the agency to take a "satisfactory" profit. The latter arrangement seems unnecessarily vague, and one wonders how it was handled without friction. On this point no information is available except that the plan was used for many years with success.

The Ayer firm offered these two open-contract plans before 1900 because there was a wide variation in the size of the accounts handled. Ayer had settled on 15 per cent of the net cost of space used as his charge, but many advertisers — particularly schools, colleges, and seed and nursery houses — made such small annual expenditures that 15 per cent would not cover the agency's cost of handling their business and still allow a reasonable profit. Ayer, therefore, made an arrangement which would permit him to obtain a larger margin — with the publishers' card rates as the upper limit.

The contract-without-commission plan gradually disappeared after 1900, the last agreement of this kind terminating in 1909. Thereafter, the Ayer agency placed advertising on either the contract-plus-commission or the order basis. The amount of business handled on the contract-without-commission plan cannot be determined from the ledgers, but it was apparently not large. A number of factors contributed to its abandonment. Publishers began to insist, after 1900, that agencies uphold their card rates, so that any advertising which the Ayer agency handled on this basis became, in fact, fixed-price advertising. At the same time the need for three plans ceased to exist: the Ayer management had, by 1905, stopped altogether the limited amount of bidding in competition which it had done in earlier years. If an advertiser needed continuous agency service, the contract-plus-commission plan was the better arrangement for him and for N. W. Ayer & Son. If, on the other hand, he did not need such service, the agency could handle his advertising on the order or fixed-price basis.

In other words, the contract-without-commission business merged with the straight order basis. Such business comes mainly from educational institutions, seed companies, and similar enterprises whose advertising is limited in amount, seasonal and routine in character, and simple to plan and prepare. After about 1905 the Ayer management usually handled on the order basis the advertising which showed no promise of exceeding $5,000 in amount per annum.[4] In 1912 the accounts handled in this way actually averaged approximately $750.[5] In recent years the average size has increased somewhat, but the number of such accounts has diminished, and the fixed-price advertising is of minor importance in relation to the total volume.

Today (1949), as before, order-basis business is not competitive in the matter of price, but is distinguished from the agency's regular business in that the agency does not have an open contract and a full client relationship. The only kinds of business handled on this basis today are advertising for publishers and schools and an occasional special situation in which the agency decides, as a matter of convenience to the advertiser, to handle a campaign on a one-shot basis.

EVOLUTION OF THE OPEN-CONTRACT-PLUS-COMMISSION PLAN, 1876–1949

The nature of the open-contract-plus-commission plan, as Ayer inaugurated it in 1876, has already been explained. In view of the plan's importance to N. W. Ayer & Son and to the general development of the agency business, it is advisable to note briefly some further details about the evolution of the open contract during the years since its adoption.

The Ayer contract was, at least until the 1880's, a verbal agreement. In practice the agency always submitted written estimates to its contract customers in advance of any advertising to be done; as a result, the details of every order were put in writing and approved by the client before the agency bought space for the advertising. But the contract for continuous relations was an oral one for several years after 1876. According to F. W. Ayer, the general open-contract agreement was first put in writing when he obtained the business of Perry Davis & Son, of Providence, Rhode Island, manufacturers of proprietary medicines. The firm approved of the arrangement which he proposed, but wanted to have the understanding put into definite form. Ayer wrote out a letter of agreement, the substance of which is embodied in the Ayer contract today.[6] The firm thereafter began to use written agreements with other advertisers. The available evidence shows, however, that it also continued to make oral agreements as well during the 'nineties, some of them even surviving into the present century. Since 1912 all clients (except, of course, the fixed-price customers) have signed the same general agreement.[7]

Rival agents have often attempted to show the Ayer contract in a bad light, criticizing it as a one-sided agreement designed to further the selfish interests of N. W. Ayer & Son. Such arguments, however, have gained little ground, for the contract clearly protects both agency and advertiser, and the practice of having written agreements has spread to other agencies.

The earliest letter of agreement which has been preserved among the Ayer records is given below; it is probably similar to the first one used.

September 17, 1891

CONTRACT

N. W. Ayer & Son,
    Philadelphia.
Dear Sirs:—

I agree to place all my newspaper advertising in your hands for one year from this date, and thereafter from year to year, subject to withdrawal at the end of any year on three months' written notice of my intention to that effect, the terms on which the business is to be handled being as follows:

You are to secure the lowest obtainable price for the insertion of my advertisement in each paper, and to charge me just the amount of this net credit in each case; to these net costs you are to add fifteen per cent (15%) to cover your compensation, and profit; electrotypes are to be furnished by you at mutually satisfactory prices, carriage on electrotypes is to be charged to me at actual cost.

Under this agreement, you may expend for me during the first year about $3800.00 Dollars in advertising in the lists as furnished herewith; Payment to be made in quarterly amounts as earned; advertising to begin as soon as is consistent with best prices, unless otherwise advised in any particular instance.

If I order any additional advertising the first year, the same conditions are to apply.

(signed) Geo. H. Stahl

Accepted for
    N. W. Ayer & Son
    (signed) W. H. Marker

This and other Ayer contracts for the period (that is, before about 1898) apply only to newspaper advertising, but a study of all the contracts now preserved shows a constant extension of the open-contract-plus-commission plan to other departments of agency work. Thus in 1898 the firm began to make open contracts covering magazine as well as newspaper advertising, and in 1899 it began to handle poster and other outdoor advertising on the same basis.

Before 1898 the agency had supplied drawings and electrotypes for advertisements, sometimes at cost, sometimes "at satisfactory prices." Owing, however, to the growing importance of illustrations in advertisements and the increasing amount of work and skill involved in their preparation, the Ayer contracts began regularly to provide for a commission of 15 per cent on "any expense which may be incurred for drawing, engraving, printing, or advertisement writing." [8] Later, when the agency began to handle radio advertising, it did so on the same basis, charging a commission on the cost of the station time, program preparation, and the "talent" or radio artists used.

The percentage charged by the Ayer agency for its services on the contract-plus-commission plan at any one time was the same for all clients, regardless of the amount of their advertising appropriation or the nature of their advertising.[9] Prior to 1919 the rate was 15 per cent; but agency costs, partly owing to the addition of new services, rose during the World War to such an extent that N. W. Ayer & Son felt obliged to increase its charges. After January 1, 1919, the rate for all open-contract clients was 16⅔ per cent of the net cost.

In 1925 the Ayer agency added a new clause to its contract which provided a minimum fee of $3,000 for its services during the first year of the contract's duration. This new provision was designed to ensure some compensation for the work which the agency does for its clients before any advertising is actually launched. The charge affected only a few clients, for unless an account involved an expenditure of less than $21,000 during the first year ($18,000 in media charges, plus the 16⅔% commission or $3,000), the minimum charge clause made no difference, and very few accounts failed to exceed that amount even during the first year of the relationship.

After trying the minimum charge for several years, the Ayer management decided to abandon the provision. It believed that some new clients were inclined to expect too much in the initial stage as a result of the charge. It also concluded that the minimum charge tended to encourage the Ayer solicitors to bring in the wrong kind of clients; that is, that members of the business-getting staff were more disposed to seek new accounts because they produced immediate revenue, rather than to scrutinize accounts from their long-run growth possibilities. In 1933, therefore, Ayer management decided to eliminate the minimum charge and to examine more closely the accounts which were offered to it on the open-contract plan. Its acceptance of an account, thenceforth, depended not only on the character of the advertiser's business, but also on the likelihood that his advertising would develop into a large account for the agency. Today the Ayer firm considers the current size of a prospective account, as indicated earlier, much less important than the character of the client's management and the potential development of the business.

The form of agreement in use in 1933 follows:[10]

Town........ State........ Date........

N. W. Ayer & Son, Incorporated,
 Philadelphia, Pennsylvania
Gentlemen:
 This letter states the arrangement under which you are to handle our advertising.
 You are to place all of our newspaper, periodical, radio and outdoor advertising, as ordered by us, during the period of this agreement.
 For newspaper, periodical and radio advertising, you are to charge us the net price to you, plus your commission of sixteen and two-thirds per cent ($16\frac{2}{3}\%$). For outdoor advertising you are to charge us the gross rate charged by the plant-owners.
 In the event of our wishing such service, you are to prepare advertising copy, ideas for posters and painted signs, and radio advertising announcements, for use in the advertising you place. For the work of artists of your staff, the services of your Printing Department on advertising copy, and writers of your staff in the preparation of entertainment and educational radio scripts, you are to make a reasonable charge. For any expense incurred in such service outside your organization, and for engravings, electrotypes and other cuts, and for talent for radio programs, you are to charge us the net price to you. To all such charges you are to add your commission of sixteen and two-thirds per cent ($16\frac{2}{3}\%$).
 Should we wish to use any forms of advertising and materials not herein provided for, you will assist us, if desired, in their consideration and preparation — the charge for same to be determined by estimate or special agreement.

Expenses incurred for the carriage of advertising matter or material, and in the purchase of wrapping or boxes for same, will be charged to us at the net price to you.

We are to receive the benefit of all cash discounts allowed you, provided you receive payment from us within the discount period.

Payments are to be made monthly as earned.

Except for very minor changes, the Ayer contract remained the same for more than half a century. This contract established (1) a fiduciary relationship continuing over a period long enough to permit agency service to be effective; (2) the principle that N. W. Ayer & Son, Inc., was working for the advertiser rather than for the various media which allowed discounts or commissions to agencies; and (3) a basis of compensation involving a commission to the agency, determined by agency and client, based on certain expenditures of the advertiser.

It was not until 1949 that this open-contract-plus-commission plan was modified in any significant respect, so that in essence it endured seventy-three years. And the change which finally came about affected only the third aspect noted above, namely, the basis of compensation. Developments in the field of advertising, not anticipated seventy-three years ago, had made it increasingly difficult to maintain the traditional basis used by the firm in computing its charges to advertisers.

Nearly all publishers allowed a commission on space, the percentage varying widely in the early years, as we have seen. Later the rate became fairly well stabilized, with the result that, when this commission (usually 15 per cent) was accepted by Ayer, credited to the client, and a new commission was figured at 16⅔ per cent on the net, the final result was usually a fraction less than the standard card rate. However, certain expenditures involved no provision for a commission to the agency, such as art work, printing, plates, and so on. On these items the Ayer charge of 16⅔ per cent was higher than that of nearly all rival agencies, whose charges on non-commissionable media usually ranged from zero to 15 per cent. For printed advertising, the cost of space was likely to be many times greater than the cost of the expenses incidental to using the space; hence, on business handled by Ayer, the savings on commissionable space were likely to offset the higher charges on incidental items.

As radio became a major medium, however, a new pattern began to emerge. The costs incidental to the use of time came to be much greater than those incidental to the use of space. The cost of a radio show might equal, and in many cases exceed, the charges for time alone. And television, in its early stages at least, has extended this pattern considerably. Show-production costs in television may equal 70 per cent to 80 per cent of the entire cost of the program.

A commission is allowed to agencies on charges for station time. But there is no such commission on the costs for talent and production. As a result, on a major part of a radio advertiser's budget Ayer found itself quite unintentionally penalizing the advertiser by making its regular charge of 16⅔ per cent on talent that any other agency would have purchased for 15 per cent.[11]

Thus the traditional method of compensation for Ayer finally ran headlong into the new problems created by radio and television. And in this field the standard method of compensation proved itself to be a method definitely unfair to certain advertisers and a handicap to the agency. No longer could Ayer contend that it employed a *uniform* system of charges without regard to the media involved. For no matter what the theory, the facts were that a radio advertiser was likely to pay relatively more for the service of the agency than an advertiser using printed media. Thus, a second basic Ayer policy — that of uniformity in charges to all advertisers on the amounts spent on their behalf — became involved.

Ayer management has found only one solution to the difficulties: the method of compensation had to be changed, and Ayer adopted for itself the system which is at present in almost universal use — charging advertisers the card rates and retaining the commission on commissionable items while adding 15 per cent commission to non-commissionable items. To revert to 15 per cent on the net cost of all items would have made serious inroads on the profit margin when agency operating costs had already risen, and it would have embroiled the agency with media owners, who would consider 15 per cent on the net as rate-cutting. Discussions

with clients revealed that to charge 16⅔ per cent on commissionable media and 15 per cent on other expenditures was confusing and difficult to explain. The Ayer management decided to
cut the Gordian knot and, in effect, adopt the method of compensation used by most other agencies and now accepted by most advertisers without question.

The old method died hard, for Ayer management was deeply
reluctant to surrender a long-established policy. And this one had
special meaning for the firm because it was, in fact, the living
residue of an early and extremely important action taken by the
founder. Perhaps hardest of all to swallow was the fact that the
traditional method of charging, based on net cost to the advertiser, had the appearance of proving the Ayer contention that
the agency really worked for the advertiser and not for the pur-
veyor of space or time who allowed the commission.

It should be remembered that in the days when this policy was
adopted commissions were not standardized, and there was considerable incentive for the agent to recommend those publications
which allowed the largest commissions. But that time has long
since passed. Commission rates on the various media have been
standardized at 15 per cent for more than a quarter of a century.
Further, the fact that clients and agencies generally have accepted and adapted themselves to what is now the usual plan of
agency compensation has deprived the original Ayer logic of much
of its force.

Of course the provision for "16⅔ per cent on the net" in contrast to "15 per cent on the gross" was not what made the Ayer
agency work for the client. Ayer worked for its clients as a matter
of policy. This policy reflected an attitude which was deeply rooted
in the business and long manifested in operations. A technical adjustment in the contract itself has not changed this basic Ayer
policy. In fact, in making the change the agency emphasized its
historic policy of arranging its compensation with the client and
not the media owner. Ayer is not "accepting" a commission from
media; it is billing clients for space or time such amount as will
make the net cost to Ayer eighty-five per cent of the agency's
charge to clients.

Thanks largely to the growth of radio advertising, strict adherence to the method of compensation adopted more than sev-

enty years ago placed the Ayer firm in the position of charging substantially more than other agencies were receiving for similar services. Until broadcast advertising became a major medium the Ayer management, for the sake of upholding a tradition, was willing to tolerate the situation. The advent of television and the mounting proportion of non-commissionable expenses related to broadcast and telecast programs made a change essential.

Some observers may see in this change the abandonment of principle for profit, but one who examines the total situation is likely to see instead the impact of technological change and management adjusting policy to new and materially different circumstances.

Some General Comments on Advertising Agency Compensation

The general features of the Ayer open-contract-plus-commission plan are noteworthy because they are logically and economically sound and because they have seldom been embodied in the agreements used by other agencies. Although advertisers are sometimes reluctant to make agreements which bind them to one agency for a year, even this length of time is barely sufficient to allow an agency to analyze an advertiser's problems, to plan and launch an advertising campaign, and to show some results. Unless, therefore, an agency is assured of this minimum period of time, it cannot hope to approach its work with anything like a professional spirit. An agency is (or should be) like a physician who is allowed to diagnose and treat an illness in his own way before another doctor is called in. Few advertising agencies, however, have had the courage to insist upon this consideration.[12]

The outstanding feature of the Ayer contract, as already indicated, was the fact that it explicitly made the agency's compensation a matter of agreement between the agency and the client. This principle distinguished the Ayer basis from that governing the majority of agency-client relations. The best information available indicates that, in 1932 and 1933, about 80 per cent of all advertisers were placing most of their advertising with agencies in such a way that the agencies' compensation was determined by the media owners and not by the agencies and advertisers themselves. That is to say, most agencies charge the advertiser the prices which the owners of media have established and receive as their compensation the discounts which the owners of media allow to agencies.[13] Since 1949 this has been true of N. W. Ayer & Son.

In other words, while the modern advertising agency unquestionably works directly for advertisers, most agencies (Ayer was long a notable exception) are compensated by an arrangement which evolved when advertising agencies worked directly for media. The agency's function changed long ago, but the old method of compensation persists.

If the agencies were independent middlemen, this traditional method of remuneration, though illogical, might be quite acceptable on practical grounds. But advertising agencies are not independent as to function, whatever their exact legal position may be. They are hired not merely to purchase the means by which advertising is done but also to give expert counsel in its use as one part of the client's business operations. Hence the basis of compensation should be one which does not interfere with impartial judgment either of advertising as a general tool for promoting a client's business or of particular media as the appropriate means to be employed.

If, however, the remuneration of the agency depends on the margin allowed to it by the media owner, so that it stands to receive 10 per cent from one medium, 15 per cent from another, and none at all from a third, the agency is subject to the temptation to recommend those media which will be most profitable to itself, regardless of their value to the advertiser. Many considerations will, of course, deter the agency from yielding completely to that temptation, but it unquestionably introduces an element of bias which should not be present.

The Ayer contract was designed to eliminate this bias, and wide recognition has been given to both the wisdom of the Ayer point of view and the inherent unsoundness of the arrangement which most agencies continue to use.[14] The traditional arrangement, however, stubbornly persists. One reason it does, as shown above, is the fact that the discount or commission has long been standardized and the entire advertising industry has become adapted to it. Indeed, the usual basis of agency compensation is so deeply engrained that it is no longer true (except in highly abstract theory) that agency compensation is determined by the media owner. It is determined by custom and market forces, just as other prices are usually determined.

The Ayer contract, however, left the agency still subject to one element of bias in that, along with the great majority of agencies, N. W. Ayer & Son received remuneration strictly in proportion to the amount of money spent on the client's advertising. Theoretically, in consequence, there exists a temptation to urge upon the client a greater expenditure for advertising than his business situation really justifies. How much of such urging actually does take place is a matter of argument. N. W. Ayer & Son (and probably a number of other agencies) can cite numerous instances in which it has refused to approve expenditures for advertising which, in the agency's opinion, would not bring satisfactory returns to the advertiser. But those who criticize the commission system on theoretical grounds hold that such instances are further proof of the need for modifying the traditional arrangement: that an agency is entitled to compensation for the time and expense involved when it investigates a client's situation and finds that advertising will not yield the desired results.

It must be said at once that this problem of establishing a sound basis for remunerating agencies is one which confronts the entire advertising industry rather than any one individual agency. It is not a new problem by any means. Discussions of the commission method of compensation began to appear in *Printers' Ink* within a year of its founding (1888), and since then few numbers have appeared without some reference to the problem. The same is true of other publications which deal with the advertising industry. This is not the place for an extended treatment of the opposing points of view, but it is probably fair to summarize by saying that those who have condemned the commission method have done so on the ground that it creates the biases already mentioned and that, in view of the widely varying services which different advertisers need, it is too rigid to be fair; while those on the other side have defended the system largely on the empirical ground that, whatever its shortcomings may be, the commission method has worked reasonably well over a long period of years. Certainly it is the product of a natural evolutionary process, and there is evidence that the system is being modified to suit changing circumstances. Indeed, it is probably safe to say that much of the debate on this subject has been engendered by attempts, such as the NRA code which the agencies proposed, to block by artificial means any material change in the prevailing method of compensation.[15]

A MATTER OF PRINCIPLE RATHER THAN DOLLARS

Through developments in the advertising industry the Ayer plan lost one distinctive feature because the amount of commission charged under the Ayer contract resulted in space rates which were, in most cases, practically identical with the card or gross rates charged by rival agencies. Originally, as we have seen, there was a considerable difference between the two because the discounts or commissions allowed by media owners varied widely. If less than 13 per cent, the net cost plus the Ayer commission of 15 per cent totaled more than card rates; if more than 13 per cent, the total Ayer price would be somewhat below. When Ayer first set his commission at 15 per cent, the discount which publishers typically allowed was more than 13 per cent and frequently as much as 25. By 1900, newspapers usually allowed 15 and magazines 10, so that Ayer prices were low on newspaper space and high on magazines.[16] After World War I, however, the owners of the various advertising media (including outdoor and radio advertising) have generally tended to standardize the discount at 15 per cent, with 2 per cent additional for cash. (There are exceptions to this, but they seem to be of minor importance.) The result was that the charges made by Ayer to clients differed little from those charged by agents operating on the traditional system.

The similarity of charges calculated on the two bases was not necessarily the result of any deliberate effort on the part of N. W. Ayer & Son. It decided to increase its rate to 16⅔ per cent, effective January 1, 1919, when other agencies were generally receiving but 13 per cent discount from publishers.[17] It is possible that the Ayer firm was merely conforming to a change in media discounts which had already started, for as early as August, 1918, several magazine publishers announced a change in the agency allowances from 13 per cent, plus 3 for cash, to 15 and 2; while other agencies were urging a general increase.[18] Whatever the explanation, the widespread standardization of agency discount which subsequently took place made the charges calculated by the two methods so nearly alike that advertisers have tended to overlook the fundamental difference in the principle involved.

To some observers this difference in principle is of first-rate importance: it explicitly recognizes that the agency works in the interests of the advertiser, and it makes compensation a matter of agreement between the agency and its client. Of interest in this connection are the conclusions of the report on agency compensation which Albert Haase prepared for the Association of National Advertisers. That report challenged on legal and theoretical grounds the traditional arrangement under which agency remuneration is determined by the owners of advertising media. While insisting upon the impossibility of standardizing agency compensation in view of the highly unstandardized nature of the agency service,[19] the Haase report concluded by advocating the essential principle of the Ayer plan as a basis for agency agreements.[20] The difficulty has been that clients have not considered that principle important, and new advertising media, radio and television, have forced Ayer management to reconsider its position. Perhaps the important point today is that the policy so long upheld by Ayer forced the matter of compensation into the open and brought about a better understanding of the relations between client, agency, and media owners.

CHAPTER XI

THE PLANNING OF ADVERTISING CAMPAIGNS

AFTER the letter of agreement has been signed by the client or advertiser and accepted by the Ayer management, the staff of the agency goes to work on the account. The operations which subsequently take place within the firm have, of course, varied with the development of Ayer services and general marketing technique. While a detailed and complete description of these operations cannot be set forth in the space available, the material which follows may convey some conception of the principal objectives and practices which the agency has followed.[1]

ABSENCE OF PLANNING IN EARLY CAMPAIGNS

Until about 1890, as we have seen, the details of the advertising which the agency handled were determined mainly by the advertiser rather than by the agency. The advertiser knew his own product and something of its market, and the agency knew how to buy space to the best advantage; but, in the planning and preparation of advertising, neither employed any methods which might be called scientific. This was inevitable, since the accumulated body of knowledge about the principles and technique of marketing was extremely limited.[2] The general run of competition in selling, moreover, was neither very rapacious nor very intelligent; and even crude advertising, if handled with a fair amount of common sense, brought reasonably satisfactory results.

Since the advertiser, in these circumstances, was presumed to be competent to decide for himself the kind of advertising his business needed, and since, in any case, advertising and advertising agents were relatively new and untested adjuncts of business in which business men had only limited faith, the advertiser did for himself much of the work which is now the most important part of the agency's function. He decided for himself the sum of money which he would devote to advertising. He wrote his own advertisements, chose his own brand names and trade-marks, purchased electroplates or woodcuts, and chose the papers which he wanted to use. The agency occasionally gave some help and advice in these matters, but such assistance was incidental and subordinate to its main work of dealing in space.

Under the Ayer open-contract arrangement, however, the advertiser's list of papers was tentative until the Ayer firm had negotiated with the publishers about the space desired. Some papers would be used even if the agency had to pay the regular rates, but others would be given the business only if they accepted the prices which the agency offered to them, often a half or third of the price published by the owners of the media. In the course of thousands of transactions the Ayer space-buyers naturally came to know approximately what price any publisher could be induced to accept and became adept at bargaining with him to the best possible advantage.

The purpose of such bargaining was twofold: Ayer, like his competitors, claimed to save money for his customers; if he did not bargain for bottom rates, some rival agency could handle the advertising at a lower price and win his customers away from him. Moreover, the lower the rates were on the individual papers, the larger the number of papers which the appropriation could be made to cover, the greater the total circulation of the advertising, and the greater the likelihood of profitable results. In the days before markets were flooded with goods and the public calloused by a ceaseless barrage of advertising from all directions, this line of reasoning was approximately correct.

As soon as the Ayer firm had received replies from its offers to publishers, it settled on a list which, when the agency's commission was added to the cost, would use up the sum of money appropriated. Thus, the plans of the advertising campaign, determined mainly by an arbitrary sum of money and the rates obtainable for space, was then complete and ready for execution.

The Rise of Planned Advertising

Since about 1890 the work of preparing an advertising campaign has become much more scientific in method and more involved and difficult in formulation. The campaign has been determined less by the money available and space rates charged than by the nature of the job to be done. And by general consent the agency has gradually taken over and developed the task of ascertaining the nature of that job. The increased attention to the planning of advertising campaigns came out of the growing struggle between advertisers to capture business, a struggle in which intelligent strategy played an increasingly important part in every aspect of marketing. As early as 1893, one of N. W. Ayer & Son's self-advertisements referred to this new emphasis: "Increasing competition in this line [newspaper advertising] makes well-defined plans and well-organized efforts more and more essential." [3]

In many respects, advertising is a voyage of discovery and missionary work. The advertiser who undertook this voyage before the 1890's determined for himself the occasion and direction of his travels. He had, however, only a vague idea of the destination which he desired to reach, and he allowed it to be determined mainly by the travel allowance, which he had arbitrarily settled upon, and by the cost of transportation. Today the advertiser budgets his travel allowance more carefully than ever; but, before he fixes its amount, he decides upon a goal, studies all the ways and means of getting there, tries to anticipate all the things which must be done to make the journey a successful one, and charts his entire course before he starts. This done, he is in a position to consider the costs and the means of making his income cover the expenses of the journey. Through all these preliminary steps, however, he leans heavily upon the agency which is to conduct him in his travels.

DECIDING WHETHER TO ADVERTISE

After the signing of the Ayer contract, therefore, the first concern of N. W. Ayer & Son has been to determine intelligently whether or not the advertiser really should travel at all and, if he should, to ascertain the destination and the kind of journey he should take. That is to say, the agency has had to dig out and assemble all the available information about the problems and objectives of the business with which advertising and public relations counsel might help. After analyzing the collected data, it is then better able to define the object and method of the advertising which the particular situation demands.

In the years between 1915 and 1936, roughly, the Ayer inquiry usually started with the product to be sold.[4] Here are a few of the points touched on. What are the chief uses of the client's product? Is it a luxury, convenience, or necessity? Are there similar articles on the market competing for buyers? If so, how does the client's product compare with them as to advantages, disadvantages, quality, and cost? What is its price and unit of sale? Is the package appropriate, convenient, and distinctive? Can it be readily identified by means of a brand or trade-mark? Are the name and trade-mark effective, and are they properly established and protected? Is there an established demand for a product of this kind?

In the 1930's, and especially after 1936 when the Ayer planning activities were reorganized into the present Plans-Merchandising Department, the questions began to start at a different point — particularly when the client was a well-established advertiser with a product which had gained wide acceptance: What is the client's problem? Is it to develop a reputation for quality, style, or scientific progress? Is it to increase the pride of employees in their work by explaining to them and to the public the importance of their contribution? Is it to acquaint the public with facts about prices, wages, or profits?

In general the Plans-Merchandising Department seeks to work out first an over-all strategy as a basis for tactics in sales promotion, advertising, and public relations. It tries to obtain a genuine understanding of the problems of the business in terms of the ambitions and policies of the client's management. Ultimately it must develop specific answers to three basic questions: (1) What are we going to accomplish? (2) What have we to say? (3) To whom do we want to say it?

By such an analysis the agency staff finally reaches definite conclusions as to the objectives, scope of the task, its probable cost, and the results which may be reasonably expected. It is then in a position to say whether or not the client should spend any money in the area. If it thinks he should, it has a basis upon which the Media, Copy, Radio, and Public Relations departments can work out detailed plans, plans which integrate and harmonize with the aims and operations of the client.

Today Ayer clients frequently have advertising objectives related to the creation of a favorable public attitude toward the company, or the industry of which it is a part, or toward private enterprise, rather than to the sale of a product. During World War II, and again during the winter of 1947–48, oil companies actually advertised to *discourage* the consumption of oil and gasoline as a fuel conservation measure. But most advertising done by the Ayer agency still relates to selling products or services, and what follows indicates the kind of analysis which the Ayer staff makes.

ANALYZING THE PRODUCT FOR ADVERTISING PURPOSES

The nature of the product throws much light on the kind of advertising which must be used: there is not much to be gained by advertising farm machinery in the *New Yorker* or cosmetics in the *Iron Age,* and there are other less obvious distinctions which must be recognized.

The study of the product, moreover, frequently enables the agency to recommend new uses, improvements in quality or design, or changes in the packaging. In the course of its history N. W. Ayer & Son has made many suggestions to clients about their products, and Ayer clients have adopted with profit a substantial number of the agency's recommendations.

Responsibility for the product always belongs first of all to the producer. But, just as the advertising agency must interpret the manufacturer and his product to the public, so it must interpret the public to the manufacturer. A part of the Ayer agency's regular work has been to study and understand consumer habits, tastes, and needs. If a product is not adapted to sell readily, it is the business of the agency to discover the faults and have them corrected before it launches any advertising. A poor product has wrecked many an excellent advertising campaign. By making a check in advance the agency has reduced the risk of wasting a client's money and hence injury to its own reputation as well. N. W. Ayer & Son began to realize the importance of this fact

in the 1880's; and, especially after 1900, it made increasing
efforts to consider the client's product critically from all points
of view before spending money on appeals to the public.

Analyzing the Market

With information about the product in hand, the Ayer agency
makes a study of the market for the product or service which the
client has to sell.[5] Is the market concentrated in one area or
scattered over the entire country? Do sales promise to be large
enough over a period of time to support advertising? What kind
of people buy the product — wealthy or poor, educated or manual
workers, city folk or farmers? Where are they located geographically? In what circumstances do they ordinarily buy the product
— in the home, on the way to the office, with or without much
forethought? Who influences the purchase and what factors determine the choice of product and brand? What is the greatest
possible consumption of the product per year in this country? Is
it likely to increase or decrease? Is the purchase or consumption
seasonal in character? How are consumption and sales affected
by trade and economic conditions, changes in style, or other
variable circumstances? What is the attitude of the general public
toward the client company or its product? Are any problems
raised by the attitude toward the product of particular sections
of the public, such as racial, professional, or religious groups?
What is the nature and amount of competition?

Armed with facts about product and markets, many of which
are obtained by field investigators, the Ayer staff is able to make
a critical study of the channels of distribution through which the
client's product must move on its way from the factory to the
consumer, comparing the ones in use with those which would be
ideally adapted to the particular product and its market. The
agency asks questions like these: Does the client sell directly to
the public, to retailers, to wholesalers and jobbers, or through
other types of middlemen? (Occasionally N. W. Ayer & Son has
uncovered and eliminated serious conflicts of interests among
these dealers.) What are the average distribution costs of the
client and the middlemen used, and how do those costs compare
with the gross margins of profit which they receive? (In several

instances the agency has discovered that the margin allowed failed to cover the normal expenses of dealers.) What are the price policies and selling terms? What is the attitude of dealers toward the client and his product? What selling problems or sales resistance has the client encountered? (Advertisers have frequently sought Ayer advice about such issues as price-cutting and fads in consumption.) Have there been any changes in the methods or organization of the factors of distribution affecting the client's sales, such as the formation of chains of retail stores or the elimination of wholesalers?

STUDYING THE CLIENT'S ORGANIZATION

While studies of the product, market, and the distributing mechanism are in progress, the agency also directs attention to the client company itself. What is its history? How is it now organized? How does it differ from competing companies? How does it rank in its industry? What is its financial structure and position? What are its production methods and facilities, and how do they compare with those of competitors? What is its total plant capacity, and what rate of production is necessary for profitable operation? What have its total volume and profits been during recent years? How is its salesforce organized and controlled? How are its salesmen trained and paid? What are the territorial sales divisions? Where are the branch offices and warehouses located? What has its sales record been for recent years, classified according to product, brands, territorial divisions, and types of purchasers? What has its advertising experience been? What are the principal problems which the company faces at the present time?

The above summary oversimplifies in many respects the agency's research, but it suggests the main character of the work done. The general significance of all these inquiries is that N. W. Ayer & Son has long regarded advertising not as an independent selling device but as one part of a general marketing effort, a part which must be carefully integrated with the activities of salesmen and dealers.

Obviously the advertiser himself should have information on all these points without any urging from the agency. To some extent he usually does. But the advertiser's point of view is often too limited to permit him to see his own situation clearly. To some facts he is quite blind, and his own observations are in general colored by his bias. He may not see that his product is obsolescent; possibly his close attention to production has prevented him from noticing the growing menace of a rival firm or the advent of improved methods of distribution; or he clings blindly to long-established but ineffective selling organization and policies. He needs the assistance of an outside point of view in order to obtain a new picture of the consumption and distribution of his product, both actual and potential.

Sources of Information

Some of the desired information has usually been uncovered by the preliminary survey which the Ayer Business Development Department made as a part of its endeavor to win the advertiser's business; in preparing its plans, therefore, the Ayer agency has made a practice of reviewing the records covering its solicitation of the account. Many facts, of course, can be supplied only by the client, and the agency has tried, therefore, to inspire sufficient trust to obtain the release of very confidential material.

It has also gathered information from independent sources, such as market data made available by governmental offices, commercial research organizations, and students of marketing. Moreover, it has drawn upon the valuable fund of information which has been accumulated out of its own vast experience and has been preserved in the minds of its staff members as well as in the extensive files which it maintains.

Frequently, too, the Ayer firm has found it advisable to conduct field investigations among dealers, users, and others familiar with the product or the client's company. In recent years there has been a tendency to make more searching inquiries among consumers themselves, for experience has shown that neither the manufacturers nor their dealers, nor even the advertising men, are able to judge, without carefully conducted interviews, what the consumer's wants and buying habits really are. As a result, this part of the agency's work has steadily grown in importance and scope.

The Ayer firm has sometimes employed independent technical experts to give the product a scientific test, designers and package specialists to make improvements upon the product or its container, and market analysts to help with the collection and analysis of market data.

In recent years there has been a significant change with respect to research projects handled by the agency. Until the late 1930's most of the product and market surveys were undertaken by the agency itself. Many of them were excellently conceived and well executed, while some were carried out in a rather perfunctory and uncritical way. This unevenness seemed to be characteristic of all the agencies;[6] and it is scarcely surprising when one recalls that they were not usually paid for this all-important preliminary work but only for the advertising (if any) which followed it. Within the past three decades there has been a growing recognition of the necessity for making careful product and market analysis, and some advertisers have been willing to pay for having a thoroughgoing job done. There still remains, however, an inclination to expect advertising agencies to handle such work as a part of the services regularly performed to earn the usual compensation. Agencies cannot afford to spend much money on market surveys unless they are reasonably sure that the client concerned is eventually going to spend a large sum of money on his advertising.[7] The only generalization the historian can safely make is that, according to advertisers who are in a position to know, Ayer research compared favorably with that of the leading rival agencies.[8]

Since the late 1930's a number of very competent, independent research agencies have established themselves, and both the agency and its clients have increasingly made use of their services. No longer does the agency attempt to conduct, at its own expense, major research projects in the client's interest. Where the research is intended to produce information which the Ayer management would normally expect from the client, it recommends the project and coöperates closely in carrying it out, but it expects the client to pay the cost. When research is intended to benefit the technical performance of the Ayer staff itself, the agency bears the cost. The Ayer management believes that this method brings better results and is less expensive both for the agency and for its clients. Today it recommends a direct arrangement between the client and the research organization which it proposes. Members of the agency staff maintain close contact with the project as representatives of the client. This helps because the agency has a good understanding of the client's business and its requirements, and it also understands the problems which confront the research organization.

This change in Ayer policy on research projects has come about for two reasons: first, the agency now recognizes that independent research agencies have available the entire American scene in which to operate, can maintain a permanent, trained, and experienced staff, and can spread the cost of the research organization among many business concerns. The agency, on the other hand, has only a relatively limited number of clients with which to support a staff of field investigators, and the scope of investigation would necessarily be somewhat restricted. Secondly, client organizations have changed their point of view. They understand the importance of independent field investigations of high quality, and they no longer expect to obtain major research projects free of charge from an advertising agency. Ayer management takes the view that it is better off with no such field research when the advertiser does not choose to make funds available for an adequate investigation. It would rather depend upon the combined experience and judgment of its staff than upon a superficial field study.

The significant thing is that N. W. Ayer & Son was among the first to undertake field research projects and that it has, to an extent which has steadily increased during the last quarter of a century, applied the scientific method to its activities. It is unmistakable that both the need and the tendency of the agency have been to study and assist in the solution of its clients' problems of management as a whole.

By the time such a survey on many fronts has been completed, N. W. Ayer & Son possesses a fairly accurate and comprehensive view of the client's product, business organization, and opportunities upon which to base its recommendations. Not all its basic analyses proceed upon these same lines. When the client is one whose product is well established throughout the country and whose salesforce is known to be well organized and managed, the Ayer approach is of course different from that employed when the product is a new one, or the particular market undeveloped, or the client not experienced with modern advertising. The survey, like the advertising plan to follow, has had to be adapted to the particular client and his situation.

Making Use of the Assembled Facts

It is of the utmost importance to have a penetrating survey of a client's entire business, actual and potential, before any advertising is done. Any survey is worthless, however, unless the facts uncovered are interpreted and used with intelligence. This is an obvious truism, perhaps, but advertising agencies have been known to conduct elaborate investigations which yield masses of figures and opinions, impressive to look at but of no significance; or, if significant, still unused because the findings conflict with the preconceived ideas of someone in the agency's or the client's organization. Maps alone do not win battles or complete safe voyages. Those in command have to use the available information with intelligence and resource, drawing up plans in advance of any action. The same is true of advertising campaigns. The Ayer surveys have been merely the basis of Ayer strategy, a procedure for finding the consumer, learning about his buying habits, and analyzing the problems encountered by the client in communicating with him.

The agency's next step has been to lay out a program of action in the form of a detailed written report, summarizing and interpreting the conclusions reached from its studies, and setting forth a series of recommendations founded upon these conclusions, touching upon all phases of the client's business. This plan relates specifically to the client's activities for the ensuing year, but it also takes future developments into account.

Ordinarily the Ayer agency's recommendations have dealt first with the various steps which should precede the launching of a campaign of advertising, such as changes in the product or its package. The Ayer agency has also advised clients to alter the prices charged for their products. Sometimes it has recommended an increase, in order to provide for an advertising allowance or larger margin to the middleman — usually with the idea of lowering the price as soon as the volume has increased enough to make a reduction in price possible. More frequently it has recommended a scaling-down of prices in order to stimulate sales and increase the client's total volume.

Invariably N. W. Ayer & Son has given a great deal of attention to the client's selling force and advised changes of importance. In contrast with many agencies which have attributed unlimited power to advertising, the Ayer firm gave recognition, as early as the 1880's, to the view expressed in a recent report to a client: "Advertising can help good sales work to accomplish much greater results than could be done without advertising. But advertising can never take the place of good sales work." At least since about 1910, in keeping with this view, the Ayer reports have made specific recommendations to clients, designed to improve the effectiveness of their selling efforts as a whole. It has presented plans for sales quotas and records of performance, outlined methods of training and managing salesmen, and advised payment of salesmen by both salaries and commissions or bonuses, in order to maintain proper control over their work while preserving an adequate inducement to effective effort.

The purpose of these preliminary recommendations has been to make reasonably sure that the client's product would be efficiently distributed before any advertising went out to the public. All such precautions seem to be too obvious to require mention. Yet even today supposedly competent agencies waste money by placing advertisements in the hands of the consumer without first making sure that the product advertised is readily obtainable from retailers. Convinced by the advertising, the consumer tries to buy the product and fails. He seldom makes a second attempt. N. W. Ayer & Son's care in this respect is another indication of the fullness of its service.

After giving proper attention to the client's arrangements for distributing his product, N. W. Ayer & Son has focused its energies upon the advertising itself. With the basic facts as a guide, the agency has determined the purpose, nature, and scope of the advertising effort to be made and then worked out in all particulars the methods and details to be followed.[9]

DECIDING THE PURPOSE OF THE ADVERTISING

The purpose or object of Ayer campaigns has of course varied widely according to clients and circumstances. To be sure, the primary one is usually to sell goods, but it may be necessary to do this indirectly. Thus the particular object may be to locate prospective buyers by persuading people to send in coupons or make inquiries which will supply the advertiser with "leads." The Ayer advertising for schools has always been of this type. The agency has also launched campaigns designed to pave the way for personal selling efforts — to assist the recognition or acceptance of a brand or product by the public, or to give status to salesmen who might, as the unheralded representatives of unknown companies, receive no hearing at all. Again, advertising is designed to encourage dealers to stock the client's product and coöperate in selling it to the public.

It is to be noted, however, that, while the coöperation of retail and wholesale distributors is essential to good distribution, the producer frequently competes with them for control over consumer demand. Some remarks of H. N. McKinney in 1905 on this point are interesting in view of the decline in the wholesale dealer's importance in subsequent years:[10]

The most dissatisfied man today is the manufacturer. The day of the jobber is passing. The manufacturer finds that he is helpless in the hands of the jobber. He does not sell his goods or make a reputation for himself, but he makes it for the jobber. The manufacturers are waking up to that fact; and our great business is to show the manufacturer that he ought to own his own trade by making the demand direct from the consumer.

As might be expected, pioneering campaigns bulked large in early Ayer history, but those of a competitive nature have demanded an increasing share of the agency's attention since the 1890's. Nearly every advertiser, after getting established, has found it necessary to fight for existence against other concerns offering similar goods or services, and in most cases he has had to employ advertising as one of his weapons in the battle. In giving credit to advertising as an instrument of material progress, we must remember that advertising is also used to defend established interests against change. Like real weapons in actual warfare, advertising is used both in offensive and in defensive movements; the agency has to decide, in making its plan, the kind of tactics that the situation demands. If defensive, the plan may be merely to keep the client's product or name before the public by means of periodical, billboard, and other visual advertising, and by sponsored radio programs. Usually, however, such campaigns have gone further and have actively attempted to discourage the substitution of other products or brands, or else to combat some idea, accepted by the public or fostered by a rival concern, which is interfering with sales. Thus, in 1919 the Ayer agency handled a campaign which was aimed to assure the public that coffee did not cause all the ills which have been attributed to it; and in 1934 it placed advertising for the Ford Motor Company which, by urging the advantages of solid front axles on motor cars, helped to offset the propaganda of rival manufacturers in favor of independent front-wheel suspension.

In general N. W. Ayer & Son has planned competitive campaigns to defend by taking the offensive. In doing so it has tried to avoid direct attacks upon the goods of the client's competitors, stressing rather the merits of what the client has to sell.

From the consumer's point of view advertising might be more helpful and interesting if manufacturers were to "debunk" one another's sales arguments in public; but, because the border line between correction of statements and disparagement of products is a hazy one, such action would soon lead to trouble. It is largely for this reason that it is unethical in advertising to attack competing merchandise.

N. W. Ayer & Son has attempted, by various means, to increase the consumption of the client's product among existing users, to encourage users of competing products to change to that of the client, and to develop new uses which will bring about increased consumption all around. In considering the purpose of a campaign, the agency has to study the client's line of products in order to determine which of them should be featured in the advertising. The modern manufacturer ordinarily produces a large number of commodities — sometimes hundreds of items. It is not feasible to advertise them all, and the usual practice is to select one or two as the basis for a campaign which will establish the brand name for the entire line. Obviously the selection is one which requires careful consideration from many points of view.

Lastly, Ayer plans have frequently had as their general purpose the building of prestige of the client. Such advertising is usually referred to as institutional, and it is devoted not so much to selling a product or service as to explaining a client's general policies or methods, describing his business and its history, or in some other way to creating goodwill with the public. The advertising which Ayer has done for the American Telephone and Telegraph Company is perhaps the most familiar example of this type.

Few of the Ayer campaigns fit neatly into this general framework of purposes. Some of them combine several objects; some shift constantly from one type to the other; and others have an ulterior or secondary purpose somewhat removed from the ordinary field of marketing. Occasionally, for example, Ayer plans have called for advertising which has been ostensibly competitive or institutional in character but which has been intended, to a large extent at least, to foster pride or bolster working morale among the client's own staff of employees. Or the purpose may be to impress investors in a company's stock rather than to interest consumers in its product. The advertising which the Ayer firm handled for a western railroad in 1926 had as its avowed purpose the encouragement of settlement along the railroad's right of way, the development of passenger traffic over the line, and the spreading of information generally about the region served by the system. It is evident from the correspondence between the agency and the receivers, however, that the campaign was also intended to impress the investing public with the importance of the railroad, in order to facilitate reorganization.

SCOPE OF THE CAMPAIGN

The general purpose of the campaign having been determined, the agency has proceeded to the question of its scope. Before about 1930 the procedure often was to launch the advertising in a few selected cities as a trial effort, getting the client's product well established, the salesforce effectively organized, and the general selling plan thoroughly tested. After the methods used had proved their merit, the campaign was then advanced into adjacent territories in a systematic manner, as rapidly as production facilities, dealer coöperation, and the sales organization could be expanded. This slow, piecemeal progress permitted the agency and its client to experiment, correct mistakes, and make improvements before engaging in a comprehensive and expensive campaign on a wide front.

These methods are still used when appropriate, but today, in serving well-managed clients who have established products, there is less need for "market testing." At the same time a market-by-market expansion program may be desirable in order to spread expense and man power over a period of time. The scope of the effort and the point of attack depend largely upon the stage of development which the client's business has reached and the problems it has encountered.

Another important part of the typical Ayer plan is an analysis of the audience to be reached. Some advertisements are directed to the general public; others concentrate upon a particular group or combination of groups within "the public." The great mass of population which we glibly call "the public" or "the market" really consists of many races, many classes, and people of widely varying tastes, interests, habits, and income — often overlapping segments. Thus a campaign may attempt to reach the dealers who handle the product (e.g., retail druggists or hardware wholesalers), or technical or professional men (such as doctors or engineers) who are consulted about its use, or certain ultimate consumer groups. The purchasers of Boeing airplanes, Cannon towels, and Hess & Clark stock tonics are rarely the same people. A plan must work out the audience to be reached from two points of view. First, the product or the company's interest may automatically restrict the group or groups to be reached. Secondly, the agency must consider budgetary limitations. Reaching the national audience is so costly that relatively few advertisers can afford the bill. Where wide coverage is desirable, therefore, the

agency tries to define the audience by groups in order of importance to maximize the results according to the available funds.

METHODS OF REACHING THE PEOPLE

Having settled the purpose, scope, and audience of the campaign — the main strategy — the agency has turned to the question of methods — the particular tactics to be used. What kind
of selling appeal or basic copy theme is likely to be most effective? Which of the various media — newspapers, magazines,
radio, trade papers, or other types — offers the best means of
conveying the message to the desired audience? If several are to
be used, how much of each and in what way are they to be co-
ordinated to obtain the best results? And what is to be the exact
timing and sequence of the various steps of the campaign?

The choice of appeal brings into the plan the element of psychology and art, an element which has steadily grown in advertising. Especially in the period since 1900, the competition between products has tended to develop into competition between
ideas about them. Advertising's function as a signpost has largely
been superseded in importance by its function as an active force
influencing people. The agency has to create a demand for the
product of its client by turning out ideas which will make people
want it or, if it is one for which there is a well-established demand, make them prefer brand A instead of brand B. By skillful
appeals to vanity, fear, pride of possession, economy, or other
motivating forces, the advertising can surround a product with a
subjective value for the consumer. Since that subjective value
often looms larger in the consumer's mind than the objective value
of the product, the selection of the advertising ideas which create
it is of the utmost importance. The central problem is how best to
get the attention of consumers, what ideas to emphasize in order
to have the effect on them which is desired, and how to express
the entire message convincingly. To some extent this is a matter
of common sense and human psychology, but in its final form the
solution depends upon graphic art and literary skill.

Should the advertisement be illustrated or in type alone? If
illustrated, what subject? And what method of illustration —
photograph, sketch, or painting? Should it be in black and white,

two colors, or more? The answers to such questions depend largely upon the nature of the product and its market, the kind of media used, and the money available. In any case the decisions are important, and the special knowledge and extensive experience of the agency is of the utmost aid in reaching them.

Other means of stimulating demand are also considered — such devices as prize contests, free samples and souvenirs, and spectacular stunts of one kind or another. If the agency decides to recommend something of this sort as a part of the campaign, it must work out the scheme in detail.

The agency likewise has to give counsel about the use of various supplementary advertising devices as a part of the plan, even though it may have little or nothing to do with their preparation: special introductory offers to dealers and consumers, window and counter displays, and other so-called dealer aids. These must tie in with the rest of the campaign.

PUBLICITY AS A SUPPLEMENT TO ADVERTISING

The public is usually interested in news stories relating to companies and their products. Recognizing this fact, advertisers and their agencies frequently prepare and release items of news, feature articles, and photographs. The purpose of such material is to develop knowledge and goodwill among the public and to create a background of interest in the product or company.

Unlike advertising, publicity brings no direct revenue to the publishers (apart from exceptional instances where some agent or his principal provides secret subsidies), and ordinarily it is printed by them, in spite of its commercial value, because of its genuine news interest. It contains no direct selling appeal, and it usually concerns industries or types of products more often than particular firms or brands of merchandise. From the point of view of the public, considerable danger lies in the fact that publicity, unlike advertising, carries no surface indication of its source or purpose: publicity cannot assume the responsibility which it should bear for its message. The public, however, unquestionably wants news about commercial enterprises and their wares, and the advertiser is therefore frequently able to benefit himself by catering to this interest, superintending the preparation of any news relating to his company, and releasing it at times best suited to his own interests.

Because of the assistance which publicity can give to an advertising campaign, N. W. Ayer & Son, like many other advertising agencies, has undertaken to prepare and release publicity material as a part of its regular work. But it regards publicity as complementary to, rather than a substitute for, avowed advertising; and it recognizes that for many clients publicity can be of no real value. The agency's plans, consequently, weigh the question in each case as to whether any publicity efforts would be advantageous in connection with the other selling efforts, and if so, they outline the general nature of the publicity which might be prepared.

SELECTION OF PARTICULAR MEDIA

Today most Ayer plans are drawn up in the form of a general outline of sales strategy, the details to be worked out after the client has agreed to the major objectives and the methods proposed for attaining them. Until about 1910, however, a plan consisted of little more than a detailed schedule of publications, space allotments, and dates for the appearance of advertisements. Today, of course, the first decision the agency has to make about media is the type to use for the client concerned — whether radio, television, magazines, newspapers, outdoor posters, motion pictures, and so on. As the number of possibilities increases, the decision becomes more complicated: it is a question not only of cost per person reached, but also of the effectiveness of the particular medium upon that person. The important point is that the decision as to types is reached by an impartial group within the agency in terms of the client's needs as ultimately defined. For certain media — especially radio — this represents a change in approach. During the early 'thirties the Radio Department was likely to say in effect, "Here is a program for sale. What client can we persuade to buy it?" Some agencies still operate in that manner. Today the Ayer Plans-Merchandising Department asks, "Which media, or combination of media, will best reach the audience we want, at an economical cost?" If the answer includes radio, then, and only then, is the Radio Department asked to provide specific ideas as to creative programs, hiring talent, and obtaining network coverage to fit the needs as defined.

Once the Plans-Merchandising Department has decided upon the types of media to be used, it turns the details over to specialists on the particular types — to the Media Department for the selection of specific newspapers and magazines, to Radio for choice of times and stations, and so on.

The publications differ widely among themselves in respect to the type of people reached. *Life* and the *Saturday Evening Post,* for example, reach a large number of people of almost all ages and classes. Others (e.g., *Foreign Affairs* and *Vogue*) circulate among a comparatively limited number of people having very special tastes or interests. Some newspapers of general appeal have a wide suburban circulation, while others go mainly to readers who are especially interested in financial or sporting news, and hardly ever circulate beyond the business district of the city. One paper may have a large circulation gained principally by the offer of premiums, prizes, or other special inducements, while a competing paper of small circulation is bought for its contents and is therefore likely to be a more carefully read and valuable advertising medium.

Circulation data are more readily available and dependable now than during the early years of agency history, but it is still advisable for an agency to check and interpret with great care the statistics given out by media owners and by such commercial gatherers of data as the Audit Bureau of Circulations. The agency has had to consider not only the quantity and location of a paper's circulation but also the incomes, education, and interests of the majority of its readers. And it has had to weigh such intangible factors as the extent of the paper's influence upon those readers, its political or economic leanings, and its general importance, as well as such mechanical factors as size, typography, and the time of issue. In selecting media for advertising campaigns, N. W. Ayer & Son has had to take cognizance of these and many other special qualities, some of them involving quite subtle differences. It has then had to gauge the implications of such qualities with respect to the advertising of particular products and to select the media best suited for the task at hand.

In the preparation of radio plans the problem is more complicated than in the selection of printed media, for in radio the advertiser (through his agency) has to provide the entertainment as
well as the advertising message to accompany it. With newspapers
and periodicals the advertiser is, of course, responsible only for
the advertising; the publisher supplies the editorial content.
Hence, in working out the choice of stations, the Radio Department has to consider the type and length of programs. And, because the radio industry does not yet offer any uniform data on
station coverage like those of the Audit Bureau of Circulations,
the Radio Department must develop a large proportion of its own
data governing the selection of stations and network. Moreover
decisions are influenced by such factors as the time of day when
the program can be broadcast, the character of the programs immediately preceding or following it on the network, and the programs at the same hour on other networks which will compete for
attention.

OBTAINING THE CLIENT'S APPROVAL

The best brains of the Ayer agency and the combined resources
of its principal departments are brought to bear on the preparation of advertising plans for its clients. Although a vast organization of specialists closely integrated with the mass production of
standardized goods, the agency itself cannot use the methods of
the factory, for its product is never a uniform one and few of the
parts of that product can be standardized. Each advertising campaign forms a special problem, and N. W. Ayer & Son has long
regarded it as such. To define and solve that problem the agency
calls upon the services of many specialists — market analysts,
copywriters, and experts in media, but their contributions must,
of course, be welded into a harmonious flow of ideas and results.
To this end the management has maintained a flexible organization which permits frequent conferences among the staff members
and many reviews of the work in process. To a large extent the
plan is evolved rather than created.

When the Ayer management is finally satisfied that the completed plan is the best possible for the purpose at hand, it submits

its report, together with cost estimates and alternative suggestions on some points, for the approval of the client. This step is often a delicate one, a task of explanation and persuasion which sometimes taxes the agency's best abilities. The agency, of course, has been in close consultation with the client throughout and knows his views about the kind of advertising which should be done. At some points, however, its conclusions may conflict with the client's ideas. Every plan contains decisions and proposals about which legitimate differences of opinion are bound to arise, and some sort of agreement must be reached before the agency can go ahead. Perhaps the majority of plans ultimately embody a compromise between the views of the client and those of the agency. In a few instances, however, the client has clung to ideas which N. W. Ayer & Son felt would seriously jeopardize the success of the advertising, and it has withdrawn from the relationship rather than execute a campaign which it regarded as bound to fail.

BRIEF APPRAISAL

For the most part, the Ayer attitude in planning advertising campaigns seems to have been unusually frank, honest, and intelligent. The advertising manager of a firm which spends more than $3,000,000 annually through N. W. Ayer & Son wrote an unsolicited letter of appreciation at the end of eight years of Ayer service. One excerpt from it summarizes what many clients have said:[11]

We always feel free to pass along anything, regardless of how large or small it may seem — and we know that in accepting our suggestions you always treat them on the basis of their face value. You know many agencies do things to please their customers and in this respect our working contact with N. W. Ayer & Son has been so different — that is, if our thoughts and suggestions are worth while, they are accepted, if not you are so frank to tell us the situation and to go ahead with your original ideas and plans. This works both ways for we, regardless of any feelings, try to give you that which we believe to be in the best interests of the business. . . . We know you will continue to call "a spade a spade" regardless of whether you believe you will please us or not.

The charge has often been made that advertising agencies waste money by overemphasizing advertising in the client's general selling program. There is no absolute standard by which to judge performance in this respect, but I have been unable to discover any evidence of obviously excessive recommendations by the Ayer agency. On the contrary, I have found a number of clear instances in which Ayer executives have had to go to some lengths in persuading a client to spend less money on advertising than he wanted to. The long-standing success of N. W. Ayer & Son and of a great many of its clients is one indication that the general run of Ayer planning has been of high quality. While some of it has undoubtedly fallen short of perfection, the available evidence shows that N. W. Ayer & Son has corrected serious flaws in the sales organization and technique of many clients, in addition to improving their advertising materially. Indeed, its success in giving counsel on all aspects of a client's activities suggests that the Ayer agency will develop further in this direction. Certainly it has long outgrown the scope and name of advertising agency.

CHAPTER XII

CAMPAIGN EXECUTION AND GENERAL SERVICE

As soon as the client has agreed upon the final plan and authorized the expenditure of money, the Ayer staff goes into action to
convert ideas and plans into realities. The service representative
has to maintain close contact with the client and see both that his
wishes are correctly understood by the Ayer staff and that the
agency's work is properly interpreted to him. The Copy Department has to prepare material for the advertising message and its
reproduction; the Media Department to buy space; and so on
through the entire Ayer organization. Thus, as the campaign gets
under way, the problem of the Ayer management shifts from fact-
finding, analysis, and reasoning to direction, correlation, and efficiency in execution.[1] Without effective follow-through, of course,
the best conceivable plan comes to nought.

Preparation of Advertising Copy

We have already had a glimpse of the work which the agency
does in preparing advertisements for its clients, and a later chapter will deal with the subject at some length; but it may be well to
note here a few brief details of the Copy Department's work.

As the reader will recall, N. W. Ayer & Son had very little to
do with the preparation of copy until 1892. Since that time, however, it has acquired a large staff of employees to specialize in
this kind of work. Especially after 1900, copy production as an
agency function grew in importance and complexity, demanding
ever greater skill, experience, and cleverness. Apart from broadcast programs, the finished advertisements are the only product
of the agency to appear before the general public; they are the
ultimate object of most of the agency's work, the actual means of
bringing the client's company or goods to the attention of possible

customers, and they form almost the only tangible basis upon which the client can judge the value of the agency's services. If they are poor, the advertising space — once the agency's principal stock-in-trade — is largely wasted. Small wonder, then, that the Copy Department has become one of the most important parts of the Ayer organization.

The advertising plan merely outlines the nature of the copy to be used. The Copy Department has to transform the outlines into finished advertisements — write the text, prepare rough sketches of the illustrations to be used, and design layouts to indicate how the headlines, text, display, and other parts of the advertisement are to be arranged. If each advertisement could be considered as an isolated problem, this would be a comparatively simple matter, but many external factors make it exceedingly complex and difficult.[2]

The advertisement must be quite distinctive as well as attractive and interesting: it must have a character of its own, or it will resemble those of other companies and make no impression upon the consumer. And, at the same time, it must not depart too much from the prevailing style of advertising copy or it may appear ludicrous or grotesque and have an undesirable effect upon the reader. Indeed, the problem is often further complicated by the necessity of creating and maintaining an individual style for copy which will suggest, by its very atmosphere alone, some quality of the client's product or organization. To preserve this atmosphere, while introducing sufficient novelty and variation to avoid monotony, presents a severe challenge. Yet the Ayer writers have succeeded in this difficult task for many clients. Witness how the Yardley advertisements of cosmetics and toilet goods in recent years have preserved an air of dignity and refinement and a flavor of Old England, while featuring different products with variations in art work and appeal. Witness, too, how the advertisements of the American Telephone and Telegraph Company have maintained, since 1908, an atmosphere reflecting progress, stability, and public interest. And, to prove that Ayer talents are not restricted to this somewhat sober vein, there are the gay, sprightly, and stylish Cannon towel advertisements; the French Line copy in which the agency managed to impart an attractive flavor of

French sophistication, epicureanism, and wit; and the copy for Prince Albert smoking tobacco of about 1920 with its friendly air of masculine cheer, homely philosophy, and simple comfort.

Each advertisement is prepared for a specific purpose; it is designed to fit rather precisely into the advertising program of a particular client. And that advertising program must be designed to dovetail neatly into the client's over-all business strategy. Each advertisement — whether it appears in a newspaper or magazine, as a commercial radio announcement, as a promotional piece for dealers, or as a direct-by-mail communication — must achieve its purpose quickly, economically, and in the right way. It must attract the attention of the persons to whom it is addressed. It must hold their interest long enough to deliver its message, even when many other people, activities, and interests are competing for notice. It must do these things in such a way that the persons reached are impressed in the way that the advertiser intends. It must inform and create belief; and it must influence action.

The text, sketches, and layouts, completed to the agency's satisfaction, are then submitted to the client. And, when his approval has been given, the agency proceeds with obtaining the materials and services necessary for the physical reproduction of the finished advertisements. The Art Bureau engages the artist or photographer whose particular talents seem best suited for the finished illustration desired. The Engraving Bureau orders the proper engravings and plates. The Printing Department sets up the advertisement and runs off proof to show publishers exactly how it is to appear in final form. Each operation demands the technical skill and wide experience which can be made available only in a large organization.

At the same time the Copy Department starts the preparation of text; when it is done, the layout artists prepare sketches. After the client has approved the layouts, the Art Bureau buys finished art work for any posters, packages, booklets, sales portfolios, catalogues, or other supplementary advertising material which may be required.

The work of copy preparation, whether for printed advertisements or for radio, calls for the highest skill, imagination, and creative talent. While it can be planned and systematized, it cannot be reduced to routine; and, unlike market surveys and merchandising, it is far removed from the regular work of the client's own organization. This part of the advertising process seems, moreover, to be peculiarly the province of independent specialists, and there is reason to believe that it is the most valuable of the services which the agency renders to its clients.[3]

BUYING SPACE AND FORWARDING ADVERTISEMENTS TO PUBLICATIONS

While the advertising copy has been in preparation, the Media Department has been engaged in reserving and buying space in the various publications. While the preparation of copy has grown in complexity and importance since 1892, the work of space-buying has become simpler in many respects during the same period. As one member of the staff expressed the change, "We used to buy space. Now the publishers sell it to us." In saying this he was emphasizing the change in the publishers' attitude which practically put an end to the shrewd bargaining which agencies had done in earlier years. Rates have become stabilized, circulation figures have lost much of the fog of secrecy and ignorance which formerly surrounded them, and the purchase of space has become more routinized. In spite of these changes, the work of the Media Department retains much of its early prominence in the agency. It continues to demand special knowledge, wide experience, and critical judgment at many points, without which the client's money may be wasted.

The savings which N. W. Ayer & Son obtains for clients in buying space today are not, as they were fifty years ago, the result of special rates gained through bulk purchases and sharp bargaining. Until the 'nineties, advertisers bought their space through agencies primarily because it was cheaper to do so. Some light is thrown on the extent of the difference by a study which the Ayer agency made in 1893. At that time the Royal Baking Powder Company was placing its advertising directly with newspapers and claimed to save money by doing so because many publishers allowed it the agent's discount. The average rate which the company paid, according to the statement of its advertising manager, was $2.50 per inch per 1,000 circulation per year. Applying this rate to the advertising schedule which it was handling for the N. K. Fairbanks Company, the Ayer management found that the cost, according to the Royal rate, would have been $20,839.31. The amount which the N. K. Fairbanks Company actually paid, including the 15 per cent commission to Ayer, was $17,151.17, or 17.7 per cent less.[4]

Nowadays, publishers ordinarily allow the agency discount only to agencies, so that an advertiser pays approximately the same price for space, whether he deals directly with the papers or buys through an agency. Of course, when he buys through an agency he receives, at no extra cost, many services which he would otherwise have to perform for himself. Thus the savings which N. W. Ayer & Son obtains for him now come largely in the form of services rather than cash differentials won by the space-buyers.

But while it is true that the proportion of savings which the Ayer space-buyers can achieve through superior knowledge and bargaining power has declined, the great increase in the amounts of money involved in modern advertising campaigns has made those reduced economies of great importance in terms of dollars and cents. It is still possible for an agency to save money for an advertiser by obtaining less than card rates from many newspapers; and additional savings are possible when the space-buyer finds loopholes in the complicated rate structures or takes advantage of the concessions which many publishers offer on large orders. For example, owing to the somewhat fortuitous way in which the quantity discounts run, it is sometimes possible to buy 10,000 lines of space in a paper at a lower total cost than 9,500 lines, or 20 insertions for less than 16. Thus, by using what space-buyers call "rate-makers" (small additions to an order to gain a better rate), the agency can get more space for a client while saving him substantial sums of money. Such savings, however, cannot be won by routine work; they are the result of wide knowledge, experience, and close attention to duty.

The space-buying division also achieves large savings for clients by taking steps to protect them against increases in rates. Especially in the period after World War I, N. W. Ayer & Son found numerous opportunities to buy space for its clients in anticipation of their needs, contracting for the space at the rates prevailing before the increases became operative.[5] During the period 1930–33, on the other hand, it saved money for clients by close attention to decreases in space rates.

One must not, in this connection, overlook the fact that such savings for the client mean decreased revenue for the agency, since its commission is computed on the final net cost. The frequency with which N. W. Ayer & Son has discovered and taken advantage of ways of saving money for its clients, however, is evidence of both its alertness and its integrity. Clients are seldom aware of many of the economies which the agency obtains for them; but many publishers have, with mingled rue and admiration, testified that the typical Ayer space-buyer remains courteous but unmoved in the face of the best salesmanship of their representatives, that he weighs the facts impartially, and makes purchases with an efficiency and economy which is unsurpassed by any other agency.[6]

Since the 1930's one of the main contributions of the Media Department has been the selection of printed media to be used — an operation which necessarily precedes the purchase of space. Increasingly the effort has been to analyze all publications with regard to every characteristic which has any bearing on their suitability as bearers of advertising messages — not only the size and location of their circulation but also the make-up of their readers as to sex, age groups, occupation, and income, their editorial appeal and influence, and so on. All this is essential today because of the wide choice of media for reaching various segments of the public; and, in addition to choosing economical media, the agency staff must try to obtain the most appropriate ones in terms of the "atmosphere" in which the advertising of specific clients is to appear. Consequently the Media Department must keep up to date a greater variety of data than ever before about all types of publications. In this connection the Ayer Media Department is responsible for the development of complete data books now in use by a large number of leading magazines, trade and business papers, and some newspapers. These data books are virtually encyclopaedias, based on suggested outlines furnished to the publisher by the Media Department to answer all conceivable questions concerning their relative merits as an advertising medium.

The selection staff, who devote their full time to the analysis of all publications, must use expert judgment and all the data available in solving the problem of which media to use for particular purposes. That problem has become so intricate and the possible combinations so many that the work of media selection is beginning to be virtually a creative agency activity.

As soon as the Media Department has selected and ordered the space, the Business-Production Department checks closing dates and assigns deadlines to be met by the Copy, Art, Engraving Bureaus and the Printing Department. An outside foundry ships plates to the publication in time to meet closing dates. The forwarding work is complicated because the materials sent out must conform to the mechanical differences among publications—variations in size of pages, press equipment and quality of paper. The number of details requiring careful attention fairly staggers the imagination.

Checking the Published Advertising and Paying the Bills

After the agency has forwarded the advertising material to publications, it has to see that the advertisements appear as ordered — another routine clerical job of colossal proportions. Since 1874, if not earlier, N. W. Ayer & Son has had a special division, now known as the Checking and Auditing Bureau, to do this checking. Throughout its history the dominating purpose has been to make sure that Ayer clients receive everything they actually pay for.[7]

The sheer bulk of the material handled by the "C and A" Bureau of N. W. Ayer & Son indicates the magnitude of the checking work. The usual Monday morning consignment of voucher copies from publishers totals between 3,500 and 4,000 separate publications which fill from 15 to 20 mail sacks. Some agencies accept as proof of publication merely the page bearing the advertisement; except during the recent paper shortage, Ayer has insisted upon seeing the complete issue, in order to inspect the position of the advertisement in the paper as a whole. The number of voucher copies received by N. W. Ayer & Son each week averages about 8,000 pieces. These have to be opened, sorted according to geographical source, and then checked for advertising. Later they are filed for reference, all newspapers being kept for five months; magazines, on the other hand, are retained for a whole year.

The C and A Bureau receives a schedule of insertions, copy of instructions, and proofs for every Ayer campaign as a basis for checking. It then examines the papers sent in by publishers to see not only that the clients receive the correct size of space and number of insertions on the dates specified, but also that the

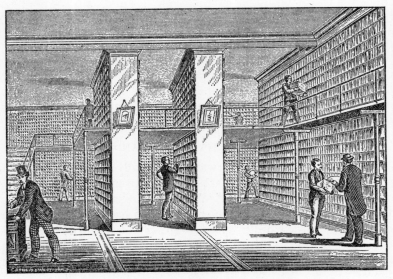

REGISTRY DEPARTMENT, N. W. AYER & SON, 1878
Showing files of periodicals used for checking the appearance of advertisements placed by the agency.

printing results are satisfactory. If the printer uses the wrong copy, or makes a typographical error, or if the advertisement is poorly reproduced, the agency immediately requests an adjustment, just as it does when an insertion is missed or an advertisement cut down in size.

The Registry Bureau, moreover, checks the appearance of an advertisement in relation to competing copy or display. Some of the agency's orders designate the position of the advertisement —

top of column next to reading matter, on the sport page, or some other definite location. The rates for special positions are usually higher, and the agency must see that its directions are explicitly followed. For other orders the agency expects good position, and it files a complaint with the publisher if the ones given are unsatisfactory. Thus, when Kellogg advertisements appeared alongside those of competing cereals, the agency held that the value of its client's advertising was impaired and obtained an adjustment from the publisher. It has taken similar action when the page opposite bore competing copy, or when, contrary to instructions, a client's advertisement appeared beside patent-medicine copy.

SECTION OF THE AYER REGISTRY BOOK, 1878

By means of this record the agency checked the insertion of advertisements. The symbols used indicated the first appearance, subsequent correct insertion, out of position, short space, omission, no paper of that date received, and so on.

This check upon the final appearance of Ayer advertising has, from the firm's beginning, been the basis of payments for space. The bills which the agency receives from publishers have always been compared with the checking records before being approved for settlement. Here, especially, the Ayer precept, "Spend the advertiser's money as if it were your own," has been scrupulously observed. For about fifty years — possibly longer — the Ayer agency has permitted clients to inspect its books in order to check their charges against the payments to media owners; and the pride of Ayer payment clerks in their accuracy has long been supported by the testimony of the most punctilious auditors. Whatever else he may complain about, no client has ever been able to say that N. W. Ayer & Son charged him for space or materials which he failed to receive.

It is impossible to estimate the cash value of the errors prevented or corrected by the C and A Bureau. Its worth to advertisers, however, is beyond question, as one example alone illustrates. In 1921 N. W. Ayer & Son began to serve a client who, as one of the largest advertisers in the country, had formerly spent $15,000 annually in checking his own advertising and bills, despite the fact that his advertising was placed through an agency. In fact, three different agencies had handled his business and had overlooked so many mistakes that the errors caught by his own checking department more than paid for its cost of operation. His staff continued checking for a few months after changing to N. W. Ayer & Son; but, after finding that the Ayer C and A Bureau was catching all the errors discovered by his own department, the client abandoned it and reduced his advertising expense by $15,000.

The Outdoor and Radio divisions make a similar check on the execution of orders which they place.

GENERAL SERVICING OF ACCOUNTS

While the material for periodical advertising is being prepared and placed with publications, the Outdoor, Radio, and Public Relations departments of the agency are at work with their respective rôles in the campaign. The Outdoor Department has had the posters printed and sent out to the billboard owners with whom it has contracted for space. The Radio Department prepares material for broadcasts, hires talent, rehearses performances, leases time on the air, and supervises the actual production of radio programs (see the following section). The Public Relations Department prepares and releases for publication news articles, feature stories, and photographs, arranges for interviews and publicity stunts, and gives advice to clients as to ways and means of obtaining favorable public notice.

The Ayer agency's work is not finished when material has been sent to publishers and billboard owners or when a series of broadcasts has been launched over the radio. Nor does it end, as it usually did in the 'seventies and 'eighties, when the agency has checked the fulfillment of orders to media and paid the bills. Soon after the advertising has begun to appear, members of the Ayer staff begin to study the results by examining sales reports and statistics and by making inquiries among dealers and consumers.

Apart from mail-order business, it is impossible to measure the effect of advertising on sales with any precision, particularly when the client has been advertising over a long period. Neither the cumulative effect nor current business situations can be weighted satisfactorily. A Plymouth advertisement in the newspaper today may lead John Jones to the nearest dealer for a new car, but one cannot even guess how much of his decision is derived from past advertising or from the performance of the car itself in his neighbor's hands or from a recent increase in his income. In some cases a long time must elapse before advertising begins to bring in sales; and it is extremely difficult to trace the tangible results of an institutional campaign.

One early attempt to relate sales to advertising may be of interest here. In 1892 and the early part of 1893, the Ayer agency placed mail-order advertising for Lawrence, Butler & Benham, a firm in Columbus, Ohio. This firm succeeded in tracing 60 per cent of its sales during the period to individual papers, as shown in Table 7.

Since the agency charged $1,300 for the first order and $1,400 for the second (obviously this advertising was not placed on the open-contract plan), the advertiser obtained at least $21,000 worth of business (the $12,621 plus the 40 per cent not attributable to particular papers) with expenditures of $2,700 in advertising. While such checks are easily and fairly accurately made for clients who conduct their business by mail, they are not applicable to goods sold over the counter. In recent years, however, a number of methods have been devised by which the effectiveness of advertisements can be checked with some success.[8]

While it cannot connect sales exclusively with advertising, the Ayer agency has to observe closely the progress of a campaign in order to revise it if any unforeseen difficulties occur or conditions change. The advertising has to be extended or altered in one territory, or a special campaign launched in another, or some other change made in the third. On one occasion, when it became

TABLE 7

ANALYSIS OF ADVERTISING RESULTS, 1892

A. *Returns on Advertising Order of July 9, 1892*

Paper	Published	Location	Lines	Times	Gross Price of Space	Sales Traced
Comfort	Monthly	Augusta, Me.	18	6	$486.00	$1,113
Delineator	"	New York, N. Y.	"	"	162.00	3,143
Demorest's Magazine	"	" "	"	"	45.00	239
Ladies' World	"	" "	"	"	145.80	354
Housewife	"	" "	"	"	77.75	164
Household	"	Boston, Mass.	"	"	55.00	99
Housekeeper	Semi-Mo.	Minneapolis, Minn.	"	"	72.00	213
Home Magazine	Monthly	Washington, D. C.	"	"	170.00	520
Ladies' Home Companion	Semi-Mo.	Springfield, Ohio	"	"	68.00	435
Ladies' Home Journal	Monthly	Philadelphia, Pa.	"	"	324.00	3,400
Leisure Hours	"	" "	"	"	27.00	20
					$1,632.55	$9,700

B. *Returns on Advertising Order of October 19, 1892*

Paper	Published	Location	Lines	Times	Gross Price of Space	Sales Traced
Century	Monthly	New York, N.Y.	18	6	$151.20	$ 198
Scribner's Magazine	"	"	"	"	113.40	179
Godey's Lady's Book	"	Philadelphia, Pa.	"	"	50.00	28
Home Queen	"	"	"	"	19.13	20
Arthur's Home Magazine	"	"	"	"	18.00	20
Great Divide	"	Denver, Colorado	"	"	43.20	32
St. L. Mag. [sic]	"	St. Louis, Mo.	"	"	18.00	12
Harper's Bazaar	Weekly	New York, N.Y.	"	13[a]	165.00	199
Club	Monthly	"	"	6	40.00	4
La Mode	"	"	"	"		
La Couturière	"	"	"	"	29.16	42
La Mode de Paris	"	"	"	"		
Paris Album of Fashions	"	"	"	13[a]		
S. S. Times	Weekly	Philadelphia, Pa.	"	6	234.00	255
Vick's Ills. Mag.	Monthly	Rochester, N.Y.	"	4[a]	108.00	152
Youth's Companion	Weekly	Boston, Mass.	"	1	278.00	1,474
Youth's Companion	"	"	33	2		
Vick's Fireside Visitor	Semi-Mo.	Augusta, Me.	18	2		
Happy Hours	"	"	"	1	108.00	300
Hearth & Home	Monthly	"	"	1		
Good Stories	"	"	"	1		
Jenness Miller Monthly	"	New York, N.Y.	"	6	40.00	6
					$1,515.09	$2,921

a Every other week.
SOURCE: Memo. dated Mar. 1, 1893, A. C.

[283]

evident that the agency had diagnosed the advertising problem wrongly, it did not hesitate to declare its entire plan a mistake and start afresh on a new one.

For the most part, the agency's work goes on without any break once the first advertising is launched; thereafter the study and analysis of the client's sales is a continuous process. And the successive advertising plans are, for the most part, variations on the first theme, with such revisions and extensions as experience dictates and facilities permit, together with changes in copy ideas, selling appeals, and general presentation in order to maintain the attention and interest of the consumer.

There must, of course, be periodic checks to determine whether the fundamental marketing and competitive position has changed, or whether the advertising continues to perform its proper work, or whether the choice of media or copy technique can be improved. And special problems constantly arise to engage the attention of the Ayer staff. Generally, however, its chief concern, for some time after an exhaustive diagnosis, has been to propose attractive and effective advertisements along the lines originally laid down.

Since it handles the work of many firms, N. W. Ayer & Son is often able to arrange for coöperative efforts between them, in sales and publicity as well as in advertising. For example, Cannon towel advertisements have sometimes featured certain hotels (Ayer clients) which use Cannon towels throughout; and beverage advertisements have included illustrations of glasses or other equipment sold by other Ayer clients. Similarly the agency arranged for the marketing of a package combining towels and lavender, the products of two clients; and it was instrumental in having one client — a distributor of automobile supplies — handle the anti-freeze preparation manufactured by another. Publicity material, particularly articles on food and cooking, has likewise worked in the products of two clients — describing, for example, the cooking of the food product of one on the electrical equipment manufactured by the other.

Radio as a Part of the Advertising Campaign

In Part I we saw something of the place of radio broadcasts in advertising and of the contributions made by N. W. Ayer & Son to the development of this new medium. A few additional remarks are appropriate here to show more concretely how the Ayer agency handles radio advertising.

Broadcast programs, as already indicated, were initially regarded as a means of developing public goodwill. Since about 1929 radio has been used increasingly as a device for the direct promotion of sales. To the Ayer agency this shift of emphasis has led to a change in the approach to the subject. In the 1920's the principal question was, "Does the program provide good entertainment which will result in a favorable public attitude toward the client's company and product?" In recent years the main question has been: "Can a program be developed which will fit effectively into the client's merchandising plan as a whole?"

The established Ayer policy is that radio is not to be recommended to any client unless it can reasonably be expected to contribute adequately to the ultimate sales goal, and that it is to be regarded not as an independent promotional unit, but rather as an integral part of the client's entire selling plan. The decisions of the Ayer Plans-Merchandising Department on the use of radio are those of a general board of strategy. Representatives of various departments — including experts in newspapers, magazines, radio, and outdoor advertising — are available for consultation, but the Plans-Merchandising Department is responsible for deciding whether or not radio, or any other medium, is appropriate for solving the advertising problem of the client. Thus the decision is as objective as the agency can make it.

When it has been established beyond doubt that radio should be used in the particular campaign, the head of the Radio Department holds a meeting which has come to be known as a "hash clinic." Those attending include his chief of production, program directors, the head of his writing staff, chief commercial writers, musical experts, and others whose experience or judgment seems likely to be helpful.

To this group the head outlines in detail the selling aims, the budget available, *and the collateral efforts which are to be made in other media.* The meeting then becomes an open forum, in which each person present gives his first reactions. No idea is too strange to obtain a hearing, for experience has shown that useful results grow out of indirect associations. After considerable discussion, the men in charge of the various subdivisions of the Radio Department are asked to meet with their staffs and return on a specified date with detailed recommendations for their part of the plan. While they are working out specific proposals, the men concerned confer with one another frequently so as to develop a well-knit, consistent plan.

Meanwhile, the time and contracts division has begun to devise a schedule of stations and networks. They must use the funds apportioned to them to the best advantage, choosing geographic markets wisely, determining whether day or night time is indicated, and calculating (on the basis of known listening habits) the most desirable audience in terms of age, sex, sets available, and so on.

When the second meeting is held, the various formulated proposals are subjected to a thorough discussion, after which final recommendations are written and assembled into a "presentation" which is considered by other Ayer departments and ultimately by the client himself. This presentation gives both an outline of the program and the reasoning behind it.

The actual program in many cases is built completely by the agency, including idea, script, and production. In some cases, however, it may be built in coöperation with a "package producer" or selected from the wide variety of available shows created by package producers or networks, which are constantly under review by the agency's program division.

In this way the type of show recommended to the client is evolved out of the needs of his selling problem as the agency sees it. The determining factor is not an established program which someone wants to sell, nor a famous star performer who is available for a leading rôle, but rather a specific job to be accomplished as part of the client's total promotional plan.

PUBLIC RELATIONS WORK

Since 1930 N. W. Ayer & Son has undertaken a new service to its clients, one which is closely related to the agency's publicity work and really emerged from it, namely, public relations counsel. Publicity relates chiefly to the product itself. Public relations work is concerned with the attitude of the public toward the company and includes the subject of industrial relations — the promotion of satisfactory relations between the company and its employees.

In some respects the Ayer agency entered the field of public relations about 1900 when it began to handle the advertising of such large concerns as the National Biscuit Company and the Standard Oil Company, for it soon had to take account of the attitude of the public toward these "big business" institutions. The agency strove to obtain public goodwill principally by the use of advertising, but inevitably it was compelled to prepare publicity material as a part of its regular work and also to prepare news releases. By 1920 the firm had a well-organized publicity bureau which became increasingly important during the next decade. Its function was not merely to get news material into the papers; sometimes it had to restrain the client's desires in that direction. On the whole, it was trying to guide the client in his relations with the Press.

Shortly after 1930 the emphasis began to change to assisting the client in his relations with the public at large, not merely in so far as the Press was concerned but on all possible fronts. The agency's previous work had been to place the client's product and organization in a favorable light. As the depression deepened, something more fundamental had to be done to repair the damaged reputation of business in the eyes of labor and of the entire American public. It was not enough to interpret business to the public. The agency had to reverse the procedure and interpret public opinion to its clients. That meant making careful inquiries into public attitudes, diagnosing individual situations, and prescribing measures for clients to apply in their own internal affairs — constructive action rather than mere words to the public.[9]

The Ayer agency had been moving toward this sounder program before the dark days of 1932 and 1933 came upon us, but it had done little to urge the value of the service it could render until 1936 when it launched an unusual series of advertisements emphasizing the need for a better understanding between industry and the public.[10] It was prepared, therefore, to serve intelligently when, in 1937, American business leaders began to understand the connection between labor policies and public relations and started seriously to seek advice. The Ayer philosophy of public relations was outlined in a speech made by President Batten early in 1937, the core of which follows:[11]

Too many manufacturers think of Public Relations as a temporary dose of medicine, rather than as a fundamental system of business hygiene. Instead of watching their diet, and exercising in order to keep well, they neglect their corporate health and then scream for the Public Relations herb-doctor around the corner. Others use it as a means of giving public expression and visibility to their own personalities. . . . Still others . . . employ Public Relations as a species of conscience-fund.

None of these measures does any real good; and indeed none of them is really Public Relations at all. For Public Relations is a long-term thing and a constructive thing. It is a builder, not merely a mender. And it involves *not only the public portrayal and representation of the business, but the actual molding and shaping of business itself.*

Any Public Relations worthy of the name must start with the business itself. Unless the business is so organized and so administered that it can meet at every point the test of good citizenship and of usefulness to the community, no amount of Public Relations will avail. . . .

If you are not going to tell the truth in life and in business you might as well give up now, because you will inevitably be found out and discredited. But if you are going to tell the truth — if you are going to paint a faithful portrait of your business — then it is essential that the business itself be worthy of the painting.

This branch of Ayer service is handled primarily by the Public Relations Department, but other divisions frequently coöperate, especially the Copy and Radio departments.

MISCELLANEOUS ASSISTANCE

Far from confining its attention strictly to advertising, N. W. Ayer & Son has constantly acted as general counselor to its clients on every phase of their business affairs. Clients have come to the agency for advice on business conditions, financial matters, production and distribution problems, and a host of miscellaneous questions. Thus the agency, in 1928, urged one client to buy a part of his goods from other producers rather than expand his own manufacturing facilities before a continuous demand was assured. It has frequently given advice to clients about handling their finances, and no end of perplexing sales and merchandising questions come up for its consideration. One client wants the agency's help in missionary sales work or its influence in obtaining certain dealer connections. Another wants to know whether he should accept an order for private-brand merchandise which will be sold in competition with his own brand, or he asks advice about meeting chain-store competition. A third gets the agency's opinion about buying out a troublesome competitor or disposing of a surplus factory of his own. Others bring questions of participation in parades or trade exhibits, or want assistance in filling vacancies on their staffs. And an astonishing number of legal questions about sales practices, advertising copy, trade-marks, and prize contests come regularly before the Ayer staff for disposition, especially since the recent increase in governmental regulation.

Some of these matters require only the attention of an intelligent employee. Some involve only the time and thought required for an Ayer executive to write a letter of advice. But others necessitate special inquiries or the combined efforts of several departments. Yet, because its assistance fosters goodwill and frequently contributes to a client's general success, N. W. Ayer & Son has given careful consideration and generous help whenever it could reasonably be expected to do so. Indeed, the extent of its service seems to be limited only by the willingness of the client to accept proffered help. On the other hand, the Ayer management has repeatedly rejected requests which meant practically running a client's business for him or at least selling his goods. It has quite properly tried to stick to its own last and, in matters outside the field of advertising, to confine its assistance to giving information and advice.

When one reviews the service rendered by N. W. Ayer & Son since 1869, an interesting contrast is apparent between the evolution of different functions and their logical — even chronological — order in the advertising process. Historically the Ayer agency began with space-buying, formally took over the preparation of advertising copy in the 'nineties, systematized the preparation of advertising plans after 1900, began to make market analyses as a part of its regular procedure about 1910, has emphasized product analyses only since 1920, and did not really study the client's needs for advertising in the broad sense (going beyond selling problems as such) until after 1936. The present order of the agency's attack upon a client's advertising problems is, as shown above, exactly the reverse of this succession. In the agency business, as in many other walks of life, man has undertaken the work which was concrete and of immediate practical importance before proceeding to less obvious but basically more important considerations.

In this order of development lies hope for the consumer. Economists, together with other critics with a strongly developed consciousness of social welfare, have long attacked advertising for working against the interest of the consumer and taking advantage of him at every turn. Their criticism, though one-sided, has undoubtedly contained a large element of truth. But, as agencies like N. W. Ayer & Son move toward a scientific study of the consumer's real wants and buying capacity, the business man will be led toward a program of activity more far-sighted and, therefore, more valuable from a social point of view.

SOME EXAMPLES OF AYER SERVICE

A few illustrations may serve to round out the picture of the work done by N. W. Ayer & Son for its clients. Admittedly the picture must be incomplete because it is impossible to describe here the many types of campaigns which the agency has handled. It must also be a distorted one in that it contains no examples of failure on the agency's part. This flaw is unfortunate but impossible to avoid: like most other business concerns, the Ayer agency does not record its mistakes. It has some mediocre work to its credit, of course; but the fact is not significant because there is, if anything, less of it than one would expect to find in a business enterprise of comparable size, and we must judge by general performance rather than by isolated incidents. The three examples of Ayer service which follow are intended, therefore, to suggest high lights and bright colors rather than to present a complete portrait.

Before N. W. Ayer & Son became the advertising agency of Steinway & Sons in 1900,[12] the latter firm had used only a limited amount of advertising. It had relied upon the frequent appearance of its pianos at concerts and recitals to keep its name before the public. The agency pointed out that such publicity reached only the people who were already interested in music. On the other hand, a great market lay waiting in the large part of the public who had not yet developed a taste for music. A trial soon proved the correctness of this view. Although the copy used was not particularly educational or strong in its appeal, the Steinway sales immediately responded; and increased advertising appropriations brought still better results to the clients in sales and profits.

After World War I it became evident that efforts to sell pianos would have to improve or the industry could not survive the competition of new products. Pride in the parlor piano was giving way to pride in the family car; and within a few years the radio cut into piano sales still further by offering superior entertainment to all but the really earnest lovers of music. While recognizing the difficulties it faced, the Steinway Company refused to compromise its prestige and dignity by resorting to any cheapening of its product or to high-pressure selling methods. N. W. Ayer & Son soon showed that these measures were not necessary to success. It provided a striking but artistic series of rotogravure advertisements in metropolitan newspapers, emphasizing the importance of musical training in the education of children. In carefully chosen magazines the agency also placed a now-famous series of advertisements in color, featuring portraits of famous musicians, scenes from well-known operas, and graphic interpretations of distinguished compositions. This method of attack stimulated an interest in music, brought Steinway pianos to the attention of a large public, and, without any of the usual commercial appeal, increased sales to a remarkable extent. By 1929, although the piano industry as a whole had dropped below its 1921 capacity, Steinway sales were 69 per cent above those of 1921.

In 1930, following the financial crash, N. W. Ayer & Son advised the Steinway Company to reduce its advertising expenditures drastically, restricting its efforts to small space in selected metropolitan newspapers. This space was used to keep the firm's name before the public, to announce price reductions as soon as lowered production costs made them feasible, and to stress the maintenance and importance of Steinway quality. In 1933 the agency and its client felt warranted in expanding the advertising somewhat. Still using comparatively small space in both newspapers and magazines, the agency provided some illustrations in a new artistic technique to assist in explaining the craftsmanship and mechanical excellence which is embodied in Steinway pianos. Steinway sales for 1933 were nearly 57 per cent above those of 1932.[13] Not all credit for these results can be given to Ayer advertising — business recovery, the merits of the Steinway piano, and the work of the Steinway organization were undoubtedly major factors, but N. W. Ayer & Son is entitled to recognition for a substantial part of the success.

The Ayer treatment of a different kind of advertising problem is well illustrated by its work with Hills Bros. coffee. When N. W. Ayer & Son first became the agency for the firm, Hills Bros. were distributing their coffee in eleven western States. Since 1923 the Ayer agency had assisted in a steady drive toward eastern markets which proceeded at the average pace of one State per year. In 1930 the agency and its client attacked the Chicago area. They studied the market and laid their plans with care. The first open move was a postcard to grocers announcing that Hills Bros. coffee was entering the city. Other cards told grocers about the company, its sales policies and plans, and its product. With the way thus paved, the company's salesmen had little difficulty in obtaining a courteous hearing from dealers. In the first two weeks they made 1,839 calls and obtained 1,063 orders. A short time later half-pound packages of coffee went out to telephone subscribers, and again dealers were informed of the procedure. Lastly, with the dealers stocked and consumers interested, a series of full-page newspaper advertisements went out, and the coffee immediately began to move off the dealers' shelves. Tests made eleven months later indicated that Hills Bros. coffee was leading other brands in sales in the Chicago area. Here, again, advertising and the Ayer agency contributed only a part of the success, but it was an important part.

I cannot refrain from noting that, although Hills Bros. coffee was vacuum-packed in sealed tins long before its leading competitors were using this device, the Ayer advertisements made no attempt to attribute any human ills or discomforts to the use of stale coffee. Nor did they try to insinuate that coffee possessed mysterious aphrodisiac properties. Instead, in an interesting and dramatic way, they featured quality coffee, expert roasting, and good flavor. N. W. Ayer & Son had again demonstrated that sound economic methods need no sensational appeals as support.[14]

The third example shows how N. W. Ayer & Son handled an emergency order. On October 31, 1929, the Ford Motor Company decided to announce a price reduction on its cars. It took up the matter with the Detroit branch of N. W. Ayer & Son; and the branch office and the Ford advertising department worked out the wording of the copy. At four forty-five in the afternoon, just fifteen minutes before its usual closing time, the agency in Philadelphia received a telephone message relaying the content of the advertisement and requesting its publication in every daily newspaper in the country on the following day.

The Ayer management hastily arranged for members of the Media Department and Printing Department to work overtime, and notified the telegraph office to be prepared for a flood of messages. In forty-seven minutes the advertisement had been set in type, revised, and proofs run off in finished form, in sizes varying from tabloid sheets to standard eight-column pages. Meanwhile, other members of the staff had prepared a list of over nineteen hundred newspapers in the United States and Canada in which the advertisement was to appear, together with the exact wording of the telegraphic message embodying the text and instructions for setting it up in type.

By eight o'clock the completed telegrams were in the telegraph office and 75 operators were busily sending them over the wires. Each telegram contained 588 words and, to ensure strict accuracy in the price quotations, was repeated back to Philadelphia by the receiving office before delivery to publishers. The telegraphic facilities of the entire country were, as a result, jammed to the limit, and at some points there were unavoidable delays.

Of the entire list of papers approximately sixteen hundred and fifty printed the advertisement on the following day, November 1. Some two hundred and seventy-five, mostly morning papers, were unable to include the copy in their morning edition; some had gone to press before the message reached them; others were unable to finish the composition and plating of so large an advertisement in time to get it into their early editions. But, within twenty-four hours of the receipt of the telephone message from Detroit to Philadelphia, the announcement of Ford's reduction in prices had appeared in morning and evening papers with a combined circulation of over thirty million copies. This was an achievement which needs no comment.[15]

CHAPTER XIII

SOME DEVELOPMENTS IN AYER COPY

ADVERTISEMENTS constitute the most immediate and tangible product of the work which an agency does for its clients. During the eighty years of Ayer history there have been many notable changes in the nature of advertising copy — so many, indeed, as to justify saying that within this period a revolution has taken place in the art of selling in print.

Some of the changes were apparently introduced by N. W. Ayer & Son; some originated with publishers; and some came from rival agencies, independent writers and artists, and other outside sources. Most of them are to be characterized as the embodiment of general developments in salesmanship, knowledge of human psychology, popular tastes and styles, graphic art, and the techniques of mechanical reproduction and printing. Whatever their origin, all the innovations and refinements have found their way into the Ayer agency and so into the advertisements which the firm has prepared for its clients. A complete history of Ayer copy would thus provide a fairly adequate story of the development of advertising copy in America generally for the years since 1869.

This aspect of N. W. Ayer & Son's history can never be fully treated, however, partly because much of the early copy has been destroyed, partly because of the tremendous amount of copy turned out. To present an adequate cross section of the agency's copy production in any one recent year would require a large volume in itself. Inevitably, therefore, any attempt to describe within a single chapter the Ayer advertisements turned out during three-quarters of a century must be incomplete, sketchy, and unsatisfactory from many points of view. The following presentation must, therefore, be regarded as a rapid survey, intended to indicate merely a few of the principal developments.[1]

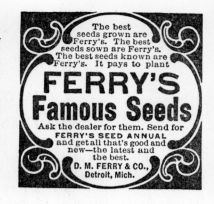

EXAMPLES OF EARLY COPY PLACED BY N. W. AYER & SON

FERRIS'
PATENT
GOOD SENSE

Style 210
FOR INFANTS.

Style 219.
Ladies' Medium Form, Long Waist.

Style 212,
CHILDREN, 4 to 6 years.

Style 216,
MISSES, 7 to 12 years.

Style 217,
MISSES, 13 to 17 years.

CORDED CORSET WAISTS.

BEST FOR HEALTH, COMFORT, WEAR AND FINISH.
EVERY PHYSICIAN WILL RECOMMEND THEM!
SUPERIOR WORKMANSHIP THROUGHOUT.

BUTTONS·FRONT instead of Clasps, thereby avoiding the injurious stiff steels in ordinary corsets.
TAPE-FASTENED BUTTONS are used together with our DUPLEX CORD EDGE BUTTON HOLES.
CORDS are placed in a special manner for stiffening instead of *Bones,* thereby leaving the garment
    pliable and flexible throughout.
SHOULDER STRAPS are adjustable, and being curved and broad at the back, are comfortable, supporting
    the *skirts* and *stockings* directly from the shoulders.
Physicians affirm that such support is *essential* to health.
SUPERIOR SHAPE.—These Corsets are not made after any "French Patterns," but are made to conform
    to the natural beauty of the figure, and with regard to the most approved rules of health.
CAN BE WASHED without losing the shape or causing any damage, as all the steels may be easily removed.

EVERY MOTHER SHOULD BUY "GOOD SENSE" CORSETS FOR HERSELF AND DAUGHTERS.

☞ The large demand for "GOOD SENSE" Waists gives an opportunity to unprincipled dealers
    to offer inferior imitations under various names, upon which they can make a larger profit, saying
    they are "about as good as the 'Good Sense' Waist." They are not as good.
The genuine "Good Sense" Waists are each stamped inside with the Trade Mark "GOOD SENSE."

FERRIS BROS., Sole Manufacturers, New York City.
FOR SALE BY FIRST-CLASS RETAILERS IN THE UNITED STATES, ENGLAND AND CANADA.

FERRIS BROS., 1888

[297]

Early Copy Placed by N. W. Ayer & Son, 1869–1890

When F. W. Ayer first opened his agency, American advertising copy was emerging from the stage in which nearly all advertisements were set up in agate type, single column, in the uniform and prosaic manner of today's classified advertising. The introduction of the cylinder press (1846) and the use of curved stereotype plates by newspapers (1861) had made the reproduction of illustrations extremely difficult and expensive. Publishers, moreover, were inclined to restrict the amount of space used by any one advertiser, on the theory that the greater the number of individual advertisements they could squeeze into their pages, the greater the appeal to readers. Many of them also refused to permit the use of illustrations in advertising, on the ground that the user would gain an unfair advantage over those who for any reason clung to type alone.[2]

In the late 1860's the ban against display (illustrations, fancy borders, and other special devices for catching the reader's eye) began to break down. The gray mass of closely printed advertisements was more than the average reader would digest, and individual advertisers insisted on using larger space, display material, and a variety of type faces, in order to break up the monotony and to make their advertisements stand out. Illustrated advertisements were more interesting for the readers and more profitable for their sponsors, and, as the mechanical difficulties of reproducing them were gradually overcome, they began to appear in large numbers.[3]

Three of the advertisements reproduced on page 296 are fairly representative of the copy placed by N. W. Ayer & Son between 1869 and 1880. The illustrations used in the pump and face-cream advertisements reveal both the crude commercial art work used at the time and the primitive technique of reproducing pictures for the commercial printed page before the advent of half-tone engraving. The originals were evidently woodcuts, reproduced by means of an electrotype. The Compound Oxygen copy shows the generous use of bold-faced Gothic type which was often used, in the absence of an illustration, to attract the reader's attention. It is a mild sample of the patent-medicine advertising which

James A. Garfield.

"If the power to do hard work is not talent, it is the best substitute for it." If you are not talented, don't fret, you can obtain power by eating the peerless

H=O Hornby's Oatmeal.

Uneeda Biscuit—a new form of Soda Biscuit, crisp, tender and delicious. Serve with every meal; take a box with you on your travels; splendid for sandwiches; perfect for picnics; unequaled for general use. Good food for everybody. Made to eat, not to keep.

Five Cents a package.

"Uneeda" is our Trademark. Moisture spoils biscuit; to preserve and deliver to the consumer our new and splendid **Uneeda Biscuit** as crisp, tender and delicious as when fresh from the oven, we have originated this moisture proof package. Carefully remove the wrapper; serve in this package. After the biscuit are eaten, you have a lunch box for school children. Patents pending.

NATIONAL BISCUIT COMPANY, 1899

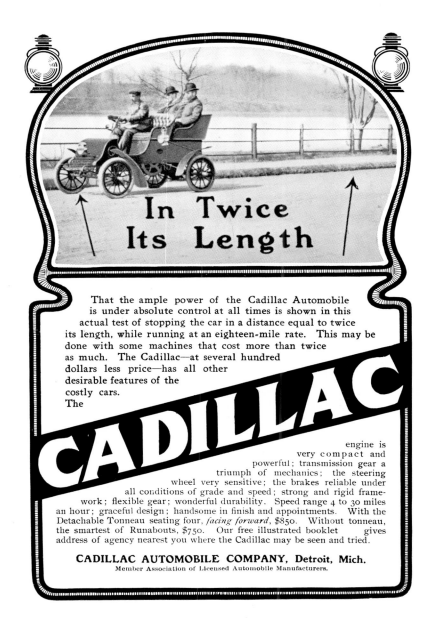

In Twice Its Length

That the ample power of the Cadillac Automobile is under absolute control at all times is shown in this actual test of stopping the car in a distance equal to twice its length, while running at an eighteen-mile rate. This may be done with some machines that cost more than twice as much. The Cadillac—at several hundred dollars less price—has all other desirable features of the costly cars. The

CADILLAC

engine is very compact and powerful; transmission gear a triumph of mechanics; the steering wheel very sensitive; the brakes reliable under all conditions of grade and speed; strong and rigid framework; flexible gear; wonderful durability. Speed range 4 to 30 miles an hour; graceful design; handsome in finish and appointments. With the Detachable Tonneau seating four, *facing forward*, $850. Without tonneau, the smartest of Runabouts, $750. Our free illustrated booklet gives address of agency nearest you where the Cadillac may be seen and tried.

CADILLAC AUTOMOBILE COMPANY, Detroit, Mich.

Member Association of Licensed Automobile Manufacturers.

CADILLAC AUTOMOBILE COMPANY, 1903

Steinway Pianos

WHEN purchasing a piano, no matter what consideration may be paramount, it is invariably best to buy a Steinway, for no other piano stands for the same high standard of piano construction.

If it is a question of quality and permanency of tone, of superior materials and workmanship, of proven durability—then the recorded judgment of the world's most eminent musical and scientific experts declares the Steinway the Standard of the World.

If it is a question of cost—then, all things considered, the Steinway is the greatest piano value for the price paid.

If it is a question of durability—then experience has proven that a Steinway Piano actually appreciates in value for the first ten years, and after that depreciates less both in intrinsic and market value than any other make.

For visible, tangible proof of Steinway primacy, examine a Miniature Grand at $800, or a Vertegrand at $550.

Each piano the criterion of its class.

**VERTEGRAND
PRICE $550**

**MINIATURE GRAND
PRICE $800**

Steinway Pianos can be purchased from any authorized Steinway Dealer at New York prices, with transportation cost added. Illustrated catalogue and booklet, "The Triumph of the Vertegrand," sent on request and mention of this Magazine.

STEINWAY & SONS
Steinway Hall
107 and 109 East 14th St., New York

Ayer handled in large quantities at that time, and it contains a prominent politician's endorsement, a forerunner of modern advertising practice.

The headline of the face-cream advertisement is an example of the "literary" turn which misguided copywriters often gave to advertisements of the period.[4] Considering the wild exaggerations of contemporary advertisements, we must conclude that the use of a physician's back-handed recommendation of the cream as "least harmful of all the skin preparations" shows amazing restraint. Then, as today, cosmetic advertisers hoped, by throwing in a few French phrases — no matter how awkwardly they might fit — to stimulate visions of Parisian style and beauty and thus to surround their products with an alluring atmosphere.

All three of these early examples are typical of the period in that they are crowded full of type of odd sizes and faces, even to the extent of running in lines vertically so as to fill some of the space left by the illustration. The judicious use of white space was plainly not appreciated, and the dominating idea seems to have been to buy the minimum amount of space and to cram it to the utmost with printed material. Such advertisements caught the reader's notice by hitting his eye with a mass of black ink, instead of attracting his interest by means of an impressive or arresting headline. The selection and arrangement of type was done in the Ayer printshop, but the agency probably had little or nothing to do with the text.

The advertisement on page 297 reflects the progress made between 1880 and 1888 in advertising copy. While the art work is not attractive, it was adequate to illustrate the product, and its reproduction is superior to earlier electrotypes. The entire effect is crowded and heavy, but it is less so than typical advertisements of the previous decade. Like most copy of the period, the Ferris advertisement contains several headlines and many factual details. The result was a diffusion of emphasis which probably left the reader with no lasting impression of the name or particular merits of the product.

One noteworthy feature of the advertisements which appeared before 1900 and even later was the general absence of strong primary selling appeals. It was usually assumed that the consumer would at once appreciate the value of a product the moment it was described or illustrated, and little attempt was made to stimulate a desire or induce the reader to act. In effect the advertisements were addressed to people who had already decided to purchase medicine, machinery, or clothing and were merely hesitating over which of several brands to buy. Men took demand for granted, apparently not realizing that people could be induced to recognize unfelt needs or feel new desires. As a result, the strongly persuasive note in modern advertising was absent. For the most part, the advertisements of the 'seventies and 'eighties constituted mere announcements that certain brands of merchandise were for sale. The accompanying illustrations, fancy borders, and other display devices were little more than signposts to draw attention to the announcement. The modern technique of creating an atmosphere or stimulating desires by means of imaginative art work was rarely if ever in evidence.

IMPROVEMENTS IN AYER COPY, 1890–1905

As we have already seen (pages 77–80), N. W. Ayer & Son was offering considerable assistance in the preparation of the copy used by its customers in the 'eighties, and by 1892 the firm had hired a man to devote his entire time to this work. To such specialists much credit is due for the improvements in copy which followed, though many other forces contributed — especially a growing recognition of the profits to be derived from effectively prepared advertisements.

It is evident, however, that the Ayer agency, like others of the time, was not content to obtain copy from a single source. In 1891 and again in 1894, the firm offered prizes for the best copy submitted to it for use in advertising the products of the N. K. Fairbank Company (makers of Fairy Soap and Gold Dust Washing Powder).[5] By such means the agency profited from the ideas and experience of many men as to the kind of copy which appealed to the public. From the clippings of advertisements and of articles on advertising copy which have been preserved in the Ayer scrapbooks, it is evident that men on the Ayer staff were attempting to check the methods of other advertising men against their own. To prepare the simple announcements of earlier advertising required no great talent or experience, but copy which would induce people to act called for ingenious ideas and skill in presentation; and advertising men in effect pooled their experience by studying one another's work.

One of the notable developments of the advertising copy of the 'nineties was the increased use of pictures of human beings, particularly children. In part this tendency may have been the result of a desire to make advertisements more interesting. Another factor was the development of the photo-electric process of engraving which made possible the inexpensive reproduction of pictures.[6] As late as 1888 woodcuts were the preferred medium of illustration for better copy,[7] but in the 'nineties half-tone reproductions of photographs and wash drawings were used for all types of advertising.[8] Among the Ayer advertisements of this period perhaps the best-known figures were the curly-headed boy who enthusiastically waved a mug of Hires' Root Beer for all to see, the winsome girl who advertised Fairbank's Fairy Soap by asking, "Have you a little fairy in your home?" and the strapping youngsters who demonstrated the health-giving qualities of Mellin's Food. Even more familiar, perhaps, was the boy in oilskins, created by the Ayer copymen in 1900 to dramatize the protective packaging of Uneeda biscuits.

Some of these developments in Ayer copy are evident in the advertisement on page 299. Although the text is brief, the fact that it is spread over two columns permitted it to be set in large, well-spaced type without any heaviness or crowding. The reader's desire for the product is still taken for granted, but interest is aroused by the quotation and picture of Garfield. (Another advertisement in this series featured Admiral Peary's picture — thus connecting polar exploration with commercial advertising more than three decades before the much publicized Byrd expeditions.) The illustration is from a line-cut, but two years earlier (1892) the Ayer Copy Department had turned to photographs and wash drawings for illustrative material, using half-tone engravings to reproduce them. In contrast with the earlier examples, the Hornby advertisement emphasized the trade-mark so that the reader was likely to remember the brand when he went to the grocery store. The Ferry seed advertisement on page 296

The Telephone's Burden

*E*VERY *day brings a new use—a new requirement. It is the Telephone's Burden not only to keep pace with business development, but to camp constantly a little across the frontier.*

Can you imagine a city, as cities once existed, made up of several "quarters," to each of which was confined a population which spoke a separate language?

You, as the average citizen, would be forced to learn several languages, or to go about the city with an interpreter - a process that would seriously interfere with your business.

If, instead of using different languages, the people of a city used *different telephone systems*, the result would be exactly the same. You would have to keep *each particular brand* of telephone. It is nobody's *fault* that this is so. The Bell companies are not responsible for the fact that a nation's convenience demands the use of one telephone system, any more than they are that *one language* for a nation is better than a collection of provincial dialects.

The associated Bell companies, with their singleness of purpose and unity of service, *are* responsible, however, for doing their utmost to *provide the system that wholly fits this recognized condition*—that prevents the endless and expensive confusion of many systems.

The Telephone's Burden is to embrace in *one* comprehensive system all that a city, or the whole country, needs in the way of telephone service. *This has made the telephone universal.*

To-day's work of carrying sixteen million messages—some of business, some of joy and some of sorrow—is not all of the *day's burden*, either.

Preparing for to-morrow's quota of message-passengers on this great national highway of speech is a labor quite as heavy as to-day's actual work.

For in the Bell service to-morrow never comes.

The associated Bell companies' eighty thousand workers are *always* preparing for it—always working to keep pace with the new requirements, forecast by to-day's routine.

People have rapidly developed this *new sense*—the sense of projecting speech. As the sense develops they are learning more about the telephone's possibilities. Twenty million minds are constantly finding new uses for it.

We must immediately adapt the entire Bell system to these new uses.

A realization of this widespread work should clear your mind of doubt, if any exists, that the associated Bell companies are working *with* and *for* the public, striving by the most progressive methods to provide a telephone service that will take your voice anywhere that your thought goes, or your friend goes, or your letter will travel—sometimes even farther than your imagination will carry you—, whether it is half way across the town or half way across the country.

The Bell service is diligently keeping pace with the country's progress, in full knowledge of existing conditions and the necessities of the future.

It goes to the public with such statements as this, in order that all telephone subscribers may understand the position it occupies as a utility, may make their demands on the service intelligently ; may readily see that rates must perforce be regulated and continue on an equitable business basis in order to provide the maximum number of subscribers—to make the system universal ; that they may fully understand that co-operation of subscriber and telephone company is the *surest guarantee* of good service.

American Telephone & Telegraph Company

And Its Associated Bell Companies

LOCAL AND LONG DISTANCE TELEPHONE

One Policy—One System Universal Service

UNITING OVER 4,000,000 TELEPHONES

AMERICAN TELEPHONE AND TELEGRAPH COMPANY, 1908

shows an attempt to obtain distinction within small space by means of a heavy, fancy border — a device which became increasingly popular in the 'nineties. The selection and arrangement of type show a substantial advance over the small advertisements of earlier decades, and the advertiser's name is prominently displayed to make a deeper impression on the reader.

No. 2 of the first series of advertisements promoting Uneeda biscuit is shown on page 300. It not only exemplifies the steady advance in advertising typography but shows that the Ayer copymen were acquiring a feeling for the effective arrangement of text and display — layout, in modern parlance. The fancy border reproduced the decoration of the package featured. The diagonal position of the package across the copy would naturally attract attention and differentiate the advertisement from others in the publication which used the conventional horizontal arrangement. Both the display and the text emphasized the brand name. This piece of copy thus has a unity which earlier efforts usually lacked. It is noteworthy, too, that the text attempted to sell biscuits in general, as well as the Uneeda brand, presenting this primary appeal by reference to appetizing qualities and convenience in serving, while pointing out the chief distinguishing merit of Uneeda biscuit: the new package which preserved their freshness. That is to say, the copy did not stop with urging people who were on the point of buying to choose Uneeda, but went on to arouse in others a desire to eat soda biscuits, attempting thus to increase the total consumption. The theory of this approach is that people who respond to the primary appeal to purchase biscuits will also be likely to respond to the secondary appeal to patronize the Uneeda brand, so that the increased consumption will reward the advertiser for making the broader appeal.[9]

In the early automobile advertisement opposite page 300 are evident the developments in typography and layout just after the opening of the present century. In response to the growing demand for realism, a photograph of the product in use was reproduced by means of a half-tone engraving. It is evident that the commercial photographer had not yet learned the art of dramatizing his subject convincingly; but the type is well chosen, and the advertisement succeeds fairly well in showing graphically one of the chief merits of the car that is featured. The decorative border represents an attempt to frame the picture and bind it to the trade-mark and text. Although the general effect is rather ponderous, there has been a definite attempt to give the advertisement symmetry and balance. The message of the text is mainly descriptive, containing no primary appeal to buy a car and only one weakly presented secondary appeal for patronage on the ground that the Cadillac had some features which were found in more expensive cars. It is apparent, however, that copywriters were learning to concentrate upon a single idea or feature which the reader could understand and remember, rather than confusing him by an attempt to emphasize several points.

The use of color in magazine advertising was an important innovation of the 1890's. Its first appearance in an American periodical was in the reproduction of Perrault's "The Awakening of Cupid," lithographed on the back cover of the *Youth's Companion* for May 4, 1893, to advertise Mellin's Food. Although the idea of printing the picture in color may have originated with the advertising department of *Youth's Companion,* the advertisement was placed by N. W. Ayer & Son. The cost was $14,000, which is said to have stood for ten years as the top price for one insertion in a single publication.[10] The Ayer agency scored another "first" in April, 1895, when it persuaded several leading magazine publishers to permit two-color inserts in their advertising sections, bearing the announcements of several products made by the N. K. Fairbanks Company.[11] Thereafter advertisements began to appear frequently in chromolithograph form. But, as Ayer pointed out at the time, "the wide use of color printing . . . awaits the overcoming of mechanical and financial obstacles,"[12] and it was not until about 1910 that the half-tone two-color and three-color processes were used extensively for advertising work. The colors were usually raw and glaring, and the art work was surprisingly amateurish, but improvement came with increased use. Color not only provided a new device for attracting attention but also made it possible to illustrate products and trade-marks more realistically and to create an atmosphere of richness and splendor which was particularly useful in advertising luxury products.

On the whole it is evident from the copy of the period 1890–

YOU Can Rise to a Position of Power

To hold a position of power you need to know more about *your particular business* than the men working beside you.

The secret of power and success is to KNOW EVERY-THING ABOUT SOMETHING.

Right along these lines the International Correspondence Schools train men for Positions of Power.

The I. C. S. gives you "concentrated" knowledge—specialized training —that enables you to *master* easily and quickly everything you need to know to work up to the Position of Power.

If you can read and write, the I.C.S. can help you to succeed in the occupation of your own selection. To be convinced of this, just mark and mail the coupon—the I. C. S. will send you detailed information as to just how you can be qualified to advance higher and higher.

Marking the coupon involves no obligation on your part—do it now.

GOETZ
All Silk Satin

A GOETZ* All Silk Satin lining lends tone and distinction to a suit or coat and gives unusual wearing service.

Rich, solid colors, an exquisite sheen, the soft smoothness of its weave and the name GOETZ woven in white on the selvage distinguish GOETZ All Silk Satin.

It can be bought by the yard at many of the better shops. It makes up beautifully into serviceable waists, dresses and petticoats.

GOETZ SILK MFG. CO.
Madison Avenue and 34th Street
New York

* "Gets"

GOETZ SILK MANUFACTURING COMPANY, 1916

1905 that the advertising industry, like the rest of the world, was making speedy advance in mechanical technique but was slow in learning to utilize fully the potential advantages of its technical achievements. And yet, when a comparison is made with the work of only twenty years earlier, it is clear that definite progress had been made on all fronts.

ADVERTISING COPY, 1906–1920

By 1906 advertising copy was fast reaching the form which is familiar to us today. To an increasing extent advertisers were using large space; full-page advertisements were becoming common; and illustrations were generally accepted as a necessary adjunct of copy. The advertisements of the decade before World War I appear crude and quaint today; but the advance lies more in the closer adaptation of technique to purpose and in the refinement of method than in fundamentals.

For example, the arrangement of the Steinway advertisement, opposite page 301, is frequently used today. While the decoration of the heading leaves much to be desired, it represents a proper attempt to adapt art work to the subject matter so as to create a suitable background for the product. Much art work was (and some still is today) merely tacked on to an advertisement, a pretty picture bearing no relation to the text. But copywriters were beginning to achieve a unity of text and decoration. The time had passed when the artist had merely to produce a picture. He had to provide art work for a specific piece of copy having a specific job to achieve in communicating an idea.[13] The heavy border of earlier advertisements was dropped, supplanted by generous use of white space, and the whole appearance is attractive, fresh, and clear. Like most automobile copy of today, this advertisement assumed that the reader did not need to be persuaded to buy the product, but merely stressed the merits of the Steinway piano compared with others. In the era before the widespread possession of motor cars, the ownership of a piano gave so much economic and social prestige that the assumption may have been sufficiently correct.

Possibly as a reaction to the "trust-busting" and "muckraking" era, large business firms began after 1900 to use adver-

CAMEL CIGARETTES

Are Here!

To cigarette smokers of America who smoke 5c, 10c, 15c, 20c, or 25c cigarettes:

Here are Camels — 20 cigarettes for 10 cents — a choice blend of specially selected Turkish and domestic tobaccos!

No man's money can buy a more delightful cigarette at any price.

High grade tobacco and expert blending gives *you* a cigarette that *will not* bite the tongue and leaves no *cigaretty* taste (you know what that means!) in the mouth.

Every time you buy another brand you're simply wasting money and pleasure.

On sale all along the line — 20 for 10c.

If your dealer can't supply you, send 10c for one package or $1.00 for a carton of ten packages (200 cigarettes), postage prepaid. After smoking one package, if you don't find CAMELS as represented, return the other nine packages and we will refund your money.

R. J. REYNOLDS TOBACCO CO., Winston-Salem, N. C.

Don't look for premiums or coupons, because the cost of tobaccos prohibits their use. You haven't enough money to buy a more delightful cigarette!

20 for 10 cents

R. J. REYNOLDS TOBACCO COMPANY, 1914

peach time

Every jar of preserves you put up saves buying expensive winter foods. Preserves are high in nutritive value and add variety to any meal.

The importance of the right sugar in preserving is great—order "Domino Granulated", which comes in sturdy cartons and strong cotton bags, free from the contaminating touch of flies, ants and dust.

SAVE THE FRUIT CROP

American Sugar Refining Company

"Sweeten it with Domino"

Granulated, Tablet, Powdered, Confectioners, Brown, Golden Syrup.

AMERICAN SUGAR REFINING COMPANY, 1920

tising as a means of developing a more favorable attitude toward their enterprises. One of the first pieces of institutional copy used for the American Telephone and Telegraph Company appears on page 304 and affords a good example of the way in which advertising was employed to educate the public. No one can be forced to read an advertisement; the copywriter must prepare his material in such a way that those who see it will be impelled to read it and carry away a favorable impression. This feat may be difficult when the subject is an institution rather than a product. The people to whom the message is addressed are often indifferent and absorb information only when it is handed out in small, appetizing doses. The caption "The Telephone's Burden" quickly drew attention to the copy and aroused a certain amount of curiosity as to what followed. The text told a story in a simple, convincing, and readable style. Its purpose was not so much to sell a product or service as to inform and explain, in order to calm any fears that people might have had regarding the growth of a telephone monopoly. Since the chief emphasis was to be on the message rather than on a trade-mark or product, the display material consisted of only a small, easily reproduced line sketch, and the company's trade-mark and signature were likewise subordinated.

Just as advertising men were learning to write copy text which appealed to human buying motives, both rational and emotional, and tended to induce action, so they were beginning to appreciate the value of atmosphere in an advertisement — to realize that text and illustration could be designed to relate a product to familiar or easily grasped concepts so as to give it, by association, an intangible but appreciated value, such as luxury, beauty, or success. The International Correspondence Schools' advertisement reproduced opposite page 306, for example, suggests the importance of business achievement and connects correspondence study with it.

A similar attempt to create atmosphere is to be seen opposite page 307. A model, wearing stylish garments made of the satin which the advertisement features, is shown reflected in a mirror of fashion. This example also illustrates the novel photographic effects which were popular in advertising before the copywriters

When You Hear a Little Cough

suspect worms. Hogs and shoats are afflicted with worms much more generally than most people suppose. Drive out the worms and tone up your hogs' systems at the same time by feeding Dr. Hess Stock Tonic.

It will start the runts and scrubs to growing better — gives them a chance to do their best. Feed it to your brood sows to relieve constipation. Stock Tonic is a conditioner and a true tonic. It makes hogs thrive.

Buy 2 pounds for each average hog, to start with. A responsible dealer in your town will sell it to you at an honest price and will refund your money if it does not do as claimed.

Why Pay the Peddler Twice My Price?

25-lb. Pail, $2.25; 100-lb. Drum, $7.50
Except in the far West, South and Canada
Smaller packages in proportion

DR. HESS & CLARK
Ashland, Ohio

Dr. HESS POULTRY PAN-A-CE-A
will start your pullets and moulted hens to laying

DR·HESS STOCK TONIC

Dr. Hess Dip and Disinfectant Kills Hog Lice

DR. HESS & CLARK, 1920

had learned to use photographs for effective illustration rather than eye-catching photographic tricks.

The copy in the advertisement on page 308 is interesting because it was the first of the series of newspaper advertisements which introduced Camel cigarettes to the American public. It followed a series of "teaser" advertisements which featured the headline, "The Camels Are Coming," with an illustration of the camel which was to be the trade-mark. The first copy, giving no inkling as to the product involved or the meaning of the advertisements, aroused widespread public curiosity and interest. Readers watched for the successive advertisements which solved the mystery, and the campaign accordingly impressed upon their minds the identifying trade-mark and brand name.

Trade-marks and brand names are also stressed in the pieces of copy shown on pages 309 and 310. In these advertisements, too, we have examples of the hand-lettered headlines which became common as advertisers used larger space and sought new ways of giving individuality to their copy.

The use of trade names and slogans is one development of the advertising agency's work which came into prominence during the years before World War I. These devices had originated long before, of course; but it is probably correct to say that they did not reach peak popularity until after 1905. The Ayer agency has created thousands of names and slogans, some of which now have great commercial value, while others quickly disappeared. Apparently it is impossible to determine beforehand whether a coined name or phrase will catch hold or fall flat; and advertising men, in order to give a product a distinctive verbal handle, are obliged to try almost anything.

Rise of Art in Advertising Copy, 1920–1939

Long before World War I the Ayer agency, like many others, was devoting considerable attention to the artistic side of the advertising which it prepared. As early as 1898 it had hired a commercial artist to assist with copy preparation, and in 1910 it had appointed an art director who was primarily responsible for the design and illustration of all the advertisements turned out. For many years, however, advertising art was an euphemistic

CANADA DRY GINGER ALE, INC., 1924

LIFT UP YOUR EYES !

How long ago did Wilbur Wright circle the drill field at Fort Myer while a few score of astonished witnesses stared open-mouthed at the sight of this first man to fly with wings for more than an hour? . . .

How long ago did the intrepid Bleriot hop in his flimsy, scorched monoplane from France to land precariously on the cliffs of Dover? . . .

How long ago did Graham-White circle the Statue of Liberty, struggling dexterously with his hands to maintain equilibrium? . . .

It seems only yesterday!

Yet in the few brief years since then man has learned a new technic in existence. He has explored the earth's atmosphere, his noble machine climbing on after human faculties had failed. . . . He has skimmed lightly over the impenetrable ice barriers of the polar regions. . . . He has taken in his flight not only the gray, fog-blanketed waters of the North Atlantic, but the empty blue seas of the South Atlantic—the Mediterranean—the Pacific—the Indian Ocean—the

Gulf of Mexico. . . . He has soared confidently over the sands of Sahara and the Great Arabian Desert, where only the camel had dared venture before. . . . He has skimmed the terrible dark jungles of the Amazon, and scaled high above the silent places of Alaska. . . . He has flown in squadrons from the Cape of Good Hope to London. . . . In squadrons he has circled South America. . . . *In squadrons he has circumnavigated the globe!*

And in the ordinary routine of transportation service he travels on fixed schedules over airways that streak the skies of Europe and North America. Mail. Passengers. Express. The world is rapidly assigning special duties to this safe vehicle that cuts time in two.

Is there any epoch in all history that has been so sudden in growth from birth to universal achievement? . . . so dramatic in its nature and accomplishments? . . . so rich in promises for the future?

Perhaps the most significant thing in

the great accomplishment of young Colonel Lindbergh is that in him the world sees *the first outstanding example of a generation that is born air-conscious!* Just as the past generation was born to steam, accepting railway transportation as an accomplished fact—and just as the present generation has accepted the automobile as a customary vehicle—so does the rising generation lift up its eyes to the skies! It may be hard still for many of us to accept the fact, but it is certain that the aeroplane will give as great an impetus to advancing civilization as did the automobile.

In this firm belief the Ford Motor Company is devoting its activities and resources to solving the problems that still face commercial aviation. In factory equipment, in laboratory experiment, in actual flights, the Ford Motor Company is establishing a foundation for one of the greatest industries the world has yet known. Within the last two years pilots have flown over the established Ford air routes, carrying freight, on regular daily schedules, a distance of more than 700,000 miles.

FORD MOTOR COMPANY

It is gay and brilliant at Buckingham Palace tonight . . . England's fairest daughters are being presented to Their Majesties' Court. Lady Ellen Parton,* daughter of the Dowager Countess of Wessex, arrives at the palace, wrapped in a coat of snow-white fur. A young lady blessed with exquisite beauty—blessed, too, with a complexion velvet-smooth, and a fresh and fragrant charm. ꘠ ꘠ The task of keeping her skin so lovely does not worry Lady Ellen. Ever since she can remember, her Countess-mother has taught her to use but one delightful toilet soap. Yardley's Old English Lavender. (We are told it is used by smart Parisian women, too.) For, in all the world there is no other soap, however rare, that will better cleanse, soothe or preserve the beauty of a fair skin than this. ꘠ ꘠ Seeking further acquaintance with the lovable fragrance of this soap, Lady Ellen has found it again in each of the Yardley products. England's best, they are—Old English Lavender Soap, "The Luxury Soap of the World," box of three cakes, $1, or 35c the cake; Lavender Water, $1; Face Powder, $1; Compact, $1; Talc, 50c; Sachet, 25c; Shampoo, 15c the cartridge; Bath Salts, $1; Bath Dusting Powder, $1.50. Yardley, 8 New Bond Street, London: 15-19 Madison Square, North, New York; also Toronto and Paris.* *Out of deference to our clientele we have refrained from using actual names.*

Yardley's Old English Lavender Soap

Established in 1770.

YARDLEY & COMPANY, LIMITED, 1928

phrase expressing more hope than reality in American advertisements. The work of such recognized artists as Jules Chéret and Toulouse-Lautrec had introduced genuine art into European poster advertising before 1900, and some of it had filtered through to the covers of American magazines; but, for a number of reasons, most of the art which went into periodical advertising in America continued to be amateurish, pedestrian stuff — often adequate, occasionally attractive, but never inspired. One difficulty was that few competent artists were willing to accept advertising commissions. Another obstacle was that the satisfactory reproduction of illustrations in color was not achieved till about 1910. Good work was possible in black and white, of course, but advertising men seemed to think of good art work mainly as pictures in color. Perhaps a more important factor was the limited demand for talented artists in advertising. The ultimate purpose of advertising is to convey a message, not to entertain the public or promote art; and both advertisers and agents were slow to realize that superior art work might be a means to this final goal by making their advertisements more effective.

By 1915, however, the business world was beginning to appreciate the commercial value of beauty. As it did so, advertising improved in aesthetic quality. A number of influences contributed to this change. The artistic taste of the entire nation had been improving. Sincere and able artists were finding a real challenge in commercial work and were learning how to adapt their skill to the purposes of advertising. The art of printing had improved to the point where good work would not be marred in the process of reproduction. Even the increasing circulation of periodicals was a factor, for space rates rose accordingly; and, when a business firm regularly had to spend hundreds of dollars for space in a single issue, it soon recognized the importance of putting into that space the best copy obtainable. Weak text or poor illustration might waste the entire investment.

There was, and still is, some confusion between advertising art and fine art. Many an advertiser has paid dearly for a drawing or painting which, though of real artistic merit, was of little worth as an advertisement. Fine art is not valued primarily for its usefulness or practicality. It is self-contained and its function is to express an artist's ideas, in the course of which it provides immediate aesthetic pleasure. Advertising art frequently affords the observer pleasure of a high order, but that is not its ultimate purpose. It is a commercial tool. It must attract attention, impress the observer with an idea, and (with some exceptions) stimulate him to action; and ordinarily it must do so not of itself but as a part of a complete advertisement. Thus the artist is not wholly free to express his own ideas in his own way: he has to present a point of view defined beforehand by someone else. An able artist may be given considerable scope for his imagination, but often his job is essentially to finish a rough sketch prepared by the agency's art director and layout man after numerous conferences with the client's advertising manager, the agency's account representatives, and the copywriter. Whatever art emerges from the composition and design depends upon its functional fitness.

Fine art may be simple or esoteric, but advertising art must be easily and quickly understood. Unlike a painting, the ordinary advertisement receives little more than a glance. Unless it accomplishes its purpose in that brief interval, it fails. Hence, good advertising art usually eliminates useless or unimportant details in order to aid the reader: it tries to picture the essence of its subject, not the exact appearance; to suggest and interpret rather than to give a literal representation of nature.

Advertising art resembles much fine art in that it frequently turns the mind away from immediate surroundings to some imagined and possibly more desirable world — from what one has to what one might have. And, like many examples of fine art, advertisements are sometimes criticized because they arouse discontent rather than ambition, or because they are sensual in their appeal, or because in striving for effect they depart from strict and detailed truth. The problem of realism versus romantic or idealistic treatment is as much vexed in advertising as it is in art.

Unlike fine art, advertising has to be popular at the very outset. It must interest people in the mass, must put before them the kind of words and pictures which, judging by their responses, make an impression upon their minds. A good artist is ahead of his times: he is concerned with posterity. But not so the adver-

You won't find a Recipe in your Cookbook for Making Six-Foot Waffles

❧ And you'll never find Hills Bros Roasting Coffee in Bulk. Instead they Roast a few Pounds at a time by a Continuous Process

MEASURING and mixing the ingredients—controlling the heat—can be done much more exactly when you make several small waffles than mammoth ones.

As you follow this principle, in cooking all food, so Hills Bros. apply a similar rule to roasting coffee. They roast their coffee a few pounds at a time by a continuous process instead of in bulk. As a result every berry is roasted evenly and the rich flavor of the rare blend is developed to the utmost.

No other coffee can taste like Hills Bros. because none is roasted the same way. Controlled Roasting is Hills Bros.' process exclusively. And the full-bodied flavor and rich aroma come to you in all their fulness because Hills Bros. Coffee is packed in vacuum.

Coffee-lovers everywhere overwhelmingly prefer Hills Bros. Coffee. Ask for it by name and look for the Arab, Hills Bros.' famous trade-mark, on the can.

Fresh from the original vacuum pack—easily opened with the key.

HILLS BROS COFFEE

© 1929

HILLS BROS. COFFEE, INC., 1929

IT'S A CINCH

FOR THE "CATERPILLAR"

Rough going the whole stretch, moving thousands of tons of blasted granite to form a dam! But the wide tracks crawl surely over the rocky fill and anchor the dump-wagon as it drops the load. Other "Caterpillars" move nimbly across soft fields, conquer the weather for increased profits. Build highways, grade roads. Speed things in the logging camps. Extra power, easy mobility, greater efficiency —"Caterpillar" track-type Tractors (there are five different sizes)— bring all these in one package.

•

Prices—f. o. b. Peoria, Ill.

TEN $1100
FIFTEEN 1450
TWENTY 1900
THIRTY 2375
SIXTY 4175

CATERPILLAR TRACTOR CO.
PEORIA, ILLINOIS and SAN LEANDRO, CALIFORNIA, U. S. A.
Track-type Tractors • Combines • Road Machinery
(THERE'S A "CATERPILLAR" DEALER NEAR YOU)

CATERPILLAR
REG. U. S.   PAT. OFF.
TRACTOR

Caterpillar Tractor Co., 1930

tising man. His product is usually as ephemeral as the radio programs and periodicals that carry it. A good advertising man has to look beyond the immediate present, but rarely does his job call for considerations extending much beyond next year. Like Hollywood's producers, he has to think of today's public taste; and, if the results seem obvious or vulgar at times, that is because they reflect the audience at which he has aimed, an audience whose cultural standards are not very high. But, in view of the very substantial progress in advertising copy since about 1910, it is a mistake to emphasize this aspect. The best advertising art is slightly ahead of the average person's taste, just as the best style in clothing is a little in advance of what the masses are wearing.

But let us turn to specific examples in which the progress of advertising art (including text, layout, and illustration) is evident. One of the first advertisements of Canada Dry Ginger Ale is shown on page 314. The effectiveness of the black and white art work and its adaptation to the text are noteworthy. So is the skill with which the copywriter dramatized his subject and gave it not only an attractive atmosphere but also a convincing reputation for quality.

Both the illustration and text of the Ford copy facing page 314 tell an interesting story in an impressive way. Only the shadow of an airplane is needed to convey the idea of the advertisement, which was to promote interest in aviation. The rest of the picture effectively portrays a sudden innovation in modern transport. The artistic skill with which the public was informed about progress in aviation, by means of this and other advertisements, contrasts strongly with the fumbling efforts of early advertising in support of the automobile.

The Ayer organization achieved some noteworthy art in connection with the Steinway advertising of the period of 1926–30. Many famous artists — among them Everett Henry, Rockwell Kent, N. C. Wyeth, Boris Anisfeld, Sergei Soudeikin, Ignacio Zuloaga, Pierre Brissaud, and Miguel Covarrubias — were commissioned to portray great musicians or paint interpretations of their music. These pictures were embodied in a series of color advertisements intended to stimulate public interest in music. By this strategy the Steinway Company was able to provide a rich and distinguished atmosphere for piano advertising as well as to tap a new source of sales — people who had not previously been actively interested in music. Space limitations and inability to reproduce in color made it inadvisable to include any examples of the series here (the original paintings may be seen in Steinway Hall, New York City), but opposite page 319 is shown a later Steinway advertisement which used fine photography to suggest the value of the piano in the education of children.

The copy reproduced opposite page 332 reveals a dignified appeal to a sophisticated audience. Throughout the Yardley advertisement there is an atmosphere of refinement, luxury, style, and beauty, well suited to the suggestion of exclusiveness contained in the text. The illustration gives a good example of the imaginative simplicity of modern advertising art. The Cannon advertisement (opposite this page) employed a somewhat similar approach, but it solved a more difficult problem in arousing interest in the ordinary household towel which offers less scope for imagination. The modernistic illustration did much to emphasize the style of the product and support the appeals to pride of possession and pleasure in the use of a product. Sex appeal is evident, too. The unashamed portrayal of the female figure here contrasts with the conscious modesty which is evident in the Ferris advertisement (page 297).

In the advertisement of Hills Bros. coffee (opposite page 316) we have a good example of modern newspaper copy. Both the headline and illustration are arresting, and the trick photographic effect serves a very definite purpose in driving home the idea embodied in headline and text.

The Caterpillar Tractor advertisement (opposite page 317) shows copy for an industrial product. The photograph gives a striking picture of the product in use, and the headline has been made into a partial frame in a manner which contributes force and variety to the layout. The brevity and simplicity of the text illustrates another tendency in modern copywriting.

The French Line copy (page 320) reveals a new note which began to appear in the advertising copy of the late 1920's, that of sophisticated humor. The headline parodied the popular title of

SO FAIR ... BUT NOT SO FRAIL

Look a little beyond the very evident smartness of the new Cannon towels you buy . . . to their softness and their gentle efficiency, to their long and faithful service at the lowest wages you ever paid to towels. Isn't it nice to know that the things you select for their color and good design excel on the practical side as well—that your most thrilling fancies are backed by the facts? ✷ Cannon towels are made for work and wear—and charm. The latest styles simply make bathrooms over—bring new light and new life. Their patterns are equally clear and decorative on both sides. New designs and shades were suited to new ideas in tubs and tiling and color schemes. There are Cannon face cloths and bath mats to match the new towels, purchasable singly and in ensemble sets. How easy now to have perfect harmony—in one room at least, without gambling your time and trouble and money ✷ Cannon towels are thrifty. The prices of the advanced styles are kept down by vast output in the standard grades. Millions are made every week—more than the totals of all other towels combined. The result is low cost for high quality, always. Whenever you find the Cannon label you have found a real bargain in beauty and service. . . . Cannon Mills, Inc., 70 Worth Street, New York City. *The producers of* LAVENLAWN, *the finest sheet in the world.*

1: *Absorbency Facts.* Small squares of fabric were cut from various makes of towels of equal grades. The Cannon materials soaked up water and sank to the bottom of the glass almost at once. Others took much longer—in some cases, as much as ten minutes more. **2:** *Service Facts.* A great hotel sewed together typical towels of all the leading brands—then laundered the "sheet" a hundred times. Cannon towels showed far less wear at the end of this strenuous test than any others. **3:** *Value Facts:* Shoppers visited leading stores in twelve major cities and bought towels by pairs, one Cannon towel and one other towel of similar style and the same price. All were weighed on delicate scales—and the balance in favor of Cannon was more than 7%. Thus, every 92 cents you spend for Cannon towels brings you a full dollar's value.

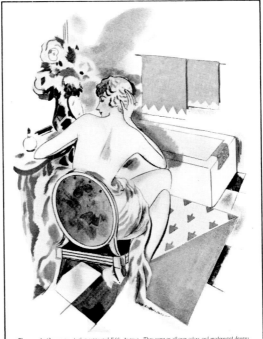

These are the Cannon towels that captivated Fifth Avenue. They come in all-over colors and modernized designs. They have two right sides, two bright sides—both equally decorative. New colors are rose, peach, turquoise, jade, maize, orchid—guaranteed fast. Typical Cannon values—75c and more for the bath towels—at your own store or shop . . . now. There are Cannon face cloths and bath mats to match—sold singly and in ensemble sets. Cannon towels may be had in many other styles, to suit any taste, at prices from 25c to $2.50.)

CANNON TOWELS

CANNON MILLS, INC., 1930

STUDY OF A CHILD AT THE PIANO, BY ANTON BRUEHL

Song at Morning

To A CHILD all things are lovely . . . and music, like some golden dawn, glows with a strange delight. The song of a thrush . . . a melody in the air . . . a voice singing . . . the morning of life is filled with enchanted sounds.

That music shall continue to illumine the child's inward life is the aspiration of all intelligent parents. And upon parent, rather than child, devolves that responsibility. Thus, instruction should be early and continuous . . . the teacher accomplished, and sympathetic. And the piano, which daily shapes and fashions a child's perception of tone, should, above all, be wisely and thoughtfully chosen.

Your children deserve a Steinway. Richly associated with the creative and interpretative history of the art, this instrument, pre-eminently, should foster their musical education. Wagner and Liszt used the Steinway in their time. . . . Paderewski, Rachmaninoff, Hofmann and Horowitz use it today. Its brilliant voice sounds through the great conservatories of Europe and America . . . comes, clear and strong, from the foremost radio broadcasting stations. In concert hall and private home alike, the Steinway stands superbly and triumphantly alone.

Yet the Steinway, which will serve your children and their children after them, is really not an expensive piano. It belongs, and has always belonged, to the home of modest income. You can have a Steinway delivered at once simply by making a small down payment on the purchase price. The balance will then be extended over a convenient period.

THE NEW STEINWAY ACCELERATED ACTION
The Steinway has long been pre-eminent among pianos for its rare tone and exquisite perfection of action. Yet the Steinway with Accelerated Action is even more sensitive, richer in tone quality, than its distinguished predecessors! See . . . hear . . . play this piano today! You will be astonished that even the most difficult passages can be interpreted with incredible lightness and precision of touch . . . that for child and concert artist, playing is so much easier, and requires so little effort.

THE STEINWAY BABY GRAND FOR AS LITTLE AS
$1175 SMALL DOWN PAYMENT
BALANCE CONVENIENTLY DISTRIBUTED
ALL PRICES PLUS TRANSPORTATION

There is a Steinway dealer in your community, or near you, through whom you may purchase a new Steinway with a small deposit — the balance distributed over a convenient period. Used pianos are accepted in partial exchange. STEINWAY & SONS, Steinway Hall, 109 W. 57th Street, New York City, just west of Sixth Avenue.

THE INSTRUMENT OF THE IMMORTALS
STEINWAY

STEINWAY & SONS, 1934

the day. This, with the simple, crude, almost grotesque cartoon, provided a light touch which stood in contrast not only with other steamship advertising but also with the depression in public spirits in 1933. This kind of copy is difficult: it must be extremely good or it will fall flat. By employing the well-known member of the *New Yorker* staff, the Ayer agency assured itself that the illustration would be effective.

Shortly after 1930 the American public heard for the first time about the surrealist school of artists. The first exhibitions puzzled some spectators and shocked others, but the technique made a lasting impression. The Ayer agency lost no time in applying it to the illustration of certain advertisements which presented opportunities for unusual treatment. One striking example by A. M. Cassandre is shown opposite page 320. The effect of the original is partly lost in the reproduction in black and white on reduced scale, but there is no mistaking the clever way in which apparently contrasting elements of the design were unified neatly and simply to illustrate the headline. Here surely is modern art of the first rank, modern advertising of the best.

Another example of the same type of approach is to be seen opposite page 321. The artist took a drab industrial subject and dramatized it in a most vivid and original fashion. Note the reversed perspective of the box which at once catches and holds attention. In this illustration, as in the Cassandre painting, one sees plainly the studied simplicity, the incisive symbolism, and the forceful clarity of good advertising art. Such advertisements do more than is often realized to familiarize the public with current developments in fine art, without neglecting their primary selling work.

The Ford advertisement opposite page 322 provides a good example of modern institutional advertising. It stresses personalities and public service, and because it was based upon a wide knowledge of public opinion, it carried conviction. The same is true of the Bell Telephone advertisement opposite page 331. In the latter, however, there is less need for text, and the chief reliance for effect is upon the photograph, which tells almost without explanation the story of the Telephone Company's efforts to catch up with the postwar problem of expanding telephone facilities for civilians.

I AM A FUGITIVE

from Chilblains!

"THEY say he has no weakness" . . . but "Here's a study for you, Doctor —he faints". . . yes, at the very thought of spending a stricken winter in this bleak land of ailing antrums, damp soles, and chilblains.

So here he is in North Africa, soothing his sinuses with balmy air and vitamin D . . . a fugitive sun-worshiper whose wintry complexes are sublimated with a French Line Mediterranean Cruise. For snowplows have no place in the picturesque bazaars of Algiers; there's no ice-skating on the Bay of Naples; the golden Riviera does not induce "codes id de head"; and they never wear galoshes in Majorca.

He has escaped! . . . And the *De Grasse,* his Argosy, is an ideally comfortable home for cruising. Its salons are charming and airy . . . its French Line cooking is world-famous . . . its English-speaking stewards are perfectly trained to know what you want before *you* do . . . and the ridiculously low rate of $365 and up, *makes winter cost you almost as little, as $10-a-day!* It's economical; it's restful; and it's diverting. So we're reminding you now to see your nearest travel agent right away. He'll gladly arrange (without charge) to make you a French Line fugitive from winter. . . . French Line, 19 State Street, New York City.

French Line

NORTH ATLANTIC SAILINGS: ILE DE FRANCE, April 8 • PARIS, January 20, February 10, March 4 and 24 • CHAMPLAIN, February 18, March 11, April 1 • LAFAYETTE, January 28, March 18 • ROCHAMBEAU, March 25

2 Mediterranean Cruises • 36 days February 4 and March 15 • $365 up

Vigo - Lisbon - Casablanca - Gibraltar Algiers - Naples - Ajaccio - Monte Carlo Marseilles - Cannes - Majorca - St. Michael

(Shore trips arranged with Thomas Cook & Son)

FRENCH LINE, 1933

[320]

A. M. CASSANDRE 36

PINEAPPLE JUICE FROM HAWAII

Hawaiian Pineapple Company, Ltd., 1937

HARMONY

Men,
materials
and methods
synchronized for
the production
of better paperboard
packages

zepf

CONTAINER CORPORATION OF AMERICA

Recent Copy, 1939–1948

The past decade has seen no major innovation in advertising copy, but the few examples of Ayer work reproduced here for the period reflect continuous progress and refinement in the art of communication through the printed advertisement. The layouts are simple and clear-cut, making generous use of white space. The headlines are incisive and brief, and the illustrations are fresh and cogent, with an increasing use of color photography. The text is straightforward, interesting, and short. In general there has been a tendency to concentrate on presenting a single theme effectively, rather than to attempt covering a number of ideas.

The advertisement for Comptometers (opposite page 323) illustrates one approach to the problem of drawing the reader's attention to a product which is not outwardly of interest to the average person. By humorously portraying an obsolete character type, the copy arouses interest and holds it to the end. The text is brief, amusing, and easily read. Note the simple, open, and balanced arrangement of the layout. Despite the minuscule display given the names of the product and its manufacturer, readership tests have proven that a high proportion of readers noticed the advertisement and correctly associated it with the Comptometer.

In the advertisement of the National Dairy Products Corporation (opposite page 328) we have another example of institutional advertising for a rather prosaic commodity — milk, which was made more interesting because it was related to the war effort. The picture and the headline tell the story at a glance, while the text quickly elaborates and amplifies the message to be conveyed.

Two examples, the advertisement for De Beers (opposite page 324) and that for Yardley (opposite page 332) show recent treatments of luxury commodities. The object of the De Beers copy is to enhance the prestige of diamonds in the public mind and to give support to reputable jewelers as the agency from which to buy diamonds. The Derain painting (reproduced in color), the headline, and the text combine admirably to this end. Here again the simple, clear-cut layout and the open-set, modern type contribute to the effectiveness of the advertisement. The Yardley advertisement — by a deft combination of a photograph and art

work, reproducing color accents against a gray background —
blends the atmosphere of London's Bond Street with the picture
of an attractive, well-groomed woman so as to identify Yardley
products with cosmopolitan good taste. The layout is simple and
fresh, yet it is less obtrusively modern and formal than the De
Beers copy. Even the choice and arrangement of type faces has
been made to enhance the total effect: note how the starkly
modern type of the De Beers advertisement, set flush at the margins, differs from the more conventional type face of the Yardley
copy, which has been set with uneven margins to soften the effect of the type block. The average reader is unconscious of such
subtleties, and yet they do contribute to the total impression that
he receives. By comparing the recent Yardley copy with the example for the same firm twenty years earlier (opposite page 315),
one can again note advances in copy technique.

The Boeing copy (opposite page 325) is fairly typical of good
war-time institutional copy. The easily understood photograph,
the simple title with an unusual twist, and the small but impressive display of the advertiser's name quickly make an impression
on the reader, and the text amplifies the communication. By comparing this example and the Ford advertisement for aviation (opposite page 314) — particularly as to text — one can see progress
in the form of sharper, simpler presentation. One may also usefully compare it with the advertisement for the U. S. Army Recruiting Service (opposite page 330). The layouts are similar in
their arrangement and simplicity, but the recruiting advertisement (using a color photograph) had an immediate selling job
to do instead of a long-run institutional objective. Hence its headline is aimed directly at male readers, and the text is both persuasive and informational in its emphasis upon men of quality.

Automobile advertisements present special difficulties because
it is hard in printed copy to set forth in easily grasped terms the
distinctive, technical merits of a given make of car. This problem
was aggravated during World War II, when no cars were manufactured for civilian use and yet manufacturers wanted to keep
their names before the public. The Plymouth copy (opposite page
329) shows one Ayer solution: a homely, humorous illustration,
effectively reinforced by an expressive headline, which struck a

The Fords Tell Their Plans
for 1939

Henry and Edsel Ford, on the occasion of the 35th anniversary of the founding of the Ford Motor Company, June 16, 1938

IF WE KNEW anything better we could do for the country than make good motor cars, we would do it.

By every one doing his best in the job he thinks most useful, this country is going to do regain its momentum. We have tried to do our best in our job.

When business was suddenly halted in its recovery more than a year ago, we determined that we should keep going anyway, if not at full-volume motor car production, then at getting ready for greater motor car values that would help future production.

EXPANDING FOR THE FUTURE

We began to build 34 million dollars' worth of new plants and equipment. We felt that if we could not employ all our men building motor cars, we would employ as many as we could building better production facilities.

We were told, of course, that this was no time for expansion, that a wiser business policy would be to "hold everything"—which means, stop everything. But no one ever got anywhere standing still.

Besides, we are not defeatists. We do not believe this country has seen its best days. We believe this country is yet in the infancy of its growth. We believe that every atom of faith invested in our Country and our People will be amply justified by the future. We believe America is just beginning. Never yet have our People seen real Prosperity. Never yet have we seen adequate Production. But we shall see it! That is the assurance in which we have built.

Business is not just coming back. It will have to be brought back. That is now becoming well understood in this country; for that reason 1939 will be a co-operative year. Manufacturers, sellers and buyers will co-operate to bring back the business that is waiting to be brought back.

This construction program is almost completed. It has increased activity and payrolls in a number of related industries. It has given us better facilities for building better cars and trucks, and eventually our new tractor which is being perfected.

THIS MEANS MORE VALUE

The current program has provided a new tire plant, which will turn out a part of our tire requirements . . . a new tool and die plant that will help us cut the cost of dies . . . and a steel-press plant that will enable us to make more of our own automobile bodies. These are in addition to the plants we already had for producing glass, iron, steel, plastics, and many other things.

We don't supply all our own needs, of course, and never expect to. The Ford engine is one thing that no one's hand touches but ours. Of nearly everything else we use we build some quantity ourselves, to find, if possible, better and

more economical ways of doing it. The experience and knowledge we gain are freely shared with our suppliers, and with other industries.

We take no profit on anything we make for ourselves and sell to ourselves. Every operation, from the Ford ships which first bring iron ore to the Rouge, is figured at accurate cost. The only profit is on the finished result—the car or truck as it comes off the line. Some years, there is no profit for us. But we see to it that our customers always profit. A basic article of our business creed is that no sale is economically constructive unless it profits the buyer as much as or more than the seller.

Our new plants have helped us build more value into all our cars for 1939. That means more profit on the purchase to the purchaser.

We have not cut quality to reduce costs.

We simply will not build anything inferior.

NEW TESTING EQUIPMENT

While we were putting up new plants to produce them, we constructed new equipment to test them. The first weather tunnel of its kind ever built for automobile research went into operation at our laboratories this year.

It makes any kind of weather to order. The weather it delivers every day would take months to find in Nature. Our cars are weather-tested to give you good service in any climate anywhere.

In other tests, every part of the car is punished unmercifully. Then our engineers tear it down to see if they can find abnormal wear or any sign of weakness.

The money we spend on tests saves you money on repairs. And your family car is safer and more dependable when we put it in your hands.

THE NEW CARS

We have two new Ford cars for 1939—better and better looking—but we also have an entirely new car.

It's called the Mercury 8. It fits into our line between the De Luxe Ford and the Lincoln-Zephyr. It is larger than the Ford, with 116-inch wheelbase, hydraulic brakes, and a new 95-horsepower V-type 8-cylinder engine.

We know that our 1939 cars are cars of good quality. We think they're fine values in their price classes.

With new cars, new plants, new equipment, the whole Ford organization is geared to go forward.

FORD MOTOR COMPANY, Dearborn, Michigan

Uncle Ira
is a screwball !

Remember Uncle Ira?

Everybody used to say he was a genius. He had a head for figures—"The Lightning Calculator," he used to be called.

When we were kids, we'd say, "Uncle Ira, how much is seven hundred and thirty-one times twenty-six?"

"Nineteen thousand and six point zero!" Uncle Ira would say, right off.

And then we would figure it out on paper, and sure enough, the answer was 19,006.

Today, everybody says Uncle Ira is just a harmless old screwball. He's bitter and cantankerous, and he doesn't mind telling you why.

"Look at me!" says Uncle Ira sadly. "A genius! A man the Almighty blessed with a great gift! But what good is it, in this allfired crazy world?

"Why, any young snip of a girl can set down to one of them new-fangled* Comptometers, and calculate faster than I can! With a machine, mind you! Add, subtract, multiply and divide by finaglin' with buttons! It ain't *human!*

"Why, those consarned contraptions even got a jigger** that eliminates errors! I tell you, the folks*** that make them Comptometers had ought to pay me damages!"

---

* *Anything younger than himself is new-fangled to Uncle Ira. Comptometers have been serving Business and Industry for 54 years.*

** *The Controlled-Key, which positively checks all imperfect keystrokes, and helps to make possible the Comptometer's remarkable first-time accuracy.*

*** *Felt & Tarrant Mfg. Co., Chicago, Ill.*

FELT & TARRANT MFG. CO., 1940

responsive chord in every prospective car-buyer's heart and stamped the name Plymouth in his mind.

In the Kellogg advertisement, page 334, we have an example of recent newspaper copy dealing with a new breakfast cereal. It employs the cartoon technique so popular in recent years, but avoids the blatant sex appeals and cheap sensationalism which have marred so much of this type of copy. It is informative, readable, and very much to the point, without resorting to exaggerated claims on behalf of the product.

The next-to-the-last selection, the Carrier advertisement (opposite page 333), shows a new illustrative technique used imaginatively to promote air conditioning and refrigeration equipment. The object was to convey the idea of air conditioning, rather than the machinery which does it. The photogramatic plate effectively communicates at a glance some familiar symbols of spring — and does so by a new technique which effectively distinguishes the advertisement from the usual run of advertising copy which would be its normal accompaniment in a magazine.

It is impossible to show here advertisements in their context, surrounded by other advertisements in black and white and in color, promoting all types of products. Yet that context must be kept in mind in appraising the effectiveness of advertising copy. The De Beers advertisement is inherently distinctive, but it was even more distinguished in its proper background because it appeared when most other advertisements, in the interests of realism and economy, were illustrated by means of color photography. Similarly the Carrier advertisement was unusually effective because it appeared in competition with many advertisements in the tabloid or display style of copy, combining numerous photographs, blatant headlines, and tag-indicators. Thus, one of the major problems of the art director is to obtain layouts and art work which not only make an advertisement attractive in itself, but also give it strong individuality when it appears beside competing advertisements.

Awards for Advertising Copy

It would be both interesting and helpful to evaluate the relative merits of Ayer copy over a long period, but the judgment of a

TABLE 8

POINTS SCORED BY AGENCIES FOR ADVERTISING COPY, 1928[a]

According to Four Independent Judges

Agency	Number of Advertisements Given a Place[b]	General Advertising Effectiveness	Points Awarded by Judges[c]				Total	Average per Advertisement Placed
			Copy	Art	Layout	Typography		
N. W. Ayer & Son.........	13	199	42	41	40	26	348	26.9
Batten, Barton, Durstine & Osborn............	9	99	25	18	13	14	169	18.8
The Blackman Co...........	6	90	14	23	17	13	157	26.2
Young & Rubicam..........	6	87	18	20	17	15	157	26.2
Calkins & Holden..........	6	78	15	18	14	11	136	22.7
Lennen & Mitchell.........	5	78	20	15	16	11	140	28.0
J. Walter Thompson.......	5	65	13	15	12	8	113	22.6
Charles Daniel Frey.......	5	58	7	13	11	4	93	18.6
MacManus.................	5	46	8	8	10	7	79	15.8

[a] Only the agencies which won at least five places in the final selection have been included in the table.

[b] This does not include the advertisements which were given honorable mention.

[c] The model score was 5 points for general advertising effectiveness, 1 for copy, 1 for art, 1 for layout, and 1 for typography, making possible a total of 9 points from each judge or a grand total of 36 points for a given advertisement.

SOURCE: *The Advertising Parade*, Robert Hunt, editor (N. Y., 1930).

SONG AT CHRISTMAS ✳ Of stars—and candle-flames—and crystals of snow—and tinsel gleams. . . . Of all the small and lovely lights that prick the sky and deck the world in joyous celebration of this holy day, there is one which, once part of your Christmas treasure, will never be extinguished. ✳ Throughout the year—and all the years to come—the light of the diamonds you receive will

PAINTING BY ANDRÉ DERAIN, FROM THE DE BEERS COLLECTION

Comparative sizes of Unmounted Quality Diamonds. (Exact weights shown are infrequent.) Size alone does not determine values. Purity, color and excellence of cutting affect the price.

This is one-half ⬤ carat

One-carat diamond ⬤ is actual unmounted size

Two carats ⬤ shows as it appears before mounting

Three carats ⬤ (All brilliant cut)

shine forth . . . a precious message of devotion from one who loves you. ✳ If you are asked to participate in their selection, or if you intend to make this gift of gifts to other loved ones, see that the diamonds that compose it are as notable for pure color, absence of imperfections and for exquisite cut as they are for size. Make a trusted jeweler your adviser for such important purchases. De Beers Consolidated Mines, Ltd., and Associated Companies.

DE BEERS CONSOLIDATED MINES, LTD.,
AND ASSOCIATED COMPANIES, 1940

Bombs for Breakfast

As the man says: whatever goes up must come down. In the case of airplane-planted bombs, the all-important question is *where*.

By official count, a remarkably high percentage of the bombs released from Boeing Flying Fortresses* come down where they'll raise the most hell with Axis hopes: at sea, on battleships, cruisers, transports, destroyers, aircraft carriers; on land, atop factories, arsenals, railroads, power-plants, munitions dumps, docks, canals and vital supply centers.

There are two things that make the Flying Fortress a mailed glove on Freedom's aerial fist.

One is *quality*: the ability to fly a swift, straight course to the target in spite of enemy interceptors . . . and, by virtue of great flight-stability, provide a perfect (and heavily armored) "platform" from which to let loose several tons of death and/or destruction. Score one for Boeing engineers.

The other is *quantity*: the rate at which these heavy bombers are built under the concentrated short-flow multiple-line factory system which results in "production density". . . maximum output per man, machine and unit of plant space. Score one for Boeing production men.

There'll come a V-day when Boeing engineering and "productioneering" will turn from paths of war to paths of peace . . . from making the world unsafe for tyranny to making the new, free world a better, brighter one in which to live.

For in designing and building Flying Fortresses, Stratoliners, globe-girdling Clippers and other airplanes, Boeing continually acquires new "know-how" in many fields of engineering: electrical, structural, soundproofing, heating, radio and a score of others. It's the kind of "know-how" that helps to win wars, and will some day help to make peacetime products better and cheaper.*

BOEING AIRPLANE CO., 1943

single person is of very limited value. Nowhere do personal opinions differ more widely than in the estimation of advertising copy, even among advertising men themselves. It would therefore be exceedingly difficult to obtain a reliable opinion of Ayer copy as a whole in comparison with that of other agencies. In recent years, however, there have been attempts to appraise both advertising copy and advertising art, and the judges' decisions indicate that N. W. Ayer & Son stands among the leaders in the production of effective copy.

The results of one appraisal of copy for the year 1928 are partially summarized in Table 8. Several men interested in advertising made a preliminary selection of what seemed to them the best advertisements of the year. Nearly three hundred pieces of copy were thus chosen and submitted to four independent judges, who were asked to select the best of them and grade their merits. The final selection included only the advertisements which had been chosen for merit by at least two of the judges and totaled 146 pieces of copy. As the table shows, N. W. Ayer & Son placed more of the advertisements finally selected than any other agency by a substantial margin, and it received high scores on all accounts. Unfortunately Table 8 covers only a single year's work and gives no clue to the effectiveness of the Ayer Copy Department over any considerable period of the firm's history.

In 1921 the Art Directors Club of New York began holding annual exhibitions of advertising art, and the awards for merit which have been made each year indicate achievement in one important aspect of advertising copy. Table 9 presents a ranking of the leading agencies according to the awards conferred by the Art Directors Club for art work which they handled. Taking the entire eighteen exhibitions, N. W. Ayer & Son stood well in the lead in the number of medals, honorable mentions, and total awards received.

In one sense Table 9 is misleading, for the awards are for the art work itself; and the chief recognition belongs to the artist who prepared it. It must be said, however, that an agency not only chooses the artist but also has a considerable voice in the final form of his work, and it is therefore entitled to share in any honors which the finished art work happens to win. Moreover,

TABLE 9

AWARDS FOR ADVERTISING ART, 1921–1948[a]

Annual Exhibitions of the Art Directors Club of New York

Agencies[b]	1921		1922		1924[c]		1925		1926		1927		1928		1929		1930		1931		1932		1933		1934		1935		Totals 1921–1935		
	M	O	M	O	M	O	M	O	M	O	M	O	M	O	M	O	M	O	M	O	M	O	M	O	M	O	M	O	M	O	T
N. W. Ayer & Son, Inc.	–	–	–	–	2	1	–	–	2	2	–	6	1	4	1	1	2	2	1	4	2	1	1	4	–	3	–	–	13	28	41
J. Walter Thompson, Inc.	–	2	1	2	2	2	1	3	1	2	2	5	–	–	2	1	1	3	1	1	2	1	1	–	4	1	1	3	11	31	42
Young & Rubicam, Inc.[d]	–	–	1	–	1	1	1	1	1	–	1	–	–	–	2	1	3	–	–	–	3	–	2	–	2	1	2	1	2	9	11
George Batten Co.	1	–	–	–	–	–	–	1	–	–	–	1	1		1		2	–	3	–	3	–	1	–	1	–	2		3	21	24
Barton, Durstine & Osborn.	2	–	–	–	2	1	2	–	–	–	–	1			1	2	1	2	–	3	–	3	1	–	1	–	1	–			
Calkins & Holden.	1	–	–	–	1	2	1	1	1	1	1	1	1	–	1	2	4	1	2	–	–	1	1	–	1	–	1	–	10	13	23
McCann-Erickson, Inc.	–	–	–	–	–	–	–	–	–	–	–	–	–	–	–	–	1	–	1	–	1	–	–	1	–	1	1	–	1	1	2
Compton Co.[e]	–	–	–	1	–	–	1	–	1	–	1	–	–	–	1	–	1	1	1	1	1	3	1	1	1	1	1	–	4	8	12
Newell-Emmett Co.	–	–	1	2	–	1	2	–	–	–	1	–	–	–	1	–	–	1	1	–	3	–	1	–	1	–	1	–	1	9	10
Foote, Cone & Belding, Inc. (Formerly Lord & Thomas)	–	–	–	–	–	–	–	–	–	–	–	1	–	–	–	1	–	–	–	1	–	1	–	–	–	1	–	2	–	5	5
Campbell-Ewald Co.	–	–	–	–	–	–	–	–	–	–	–	–	–	–	–	1	–	1	–	1	–	1	1	1	2	1	3	–	3	4	7
Federal Advtg. Co.	–	–	1	1	–	–	–	1	–	2	–	1	1	–	–	–	–	–	–	–	–	–	–	–	1	–	1	–	1	5	6
Lennen & Mitchell.	–	–	–	–	–	–	–	–	–	–	–	–	–	–	–	–	–	–	1	–	–	–	–	–	–	–	1	–	1	–	1
J. M. Mathes[f]	–	–	–	–	–	–	–	–	–	–	–	–	–	–	–	–	–	–	–	–	–	–	–	–	–	–	–	–	–	–	–

TABLE 9 (continued)

Agencies^b	1936 M	1936 O	1937 M	1937 O	1938 M	1938 O	1939 M	1939 O	1940 M	1940 O	1941 M	1941 O	1942 M	1942 O	1943 M	1943 O	1944 M	1944 O	1945 M	1945 O	1946 M	1946 O	1947 M	1947 O	1948 M	1948 O	Totals 1936–1948 M	O	T	Grand Totals 1921–1948 M	O	T
N. W. Ayer & Son, Inc.	–	4	3	–	1	4	2	4	2	3	–	–	6	–	2	2	3	–	2	9	–	2	2	1	–	–	11	41	52	24	69	93
J. Walter Thompson, Inc.	–	–	2	1	1	1	1	1	–	1	1	–	3	1	1	1	1	1	–	3	2	–	1	–	–	–	11	8	19	22	39	61
Young & Rubicam, Inc.^d	1	1	8	–	–	3	–	–	1	4	1	5	1	1	1	2	–	–	–	–	–	–	–	–	–	–	4	24	28	6	33	39
Batten, Barton, Durstine & Osborn	2	–	–	–	–	1	1	–	–	–	–	–	1	1	–	–	–	–	–	–	–	–	–	–	–	–	1	4	5	4	25	29
Calkins & Holden	–	–	–	–	–	–	–	–	–	–	–	–	–	–	–	–	–	–	–	–	–	–	–	–	–	–	–	–	–	10	13	23
McCann-Erickson, Inc.	1	1	1	1	1	–	1	–	1	1	–	–	1	1	–	–	2	2	2	1	–	–	–	–	–	–	8	9	17	9	10	19
Compton Co.^e	–	–	–	–	–	–	–	–	–	–	–	–	–	–	–	–	1	1	–	–	–	–	–	–	–	–	1	1	2	5	9	14
Newell-Emmett Co.	–	–	–	–	–	–	–	–	–	–	–	–	–	–	–	1	1	–	–	–	–	–	–	–	–	–	1	–	1	2	9	11
Foote, Cone & Belding, Inc. (Formerly Lord & Thomas)	–	–	–	1	–	–	–	–	1	–	–	–	–	–	–	–	1	1	–	–	–	–	–	1	–	–	2	2	4	2	7	9
Campbell-Ewald Co.	–	–	1	–	–	–	–	–	–	–	–	–	–	–	–	–	–	–	–	–	–	–	–	–	–	–	–	1	1	3	5	8
Federal Advtg. Co.	–	–	–	1	–	–	–	–	–	–	–	–	–	–	1	–	1	–	–	–	–	–	–	–	–	–	2	–	2	3	5	8
Lennen & Mitchell	–	–	1	1	–	1	–	–	–	–	–	–	1	1	1	1	–	–	–	–	2	5	–	–	–	–	2	5	7	3	5	8
J. M. Mathes^f	–	–	–	1	–	1	1	1	3	1	3	1	–	–	–	–	–	–	–	–	–	1	–	–	–	–	4	4	8	4	4	8

a Awards shown for each year refer to copy produced in the preceding year. M indicates medals; O includes other awards, the nature of which changed several times during the period covered; T combines all awards for the period indicated.
b Only the agencies which received at least eight awards for the period 1921–1948 have been included.
c No exhibit was held in 1923.
d Firm began operations in 1923.
e Until 1937 the firm name was the Blackman Co.
f Firm began operations in 1933.
SOURCE: *Annual of Advertising Art* (N. Y., 1921–48).

not all agencies submit material regularly for the exhibits. The Art Directors Exhibit, however, is representative of the country's best advertising art, even though it does not have complete coverage. N. W. Ayer & Son's consistent record of awards over the period since 1921 is therefore convincing evidence of the agency's leadership among agencies in the production of the highest type of advertising art in the United States.

Whether this means leadership in effective advertising is another question, for the standards of the men who judged the exhibitions were not necessarily those of the public at large. The exhibition for 1935, for example, was shown to the public in the galleries of R. H. Macy & Company, and those who visited it were asked to record their preferences. The results of this ballot indicated that the majority did not concur in the judges' verdicts, but preferred unsophisticated art embodying a rather elementary type of human interest and humor.[14]

The Harvard Advertising Awards which were made annually from 1924 to 1930 might have provided a broader basis for judgment, since the principal criteria related to the advertising effectiveness of a complete campaign rather than a single piece of copy. Comparison is invalidated, however, by the fact that the Ayer management declined to submit material, on the ground that clients, not agencies, should compete when cash prizes are offered. Even so, the limited number of advertisements which Ayer clients submitted won five awards during the period, a total that was surpassed by only one other agency.[15]

In 1935 these annual awards were revived without the cash prizes, under the sponsorship of *Advertising & Selling,* and N. W. Ayer & Son has sent in material for consideration. Table 10A shows the standing of the agencies which won five or more awards during the period 1935 to 1947. Here again the results indicate the excellent quality of Ayer copy as judged by committees of experts. This evidence, however, is not conclusive, for there are men in the advertising field with opinions entitled to respect who argue that the real test of merit is not what a jury of experts may think but whether the copy is effective in doing its job. In most cases this means its ability to stimulate sales. In view of the impossibility of relating sales to specific advertisements, to say

The army moves at dawn

It was cool in the field last night.... The army gets up reluctantly, at the command of a twelve-year-old sergeant. Steam rises from each warm patch of earth. Slowly the column forms and trudges toward the barn.

It's not a very big army, but it's important to America's military strength. For milk is this country's most valuable crop. Milk is nature's most nearly perfect food. And milk products make up about 25% of the food consumed by the average American.

Well-fed civilians work better. Well-fed soldiers fight better. *And the nation's dairy farm families* — toiling long and hard to lick the shortages of manpower, machinery and stock feed — *are making a major contribution to victory.*

As our forces overseas increase, huge supplies of *all* foods must follow. As the starving peoples of ravaged lands are freed, they'll need food from us until they can grow their own again. *Every* American can save *lives* by saving *food.*

National Dairy is proud to have a part in this big job. We delivered $96,000,000 worth of milk products for direct-war purposes last year. And our research laboratories helped develop new products for the Army and Navy that will be as beneficial in peace as they are valuable in war.

Dedicated to the wider use and better understanding of dairy products as human food . . . as a base for the development of new products and materials . . . as a source of health and enduring progress on the farms and in the towns and cities of America.

NATIONAL DAIRY
PRODUCTS CORPORATION
AND AFFILIATED COMPANIES

NATIONAL DAIRY PRODUCTS CORPORATION
AND AFFILIATED COMPANIES, 1944

Just wait till you get your hands on the wheel—

of the Latest, Greatest PLYMOUTH

PLYMOUTH Division of CHRYSLER CORPORATION   Buy Victory Bonds . . . to Have and to Hold!
Remember Thursday Night! The Music of Andre Kostelanetz and the musical world's most popular stars—Thursdays, CBS, 9 P.M., EST.

PLYMOUTH DIVISION OF CHRYSLER CORPORATION, 1945

nothing of getting coöperative scores for the agencies concerned, no ranking can be made on that basis. The next section of this chapter presents evidence to support the view that Ayer copy scores high likewise in getting its messages across to readers as well as to judges. Certainly we are justified in regarding the Advertising Awards as one indication of copy excellence.

During the years 1943–45, inclusive, *Advertising & Selling,* because of war conditions, did not make the usual advertising awards. Instead the committee of judges selected a special group of one hundred advertisements each year which they considered to be the best war-time copy. Table 10B shows how the agencies listed in Table 10A scored in this evaluation. Ayer, though not placing the highest number, again showed up very well.

All things considered, there can be no doubt that the Ayer agency has a long record for producing copy of outstanding quality. That quality relates not only to the advertisement as a whole but also to its component elements — art work, text, and layout. It extends, too, to subtle details of typography; the Ayer organization has long had a national reputation for artistry in the selection and arrangement of type. And it includes painstaking efforts to assure excellence in the finished advertisement which finally reaches the reader, by exacting care in buying plates, providing detailed instructions to printers about ink and paper surfaces, and by constant efforts and research to get the finished advertisement before readers in precisely the form and color visualized by the copy experts.

Copy Testing

Any discussion of recent advertising copy would be incomplete without some mention of copy-testing methods. Prior to 1929 very little had been done to determine by scientific methods the effectiveness of individual advertisements. The chief reliance had been upon the opinion of men who had had experience with advertising and presumably knew a great deal about the results obtained by different types of copy and selling appeals. Since 1930 there has been a great deal of investigation and debate about the subject of copy testing. Some observers have refused to concede any merit in it at all. Others have regarded it as a device of enormous accuracy and value, without which copywriting is a guessing game.

As late as 1935 the Ayer management was still skeptical about testing, but as methods improved it increased its interest and began to use tests of various kinds. The firm's view today is that, within certain limits, copy testing can be exceedingly helpful in enlarging the basic knowledge which underlies the agency's creative activities as a whole. The present Ayer policy is to use testing to the full extent possible within those limits. One test, of course, is whether or not the copy sells the goods. But many elements influence sales, and other methods have been devised to assist in determining which advertisements are unusually effective and why. Among the important tests are:[16]

Reader Recognition	Sales Area Test
Unaided Recall	Psychologic Scoring
Consumer Jury	Spontaneous
Coupon Return	Buried Offer
Split Edition	

Some agencies rely chiefly upon one or two of these methods for testing copy. N. W. Ayer & Son, however, believes that no one of them is wholly dependable as a guide. Each has its elements of strength and weakness, and the agency prefers to use the one which seems most appropriate for the particular copy to be tested, frequently using several different tests in order to obtain a satisfactory cross-check. The Ayer staff also checks the copy produced by other agencies. By studying the results, the Ayer Copy Department is able to draw certain general conclusions concerning the relative current effectiveness of various types of copy appeal, layout, size of space, position, and so on, under given conditions and for given types of products.

During the past ten years the Ayer agency has made increasing use of readership surveys. These are designed to measure the number of people who notice an advertisement and the number who read it and its various parts. The data derived from such surveys provide a useful factual basis for estimating the performance of published advertising — how many people they suc-

Will you measure up to these men?

Ski trooper . . . flight sergeant . . . parachute infantryman . . . tankman . . . they're Regular Army soldiers all. Look them over. See how they carry themselves, each proud of his uniform and what it represents.

It takes men — *real* men — to meet the high standards of your new Regular Army. Excellent physical condition and stamina are among the requirements. But keen, quick-thinking brains and sound character are equally necessary. For *quality* counts as never before in this modern, streamlined Army.

Here is a force that must be capable of handling the most intricate machines, the fastest aircraft, the hardest-hitting weapons the world has ever known. Capable, too, of carrying forward scientific research on a gigantic scale — discovering and developing new benefits for all mankind.

That's why the Regular Army offers such a thrilling challenge to the picked young men of America. Are you strong enough, intelligent enough to meet those standards? Have you the stuff it takes to make the grade? If you are qualified, there's a real future for you in the Army, with the finest

kind of training and experience in one or more of many interesting, useful fields of work.

Enlistments are open to men from 18 to 34 inclusive (17 with parents' consent). New high pay scales, the opportunity for advancement, education, travel — and a retirement plan that has no equal—make this one of the most attractive careers offered today. Details may be obtained without obligation at the nearest Army Recruiting Station

Listen to "Warriors of Peace," "Voice of the Army," "Proudly We Hail" on your radio.

U. S. ARMY RECRUITING SERVICE

YOUR REGULAR ARMY SERVES THE NATION AND MANKIND IN WAR AND PEACE—CHOOSE THIS FINE PROFESSION NOW

U. S. ARMY AND U. S. AIR FORCE RECRUITING SERVICE, 1946

TELEPHONE
MEN
WORKING
ON A
RUSH JOB

We are working on new cable for the thousands of telephones the public wants. The war put us behind — in buildings, switchboards, telephones and other equipment — but we are beginning to catch up now.

Catching up on two million telephones and putting in two million miles of Long Distance circuits is a big job but we are hurrying it with all possible speed. We shall not let up until you can again have all the service you want.

BELL TELEPHONE SYSTEM

AMERICAN TELEPHONE & TELEGRAPH COMPANY, 1946

TABLE 10

A. Annual Awards for Advertising Copy, 1935–1947[a]

	1935		1936		1937		1938		1939		1940		1941		1942		1946[b]		1947		Totals		
	M	HM	M	HM	M	HM	M	HM	M	HM	M	HM	M	HM	M	HM	M	HM	M	HM	M	HM	T
N. W. Ayer & Son, Inc.	1	2	—	3	3	3	2	2	—	6	1	2	1	3	1	3	1	2	1	2	11	28	39
Batten, Barton, Durstine & Osborn, Inc.	4	3	1	5	2	—	2	3	1	2	2	—	2	2	—	1	—	1	1	3	15	20	35
Young & Rubicam, Inc.	3	3	2	2	2	2	3	3	3	—	—	2	—	2	—	1	—	3	—	2	13	20	33
Newell-Emmett Co.	1	—	1	1	1	1	—	1	—	2	—	2	1	1	1	1	—	—	—	—	5	9	14
Foote, Cone & Belding, Inc. (Formerly Lord & Thomas)	—	1	—	—	—	—	1	1	—	—	—	4	—	1	—	1	—	1	—	1	1	10	11
McCann-Erickson, Inc.	—	—	—	2	—	1	—	—	—	1	—	—	1	1	1	—	—	—	2	2	4	7	11
Fuller & Smith & Ross, Inc.	—	1	—	1	—	—	—	2	—	1	—	1	—	—	—	—	—	—	—	—	—	6	6
Kenyon & Eckhardt	—	—	—	—	1	—	1	—	—	—	1	1	1	—	1	—	—	—	—	—	5	1	6
Erwin, Wasey & Co.	—	—	—	—	—	1	1	1	—	—	—	—	—	—	—	—	—	—	1	—	2	3	5
J. Walter Thompson, Inc.	—	—	—	1	1	1	1	—	—	—	1	—	—	—	—	—	—	—	—	—	3	2	5
Rickard & Co.	1	1	1	1	—	—	—	1	—	—	—	—	—	—	—	—	—	—	—	1	2	3	5

[a] This table refers to the awards made annually since 1936 under the auspices of *Advertising & Selling*. The dates indicate the years in which the advertising appeared and not the years in which the awards were made. Thus 1935 copy was judged in 1936, and so on. Only agencies which have received a total of at least five awards have been included. M refers to medals given; HM stands for honorable mentions; T combines both medals and honorable mentions.

[b] In 1943, 1944, and 1945 *Advertising & Selling* did not make the usual Annual Advertising Awards. Instead they selected a special group of 100 wartime advertisements for each year. For the number of selections made from the work of the above agencies see Table 10B.

SOURCE: *Adv. & Sell.*, Annual Advertising Number, 1936–48.

TABLE 10 (*continued*)

B. WARTIME ADVERTISING AWARDS[a]

	1943	1944	1945	Total
N. W. Ayer & Son, Inc...............	7	10	10	27
Batten, Barton, Durstine & Osborn, Inc...	3	10	10	23
Young & Rubicam, Inc................	10	13	12	35
Newell-Emmett Co....................	6	6	8	20
Foote, Cone & Belding, Inc. (Formerly Lord & Thomas).........................	6	2	2	10
McCann-Erickson, Inc................	16	7	12	35
Fuller & Smith & Ross...............	—	3	2	5
Kenyon & Eckhardt..................	5	6	3	14
Erwin, Wasey & Co...................	—	—	—	—
J. Walter Thompson, Inc.............	5	6	3	14
Rickard & Co........................	—	—	—	—

[a] This table shows, for the agencies listed in Table 10A, the number of advertisements selected by *Advertising & Selling* as the best 100 wartime advertisements for each of the three years in which the Annual Advertising Awards were not made.

SOURCE: *Advertising & Selling*, 1943–45.

ceeded in talking to. An analysis of the data, moreover, provides a valuable guide to the preparation of *future* advertisements by revealing why some pieces of copy were more successful than others. Since 1938 the analysis and interpretation of magazine readership surveys made by Daniel Starch and his staff has formed an important part of the research activities of the Ayer Copy Department. In the area of newspaper advertising the Ayer organization, since 1939, has been using data supplied by the Advertising Research Foundation, the Starch Newspaper Service since 1945, and B. H. Grant Research Associates (a continuation of the Clark Newspaper Service) since 1939.

That Ayer copy is effective is indicated by the readership data. For example, a study of the ratings for 806 advertisements, one-half page or larger, placed by Ayer during 1946 in seven magazines (*Collier's, Life, Saturday Evening Post, Time, Good Housekeeping, Ladies' Home Journal* and *McCall's*), showed that the average Ayer advertisement was seen (and associated with the advertiser's name) by 29 per cent more persons and was read

Its lovely lady air haunts boulevards and byways with memories
of beauty that stir anew each day. For the romantic charm
of "Bond Street" is unmistakable, and shared by women of
dramatic taste and noble poise everywhere in the world.
"Bond Street" Perfume, $2.50 to $15. Toilet Water, $1.50 and $2.50. Plus tax.

 by YARDLEY

Yardley products for America are created in England and finished in the U. S. A. from the original English formulae, combining imported and domestic ingredients. Yardley of London, Inc., 620 Fifth Avenue, N.Y.C.

YARDLEY OF LONDON, INC., 1947

Spring will last all summer

A new Carrier Room Air Conditioner takes hot, sticky months right out of the calendar . . . gives you cool, bracing weather to enjoy the summer through. One of these handsome, efficient units will let you relax in pleasant comfort in your living room . . . keep your bedroom cool as a mountain lodge. And in an air-conditioned office you'll work better, tire less. There's a model for any size or type of room or office. Carrier Room Air Conditioners are produced by the same pioneering skill that has made Carrier the leader in air conditioning for almost half a century. Call the Carrier dealer listed in your Classified Telephone Directory. Carrier Corporation, Syracuse, New York.

Carrier AIR CONDITIONING · REFRIGERATION

SPRING—A PHOTOGRAMATIC INTERPRETATION BY MEDNICK

CARRIER CORPORATION, 1948

thoroughly by 58 per cent more than the average for all advertisements appearing in the same magazines. Another study of the same seven magazines for the three-year period from 1944 through 1946 covered over fourteen thousand advertisements placed by the five leading agencies (N. W. Ayer & Son; Batten, Barton, Durstine & Osborn; McCann-Erickson; J. Walter Thompson; and Young & Rubicam). The average ratings for advertisements noted and advertisements seen and associated with the advertiser were substantially higher for Ayer than those of any of the four other agencies. Ayer and one other agency were virtually tied for leadership in the ratings as to advertisements read most. Here, then, is evidence that Ayer copy is of top quality not only in the eyes of expert juries who have given it the awards indicated previously, but also in the judgment of the public to which it has been directed. What is of even greater importance for the future is that, according to the readership data, Ayer copy has been showing substantial improvement in this respect during the past decade.

In commenting on the advertisements reproduced in this chapter the author has necessarily given his own reactions; others might like them less or better. It is also true that one could find both poorer and better individual pieces of copy among the tremendous number of advertisements produced by the Ayer organization in the course of its long history. What I have tried to do has been to set forth a *representative* group of advertisements which would illustrate changes in copy through the years and at the same time give the reader a notion of some of the tangible end-products of the Ayer agency. Since I have found much to praise I may be accused of favoritism. Actually I have tried to be scrupulously fair. The quality of Ayer copy, as appraised by various independent judges over a period of twenty-eight years, is unquestionably very high, so that on the whole it is Ayer's performance, not the writer's bias, which is responsible for the overall conclusion. It is readily apparent, too, even from the limited number of examples reproduced here, that Ayer advertising copy has improved tremendously during the past seventy-five years — in text, art work, layout, typography, and total effectiveness in

Gee....but we're a whiz together

Sally **CORN** for flavor and energy

Sammy **SOYA** for more body-building proteins than in any cereal

Sammy: What a team of tastiness and nourishment we are, Sally . . . that's why Corn-Soya is such a favorite.

Sally: Right you are, partner. How proud I am when I hear the ladies talking about how easy ready-to-eat Corn-Soya is to serve.

Sammy: I like the way the men-folks cheer our crispness . . . say we're mighty satisfying.

Sally: People everywhere are calling us the nourishing way to start the day.

Sally Corn, the flavor and energy queen, and Sammy Soya, the prominent protein, make a great new cereal combination. Crisp, light, delightfully flavorful, Kellogg's Corn-Soya is toasty, tasty, tempting. **It took Kellogg's 20 years** of courting, with endless work and experiment, to arrange the wedding of these two nourishing "naturals."

From the very first bite, you're in for a treat . . . these crunchy shreds stay crisp in milk . . . and they bring you vitamins, minerals, and proteins. Fact is, the protein value of one ounce (about ⅔ cup) of Corn-Soya with four ounces of milk equals that of one egg with three slices of bacon. Stop in and get Corn-Soya at your grocer's today.

Kellogg's CORN-SOYA *New* SHREDS

Kellogg's THE GREATEST NAME IN CEREALS BRINGS YOU THE IDEAL MARRIAGE OF FLAVOR AND NOURISHMENT

KELLOGG COMPANY, 1947

[334]

communicating ideas to the public, as well as in the mechanical techniques upon which printed advertising depends.

It is not possible to present the evidence in a book, but a similar improvement has, in the writer's judgment, taken place in the advertising which N. W. Ayer & Son has prepared for transmission by radio and television.

CHAPTER XIV

PROBLEMS AND POLICIES IN DEALING
WITH ADVERTISERS

IF BUSINESS were conducted upon an entirely reasonable basis
and always followed the normal course, there would be little need
to go further in this study of the Ayer relations with advertisers.
Business, however, is never completely rational: it is subject to
the ever-present conflict of principles, the senseless whims of circumstance, and the idiosyncrasies of men. As a result of non-logi-
cal and accidental forces, many problems have arisen out of the
routine relations between agency and advertiser to disturb the
normal methods and arrangements of the Ayer firm. A description
of those problems and of their disposition is of the very essence
of business history, and, while an exhaustive analysis is manifestly out of the question, it has been possible to summarize some
of the main recurrent problems which N. W. Ayer & Son has had
to solve.

Perhaps of even greater importance than the problems themselves are the agency's ways of handling them; for, with business
concerns as with people, the true character reveals itself most
clearly in unusual situations. The day-to-day decisions, though
not always consistent with one another or related to broad principles of management, combine to form patterns of action which
constitute for us the key to the business policy of an enterprise.
We shall consider here those problems and policies which concern
the relations between N. W. Ayer & Son and the advertisers who
are actual or prospective clients.

On the whole, the resulting pattern is highly creditable to
N. W. Ayer & Son. Mistakes have been made, of course, and there
are aspects of firm policy which an outsider is likely to criticize,

but the entire record compares favorably with what we know about the other agencies of the country.

Selecting Desirable Accounts

N. W. Ayer & Son has encountered a number of difficulties as a result of its desire to have a carefully selected clientèle. As we have seen, the firm exercised no discrimination whatever in the beginning; but gradually the Ayer management began to see that the advertising of some commodities was objectionable from a social point of view or because it might bring the name of Ayer into disrepute. Indeed, the firm gradually adopted the view that the sacrifice of immediate profit from certain sources would eventually lead to a greater volume from other, more desirable sources.

To rule out lottery and "secret disease" advertisements was a comparatively simple matter, and so with liquor advertising. But the further application of a selective principle soon raised important issues. What is objectionable advertising? Where should one draw the line between desirable and undesirable products?

The criterion of ultimate profit to the firm might decide some cases but not all. And, after a decision has been made, time and changing forces outside the firm sometimes undermine it. Thus, the Ayer management spent nearly a decade in deciding to exclude all patent medicines of the old-time nostrum variety; but it had been rid of this type of business only a few years when the selling appeals used for such standard pharmaceutical products as tooth paste, milk of magnesia, and the like, began to take on some of the features which had made patent-medicine advertising objectionable. Moreover, advertisers subsequently began to exploit even food products like yeast, coffee, and bran in a similar way, using sensational copy and making exaggerated and misleading claims about the benefits to be derived from their use. If N. W. Ayer & Son was to be deterred by fear of the odium which this kind of advertising incurs, it would plainly have to abandon the advertising of all foods, drugs, and cosmetics, that is, several of the major sources of agency business.

Changes in companies resulting from the integration and diversification of American industry have further hindered the application of a clear-cut policy. Firms which were manufacturing the most desirable and blameless products have added others to which exception might be taken; witness the recent entry of drug, soft-drink, and grocery manufacturers into the liquor business.

Amid this constant shift of products and public opinion, no firm can lay down a hard and fast policy. Rather it has to consider each client or each line of products separately. Thus the Ayer agency has, within recent years, refused to handle the advertising of a liver pill, the appropriation for which was over a million dollars per year; while, at the same time, it handled the advertising of an inhalant for the relief of colds, as well as that of a well-known saline laxative. And, although it steadfastly refused to modify its stand against the advertising of liquor after the repeal of prohibition, the Ayer firm, as we have seen, did not always succeed in keeping the lure of alcoholic beverages out of its advertising for other clients.[1]

In recent years an attempt to avoid the advertising of commodities or enterprises of a speculative nature has created similar difficulties. Both land and securities fall into this class. N. W. Ayer & Son has often advertised both, and no one could reasonably expect it to eliminate them entirely. Yet, how are we to distinguish between risky investments and "comparatively safe" speculations? Here again, the Ayer management has considered individual cases. It refused to advertise lots in an elaborately landscaped cemetery because the whole project was still in the blueprint stage and might easily fail to materialize, regardless of the sincerity of the promoters. But, at the same time, N. W. Ayer & Son conducted a large campaign for the Coral Gables Corporation, reasoning that, while Florida land might be a risky investment, the city of Coral Gables, which the agency was to advertise, was actually in existence — a physical fact of which the prospective buyer might judge for himself. That this reasoning was sincere is beyond dispute: greatly impressed by the beauty of the "American Venice" and the blandishments of its sponsors, the Ayer management eventually extended unusually large credits to the Coral Gables Corporation; and, when the Florida boom collapsed, N. W. Ayer & Son was among the losers.

Since 1906, if not earlier, the Ayer agency has generally refused to handle any advertising in which its management might

not reasonably take personal pride; and there is ample evidence
to prove that in applying this policy the firm has shown itself to
be more circumspect than most of its rivals. Indeed, the comment
of those rivals that N. W. Ayer & Son is high-toned and old-
maidish about advertising is additional testimony in support of
its integrity and ideals.

Further, as shown in Chapter VIII above, the firm has scrutinized accounts since 1941 with regard to their impact upon the
agency itself: it now recognizes the need to safeguard its own independence and professional integrity, in the interest of both the
Ayer organization and the clients it serves. The Ayer management
wants large accounts, but it regards them as dangerous unless
sufficiently balanced by other business to enable the agency to
withstand the loss of a large account without serious embarrassment. It is now fully aware, too, of the importance of what it calls
a good counseling relationship. Hence it will not accept an account unless there is a reasonable expectation at the outset that
the two organizations can work together in confidence and harmony. Only with such a basis is professional service possible.

Tʜᴇ Dᴇᴄɪsɪᴏɴ ᴀɢᴀɪɴsᴛ Cᴏᴍᴘᴇᴛɪɴɢ Aᴄᴄᴏᴜɴᴛs

The desire to have a respectable business creates only a small
proportion of the difficulties which the management has to face:
far more time is taken up by problems arising out of circumstances or caused by the advertisers themselves. Of such problems one of the most perplexing emerges when the agency attempts to serve two clients who are engaged in the same line of
business — when, to use the vernacular of advertising men, it has
two competing accounts. One of the clients threatens to cancel
his contract unless the agency gets rid of the other, and the
agency at once has to decide which account it prefers to keep.

Such conflicts between accounts belong chiefly to the period
from 1900 to 1925. Before 1900 N. W. Ayer & Son handled advertising for a large number of firms who were in direct competition with one another;[2] and, until it began to prepare plans and
copy for its customers, no one thought of objecting to the practice. But, as soon as the agency began to supply important services along with the space it sold, it placed itself in the position of

providing strategy for both of the opposing armies in a commercial battle.

Apparently the issue first arose shortly after N. W. Ayer & Son had begun to place advertising for the National Biscuit Company (1899). When Ayer executives consulted the Biscuit Company about accepting the advertising business of a competing concern, the company objected. Probably it took the reasonable view that it alone should receive all the useful copy and marketing ideas about soda crackers which the agency could evolve. Other customers now began to reach similar conclusions; and by 1905 the question of competing accounts formed one of the principal topics of discussion at a meeting of the Ayer solicitors. On that occasion McKinney stated, as the policy of his firm, "that we would not agree not to take a competing line, but that we would not do so if we felt it jeopardized their [the client's] interest." [3]

The Ayer management then held the view to which it clung for many years, that it could serve competing accounts perfectly well; that it would, indeed, benefit both by avoiding the vicious advertising battles which frequently break out. Referring to a particular case, an Ayer executive expressed the firm's attitude in 1923 as follows: [4]

. . . the agency handling both [accounts] as a result will know more about the [steel] safe business and, therefore, make fewer mistakes in each case and be better able to serve each account.

Neither campaign should be a knocking campaign, but each should tend to build a market for a protection of records, valuables, etc.

If N. W. Ayer & Son handled both accounts, both campaigns would be business-building campaigns and neither would be negative. This would not only be true in connection with the advertisements but with the entire advertising, selling and merchandising thought and plan which might be developed by the agency.

There is undoubtedly an element of truth in the view put forth, and it convinced many clients. But an increasing number of advertisers have felt that the advantage of this arrangement does not offset the obvious objections: there is too great a chance that confidential information might find its way into the hands of the competing client; and, if the agency were honest and fair with both, it would be compelled to give them practically the same service and advice, whereas the value of such assistance often depends upon its being exclusive. Certainly, if an agency really attempts to give its clients effective advice in their selling problems, it is bound to face an impossible situation whenever it is called upon to assist two firms which are struggling to control the same market. Both cannot win, and the agency must either help one to get the better of the other, or be of so little use that the clients will have to engage other agencies in order to avoid losing ground.

The Ayer firm occasionally argued that it could organize separate groups within the agency to handle competing accounts; but, no matter how independent such groups were, their work had to be reviewed from time to time by the same executives. Hence their plans and policies for the two accounts could not be formulated altogether independently. The management of any agency eventually has to recognize that there is no way out of this dilemma: either it must cease to handle accounts which compete directly with one another, even when the clients consent to the arrangement, or else it must stop giving help with the selling and merchandising problems of its clients. Of course, there can be no defense of any attempt by the agency to handle competing accounts without the knowledge of both clients concerned. For reasons which are not wholly clear, N. W. Ayer & Son was guilty of this at least twice before 1930.[5] The firm's usual policy, however, was to discuss the matter with both the companies concerned as soon as the situation arose.

Difficulties in Avoiding Accounts That Compete

But a blanket decision not to handle any competing accounts did not remove all the difficulty. To determine whether two clients are really competing is not always a simple matter and can easily become the subject of disagreement. For some years the Ayer agency handled the advertising of two coffee firms, one selling in the East, the other in the West, between which there was at first no competition. Trouble arose, however, when the western client began to penetrate eastern markets. Further complications developed when a third client, a cereal manufacturer, began to prepare a de-caffeinated coffee and sell it over a large part of both regions. The Ayer executives could contend that the accounts did not compete because de-caffeinated coffee would be bought only by people who were unable to drink ordinary coffee; but, so long as its advertising might encourage the public to change from ordinary to de-caffeinated coffee, there was a definite conflict. In order to meet the objections which were made, the Ayer management persuaded the cereal manufacturer to advertise his new product through another agency, while leaving the rest of his advertising in the hands of N. W. Ayer & Son.

The same problem has also arisen in another form. In nearly every field of enterprise, different firms tap different price divisions of the market, and competition between these firms is potential rather than actual. But there is always ample room for a difference of opinion as to the point where real competition begins. Sometimes this doubt has occasioned disputes, but at other times the clients have been able to agree. Thus, for a period the Ayer agency advertised at the same time a low-price, a medium-price, and a high-price motor car without objection from the clients concerned.

It is not only a question of avoiding conflicts between vendors of the same kind of goods. Some clients have felt inclined to press objection still further and protest, for instance, against the advertising of steel by the Ayer firm when it is also promoting the use of wood. How far can such protests be considered? Radios and cars compete with pianos, gas with electricity, bonds with insurance. Clearly no sharp division can be made. The Ayer management must continue to do as it has done: consider each case strictly on its own merits.

This problem of competing accounts would be less perplexing if it were not that every advertising agency must be continually seeking new clients. Advertisers are constantly changing from one agency to another, frequently for no other reason than the greener appearance of the other pasture. Within what limits is an agency's search for new business to be conducted? Is the fact that one of the agency's clients is a hosiery manufacturer to prevent it from cultivating relations with other hosiery manufacturers? If so, it may pass over chances to obtain new accounts, only to lose through no fault of its own the one which it already has. If the agency were to wait until the first client canceled his account before soliciting others in the same industry, much valuable time would be lost and the whole problem of management vastly complicated. Thus, a policy of excluding all competing accounts from consideration, if consistently adhered to in all parts of the business, would so circumscribe efforts to get new clients that effective solicitation would be impossible.

On the other hand, when the agency does develop contacts with a competing advertiser and is (sometimes unexpectedly) awarded his contract, it has to deal with the resulting conflict. Which account should the agency serve? In general, N. W. Ayer & Son has tried to favor the older client, but mere priority cannot always decide the matter. So long as advertisers drop one agency for another in a perfectly cold-blooded way, the agency cannot ignore its own interests. But neither can it be too ruthless, for no advertiser wants to engage an agency which may with little warning throw out his account in order to take on a more profitable one. The dilemma was plainly expressed by one Ayer executive in a letter to another:[6]

We are not forgetting in this discussion the necessity for the House to procure as much national business as possible and as many large accounts as they can; yet, if this is to be the sole basis for deciding whether or not an old customer is to be retained, I am inclined to believe that we will defeat the very purpose that we are striving for; namely, to build and maintain a big volume of business. Surely we would not have it said about N. W. Ayer & Son that regardless of the standing of a customer in the House, their future possibilities, and the pleasant relationship that exists, that we will, without the slightest consideration, turn them out because we are in a position to take on an account with larger billings.

During the past ten years the problem of actual and potential conflicts has been less troublesome for the firm because its solicitation of new business has been much more selective than before. Occasionally, however, the issue continues to rise unexpectedly. In 1947, for example, a company which had dropped the Ayer agency in the uncertain days of 1937–40 asked the Ayer management, without any preliminary contact, to take back its advertising, with a current annual volume in excess of six million dollars. To accept meant that N. W. Ayer would have to drop another account with a current volume of about three million. Ayer executives reviewed their relationship with the smaller client, decided that it was fundamentally sound for the long run and, within 24 hours, refused the offer. The question on which the decision was made was not the relative profitableness of the two accounts but whether the agency's relationship with the smaller account was on a basis which permitted the organization to do its best for the client. In some agencies the resulting decision would have led to discontent among bonus-minded executives, but in the Ayer organization the response was well stated by one of the men who stood to gain directly from increased profits:[7]

I have been around here for twenty years and it certainly made me feel good to see the speed and certainty, the complete lack of hesitation, with which the decision to reject three million dollars of added billings for next year was arrived at.

That executive, like his colleagues, was very ambitious for himself and for the firm, but he also adhered to high standards of professional integrity.

SPLIT ACCOUNTS

N. W. Ayer & Son is just as reluctant to share a client with another agency as the client is to share the Ayer agency's service with a competing advertiser. Advertisers frequently want to divide their advertising appropriation between two or more agencies, apparently on the theory that the keen competition and immediate comparison of results will produce better advertising. In the days when the Ayer firm sold space alone, the practice was quite common, and no one could raise any serious objection to it.

Since about 1895, N. W. Ayer & Son's general policy has been against splitting an account with a rival agency in this way, although the policy has been somewhat modified in recent years. The reason for this attitude is not merely a selfish desire to have the whole rather than a part of the business. When the decision against splitting an account was first established, its purpose was mainly to improve the agency's bargaining position with publishers, as McKinney once explained to an advertiser:[8]

Our experience has taught us that where more than one agency represents an advertiser, that fact is speedily known to the newspapers at large, and this fact of itself conveys to them the idea that there is no one agency who is the advertising department of that house, and the division of the business suggests possible changes in the future, and that another year a newspaper may be able to get a better price from somebody else than the agency who offers it this year, and these uncertainties tend to increase the cost of the advertising.

Our experience has thoroughly satisfied us that in order to get the lowest rates, some agency must be the advertising department of the house they represent, and must have absolute say upon the advertising matters, must be in position to say of every newspaper that they are not obliged to give them that contract, that it cannot be obtained anywhere else, and that under no circumstances will it be given to them unless rock bottom prices are allowed. Our rule that we must handle the entire business of an advertiser, when we take it upon our open contract plan, was adopted simply because our experience has abundantly proved that this was the only way to render our client the best service, and if we failed to render him that, our interests as well as his suffered in the end.

Today N. W. Ayer & Son recognizes that every advertising campaign requires a unity in conception and execution which is difficult unless a single agency is in complete charge. No two agencies can be expected to agree about the allocation of the advertising funds, the type of copy, the selection of media, or any other part of a campaign; recrimination and evasion of responsibility about results are only too likely to follow. Hence the policy against split accounts.

Circumstances have, however, altered the prevailing concept of what constitutes splitting. A single company, especially in the period since 1920, often comprises several separate divisions or subsidiary concerns, each with its own sales organization. As far as advertising is concerned, each unit may be regarded as a separate account; and, if the client insists upon parceling out the business among different agencies, the Ayer management usually consents. A part is better than nothing at all, and handling it well may lead eventually to getting the rest. The need to avoid competing accounts is sometimes the occasion for such a split. A company may sell both drugs and cosmetics, for example, and, if the agency already is handling a drug account, it will be offered (or can accept) only the cosmetics division as an account. So long as such an arrangement does not violate the principle of unity, it is not considered as splitting an account.

There is another type of splitting of accounts to which the Ayer firm has sometimes agreed; namely, dividing the account among several agencies according to the different media to be used. Thus, many Ayer clients place their outdoor advertising through another agency, owing to the fact that between 1915 and 1931 N. W. Ayer & Son handled no outdoor business. Some clients place their radio advertising through a separate agency; and, in at least one case, the Ayer management consented to an arrangement by which it handled only the magazine advertising of a client, while another agency placed the advertising in other media. Such exceptions to the general policy have been dictated by special circumstances; and, to prove that the policy is not an empty form, there are many instances in which N. W. Ayer & Son has turned down substantial amounts of business rather than split the account in a way which seemed bound to lead to dissatisfaction.

The Ayer management is convinced that the client who splits his account by media thereby makes it impossible for the agencies concerned to give professional service. In effect (and sometimes by intent) he places the agencies in direct competition with one another in handling his business. This, in turn, tends to make the agencies concentrate on the question of what will appeal to the advertiser (who is, after all, not technically competent to judge) rather than what will best accomplish his purposes. In these circumstances mutual confidence and objective thinking are inevitably impaired, to the advertiser's loss.

PROBLEMS OF PERSONAL INFLUENCE

Probably the most baffling difficulties which the Ayer organization has to face are those arising out of personal influence. When competition is keen and the difference in price or quality is small, the business man allows personal likes and dislikes to influence his decisions. As many an unemployed man learned during the depression, family connections, social contacts, and other forms of influence frequently take precedence over merit. Every agency has often lost business because the advertiser had some personal connection in a rival agency. In one rather involved case a manufacturing concern was unable to consider N. W. Ayer & Son, not because of the management's opposition, but merely because the sales manager of the firm which took a large part of its output was under a social obligation to another agency, and the management of the manufacturing concern could not afford to oppose his wishes. Again, a person holding a large financial interest in a firm has, at times, influenced its choice of an advertising agency for the sake of a friend, relative, or business connection. Occasionally the Ayer representative has made progress with one executive in a company, only to fall foul of petty politics and jealousy within the organization.

Such irrational situations, of course, cut both ways; and N. W. Ayer & Son has frequently benefited by them. The firm's general policy, however, has been to use personal influence merely as an entering wedge, and to found its connection with an advertiser upon the less capricious basis of sheer business merit.

It is notorious, of course, that wine and women play a part in the winning of many advertising accounts. The extent to which they do so has been exaggerated on the stage and screen, and in novels; but the fact remains that a considerable number of business men are swayed by lavish entertainment. The Ayer management has always frowned — one might almost say glowered — upon such questionable methods of solicitation. It is opposed to any attempt to win business through sensual influence, not only on moral but also on practical business grounds; for accounts which are won by such means are usually lost by the same route. Nonetheless, the evil is one which must be reckoned with in the modern competition between agencies.[9]

N. W. Ayer & Son has lost business because a client's advertising manager liked the gay evenings which the representatives of other agencies provided; and I have reason to believe that, despite the strict opposition of the management, occasionally some Ayer representative has curried favor with customers by similar tactics. No firm can exercise complete control over its staff members in the field, especially as social and convivial entertainment has become an accepted part of the selling efforts in many lines of business. One must recognize, too, that an employee is judged by the business he obtains for his firm; and, if wild parties sway prospective customers' decisions, he may decide to pay for them out of his own pocket as an investment leading to promotion. It is quite clear, however, that solicitation by means of revelry is contrary to Ayer policy, and the testimony of clients is that N. W. Ayer & Son has a specially good record in this respect.[10]

Still another problem of personal influence arises — one which might appropriately be called a racket. Because of his experience or personality, some one person in a firm succeeds in obtaining so much influence over its advertising department that he can practically dictate how its advertising business is to be disposed of. Occasionally the man who gets control is an employee of the agency which has been handling the account. Such a man is said to have the account in his pocket, and he frequently attempts to turn his influence into cash. N. W. Ayer & Son has repeatedly had an opportunity to win a new account, provided that it would hire the man in control — of course, at a handsome salary. To such proposals the Ayer management has turned a deaf ear, even when the man concerned would have been a useful addition to the Ayer staff. It knows full well that business won in this way is likely to remain in the control of the person who brought it, and that it is usually lost as soon as another agency makes a higher bid.

For many years the organization and integration of the various phases of Ayer service have been deliberately arranged to prevent any one person from gaining personal control of an account. Even before the signing of the contract a number of specialists from the agency meet with representatives from the advertiser's organization, and the client soon learns to recognize these specialists as authorities and even insists upon contact with them individually, within their specialized fields, rather than to look upon any one person as the dominant factor.

GEOGRAPHICAL AND FINANCIAL FACTORS

Ever since it expanded beyond the Philadelphia area, N. W. Ayer & Son has had to face problems created by its geographical location.[11] Although the firm was centrally situated for its customers of the 'seventies, today the Philadelphia headquarters is a long distance from many of the country's large advertisers, and this fact often enters into the choice of an agency. A manufacturer in Chicago or Cleveland, in order to have the assurance of quick communication and service, may give his business to a local agency. If the local agency is one with an adequate national organization, there is much to be said for the arrangement; and all that the Ayer representatives have been able to do is to point out that accessibility is a relatively poor criterion by which to judge an agency. If the local agency is small, on the other hand, they have emphasized the importance of the wider experience, the greater influence with advertising media, and the larger staff of expert specialists which N. W. Ayer & Son makes available. Since 1900, too, the Ayer management has met this problem of location by the establishment of branch offices in Boston, New York, Detroit, Chicago, San Francisco, Hollywood, and Honolulu. The Ayer firm, moreover, makes generous use of telephone, telegraph, and teletype messages, and its representatives, both from the central office and from the branches, make frequent visits to clients. Thus, though sometimes mentioned as a disadvantage, the location of the Ayer headquarters in Philadelphia has ceased to be a real handicap, especially since every other large agency has to contend with the same kind of competition from local agencies.

A number of advertisers, however, have favored the local agency because of its very smallness. This policy, they believe, ensures closer attention and more personal service. They are afraid that their advertising will be neglected in a large organization when the details of their campaigns are divided among many employees. Again, there is something to be said for this view; but the Ayer representatives never fail to remind the advertiser that small agencies are not small by choice; they grow as fast as they can. The small agency, moreover, cannot possibly provide at a reasonable cost the expert specialists who are on the staff of the large agency, and its work must therefore lack something in quality to offset any possible gain in personal attention. And it is not an established fact that the small agency can really devote closer attention to its clients. Frequently its few employees are swamped with detailed work, and its head must be a jack of all trades, trying to ply several of them at the same time. As we shall see presently, too, the Ayer staff has long been organized to ensure personal interest and responsibility as well as the attention of experts.

Occasionally N. W. Ayer & Son has encountered business-getting problems of a financial nature. Throughout its history there have been enterprises which were willing to become Ayer clients provided that the firm would give them financial assistance. Some agencies have made a practice of doing this,[12] for it gives them a hold upon the advertiser's business which is not easily broken. During the 'eighties and 'nineties N. W. Ayer & Son extended liberal credits to many customers, to enable them to advertise. From time to time, also, the firm has held stock in the enterprises of clients; but the amounts have never been large and, in all but two or three instances, these have been the result of settlements for money owed to the Ayer agency. None of the investments was made out of any desire to acquire influence over the management.[13] Although the firm has occasionally extended unusual credit privileges (always charging interest, however), the Ayer policy is now, and apparently has always been, to refuse to lure advertisers by using financial assistance as bait. The management has long recognized that such assistance is a matter for a bank rather than an advertising agency to handle. It has felt, too, that financial interests of this kind are bound to warp the agency's judgment, leading to a preferred list of clients who receive unusual attention and service at the expense of other customers.[14]

In dealing with all its problems of solicitation, N. W. Ayer & Son has attempted to adhere to the general policy of winning clients through the value of the service it has to offer, rather than through any external or irrelevant considerations, and thus to get business on a basis which would permit its organization to give intelligent, unprejudiced, and unified service. And, in practice, the firm has applied that policy with remarkable consistency and courage.

PROBLEMS AND POLICIES RELATING TO THE AYER CONTRACT

For many years after the inception of the open contract, the Ayer agency had some difficulty in getting advertisers to accept the arrangement. Afraid of what it might entail, many preferred to continue giving their business to the lowest bidder. The agency itself was not always sure whether or not to offer its new plan. In 1906, for example, the Ayer solicitors met to discuss with the management the following questions:[15] "Under what conditions should the open contract plan only be presented? When is it preferable to take business on a definite order: i.e., on the order or fixed-price basis? In case a contract is not obtainable, when is it wise to decline the business as a definite order?"

These questions, as we have seen, have long since been answered within fairly definite limits. Schools and camps, because of the special nature of their advertising problems, are all handled on the order basis through the Educational Department, with its own plans and copy staff. Occasionally, too, a single-shot or short-term campaign will be handled on the order basis. Advertisers who need agency counsel and service, regardless of the size of their appropriation, are taken on the open-contract plan.

The recent decision (1949) to abandon the provision providing for the net cost plus commission on all expenditures removed one source of confusion for clients. The difference in cost between net cost plus commission and the gross price was so slight that few advertisers, despite the difference in principle, could see any point to the traditional Ayer principle.[16] They began to note a difference, however, when the expenditures for non-commission items (particularly expenditures for radio and television talent) began to reach substantial size. Under the old arrangement Ayer had added its commission of 16⅔ per cent to such items, whereas most agencies charged 15 per cent, taking the same rate as most publishers allowed. The difference of 1⅔ per cent, when applied to a hundred thousand dollar expenditure, began to be a consideration in the selection of an agency, thereby working to Ayer's disadvantage. The current plan has eliminated this difficulty.

Occasionally, the time clause creates difficulty. In one case a producers' association wished to put on an emergency campaign for which $200,000 was available. The campaign, however, was to be completed within three to six months of its start; and, since the association did not contemplate any further advertising during the year and might even cease to exist within that period, it was unwilling to commit itself beyond the one campaign. The committee in charge, therefore, objected to signing the Ayer contract with its provision for a duration of one year, plus the required notice of three months for termination. The particular point was of no great importance, but, because the Ayer management was determined not to make any special concessions in order to get business, it debated the matter for a week in numerous telegrams and letters before consenting to the slight variation in the contract which would permit the relation to terminate at the completion of the campaign.

Legal Disputes

Only one serious dispute has arisen over the legal interpretation of the Ayer contract.[17] Briefly, it was as follows. During 1916 and 1917 the United States Rubber Company entrusted the newspaper and magazine advertising of all its divisions to N. W. Ayer & Son. Early in 1919 the Rubber Company appointed a committee to review its advertising and decided to place that of each division separately. Upon learning of the decision to review, the Ayer management voluntarily offered to terminate its contract with the completion of the orders which it had on hand, so as to relieve the committee of any possible embarrassment during its investigation. Within a few months this offer was accepted by the Rubber Company on behalf of the Footwear and Clothing Division and the Mechanical Goods Division, but the Tire Division announced that no immediate change of agency was contemplated. Accordingly, N. W. Ayer & Son proceeded with the preparation of tire advertising for the year 1920; and when, in November, 1919, a general increase in newspaper advertising rates was announced by the publishers, the agency made contracts for the Rubber Company with over a thousand newspapers in the United States, in order to obtain the rates prevailing before the proposed increase. The agency also made space reservations in various magazines so as to obtain preferred positions and guard against expected increases in magazine advertising rates. The space thus engaged by the Ayer firm — with the Rubber Company's authority — was valued at over $940,000. Soon thereafter, by a letter dated December 15, 1919, the Rubber Company gave notice that it would terminate its contract with N. W. Ayer & Son on January 1, 1920. To sever relations on that date did not allow for the three months' notice required by the original agreement, nor did it permit the agency to complete the orders then on hand. To the Rubber Company's letter, therefore, the Ayer management replied that the agreement between the two parties provided for the completion of all orders held by the agency at the time of the notice, that it had gone to all the work and expense of preparing plans and obtaining space for 1920, and that it accordingly expected to receive a commission on the space used. The Rubber Company refused to pay, on the grounds that its new agency was to prepare and forward copy and would hence do the actual placing for which a commission was payable.

In the court trial which followed, it was shown that the Rubber Company had made use of the space for which N. W. Ayer & Son had contracted, and that it had received the benefit not only of savings in rates but also of preferred positions because of the advance contracts which the Ayer agency had made with publishers. The jury decided that N. W. Ayer & Son was entitled to the full amount of its commission, even though part of the advertising was published after the expiration of the required three months' notice. The sum awarded to the agency was the amount of the commissions due, plus interest from January 1, 1921, to the date of the decision (April 18, 1923), a total of $178,620.87.[18]

In this instance, the nature of the disagreement and the amount involved were such that the firm felt compelled to insist upon its rights. Ordinarily, however, the Ayer management has pursued a policy of treating clients with generous consideration in any case of reasonable difference of opinion, avoiding disputes by not insisting upon the exact letter of the law. Once, for example, the question arose as to whether the firm should refuse the request of a client who wished to be released from the contract before the earliest legal date of expiration. The view of the management in Philadelphia was as follows:[19]

It is our feeling here that this could only be looked upon largely as a technical recourse, and it has never been our policy in conducting business to follow such methods for holding an account. Our dealings with people have always been on the basis of mutual satisfaction and co-operation and respect. If these people cannot command our respect and cannot co-operate with us here, it seems to us that the best thing for all concerned is to sever our relationship and forget the whole incident.

DEMANDS FOR PRICE CONCESSIONS

The Ayer management received many requests for exceptions to the charge of 16⅔ per cent of the net cost of the advertising space. Some clients bluntly demanded a reduced rate of commission or a rebate, without any reduction in the amount of service expected. Others wanted to omit some of the service and pay a smaller commission. Still others took the more diplomatic course of asking for extra services without additional charge: advertisers offered, for example, to hire the agency if it would employ (and pay) a number of men, nominally research workers on the agency staff, but actually to do active sales work for the advertiser.

N. W. Ayer & Son stood firm, however, and stoutly refused to make the slightest concession, either by reducing the rate of commission, by promising extra service, or by making any special allowances. On one occasion the manager of an Ayer branch office himself suggested that the firm charge a client no commission for space on which the publisher allowed no discount (certain trade papers and business publications do not grant discounts to agencies). If the usual charges were made, the space would cost 16⅔ per cent more through N. W. Ayer & Son than it would if the client bought it directly from the publisher. If, as was suggested, no commission was to be charged, the agency would receive no compensation at all for handling the transaction. The only reason for making the proposal was that the client was one whose annual expenditure for advertising was very large; and, since he seldom used non-commission media, the allowance would be so slight as to be merely a friendly gesture. The reply from the Ayer headquarters was firm and to the point:[20]

If we handled a situation of this kind for a client and did not bill him commission, would it not be the most natural thing in the world for him to ask himself how far we go in handling matters for other clients for which we make no charge? . . . You have a beginning in a procedure of this sort but you cannot see the end. As you know, we treat everybody alike. We bill them the net cost of the space plus our commission. That is our policy. We cannot charge one client commission and not charge another.

In another case, during the 1930's, a client, whose annual expenditure for advertising usually far exceeds $2,000,000, sought to have the rate of commission lowered to 10 per cent, since he did not want the Ayer staff to prepare any of the copy. An immediate order for $500,000 worth of advertising was at stake, valuable at any time and especially tempting during the depths of the depression; but the Ayer management again refused to alter its policy. After pointing out that the agency could not lower the charge without breaking faith with publishers who expect agencies to maintain card rates, the Ayer reply gave a statement of its policy regarding agency services, as follows:[21]

Our charge to all our customers is on the placing basis. In addition to this service, our volume enables us to maintain numerous plus services in creative, merchandising and other phases of the business. Sometimes customers use none of these plus services, others use some, but they are available to all customers. In our agreement with you you will find that we did not obligate you to use advertisements which we prepared, because it reads: "In the event of our wishing such service, you are to prepare advertising copy, etc." You will see we obligate ourselves to give you our full service, but we do not obligate you to take it.

In this instance the client finally agreed to the usual Ayer terms, but on several other occasions clients have canceled their contracts and given their business to agencies which presumably agreed to accept less than the usual agency compensation.

The Ayer policy of charging a uniform percentage of the cost of the advertising handled was open, of course, to the objections raised in Chapter X to the arrangements for compensation used by most agencies today. It tended to bias the agency's judgment in favor of large advertising appropriations, and it was relatively rigid in view of the wide variation in the amount and kind of agency service required by different clients, even when their expenditures were about the same. A great deal can be (and has been) said for and against a uniform system of compensation for all clients regardless of circumstance or size of advertising appropriation. But the problem belongs to agencies as a group, and N. W. Ayer & Son cannot be singled out for special consideration in this respect. The main point to be remembered here is that the arrangement occasionally creates friction between the agency and a client. To be sure, it is highly unlikely that any system of compensation could be devised that would eliminate such friction entirely. Certainly the desire of the Ayer management to avoid discrimination between clients is sincere and sound.

The Agency's Difficulties in Making Preliminary Studies

N. W. Ayer & Son has frequently encountered problems connected with the various analyses which it makes in preparation for a program of advertising. To determine whether a product is readily salable or not calls for shrewd judgment, intelligent fact-finding, and a careful study of market data. But how much further should the agency go with its analysis? Should it attempt to have scientific tests made as to the quality and value of the product from the consumer's point of view? N. W. Ayer & Son has done so in some cases, with results that have been far from satisfactory. The firm cannot itself make adequate tests, for no agency can afford to maintain the expensive apparatus and staff of technicians which testing involves. As a substitute, it has frequently had members of the Ayer staff use clients' products in order to gain an idea as to the wearing qualities and fitness of purpose; but such tests are too unscientific to be of great value. Many clients test their own products and do it very well, but their opinions are necessarily biased. Unfortunately, when the agency has sought the opinion of an independent laboratory or scientific authority, the results have often been too inconclusive to be of much use. Experts have a way of disagreeing on nearly every point, and they seldom take such a thing as marketability into consideration. Thus, to correct what they regard as a flaw in a product would often make its cost prohibitive to the ordinary consumer.[22] In consequence, the Ayer firm ordinarily has to be content with an analysis which merely gives a general idea about the nature of the product and its probable appeal to the public.

Another difficulty is the fact that manufacturers change their products so often that the results of testing are soon out of date. On one occasion, a least, the Ayer firm prepared and executed an advertising campaign on cigars, based upon the opinion of staff members about samples supplied by the client. The campaign failed; and, when the agency began to investigate the reasons for the failure, it discovered that the client had deliberately lowered the quality of the cigars after agency employees had tried them, to such an extent that the public would not continue to buy them. Fortunately N. W. Ayer & Son has not often been a victim of this kind of practice.

The market surveys, too, are fraught with difficulties. Often the client does not have the facts about his own business which the agency requires, and he is occasionally unable or unwilling to take the trouble to get them. In a few instances the client has had the information, but refused to entrust the Ayer staff with it. And, again, there is always the problem of false or misleading data. Clients have sometimes supplied statistics about costs, sales, and markets which have contained important but hidden errors. In a few cases the falsity has been deliberate. One client, for reasons which are not clear, misrepresented to the agency his marketing setup. A brief check by the agency among dealers uncovered the deceit; further investigation showed that, although the existing arrangement was unsound, the client would not change it. The Ayer management immediately canceled its contract.

In general, however, N. W. Ayer & Son obtains excellent cooperation from its clients, and difficulties commonly arise not because clients are dishonest or cunning but rather because they (as organizations) are complacent or gullible. A corporation is no cleverer than its staff members, and the executive at his desk in headquarters has difficulty in checking the reports which come from the field. His subordinates frequently omit or gloss over facts which might not be to their credit and play up the favorable material. Information which they supply is used by the advertising agency and any errors which it contains may impair the agency's work. N. W. Ayer & Son's problem is essentially one of piecing together information from a number of different sources, in order to obtain the best possible picture of the client's market.

The client is not always the only one at fault when difficulties arise. Beyond question, before the formation of the Creative Production Board, the Ayer agency was careless at times about keeping in touch with the marketing situations of its clients, particularly after it had handled an account for several years with fair success. There is a natural tendency to become complacent after the initial effort and to neglect the continuous study of products and distribution, which is necessary if succeeding campaigns are not to be built upon obsolete facts. Thus, in 1926, N. W. Ayer & Son was handling the advertising for one client from whom it had obtained no sales data since 1919, and for another whose last detailed information about sales dated from 1917. In both cases, obviously, the client was somewhat to blame for overlooking the agency's carelessness; but the Ayer staff was, of course, guilty of neglect because of its failure to insist upon up-to-date information and new studies of the clients' problems at proper intervals. This is one of the problems that the Creative Production Board was designed to prevent, and five years of experience have shown that the Board can eliminate it entirely.

Slips and oversights are, of course, fairly common in big business. A corporation may have wise policies, able executives, and a well-trained staff, but at best it can never completely eliminate errors which are due to the human factor or which occur because a routine system of operation can never comprehend all possible contingencies. Big business, as is too seldom recognized, breeds the bureaucracy and red tape which are supposed to thrive only in the backwaters of government service. Obviously, however, N. W. Ayer & Son could not maintain its present position in the industry if the occasional lapses mentioned here were characteristic of its work.

Problems and Policies Connected with Planning Campaigns

Apart from the usual problem of devising a successful advertising campaign, most of the difficulties which N. W. Ayer & Son has encountered in planning seem to be the result of human prejudices and weaknesses. When both the agency and its client face their advertising problems in an intelligent and coöperative manner, few serious difficulties can arise. But when one or the other plays favorites or is unable to recognize the logic of facts, trouble inevitably occurs.

The Ayer agency, as we have seen, sometimes recommends changes in the client's selling or distributing arrangements as a part of its plan for improving sales. Occasionally, however, the client is unwilling to accept the recommendations. It is human, of course, to balk at innovations or changes in the established régime, and the agency's best efforts at persuasion sometimes fail to influence a client to act for what seems to be his own best good. Thus, N. W. Ayer & Son was unable to convince one client that he should maintain his prices and not make secret concessions to customers. Another had encountered sales resistance which was mainly the result of too high prices, but the agency could not persuade him to reduce them to a reasonable level.

Because of its insistence upon having a sound basis for advertising, the Ayer agency has lost valuable business. In 1926 it warned a manufacturer of long black stockings for children that changes in the general style demand were steadily undermining his business, and that, unless he would add half-hose and colored patterns to his line, he would eventually lose ground to competitors. Being unable to make the change in production and recognizing the futility of trying to stem the flow of public taste, the client decided to stop advertising. Another client promised to change his selling organization in accordance with Ayer recommendations, but he failed to take any action, and the advertising which the agency prepared brought unsatisfactory results. The agency again urged the necessity of changes and even worked out a detailed plan for improving the sales organization, proposing that consumer advertising be curtailed until proper distribution was established. This time the client rejected the recommendations; whereupon the Ayer management, to his surprise and dismay, canceled the contract.

There is, of course, ample room for a difference of opinion as to what really is best for the client in the long run, and, if the client presents sound arguments for opposing the agency's suggestions, the Ayer staff has reconsidered its judgment rather than tried to force its ideas upon the client. In most instances there has been a frank exchange of ideas and excellent coöperation in preparing ground for a campaign. It seems probable, therefore, that the advertiser who complained that N. W. Ayer & Son had "the reputation of mixing into sales matters in an objectionable way" was testifying to the agency's solicitude for the good of its clients' sales as well as to his own unwillingness to consider alternative ideas and well-meant advice.

The same type of problem hampers the formulation of the advertising plan itself. The Ayer firm makes recommendations which it regards as sound, and the client may oppose them. Sometimes his opposition is the result of his instinctive distrust of unfamiliar ideas and methods. At other times he wants to incorporate details in the plan which would endanger its success. The agency must then obtain a compromise, refuse to handle the business, or make the client accept full responsibility for the results of his proposals. One client, for example, succeeded in persuading the Ayer agency to launch a campaign before, in the agency's opinion, adequate distribution of the product had been obtained. When the results proved that the agency's view was well founded, an Ayer executive wrote to the client with characteristic candor:[23]

You know that much against our advices towns were added to carry this advertising. Instead of waiting until the whole plan had proved itself as we wanted to do, your men would go to a jobber and on the strength of the advertising portfolio and the promise of running this advertising, would extract an order. Then long before the goods had reached enough outlets so that women could conveniently buy them, the advertising was started and I think you will bear me out when I say against our advices.

Sometimes more embarrassing for N. W. Ayer & Son is the situation in which two or more members of the client's organization have coördinate authority in the advertising which is done. The likelihood of disagreement is, of course, increased, and the agency frequently has a diplomatic problem of reconciling the opposing views of the executives of the client's organization. Thus, the Ayer firm has won the advertising manager to its point of view only to encounter the determined opposition of the sales manager, who was jealous of his authority and refused to allow any changes in the organization of his salesmen when proposed from the outside. Again, the client's treasurer condemns a plan as costing too much money, or the president may criticize it because he wants to see his own or the firm name emblazoned prominently over a large and sensational campaign, instead of the less ambitious plan recommended for a long, steady pull.

Problems Caused by Clients' Dealers

Difficulties have been caused, too, by the dealers who handle the client's goods. Early in the agency's experience dealers often exerted pressure upon the manufacturer to do local advertising featuring their names rather than his product. They even tried to condition their purchases upon service of this kind, with the result that the manufacturer occasionally felt obliged to yield to their demands. On this point the Ayer agency felt so strongly that it would refuse business rather than prepare the kind of campaign the dealers wanted. In 1903, for example, the firm wrote to a customer as follows:[24]

. . . . To our minds an advertising plan where the local dealer is a prominent factor possesses inherent weakness. The real object of newspaper advertising should be to convince the consumer of the value of your product. That done, some dealer will have to keep it. When advertising is done to please the dealer, or to induce him to purchase, your effort fails before it reaches the proper mark. Even if you succeed in getting the dealer's good will, you are not yet in touch with the consumer, and have no guarantee that the dealer will not drop your goods for those of another whenever he sees fit to do so. If, on the contrary, you had the good will (which good advertising produces) in the minds of many consumers, no dealer could come between you and them. . . .

We want business very much, and we would greatly value yours, but we would rather go without anything we cannot do to our own credit or to the real advantage of the advertiser. If you will undertake a campaign of education, without the local complication, we see no reason why you cannot in time create a valuable good will for the Andes stoves and ranges. This good will will reside with the women who have read of them, and tried them and believed in them, and not with any dealer anywhere. Moreover, in working in the regular way we could do more, perhaps as much again more advertising, for the same amount of money.

Since 1903 the problem has changed somewhat. Dealers now exert pressure to obtain a campaign which will include liberal allowances to them (that is, cash or concessions in the price of the goods they buy) for their local advertising in which the manufacturer's name or product is given a prominent position. On this point the Ayer attitude in 1929 was summed up as follows:[25]

The so-called "advertising allowance" is nothing more or less than a method by which chains and department stores seek to gain an added discount and once they have been given it, they are more anxious from year to year to get more.

In all our experience, we have found that the wisest advertising policy is for a manufacturer to control and direct his own advertising expenditures. When he embarks upon advertising allowances and the usual fifty-fifty plans, he has no control whatever over his advertising or what is said in it. You will appreciate that this is true because the retailers simply want to take the advertiser's money to help pay for the space, and how that money is spent and what is said is always determined by the retailer and not the manufacturer.

Another communication throws further light on the Ayer policy with regard to advertising allowances to dealers:[26]

It is the manufacturer's job to build consumer demand on his product through well planned and aggressive advertising. It is the retailer's job to cash in on that demand by mentioning the advertised product in his own local ad — and the retailer should pay for this mention.

This attitude towards advertising allowances must not be confused with the agency's general policy with regard to trade middlemen. N. W. Ayer & Son has recognized for many years that a manufacturer's selling organization cannot be effective unless it has the coöperation of the dealers who handle its products. Hence the agency has emphasized the need for obtaining support in the trade for any campaign that it handles, and it makes a definite effort to see that every client's relations with his dealers are on a proper footing.

Handling Association Advertising

The development of association advertising raises a different type of difficulty. When a group of manufacturers agree to coöperate in advertising to promote their industry as a whole, the individual client's advertising dollar must be split two ways. One part goes to join the funds supplied by his competitors to promote the sales of the entire group. The other part is devoted to the client's struggle to get for himself as large a proportion as possible of those sales.

The trouble is that it is almost impossible to keep the members of a voluntary association in agreement upon a definite project; moreover, it is usually impossible to get all the members of an industry to contribute to the cost, for one or two hold back in the hope that they can benefit from the results without any expense.[27] When the issue has arisen, N. W. Ayer & Son has often advised its clients against participating in coöperative campaigns, on the ground that they were not likely to receive an adequate return for their money, or that they would save themselves the trouble of getting into disputes and entanglements which such undertakings frequently engender. In spite of its pessimism where individual clients have been concerned, however, the Ayer agency has gladly solicited the advertising of associations and assisted in launching their campaigns. From a perusal of the firm's correspondence, indeed, one is bound to infer that the only association campaigns which are likely to succeed are those handled by N. W. Ayer & Son! Perhaps the Ayer views on the subject were influenced a little by the natural desire to see advertising dollars spent through N. W. Ayer & Son instead of through a competing agency.

However that may be, it is interesting to observe the principles and purposes which N. W. Ayer & Son believe should be embodied in an association campaign. These were summarized in a letter to an association for which the agency hoped to place some advertising:[28]

You should assure yourselves that
 (a) The membership as a whole is behind the movement and pledged to contribute to its success.
 (b) A financial plan has been adopted providing sufficient funds to carry on the movement uninterruptedly for at least three years.
 (c) The national program is placed in the hands of a small committee with full executive powers — able to make decisions quickly and to co-operate with your national advertising counsel in the fullest possible manner.
 (d) Advertising counsel is equipped with men, resources and experiences that will assure you an effective national service.

The purpose of the advertising:
 (a) To increase the number of users of ... [the product].
 (b) To increase the general quality of ... [the product]. In other words, to establish and maintain a high standard as a qualification of membership.
 (c) To combat the serious inroads of substitutes.
 (d) To protect your industry against competition, particularly against unfair and prejudiced competition.
 (e) To secure public recognition of the high standard of service rendered by members.
 (f) To obtain public preference for concerns using the emblem.

The agency also touched upon the methods employed by associations to raise their funds for advertising:[29]

Usually an equitable rate is struck on the basis of volume which is added to the production cost of the commodity, such as one cent per square yard; three cents per case; one-fiftieth of one per cent of the gross sales, etc.

In one case an association provided the funds, using sales as a basis, as follows:

½ of 1% of 1920 sales provided appropriation for 1921
¾ of 1% of 1921 provided appropriation for 1922
1% of 1922 sales provided appropriation for 1923

Assessments are, as a rule, paid monthly, quarterly, or semi-annually in advance — each contributing member agrees to maintain his payments over a full period of three years.

On the whole, N. W. Ayer & Son's difficulties with planning are mainly those of convincing the client, whether an individual firm or an association, of the soundness of its advertising ideas and methods and of persuading him to use them. An impartial observer might feel at times that the agency had been overly enthusiastic about its own views, but this is only to be expected. Of the Ayer desire to promote the best interests of its clients, even when adherence to this desire means a loss of profits, there can be no shadow of doubt.

Problems with the Preparation of Advertising Copy

The difficulties connected with the preparation of advertising copy, even more than those of planning, have arisen largely out of personal tastes, whims, and prejudices. Other parts of the agency's work are intangible but largely subject to reason and based upon well-tested principles of action. But a piece of advertising copy is something concrete which can be readily compared with other advertisements for beauty, atmosphere, and appeal. Many of the theories upon which it is based are still not subject to conclusive proof; and whether it is good or bad, therefore, depends less upon established standards than upon the taste of the person who looks at it. As in the realm of pure art, it is a matter of subjective rather than objective values; and getting agency and client to agree as to what constitutes good advertising copy is closely akin to the difficulty of getting two people to agree on the merits of a painting or a piece of sculpture.

We are dealing here, of course, with problems other than the task of creating copy which will express the ideas agreed upon as desirable. To embody those ideas in a convincing graphic form is a problem which an agency regularly has to solve, and the difficulty of doing this need not be emphasized.

The obstacles which arise from the outside to hamper that achievement are of a different and more perplexing nature. They depend upon the idiosyncrasies of clients and the exigencies of competition.

One source of difficulty lies in the restrictions under which the Ayer Copy Department sometimes has to work. Some clients have prescribed what they want within such narrow limits that the copymen have had no scope for effective writing or art work. A firm of jewelers, for example, insisted upon austere, dignified copy, with small and ultraconservative illustrations and brief texts from which anything in the nature of sales appeal was barred. Within this narrow limitation the staff could prepare only commonplace and comparatively uninteresting copy.

Other clients have had to guard against censorship by some outside body of authority. Thus, long before the present federal legislation about security advertising, the Ayer agency found difficulty in preparing for a brokerage house copy that would meet with the approval of the New York Stock Exchange. In advertising pharmaceutical products the agency has had to guard against making claims which might antagonize the American Medical Association. And it has likewise had difficulty with copy containing statements to which the National Better Business Bureau and publishers might take exception, for both groups attempt to eliminate from advertisements any material which too plainly "knocks" the products of a competitor or which promises too much to the purchaser. N. W. Ayer & Son has always endeavored to maintain high ethical standards on these matters, but there is, of course, plenty of room for dispute as to where to draw the line. The mere fact that copy is censored by outside organizations places limitations upon copy preparation which sometimes chafe.

Trouble arises from outside pressure to put objectionable material into the copy, as well as to keep it out. Thus, before World War I clients often insisted upon having their names and pictures appear in prominent positions in the advertising, and it was difficult for N. W. Ayer & Son to persuade them that such sops to vanity hindered the work of advertising. In recent years the firm has encountered another form of the same type of problem: a number of clients have asked it to incorporate in their advertising purchased endorsements from film stars and other people prominent in the public eye. The Ayer agency, however, has consistently refused to use testimonials from any but genuine and well-informed users of a product; and this policy has occasionally caused some strained relations. On one occasion, to the writer's personal knowledge, the Ayer management had to inform a valued client of long standing that it would cancel its contract with him rather than comply with his request to buy a testimonial from a person who obviously could have no knowledge of the product concerned.

GETTING THE FINISHED COPY APPROVED

To obtain the client's approval of copy, once it has been nursed past these initial obstacles, forms another type of problem. Sometimes a client expresses objections which are based upon quite reasonable differences of taste and reaction to which the agency must yield. Frequently, however, his criticisms are merely captious. Clients have approved the typewritten text of an advertisement only to find fault with it in printed form; or they have expressed enthusiasm about the sketches and layouts and then complained about the finished advertisements. One client took the agency to task because the illustrations showed models of his products which he said were badly chosen and out of fashion. The models were of his own choosing.

When an agency has to satisfy the tastes of several persons in the client's organization instead of one executive alone, its difficulties seem to increase in a geometric ratio. A committee, for example, may be well pleased with a piece of copy at first inspection, and then, upon closer analysis, pick it entirely to pieces. One man suggests a different word or phrase; another wants to alter the lines of the illustration or to use another variety of type; the third decides that a slight rearrangement of the headlines and illustration would improve the layout. Each suggestion brings forth another until the copy is no longer recognizable — its unity destroyed, its atmosphere muddled, and its general effect made ragged and lifeless.

On the other hand, if the authority for approval of copy is concentrated in a single person, the agency may be embarrassed by

his poor judgment. An excerpt from a letter from one Ayer executive to another illustrates the issue as it arose in connection with
a radio program:[30]

> . . . we are held responsible by the —— —— Company for the direc-
> tion and production of their broadcasting, while at the same time we
> allow the contact with our client in this work to be limited to one in-
> dividual. . . . We leave ourselves in a manifestly unfair position when
> our work is subject to the approval and dictation of a man who has
> shown himself so fully lacking in appreciative faculties, in discrimina-
> tion and in judgment, and a man who is so readily repudiated by the
> higher executives of his company as we have had occasion to note at
> times to our sorrow.

A certain amount of revision by the client is expected as a matter of course: no copy can be above criticism. On the whole, however, the problems in this area are less serious than the above
paragraphs might indicate. During the past two decades, moreover, advertisers have increasingly recognized the complex and
technical nature of copy preparation, and they have accordingly
been more inclined to respect the judgment of experts. In recent
years, too, copy-testing data have helped to eliminate the element
of personal opinion, thereby putting copy approval on a more
objective basis. Today this phase of agency work is not regarded
by the Ayer organization as presenting any serious headaches.

RUSH ORDER DIFFICULTIES

The time required to produce advertising often creates difficulties. It takes time to write good copy and to prepare satisfactory illustrations; it takes still more time to prepare good engravings and plates for their reproduction. A rush order for copy
means hasty work, unsatisfactory copy, inferior plates, and extra
expense for overtime work. The agency makes every effort to
avoid eleventh-hour demands, but some clients habitually delay
their decision to launch advertising until it is too late to meet the
desired publishing dates without excessive haste. In other cases
the rush is the unavoidable result of an emergency — the outbreak of a bitter trade war, a sudden change in style, or some
other unexpected event.

Not only is rushed work often unsatisfactory, but it frequently causes friction and misunderstanding. Of course, the agency can allow the client only a brief time for examining and approving emergency copy. The client has often complained later that he would have caught errors or made improvements if he had been given more time to review it, even when he himself was the cause of the haste. And, after he has returned the corrected copy, the agency has to strain every resource in order to get proofs and plates to the printers before the presses start. Recriminations are bound to follow. To be sure, such rushes are inherent in modern commerce, particularly when the product advertised happens to be the subject of sudden changes in fashion or fad. But magazine advertising usually has to be prepared several months before it reaches the public, and this time requirement, plus the importance of styling in modern business and the speed of the modern style cycle, gives the agency additional reason for being alert.

Keeping Secrets

The plans and copy of a client must, of course, remain a secret until the campaign is launched, and to prevent news of them from reaching competitors beforehand often calls for special arrangements. All Ayer copy is regularly guarded from the eyes of outsiders, and, if the information contained is of special strategic importance, the copy is kept under lock and key. On one occasion before this practice was adopted, copy which was designed to steal a march on a client's competitors was filched from the agency some weeks before the campaign was to begin. The agency had at once to junk all the materials and plates which it had prepared and start with new plans. Emergencies of this kind are rare, but the need to prevent confidential information from leaking out is very real, and the agency takes its responsibility seriously.

The Ayer agency has a special advantage in guarding confidential material in that its creative services are all performed in one building, from the writing of text to the pulling of proofs on the finished advertisement. Many agencies have their layouts prepared by outside artists, and the great majority send their work to an outside printer. In such circumstances, secrecy becomes difficult, and details of strategic importance often leak out well in advance of the publishing date. By having all work done under one roof, the Ayer management has long avoided this danger.

PROBLEMS AND POLICIES CONNECTED WITH PUBLICITY

In recent years the craze for notoriety, together with a very general and natural desire among advertisers to get newspaper space for nothing, has complicated the publicity work of N. W. Ayer & Son. Some clients want the agency to prepare publicity for them when they have no possible chance of material benefit. Others feel that publishers should, as a matter of course, print news articles about them merely because they advertise on a large scale. Still others can benefit by good publicity but want the agency to prepare articles or arrange public exhibitions of a type which can be of no value. And, occasionally, a client wants the agency to prepare political or tariff propaganda for dissemination among newspapers and magazines.

On all these points N. W. Ayer & Son long ago took a firm stand, the general policy appearing in the following excerpt from correspondence with a client:[31]

With complete sympathy for the position of the publishers, regarding this unhappy practice of trading paid advertising for a certain amount of "press agency" stuff, we inaugurated our policy of preparing publicity which should be acceptable to publishers solely on the intrinsic merit of the writing and its inherent interest to the readers of the news and editorial columns of the publication.

At that time we made it a fundamental policy of this business to give the publishers our pledge that they were entirely at liberty then and always to consign any part or all of this material to the wastebasket, instead of prejudicing their interests in the slightest with us. And we also determined that not a soul, either in or out of the publishing business, should be able to say that N. W. Ayer & Son endeavored to "make a profit on free advertising."

To this policy the Ayer firm has adhered with remarkable consistency. In every instance, when the question of using publicity has come up, the agency has first considered whether or not the client's business presented any news of general interest. It has also tried to determine whether or not the client concerned was sufficiently important in his field to reap the benefit of any aroused interest. Obviously most publicity material can feature only a general product rather than a particular brand; therefore, a small producer has little chance of benefiting from publicity about his industry. The Ayer agency has repeatedly informed clients that it was unable to give them publicity service until there was some prospect of results commensurate with the expense involved.

To clients who have felt entitled to news and editorial space as a special premium for their extensive use of space, the Ayer firm has been quick to point out that the only publicity of any value is material which is inherently interesting, a quality which bears no necessary relation to the size of an advertising appropriation. Even though they start with this policy in mind, however, clients have seldom been content with mere general news about their product, and several have expressed a belief that their products should be mentioned by brand name or that sales arguments should be worked into the material. Such material plainly belongs in the advertising columns, and N. W. Ayer & Son has not hesitated to say so. Thus, when a client complained that his name appeared too seldom in the publicity articles, the Ayer Public Relations Department's comment was:[32]

The real point in all this as I see it is not whether any of our clients are mentioned by name in any publicity releases, but whether such mention is of a sort that is in accord with the highest standards of journalistic, advertising, and publicity practice.

The Department stopped giving publicity service to another client because "Obviously we cannot continue indefinitely to produce publicity which has no other merit than that it presents the sales arguments in favor of . . . [the product concerned]." [33]

N. W. Ayer & Son is not opposed to stunts arranged to attract public notice to a product or firm, but it refuses to recommend such devices if they serve little useful purpose. Thus it helped to arrange airplane flights to provide publicity for a spark-plug manufacturer, and a pajama parade for a client who manufactured pajamas. It advised several clients, on the other hand, not to make presentations of their products to Queen Marie of Rou-

mania during her tour of the United States. In the agency's opinion the cost of arranging for such occasions was too high, and it
felt that, in any case, so many firms were attempting to draw
attention to their wares through Queen Marie that the country
was becoming bored by the pother — probably a correct estimation of the public's attitude.

Because it instituted its public relations work to provide news
material which might aid sales, N. W. Ayer & Son has rejected
proposals to have it assist with propaganda for political or tariff
purposes, though the agency has many connections in Washington
which enable it to help clients who have occasion to deal with
government officials.[34] While publicity is still a major function,
over the years the activities of the department gradually evolved
into the broader field of public relations, involving helping clients
in their relations with stockholders, employees, and the public.
With this change in the character of the work, the original policy
of operating the department without profit was changed to one of
earning a reasonable profit.

FAULTS IN THE CLIENT'S ORGANIZATION

Many difficulties are not related exclusively to a single phase
of the agency's work. They are matters, rather, which complicate
the general routine of handling an account, and frequently they
cut across planning, copy preparation, marketing counsel, and
some of the problems we have already considered. Because of
their heterogeneous nature, such problems can seldom be treated
according to a fixed policy; yet the handling of them, of course,
reflects both the strong and weak points of managerial policy.

One of the most serious general difficulties encountered is an
inefficient or badly organized management in the client's organization. In several instances two men of different ideas but equal
authority have had charge of the advertising. One prominent company, for example, divided activities between two plants, one in
Chicago and one in the Boston area. Executives in both places
attempted to direct the advertising — one through the agency's
Chicago branch, the other through the Boston office. In such circumstances constant friction and disagreement were inevitable,

and the Ayer firm was compelled to make a frank request for centralization of authority.

On another occasion the president of a large and supposedly well-organized firm complained that the Ayer representative failed to consult with him about advertising. The agency was obliged to point out that it was supposed to work with his advertising department and that to go over the advertising manager's head would simply invite trouble.

A client's managerial inefficiency or carelessness has often been the source of trouble for the agency. In spite of the agency's best efforts, it has been impossible to get results for some clients simply because they have been unwilling or unable to assimilate new ideas. In some instances the client has been content to drift and has not actively caused concern, but of course his lack of progress and initiative has thrown a burden upon the agency which it should not have had to bear. Fortunately problems of this sort have arisen less frequently during recent years.

Excessive Demands upon the Agency

With certain clients, however, the trouble has been that the management deliberately tried to unload upon the agency work which was not a part of its function. The agency is somewhat to blame for situations of this kind. The line between advertising and active selling is particularly difficult to draw in any case, and the agency has aggravated the difficulty by offering so much assistance that clients have been led to expect too much. Thus, as early as 1905, McKinney urged the staff to discriminate in the accounts they accepted and the service they offered:[35]

I think we are all apt to sometimes get a wrong idea of the right service for a particular case. I do not think it is possible to get our standard too high. . . . [But] when we get an advertising contract, we should stop and think what we can afford to do on that contract. If there is but $100 profit on the order, we had better refuse the business than spend $150 in the handling of it. . . . We ourselves, more than other houses, are adding to the expectations of the advertiser beyond what he really has a right to look for. We talk about our good service until we get the advertiser to expect so much that he is dissatisfied even with what we do give, and he will perhaps leave us and take inferior work and because he pays a less price does not expect so much.

Ayer service has greatly expanded beyond that of 1905, but the firm still has to contend with unprofitable accounts and clients who expect too much. When a client has demanded help with the actual selling of his product, however, the Ayer management has been forced to draw a definite line. It defined its work, on one such occasion, as follows:[36]

We are an advertising agency. Our primary function is the application of advertising as a definite selling force to assist in the expansion of a business.

In order to check our own recommendations and to be of greater service to our customers, we maintain a very complete Merchandising Department. This department is equipped to give advice on many phases of a sales program, but it cannot, nor should it be expected to, plan the details of a sales program as thoroughly as a manufacturer's own organization.

This view was amplified somewhat in a discussion about a different client:[37]

Our work is to prepare advertising and to contribute to defining a sales policy that will work in harmony with advertising plans. If there were a question regarding how the —— should be advertised in any one section that we could not solve without making a personal visit or investigation, we would do that. But we do not hold ourselves responsible in any way for the conduct of their sales organization in any city, and we will not assume the duty of checking up on their sales organization.

These statements may leave something to be desired in style and grammar, but their candor and firmness in the face of unreasonable demands from clients are noteworthy.

Occasionally friction has arisen because of plain ignorance on the part of the client. One, for example, complained bitterly about the results of the advertising placed by Ayer. However, the statistics which he himself quoted proved that, whereas sales had been dropping off before his connection with N. W. Ayer & Son, they had subsequently shown steady and substantial improvement. This sort of difficulty belongs mainly to the period before 1930.

One interesting problem emerges from the modern way of organizing and managing large business enterprises. However much business men may be inclined toward handling affairs on a personal basis, in the large corporation of today transactions must be conducted through designated channels and the personal element thrust into the background; otherwise, the machine will break down from the combined weight of volume and frustrated specialization. Clients have occasionally been unwilling to recognize the necessity for impersonal system in the agency. Thus, N. W. Ayer & Son encounters difficulty because an advertiser frequently prefers to have his contacts with the agency maintained by the representative who originally persuaded him to use the agency. It is obvious, of course, that the men best adapted for getting business are not necessarily qualified to handle the subsequent creative work in a satisfactory manner. In any case, if the Ayer management allowed its solicitors to service the accounts which they won, their time would soon be so taken up that efforts to get new business would necessarily cease. So far as possible, the firm has tried to have in liaison positions men with whom the client prefers to deal; but neither this nor the practice of having men specialize strictly in the search for new business can be followed without compromise.

Appraisal of Policy of Handling Clients

Two situations arose which revealed weaknesses in the Ayer policy used before 1932: one when two accounts began to conflict; and the other when the expenditure on an account was so small that the commissions earned did not cover the cost of handling the business.

As early as 1900 the agency began to experience the temptation to hold back the development of one client in order to avoid a conflict with another. At that time one solicitor referred to the problem in a report of his activities. Discussing the advertising of a client who manufactured corsets in a small way, he wrote:[38]

The extent to which this advertising can be developed depends very largely upon how far we find it may interfere with our advertising for the Ferris Bros. Co. — it is therefore quite as much a question of how far it is policy for us to develop them as advertisers as it is of their ability to advertise.

With the tendency of modern firms to expand operations and enlarge their line of products, this problem of growing conflict became more difficult to handle, as we have already seen in the preceding discussion of solicitation problems. Thus, the Ayer management felt obliged to caution a representative not to encourage one client to seek a market for glass dishes in the hotel field because his account would then conflict with that of a china manufacturer who was working the institutional field intensively with the agency's help. In several cases the possibility of conflict was avoided by definite agreement with the clients involved. The agency, for example, was placing the advertising of a manufacturer of crystal tableware and, at the same time, that of a manufacturer of plain glassware. When the latter firm began to expand into the manufacture of crystal ware, the agency pointed out the possibility of conflict and obtained an understanding by which the agency was not to be asked to assist with the new line.

The Ayer agency keeps no exact account of the cost of handling the business of individual clients, but the management has an approximate idea of the profitableness of accounts in relation to their size. Occasionally in the past it felt obliged to cut down on the service given because the volume was reduced to the point where the commissions did not cover the estimated cost. In most, if not all, instances of such limitation of service the matter was arranged by agreement with the client. In several cases advertisers agreed to prepare their own copy and illustrations in order to have N. W. Ayer & Son handle the rest of their work at a reasonable profit. One client agreed to place his own trade-paper advertising so as to relieve the agency of this unprofitable part of his business. In other instances the agency transferred accounts from the contract to the order basis so as to eliminate the excessive costs. With the policy of selectivity, which has been pursued since about 1940, accounts which do not pay their way on a full service basis have been eliminated.

On the other hand, until N. W. Ayer & Son agreed with a client to curtail its service, its policy was to give whatever assistance is essential for good advertising. The following statement from one Ayer executive to another seems to be typical of the firm's attitude for many years:[39]

I notice in the last paragraph of the attached report on . . . [an Ayer client] that we are called upon to make various surveys in sales territories and that in Mr. H. . .'s opinion if we continue to make them whatever profit there is in the account will be gone.

As long as we are serving this business, we will do anything necessary in connection with the account to enlighten ourselves as well as the client regardless of our profit, as of course you know this is the policy of our house.

I should think that Plans Department should decide the necessity of making the surveys. If it is necessary to do this work, we should certainly do it regardless of our cost. In other words, so long as we are serving an account we must serve it to the very best advantage regardless of the expenditure.

In all its relations with advertisers N. W. Ayer & Son has, on the whole, pursued a consistent policy of enlightened self-interest. It has sought to make a profit by providing to clients the best service it has known how to give. In keeping with this aim it has, since 1876, identified its own interests with those of its clients. An outsider may question whether any agency should attempt to help with so many phases of a client's business. The Ayer firm seems to do too much work for the credit received, possibly more than is needed. At any rate, its record of actual performance has squared with its avowed policy of "making advertising pay the advertiser" and "spending the advertiser's money as if it were your own." There have been occasional mistakes and shortcomings, of course, but these have arisen out of oversight or mistaken judgment, not of wrong principle. They are but slight deviations in a long career of uniformly high service to advertisers.

WHY ACCOUNTS HAVE BEEN LOST

As a result of the welter of problems encountered in the relations between the agency and its clients — and often because of Ayer policies in handling those problems — N. W. Ayer & Son occasionally loses an advertising account. The turnover of clients, indeed, is one of the most perplexing problems which the modern advertising agency has to face.[40] Lost clients must be replaced if the agency business is to survive, and getting new clients is often a long and expensive process. The cancellation of an account, especially if it takes away a substantial portion of an agency's total business, necessitates readjustments in the agency's organization which are not easily made. The business of a single client has sometimes constituted more than a tenth of the total Ayer volume, and any concern which may lose so large a proportion of its business at one stroke of the pen is in a highly vulnerable position.

The forces which bring about this migration of business from one agency to another, although obviously of the greatest importance, are extremely difficult to trace with precision. Agency men have little difficulty in generalizing as to the major causes of the turnover as a whole. But any attempt to analyze particular cases soon bogs down: no two persons will agree as to why an account has been lost, and it is surprisingly difficult to reconcile their views.

Those within the agency itself disagree in their explanations, partly because no man likes to advance reasons which might involve his own culpability, partly because there are usually ample grounds for an honest difference of opinion. Sometimes, too, executives find it advisable to conceal the true facts even from trusted subordinates. The agency as a whole, moreover, is naturally reluctant to admit that there have been flaws in its work, and seeks explanations from the outside.

The client himself can give the historian little help in the matter. If he has found the agency at fault, he ordinarily prefers to keep his opinions to himself: the business man seems instinctively to shun frank criticism in his own sphere of private enterprise. If the advertiser has changed agencies because of any personal or irrational motives, he is still less inclined to give out the true explanation. Indeed, he may not be conscious of the real reason, feeling instead an unidentified dissatisfaction with the service that he has been getting. Rival agencies, of course, are only too willing to plant and cultivate the seeds of such discontent. Many an advertiser undoubtedly rationalizes or invents reasons after he has decided upon a change.

In an effort to throw some factual light on this matter, an attempt was made to analyze all the canceled contracts in the Ayer files to 1932. These were over 1,100 in number and dated from 1895. At best, a study of them could yield only a limited amount of information: many of them contained nothing more than a notation that the account was canceled; others listed brief explanations which may have been wrong or only half true. Even the letters which related to many of the cancellations revealed little about the cause of friction or complaint; for, in advertising as in many other lines of business, a great deal of negotiation is conducted by means of personal conferences, particularly when it concerns important agreements or policies or strained relations. As a rule, therefore, only the final decisions or conclusions become a matter of written record. While such obstacles form an insurmountable bar to a nice statistical analysis, the evidence which could be pieced together from canceled contracts, correspondence, and (where recent cancellations were concerned) personal interviews suggests some of the major factors in the constant shifting of Ayer clients.[41]

In the early period of the Ayer firm's history, price was of course one of the most prominent causes of the turnover of accounts. Advertisers frankly sought bargains, agents bid for their business openly and without shame, and many an advertiser took his business away from N. W. Ayer & Son when he found that he could get the space he wanted for less money elsewhere. Now that space rates and commissions have become fairly well standardized and any reductions from them are regarded as unethical, price is almost never mentioned as a cause for change. An advertiser who changes his agency in order to take advantage of any special price arrangement usually disguises the fact by citing other causes for cancellation. During the period 1930–39, however, hungry agents and economizing advertisers became more daring in their defiance of standardized prices. To the writer's personal knowledge, at least two important national advertisers frankly demanded price concessions from N. W. Ayer & Son. Fully aware of the probable consequences, the Ayer management refused to alter its terms and had to watch several million dollars' worth of advertising go to other agencies.

Closely connected with price as a factor in the turnover of clients is the service given by the agency. Indeed it is seldom possible to consider the two separately. A substantial number of advertisers have objected to the Ayer price, not because Ayer service has not been considered worth the cost but rather because they did not want or could not use all the services to which that price entitled them. On the other hand, Ayer clients have occasionally canceled their contracts in order to use a cheaper agency, only to find that the service given by N. W. Ayer & Son was ultimately less costly in comparison. This was particularly true in the days of unstable space rates, when the ability of N. W. Ayer & Son to save money on the price of space usually more than offset any difference between its remuneration and that of rival agencies.

Some cancellations can be traced directly to the client's dissatisfaction with the work done by the agency. Whether their complaints, on the whole, were justified or not it is impossible to say. In some instances there is fairly clear evidence of carelessness or neglect by the agency. In others the client was plainly unreasonable in his expectations. One, for example, canceled when the agency very properly turned down his request for special favors at the expense of other Ayer clients. As might be expected, there is some evidence to show that advertisers are more critical of agency work in times of difficulty than in periods of prosperity.

Another important cause of cancellation in the period since 1920 has been the failure of client and agency to agree as to the proper method of advertising. Here the difficulty is not so much dissatisfaction with service as an honest difference of opinion about the kind of advertising which the client's business requires.

Every agency, of course, loses business because clients become dissatisfied with its work, and there is no reason to believe that N. W. Ayer & Son has suffered more on this score than any of its rivals. Certainly the fact that it will risk losing business rather than agree to a campaign which it regards as wrong indicates a high degree of commendable professional integrity.

Changes in ownership through company mergers and other combinations of business concerns have constituted another important factor in the loss of accounts, especially since 1900. When corporation A takes over companies X and Y, its management frequently places their advertising in the hands of an agency which it has been using or which it happens to know better, no matter how satisfactorily the work has been previously handled.

Changes in personnel, too, have been an important factor. In repeated instances a new executive in the client's organization has transferred the advertising from N. W. Ayer & Son to an agency of his own choosing. More frequently still, the client's advertising manager resigns to join the staff of another agency or to form one of his own, and, because of his personal influence with the concern, he is able to obtain its advertising business, even though the Ayer service has previously given satisfaction. In a few instances the new agency thus formed is really a subsidiary of the client's company, formed to enable the company to handle its own placing while complying with the publishers' requirements for recognition as an agency entitled to the agency discount. From the time of the founding of the Ayer agency down to about 1910, publishers could often be persuaded to grant the agency discount to large advertisers who wished to place their own advertising, and the agency occasionally lost business when a client decided to try his own hand at the work.

Changes in the Ayer organization itself have sometimes caused clients to cancel their agreements. Such changes occur when a member of the agency staff has been shifted to another position, or when he has been dropped, or when he has resigned to join another firm. From the point of view of the Ayer firm such changes are usually unavoidable and often bring about improvement; when, however, they deprive a client of the services of a man whom he has regarded with special favor, friction may result. This difficulty most frequently has developed around the

Ayer representative who acts as liaison man between the agency and the client. The responsibility for interpreting the client's ideas and needs to the agency, explaining the agency's plans and copy to the client, and keeping the advertiser satisfied rests largely upon him; and, for personal reasons alone, one such representative sometimes fails where another has attained marked success. The Ayer management has always attempted to give proper consideration to the wishes of clients in this matter, but there are obvious limits to what it can do, and it has firmly resisted any attempt on the part of a client to dictate what its internal organization is to be.

The reason for cancellation most frequently recorded by Ayer clients before 1932 was the desire to change to a local agency. Underlying this explanation, of course, are other factors which have already been discussed. The client may be offered special price concessions by the local agency, he may have acquired a personal or financial interest in it, or he may believe that it will provide him with advertising service which, in some respect, will be more satisfactory than that given by N. W. Ayer & Son.

WHY THE AGENCY SOMETIMES RESIGNS ACCOUNTS

It must not be supposed, however, that the client always takes the lead in severing relations with the agency. The agency itself often does the canceling. Indeed, of the 1,164 old contracts studied, 581 were canceled by the agency, compared with 391 canceled by clients and 192 in which the canceler could not be ascertained. These figures may be somewhat misleading, for it is clear from the correspondence that the Ayer management has sometimes given hasty notice of termination as soon as it has received indirect word that another agency has won the account, hoping by this means to put a better face on the situation from its own point of view. Despite this fact, however, there have been many instances in which the agency plainly wished to get rid of an advertiser whom it had contracted to serve.

In the majority of such cases the agency canceled because the client had stopped advertising altogether or had reduced his appropriation to a very small figure, and the agency wished to be quite free from entanglements which might hamper its business-getting efforts. Often the agency took its action because the client had ceased to be a good credit risk or had gone into bankruptcy, or because he was going out of business. Such cases are mainly the result of ordinary business mortality. They may possibly show that advertising is no guarantee against failures, but, since it is impossible (owing to the lack of adequate information) to determine any definite relation between them and the agency's work or advertising in general, they have no special significance for us here.

Of far greater importance is the fact that the agency has canceled accounts with clients because the Ayer management decided that their business showed no promise of developing from an advertising point of view, or came to the conclusion that it was undesirable with reference to Ayer policy. The agency has, moreover, canceled contracts because the advertisers concerned were competing with clients whose business the Ayer management regarded as more valuable. Most significant of all, perhaps, it has canceled accounts because it was dissatisfied with the attitudes of the clients: some of them habitually made unreasonable demands of the agency, some were unwilling to give proper coöperation in making the advertising program effective, some insisted on sales or advertising policies of which the agency could not approve. If the available data are dependable, the agency canceled 42 of the accounts analyzed primarily because it was dissatisfied with the attitude of the clients, a figure which closely matches the number of clients, 44, who were dissatisfied with Ayer service.

Average Life of Ayer Accounts

The subject of the turnover of accounts necessarily involves some consideration of the length of time during which the agency keeps its clients. Here again no nice statistical analysis of the agency's record is possible. The accounts which have been with the agency for the longest period cannot be included in the calculation of any average because they are still clients and may continue to be for many years to come. All that we can do is obtain an average of the contracts which have actually been canceled and take that figure as an approximation of the true average. But even this result is somewhat misleading, for the average must necessarily be based upon the recorded dates of expiration, whereas the actual business relations between agency and client have sometimes ended weeks and months before the legal termination of the contract. Subject to these qualifications the Ayer files of canceled contracts reveal the following facts. For all the 1,164 contracts the average duration was 3 years, 7.6 months. For the 699 contracts canceled before the end of 1920 the average was 3 years, 5.2 months; and for the years from 1921 to 1932, inclusive, the average was 3 years, 10.9 months. Since the dates of termination in the latter period were much closer to the dates when relations actually ceased than in the early period, the average life of an Ayer contract apparently lengthened in this period by about 15 per cent. It is impossible to say, however, whether this increase means that the agency lost more clients of long standing after 1920 than before or that it was more successful in holding its customers.[42]

At all events the agency is proud of the fact that the first advertiser to agree to the open contract in 1875 was a client until the firm went out of business over seventy years later, also that several important clients have been with the agency continuously for over a quarter of a century. A study of the accounts currently being handled at the end of 1947 shows that 50 per cent had been dealing with N. W. Ayer & Son nine years or longer, 25 per cent 16 years or more, and 10 per cent in excess of 30 years. That large and experienced advertisers are satisfied with Ayer service for such long periods is further evidence that Ayer service has been of high quality.

CHAPTER XV

THE AGENCY AND ADVERTISING MEDIA

AN ADVERTISING agency is not only a seller but also a buyer. Thus far in our detailed study, we have focused attention primarily upon N. W. Ayer & Son in its dealings with the clients to whom it *sells* service. We must not neglect those from whom the firm, as a result of its work for advertisers, must *buy* service. A complete list of such concerns would include artists, photographers, style experts, engravers, publishers, and a host of others. But by far the most important are those who present the advertising message in its final form to the public — the publishers of newspapers and periodicals and the owners of billboards, radio broadcasting, and television stations. It will amplify our picture of the advertising agency to examine in some detail the relations between N. W. Ayer & Son and this group.

EARLY RELATIONS WITH PUBLISHERS, 1869–1900

When F. W. Ayer first opened his agency, he was, as we have seen, a seller of advertising space which he had bought from the owners of religious weekly newspapers published in Philadelphia. Almost immediately he began to enlarge the scope of his work, until he was selling space in papers, both religious and secular, daily and weekly, all over the United States. The bulk of this space was in publications from which Ayer, anticipating the needs of his customers, had leased the advertising columns in entirety or bought large blocks of space. In the remaining papers with which he dealt, he bought space from time to time as he received actual orders from advertisers, bargaining for the lowest space rates obtainable.

The significant thing is that Ayer was essentially a space jobber and wholesaler: he was in no sense the agent of the advertiser, and it was only in a distinctly Pickwickian sense of the term that Ayer could be said to have been the agent of the publisher. His business was to buy advertising space at a price which would permit him to resell it at the greatest possible profit to himself.[1]

Bargaining about the price of space and the "commission" or discount to be received by the agency was, in consequence, the outstanding activity of an agent. Indeed, it provides the key to relations between N. W. Ayer & Son and publishers and to agency-publisher relations in general during the period 1869 to 1900. We catch a brief glimpse of this in a letter from F. W. Ayer to his father, written in 1872:[2]

The Pat[ent] Med[icine] adv[ertising] of Wenzell's [an early Ayer customer] is coming back pretty lively. They [the publishers] can't swallow my low figures. Will try & fix them up satisfactorily however. Went to Bato. [Baltimore] Tuesday morning, came back yesterday. Made good terms with "Epis[copal] Meth[odist]" & "Cath[olic] Mirror" of Bato. for pat. med. adv. also with Wilmington "Com[mercial] & Tribune" for Evans' [another Ayer customer]. The latter was $100.00 gross trade. Could not come to terms with the "Meth[odist] Protestant" but may yet. They want double rates for pat. med. advs. which I am not inclined to pay. . . . I quite improved our arrangement with *The Epis. Methodist* and they will publish us as their Phila. agents. . . . Since returning from Bato. "The Epis. Register" have accepted the offer which I made them on Monday after writing you. It is $3600.00 per yr for 3 yrs we to have exclusive control of *all* their advertising.

In the last deal mentioned, Ayer was, of course, arranging to take over the management of the advertising columns as a whole. This required a considerable amount of working capital, and the number of publications with which it could be done was therefore limited. Whenever his business with other papers was sufficient to justify doing so, he bought space by the column in order to obtain advantageous prices. Thus, in 1876, Ayer advertised special bargains in space in fifty Philadelphia suburban papers, with the following explanation of the low rates quoted:[3]

An inch advertisement, one month, in an advertiser's choice of ten papers from this List (dailies and weeklies in proportion), would in the ordinary contracting cost at least fifty dollars; but our method of buying a whole column, and in some cases two or three columns of space by the year, enables us to offer an inch, one month (four times in weeklies and twenty-four times in dailies), in the entire List, for

FIFTY DOLLARS

The Ayer agency was clearly the special advocate of a limited number of papers at this time, urging upon the advertiser the merits of those in which it owned blocks of space.

As we have already seen, however, circumstances made it difficult for the advertising agent to restrict his activities to representing a few papers. In order to sell space effectively, he found it necessary to show merchants and manufacturers how to advertise. Before urging the merits of given advertising media he had to convince them of the value of advertising at all, and afterwards he was practically compelled to assist them with every phase of the work in order to make their advertising produce results. Especially did his customers expect advice and assistance when it came to choosing the papers to be used in carrying the advertising message to given market areas.

Looking back from the present, we can see that there was an economic need for two types of middlemen in the advertising field, one to develop advertisers and help them to use advertising in their selling work, the other to help the individual publisher to sell his advertising space. But it was years before this difference in function was recognized. In the meantime, the agent fell between two stools and all parties concerned worked at cross purposes. Believing that to increase the number of agents would bring an increased volume of business, the publishers (save those who had sold out to one agency) readily allowed commissions and accepted orders from every man who proclaimed himself an agent. The multiplicity of agents, in turn, compelled each to seek advantage by sacrificing part of his commission to the advertiser and by bullying publishers into granting him special low rates. And the advertiser, seeing the frantic scramble for his business, gave impetus to the competition by forcing the agents to bid against one another for his custom. The result could be only vicious competition, sharp practice, and dissatisfaction all around.[4]

It was in order to avoid this confused conflict that F. W. Ayer inaugurated his open-contract plan in 1876 and threw in his lot with the advertiser. And, in 1880, as he himself expressed it,[5] "In order that I would have no axe to grind, no special list identified with the business of N. W. Ayer & Son, the religious paper list we had controlled was taken out of our office and run under a separate organization." Some years after this offshoot had been incorporated as the Religious Press Association, a rival agency put out a circular to spread the impression that N. W. Ayer & Son and the Religious Press Association were identical. Ayer at once issued a pamphlet in reply, in which his altered status with regard to publishers was plainly set forth. He admitted that he personally owned stock in the Religious Press Association, but he emphatically denied that his advertising agency had any control or influence over the Association.[6] He also denied that his agency received any favors from the Association and proceeded to state the firm's policy with regard to lists:[7]

Since the incorporation . . . we have never, despite the most diligent effort, been able to secure a special price on any of its papers, or a better discount than that which is announced as regularly allowed to all accredited agents. . . .

As we look at it the advertising firms who have the special agency of a paper, or who control the space of certain papers for which they must pay, whether it is used or not, can never be safe advisers to their customers. Anxiety to use that space is bound to warp their judgment; indeed, the warping of their judgment is just what was intended by the publishers when the special agency was given or the space sold.

We therefore make it a rule of our business to have no "Special Lists" or "combinations" of papers, religious or secular, nor are we ever bound to secure a certain amount of space for any particular paper or papers. On the contrary, our constant aim is to maintain such relations with the publishers of all newspapers that we can at all times give an unprejudiced opinion as to the value of different mediums for any given line of advertising.

The "special agency" referred to here was, of course, the advertising middleman who refused to follow the Ayer agency's lead in becoming an avowed assistant to the advertiser. He preferred to cling to the agent's original work of selling space. The spread of the Ayer idea, however, compelled him to devote himself more narrowly to that function, and gradually he confined his activities to representing only a few papers which, located in different cities or reaching different groups of readers, did not compete with one another.

N. W. Ayer & Son, meanwhile, steadfastly pursued its policy of working explicitly for the advertiser. But, while this policy meant doing away with the space concessions which the agency had owned, it did not, for many years, put an end to the wholesale purchases of space which had formed an important part of the firm's activities. To some extent such purchases gave N. W. Ayer & Son some special interests of the kind it was trying to avoid; but, so long as publishers were willing to make substantial price reductions on large orders, competition with rival agencies compelled the Ayer firm to buy large blocks of space in advance of its current needs in order to get the low prices which its customers demanded.

Among the papers preserved in the Ayer files is a bundle of old contracts with publishers, the provisions of which reveal a fairly clear picture of the way in which agencies bought space in the period from 1882 to about 1897. The general tenor of these contracts is especially worthy of note: N. W. Ayer & Son plainly sought to gain advantageous prices through special agreements; indeed, many of the contracts specified that no other agency was to be given equally low rates. In order to avoid the chance of loss, through inability to use space before a particular date, the contracts usually provided that the space was to be "good till used." Ordinarily, too, there was a promise of strict secrecy on both sides, made in an effort to prevent other agents from demanding equal treatment. The Ayer firm, however, reserved the right to make the rates known to its open-contract customers, thus permitting it to comply with the provisions of its open contract. In its effort to get exclusive advantages, however, the agency sometimes made agreements which, at least on the surface, gave it a special "axe to grind" — a bias in favor of particular papers. These points are well illustrated by the following summaries of selected contracts typical of the entire lot which have survived for the period:[8]

A contract with the *Nebraska Farmer*, Feb. 8, 1882, provided for the sale of 1,000 inches of space to Ayer for $625, good till used.

By agreement dated Feb. 12, 1886, the *Christian Union* sold Ayer 16,000 agate lines for $2,400, good till used, with the provision that each line of reading notices (advertisements disguised as editorial matter) be regarded as two lines.

The *Home Magazine* of Washington agreed, Nov. 11, 1892, as follows: "In consideration of the assurance of N. W. Ayer & Son that they will advise the use of the 'Home Magazine' whenever they think it consistent with the best interest of their clients [a small concession on the part of the agency] we agree to allow them a commission of 25% (other agents 15%) for one year from this date." This agreement was amended on Jan. 10, 1893, as follows: "The party of the second part N. W. Ayer & Son agrees not to sell any of this space at less than card rates, less agent's commission, except to their open-contract customers, but with such customers, this rate is not used in competition, and is given only to those who place their entire business in the hands of N. W. Ayer & Son." This exception in favor of open-contract customers was expressed or implied in most, if not all, of the contracts in which the agency agreed not to quote less than card rates.

The *Home and Farmer* of Louisville, Ky., agreed, Jan. 25, 1886, to allow N. W. Ayer & Son a discount of 25 per cent from card rates (all other agents were allowed only 12½), on the condition that the agency send at least $900 of business per month for 12 consecutive months and not cut the rates in selling the space to advertisers.

On Sept. 24, 1889, the *Delineator* contracted to sell 2,500 agate lines to Ayer for $2,500 although the card rate was $1.50 per line. If any space was unused on or after January 1, 1891, the paper was to have the option of canceling the agreement and refunding the money.

The contract of Aug. 21, 1890, with the *Farmer's Call* of Quincy, Ill., provided for the following rates to Ayer: $1.25 net per inch per insertion for orders running less than three months; $1.00 net on orders running three months or more. The paper was not to be quoted on the agency's estimates at less than $2.00 net. In return the agency promised to send advertising to the paper whenever it was at liberty or under instruction to place it in the paper's territory.

The contract by which the *Constitution* of Atlanta, Ga., agreed, Dec. 4, 1891, to give a special rate to N. W. Ayer & Son provided that the rate was not to be made known by any advertiser to any other agent; if made known to any agent, the contract could be canceled.

The *Farmer's Home* of Dayton agreed, Dec. 17, 1891, to give Ayer & Son 15 per cent and 15 per cent, and guaranteed that no other agent would be given more than 15 per cent discount. The resulting special rates were not to be stated on any competitive estimates prepared by the agency, nor any information about them to be given to Thos. Childs of New York or T. B. White of Chicago (special agents, presumably representing the *Farmer's Home*).

A contract with the Boston *Pilot*, Feb. 1, 1892, provided that, if the business sent to the paper by Ayer during 1892 reached $1,000, the publisher would make a cash rebate on the basis of a 30 per cent commission instead of 25 per cent; if $1,500, 33⅓ per cent; if $2,000, 35%.

The *House Keeper* of Minneapolis contracted, Feb. 4, 1892, to sell 15,000 lines to N. W. Ayer & Son at a special rate of 40 cents net per line and agreed not to sell space to other agents at a lower rate. The publisher stated in the agreement that, apart from N. W. Ayer & Son, the only agents to get his space at better than published rates were J. Walter Thompson and J. L. Stack.

The *Kansas Farmer* promised, May 27, 1892, to give a rebate to Ayer on acceptable advertising, based on the rates current for 1892, of 5 per cent for $500 worth of business, 10 per cent on $1,000 to $1,500 worth, and 15 per cent on anything over $1,500.

Godey's Lady's Magazine stated, August 22, 1892, that its regular rate was $1.00 per line, that it was making a special offer to agents of 75 cents per line until January 1, 1893, but agreed to sell space to Ayer for 45 cents per line for all business.

The *Domestic Monthly* of New York gave the Ayer agency (Dec. 29, 1892) a net rate of 21 cents per line for all business to January 1, 1894, and stated that the lowest rate given to others was 25½ cents per line net, except Lord & Thomas who had a contract running at 22.95 cents per line.

An agreement with the *Farm-Poultry Monthly* of Boston, November 1, 1893, stated that, since the paper had received 2,000 lines of advertising from Ayer, it would allow the agency a discount of 15 per cent and 20 per cent "on all first class, clean advertising." A rate of 10 cents a line net without further rebate was allowed for seed advertising, on the condition that the paper receive a liberal share of every seed account placed by Ayer for the season of 1894.

The *Union Gospel News* of Cleveland agreed, Dec. 16, 1892, to an extra large discount for cash in advance, conditioned as follows: "Referring to the order of this date for Dr. Williams Med. Co., and the Gold Dust advtg. if placed with the Gospel News, Mess. N. W. Ayer & Son are to have privilege of prepaying both orders at disct. of 10%. If, however, Gold Dust is not placed with Gospel News there will be no cash rebate on the Dr. Williams advt."

The form of agreement which the Ayer agency asked publishers to sign (and, in many cases, succeeded in its effort) between 1892 and 1897 was as follows:[9]

AGREEMENT, made this ...... day of ...... between .... party of the first part, and N. W. Ayer & Son, of Philadelphia party of the second part.

In consideration of the party of the second part agreeing to use their best efforts to secure business for the publications of the party of the first part, the party of the first part hereby agrees to allow the party of the second part a commission of Twenty-six (26%) per cent on all their publications, and to allow other agencies a commission of not more than [fifteen] (15%) per cent.

All orders from the party of the second part are to be sent at Fifteen (15%) per cent commission, and all bills are to be rendered by the party of the first part at fifteen (15%) per cent commission. The difference between fifteen (15%) per cent and twenty-six (26%) per cent to be repaid by the party of the first part whenever settlement is received for each bill rendered.

This agreement is to continue in force three years from this date, and indefinitely thereafter, subject to cancellation on ninety (90) days' notice from either party.

It may seem curious that publishers were willing to make such concessions to Ayer. The following excerpt from one publisher's letter probably expresses the typical attitude:[10]

We desire that you shall understand our object in giving this rate. With our intercourse with Advertizers, we have become aware of the amount of Adv'g handled by you, and feel assured that if attention is paid the Bulletin our business from you can be raised three or four times the Amount ever received from you. To secure this effort in our behalf we are willing to discount all business recd.

Another common motive is clearly shown in the following un-solicited offer from a publisher:[11]

I want six hundred ($600.00) dollars, cash in advance, for one thou-sand (1000) inches advertising space to be used within 1 yr. or 15 mos.
No space is or shall be sold at less than 6¢ net per agate line while your contract runs. — This I guarantee.
I talk right to the point because I can use the money just now — also because I know I have been left out of quite a number of good orders as you did not own space in the paper.

In addition to making these wholesale purchases, N. W. Ayer & Son filled the specific orders which continually came in from advertisers by buying space in small lots from papers through-out the country. The usual practice was, as explained in Chapter II, for the agency to send out an "advertising proposal," stating the size of the advertisement, the position, and the number of insertions desired, and offering the publisher a definite price for the order. Ordinarily the amount actually to be paid was the sum named "less agent's usual commission," a discount which, until the 'nineties, was usually 25 per cent.

The amount offered by the agency in its proposal was seldom as much as the paper's card rate. Indeed, it was sometimes so much less that the publisher flatly refused to accept it. When this happened, the agency usually bargained with him until terms could be obtained which were satisfactory to both. Some publish-ers took this procedure as a matter of course; others were irri-tated by it and their ire sometimes led to public rebukes like the following:[12]

Nov. 19.
November 19.
Monday, Nov. 19.
Monday, November 19.
Forms close Nov. 19 at noon.
Advertisers sending orders through Ayer's Agency should allow two weeks lee-way so that the usual monkey business (attempting to cut our rates) can be gone through with by Ayer before our forms close. Our

relations with the J. L. Stack agency have always been pleasant and quite extensive. Their clients can congratulate themselves on being properly represented.

In so far as this notice singled out Ayer, it is not significant, for all accounts of early agency activities agree that the bargaining for favors was universally practised. It is probable that the Stack agency instigated the attack and paid for it in one way or another. But the excerpt fairly reflects typical outbursts of small-editor temper which were sometimes caused by the Ayer proposals. Among agency space-buyers, however, there was a feeling that the publishers who complained the loudest were the ones who were most likely to accept less than card-rate offers. Of course, the bargaining process, by reducing the cost of space, likewise reduced the agency's commission from clients.

Not all space was bought for cash. Many orders were payable only in commodities offered by the Ayer agency or its customers. That is to say, the Ayer agency (and others) acquired much space by means of barter transactions. To modern observers it is somewhat surprising to find this primitive exchange arrangement existing in an industry which ordinarily has made a fetish of the most up-to-date methods and products. But the advertising agent has had to take the business man as he has found him. In the 'seventies and 'eighties there was evidently a shortage of working capital among many firms which wanted to advertise. Unable or unwilling to pay ready cash for the purpose, they would advertise only if they could settle the bill by means of the products which they had to sell.

Thus, one of the earliest of F. W. Ayer's letters now extant is in reply to a Philadelphia merchant who wanted to exchange an office safe for advertising in the *National Baptist*.[13] And during the Centennial Exhibition of 1876 the Ayer firm sent out proposals which read in part:[14]

We are authorized to offer the above advertisement of THE FRANKLIN HOTEL, (Centennial grounds) . . . Charge us . . . . Dollars less usual commission, payment to be made in board or lodging at the hotel.

We will send you their due-bill for the gross amount at any time, and you can use it or sell it. . . .

Please notify us at once whether you accept or decline. We would much rather send you this as a cash order, but they decline to do any more cash advertising. They think everybody is coming to the Centennial, and that their due-bills are about as good as money.

Another proposal, sent out this same year, offered to publishers the advertising of Miller's Bible & Publishing House at rates minus commission:[15]

payable on demand in their Trade Bibles, or Photograph Albums at list price . . . less forty per cent, discount. This discount brings the books down to a money basis, inasmuch as if unable to use them yourself you ought to be able to turn them right over to any bookseller, at just this price. . . .

We would much prefer sending it to you as cash order, . . . but found it impossible, inasmuch as Mr. Miller had decided to do no advertising whatever this Spring.

Ascertaining that they had a large overstock on hand, we proposed to them the offering of the advertisements in this way, and finally obtained it.

The form of due-bill which was apparently the most often used in these barter transactions was the following:[16]

$. . . . .   Philadelphia,. . . . . .187. .
    For Value Received, we will pay to the Publisher of
. . . . or order,
. . . . Dollars,
in Merchandise from our Store at cash prices, upon presentation of this Due-Bill, approved by Messrs. N. W. Ayer & Son, to whom we have charged this amount on Advertising Account.
                                        Signed. . . . .
Approved by. . . . . No. . . . .

The principal goods handled in this way were Bibles, dictionaries, and other books, but the Ayer agency also sent out proposals for advertising payable in hair tonic, patent medicines, clothing, board and lodging, and even musical instruments.[17]

In addition to the space which was paid for with the goods advertised, the Ayer agency used space which was obtained by two other types of trade agreement. One was the exchange of advertising space in one medium for space in another. Thus, in 1875 N. W. Ayer & Son sent out proposals offering advertisements for the *Saturday Evening Post* (long before Curtis acquired the weekly) at publishers' rates without commission, payable in exchange for advertising in the *Post* at cost prices.[18] And, as we have seen, the agency acquired space in newspapers by exchanging for it advertising in the *Advertiser's Guide, Ayer & Son's Manual of Advertising,* and the *American Newspaper Annual* — media which the agency itself published.[19]

Still a third method of buying space involved payment in the form of printing materials which the agency itself bought for the express purpose of such trades. The following proposal shows a typical transaction of this sort in the negotiation stage:[20]

AN ADVERTISING PROPOSITION
     From N. W. Ayer & Son,
         Advertising Agents,
Times Building,   Philadelphia,   January......1881.
Publishers.......................

Dear Sirs: — We have authority from a firm engaged in the manufacture of an Agricultural Implement to offer you their advertisement on the following terms:

Advertisement will be 21 inches, 7 inches triple column, all electrotyped (so that there will be no composition), for 8 weeks in your Weekly, *run of paper.*

The aggregate space is equal to about the same as three inches one year. For it we have authority to offer you

($........)....................................... Dollars, Less agent's usual commission of 25 per cent, payable in Printing Material of any kind.

The matter is an entirely open one with us. We have no contract for any particular paper, but shall place the advertising wherever our offers are accepted. While not expecting to secure insertion everywhere, *we would be glad to include your paper in the list.*

One word in reference to our mode of payment:

We offer Printing Material because the small profit we make on it enables us to secure insertion in many papers which the limit of the advertiser's price to us would prevent our using were we to pay cash only.

For your purposes the Material is the same as cash, because

We sell Page's Wood Type — the best in the market — at factory prices.

We are Special Agents for Wade's celebrated Job and Colored Inks, universally recognized as the best.

We also make a specialty of the best Imported Gold Bronzes, quality guaranteed.

We handle best grades of News Inks, made especially for our own select trade, and guarantee price and quality every time.

We are also prepared to supply the best quality of Metal Type, Furniture, etc., in fact, anything made in the Printing Material line at manufacturers' prices.

For Western Trade, we supply Woodworth's News Inks shipped from Cincinnati, and fill our orders for Metal Type, etc., from the foundry of Marder, Luse & Co., Chicago.

As we desire the insertions to commence at once, it is very important that we hear from you immediately *whether you accept or not.*

We therefore inclose postal, so that you can reply without cost, and request immediate consideration.

In view of the cryptic explanation given for the offer of printing materials, it is interesting and a little puzzling to note that two sets of proposals were often sent out relating to a given advertising contract, the one payable in materials, the other payable in cash. A possible explanation is that an exchange agreement was not even to be hoped for from certain valuable papers. It is significant, in any case, that the agency ordinarily made no attempt to get less than card rates when it offered goods instead of cash. Evidently the exchange of goods was an alternative to bargaining for a better price.

By 1900 the purchases of space in wholesale lots and the acquisition of space by the exchange of goods were both obsolescent practices. But even today much of the hotel and resort advertising which is done through agencies is paid for in due-bills redeemable in hotel accommodation. And occasionally, even since 1929, the publisher of a country newspaper has neglected to send in his bills to the Ayer agency, allowed the amount due to accumulate, and then suddenly turned up at Washington Square with a request that the agency settle accounts by paying for the piano or suite of furniture which his wife has selected in a Chestnut Street store. Since World War I, however, such trade arrangements have been unimportant exceptions to the general procedure.

The relations between N. W. Ayer & Son and publishers have, on the whole, been marked by mutual coöperation, consideration, and respect. But occasional misunderstandings are bound to arise in all lines of business, and in the period before 1900 friction sometimes developed between the Ayer agency and a publisher. Perhaps the most notable instance was a disagreement between the agency and the publisher of the *National Stockman & Farmer* of Pittsburgh, Pa., a disagreement which lasted from 1893 to 1898. The publisher had agreed to a series of rebates varying with the volume of business sent by the agency. Almost immediately a question arose as to whether the agreement applied to all business sent, or only to advertising which the paper had not previously had. The agency and the publisher clung to opposing interpretations of the agreement and of the pertinent facts; and, while business relations did not entirely cease, the two firms remained at odds for five years. The publisher allowed Ayer no commission on business sent, and Ayer sent as little as possible, urging any customers who wished to use the *National Stockman & Farmer* to place the advertising directly. The volume of business sent to the paper by the Ayer firm dropped from $5,518 in 1892 to $2,213 in 1895, and almost disappeared in the next year. Exasperated at this treatment, the publisher launched a crusade against rebating in general and the Ayer agency in particular, despite the fact that he had been willing enough to promise rebates in previous years. At every opportunity the publisher made attacks upon "the big private rebate agency of Philadelphia." He also wrote to Ayer customers charging that the agency discriminated unfairly against his paper and even insinuating that it did not pass on to open-contract customers the rebates which it obtained from publishers.

The charge of discrimination was too well founded to be denied, but the Ayer management, of course, emphatically denied the insinuation which accompanied it. So did a number of Ayer

customers. One of them wrote to the *National Stockman &*
Farmer as follows:[21]

I pay Ayer & Son 15% commission for placing my business; other
agencies have offered to do the business for from 33⅓ to 50% less
than I pay Ayer. I pay Ayer his price for the reason that I have confidence enough in them to feel that they give me a square deal. . . .
Now gentlemen, I will pay you $100 for every paper that you can prove
to me has been charged up by Ayer at a higher rate than net cost of
same to Ayer & Son.

Silas Paine of the Standard Oil Company and W. Atlee Burpee
of the Burpee Seed Company replied to the publisher's letters by
saying that they felt his attacks unwarranted and ill-advised.
Eventually, in 1898, friendly overtures were made and business
relations resumed, but the terms of reconciliation have not been
recorded.[22]

In marked contrast with this episode is the story of the relations between F. W. Ayer and Cyrus Curtis when the *Ladies'*
Home Journal was getting under way in the late 'eighties. Curtis
wanted to advertise his magazine but lacked the necessary money,
and he discussed the matter with the agency. Here is the story in
Cyrus Curtis' own words.[23]

I wanted to do a little advertising and I went to Mr. Ayer and wanted
a credit for four hundred dollars. Mr. McKinney came to me a little
later and said, "Mr. Curtis, we don't know much about your resources,
we don't think you have any to amount to much, but we are going to
take a chance on you; if you make good, all right; if you don't, four
hundred dollars won't break us anyhow. All we ask is that you let us
spend it where we think it will do you the most good."

That four hundred dollars was spent in three publications, two of
which did not allow commissions to advertising agents, and the third
one, which I have forgotten now, allowed the usual commission, but
there was very little profit on that for Ayer & Son. However, the results
were such that we went on from time to time spending money until I
spent hundreds of thousands of dollars a year. This was the beginning
of that practical friendship.

Later there came a time when I wanted a good deal of credit; when

I had plans for enlarging the Ladies' Home Journal, of which no one else approved, not a soul, not even my own family. I went to Mr. Ayer with my plan of what I wanted to do. To carry out these plans, I had in mind an advertising campaign that would cost a great deal of money, and he said, "Mr. Curtis, how much credit do you want?" I hardly dared to name it but I did; I said, "Two hundred thousand dollars." He said, "That doesn't scare me," so we went through with that campaign; but before we got through with it, Mr. Ayer sent for me one day and said, "You will require credit at a certain bank; I will see the bank," and he did. Then he said, "Now, if I am going to give you a credit of two hundred thousand dollars, your paper maker should give you a credit of at least one hundred thousand dollars." Well, we had not been dealing with those people very long at that time and they didn't know me, and they decided they would not extend me the credit. Mr. Ayer suggested that we go to Boston and meet them there — they were from Pittsfield, Massachusetts; they came to Boston to meet us. They said on the start, "You have requested this interview and of course we are courteous enough to give it, but we tell you right now we are not going to grant what you ask." We talked and argued for some time and finally Mr. Ayer said, "Mr. Curtis, I would like to see these gentlemen alone a few minutes." I went downstairs in the Parker House and lit a cigar and waited. Finally I was sent for and, when I went into the room, the senior member of that paper firm put out his hand and said, "You win." Well, I did not know what had happened in that room, but they decided to give me the desired credit. We came home and Mr. Ayer said nothing about it, and for many years afterward. I never knew what had happened that day until Mr. McKinney, just before he died, said to me, "It is so long ago I do not know that there is any harm in telling you now, Mr. Ayer guaranteed your notes."

Many another publisher can tell a similar tale of Ayer help in times of difficulty, usually in the form of a large purchase of space for cash. Thus the publisher got much-needed funds and the agency acquired space at exceedingly favorable prices. The danger, of course, was that the interest thus acquired in the future of a publication might influence the agency's recommendations to clients. Today such assistance to the owners of advertising media would be contrary to the Ayer policy. In the period before 1900, however, advertisers were not so concerned about the agency's strict impartiality in regard to advertising media, and most publishers looked upon N. W. Ayer & Son as a source of help in times of stress. It is almost certain, too, that this intimate and coöperative relation between the agency and publishers ultimately redounded to the benefit of the agency's clients, in the form of lower prices for space or better service or both.

MEDIA AND AGENCY COMPENSATION

The gradual separation of advertising middlemen into two groups, that is, general agents and special agents (publishers' representatives), threw doubt and confusion around the matter of agency compensation. The relations between publishers and their special agents or representatives were clear enough: these representatives sold space in particular papers and magazines, and no one questioned their right to a commission for the work.

But the position of the general agent was quite different. Ayer (as well as the agents who imitated his plan) explicitly stated that he was working for the advertiser, and he charged the advertiser a commission for his services. This, and the fact that many publishers now possessed their own representatives whom they paid by means of a commission, led to a feeling that the general agent was not entitled to the discount or commission which publishers had previously allowed to all agencies. Some media owners, indeed, discontinued the allowance. Hence there was a period in which special representatives sometimes competed directly with general agents for the orders of an advertiser. And, thanks to their closer connection with publishers, such representatives sometimes gave the advertiser lower space rates than the general agent could give him. Out of this situation arose the "direct advertisers," who dispensed with the general agent's services and bought space from the publisher or his representative. A few of these direct advertisers have survived to recent times and may still get their space at less than gross rates.[24]

This sporadic competition between special and general agent, however, lasted only a comparatively short time. Before 1900 most publishers had agreed to two commissions or discounts from their gross rates: an allowance of about 15 per cent of the gross price to the general agent, whether he bought space direct or through publishers' representatives, and to the representatives a further allowance of 10 or 15 per cent of the net price of the business obtained by them. The force which dictated this change was probably the necessity of organizing on a sound business basis, a need which arose from the growing size of the financial investment entailed in the daily newspaper. In their constant search for devices to boost circulation, publishers had to add telegraph and cable service, more elaborate organizations for news-gathering, cartoons, and expensive printing presses. Without stable rates and more careful management of advertising departments, this increase in overhead costs would have been ruinous.[25]

The commission arrangement has endured down to the present day. As a result of it, both groups of space middlemen — the general agents who buy and the special representatives who sell — usually receive compensation which is determined, or at least protected, by the owners of advertising media.[26] So far as national advertising is concerned, the advertiser must pay the gross rates established by the publisher even though, dispensing with the middlemen, he buys space directly from the media.[27] It is not difficult to understand why the arrangement should be made for the special representatives who work for the media, but to maintain it for the general agents who work for the advertiser is a matter requiring some explanation.

The newspaper and magazine owners finally decided to allow commissions to the general agent because they found a direct pecuniary advantage in doing so. By 1891 the advertising industry seems to have agreed that the general agent performed an essential function which neither publisher nor representative could fulfill. He alone could promote the cause of advertising as a whole. His wide experience, his judgment, and his lack of bias about particular papers caused him to be the logical person to take the leading rôle in making advertising profitable for advertisers. He was in the best position to discover new advertising possibilities and to help advertisers with their sales publicity. Everything he did to stimulate the use of advertising would benefit publishers and their representatives.

Probably the attitude of the space-sellers was based less upon reason than upon immediate practical considerations. The general agent held the advertiser's confidence, and during the 1890's special representatives often found that the easiest way to the order they sought was not to approach the advertiser directly, but rather to bring the merits of their papers to the notice of his general agent. The general agent, moreover, already possessed the requisite facilities for handling the staggering amount of clerical work involved in placing advertisements; he could save both publisher and representative considerable trouble and book-keeping expense. More important still, he ordinarily took over the credit risks involved in dealing with a host of customers who were widely scattered and, for the most part, of little-known commercial standing.[28]

To the extent that the general agent saved the publisher tangible expense, he expected — and the publisher was well advised in granting — a lower price for space than the advertiser could get when buying space through a special agent or from the publisher direct. He also demanded additional consideration in price because of the service which he gave to space-sellers indirectly by developing new advertisers and helping old ones to grow. In short, while he was working directly for the advertiser, the general agent performed tasks which gave both direct and indirect benefits to publishers and their representatives. More than any other factor, this inescapable mixture of economic services to both sides of the advertising media market has confused and bedeviled the question of agency compensation ever since.

Had the media owners been less dependent upon the general agent, they might have cut through the tangle of benefits and obligations by discontinuing the commission allowed to him or by reducing it sharply to a figure which would cover the direct benefits received. But for some years before 1900 it was almost impossible to draw a sharp line between general agents and special representatives; and, even when it was possible, few publishers could afford to risk antagonizing the general agent. The national advertising handled by a great many papers was too small to justify hiring a special representative. It was clear, too, that the representative who was selling space for only six or eight papers could not possibly cover so much territory as the general agents who sought business for all, even though he was more aggressive on their behalf. Also, there was apparently a feeling that unless the newspaper publishers continued to allow a sizable commission to the general agent he would be found to turn against them, favoring magazines, outdoor signs, and other advertising media which were coming into general use. Experience had certainly proved that the general agent would discriminate against any individual publisher who refused to allow him a commission, and consequently few media owners dared to withdraw the agent's commission until assured of support by their fellows.

The situation called for a united front which publishers were not long in forming. The American Newspaper Publishers' Association, organized in 1887, tackled the problem in 1889 by drawing up a list of the firms which it would recognize as approved general agencies. Strong opposition was expressed against agents who, while professing to be impartial middlemen, bought up the space of particular papers and in effect came into competition with publishers. And at the Association's fourth convention (1890) the discussion so strongly reflected a fear of advertising media other than newspapers that one enlightened member sarcastically moved that all advertising, except in newspapers, be abolished. The significant thing is that, in spite of a widely expressed opinion that the general agent should be paid directly by the advertiser — thus supporting the Ayer viewpoint — no action was taken to terminate the commission which publishers allowed him.[29] Indeed, in 1893 and 1894 the Association passed resolutions against allowing the agent's commission to advertisers or their employees, thereby expressing its belief that the general agent should be protected.[30] Thus by the early 'nineties the newspaper publishers were agreed that the general agent did not compete with their representatives, that on the contrary he supplemented the special representatives' work, and that their own best interests were promoted when the agent was protected in his selling efforts by a substantial advantage in price.

Magazine publishers went still further in their efforts to curry favor with the general agent. With the newspaper holding a well-entrenched position, they were having some difficulty in gaining wide recognition for periodicals as advertising media. Moreover, unlike the newspaper publishers, they had no solid foundation of local business to supply revenue; they were entirely dependent upon national advertising, and had therefore to lean heavily upon the general agent. Leading agents had long complained because the cutting of rates and rebating of commissions had injured their profits. Evidently reasoning that the agent should be protected from unscrupulous competitors as well as from short-sighted media owners, the magazine publishers threatened to withdraw recognition from any agent who shared his commission with his customers. Nor was the threat without results. In 1897 N. W. Ayer & Son, through one of its clients, obtained estimates on two magazines from twelve leading agents. Of the twelve, seven quoted less than card rates on the *Ladies' World,* but only four dared to cut the rates of the *Ladies' Home Journal.* Its publisher, Cyrus Curtis, had taken the lead in the battle to protect card rates.[31]

One must recognize that, in protecting the agent's commission, publishers were trying to put an end to the demoralization of their own rates as a whole, but this was not the sole object. In 1901 the Curtis Publishing Company put into effect a contract by which it bound agents not to cut rates, under penalty of losing the commission, and bound itself not to allow the agent's commission to any advertiser. The avowed purpose of this, as well as of the many similar agreements insisted upon later by other publishers, was to protect the agent's commission so that he could provide the service which was essential to a successful advertising campaign.[32]

As far as media owners are concerned, no major change has occurred in the arrangement for agency compensation since 1901. Since that time it has been adopted by the owners of both outdoor and broadcast advertising media.[33] The American Newspaper Publishers' Association, the Periodical Publishers' Association, the National Association of Broadcasters, and similar organizations of media owners have established certain general standards which agencies are supposed to meet in order to obtain the recognition which entitles them to receive commissions. The points usually emphasized for consideration are that the agency should have a satisfactory financial condition, should be independent and impartial with regard to both media and clients, should not give rebates or cut below the rates established by media owners, and should be technically competent to provide the advertising service which advertisers need. However, members of the various associations of media owners are not bound to accept the recognition given by their organizations: a publisher, for example, may refuse to accept business from an agency to which his association has granted recognition, and he may accept orders from an agency which his association has refused to recognize. In general, recognition is essentially a matter of credit rating and outward conformance to established trade practices. Ultimately, the person who determines whether a firm shall be an advertising agency is the advertiser, and he is also the final judge as to competence.[34]

The experience of N. W. Ayer & Son with outdoor advertising throws some light — perhaps false light — upon the question of commissions allowed by media. The Ayer firm arranged in 1898 to handle billboard and other outdoor advertising (see above, page 81). In order to place their services upon an organized and closely controlled basis, the owners of these media had formed the Associated Bill Posters and Distributors of the United States and Canada. Indeed, so effective was their organization that they soon had a fairly complete monopoly of outdoor advertising, and they began to take advantage of it. Ayer had begun by handling outdoor business for clients at net cost plus 10 per cent,[35] but in 1900 the Association decided to accept business only from "licensed representatives" who charged the gross rates and took as their reward the 15 per cent commission allowed. Ayer was the first, and for a while apparently the only, general agent to be so licensed; and between 1901 and 1913 all Ayer contracts specified that clients would pay the gross rates set by the billposters.[36] This part of the Ayer work, accordingly, did not conform to the Ayer policy that compensation should be a matter for the firm and its clients to decide.

By 1910 there were 43 "official representatives" of the outdoor association, each of whom, like Ayer, paid $1,000 a year for a license. The Association seemed to feel, however, that few agencies were worth the 15 per cent commission that it allowed: in 1911 it arbitrarily reduced the number of licensees to 10; and in 1913, when the Association finally decided on direct independent solicitation of business, N. W. Ayer & Son was forced to abandon its outdoor division.[37] Almost immediately the billposters got into legal difficulties because their organization was held to violate the Sherman Anti-Trust Act,[38] and a number of advertising agencies formed the National Outdoor Bureau and again began to place outdoor advertising for clients through it. N. W. Ayer & Son, however, did not revive its Outdoor Department until 1931, when the outdoor interests had thoroughly reorganized along the lines of the publishing industry, having representatives but regularly allowing commissions to agencies. This outcome has been held by some agents to prove the wisdom of the traditional method of compensation. I suspect that it proves more about the value of the advertising agency than about the proper method of compensation; but clearly no generalizations can be made until the details of the whole episode have been collected and studied.[39]

Ayer Attitude toward Commissions Allowed by Media

Now let us turn to the opinion of the Ayer agency on these matters. F. W. Ayer had declared in 1876 that he would work for the advertiser, but there was no thought in his mind that his agency thereby ceased to be of service to publishers or that publishers should cease to allow him a commission. As we have seen, he sought larger commissions than the ones allowed to his competitors. His views on the general agent's function and the commission allowed by publishers were clearly set forth in a letter to a newspaper publisher in 1898:[40]

It is true that we do not specially represent any paper, nor would we, under any circumstances. . . . Our conception of the function of an advertising agent is that he should, by all means in his power, CREATE newspaper advertising, familiarize newspaper advertisers with the facts concerning newspapers, and put them in position to select mediums most suitable for their best service. . . . Our aim is to educate business men to the use of newspaper advertising as an up-to-date method of getting business. . . .

For some [objectionable] conditions which exist, we think that publishers are largely responsible. The giving of indiscriminate credit to advertising agents contributed to that end, as does also the refusal of many publishers to recognize that there is a difference in advertising agencies beyond the matter of credit; and, again, we think the allowance of commissions to direct advertisers, under any circumstances, is a reduction in rates, and we do not see how it can be otherwise considered.

A few months later when Frank Munsey, publisher of *Munsey's Magazine,* announced his intention of allowing no commission to advertising agents, Ayer expressed his views on this proposal in a brief memorandum to one of his partners:[41]

Referring to Mr. Munsey's announcement that no commission will be allowed advertising agents after this month, it seems to me that our policy is to decline to include Munsey's in any but O. C. [open contract] business . . . there are to my mind few cases where there is special reason to use this magazine, and unless the customer's interests would suffer by its omission, it should never be used.

In personal conference with advertisers, we can make the frank statement that Mr. Munsey leaned on advertising agents until he thought he was able to stand alone and then took the position that the advertiser, rather than the publisher, should pay for the agent's service.[42] . . . Our belief is that he thinks advertisers will insist on using his magazine, and that therefore he will get the business and save the commission. We do not wish to prevent his getting any business; but we will not guarantee accounts without profit, and we will not add the profit to the advertiser's cost unless the advertiser particularly wishes us to do so.

It is worthy of note that after two years of experience Munsey decided to return to the prevailing arrangement. In doing so he followed Curtis' example and tried to exact an agreement from agents not to cut his rates or their commission.[43] But, although Ayer had consented to the Curtis contract, he refused to sign any of the ones subsequently offered. His refusal led to a break in relations between N. W. Ayer & Son and *McClure's Magazine,* which lasted from 1902 to 1906. In discussing the matter with his staff, Ayer took this stand because[44]

it puts the control of your business and your methods of business in the publisher's hands. He says how you shall do business, not only how you shall pay him, but he reserves the right to say how you shall do business with your customers. We signed the Ladies' Home Journal contract. We did not give the matter much consideration. They came first.

They were customers of ours. We held them in high esteem. And we signed the contract. It is the only one we have signed. We have said we would not sign any more. One day along came the McClure proposition. So did others. We quickly made up our minds that the advertising business would lose its position among the businesses of the country and we would lose our own self-respect if we did not stop that thing. Once started that way and the agent becomes simply the servant of the publishers. They dictate and we follow.

The view expressed in 1905 essentially is the Ayer policy today. The firm refuses to permit media owners to dictate the terms on which it is to do business with clients. This policy, together with the philosophy behind it, was set forth by F. W. Ayer in 1921 in one of the few statements that he ever addressed to publishers as a body. His analysis of the agent's position was so clearly made that it deserves special attention:[45]

For the good of advertising, it seems desirable that there should be a clearer understanding of responsibility in the relations between publishers and advertising agents.

Some 48 years ago N. W. Ayer & Son reached the conclusions THAT agency relations were capable of a better interpretation than any then recognized; THAT we could best serve publishers and ourselves by devoting all our energies to making advertising pay the advertiser rather than in specific endeavor to secure business for any paper or papers; and THAT thereafter it should be the sole business of this agency to serve its clients. Naturally the *basis of remuneration for this service then became a matter of mutual agreement between our clients and ourselves.* None other than we could know the cost of the service. None other than the client could judge its value to him.

Forty-eight years' experience has confirmed to us the value and soundness of this principle. *No more now than in 1873[46] do we concede the right of a publisher to fix the rate of remuneration which our clients shall pay us for our services.* That is not the publisher's responsibility.

On the other hand, it has been our policy never to attempt to influence the rate of discount allowed by publishers to advertising agents. That the agent renders a service to publishers in the development of new advertising and in the assumption of credit risks, is a recognized fact, and that this service should be rewarded by a differential which gives the agency an advantage in the purchase of space is only fair and just.

But the advertising agent no longer represents the publisher. The publisher has his own representative, and some publishers have many very capable men thus employed. The agency commission has therefore ceased to be compensation for the selling of space as in the early days when no copy preparation was involved, and when responsibility for payment for an account ceased when collection from the advertiser was impracticable. The so-called agency commission is not therefore a true commission. In reality it is a differential discount to the agent because he is an agent and primarily because he assumes all responsibility for collection, and for the credit risks involved. Has it ever occurred to you that the differential discount generally prevailing is too large, and that this may be the root of some of the evils which beset the advertising business today? . . .

From our viewpoint it seems that *the agency differential should be fixed by the publisher as near as may be to measure the value of the agency to the publisher, and beyond this the agent should look for remuneration to the client whom he serves. This would confine to the publisher the responsibility which belongs to him and relieve him of the necessity of trying to fix a differential which shall cover services of varying character and value.*

To the publisher, in our opinion, solely belongs the responsibility of fixing rates for space in his publication. From time to time, N. W. Ayer & Son have been asked to join in representations to publishers regarding rates generally, but this we have refused consistently to do. The publisher is in the position of the manufacturer. He alone knows his cost of production; he alone can determine the amount which he must charge for his space. If his rates continue too high or too low, the ordinary laws of business will operate to eliminate his publication. . . . In selecting publications for the advertising of our clients, we must consider each individually for its value to do the particular work in hand. . . . Such exercise of judgment is a part of our responsibility to our clients. But that is far from treating publication rates as a group matter or attempting to say what they shall be.

The italics are mine. The parts of the letter thus emphasized lay down a basis for relations between publishers, advertising agents, and advertisers which would remove most, if not all, of the long-standing misunderstanding and confusion about the agent. It is important to note that these criticisms and ideas come, not from an advertiser who has a selfish motive in attacking the established arrangement, not from an outside observer who cannot take full cognizance of the practical business aspects of the matter, but rather from a prominent agent possessing unrivaled experience with all the issues involved.

In 1933, after a detailed study had been made of the existing commission arrangement from many points of view, the so-called Young Report on Advertising Agency Compensation was published, with its conclusion "that the method of advertising agency compensation now in force [whereby the agency receives the commission which the media owner allows] is the most practicable one for maintaining the true and long-run interests of all advertisers and all publishers." [47]

Thus ten years after Ayer's death and nearly sixty years after the institution of the first Ayer contract with an advertiser, F. W. Ayer's view of the agent's position in the advertising structure still failed to find general acceptance. The essential soundness of the Ayer principle has been widely recognized, to be sure, and even the Young Report paid tribute to its constructive influence upon the industry. But media owners, as well as other agencies, cling to the method of compensation which originated when the advertising agent was the agent of the publisher. Nonetheless, the validity of a sound idea survives the shackles of tradition and the opposition of entrenched interests. Both the methods and the conclusions of the Young Report have been sharply challenged, and for several years nearly every issue of the trade journals of advertising contained some reference to dissatisfaction about the prevailing arrangement of agency compensation. It is noteworthy that the Haase Report, which appeared late in 1934, endorsed the Ayer principle as a general basis for compensation. [48]

The decision made by Ayer management in 1948, to charge gross rates on commissionable media (such as newspapers, magazines, outdoor, and radio) and 15 per cent on the net cost of other expenditures in the advertiser's behalf, has not altered the firm's basic policy. It made the change on its own initiative, primarily in order to bring its charges for hiring radio and television talent into line with what other agencies were charging and what it felt the service was currently worth. It considered having two rates, one for commissionable media and one for other services, but it soon found that such an arrangement would be too confusing to clients. It finally adopted the prevailing plan of compensation, one which has long usage and acceptance, if not strict logic, behind it. But the firm still considers itself the agent of the advertiser and holds that its compensation is a matter to be decided between it and its clients.

SOME PROBLEMS CREATED BY MEDIA OWNERS

Although the interests of advertising agencies and owners or representatives of media are parallel in many respects, certain conflicts arise because the two groups are on opposite sides of the fence as far as particular space transactions are concerned. One must never lose sight of the fact that, with rare exceptions, both published and broadcast media exist for the profits they bring and that those profits depend largely upon advertising revenue. Consequently those who own publications are bound to be aggressive in promoting the sale of their advertising space. Much of the sales effort takes the form of attempts to prove the peculiar merits of a given paper for advertising purposes. Like all good promotional endeavor, such sales effort is educational and supplies the agency with useful facts and ideas. But, because of the obvious bias which is present, the agency must scrutinize the material presented for errors and exaggerations and guard against anything that hinders an unbiased and methodical appraisal of the media.

In the early days of N. W. Ayer & Son the agency had especially to guard against the dishonest or inaccurate reporting of circulation figures by publishers. The value of advertising space is, of course, directly related to the number of people before whom it regularly appears; though he actually contracts for space, the advertiser really wants readers who are likely to buy his product. In order to make their papers appear more attractive to advertisers, therefore, both publishers and broadcasting stations tend to exaggerate their circulation figures. One of the most important parts of an agency's work before 1900 was to penetrate this subterfuge in every way possible.[49] Gathering the facts was, however, generally a costly process, and it was to defray the expenses involved that Ayer, imitating Rowell, published the *American Newspaper Annual*.[50] The *Annual* and Rowell's *Di-*

rectory brought considerable improvement; but as late as 1898 Frank Munsey, himself a publisher, could still point to glaring dishonesty in the reporting of circulation figures.[51]

In an effort to provide more reliable information N. W. Ayer & Son completed arrangements in 1910 for a careful audit of circulations. The publishers who took the service paid a sum which was calculated to cover most of the expense involved, and the circulations thus verified were given special certification in the *Annual*.[52] Only a limited number of publishers took advantage of the arrangement, but the Ayer agency's progress with this improved method of obtaining reliable information probably hastened the formation of the Audit Bureau of Circulations which was organized in 1914. This body draws support from publishers, agencies, and advertisers, and provides an independent check for the benefit and protection of all three groups. Its existence made the Ayer audit unnecessary, and the agency promptly arranged to incorporate the "A. B. C." figures in its *Annual and Directory*.[53]

Since 1914, additional organizations have been formed — notably Controlled Circulations Audit and state publishers' associations — to verify circulation figures through an independent check, and it is generally assumed that the figures for printed media as a whole are now quite reliable. But, while it is true that most of the important newspapers and periodicals have their circulation data verified by independent audits, for many printed media no certified figures are available and the data supplied by their publishers are not altogether trustworthy. Thus, of the circulation figures for the 20,000 publications listed in *N. W. Ayer & Son's Directory of Newspapers and Periodicals* for 1939, only 14 per cent had been subject to independent audit and less than 25 per cent of the remainder were supported by sworn affidavit. By 1948 these figures had improved substantially. Of 1,873 daily newspapers published in the United States 1,016, or 54 per cent, were independently audited and 584, or 32 per cent, provided circulation figures supported by sworn affidavit, leaving 14 per cent without any certification. Of the 106 Canadian dailies 78, or 72 per cent, were covered by A. B. C. or sworn affidavits. The circulation of weekly newspapers is not so well certified. Out of a total of 10,511 weeklies published in the United States and Canada in

1948 only 686, or 6.5 per cent, were covered by A. B. C., while 6,146, or 58.5 per cent, provided sworn affidavits. In the periodical field, too, the certified coverage is still surprisingly low: of 7,000 periodicals only 2,109, or 30.2 per cent, have circulation figures supported by independent audit or affidavit.[54] In terms of advertising value and market coverage the uncertified publications are not nearly so important as their numbers might suggest; but many of them are of considerable value for national advertising, and the agency must make reasonably accurate estimates of their true circulation.

For radio and outdoor advertising the data as to the persons reached obviously present a more baffling problem. The only figures obtainable are estimates based upon sample tests and counts; and it is only since 1931 that independent organizations have been formed to gather and analyze dependable data. In the past fifteen years remarkable progress has been made, but much work still remains to be done in this direction.[55]

Thus, although the statements of coverage supplied by media owners today are much more reliable than those of fifty, twenty, or even ten years ago, N. W. Ayer & Son still feels obliged to spend considerable effort and money in order to ascertain the value received, in terms of the number of people reached, when it pays out money for its clients.

Media owners sometimes cause trouble by attempting to circumvent the Ayer policy of preserving strict impartiality toward media. A publisher or his representative hears about an advertiser who is dissatisfied with his agency, or he picks up some other bit of news which might help the agency to get new business, and he attempts to trade his "tip" for the agency's favor. The Ayer attitude toward any effort by a space-seller to gain special consideration was plainly expressed by H. N. McKinney in 1905, in reporting an interview with Thomas Balmer of the Butterick publications:[56]

Our men cannot go with your solicitors, nor can your solicitors go out and make the *Delineator* proposition as a part of Ayer & Son. And do not forget this. Your advertising world begins and ends with three publications, and they are all you are working for. No matter how you talk, the end and aim of your endeavors is to get advertising for the three papers that make your advertising world, and that is as big as your world ought to be. But do not forget, on the other hand, that Ayer & Son's world has 20,000 newspapers in it and our relation to your three papers is the same as it is to the others, and so long as we are honest, that is just the relation we will sustain to your publications. We want to give to the Balmer Trio every dollar of business we can give them in our customers' interest and not one red cent that ought to go into some other papers. Your men can go to any other agency in the United States and say to them, "I know a concern that is going to do some advertising. I will introduce you if you will take care of me," and every other agent than ourselves will say, "I am ever so much obliged to you, &c." and in return for this service, the agents will advise large expenditures in the Balmer Trio. Ayer & Son will not. Our thought would be, how can we spend the advertiser's money to best advantage, and if we do not regard the Balmer publications as the very best mediums for his use, then they will not get the business. We are glad to send you business whenever we can consistently do so, but Ayer & Son are not working for the Balmer publications.

For many years after the advertising middlemen had divided into two camps, the Ayer agency was not inclined to look with favor upon the publisher's representative. As far as N. W. Ayer & Son was concerned such a representative seemed to be unnecessary, even definitely troublesome at times, because his efforts to "sell" his publication to clients sometimes led to misunderstandings between them and the agency. As one of the Ayer staff put it,[57] "our Forwarding Department . . . is there . . . to do business with publishers. . . . We could do business without the representative of a publication. We know circulation; where the paper goes; the value of the circulation, and we can make up our list . . . without advice from the publisher."

When the representative began helping to develop new advertisers and to facilitate the handling of business between agency and publisher, the Ayer management felt that he was entitled to his place in the advertising structure. But when he merely stood between and collected his commission on orders forwarded by the agency, the Ayer management regarded him as swelling costs unnecessarily. In particular, it objected when the representative tried to thrust himself between agency and publisher, claim credit for all business sent by the agency, and persuade the publisher to increase his rates in order to provide the representative with the compensation he wanted.

An unpleasant situation of this sort confronted N. W. Ayer & Son between 1921 and 1923. The American Press Association was making a strong bid for support from country weeklies and on several occasions wrote to them claiming credit for business which the Ayer agency had forwarded. The claims were unfounded, and the Ayer firm did not hesitate to reject them when the publishers made inquiries. This denial led the Press Association to attack the agency, and the Ayer management was finally compelled to defend itself by means of general letters to publishers. An excerpt from one of its communications explains why it resented the action taken by the Press Association:[58]

From the very first this firm has been a promoter of advertising — a developer of advertising. Just now, the American Press Association professes to be interested in getting some cigarette advertising for the publishers of Iowa. Let us, therefore, refer a moment to tobacco advertising. Some thirty years ago Ayer & Son, after repeated efforts, induced the leading tobacco men of that day — Lorillard, Finzer Brothers, Blackwell-Durham, Wetmore, and others, to advertise their products in the newspapers. Some older publishers may recall the eight inch ads. which we ran at that time. More recently, we sought an opportunity to show that great and enterprising tobacco house — The R. J. Reynolds Tobacco Co. — what newspaper advertising could do to extend the sale of their products. The opportunity was given us and the results were marvelous. The "Prince Albert" campaign and the "Camel Cigarette" campaign are advertising history; but what we ask you to consider is what followed our pioneer efforts. Name for yourself the numerous other brands of tobacco and cigarette that straightway climbed on the newspaper advertising wagon, and estimate, if you can, the millions of dollars that went in consequence to the publishers of this country, some to you we hope — but which, as a matter of course, Ayer & Son never saw. With such a history, you can perhaps imagine how it sounds to us to hear that the A. P. A. is telling the publishers of Iowa that it hopes to get some Camel Cigarette advertising for them, if they will all sign up special with the aforesaid A. P. A., and if they "sit tight" they can, perhaps, make Ayer & Son pay an extra 15% for the privilege of placing that business in Iowa publications. . . .

In this letter we have mentioned the A. P. A. because they have gone out of their way to attack us. We have no quarrel with them. We wonder how they will benefit a publisher in the long run. Will they become real originators of business or will they merely hold a "skimmer" between the publisher and the advertising agents who do originate business?

If the publisher chooses to use a firm of representatives, the agency can offer no serious objection, but, when the publisher attempts to come between the agency and its clients, the Ayer management objects in no uncertain terms:[59]

We recognize the right of any publication to solicit our clients in an ethical manner. At the same time we resent an inference on the part of the publication which may plant the seed of doubt in our client's mind as to the quality of our judgment. Our recommendations to clients are made with but one major thought in mind, namely, to make the advertising pay the advertiser, and it is an extremely rare occasion when we are accused of being "unjust," and we see in the present incident no trace whatever of intentional or unintentional injustice to your publication or to our client.

It is not our purpose in this letter to justify to you our recommendation of another magazine to our client; rather, to point out to you a practice or policy of this House which we do not like to see trampled under foot, namely, that following the approval of a schedule by a client, we do resent the efforts of a publication to upset that schedule. Mr. ———'s letter carries a clear suggestion to our client that he should be dissatisfied with our recommendations.

Another type of problem arises because publishers themselves use advertising in order to sell their space, and they employ agencies to place the advertising for them. To some extent this means that the agency serves opposing interests, and unless it exercises great care the conflict may produce unfortunate results. The business which the publisher offers to the agency is well worth having, but occasionally a publisher attempts to use it as a means of obtaining more favorable treatment when the advertising schedules of other clients are made up. N. W. Ayer & Son has handled advertising for publications ever since 1869, but it has always guarded against any abuse of this kind.

Thus, in 1889 the firm received a letter from a newspaper publisher saying that he intended to spend a considerable sum of money on advertising his paper and that he proposed to give the order to the agency which sent him the largest amount of business during a specified period. To this bid for an exchange of favors the Ayer management replied:[60]

The fact that you propose to place some thousands of dollars of your own advertising with an advertising agency will not in the slightest degree influence the sending of business to your paper by us. . . .

Our customers place business with us believing that we will use all the facilities that we have, including our judgment, for their best interest. . . . Your newspaper must stand with us entirely upon our judgment of its value, as compared with other papers, to our customers; and the prospect of getting an order for $1,000,000 would not in the least change the basis of our consideration.

For many years N. W. Ayer & Son has refused to accept publishers as open-contract customers, preferring to place their business on the order basis. One reason for this is that publishers now prefer to divide their business among agencies in order to avoid any appearance of favoritism. Another is that the Ayer agency itself does not wish to incur any obligation to help in the planning of their advertising which might be misconstrued as a promise to favor the media owned by the publishers. Even the business offered by publishers on the order basis has to be scrutinized carefully. Within recent years a publisher for whom N. W. Ayer & Son was placing some advertisements attempted to trade on the connection, and the Ayer management promptly called a halt. Referring to this, one Ayer executive wrote to another:[61]

As you know, every time we get the account of a publisher we question ourselves, in the first place, as to what is his objective in coming to us — that is, whether it is a question of service to help him solve a problem or has he some ulterior motive. . . .

This morning there comes to me a portfolio containing carbons of a letter written by someone in the —— office . . . [to a number of advertisers].

There are four paragraphs quoted below from this letter.

"I recently left you an advertisement of the ——, headed 'What do the retailers read and when?' This I think tells the story completely.

"It was prepared by N. W. Ayer & Son, one of the largest and most competent agencies in America. They never proceed on theory. Facts are always determined before a campaign is launched. Always, they are careful, analytical, sure. They seldom miss their objective.

"And so, when N. W. Ayer & Son say the retailers read the ——, the retailers read the ——.

"Trust the integrity of N. W. Ayer & Son for that."

. . . the ulterior motive is quite in evidence, and it is not the kind of thing we like or care to see done.

Fortunately, occurrences of this sort have been comparatively rare in the experience of N. W. Ayer & Son. The problems which arise because of the media-owners' eagerness to sell are usually the result of unforeseen complications or chance conflicts rather than deliberate attempts to use the agency unfairly.[62] In all the instances examined, N. W. Ayer & Son has placed the interests of its clients first, and in most of them it has succeeded in ironing out the difficulties without losing the publishers' goodwill.

Coöperation by Media in Selling Campaigns

Before leaving the subject of the media-owners' efforts to sell their space, some mention should be made of the various aids which publishers give to agencies and advertisers in their advertising and selling campaigns. With a view to increasing their advertising linage, most publishers go to considerable trouble to provide detailed information about the markets which their papers reach; they furnish statistics about population, income-tax returns, schools, churches, factories, retail trade, employment, and business activity. Some publishers go so far as to assist the advertisers' salesmen in obtaining new outlets, make investigations of sales to dealers, check the stocks of merchandise on retailers' shelves, and obtain data about the acceptability of particular products in their markets. In addition, newspapers frequently sponsor cooking and housekeeping institutes and similar demonstrations in which the products of their advertisers are given considerable attention.

The extent to which this sales coöperation is sometimes given is apparent from a summary of the various aids given to one Ayer client in 1926. The newspapers held public meetings at which a dietitian gave lectures touching on the use of the client's product; they printed articles publicizing these lectures; printed publicity material about the client's factory, products, uses of the products, sales operations, radio programs, and related subjects; conducted contests offering prizes for the best use of the client's products; gave free insertions of advertising copy in trade issues; printed and mailed letters and broadsides to dealers; arranged for the distribution and installation of window displays; gave over their own windows to a display of the client's merchandise; had their representatives accompany the client's salesmen during their canvass of towns; reproduced advertisements on plain stock and mailed them to the trade; attached coupons for premiums to each copy of the regular edition; used the client's name in their advertising to promote nationally advertised products; and printed the name of the client and his products on their employees' pay envelopes.[63]

To be sure, not every publisher did so much for this client and not all advertisers receive so much free coöperation from media, but the amount of such sales assistance from publishers is surprisingly large. Some of it involves a good deal of extra expense; and, where competition between papers is unusually keen, advertisers have been quick to ask for so much help that abuses have arisen. N. W. Ayer & Son is mainly interested in genuine normal newspaper values and is opposed to buying coöperation from publishers; but, when such assistance is offered, the Ayer firm takes all it can get and has even made space contracts conditional upon the rendering of particular services.[64]

The current attitude of N. W. Ayer & Son on this matter was expressed in 1932 to publishers by the head of the Ayer Media Department:[65]

There are forms of service which prove useful to general advertisers and which publishers can render with complete propriety. There are others which should never be attempted in the name of cooperation and which result in unbusinesslike waste and often definite loss to the publisher. Such service should be limited to what the advertiser cannot well

do for himself, but which the paper can do for him at little or no extra
cost. . . .

Whatever a publisher himself needs in the selling of his market and
his paper, he can legitimately share with his advertisers without writing
an extra cost into his rate. . . .

Other types of service which entail direct outlay by the publisher if
insisted upon by an advertiser could properly be charged for on a service basis. It is inequitable to include this cost in the rate and charge
alike to the customer who does not want and cannot use such service.
But regardless of our House opinion on the subject, if a publisher is
prepared to give and does give a certain type of service to other clients
and any of our clients wants such cooperation, we dare not decline to
ask for it and expect to get it.

When the practice of giving coöperation began is not altogether
clear, but it has been widely followed since 1920. It is significant
that the code for publishers under the NRA attempted to curb
some of the abuses which have developed.

N. W. Ayer & Son, the Publishers, and Publicity

The printing of publicity material has long been regarded by
advertisers, agencies, and publishers as a special form of sales
aid which newspapers and periodicals can sometimes give. We
have already seen something of the Ayer handling of publicity
for clients (above, pages 370–372), but the matter has a bearing
on relations between the agency and publishers which should be
examined in some detail.

Although N. W. Ayer & Son did not devote special attention
to the preparation of publicity until after World War I, it has long
handled a certain amount of this material in connection with its
advertising. In the 'seventies and 'eighties, for example, the firm
sent out a great many "reading notices" which were often but
thinly disguised advertisements. Usually they were designed to
call attention to, and supplement, formal advertisements, but
some manufacturers relied on them almost exclusively. Sometimes
the publisher charged advertising rates for printing them; sometimes — especially if they accompanied a large order — he inserted them free of charge.[66] The early Ayer records indicate that,
when the first insertion of a series of advertisements was made,

the publisher could be expected to print a complimentary reading notice, of which the following is a typical example:[67]

The Osborn Cornice Co., of Toledo, Ohio, are now making the most perfect adjustable window cornice now in the market. We would advise our readers to send for illustrated price list, and call their attention to advertisement in another column of this paper.

All the evidence available for the period before about 1905 points to a conception of publicity which is quite different from the view held by N. W. Ayer & Son today. In the early period complimentary notices and other free newspaper space were sought and granted, not because the material was news which would interest readers but rather because they pleased the advertiser, gave him more space than he paid for, and (possibly) made his advertising more effective. Indeed, in offering material for complimentary insertion, the Ayer agency seldom failed to urge that its publication would help to make the advertiser increase his use of newspapers.[68] The following communication from N. W. Ayer & Son, offering publicity material in 1899, is fairly typical:[69]

We take pleasure in enclosing you herewith a copy of an opinion handed down by Judge Lacombe of New York, granting a preliminary injunction against imitations of Uneeda Biscuit. We need not comment upon the general interest of this, and its importance in supporting commercial interests, and its vital bearing upon the success of those advertisers who are most liberal in newspaper patronage. . . .

For your convenience we have incorporated in news form the facts set forth in the decision. If, however, you prefer to prepare a short article yourself, its insertion in your paper will be equally appreciated by our clients, for whom we now have an order running in your columns.

Press agents, advertisers, and agencies soon began to flood editors with articles. N. W. Ayer & Son, however, began to sympathize with the publishers who opposed the whole procedure. Realizing that many advertisers were trying to substitute free publicity for paid advertisements and thereby depriving both agency and publisher of revenue, the Ayer management was moved to protest. Touching on this point, an Ayer advertisement of 1908 complained that:[70]

Some manufacturers will move heaven and earth to get their product named in the reading columns of a publication rather than have it properly displayed and described in the advertising section where readers really expect to see it.

So fashionable is the unbeknownst-to-the-reader scheme of advertising that some agents even base their claims for business on ability to work it — and work others. They allege the possession of a mystic and powerful back-door influence by means of which they can obtain from publishers an indefinite amount of this disguised advertising.

Similar views were expressed seven years later by a representative of the Ayer firm in speaking to a gathering of publishers: "Dilly-dallying with newspapers for concessions of various kinds costs us time and money and earns no commissions." [71] At the same time he explained why N. W. Ayer & Son was nonetheless obliged to request favors: "If we do not get these things for our clients some other agent will; and as long as advertisers want such things and newspapers grant them, we . . . must ask for them . . . as a simple matter of primary self-protection." [72]

By 1919, however, N. W. Ayer & Son had recognized that there was such a thing as legitimate publicity and had assembled a staff of newspaper men (not advertising copywriters) to prepare material which would have a genuine news appeal and which, at the same time, would cultivate recognition and goodwill for Ayer clients.[73] There can be no question about the sincerity of the new policy. Members of the Ayer staff received definite instructions to explain to clients that any publicity material which the firm sent out would have to win acceptance on its own merits, unaided by promises of advertising contracts. Further, whenever an Ayer representative happened to say anything to a client which could be construed as a promise to demand or obtain free newspaper space, the management promptly corrected him.[74] In addition, every piece of publicity material sent out by the agency under the new arrangement has borne the following imprint:

Note to Editor — We submit the material on this sheet for you to judge solely on the basis of its general interest. We present it with no relation to any advertising we may have placed in your publication.

N. W. AYER & SON

To explain its policy more fully the Ayer management sent out the following statement to publishers and editors:[75]

Gentlemen:

Let us see if we cannot reduce this matter of the publicity we send you to its simplest terms and then together consider these terms frankly. It is your aim to make a living from the business of publishing a newspaper. We earn ours by making advertising pay the advertiser. The advertiser, in his turn, depends on both of us to produce the results which assure his livelihood. Thus it happens that your business, ours, and the advertiser's are closely allied. It is, therefore, common sense for us all to work together as far as we can and play the game as fairly with each other as we know how.

As we see it, there are four essential points which you have in mind in considering any publicity story we may send you.

1. Is it true?

We vouch for the accuracy of all material we release.

2. Is it interesting enough to print?

This is a matter of judgment and is entirely up to your editor to decide. We do not believe in the principle of a paper's printing anything in its news columns because of advertising it may be carrying in other columns. We therefore take considerable pains to have any story of ours go directly to the news desk and point out in a note to the editor that we want the story considered solely on its intrinsic merits and not in connection with any advertising we may place.

3. Does it take the place of advertising?

The profit that our organization makes comes from the advertising we place. For our preparation and distribution of publicity articles, our clients pay us only what it costs us to do the work. You can readily see there is no chance of our ever trying to make publicity do the work of advertising. We all know that any news or feature story in any newspaper has advertising value of a sort for somebody. Therefore, if a story is true and, judged in full competition with everything else available, is interesting enough to print, we do not see the justice of ruling against it because it will do some good to an advertiser.

4. Will it affect N. W. Ayer & Son's choice of your paper as an advertising medium?
   The answer to that is an emphatic "No." Our advertising lists are not made up with reference to the papers that use or reject the publicity articles we distribute. So you can use it all or throw it all into your waste basket with complete assurance that in either event you will not be affecting our consideration of your paper as an advertising medium.

This declaration of policy won an editorial of strong praise in *Editor & Publisher* under the heading "Correct Publicity Stand," [76] and many publishers have privately expressed their hearty approval of the position taken.[77] There can be little question that, by adopting a publicity policy which properly safeguards the publisher, N. W. Ayer & Son has won a measure of respect and goodwill for the agency which also benefits Ayer clients.

Censorship of Advertising Copy

Another subject which calls for both tact and coöperation between agency and publisher is the censorship of advertisements. For many years every intelligent publisher has carefully reviewed the advertising copy which has come to his paper, in an attempt to avoid offending either readers or advertisers. Since the agency watches his advertising columns in order to protest against any copy that might disparage the product or harm the interests of a client, it too exercises a censorial influence. This reciprocal practice of inspection provides opportunity for friction and misunderstanding.

The gains which have been made toward the wise censorship of advertising copy have come almost entirely since the founding of N. W. Ayer & Son. In the 'seventies a few editors balked at certain types of medical advertising, but for the most part both the Ayer agency and publishers (see above, pages 45–46) gladly accepted any business which was offered, regardless of its character. When, in 1880, Wilmer Atkinson announced that his *Farm Journal* would refuse all questionable advertisements and guarantee its readers against being defrauded by advertisers, he was apparently taking a stand which was revolutionary in the publishing world.[78] Other publishers also began to be more careful about their advertising;[79] and by 1890 the American Newspaper Publishers' Association was considering "the responsibility of the newspaper, legal and moral, in relation to the publication of fraudulent or improper advertisements," and took steps to uncover fraudulent advertisers.[80] The main reform, however, waited for the crusading efforts of Edward Bok of the *Ladies' Home Journal,* ably backed by his employer Cyrus H. K. Curtis. This reform began in 1892 with the Curtis Publishing Company's refusal to handle any patent-medicine advertising, and it reached its climax between 1904 and 1906 when the agitation for pure food and drug laws became nation-wide.[81] By 1910 a general movement for "Truth in Advertising" was well under way, and publishers were trying as never before to protect their readers against fraud, deceit, or indecency in advertising.[82] Although it is obvious that they still have some distance to go in this direction, the progress made has been real and substantial.

But readers were not the only ones considered when copy rules were drafted. For the sake of his advertising revenue the publisher had to prevent advertisers from disparaging one another in his pages. So long as a manufacturer praised his own product, there could be little objection; but when he tried to point out the inferiority of a competing product, the publisher had to call a halt or sacrifice the business of the manufacturer whose product was being subjected to an odious comparison. Most publishers have chosen to eliminate the "knocking" copy.

About the same time (1900–15) publishers became conscious of the need for improving the general typographical appearance of their pages and began to draw up rules governing the use of illustration, type, borders, and other mechanical details. Their desire was to make their pages more attractive in physical appearance, both to readers and to advertisers, and to obtain some harmony between the tone of the advertising and that of their publications as a whole.

Enforcing the rules about copy of course necessitated regular censorship, and, as the body of regulations grew, the task of making copy conform grew more complicated and difficult for both the publisher and the agency. N. W. Ayer & Son sympathized heartily with the general movement for improving the content and appearance of advertising, even encouraged it. Owing to the many questions of interpretation, however, there were times when the Ayer management felt moved to protest against what it regarded as unfair discrimination in enforcement. That there were many points on which reasonable opinion might differ is readily apparent from a perusal, for example, of "The Curtis Advertising Code" of 1910:[83]

. . . our prime consideration in ruling on copy is the protection and welfare of our readers. . . . Along with this is the purpose to properly protect our advertising clients, discouraging unfair, and even unmannerly, competition in our advertising columns, and safeguarding our own publications against any advertising campaigns that would tend to injure our advertising columns in their general efficiency and standing. . . .

THE LADIES' HOME JOURNAL and THE SATURDAY EVENING POST have not precisely the same editorial aim, nor the same reading public. It is evident, therefore, that the advertising policies of these publications are not to be identical. They have, however, elementary principles in common. . . .

1. Neither in THE LADIES' HOME JOURNAL nor THE SATURDAY EVENING POST are advertisements admissible the object of which is to deceive, defraud, or in any way injure our readers.

2. Extravagantly worded advertisements are not acceptable, nor those in which extreme and exceptional cases are made to appear average and representative.

3. "Knocking" copy is not acceptable — that is to say, copy which hammers at the *inferiority* of competitors' goods, in contrast with the *superiority* of the advertiser's own.

4. Medical or curative copy of any kind whatever is not acceptable for either publication.

5. Advertisements for alcoholic liquors are not acceptable for either publication.

6. We do not accept the advertising of mail-order houses doing a general merchandising business. . . .

7. Advertising is not acceptable in which installment-plan selling is made the chief feature of the advertising, or the main selling argument. . . .

8. No advertising of an immoral or suggestive nature is allowed, and representations of the human form are not acceptable in any sug-

gestive negligee or attitude. Advertisers of corsets, hosiery, underwear, etc., should consult our representatives before going to much expense in the preparation of copy and cuts for use in our publications.

9. It is desired to maintain in our advertising columns somewhat the same tone and atmosphere that prevail in the editorial sections. Copy that is unduly cheap or vulgar and advertisements that are too unpleasant, either in subject or treatment, are liable to rejection.

10. "Blind" advertising is not acceptable — that is to say, advertising which in purpose and intent is obscure or misleading. . . .

14. No advertising for boys or girls as agents is acceptable.

15. The word "free" must not be used unless the article is actually free. A thing is not free if the reader is obliged to perform some service or buy some other article in order to secure it. . . .

SPECIAL RESTRICTIONS FOR
THE LADIES' HOME JOURNAL

1. No financial advertising is acceptable.
2. No advertising of tobacco in any form is acceptable.
3. No advertising of playing-cards is acceptable.
4. No reference to alcoholic liquors is allowed — not even illustrations of wine glasses or steins.

SPECIAL RESTRICTIONS FOR
THE SATURDAY EVENING POST

1. Financial advertising is not acceptable if highly speculative.
2. We do not accept advertising for stocks, unless they are in good standing and listed on a reputable Exchange. Bond advertising is acceptable if in favor of a sound issue, put forth by a bond house of undoubted standing.
3. Financial advertisers must avoid the use of the expression "absolute safety" or "absolutely safe" as applying to any investment.
4. Cigar and pipe tobacco advertising is acceptable for THE SATURDAY EVENING POST, but no other form of tobacco may be advertised.

MECHANICAL SPECIFICATIONS

. . . . The advertiser should always submit to us an original halftone (not an electrotype). . . .

In the case of plates that are made in "line," the original zinc plate should always be sent us. . . .

Halftones should be made with 120-screen, unless minute detail is required. In this latter case a 133-screen is permissible, but nothing finer. . . .

Display type in both publications is limited to the Cheltenham family. Hand-lettering is permitted, within reasonable limits, and consideration is shown to trade-marks with individual lettering, but each instance of this must be treated as a separate case.

For body type in our advertising columns we allow Cheltenham and any good "old style" faces. "Modern" faces, so called, are not used.

Especial attention is directed to the fact that we do not use Gothic display type in our advertising columns. . . .

Ugly, disfiguring or freakish advertisements are not acceptable. . . .

For the most part such regulations are perfectly clear; but at what point does an advertisement become deceitful, extravagantly worded, or suggestive? And how far may a manufacturer go in urging the superiority of his own product before his words may be interpreted as "knocking " a competitor? The Ayer management acquiesced when a publisher struck out from a piece of copy the words "the fastest selling pipe tobacco in the world," but was naturally wrathful when the same publisher overlooked a competitor's description of his product as "the tobacco that is smoked by more millions of men than all other high grade tobaccos combined." It is difficult to avoid mistakes through oversight or difference in interpretation, and there have been occasional instances in which the censor seemed to be unduly strict in dealing with Ayer copy. Naturally the Ayer management has protested strongly against any discrimination unfavorable to its clients.[84]

The Ayer agency has taken the view, moreover, that the rule against "knocking" copy should not prevent a manufacturer from urging points of superiority which are well authenticated and of importance to consumers. Obviously a narrow interpretation of the no-knocking rule would seriously hamper the advertising of new products and improvements.

The Ayer management has not, on the other hand, hesitated to invoke the no-knocking rule when it endangered a client's interests. Thus the agency canceled contracts for advertising tobacco in publications which persisted in running advertisements for a "tobacco cure" headed "Tobacco Hardens the Arteries" and "Tobacco Causes Cancer." In its letter of protest the Ayer management asserted that it was "not our desire to appear to assume a censorship over your columns, nor to appear to wish for the suppression of honest competition." It explained, however, that it felt bound to object to questionable statements which "tend to destroy the investment which our mutual client is making with you." [85]

One glance at recent advertising shows that publishers who established copy regulations similar to those in the Curtis Code have modified them materially since World War I. Public tastes and habits change; social attitudes and taboos break down and form anew; witness, in modern advertising, the encouragement of smoking and drinking for women, the unashamed nudity in illustrations, the frank reference to such topics as constipation and feminine hygiene. Obviously the publishers' censorship regulations have to be modified in the face of such developments, and it is evident from the files of the Ayer correspondence that agency influence plays a part in bringing about that modification.

Through its ability to direct the expenditure of advertising funds an advertising agency can exert powerful pressure upon publishers. One must recognize that this force can be exerted to break down the bars of decency; something of this nature took place in the advertising generally during the years 1931–36. On the other hand, the same pressure can be — and has been — exerted to keep out of the advertising columns a great deal of objectionable copy. Sometimes the pressure has been so heavily against knocking copy that it has threatened to make advertising a meaningless collection of trade names and brands unsupported by factual statements and relevant information. Working against this tendency is the desire of every advertiser and his agency to win the public and sell goods. Hence the very interests which try to compel the publisher to curb their competitors also exert influence to prevent him from going too far with his restrictions. With opposing forces always at work something like a desirable balance is likely to prevail.[86]

The Ayer management has always recognized both the divergent and the parallel interests of agency, media, and individual advertisers. It has never lost sight of the fact, as clients sometimes do, that some censorship is essential if advertising as a whole is not to be entirely discredited; nor has it forgotten that the goodwill of publishers is of incalculable value to the advertisers. Hence all differences of opinion between the agency and media as to details of censorship and its enforcement have been settled on an amicable basis.

The Ayer Agency and Advertising Rates

For many years the general policy of N. W. Ayer & Son has been to avoid trying to take any direct part in the fixing of the rates to be charged by media owners for their space. It has always sought to get prices which, compared with those obtained by other agencies, were the most advantageous possible, and it has discouraged the use of any paper the rates of which were too high in comparison with alternative media. But, as Ayer said in the letter quoted above (page 410), the publisher alone knows his production costs and market opportunities, and to him alone must go the responsibility of deciding the amount to be charged for his advertising space. Hence N. W. Ayer & Son has repeatedly refused to accept the invitations of other agencies or of its clients to join in a concerted attempt to obtain lower rates generally. In taking this action the Ayer management has held that any move to lower rates in general would work serious injustice to a large number of publishers whose rates were already reasonable; further, that the normal working of competitive forces can be depended upon to bring about necessary adjustments.[87]

One exception to this general policy, however, has been the long-standing opposition of N. W. Ayer & Son to newspaper space rates which discriminate against national advertisers in favor of local concerns. For years newspapers have given preferential prices to local advertisers, particularly department stores, partly to favor local interests and partly because the amount of space bought by such users in a year is large when compared with that bought by national advertisers.

At least as early as 1915 N. W. Ayer & Son was contending that the local rates were too often at cost or below and maintained that, if the differential was based on the quantity purchased, it should be granted to national and local advertisers alike.[88] The

Ayer attitude on this matter was explained in 1932 to a group of publishers as follows:[89]

We are not pretending to predict how many or which newspapers in this country may now be accepting a loss on certain local linage and balancing it off with a higher rate on certain or all classifications in the general field, but the range of differential between the general and local rates in many quarters convinces us that either certain low-rate local business is unprofitable or else the high-rate business is more profitable than it would need be in justice to the general advertiser. . . .

When department store and other local retailers' linage is used as an argument with us in soliciting general advertising, our first question is — at what rates was it published? If local advertisers recognize that newspaper advertising is essential to modern merchandising and that sound circulation is a requisite of productive advertising, then they should not expect preferential rates that work inequity to general advertisers. . . .

Our position is that the two classes of rates would be equal for equivalent space. Our preference is for scale rates in the general field, just as they are quite prevalent for local advertisers. . . . With rates so paralleled the general advertiser could have no reasonable contention that he pays too much and the retailer too little and there would be far less subterfuge practised by manufacturers releasing copy to local outlets to be placed by them with the newspapers at the local rates and later to be reimbursed by the manufacturer. . . .

We have yet to see figures showing a preponderantly higher cost for the handling of general than local advertising. On the other hand it has been admitted to us that the costs are so nearly approximate as to make indefensible the wide differentials where they exist. Copy service and composition on local advertising are saved to you on general campaigns. The repeated sales calls and follow-ups locally are unnecessary in the general field. We create new business and increase current business for you. We assume all credit risks. We supply you copy in plate form, ready to print. These are factors which go far to justify rates for general advertising no higher than those in the local field.

To the general Ayer policy of not trying to influence publishers' rates there is still another exception. N. W. Ayer & Son consistently refused to allow any publisher's schedule of rates to interfere with the Ayer policy of basing its charges upon the net cost of space. In several instances this attitude led to disagreement between the Ayer management and a publisher. A single instance will illustrate both the source of the difficulty and the firm's point of view.

For many years the Curtis Publishing Company had allowed a discount of 13 per cent to agencies. That is, for $1,000 worth of space in Curtis publications an agency had to pay $870. Most agencies resold this space to clients at the gross rate or $1,000. N. W. Ayer & Son charged clients the net price, plus 15 per cent ($130.50) or a total of $1,000.50. In 1919 when the Ayer commission was increased to 16⅔ per cent, the firm's charge per $1,000 of Curtis space was $870 plus $145, or $1,015. Thus the Ayer charge was slightly above the Curtis gross price, but to this variance there was no objection.

In 1920, in response to the demand of many agencies for a larger differential, the Curtis Publishing Company increased the agency discount allowed to 15 per cent, making its price to agents $850 per $1,000 worth of space. To this net price, as usual, N. W. Ayer & Son added its 16⅔ per cent ($850.00 plus $141.667), with the result that its charge to clients was $991.667 per $1,000.00 worth of space. Technically this constituted a cut in the Curtis card rates, and the Curtis Publishing Company not only objected but refused to allow its new discount to apply to Ayer purchases until the agency had agreed to charge full card rates.

To conform to the Curtis demand meant upsetting fundamental Ayer policy and revising agreements with all Ayer clients, and this F. W. Ayer flatly refused to do.[90] Explaining his stand to his staff, Ayer said:[91]

Suppose we took it on their terms and they decided that 10% was sufficient commission and we could not charge more than their rates, then they have decided that we should make but 10% on the business. We do not decide it — we have no voice in it whatsoever. I claim that this is our perquisite, our privilege, our own business to decide that. It is not necessary that we take any business. We can go out of business, if necessary, but as long as we are in business we must set our own standards. I reserve that right to myself just as much as Mr. Curtis does to himself. . . .

We have never asked a paper to either raise or reduce its commission. The reason the commission of the Curtis Publishing Company was raised to 15% was because so many agents opposed Mr. Curtis that he overruled the judgment of his Advertising Department and the change was made. He never had any such appeal from us — it did not make a bit of difference. He need not give any commission if he didn't want to — we should not go and ask him for one. If our continuance in business is contingent upon the opinion of the publishers, the quicker we get out of business, the better. We have got to make money for the advertiser — we have got to make advertising pay the advertiser or we have no reason to live, or any excuse for living. . . .

Until 1924 neither firm would yield. Meanwhile, to conform to a strict interpretation of its contract with advertisers, the Ayer management billed clients as if the firm received the regular Curtis discount of 15 per cent instead of the 13 per cent which it actually received. On all business placed in Curtis publications, consequently, the Ayer agency received smaller compensation than it should have had. In 1924 the Curtis management decided to set a special discount of 14.285 per cent for N. W. Ayer & Son so that the Ayer charge of 16⅔ on the net price would be exactly equal to the gross card rate. Owing to the Ayer management's determination to be fair to its customers in the intervening period, the agency had sacrificed approximately $146,000 in revenue.[92]

This instance of a direct disagreement arising out of a publisher's rate schedule is a rare one in the Ayer history. The great majority of publishers, recognizing the merits of the Ayer position and the firm's unquestioned opposition to the principle of cut-rate prices, have chosen to overlook the fact that schedules of rates and discounts occasionally brought the Ayer charges slightly below gross rates. With the decision in 1949 to charge gross rates on commissionable media this issue disappeared.

OTHER ASPECTS OF AYER RELATIONS WITH ADVERTISING MEDIA

From the media-owners' point of view one of the most important aspects of an agency's history is its record of paying bills. In this respect N. W. Ayer & Son can show a particularly good performance. When F. W. Ayer said he would guarantee payment for space, he made no reservations and meant what he said. At various times in the history of his firm, customers have been unable to pay for the advertising placed by the firm; and, despite the fact that in several instances the amounts involved were large, N. W. Ayer & Son has never asked or received any abatement on this account from publishers or other media owners.

It has long been the boast of the Ayer firm that no publisher has ever lost a dollar in dealing with it. Nor has the essential truth of this assertion ever been seriously questioned. Perhaps it would be well to add, however, that probably no publisher ever received a dollar from N. W. Ayer & Son for which he had not given face value. As has already been indicated, the Ayer agency has always checked carefully to see that its orders have been properly filled before it has paid the bills.

To Ayer clients this check appears as a mere routine clerical process for catching errors, but between agency and media owners it involves a vast amount of detailed work and correspondence, never-failing judgment, and tact. From the first, N. W. Ayer & Son has politely but firmly refused to pay bills which were not supported by evidence that the advertising appeared as ordered. Whenever an insertion is missed, either it must be made up or the publisher must adjust his charges.[93] Similarly, if the Ayer agency orders a special position for certain advertising, it has to see that the position is actually obtained before the premium for special position is paid. The responsibility for correct appearance of advertisements is the publisher's, and, if there are typographical errors or if an illustration is poorly reproduced, the agency expects a re-insertion in proper form or an adjustment in the bill. The Ayer staff even checks such matters as the position of an advertisement in relation to those adjoining it or on the opposite page. If it is "buried" badly among other copy or inserted beside competing or objectionable advertising matter, the agency obtains a "make-good" or a revision of the charges.

Some idea of the importance of agency checking may be gained from the fact that in 1927 for a single client the value of the "make-goods" obtained by N. W. Ayer & Son totaled $11,000. The errors regularly caught and corrected for all clients amount to many times this sum. Inevitably the corrections and adjustments take time, and payment is accordingly delayed. As a result, a publisher occasionally complains that the agency is "slow pay." In most cases the delay is caused solely by the publisher's failure to send checking copies of his papers or to acknowledge inquiries made by the agency. In the 'eighties and 'nineties the publisher's carelessness about such details was proverbial. But even in recent years the agency has had to contend with procrastination and neglect. In 1921, for example, one publisher repeatedly sent bills for advertising which was supposed to have appeared in his paper. In spite of at least fifteen communications from the agency over a period of eight months, he failed to produce any evidence to support his claim nor did he send a single letter of reply to the agency's inquiries. In 1922 it took eight letters from the agency and four months' time to straighten out an error made by one of the country's largest newspapers.[94] Difficulties of this kind are a part of the daily grind of the agency.

On the other hand, no matter how old a publisher's claim is, if it can be substantiated, payment has been immediately forthcoming. The Ayer management attempts to settle all bills promptly, but it is not always possible to do so. Newspapers — particularly country weeklies — change hands at frequent intervals. In some cases the new owner is entitled to receive all moneys due, but in others the title to accounts receivable is retained by the former owner. Hence, N. W. Ayer & Son is obliged to wait until one of the parties has proven his claim to any amounts which it owes the paper. In a surprising number of cases the sums due have not been claimed until after years of delay. Thus far, the Ayer management has refused to invoke the statute of limitations; every just claim has been paid on demand regardless of its age. Further, in recent years the system of auditing has been improved so that payment is authorized as soon as file copies show that an order has been complied with; hence the agency no longer waits for the arrival of the publisher's bill.

In checking insertions and settling accounts the Ayer policy has always been to insist on fair, but not favored, treatment. It has been equally careful to extend fair dealing to the publishers themselves, and the firm's files contain ample evidence that N. W. Ayer & Son has not hesitated to defend a publisher against mistaken criticism or unjust treatment by a client. In short, the Ayer agency has usually stood as a diplomatic but strictly impartial mediator in such matters. In the long run, of course, this policy has worked to the advantage of all parties concerned. The publisher is assured of honest dealings, the agency gains goodwill, and clients are protected against errors and wasteful expenditure. As a result of its excellent relations with media, the Ayer agency has been able to obtain a great number of favors from publishers for its clients — extensions of the dead line on copy, favorable positions without extra charge, and willing coöperation in many directions. In making advertising pay the advertiser, N. W. Ayer & Son has never forgotten that the good-will of advertising media is essential to the process.[95]

Within the limits of this study it is impossible to touch on all phases of the relations between N. W. Ayer & Son and the various types of advertising media. In general, the firm's relations with outdoor, radio, and other media resemble those with publishers, though they belong to the recent period of Ayer history. For many years N. W. Ayer & Son showed a tendency to favor newspapers; as it extended the scope of its service to include magazine, outdoor, and radio advertising, however, the firm gave ample proof of its desire to use only the media suited to a given client's requirements. No owner of an advertising medium can expect more than this.

Before passing on to other aspects of the Ayer history, two ventures call for brief mention. In 1919 N. W. Ayer & Son instituted its annual campaign to advertise advertising. Each year, until World War II interrupted the plan, the firm prepared a series of advertisements designed to explain and arouse public interest in advertising as a vital factor in American life. These were supplied free of charge to any publisher who cared to use them. The letter which accompanied the first series said in part:[96]

To our knowledge there never has been a systematic campaign conducted in a broad way by publishers generally to increase the value of advertising. For nearly fifty years we have been striving to make advertising pay the advertiser. Inasmuch as advertising is the principal source of revenue for the publisher, we believe that it is to the great advantage of all publishers that they devote a portion of this space to increase the value of advertising. Our name is not to be connected in any way with this campaign.

You'll spend the money —Get the most out of it

Every year you spend a large proportion of the money you get. So much for clothing. So much for shoes. So much for things to eat, house furnishings, garden seeds and tools and what not.

There's one sure way to get the most for your money. Know what you want before you go to buy.

READ ADVERTISEMENTS. The advertisements you read will tell you what is new and good. They will give you the latest ideas and improvements. They will help you to live better and dress better at less cost.

If you think of it, you'll be surprised at the world of interest and the wealth of new ideas you'll find in reading advertisements.

Advertisements are the daily record of progress. They are the report to you of the manufacturers and merchants who work for you, telling what has been accomplished for your benefit.

EXAMPLE OF FIRST AYER SERIES TO ADVERTISE
ADVERTISING, 1919

BUT YOU CAN'T "PLUG"
A CAN OF TOMATOES!

Did you ever "plug" a watermelon? If so, what did that little upside-down pyramid mean when you cut it out of the melon's rind? It meant protection. With it, you could make sure you were getting what you were paying for — a good, ripe watermelon.

In most purchases, of course, you can't take that precaution. You can't, for example, cut into a can of tomatoes . . . or a box of tapioca . . . to see what's inside. But you can still protect yourself when you go to market:

You can buy familiar, advertised brands!

When you buy the things advertised in this newspaper, you are buying dependable goods. They've got to be what they claim to be in order to appear here. You'll find them as represented — and you won't have to "plug" them!

EXAMPLE OF THE 1939 AYER SERIES TO
ADVERTISE ADVERTISING

Since none of the advertisements bore any reference to N. W. Ayer & Son, the agency itself could receive no direct benefit, but the management hoped that the campaigns would help to increase the general appreciation of advertising and benefit both agencies and publishers in an indirect way. Both the use which publishers made of the material and their letters of appreciation suggest that the effort was not in vain.

In 1938, for example, 1,625 newspapers used these promotional advertisements, devoting to them space which would have cost

TABLE 11

Entries in the Ayer Typographical Contests, 1931–1948

Year	Number of Entries	Year	Number of Entries
1931	1,451	1940	813
1932	1,476	1941	1,050
1933	1,386	1942	1,326
1934	1,485	1943	1,040
1935	1,539	1944	1,180
1936	1,444	1945	1,190
1937	1,501	1946	1,206
1938	1,438	1947	1,017
1939	1,328	1948	1,914

Source: N. W. Ayer & Son, Inc.

$2,774,000 at regular rates, according to Ayer estimates. During the twenty-one years in which N. W. Ayer & Son supplied material to advertise advertising, the agency estimates that publishers devoted to it approximately $48,000,000 of space. The Ayer management estimates that the direct cost to the firm for writing, composition, printing, and forwarding the advertisements totaled about $200,000 for the twenty-one years.

In 1931 Ayer management offered for the first time the Francis Wayland Ayer trophy for excellence in newspaper typography. The purpose of this award was to stimulate an interest in the physical appearance of the printed page and encourage its improvement. Here again the Ayer agency desires no direct return from the undertaking but hopes to reap indirect benefits. That the annual contest has aroused the interest of publishers is evident from the number of papers which have entered, as shown in Table 11. More than 70 per cent of America's daily newspapers have been represented each year.

Perhaps the relations between the Ayer agency and advertising media is fairly summed up in the sentiment which has been echoed by publishers in their own columns and in letters to N. W. Ayer & Son for more than 65 years: "The House of Ayer represents the very highest and best in advertising." [97]

CHAPTER XVI

RELATIONS BETWEEN N. W. AYER & SON AND
OTHER AGENCIES

WE TURN now to another aspect of Ayer history, the relations between N. W. Ayer & Son and other firms engaged in the agency business. In this book and elsewhere the term "Ayer leadership" has often been used, and a question as to its meaning now arises: Has the Ayer agency taken any active part in coöperating with other agencies, or in encouraging them to organize, for the purpose of considering mutual problems? To this question the general answer is negative. N. W. Ayer & Son has long held a leading position in the industry, but its leadership has been in size, in general stability, and in technical excellence, rather than in any joint activities with other agencies. It has repeatedly refused to assist in forming any sort of organization of agencies or to join any such associations after others have formed them.

The history of relations between N. W. Ayer & Son and other agencies seems to fall into three periods. During the first ten or fifteen years of its existence, the firm regularly entered into business transactions with other agencies. In the second, from about 1885 to 1932, it avoided business dealings with rival firms and held aloof from all attempts to organize an association of agencies. In the third period, as a result of the National Industrial Recovery Act, the Ayer management actively coöperated with other agencies in attempting to draft a code of regulations. The failure of that attempt largely explains why the Ayer firm has long stood apart from its rivals. In spite of that failure, however, N. W. Ayer & Son has since tended to modify the attitude of aloofness which its management displayed for so many years.

EARLY RELATIONS WITH OTHER AGENTS, 1869–1885

Until sometime after 1880, N. W. Ayer & Son frequently bought space from other agents, and in turn it sold to other agents space which it owned. Such transactions arose from the fact that, as explained in Chapter II, nearly every agent at the time held some sort of exclusive control over the advertising space of certain publications. Reciprocal dealings were especially common between agents who served different geographical areas. In 1878 and 1879, for example, we find Ayer buying space from and selling it to S. M. Pettengill, of Boston; Dauchy & Company, of New York; E. N. Freshman, of Cincinnati; and Rowell & Chesman, of St. Louis. In the early 'eighties Ayer exchanged a good deal of business with two firms whose names are quite familiar today: Lord & Thomas, of Chicago, and J. Walter Thompson, of New York.[1]

Owing to the nature of the agency business, therefore, F. W. Ayer could not have followed an entirely individualistic policy, had he wished to do so. Other agents formed both a source of supply and a possible market for space; and Ayer, following the established practice, claimed a commission or discount on space which he bought from other agents and allowed a similar discount on the space which they bought from him. The rate in the 'seventies was the same as that allowed by publishers, 25 per cent;[2] but the following proposal, sent out under the heading "Confidential to Advertising Agents," shows that Ayer, like the publishers he dealt with, sometimes offered an extra incentive:[3]

We herewith hand you our Home List of Philadelphia Religious Weeklies, with revised rates for 1876, which go into effect March 1st next. . . .

As this is the Centennial Year, and Philadelphia the Centennial City, these papers ought to be highly appreciated as advertising mediums, and we have no doubt that a word of commendation from you is all that is wanting to induce many of the patrons of your Agency to advertise in them largely.

To secure your hearty cooperation, we make the following very liberal proposition for acceptable advertisements which you may send us from other than Philadelphia advertisers, viz: on all orders for two or more papers of this List, we will allow you a discount of 33⅓ per cent, from these rates.

A blind advertisement is liable to be rejected by all the papers, and medical advertisements are as a rule declined by the *Sunday-School Times, Standard and Home Journal, Episcopal Register, Christian Statesman, Friends' Intelligencer, Friends' Review,* and *Reformed Church Messenger.*

As Ayer and other agents gradually gave up their space concessions, these transactions between agents came to an end, and in 1888 Ayer indicated in a letter to another agency that his firm was opposed to them on principle:[4]

It has been for many years a rule of our house not to take business from other Advertising Agents in this country, or to deal with any one except the advertiser direct; and while we have as a matter of accommodation to some of our English friends, taken from them small advertisements to be inserted in American papers, we never have handled anything of any moment from any other Advertising Agent.

Our reason for this action is not lack of friendliness towards others in our line of business, but because we have always made it a rule to render the best service possible at the lowest prices consistent with that quality of work, and fair profit to ourselves, and this is the basis upon which we make our charges to advertisers direct. . . .

The Ayer ledgers contain clear evidence that the "many years" referred to in the opening sentence could not have been more than four at the most, but they also show that the exchange of business with other agencies was tapering off by 1880.

N. W. AYER & SON AND EARLY AGENCY ASSOCIATIONS, 1887–1916

The severing of direct business relations between N. W. Ayer & Son and rival firms after 1880 is not so significant, however, as F. W. Ayer's refusal to join in the first attempt to form an association of advertising agents. The impulse to organize this first association did not originate among the agents themselves; it came from media owners with whom they dealt. One of the first problems which the American Newspaper Publishers' Association undertook to solve, after its organization in 1887, was that of deciding which of the many space middlemen should be recognized as bona fide agents entitled to receive the publishers' commission (discount). The Association consulted a number of agents about the matter, and several of them — Erickson, Goodrich & Hull, G. P. Rowell, Lord & Thomas, and S. H. Parvins' Sons — sent out an invitation, calling a meeting of leading agents at the Astor House, New York, on April 19, 1888, to form an agency association:[5]

. . . in accordance with wishes which have been expressed by Newspaper Publishers, that there should be formed by the leading General Advertising Agencies an Association which shall by means of its organization, cause to be known who *are* considered the established and more responsible General Advertising Agents.

F. W. Ayer attended the meeting, but his ideas about the basic principles of the agency business were so much at variance with those of the others present that agreement was impossible. As he himself later described the incident:[6]

This plan of the American Newspaper Advertising Agents' Association was . . . laid out before me and I was asked to become its first President. . . . I turned to Mr. Rowell and said, "Mr. Rowell, suppose an advertiser came in and offered you an advertising contract and wanted to spend $50,000.00, more or less, and wanted you to handle it on a 10% basis, you giving him the business at cost and adding 10%. Would you take it?"

"Why, yes," he said, "I would — and I would take it quick."

I said, "Mr. Bates, would you?"

He said, "I would."

"Well," I said, "gentlemen, I would not. There is a distinction with a great difference, I think. I will go a little further than you have. If he wanted to do it at 8% you would probably take that. If you could get 12%, you would probably take that. Now, we wouldn't do either. We are trying to establish an advertising business on a self-respecting basis. You gentlemen are in the advertising business to make money. You will make more money than I do, but I hope some day to make more money than you do. I hope to have a business that will outlive me. If it does, it will be a bigger business after I am gone than it has ever been while I am in it. The basis on which you are doing business could not bring about that result."

I said, "Gentlemen, I will go a little further. I believe that the advertiser can better afford to give us 15% (which was then our commission) than he can afford to give you the business at cost. I believe I can convince him of that. I do not consider myself a competitor in that sense.

"Now, if I come into an organization like you propose and you made me president of it, I expect I would not like to say some of the things I am saying to you. I am in honor bound to say that you are 'good fellows,' that you understand the business, that you give good service. Then I have got to answer immediately 'Why do you [N. W. Ayer & Son] want 15% and they [the other agencies] only charge 10% or will take 8% if they have to?' . . . I would find it difficult to explain that and still retain my position as President of the Association or to associate with you in any way. I want a different kind of business from what you have built up. I appreciate the value of co-operation and what it has meant in a great many lines in which I have been interested — but this is service and some service is more valuable than is other service."

From all the available evidence it is apparent that as early as 1888 Ayer had decided against joining any association of advertising agents for two main reasons: (1) he was confident that he could get, by himself, recognition and any other concessions from publishers which such an association could obtain for him; (2) he strongly disapproved of the way in which most of his competitors conducted their business, and he felt that by joining with them in an association he would lend countenance to their methods and possibly cause his own to be questioned. In short, he could derive no benefits from an association and would probably lose something by joining it. Individualist that he was, Ayer preferred to carry on alone and unhampered by any obligations to his competitors.

The association which Ayer refused to join held its second convention in 1889,[7] but it dropped out of existence shortly afterward. In 1901 John Lee Mahin, a young agent, approached Ayer with a proposal to form another agency association, but again the answer was a frank refusal: the Ayer firm failed to see what it would gain from such an organization and therefore declined to show an interest.[8]

When it came time to celebrate the fortieth anniversary of N. W. Ayer & Son, the firm pointed out with no uncertain pride that in the agency business it was "Ayer & Son against the field." [9] It is plainly evident that other agents took the same view even earlier. In the published report of the third annual meeting of the American Advertising Agents' Association, held February 18, 1903, there are a number of references to the Ayer agency which indicate that the members of the Association were informally conspiring with McClure and other publishers to punish Ayer because of his refusal to sign agreements about maintaining publishers' rates.[10] Then, as in more recent years, there was a tendency among agents to resent what they regarded as a holier-than-thou attitude on the part of Ayer management. From one point of view their resentment may have been justified, for it is possible that the associations founded in 1888 and in 1901 would have enjoyed a longer and more effective life had Ayer given them his support. On the other hand, there is no indication that the associations had any constructive goal in view. Their chief object seems to have been to defend from any attack the differential allowed by publishers. With his radically different view about agency compensation Ayer was bound to withhold his support from any such program.

This clash in point of view is especially evident in correspondence between Ayer and another prominent agent in 1904. A number of publishers had reduced their discount to agents, and to some of the latter it looked as if the reduction would be general unless opposition was organized. From A. L. Thomas of the Lord & Thomas agency, Ayer received the following:[11]

The writer is very much gratified to learn from a trip of our Vice President, Mr. C. R. Erwin, to New York last week, that there was a chance of having a meeting of a few of the leading Eastern Agencies, including yours, in Buffalo on May 4th and 5th, to talk over the general situation, based on the new order of things in the way of reduction of commission, which seems to be going on all along the line with the leading daily papers.

This morning the writer is in receipt of a letter from Mr. Frank Presbrey, in which he states that the meeting cannot be effected. A meeting for the purposes we have in mind, without your house being represented, would not be nearly as effective as otherwise.

The object of this letter is to ascertain if under the new order of things you are sufficiently interested to meet with a few of the leading Advertising Agents and talk over the situation.

To this proposal Ayer gave his approval, but clearly without any enthusiasm or expectation of results:[12]

While it does not appear to me that a conference such as your letter suggests will accomplish any good in the particular direction of which you speak, I am not personally disinclined to meet the business builders among advertising agents. No matter what subjects are discussed, the conference should certainly be a pleasant one, and mutual advantage might result.

In his second letter Thomas reported that he had conferred with five other agents about the matter, had "suggested that if we could get your firm to work with us, we might perhaps accomplish something which would be to our mutual advantage," and asked if Ayer would meet with them.[13]

Before answering this invitation, Ayer asked for the opinions of his partners and then wrote as follows:[14]

. . . . The more I think about this suggested conference the less does it seem to me that there is anything to be gained by it other than a better acquaintance one with another, and I hesitate to commit so many gentlemen to what might afterwards seem to them to have been a waste of time. Perhaps I do not correctly grasp the scope of the scheme for cooperation which it is proposed to discuss. Would it not be better for two or three of us to first meet and have a general understanding of what was to be considered? If further discussion then seemed desirable we could easily arrange for it.

This reply gives little clue to Ayer's attitude, but the written comments of his partners show that the Ayer firm as a whole was opposed to joining other agents in any attempt to bring the publishers to heel. Wood noted:[15] "Mr. Thomas is looking to a general combination of agents ultimately as his 3rd ¶ shows. I do not see how we can benefit from that." Bradford preferred independent action:[16]

> The agents named in Mr. Thomas's letter have in recent years advocated a commission of 10% and 5% for cash and we have as strenuously opposed it.
>
> They now wish to get together and formulate some plan by which to head off such action by the publishers.
>
> Of course there will be nothing inconsistent on our part to meet and discuss the matter because it is along the lines of the policy we have always held. I believe we can gain as much or more independently and along lines that would better suit our convenience and profit.

McKinney disliked the idea not only because it would reverse firm policy but also because it would necessitate conferring with agents of whom he strongly disapproved:[17]

> I confess I am a good deal at sea regarding the Thomas matter. I suppose such an informal talk as he suggests would not in any way be objectionable, and yet it is so different from our past policy that it is with a good deal of reluctance that I even consider it. Perhaps the names of —— and —— increase my dislike to any such conference. I do feel very strongly that we cannot afford to give them even the apparent sanction of their methods that would come by such an informal conference. If the meeting was to be between Thomas, Batten, Presbrey and Thompson I would not at all object to it.

Notwithstanding Ayer's obvious reluctance to participate in any joint action by agents, Thomas again conferred with J. Walter Thompson and other agents and then wrote to Ayer in greater detail:[18]

> As you are aware, the daily newspapers all over the country have their association meeting in New York City once a year, and then most of the cities have their local associations, and it does seem to me as though the advertising agents as a whole, or a few of the leading ones, ought to have some sort of an understanding and work together.
>
> There are two propositions that I have been working on in the last thirty days:

First, I have made my protest against reduction in the way of commissions. The way we have been doing business, at 10% commission and 5% cash discount, it has not done us any particular good, for the reason that we have allowed the advertiser, as a rule, the cash discounts where some have been advertised by the different publications. . . .

The thought I have had along this line is something like this: If we allow the commission to be reduced by the daily papers without any protest, how long is it going to be before the leading magazines will say to us that if we are willing to work for 10% commission on a daily publication with a cash discount, that we ought to be satisfied with a 7-½% commission and 2-½% cash discount from them, and I imagine if a great many publications reduce their commissions to 10% or less that it is going to be harder work for you, or any other advertising agent, to make 15% contracts in the future than it has been in the past.

The second proposition which I have been fighting against is the payment of bills. I find that we have some 790 odd special bills to pay, on which we are allowed a cash discount if bills are paid on the 10th, 15th and so on through the month. We have been corresponding with the different publications systematically, . . . asking them to allow us to pay their bills during the calendar month after which service was rendered, and take the cash discounts allowed. Many of them have transferred their date of payment from the 10th and 15th to later on, which helps us out in our detail.

We have never refused to take a cash discount; they have come upon us gradually, and we have been glad to take advantage of them, but we are frank to say that where the leading daily papers of the country, as well as other publications, all come in (as they have since the Pettengill failure)[19] and want their money on the 10th or 15th of the month, we have either got to add a great deal of additional capital to our business, or forego the pleasure of taking some of the discounts. Besides adding to our capital, we would have to add to our force quite materially in order to get these bills out on time so that they could be checked and audited to pay. . . .

The writer had an interview with Mr. Lawson [Victor Lawson of the *Chicago Daily News*] last week, and suggested to him the idea of a classification of agents. "Class A," for instance, to be determined or defined by the amount of money they spend with the Chicago Daily News, taking it for granted that the agent who sent him — say $25,-000.00 within twelve calendar months, was the one who naturally was a producer. My suggestion to him was, that if he left his commission and discount as it will be in the future, namely 10 and 2, that a rebate

should be allowed to the agent or agency who sent him a certain amount
of business — the volume to be determined on. The proposition seemed
to interest him. His principal worry seemed to be that the "curb stone"
broker even at the new commission and discount was obtaining too
much for his services. I think without any question your house has more
influence with Mr. Lawson than any other agency in the country, and
believing Mr. Lawson to be the strongest man in the newspaper field in
Chicago, if we could get him to make such changes as we think is [*sic*]
fair and right, I believe it would be possible to get the whole Chicago
Daily Press in line.

I have some ideas of my own along organization lines that I should
have been pleased to have presented to the gentlemen had we met in
Philadelphia.

To this Ayer replied briefly:[20] "I will be glad to take up with
you the matters of which you write whenever we can arrange
for a personal conference. I do not believe I care to discuss them
in correspondence." If the two men ever held the proposed conference, nothing came of it. The Ayer firm kept its own counsel
and went its own way. The American Advertising Agents' Association disappeared; and, when a few local groups, such as the
Association of New York Advertising Agents, managed to obtain
a solid footing, N. W. Ayer & Son gave them no support.

Ayer and the American Association of Advertising Agencies

In 1917 the present American Association of Advertising
Agencies was launched.[21] Its aims and ideals have so often been
recorded that there is no need to repeat them in detail here.[22]
In general, as one writer has expressed it, "Subordination of
personal advantage to the best interests of advertising is the
principle on which the American Association of Advertising
Agencies was formed."[23] The objects of association, as recorded
in its constitution, are mainly constructive,[24] and there is nothing
in them to which a man like Ayer could reasonably take exception.
Nevertheless, N. W. Ayer & Son did not join the new association. The Ayer management was not convinced by the declared
ideals of the group. It suspected that, while a few members might
be actuated by unselfish motives, others would try to use the

organization to their own individual advantage in ways to which the Ayer firm was sternly opposed.

Subsequent events have, to some extent, justified the Ayer suspicions. Immediately after it had established an effective organization, the Association instituted a campaign to obtain an increase in the agency discount, and by 1920 it had achieved considerable success with this effort.[25] Not until 1924 did the Association get around to the formulation of its code of ethics, known as "Standards of Practice";[26] and, while concrete evidence on the point is extremely difficult to obtain, it is commonly accepted as a fact that some of the Association's members take the code lightly, to say the least.

To F. W. Ayer's policy with regard to agency associations the present Ayer management has given full support. It upholds the belief that N. W. Ayer & Son had itself established and maintained high ethical standards long before the present agency association was established, that it has little if anything to gain by membership, and that, so long as many members of the Association persist in practices which do not square with basic Ayer principles, the Association will not progress in the proper direction, and therefore N. W. Ayer & Son's contribution to the industry must be an individual one. In recent years, however, the management has shown a friendlier attitude towards rival firms, and it has coöperated in an informal way with the Association.

RECENT RELATIONS WITH OTHER AGENCIES

There have been, however, several exceptions to what we might call the non-intercourse policy of N. W. Ayer & Son. In the first place, the management has occasionally found it necessary to communicate with another agency in an advertiser's behalf. From time to time an Ayer client finds it desirable to advertise his product jointly with that of another advertiser who employs another agency — to promote, for example, the joint consumption of fruit and a breakfast cereal. The two agencies then have to communicate with one another in working out the details. The Ayer agency has also had occasion to communicate with other agencies about advertising copy to which the one or the other took exception.

Such matters are usually taken up with the advertiser direct, but to avoid possible delay it is sometimes necessary to communicate with the agency itself. In 1926, for example, a rival agency embodied in a campaign to advertise cigarettes several interviews with airplane pilots which were likely to give readers the impression that American commercial aviation was unduly hazardous. N. W. Ayer & Son, in the interest of a client, hastily called attention to the implications of the copy and obtained the other agency's coöperation in having it "killed" immediately.[27] On the whole, however, direct relations of this kind between Ayer and other agencies are rare and of little special significance.

A second exception to the general Ayer policy is the firm's willingness to coöperate indirectly with other agencies through some of the more comprehensive organizations like the Audit Bureau of Circulations and the Associated Advertising Clubs of the World. Both before and after F. W. Ayer's death, the firm held membership in these organizations, and to the second it contributed substantial amounts of money in addition to the regular subscription. According to one of the Ayer partners its specific object in doing so was:[28]

. . . to support their Vigilance Committee work. There exists a very large amount of fraudulent advertising, which works a two-fold injury by robbing advertising readers of their money, and what is far more subtle and dangerous to you and to us — robbing advertising readers of confidence in advertising. . . .

In the nature of things we do not expect a direct or visible return from our investment in this direction, but we keep it up because the organization is doing what no individual could or would do and what must be done in common interest unless advertising is to fall rather than rise in public estimation. We are therefore "going along" with this broad enterprise, wishing it increased success.

From this and other evidence it is apparent that the Ayer policy is not opposed to coöperative efforts in general but only to those particular undertakings which fail to come up to the Ayer standard of agency ethics or which the firm looks upon as matters of individual responsibility.

AYER AND THE NRA CODE FOR AGENCIES

A third and more important exception to the Ayer non-intercourse policy came in 1933 as a result of the National Industrial Recovery Act. Having learned that the Roosevelt administration intended to apply the Act to the advertising industry, the Ayer management began to consider what action it should take. It had no desire to assume the responsibility for organizing the industry; if, however, individual firms failed to take some action, it seemed clear that the Government would either draft its own code or call upon the Association of National Advertisers or the American Association of Advertising Agencies to take the initiative. In either case the Ayer point of view might receive little attention. It seemed wise, in the circumstances, for the Ayer management to avoid hanging back. Accordingly the president of N. W. Ayer & Son sent out to fifty-five organizations in the advertising industry the following letter:[29]

As has undoubtedly been the case with you, we have been studying The National Industrial Recovery Act with great interest.

The Act clearly obligates the advertising industry and those industries affiliated with it to organize in accordance with the primary purposes of the Act; namely, of creating reëmployment, shortening the working week, and increasing wage scales.

In the advertising industry, as in many others, the chief obstacle, in our opinion, to the achievement of these much desired ends lies in unfair direct and indirect trade practices.

The provisions expressed in Title I, Section 3 of the Act (see attached copy) indicate that the Government will coöperate in establishing and enforcing a code under which publishers, radio operators, billboard owners, advertising businesses and all others affiliated with the industry may profitably and fairly operate.

This legislation affords all who have stood and wish to stand for honest procedure in advertising, opportunity to coöperate in setting up a code with enabling powers, which code shall establish standards tested by time, and provide for eliminating unworthy practices from the entire advertising industry.

A frank expression from you, and through you from the members of your organization, upon this question will be appreciated. I shall value your early reply.

Without committing the firm to any particular program, this appeal promised to assure N. W. Ayer & Son a part in the discussions before any final action was taken. Although it looked toward a code for the advertising industry as a whole, it contained no concrete suggestions as to form or scope. The preliminary discussions were hardly under way before the Ayer management and others began to realize that to formulate a single code for publishers, agents, advertisers, and other related groups — the producers, middlemen, and consumers of advertising — was wholly impracticable, and that a separate code for agencies would be necessary. To this end, the American Association of Advertising Agencies conferred with N. W. Ayer & Son and several other agencies which were not members of the Association. A committee was appointed to draft a code, with ten representatives from the "Four A's" and three from nonmembers. To represent the agencies at the code hearings in Washington, four of the committee were appointed. Adam Kessler, Jr., vice-president and treasurer of N. W. Ayer & Son, was an active member of both these bodies.[30]

The meetings of the code committee were held behind closed doors, and what went on in them may never be made public; but, from the bits of information which leaked out and from the code proposals put forth, it was apparent that the agencies represented, N. W. Ayer & Son included, were mainly interested in checking the activities of "cut-rate" agencies and hoped to make them illegal by means of the code. With the details of the code as a whole we are not here concerned; but two provisions need to be mentioned because they made the code's adoption virtually impossible and because they bring to light again the fundamental contrast between the Ayer policy and prevailing practice. One of them was a clause proclaiming it to be "unfair practice" [31]

For any agency to rebate any part of its commission to an advertiser, or for any agency to be owned and operated for the financial benefit of any advertiser or group of advertisers and/or their employees, who thus directly or indirectly obtain the equivalent of a rebate and circumvent the conditions of agency "recognition" required by media-owners and/or their organized bodies.

This provision, if unqualified, would have laid the Ayer firm open to the technical charge of rebating, since the Ayer price — as explained before — was slightly below gross rates whenever the media-owner's discount to agencies was 15 per cent or more. Hence the second clause with which we are concerned, "the practice of charging 16⅔ per cent on the net cost of total advertising volume shall not be construed as rebating." [32]

Unfortunately, in its attempt to outlaw rebating and yet protect the Ayer method of doing business, the committee had impaled itself on the horns of a dilemma.

On the one hand, the second clause quoted, if allowed to stand, would give explicit sanction to a practice which was essentially different from that followed by most agencies. Worse still, it would constitute an admission that some agencies, rather than the media owners, fix the amount of remuneration for agency work, thereby opening the whole matter of agency compensation. To most agents such an admission was undesirable in any circumstances, and it was particularly unwelcome when the established practice was under heavy fire from advertisers. Certainly it would be difficult to reconcile this provision with the implication of the first, that media owners determine the amount of agency reward.

On the other hand, to withdraw the embarrassing clause would be dangerously like admitting that the agencies were working for media owners rather than for their clients. The traditional method of compensation implies as much, of course, but few agencies cared to see thus flaunted in public the breach between the fact and the logic of the prevailing practice. In its eagerness to stamp out the chiselers the committee had not adequately considered the full significance of the code which it proposed. Now it was not only trapped by the anomalous nature of the established system of agency compensation but was also unable to affirm or deny the validity of the Ayer basis without arousing a storm of protest.

It must be said that the Ayer management, too, had been caught off its balance. Even to outsiders it was apparent that N. W. Ayer & Son's interest in the code was mainly to prevent the basic principle of the Ayer contract from being outlawed. But the Ayer management soon began to realize that, with or without the safeguarding clause, the code would clash with the firm's long-established policy. If, as N. W. Ayer & Son had maintained for nearly sixty years, agency compensation was solely for agency and client to decide, there could be no talk of rebating in the strict sense of the word. Conversely, if the Ayer agency agreed to the no-rebating clause, it would bind itself to accept the remuneration fixed by media owners.

Here, as never before, the sharp difference between the Ayer point of view and that of other agencies was plainly exposed. Clearly, the Ayer agency could not possibly coöperate with other agencies in upholding a code of agency practice so long as its policy as to remuneration was fundamentally different.

The committee on the agency code made matters worse by pointing out that, while the 15 per cent commission was embodied in the provisions, the media owners and agents could get together at any time and change it.[33] This interpretation obviously gave the advertiser no voice in fixing the fees of the agent he employed, an arrangement to which both advertisers and the Ayer management had long objected. Thus, N. W. Ayer & Son would have been compelled to revise its fundamental views had the code been adopted.

For many reasons, however, the committee's recommendations never reached the stage of official code hearings. The committee itself, after making its report public, lost whatever enthusiasm it may have had for its recommendations. Many agencies, particularly those which, like N. W. Ayer & Son, did not use the prevailing arrangement of compensation, opposed the report as not representing their views. More important still, the advertisers, through the Association of National Advertisers, charged that the proposals constituted an attempt to "freeze" an outworn and illogical trade practice, to fasten upon the industry a standardized and inflexible system of remuneration for services which varied widely in kind, quality, and amount. This criticism was familiar, almost trite, but it was made with a new determination.

Faced with opposition from all quarters, the committee on the agency code withdrew provisions, put them back again, and finally withdrew the entire code for further revision. The Supreme Court gave the coup de grâce when it declared the NRA unconstitutional.

So ends the only real effort that N. W. Ayer & Son ever made to participate in anything like a trade organization. It was not so much a departure from the policy of aloofness laid down by F. W. Ayer as it was a move to safeguard the more important Ayer basis for relations with advertisers. It came to naught even before the death of the NRA because the Ayer principle, that remuneration is a matter for the agency and its clients to decide, clashed fundamentally with the arrangement used by most agents.

RECENT POLICY WITH REGARD TO RIVAL AGENCIES

The Ayer agency has been criticized for its unwillingness to join with other agents for the benefit of all. Its individualism is regarded as out of harmony with the spirit of the times, and a number of rival agents have felt that it should be modified for the good of N. W. Ayer & Son itself.[34] That there is some merit in the criticism can hardly be denied. There are a number of agencies with records as honorable as that of the House of Ayer; association with them would reflect no discredit whatever, and might be of great value in removing competitive evils and raising standards. There are many ways, too, in which agencies can coöperate to the advantage of their clients, especially in the study of markets and advertising media and in various efforts to improve advertising technique. One may feel, further, that it is the moral duty of a leading firm like N. W. Ayer & Son to do what it can to bring about better conditions in its industry, even if no other gains are to be had, and that until such a firm has done its best *within* the trade organization to correct undesirable conditions and practices, it is in no position to criticize fellow agencies.

Such criticism is valid, but it neglects important considerations. The gild and the trade association have, ever since the Middle Ages, been a weapon of the weak against the strong and of the inefficient against the efficient. The able firm can stand by itself and make progress alone in its own way. The weak, ineffective firm seeks the support of others and is ready to sacrifice progress for protection. When pioneering is necessary, the rules of the trade association hold back the leaders and handicap them in making urgent adjustments demanded by changing circumstances. The Ayer agency has always been a leader and pioneer, an effective individual firm. Common experience demonstrates the fact that the effective individual is usually a poor coöperator. But this alone does not explain the Ayer policy. The main reason is to be found in the Ayer way of doing business, in the clash of principles which was clearly exposed when the Ayer agency attempted to participate in formulating the NRA Code.

Apart from its consistent refusal to join the agency association, however, the Ayer management has tended gradually to modify its attitude toward other agencies. F. W. Ayer was almost belligerent in his isolationist policy. Fry maintained the established principle of avoiding any entangling alliances, and he hardly knew personally the head of a single rival agency; but he was at least conscious of the existence of common interests among agencies and of opportunities for coöperation in the interests of clients. Under his presidency, as we have seen, a limited amount of coöperation did take place. Since 1936 the management has been definitely more friendly toward rival firms. Unlike his predecessors in the Ayer management, Batten has personal friends connected with other agencies, and he is willing to go further than Fry did in the direction of coöperation. A specific instance of this is the national drive in 1938 to promote the sale of used cars. In this campaign the Ayer agency took a leading part and earned the sincere thanks of the other agencies that participated in the drive. N. W. Ayer & Son is still content to remain outside the agency association, but it is no longer unfriendly to competing firms.

CHAPTER XVII

DEVELOPMENT OF ORGANIZATION
AND MANAGEMENT

HAVING examined the functions of the Ayer firm and its dealings
with advertisers, media owners, and rival agencies, we may well
turn to a study of the internal structure of the House of Ayer.
During the eighty years of its existence, N. W. Ayer & Son has
grown from a one-man agency to a large organization embracing
a dozen main departments, forty-odd bureaus or departmental
subdivisions, eight branch offices, and a staff which has at times
included more than nine hundred workers. This growth, of course,
reflects the increase in the volume of business handled, the widening of the geographical territory served, and the expansion of the
functions performed. Of far greater significance than the physical growth, however, are the specialization which has accompanied it, the resulting changes in the structure of the organization,
and the development of managerial ability and technique upon
which it has depended. For the general reader the story of this
evolution can hardly be very exciting, but it is of the utmost importance to an understanding of modern business.

ORIGIN AND GROWTH OF DEPARTMENTS TO 1900

The growth of the Ayer firm may well be compared to that of
a tree: as it developed, the agency not only gained in size but put
forth branches from time to time; and both the trunk and the
main branches occasionally ramified further, producing additional
departments and departmental bureaus. At times this development seems to have been natural, unplanned, and almost unconscious; but there have been periodic attempts to introduce systematic order and method into the organization, to make it
conform to a conscious and rational design.

One difficulty in chronology should be noted. While it is possible to ascertain the exact date when a given department was formally established, the emergence of its particular function and of a specialized group to handle it usually occurred some years before that date. Thus, the Copy Department was not formally instituted until 1900, but specialized copywriters, organized as a group, actually existed within the Business Department as early

PRINTING DEPARTMENT, N. W. AYER & SON, 1878

as 1894. As a result, the dates given are somewhat misleading: they should be regarded as the time of formal recognition, rather than of actual origin.

The details of the specialization which at first took place are not known, but by 1876 the work of the agency had been largely separated into three main divisions: the Business Department sought and obtained orders from advertisers; the Forwarding Department bought space and forwarded advertisements to the papers; the Registry Department registered the advertising — checked the insertions, verified and paid the publishers' bills, and apparently did all the agency's bookkeeping. In addition, there was the less important Printing Department, which set up and printed in finished form the advertisements which were to be published and also turned out the innumerable cards, forms, notices, and miscellaneous stationery which the agency used in its own work.[1]

In 1880 took place what was evidently the first attempt to make a systematic arrangement of the agency's work, extending the principle of functional division which had already been instituted. The Business and Forwarding departments remained essentially as before, but the work of the Registry Department was divided and part of it assigned to a new department. Thenceforth the Registry Department concentrated on maintaining orderly files of newspapers and checking the insertion of advertising in them in compliance with the advertisers' orders. The keeping of all accounts was segregated in a separate Bookkeeping Department. At the same time additional departments were created, partly to take over work which the Business and Forwarding departments had been handling, partly to undertake new and related duties. One of these was the Merchandise Department, which was to handle the ink, type, and other supplies sold by the agency to publishers in exchange for space, together with the miscellaneous assortment of books, patent medicine, and general merchandise received by the agency from customers in payment for advertising. The Annual Department was created to prepare and publish the newly established *American Newspaper Annual* and similar periodicals about newspaper lists, rates, and circulation which the agency had published from time to time since the early 'seventies. To a Business-Advertising Department was assigned the work of preparing and sending out letters, pamphlets, souvenirs, and other material to publicize the business of the agency itself. Lastly, to segregate the management of the advertising departments of the religious weeklies for which Ayer owned the advertising concessions, the firm set up a new division with a separate office. It was this part of Ayer's original business which, on being incorporated in 1882 as the Religious Press Association, was permanently divorced from the agency proper.[2]

Between 1882 and 1900 there were no changes in the formal departmental organization of N. W. Ayer & Son. Within the framework, however, a number of significant developments were taking place. The total number of employees almost exactly doubled from 77 in December, 1882, to 159 in January, 1900; but the increase was by no means uniform in all departments. By 1890 the agency had given up accepting merchandise in settlement of accounts with advertisers, and it had transferred to a separate concern, the Keystone Type Foundry, nearly all the work connected with its business in type and printers' supplies. Hence the Merchandise Department had dwindled to two members by 1890 and disappeared entirely in 1898.[3] Meanwhile, the work of buying space had become simpler and more routine in character as publishers' rates became more stabilized and the agency gradually gave up its space-wholesaling activities. As a result the Forwarding Department, which had a staff of 15 in 1882, handled twice as much business in 1899 with only 7 more members. The Bookkeeping Department kept pace with the growth in volume by doubling the number of its employees. For reasons which are not clear, the Registry Department decreased slightly in size during the same period.[4]

On the other hand, several departments had grown faster than the Ayer agency's volume. Both the Annual and Printing departments had increased their personnel fourfold between 1882 and 1900, probably because both were hardly out of the experimental stage at the beginning of the period. The most significant growth, however, came in the divisions which were primarily concerned with obtaining business for the agency: the Business-Advertising Department grew from 6 to 16 employees, while the Business Department expanded from 7 to 42. Part of this increase was the result of intensive efforts to increase the agency's total volume, but much of the Business Department's growth came from a substantial and important increase in the number and variety of duties performed.

In the 'eighties, as we have seen, advertising copy itself began to play a major part in the success of advertising campaigns, and agencies were compelled to take an interest in its preparation, not only to increase the efficacy of the advertising they placed but also to aid themselves in persuading customers to advertise.[5] Since the Business Department was concerned with helping customers to advertise effectively, as well as persuading them to make the effort, the Ayer management naturally assigned to it the work of assisting with copy preparation. Indeed, the men who solicited business were themselves expected to give such assistance in the course of their canvassing. It soon became evident, however, that specialization of this work would bring some improvement: men who were effective at soliciting orders for advertising were frequently poor at writing copy, while men who were clever on paper often made lamentable salesmen for the agency. In 1892, therefore, Ayer began to appoint men who, working in close conjunction with the solicitors, were to devote themselves wholly to the preparation of advertising copy. By 1900 nine members of the Business Department were thus specialized on a comparatively new agency function.[6]

The work of the original Business Department had also expanded in another direction. As N. W. Ayer & Son's volume of business increased and the organization grew, the expeditious handling of business within the firm itself became increasingly difficult. Within the specialized departments orders might be handled quickly and well, but the operations of the separate divisions were not properly coördinated. Delays, mistakes, and misunderstandings constantly arose as work moved from one department to the other, and in 1896 we find the firm's officers and solicitors considering at great length the question: "To what extent should a solicitor be expected to follow up the execution of an order?"[7] From the recorded discussion it is apparent that the task of seeing the orders from one department to another through each stage of execution belonged largely to individual solicitors in the Business Department of this time and that the arrangement not only failed to get the work done promptly but also interfered with efforts to get new business.

With these developments in mind, the plan of departmental organization adopted by the Ayer management in 1900 will be readily understood. It was designed to bring about better coördination between the firm's activities while obtaining further benefits of specialization. From the overburdened Business Department two new departments split off. Thenceforth the preparation of copy was allocated to the Copy Department, no longer a mere adjunct of the firm's soliciting efforts but a major agency

activity existing in its own right. The second new division bore
the old name of Business Department, but it was essentially a
traffic department; its duties were solely to close the gaps between
the other departments of the agency, direct the execution of business, and generally coördinate the increasingly varied activities
of the firm. The original function of the old Business Depart-

TABLE 12

ORGANIZATION OF N. W. AYER & SON, 1900

Department	Employees
Executive...............................	3
Business-Getting.........................	10
Business................................	17
Copy...................................	9
Forwarding.............................	23
Registry................................	25
Business Advertising.....................	18
Annual.................................	4
Printing................................	28
Outdoor Advertising.....................	4
Bookkeeping {General 10, Customers 5, Publishers 6}..........	21
Janitors................................	2
Total...............................	164

SOURCE: Pay roll list for June, 1900. This list does not include the four partners of the firm.

ment, that of soliciting orders, was centered in the Business-Getting Department whose members could now concentrate their
attention and energy in one direction. Their work was in part to
seek new customers, in part to provide a constant liaison between
old customers and the agency; but in both rôles they sold advertising and Ayer service.[8]

At the same time the Bookkeeping Department was split into
three subdivisions, one to keep accounts with customers, another
to keep accounts with publishers, and a third to handle general
accounts and also the internal bookkeeping of the agency. This

arrangement gave formal recognition to the specialization of work and records which had been taking place in the Bookkeeping Department in the preceding years.

An entirely new division, the Outdoor Advertising Department, was set up in 1900 to handle the new media which N. W. Ayer & Son was adding to its line. The Forwarding, Registry, and other established departments remained unchanged. The 1900 arrangement as a whole, together with the relative size of the divisions, may be seen from Table 12.

CHANGES IN STRUCTURE, 1900–1934

Since 1900 the tendency toward further specialization has continued, and with it the policy of giving formal recognition to the division as soon as it is clear that the flow of work has carved out a definite new channel. The Ayer Copy Department is a good illustration of this development. The men who specialized in copy preparation originally had to perform a number of related but dissimilar operations. The copyman of 1898, for example, not only wrote the text of the advertisement but also worked up his own ideas for illustration, prepared the layout (showing the arrangement and relative size of the border, text, illustration, and signature or trade-mark), specified the kinds of type to be used, selected the artist, arranged for the preparation of finished art work, and ordered the engravings and plates for the reproduction of the finished advertisement. Thus he had to combine skill and experience in writing, art work, and typographical technique; and a copyman who could do them all well was rare indeed.[9]

To assist with the art work the firm hired a commercial artist in 1898, who prepared layouts and occasionally did finished drawings for advertisements. A year later the firm added a man who, in addition to writing some copy, looked after the details of buying art work and engravings. In 1902 for the first time the Department had a man who specialized in buying plates and engravings; and in 1904 the firm hired its first man to be employed exclusively on illustrations. This addition of specialists enabled the copymen to devote more time to writing, but the responsibility for originating art ideas and, to some extent, buying art work and engravings, remained with them until 1910 when an art director was added to the Department. In this way specialization went on within the Copy Department, increasing as the volume of business expanded and advertising copy gained in relative importance as an agency function. In 1912, when the entire Ayer organization was revamped, the division of work in the preparation of copy was recognized in a formal way by organizing within the Copy Department an Editorial Bureau to write advertisements, an Art Bureau to take charge of all the art work, an Engraving Bureau to buy plates and other means of mechanical reproduction, and a Stenographic Bureau to handle the typing and correspondence of the Department. In addition, the Printing Department was transformed into a bureau of the Copy Department because it was so closely related to the production of finished copy.[10]

The subdivision of work within the Copy Department caused the same sort of difficulty that the multiplication of departments had previously caused in the Ayer organization as a whole: between bureaus there were misunderstandings, delays, and confusion. To coördinate the work of the different specialists a Production Bureau was created in 1916, followed by a Detail Bureau in 1917. The members of the Detail Bureau assisted the writers in handling the printing and engraving details of their work. The Production Bureau's function was to control the flow of work through the various stages of copy preparation in all divisions of the Copy Department. All orders for copy, art work, and engravings, and all memoranda and correspondence in and out of the Department were passed through the Production Bureau, which scheduled all details of copy preparation, assigned particular jobs definitely to particular individuals to be completed at specified times, and then checked to see that all operations were performed according to schedule. Instead of a single closing date for completion of an order, there was a series of closing dates; and, as a result, work moved smoothly and systematically through various processes to its completion. By this means in the Copy Department, as in the entire Ayer organization, peak loads and last-minute rushes were greatly reduced and advertisements were completed on time. What is possibly of greater importance, creative workers were relieved of petty details and routine work, enabling them to work more effectively at their primary tasks. And, since the routine work could be done by comparatively unskilled employees, the ultimate result was better copy at lower cost.[11]

In other divisions of the Ayer agency similar expansion and division of labor were constantly taking place. By 1908 the Business-Getting Department was trying to improve the preparation of advertising plans. In the 'nineties this work had been regarded as an adjunct of the soliciting and liaison work done by the Business-Getting Department.[12] For many years it was also viewed largely as a problem of the amount of space and type of copy to be used: hence the group to deal with it was, in 1908, "to be composed of expert and experienced copymen." [13] Soon, however, the firm began to realize that the preparation of advertising plans depended to a large extent upon the analysis of markets and the recognition and solution of marketing problems. Since such work called for specialists in marketing and had only an indirect relation to the soliciting of business, the firm segregated it in a bureau of the Business-Getting Department. Later this bureau was converted into an independent Plans Department. The change increased the likelihood that Ayer advertising plans, instead of being prepared with an eye to their effect upon the total volume produced by the Business-Getting Department, would be worked out independently in accordance with clients' needs and marketing principles. At the same time it enabled the Ayer solicitors to concentrate more closely upon selling the services of the firm.[14]

Just as the Copy and Plans departments originated in and split off from the Business-Getting Department, so the Publicity Department branched off from the Copy Department, and the Radio Broadcasting Department started, in turn, as an offshoot of the Publicity Department. Originally the publicity material sent out by the agency had been regarded, as we have seen, as a kind of disguised advertising, and, as such, it was included as material to be prepared by copywriters. Gradually this work was specialized, and before 1920 a Publicity Bureau had been set up. Recognizing the essential difference between publicity and advertising, the management then began to staff the Publicity Bureau with newspaper men, but it was not organized as a separate department until 1929.[15]

Meanwhile, as early as 1922 N. W. Ayer & Son had entered the radio broadcasting field; and, regarding the new medium as a device for building up goodwill and name publicity, the management assigned it to the Publicity Bureau's charge. A group of specialists in radio broadcasting was immediately developed within the Bureau. By 1929 the technique of advertising over the air had been developed to such a point that the Ayer management organized a separate Radio Department to handle broadcast programs as advertising rather than publicity.[16] This new branch of the Ayer agency had subdivisions corresponding to some of those already used by the parent organization: a Business Department to handle details and act as a clearing house; a Plans Department to work out, in conjunction with the main Plans Department, detailed plans for broadcasting advertising; a Contract and Accounting Department to lease station time and handle the bookkeeping and money involved; and a Production Department to prepare and assemble program material, hire talent, and direct production.[17]

In the Forwarding Department, later known as the Media-Contract Department, four bureaus were established in 1914 to organize formally the specialists who had developed in rates, orders, correspondence, and cuts and electrotypes. In 1920 a Shipping Bureau was added to handle the thousands of mats and plates which the Department sends to publishers.[18]

Within the Business Department an Educational Bureau was created in 1918 to specialize in the work of advertising schools and colleges. Such advertising is largely seasonal in character, and, in order to level off the work of the Educational Bureau through the year, the management turned over to it most of the closed-order or fixed-price advertising which comes from seed and nursery houses, livestock sources, and the like. It thus became, in essence, a division for handling small orders. In 1930 this bureau was made into a separate department with its own subdivisions for soliciting business, preparing copy, and scheduling work.[19]

While the Ayer organization was thus expanding in certain directions, it was changing or contracting somewhat in others. As part of the general reorganization of 1912, the management converted the Registry Department into a bureau of the Accounting Department, thus bringing close together two divisions, one of which was essentially subordinate to the other. By 1915 the Outdoor Advertising Department had disappeared, the firm having ceased to handle outdoor media.[20] In 1931 this department was re-instituted. After existing as a bureau of the Copy Department between 1913 and 1926, the Printing Department again appeared as a separate division. The Business-Advertising Department was dissolved in 1913, part of its work going to the Business-Getting Department, part to the Copy Department, and part to a Service Bureau which was created to handle supplies, mailing, messenger service, and related duties.[21]

Adjustments, 1934–1948

In 1934 the Ayer management began to study the organization of the agency and the various functions performed by each subdivision, with a view to improving efficiency and reducing expenses. Public accountants were called in to review all the bookkeeping operations connected with the handling of business, from the preparation of estimates to the billing of clients for services rendered. The management, at the same time, scrutinized the organization from the point of view of the flow of work and the allocation of responsibilities.

The illness and death of President Fry delayed the institution of changes, but the project was by no means forgotten, and in 1937 and 1938 a number of shifts were made which eliminated a great deal of duplication, made possible a substantial reduction in personnel, and at the same time enabled the agency to improve its service to clients. The Plans Department became the Plans-Merchandising Department, the function of which is to handle all the details connected with planning a client's advertising campaign and integrating it with his selling arrangements as a whole. The Media-Contract Department was renamed the Media Department, and in it were centralized all operations relating to publications, from the selection of specific papers and preparation of estimates (formerly done by the Plans Department) to registration of published advertisements and auditing of publishers' bills (formerly handled by the Accounting Department). The Business Department was renamed the Business-Production Department, and with its former operations were merged the activities of the

Production and Detail bureaus which had previously been in the Copy Department, so that much of the timing and scheduling of work which had formerly been divided between two departments was now concentrated in one. To a large extent the new arrangement involved simply the removal of bureaus physically from one part of the building to another, in order to eliminate the relaying of instructions, but it also facilitated supervision of work, improved the coördination of activities, and made possible some improvement in service.

Between 1938 and 1948 certain other changes took place in the organization, as noted in Chapter VIII above. Apart from the closing out of the Export Division the principal shifts involved the location of various elements of the Radio and Public Relations departments. The organizational framework, after these various changes, was (summer, 1948), as shown in Table 13.

MANAGEMENT OF N. W. AYER & SON, 1869–1895

The foregoing description of the growth of departments, of course, presents merely the bare internal structure of the Ayer organization, showing little more than the order in which various parts crystallized and their position in relation to one another. We might regard it as the machinery of the agency. More important than this structure is the vital force which produced it and directed its development, namely, the Ayer management. The growth of N. W. Ayer & Son depended upon the ability of F. W. Ayer to weld his employees into an effective organization, to keep the various departments properly integrated and adjusted to constantly changing conditions, and, above all, upon his ability to create a *system* of management — to devise substitutes for the proprietor's personal supervision — as the business expanded beyond the capacity of one man to oversee all details.[22]

The term "management" has come to have a number of related but essentially different meanings. It is applied to the group of individuals who control an enterprise, to the work which they do in exercising their authority, and to the system or technique of control by means of which their work is done.[23] We have already had a glimpse of the personnel of the Ayer management — at least so far as the members of the partnership are concerned; and

TABLE 13

Organization of N. W. Ayer & Son, Inc., 1948

Department	Subdivision
Executive	. . . .
Executive Service	Philadelphia Service New York Service Boston Service Chicago Service San Francisco Service Hollywood Service Honolulu Service Detroit Service
Business Development	Philadelphia New York Chicago San Francisco Hollywood
Plans-Merchandising	Planning Marketing Statistical Library Trade Contacts Research
Business-Production	Production Traffic Filing
Educational	Service Department Editorial Department Production Department
Copy Production	Editorial Stenographic Filing Engraving Art Research
Media	Selection Purchase Production Checking, Auditing, and Filing Research

TABLE 13 (*continued*)

Department	Subdivision
Radio	Program Creation and Production Talent Copy Research Radio Clients' Publicity Station Relations Contracts, Billings and Budgets Traffic and Administration Television Motion Pictures
Public Relations	Public Relations Advice Public Relations Production Publicity Production
Outdoor Advertising	Selection and Purchase of Locations Production
Accounting	Customer Billing Auditing Suppliers' Bills Payment of Bills Collection of Accounts
Office Service	Telephones Mail and Supply Bureau Communications Bureau Cafeteria
Building Service	Engineers, Electricians, and Janitors Shipping Bureau
N. W. Ayer & Son's Directory	. . . .
Printing	Administration Composing Room Job Press| Cylinder Press Bindery and Stock Room Electrotype Bureau

Source: N. W. Ayer & Son, Inc.

we have likewise seen something of the general work in which the Ayer management has been engaged. Here we are primarily concerned with management in the third sense, as the art of executive control. To some extent this is reflected in the framework of the organization which the Ayer management has built up and through which it has run the business. Indeed, the reflections of the art of management which are revealed in the overt actions of the executives usually afford the only clues to the art itself, for it is personal, intangible, and elusive to a high degree. We are compelled, in other words, to reconstruct the strategy of management by studying its tactics. Unfortunately, in the Ayer firm as in most others, the records of executive action are almost as sparse as those providing the theory or reason underlying the action, and this account can, in consequence, present only fragments of the story.

Dividing the work of the agency into departments made possible not only the division of labor but also the division of management in an orderly and systematic way. Between 1876 and 1878 Ayer had placed McKinney in charge of the solicitation of orders and Wallace in charge of placing the business with publishers (buying space and forwarding orders); he himself continued to supervise the firm's accounts and finances and its operations as a whole.[24] To a limited extent, this arrangement specialized the work of the partners according to their particular abilities and the principal divisions of the business. It also marked the beginning of a definite system of management within N. W. Ayer & Son.

The beginning, however, was only a slight one. In the Ayer firm, as in business generally, the proprietors were still intimately concerned with the actual processes of production, and there was only a vague line of demarcation between the management and the staff. For many years, indeed, Ayer failed to recognize that the growth of his staff made absolutely essential a separation of managerial from routine duties. Apparently he believed that a simple division of the agency's work among many people was possible and desirable. This meant, of course, asking each one to bear responsibilities and make decisions when only a few were fitted by training or temperament to do so. But Ayer was opposed to concentrating discretionary powers in the hands of a few, since it placed a heavy burden upon the management, kept the subordinates from advancing, and aggravated the difficulty of replacing important staff members. He presented these views in one of the few statements of his managerial policy to be recorded.

Emergence of Management as a Separate Function, 1896–1915

In 1896 a committee of Ayer employees was appointed to improve the handling of business. They suggested having an executive to supervise and coördinate the work of the agency — in effect, to separate the managerial function from routine duties. Ayer objected that the firm's experience indicated the folly of such an arrangement:[25]

Mr. Wallace undertook to be an executive head as to the management of an order. He did this with great skill and ability, but the result was that everybody else became his assistant, and no one developed. This method besides broke Mr. Wallace down, and there was no one to take his place. . . . The way to handle our business is to cultivate responsibility and accountability in individuals. . . . The great essential is that each [employee] should be faithful, dependable, and capable. . . . The executive man proposed would be sick sometimes, absent at others on vacation, etc. . . . Perhaps the firm could have done more business and made more money with an executive man, but the others would all be pawns.

To a strong individualist like Ayer the regimentation and mechanical organization which accompany specialized management were distasteful to say the least. His employees were "members of the Ayer family," and he was interested in their future. Here we catch a glimpse of the positive and beneficent side of the paternalism which had long existed in the Ayer agency. Ayer wanted his employees to develop judgment and initiative, even if it involved a sacrifice of profits. To confine the subordinates to routine work would, he feared, stunt their development and deprive them of an opportunity to grow. In taking this stand he sought to advance the interests of his employees and his firm at the same time. Only a few months before his death he explained that his desire had been to build up his agency so that others would say:[26]

There is a well-built business. There is a business that has outlived its founder. . . . There is a business that, as it has grown in years, has renewed its youth and kept young. . . . There is a business in which the old man was not so bent on promoting himself that he could not take an interest in the development of others. There is a man who had sense enough to realize that he must grow less; that if the business was to continue, others must grow greater; that they must step into the foreground and that he must step into the background.

No one will question the need for providing a succession of trained leaders in a business concern. What Ayer seems to have overlooked in 1897 was that a staff composed entirely of leaders, actual and prospective, would be extremely difficult to manage, to say nothing of the waste of rare talent involved. He knew, of course, that only a few of his staff would rise to the top, but he did not understand at the time that the development of management as a separate function was the price of growth.

Although he only dimly recognized the fact, Ayer's chief problem between 1895 and 1915 was to segregate managerial duties, transfer discretionary power from the rank and file to the management, and find or develop men who could be safely entrusted with the work of management. Unable to draw upon any body of general theory or experience in management and confronted with a problem which came into being almost imperceptibly as his business expanded, Ayer could not have defined the issue sharply; but subsequent events made it obvious, and he eventually worked out its solution.

Within the Philadelphia organization Ayer himself really supplied the specialized management which the agency required. Aided by Wood and Bradford, he gave orders, directed operations, planned and organized the work of the various groups of specialists, helped to coördinate departments, and coached departmental heads, so as to make the Ayer organization unified and effective as a whole.

DEVELOPMENT OF SUPERVISION AND CONTROL

The one part of his business which Ayer could not supervise personally was the staff of men devoted to soliciting business. The nature of their work made direct supervision impossible, but in the 'nineties it became evident that their efforts required organization and direction from above. This was supposed to be McKinney's task; but, while he possessed some of a leader's qualities, McKinney's lack of ability as an organizer and manager deprived the solicitors of the guidance which they needed. For his subordinates he could do little besides offer suggestions and set a brilliant record for them to imitate. It was a mistake to expect him to be a good executive; but one must remember that business firms have only in recent years begun to realize that the best salesman does not necessarily make a good sales manager.[27]

Despite McKinney's shortcomings on the managerial side, there was in his department a fairly steady growth of centralization of control and direction of efforts. The Ayer solicitor of the 'eighties had been almost a free lance. His territory was only vaguely defined, he decided where and when he would solicit orders, he decided whether or not to offer the open-contract plan to customers, he was allowed considerable latitude in the price at which he would bid for orders, he determined largely for himself the credit standing of those with whom he dealt, and, in general, he was subject to the very loosest kind of control from Philadelphia. As a general rule his training consisted of working in the Philadelphia headquarters until he was familiar with lists of papers, circulations, and rates, and knew some of the elementary principles of advertising.[28]

One of the earliest Ayer solicitors recalled some of his experiences in a letter which will illustrate the general lack of administrative control over soliciting in the 'eighties:[29]

When I began my career with Ayer & Son — July 1883 — the entire staff of solicitors consisted of Jas. A. Buchanan and Joseph Bush, soliciting outside of Philadelphia, and George W. South, who solicited in Philadelphia and vicinity.

In addition to the above, Mr. McKinney solicited business, wherever his wonderful abilities seemed to be most required.

Personally I spent the first five months in intensive study of the home machinery, under the special tutorship of F. W. Ayer.

In other words, I was "railroaded" through the various departments of the home plant, to qualify me as soon as possible to operate as a traveling solicitor. My first trip in that capacity was in Dec. 1883, up in New York State.

At that time the staff of solicitors was reorganized as follows: Mr. Buchanan and Mr. Bush divided the territory west of Pittsburg between them.

Mr. South continued to solicit in Philadelphia and vicinity, and all the rest of the U. S. was specified as my territory.

In 1886 I took Mr. Ayer "right off his feet," by requesting a private interview, when I suggested the wisdom of putting another solicitor in my territory.

"Why!" — said Mr. Ayer, — "This is an unheard of thing — a solicitor asking to have his territory reduced." — This was said jocosely.

My reply was — "There are only about 300 working days in the year, and if I keep busy all the time I could not accomplish any more, if I had the entire U. S. to work in. The fact is, Mr. Ayer, the business in my territory is suffering because the ground I cover is so extensive, I can not get around to the prospective advertisers as frequently as they should be visited, and I have lost the opportunity to submit an estimate in some cases for that reason. . . ."

I advised giving [to] a new solicitor the state of New York exclusively, not including N. Y. City, which I wished to reserve for myself.

Mr. Ayer asked me who I would suggest among their employees, and I named Wm. L. Lloyd, whose father was teacher in the North Baptist Church Sunday School, where Wm. L. Lloyd was a member of one of the classes.

"All right," said Mr. Ayer. "I will do that on one condition: that you will take him around with you for one or two trips, introduce him to advertisers and break him in to the science of selling advertising."

I did so, and voluntarily turned over to him the greater portion of the business I had "dug up," in New York State outside of N. Y. City. . . .

As the volume of my sales increased . . . [I advised Mr. Ayer] of the necessity for another solicitor to operate in New England exclusively. It resulted in the appointment of Mr. Conover, who was working in Registry Dept. at the time.

By Mr. Ayer's request I took Mr. Conover around with me on an introductory and "breaking in" trip, just as I did with Mr. Lloyd, up in the State of New York. I got busy with the pruning knife again, and voluntarily transferred to Mr. Conover a readymade list of customers in New England, reserving those accounts, which for personal reasons could not be so transferred. . . .

In the 1890's both the management and the solicitors themselves began to recognize the need for planning and supervision
in the search for business. At first they attempted to satisfy the
need by having an occasional general meeting of all the solicitors
and the principal members of the Philadelphia organization, in
order to discuss problems and ideas for improvement.[30] By 1896
these meetings were being held monthly, and it is clear from the
minutes preserved that the management was feeling its way
toward a closer control of soliciting efforts. It had supplied lists of
firms which the field representatives were to canvass for business,
and it attempted to check their progress by informal reports.[31]
The notes recording one of the meetings summarize a significant
statement by Ayer, showing a definite move toward centralization of control:[32]

He wanted the solicitors to work competition only along certain lines.
Taking it where it will lead to something else, and only so long. Time
had come to turn over a new leaf. To handle the work and the men
differently. The requests for reports as recently sent to solicitors if
made as wanted would greatly help. Help us in forming judgments and
helping the men. He would like to see Mr. McKinney undertake to develop our business better, and to see all solicitors volunteer to be used
to the best end. We should work understandingly in getting an order,
and decide definitely to figure or stay away. This should be settled at
the office, not by the solicitors. Philadelphia and the office should be
more and more the centre.

Even more revealing is a paper, "Plan Suggested for Greater
Development of Our Business-Getting Department," dated May,
1897, which contains the following points:[33]

Have solicitors make out list of firms they are looking after, including
customers; state prospect of business from each when last seen, when
they should next be seen, and about time when important contracts are
usually made by each. . . .
. . . map out work some weeks ahead for each solicitor, ...
Have each solicitor before each trip prepare a definite plan in harmony with the requirements of the business, copy of plan to be in possession of both solicitor and firm, and to be adhered to except as adjustments are necessary, the firm to judge of necessity for change. As a

rule, each trip to be of short duration, and never to be extended beyond what was originally contemplated except by advice with the house.

Shortly prior to the expected presence of a solicitor in any particular section, we to correspond with other firms in the vicinity of the section to be traveled, and endeavor to secure invitations to call. . . .

As new cases require attention, distribute them among the solicitors according to the probable proximity of their other work, the several ability of the different solicitors to care for business of that particular character, and their ability to give them proper attention without neglecting other important matters. . . .

Have each solicitor report fully about each call on each firm — whom seen, what appears to be his authority, substance of interview, impression left on solicitor's mind, method of work that seems best for the future, with frank statement in case he does not think it of advantage for him to further pursue the matter personally. . . .

As far as consistent with good work, keep two or more familiar with situation of each case so that when occasion arises either can attend intelligently to what is necessary.

In 1898 the firm began to require daily reports by mail or telegraph from its field representatives, thus providing a means of closer supervision.[34] By 1905 the supervision of credit terms was centered in Philadelphia, but the solicitors and the management were still debating what to do about the embarrassing delay between the obtaining of an advertiser's business by the solicitor in the field and the approval of his credit standing and acceptance as a client by headquarters.[35]

By concentrating in special departments in Philadelphia the preparation of advertising plans and copy, and by relieving the solicitors of the details of executing customers' orders, the Ayer management greatly simplified the solicitors' work and facilitated the direction of their efforts. The establishment of branch offices was another step towards increasing managerial control over the business-getting activities. To some extent the branches decentralized control, for each had a manager who was responsible for its operations. At the same time, however, they brought supervision and control closer to the actual work of soliciting.

Such specialization is not without its drawbacks. There was danger that both the solicitor and the client would find difficulty in dealing with the organization at headquarters. How could their wishes receive prompt and effective attention when the agency's work was split up and responsibility for action divided among many people? To meet this problem the firm began, in 1905, to place a member of the Business Department in charge of each account as soon as the client had signed the Ayer letter of agreement. He thus became the special representative of the client within the Philadelphia organization and worked in close conjunction with the field representative concerned.[36] This arrangement collected the scattered responsibilities and enabled the agency to give the client both personal attention and the service of highly specialized workers.

Today the Business-Production Department discharges the same essential functions, although the methods and routines in use have, of course, been somewhat modified to meet changing circumstance. It is the responsibility of this department, through individual persons (before World War II they were men; now they are usually women) assigned to specific accounts, to keep fully informed about what is happening, to know what is supposed to be done, and to see that it is done — by the right person, in the right way, and at the right time. In short, this department clears information, issues orders, and checks the time element.

The amount and intensity of the managerial control over Ayer representatives has varied considerably, but it is noteworthy that special efforts were made in this direction in 1896–97, 1905, 1907–08, 1921–23, and 1931–35, when general business conditions made careful strategy and effective selling effort of unusual importance. Within recent years, for example, the Ayer management has increased the amount of direction and assistance from headquarters: it has made detailed analyses of industries and companies in order to determine the most desirable prospective clients and uncover new opportunities for advertising. The representative has been told not only whom to solicit but when and how to begin; he has been provided with carefully prepared material and suggestions for its use; and various measures are taken by the executives to obtain a suitable hearing for him. Of equal importance, perhaps, is the fact that the representative is not allowed to approach a prospective client, no matter how desirable his business may appear to be, until the management has had a chance to investigate and decide whether, from the long-run point of view, the firm wants him as a client. This supervision and assistance from headquarters comes now in a regular and systematic way, in contrast with the days when the representative was largely independent and got help from the management only when he asked for it.[37]

There must, of course, be a system of control by means of which the chief executives can know what is going on in the various divisions of the business and in the field, a foundation for decisions and commands. In the early years of N. W. Ayer & Son, as in other concerns of the period, the owner of the business could see for himself what was going on or could confer directly with his subordinates for the purpose of obtaining information or issuing directions. As the firm expanded, the Ayer partners had to resort more and more to other means, not only because of the increased demands upon their time but also because Ayer solicitors were traveling far afield and were available for personal conference only at long intervals.

Written communications became increasingly important. Secretaries were added to aid Ayer and McKinney in handling details; typewriters were introduced (to a limited extent they were used in N. W. Ayer & Son even before 1886); and in September, 1886, the firm hired its first stenographer — an important means of saving an executive's time.[38] By 1892 the Ayer organization was using both the typewriter and the mimeographing machine for the recording of information and as a means of internal communication.[39] The local telephone was not without its importance; and by 1898 the management regularly used telegraphic messages to maintain contact with field representatives. When the New York branch was opened in 1903, it was connected with the headquarters in Philadelphia by means of a private long-distance telephone wire.[40] By 1900 the field representatives were beginning to make written reports to the firm, but the partners still depended to a large extent upon frequent personal interviews.[41] The accounting records were improved in 1900 to provide a more complete picture of the status of the business from a financial point of view, for it was no longer possible for Ayer to see what was happening to his firm merely by examining the income and expense accounts; these were divided among four types of ledgers, and the original entries explaining the transactions were scattered in many special journals.[42] Monthly summaries had to be provided for him.

By 1920 N. W. Ayer & Son was using its present procedure of having written reports of all interviews with clients and prospective clients. These reports are drafted by the Ayer representative and forwarded to Philadelphia at the earliest moment possible after the interview. They are recorded in the Business-Production Department and then circulated among the executives concerned, together with any related correspondence. By this means the management has current information on both the activities of its own field representatives and the relations between the agency and its clients. To some extent the reports may be a source of error, for they embody the views of the representative who, to some extent, is bound to use them as a means of impressing the management with his own merit, instead of presenting an adequate and unbiased record of conversations. However, in a business in which the usual sales statistics and accounting controls are not appropriate, such a procedure, supplemented by information from other sources, is probably the best that can be devised.

Improved methods of accounting, calculating machines, motor cars, airplanes, the dictaphone, and the teletypewriter — these and a host of other mechanical devices have played their part in saving time, bridging space, supplying information, and transmitting directions. But these mechanical aids, together with specially trained operatives, are merely the means by which the central management gathers information and controls the activities of the staff as a whole. They are as charts and instruments to the captain of a ship, and they are of no value unless properly used. The real essence of management lies in the constant exercise of judgment and foresight, the formulation of plans and policies in highly dynamic situations, and the running appraisal of actual accomplishment in comparison with the goals set up. Before forming an opinion of the Ayer management as a whole, we must consider further events in the history of the firm.

Delegation of Authority

With the growth of the managerial factor in the solicitation for new business there came repeated efforts to improve the control and coördination of the rest of the Ayer organization. The establishment of the Business Department in 1900 was a major step in this direction, but the function of the new department was essentially that of handling routine work, executing the details of an order once its general nature had been decided upon. There remained a great deal of direction and coördination to be done which was not connected with actual orders for advertising: major questions of policy affecting more than one department, plans for the growth of the business as a whole, general decisions as to the work to be done by various parts of the agency. Although Ayer himself had supplied this direction during the early years of the firm, the task was fast becoming too large for one man. Further, Ayer had outside interests to attend to; he was beginning to transfer the work of central management to younger men; and the need was growing for the establishment of administrative control which would depend not solely upon a single executive.

Ayer's first solution for this problem was the creation, in 1905, of three committees of five men each, with duties and responsibilities as shown in the plan reproduced below.[43]

To some extent the personnel of these three committees overlapped. One member of the first was also on the second and another was on the third. Three members of the second committee were also on the third, and another also served on the first. This arrangement obviously promoted close understanding and coöperation between the committees, giving effective unity to their separate activities.

Business Getting Committee
Business-building plans, including work within the house; circularizing, letter-writing, &c. as well as soliciting.
Selection of lines of business which promise development through advertising.
Plan for working such lines in connection with the maintenance of our present business and its general development.
Territorial allotment to solicitors; particular lines of work for solicitors; general direction of solicitors.
Correspondence with solicitors, including necessary attention to their letters and proper advice on office happenings and matters arising through correspondence in which they are interested.

Committee
on plans
for
execution
of
business

> Decision as to the desirability of an order, in the consideration of which, credit, profit, prospects of future business must all have due consideration, as should also the relative cost of handling, including copy, placing, and care. Decision re. distribution of an appropriation; amount properly available for preparation of copy; style of copy and number of advertisements, frequency of insertions, &c. Charges to advertisers for all services of the house.
>
> Economy in operation — how to avoid needless or excessive expense in traveling; in the preparation of copy; and in the printing department.
>
> This committee should seek a profit in every transaction going through the house. Failing to find a satisfactory profit in any class of business, it should devise some means for securing it, and make the matter the subject of conference with the Business Getting Committee.

Executive

> The Business Getting Com. should be encouraged to lean on this committee for plans, both in general and in detail, for the consideration of patrons or prospective patrons.
>
> This committee should have both eyes open to discern advantages to be gained by patrons of the house through trade or local conditions, special issues, or advance orders where rates are going to change, &c.
>
> Execution of business, including methods of work and means employed.
>
> Periodical reports on condition of work in various departments.
>
> Distribution of assistants to care for work in various departments, and to meet any emergencies which may arise in any department.
>
> Assignment of assistants to the duties for which they are best fitted and readjustment of duties as experience may suggest, under direction of Mr. Wood.
>
> Careful oversight of expenditures in copy and printing departments and in providing for any unusual conditions embodied in an order or which may arise.
>
> Systematic effort to keep down expenses at all points and particularly to reduce expenses when business declines.

Two years later (1907), when Ayer was announcing some changes in this arrangement, he explained that it had grown out of "recognition of direction needs" and was designed to centralize responsibility. It had previously been difficult, he admitted, for subordinates "to find an ear" because the partners had been too busy with details of routine, and he expressed the hope that a more careful allocation of authority and responsibilities would improve matters for the entire organization.[44]

Ayer was manifestly trying here to devise a new control or managerial apex to his business, partly because it had outgrown the one-man personal supervision which he had formerly given, partly because it was dangerous to have the continuity of the firm's existence so largely dependent upon a single person, and partly because his age and his many outside activities made it imperative to transfer work and responsibility to others. He was working out the solution by a process of trial and error, and the first measures he took amounted to little more than a simple division of his work — both discretionary and routine — among his assistants. Gradually it became evident that this principle of division was not altogether satisfactory. It was too much like having an army commanded by a committee of officers, each of whom held equal power and responsibility. What was wanted was a division of the work which would give the authority and responsibility for deciding major issues and formulating general policies to one man and leave the less important duties to his assistants.

Thus, by 1911, Ayer had abandoned his committee plan and had placed a general manager in charge, as we have already seen.[45] Following close upon this appointment, there was a systematic reorganization of the entire agency in 1912. In explaining the need for revision, Ayer emphasized his own shortcomings in one of the most revealing observations he ever made:[46]

Our business has suffered from its beginning from a fact for which none of you are accountable. The lack lay in me and in my failure to recognize and remedy it early in the business's history. I never had a day's business training in my life. My father never did. I went out of the school room into this business. . . . I lacked efficiency in the things which I undertook to do. I had to feel out and find a way for everything that I did. It was a great relief to me when I got a young man who could keep the books which I had been keeping evenings. I never experienced a greater sense of relief than I did when the exactness of those

entries no longer depended on me, and so one after another of those
departments of the work which involved detail have been let go of, but
not in a well defined way, and the persons who took hold of them at
times were no better fitted for them than I was or had not had the training any more than I had. And so our business came to be a collection
of methods devised by ourselves the day it came up to be done. Now
that isn't the best way to get the best methods or to get the most speed,
or the most economical administration. Our business has, I think, always suffered, from that cause, and as a result of this laxity way back
at the beginning. . . .

This statement requires some amplification. The difficulty
which the firm encountered could not be attributed entirely to
Ayer's early lack of business experience: he had amply demonstrated his ability to cope with the managerial problems of the
period before 1900. But the growth of the agency had necessitated
a complicated organization, and this in turn called for a new type
of management. Direct personal control had to give way to indirect control through a hierarchy of subordinates organized into
a system of management. The increase in the size of the Ayer
business had not merely increased the scope of managerial duties
but had also changed their essential nature.

The qualities especially needed in the old type of business man
were courage, initiative, and a mastery of detail. The new type
of manager had to have, in addition to these, ability to coöperate
with other men, to coördinate diverse activities, to delegate responsibilities, and, above all, to formulate broad policies: mere
drive was not enough. The enterprise which became large through
successful operation and natural growth required the new type of
management just as much as the one which became large by joining with other firms. But it is usually difficult to recognize the
need for a change, and it is still harder to find men qualified to
take command.[47]

The particular difficulty in N. W. Ayer & Son could be traced
largely to the previous reorganization of 1899–1900 and to the
type of organization which had evolved earlier. The work of the
agency was divided among departments specialized in business-
getting, copy preparation, and so on. This is what is usually referred to as a functional organization. It narrows the scope of the

work of each department and individual, and yields all the high
skill and efficiency which come from specialization. As we have
seen, however, such organization requires careful coördination.
The work and the lines of authority, moreover, run mainly from
one department directly to the others instead of through the central management. As a result, responsibility is scattered, authority is somewhat vaguely allocated, and discipline tends to be
weak. One of the primary aims of the reorganization of 1912 was
to correct this weakness by defining more sharply the duties,
responsibilities, and powers of the staff. As the general manager
expressed it:[48]

The necessity has been recognized for the first time in the history of the
business of charting the business; making a map of it; getting a concrete expression of the business as it is. Arbitrarily we will assign men
and money and divisions of the business into their proper sections so
that we will have proper accounting, proper cost figures, a proper and
definite idea as to what a man or a department or a group of men or a
division of our business is costing us, what it is yielding us, and where
it is coming from. The business today is not only pitifully small compared with what it should be, but it is tremendously costful and it is
not necessary. We use too many men and too many dollars and too
many hours and make too many motions for what we get out of it, and
handling the business that we do handle this firm does not realize anything like the profit that they should realize. . . .

The assistant general manager summarized the new demarcation of authority as follows:[49]

Non-supervisory workers are responsible to and take their directions
from their bureau chiefs, who in turn are supervised by and take their
instructions from their department heads, who again in turn are responsible to the General Manager who is finally held responsible to the firm.

But someone might raise this question just now. Members of the firm
are supreme in the organization; what relation does a member of the
firm, who is also a department head, sustain in the plan of the organization? Simply that of a department head. No member of the firm has
any greater authority, as a department head, than has any other department head who is not a member of the firm. . . .

It is a business axiom that no executive can be charged with the responsibility for the performance of any duty unless that executive has been given authority commensurate with the responsibility. The firm could not logically or fairly hold its General Manager responsible for results if the authority necessary to secure those results were withheld. Likewise the General Manager must hold department heads, and department heads must hold bureau chiefs, and bureau chiefs must hold employees responsible for the best performance of their respective duties. . . .

The reorganization gave N. W. Ayer & Son what is usually referred to as a line-and-staff organization, combining the functional division with an arrangement by which definite lines of authority extended from the general manager downward through departmental heads and bureau chiefs. While it never yielded the detailed information as to costs and results which the general manager hoped to obtain, it helped to weld the various bureaus and departments into an effective, close-knit organization, and facilitated direction and control from above. Henceforth the agency received the benefit of management which ultimately centered in one man without overworking him. At the same time the subdivision of duties between the partners, the general manager, and his assistant removed the danger of a catastrophe in case anything suddenly happened to F. W. Ayer or any other individual in the managerial group.

It may be well at this point to consider briefly the alternative form of organization. A number of agencies employ what is sometimes called the group system. The work of servicing a given account is turned over to a group of people which operates much like a small agency within the larger organization. It is largely self-contained, prepares plans, copy, layouts, and sometimes even finished art work, and maintains direct contact with the client. Usually it relies on specialized departments for checking, accounting, and other subordinate details. This arrangement provides speedy, unified, and highly personal service, but it obliges the members of the group to perform a number of different functions, each of which might be performed better or more quickly by a specialist. For this reason the group system probably lacks some of the highly developed skill and resources of the functional organization.[50]

In practice, however, few agencies adhere strictly to any one form of organization for long, but vary according to existing needs. From time to time in the Ayer agency something like the group system has appeared, but it has been only a temporary arrangement.[51] The basic Ayer policy has been to draw on specialists in all fields as required and to have them work on several accounts at a time so as to keep their thinking fresh and broaden their experience at the same time.

The degree to which members of the Ayer staff are specialized in a single function must not be overemphasized. Their experience and activities are not sharply delimited. The representative must be able to talk to clients intelligently about plans, copy, and space-buying; the copyman must know a good deal about selling and merchandising; and so on through the staff. Ultimately, however, the responsibility for Ayer copy rests on the Copy Department, for plans upon the Plans-Merchandising Department, and for each other major function upon a similar group of specialists.

The Ayer System of Supervision

Many years ago the Ayer management developed a method of supervising the work of employees which has been applied in nearly all phases of the business and particularly on the creative side. In one sense it is based on the old principle that two heads are better than one. In another sense it is the idea of stretching accumulated experience as far as possible. No matter how talented or reliable an employee may be, his work is checked and supervised by a more experienced man. The arrangement has an important additional advantage in that the absence of one man cannot disrupt work on any account, because there is always at least one other man who is familiar with it.

A brief outline of the system as applied to the Ayer Copy Department will illustrate the arrangement which has been applied (with some modification because of differences in functions) to other divisions of the business. Both the writing and art staffs are under the direction of the head of the Copy Department. On the writing side there were (February, 1948) five associate copy directors and a staff of men and women copywriters. On the art side there were an art director, seven associate art directors, three art buyers, and a staff of layout men and designers.

Each of the associate copy directors is responsible for the writing of a group of accounts involving the preparation of approximately one-fifth of all the advertisements written by the agency. Responsible to him for the actual writing of the advertisements are various copywriters; but these copywriters do not work exclusively under him. In practice, many writers on the staff work with all five of the associate copy directors on a fairly wide variety of accounts.

This method of cross-contact, which is also followed in the Art Bureau, has a definite purpose. It is designed to avoid the condition that exists in certain large agencies employing the group system of organization to which reference has already been made. Under the group system the writers and artists who compose a unit usually have no other supervision than that provided by the group head, with the result that their style of writing and designing is soon influenced strongly by the ideas and preferences of the group head. The latter usually is a representative or salesman for the agency, rather than a person strong on the creative side. His natural training and inclination are to appeal to the client rather than to the client's customers — frequently with sad consequences. Of course, the group system often produces excellent advertising, but it tends to stifle the individuality of the writer or artist.

Under the Ayer system no writer or artist does enough work under any one supervisor to be unduly influenced by the latter's methods or tastes. He is, however, afforded ample opportunity to learn whatever good the supervisor has to impart.

The five associate copy directors, together with the manager of the department, constitute a critical and advisory group known as the copy board. In the Art Bureau there is a similar board composed of the art director and the associate art directors. Both groups meet regularly (but separately) for review of all creative work. Specific campaigns and advertisements are examined, and suggestions for improvement are freely offered and discussed. The object of this process is to stimulate interest and alertness in the staff, to recognize excellence, to catch inferior work, to study trends in ideas or methods, and to consider new creative techniques. To this end, the copy board frequently has as its guests and advisers at its meetings the heads of other Ayer departments, research men from outside organizations, and authorities in various economic and business fields. By such devices the Ayer management has achieved specialization plus coöperation plus supervision. Most important of all perhaps is the independent review of all phases of plans and service made regularly for each account by the Creative-Production Board (see Chapter VIII above). This Board views the account in broad perspective in terms of clients' objectives, Ayer policies and standards of performance, and general performance. It makes sure that the account does not get into a rut and that it gets the benefit of the best talent and experience that the agency can supply.

CHANGES AT THE TOP

The general system of management which was established in 1912 has been maintained in the Ayer agency down to the present without much change in form. In 1916, as explained above (pages 103–107), Fry took over the duties of general manager. Unlike the previous manager, however, he was a partner in the firm, and possibly for that reason the title of manager fell into disuse. Another explanation for its disappearance, perhaps, is that the title soon ceased to fit his position. Ayer's early partners, Wood, Bradford, and even McKinney, had served more as departmental heads than as assistants in directing the business as a whole. Ayer, and subsequently his general manager, had exercised the main powers of supervision and control almost single-handed. On the other hand, Fry encouraged the four men who were admitted to partnership between 1918 and 1923 to take part in the general administrative work as well as in the active operation of the agency. Gradually he was able to delegate to them much of the management and thus could devote more of his own attention to broader administrative questions.

Whereas Ayer had discussed problems with his associates and then formed his own decision, Fry, by 1920, was holding meetings at which all the partners were present and took active part in the decisions reached.[52] The following excerpt from the minutes of a firm meeting indicates something of the extent to which the partners assisted Fry. It shows also the way in which control over branch offices was maintained before the incorporation of the business:[53]

It was pointed out . . . that a great deal more could be accomplished at the Branch Managers' meetings if there were a prearranged program for each meeting. This idea meeting with favor, Messrs. Armistead and Thornley were appointed as a committee to arrange such programs.

At a previous meeting Messrs. Mathes and Kessler were appointed as a committee to study the Chicago Office situation and report their findings and recommendations in respect to a manager's interest therein.

Mr. Kessler reported in detail the findings as applied thereto and the committee's recommendations. It was agreed to proceed on that basis; namely,

1. A partnership — N. W. Ayer & Son of Chicago.
2. Capital — $100,000.00.
3. Manager's interest — 25%.
4. N. W. Ayer & Son interest 75%, in the name of one member, covered by declaration of trust.
5. Allowance of 4% of gross billings — exclusive of publicity billings — of all business coming through N. W. Ayer & Son of Chicago.
6. N. W. Ayer & Son of Chicago to be charged with the salaries of all persons assigned to that office, all traveling expense and entertaining expenses of such persons, rent of offices, supplies used, maintenance costs, and the expenses of such persons called from Philadelphia or other offices for service.

Mr. Fry is to have a preparatory talk with the manager. Messrs. Fry and Kessler are then to see our attorney and have agreement shaped up covering the above, and also providing for:

1. The control of the acceptance of business as to
   (a) Character.
   (b) Credit and finance.
2. Production to be controlled by and centralized in Philadelphia.
3. Territory of N. W. Ayer & Son of Chicago as to:
   (a) Personnel.
   (b) Compensation.

Fry's associates assumed an increasing share of the management of N. W. Ayer & Son in the years after 1923. They did this not only because Fry encouraged them to do so, but especially because the volume of business grew rapidly and increased the burdens of management. This development, indeed, was a weighty factor in the decision to incorporate the enterprise. Those who assisted in the supervision and control inevitably had to assume some responsibility for profitable operations. Naturally they felt entitled to a share of the profits which they helped to win. It was desirable, moreover, to make some profit-sharing arrangement as an incentive to bring out their best efforts. The firm instituted a system of bonuses with this purpose in view, but the partners soon came to feel that men in responsible positions should have a financial stake in the business; while those executives who were not partners felt, on the other hand, that they ought to have a stronger voice in the formulation of policies and the general control of the business. To enlarge the number of partners would not have been feasible because of the enormous liability which each would have had to bear as a result of the legal responsibilities of members of a partnership. The partners, therefore, decided to incorporate and allow executives of the company to become stockholders.[54]

Fry became president of the corporation, while the four men who had been his partners became vice-presidents. Almost immediately, however, the board of directors elected five additional vice-presidents to meet the growing need "of adequate official contacts" and "to bestow certain merited recognitions." [55] Others were added to the list until by the end of 1932 N. W. Ayer & Son had 14 vice-presidents on its staff, and by 1938 the total was 20.[56]

In many respects the most significant change in top management took place after 1936 — a change not in form but in spirit. In spite of all previous efforts to delegate responsibility and authority, control under the Ayer and Fry régimes had remained closely centralized at the top. Even after incorporation all major decisions and many minor ones continued to be made by the officers who owned the most stock. Essentially the firm operated much like the old partnership, with the owners holding the reins. Department heads had little to say about matters of any consequence, and, indeed, the top executives habitually cut around them without much thought about the implications. It was not an efficient way of doing business. More important, it was not a good way to develop a strong succession of executives capable of rising to the top.

As already indicated, Batten had an entirely different conception of management. He expected department heads to run their departments, and he expected them to develop strength in depth by bringing along promising people. He understood better than his predecessors that only in a limited sense can policies be formulated at the top. He encouraged employees all along the line to make their best contribution, including participation in shaping the policies they would have to execute. Having been through the mill, he understood fully how much greater that contribution could be if the people in the organization were regarded as coworkers who could rise high rather than as employees who would rarely advance much in status. The difference is one of emphasis, but it is important and it has been the principal factor in the great rise in efficiency and enthusiasm during the past ten years. It is a difference, too, which takes into account the change in attitude of people generally in the past two generations. Ayer's concept of management began to be obsolete about 1912. Fry sensed the need for a change but could not make his idealism practical. Batten has succeeded in working out a philosophy of management which is not only in keeping with democratic ideas, but is also highly efficient in getting results.

Any description of the organization and management of a firm, no matter how complete, is bound to be somewhat inadequate and misleading. An organization can never be accurately charted because it is always flexible, always in a state of adjustment to the needs of the moment. It is not a mechanical structure. It is a complex aggregation of men and women — human personalities conducting an intricate business which is perennially changing. The personal factor is always there, it is always complicated and frequently imponderable, and it is only partially amenable to reason. And so with management: it is not a system but a combination of personal leadership, principles, and methods which never remains static.

Because both the management and the organization are complicated and dynamic, any attempt to appraise them is likely to be out of date as soon as it is made. We can form only a rough judgment by examining the record over a long period of time. The quality of Ayer management as a whole is not to be judged by the general financial success of the firm. The real test is its conduct of affairs in times of trouble and its ability to adapt the business to changing circumstances. After we have examined the relations between the Ayer executives and the rank and file of employees and after we have considered the firm's financial history, we may be able to discern some shortcomings in past managerial policy. But the gradual adjustment of Ayer policies and organization to harmonize with the full implications of the Ayer open contract, the addition of marketing counsel and copy preparation to the function of space-buying, the extension of operations to include magazine, outdoor, radio, and television advertising, the survival of the loss of Ayer and McKinney, the periodic reorganization of the entire staff even to changes in executives, and the successful endurance of severe economic disturbances like those of the 1890's and the early 1930's — such achievements form concrete evidence that the management of N. W. Ayer & Son has, on the whole, been of a high order.

CHAPTER XVIII

WITHIN THE RANKS OF N. W. AYER & SON,
1870–1939

Now that the organization and management of N. W. Ayer & Son have been sketched, we may turn to a consideration of the workers themselves. It has been necessary for the firm to assemble, train, and motivate a large body of people. Since the early years of the Ayer agency there have been significant changes in the composition of the staff, its working conditions and hours, its various rewards, and its general relations with the management. These changes are naturally of great interest; and, while information about them is unavoidably incomplete, enough is available to provide a general idea of what it has meant to work for N. W. Ayer & Son at different periods in the firm's history.

Personnel

Ayer's first employees were all comparatively young, mostly came to the firm with little special training or experience, and rarely, if ever, had more than a grade-school education. Wallace was barely twenty when he was hired as bookkeeper, had only a few years' experience in business, and knew only a smattering of bookkeeping. McKinney came at twenty-five, with nine years of business experience but only two terms of formal schooling. Judging by their weekly wages, we must conclude that most of the others hired in the 'seventies began as clerks or office boys and learned the business from the bottom rung of the ladder. There was, indeed, no other way to learn it at that time. Ayer looked especially for diligence, alertness, and loyalty, as the following letter indicates:[1]

July 28 1873
Philadelphia.

Dear Uncle Geo.

I expect to make some changes in our office help this Fall and wish to find a fairly educated boy of about 16 to 18 smart as a steel trap and thoroughly reliable. He must come determined to learn our business and grow up with us and if he comes in that way we can give him in my opinion as fine a chance as could be desired. He must be willing to work early and late and for one interest. Don't want any boy who has to have everything told him but one who *sees* what needs to be done and does it. How would Aunt Laura's Charlie suit me? Would she wish him to leave home, would he do as I told him and could I depend upon his staying right along at a fair price?

A man's chances of getting hired by Ayer were considerably improved if he was affiliated with a church, and many of the early employees were members of Ayer's own Sunday School.[2] This qualification dwindled in importance as training and experience became more necessary for the agency's work; but as late as 1933 the firm continued to show some preference for applicants who participated in church work, the Y.M.C.A., or similar activities. The present management tries to be strictly neutral on the question of religious affiliations.[3]

Although N. W. Ayer & Son has continued down to the present day to engage young people and train them for work on its staff, it has long ceased to regard this procedure as an adequate source of personnel. As early as the middle and late 'seventies, Ayer was obliged to add to his staff men who had acquired specific training and experience before coming to the agency. Thus, in 1875 he began to employ qualified printers; in 1877 he acquired an experienced bookkeeper; in 1883 he hired a man who had had twenty years of general business experience, mainly as a traveling salesman, for the express purpose of having him solicit business; in 1884 he hired Bradford because he had had business experience, was known to be reliable, and was especially quick and accurate with figures; in 1886 he hired the firm's first stenographer; in 1892 he employed an experienced man to write advertisements; and in 1898 he added his first commercial artist.[4] In 1899 the Ayer management inaugurated a policy of hiring a few college graduates from time to time in order to improve its personnel. The first person so chosen was a Dartmouth man of the class of 1899.[5] By 1900 the firm was also seeking men who possessed some established contacts among business men and experience in advertising or in selling merchandise. Such men would, of course, be more effective in selling Ayer service to advertisers than those who had grown up in the Ayer organization or had come to it with only general business experience.[6]

In the years immediately after World War I the Ayer firm took on its staff as field representatives a number of men who had had experience as sales managers in various lines of merchandise. This particular background was desired for a number of reasons. Competition had become so keen and business executives so pressed for time that only men with established contacts and proven selling ability were likely to get a favorable hearing. In addition, men who had served as sales managers would be familiar with the needs of advertisers.[7] One Ayer partner explained, "We do not care whether they know anything about advertising or not. We teach them the advertising business which, added to the proper foundation gained in their respective lines, should enable them to discuss many sales problems intelligently."[8]

In recent years the Ayer agency has recruited its personnel from several general sources. Vacancies in the minor clerical positions have been filled by boys and girls still in their teens who have completed or are completing their high school work. Stenographic and secretarial positions are filled by those who have had some special training in secretarial or commercial schools. For specific talent in advertising technique the firm draws largely upon the existing supply of experienced workers to be found in the advertising, publishing, and related industries. In addition to the large number of college graduates who come to the firm by way of the business world, the Ayer management usually employs several each year fresh from the graduating classes.

In 1938 the Ayer management organized, among the employees who were recently out of college, a group which would aid in the selection of other graduates for employment in the agency. This group arranged to keep systematically in touch with many leading educational institutions, by personal contacts, letters, and

actual visits, so as to locate the young men and women who dem-
onstrate the kind of ability, character, and ambition that the management wants to have in the firm. By this means the management hopes to discover the most promising persons, well before
their graduation, to interest them in agency work, and to build up
personal acquaintance before they are actually hired. Necessarily
abandoned during World War II, this plan was resumed during
1948.

Since 1936 the Ayer management has assumed increasing responsibility for the technical training and advancement of its employees. It has adopted this course with an eye to the ultimate
worth of the individual, as well as to the enduring strength of the
firm — a view which stems directly from management's feeling
that an agency's only real assets are its people and that those
assets can be enhanced by constant planning and effort. Regarding its work as professional in character and recognizing that
there is no acknowledged course for a career in advertising, the
Ayer management feels that it must assume responsibility for
giving professional training. Regardless of a person's previous
experience, the firm regards him as a prospect until his technical
competence is proved. And it holds that he cannot reach full usefulness until he has fully absorbed the special views on advertising and agency operations which characterize the House of
Ayer. Hence it chooses its staff carefully with a view to long-run
potentialities, it provides what might be described as on-the-job
training, and it follows an employee's progress to see that he
makes progress.

Although modern advertising employs a great many women,
there were none on the Ayer staff during the first five years of the
firm's existence. The first to appear was a Jennie Waterman, who
was employed from April through July, 1874;[9] but the steady
employment of women in N. W. Ayer & Son apparently dates
from the summer of 1876 when two were hired.[10] In 1880 there
were four women on a staff numbering 43 members. By 1890
there were 40 out of a total of 109, or 36.7 per cent, and this
proportion had increased to 40 per cent by January, 1899. Then,
apparently as a result of the reorganization of the staff, a number of girls and women were replaced by men and the proportion

of women to the total staff dropped suddenly to 34 per cent. Within three years, however, the women had risen again to 38 per cent; by 1915 the proportion was 41 per cent, and in 1932 it was over 46 per cent. In 1947 the percentage of women stood at 53 per cent even after most of the men had returned from the service.[11] A comparison of these figures with those for the employment of women in the United States generally shows that N. W. Ayer & Son employed relatively fewer women than the rest of American business until after 1880, and that since 1890 it has employed a much higher proportion than the rest of the country. Recent evidence indicates that the Ayer firm employs a slightly higher proportion of women than advertising agencies as a whole, but this may also be true of other large agencies.[12]

Until the 1930's the positions held by women in N. W. Ayer & Son had been almost exclusively clerical or stenographic. It is worthy of note, however, that in every division of the agency, with the exception of the Printing Department, women have been advanced to positions involving considerable responsibility and judgment. For many years one woman has been cashier of the firm, and early in the Batten régime another was made secretary of the corporation. Particularly in the fields of radio, copywriting, public relations, and art the Ayer firm has long offered rich opportunity for feminine talent, and women, at the present writing (fall, 1948), hold some of the high executive positions in those areas.[13]

The composition of the Ayer staff could be analyzed from other points of view with very interesting results. For example, it is evident from a cursory inspection of the names on the pay rolls that the Ayer firm, in the late 'seventies, began to draw employees from the German population of the Philadelphia area. No member of the staff was of obvious German origin before 1878. In 1880, out of 43 employees, there were 6 bearing German surnames. By 1900 the proportion, again judging by names, was between 20 and 25 per cent. Other racial stocks have come in, until the Ayer staff today includes members of nearly all the European groups. Similarly the working force, which was once composed exclusively of easterners, now has members from all sections of the United States.[14]

Perhaps the most striking aspect of the Ayer staff in recent years is the remarkable variety of talent represented on it. The very nature of the agency's work makes necessary an extraordinary aggregation of occupations: there are corps of stenographers, clerks of all kinds, bookkeepers, secretaries, space-buyers, copywriters, layout men, illustrators, painters, publicity writers, photographers, style experts, market analysts, sales managers, statisticians, dietitians, chemical and automotive engineers, proofreaders, experts on typography and engravings, linotype and monotype operators and printers of all kinds, radio-script writers, program directors and producers, musicians, telephone operators, messengers, elevator operators, janitors, electricians, carpenters, steam engineers, librarians, field representatives, and general executives.

In addition to their great variety of specialized jobs in the agency, many of the Ayer workers have plied all sorts of trades and professions before entering the agency's employ. To some extent this would be true of any large body of adults today, but in the Ayer organization — particularly in the Copy Department — it is not fortuitous; it is the result of deliberate policy. The Ayer management believes that too much modern advertising has been conceived and written by persons whose basic conceptions of life have been conditioned almost entirely by metropolitan luxury and sophistication. Effective advertising is based upon a thorough knowledge of human nature, knowledge which comes largely from personal experience. To acquire a rich and varied fund of that knowledge the Ayer management has for many years pursued the policy of employing persons from all parts of the country and from all walks of life. By this means it has made its service national in spirit as well as in geographical scope.

The multifarious experiences which the staff as a body has had include teaching, manufacturing, newspaper work, farming, stock raising, mining, lumbering, shipping, aviation, banking, building construction, social work, theatrical work, play writing, poetry and novel writing, painting, drawing, selling work of all kinds, and so on through the gamut. This collective talent not only makes the group an exceedingly interesting one but also enables the Ayer agency to put a remarkable wealth of experience at the disposal of its clients.[15]

The growth in the size of the Ayer organization is amply indicated by the figures in Table 14. Several details are worthy of special note. The total working force grew at a fairly even rate until 1912. During the following four years the numbers steadily

TABLE 14

The Ayer Working Force, 1871–1932 and 1940

Year	January	July	Year	January	July	Year	January	July
1871	3	3	1892	131	131	1913	313	299
1872	3	4	1893	138	137	1914	284	280
1873	4	5	1894	131	136	1915	262	264
1874	7	7	1895	131	139	1916	266	299
1875	6	8	1896	151	144	1917	311	320
1876	11	13	1897	147	142	1918	330	352
1877	14	16	1898	151	147	1919	338	461
1878	a	a	1899	159	163	1920	496	512
1879	a	a	1900	163	169	1921	513	482
1880	43	a	1901	178	185	1922	477	495
1881	64	64	1902	193	188	1923	497	495
1882	74	80	1903	200	224	1924	511	514
1883	80	93	1904	226b	230b	1925	517	531
1884	85	89	1905	222	224	1926	579	618
1885	85	97	1906	219	231	1927	638	640
1886	95	96	1907	238	248	1928	664	671
1887	102	111	1908	263	254	1929	700	759
1888	102	116	1909	260	276	1930	823	884
1889	116	126	1910	298	306	1931	902	931
1890	112	113	1911	323	348	1932	906	796
1891	113	123	1912	350	334	1940	873	856

a No data available.

b Data for year incomplete. The figures given are for March and June.

Source: For 1871–78 the data have been taken from the expense accounts in Ledgers 1–4. For the subsequent years the printed pay roll lists have been used. Partners have been included throughout.

dropped, but in 1916 a swift rise began, a notable increase of nearly 40 per cent taking place during the first six months of 1919. The depression of 1920–21 brought a slight decrease in the staff but in 1922 the growth was resumed, rising to a peak in 1931 and falling off again as the depression became intensified. Despite adverse business conditions and rearrangements designed to re-

duce personnel requirements, the staff still numbered over eight
hundred and seventy-five in the fall of 1938.[16] These figures refer
to full-time employees and have not been inflated by adding the
personnel engaged in field research by research agencies employed
by the firm, nor do they include, as do the figures released by
some agencies, employees of other agencies affiliated for the purpose of getting or placing business in foreign areas.

WORKING HOURS AND VACATIONS

The Ayer staff of recent years has worked seven hours a day,
five days a week, and received a vacation with pay. These pleasant conditions form a marked contrast with the time spent at
work by the Ayer employees of previous generations. The change
has been gradual; and, while no single force can be put forward
to explain it, one important factor was undoubtedly the slow
realization that the hours of work could be reduced without im-
pairing the output. Indeed, there is good reason to believe that
in N. W. Ayer & Son, as in business generally, shorter hours
meant increased production. It must be said, however, that the
official working schedule is misleading as far as the administrative and executive branches of the firm are concerned, for their
members (like many others in business) stop only when the job
is done and that may be at dawn instead of five in the afternoon.

Although no record exists of the working day of the Ayer staff
during the 'seventies, it was undoubtedly from eight to six, if not
longer, with an hour off for lunch and no early closing on Saturday. Until after 1880 there was no summer vacation for anyone,
and during the first few years the working hours in summer were
apparently just as long as those in the winter. By 1875 the firm
probably closed its doors at five during the hot weeks, as it did a
few years later. The only holidays observed were the Fourth of
July, Thanksgiving, and Christmas.[17] By 1885 the summer practice was to close daily at five o'clock, with work ending at four
on Saturdays.[18]

In September, 1886, the Ayer firm announced some interesting
additions to its rules.[19] Employees were to receive an annual vacation with pay, "the limit of which shall be either a half-day or
one day, according to the grade of employee, for each full month

of employment," with a maximum of two weeks. Other rules had to do with the problem of lateness to work. For some years the management had been concerned about the fact that some of the staff were not at their desks promptly at 8:00 and 1:30 o'clock. It had attempted for a time to encourage punctuality by special citations of the employees who had not been late during each month.[20] The bestowal of praise was apparently not effective, and the firm gave notice that time lost through unexcused lateness would be taken from holiday periods or its equivalent deducted from the weekly wages. This feature is interesting in view of the fact that the employees were not paid for the overtime which they often had to work. To take the sting out of this rule a scheme of rewards for punctuality was announced: every employee would be granted one half-holiday each month, provided that he had had not more than ten unexcused latenesses during the preceding month.

In 1890 the firm revised the rules for "Premium Time," as the reward for punctuality was called. The limit on latenesses was reduced from ten to five during the month, beyond which the half-holiday was forfeited. On the other hand a full day off was given to each employee who had no unexcused absences during the month. The plan was suspended in June, July, and August, when vacations and shortened hours made further reduction of the working force impracticable.[21] This arrangement must have been a boon to the workers, especially since their normal working hours made personal shopping exceedingly difficult. Between 1891 and 1895 about 20 per cent of the staff earned a full holiday every month, and another 10 per cent earned a half-holiday every month during the nine months of the year in which the scheme operated.[22]

Although the reward for punctuality seemed to serve its purpose, the management encountered some difficulties. There were repeated complaints that the daily time slips which employees turned in were not always honestly filled out and hence premium time was being received which was not earned. Then there was the difficulty of determining what constituted an excused lateness. The frequency with which the excuses "car blocked" or "fog" (delaying the ferry service from Camden) were used in 1895 indicates that commuting difficulties and traffic jams were already complicating life for Ayer employees.[23]

In 1905 a number of departmental heads, feeling that premium time had become essentially a substitute for shorter hours, recommended that the firm recognize this fact, do away with the scheme, and shorten Saturday's working time for all.[24] The management, however, was unwilling to take any step that might relax the emphasis upon punctuality, and the abandonment of premium time was postponed until 1912, after the working week had been materially shortened for the entire staff.[25]

The pressure for shorter hours on Saturday is observable in the 'eighties, and, as we have seen, the Ayer firm was releasing its staff at four o'clock on summer Saturdays as early as 1882. This practice continued until the summer of 1888, during which the staff was allowed to stop at three on Saturdays on the condition that it take only half an hour for lunch on the same day.[26] Later, possibly because business conditions were worse, the summer week was lengthened again: in 1892 the Ayer offices closed at four o'clock on Saturdays instead of three during the summer, and then only because the staff was willing to shorten its luncheon period to half an hour on both Fridays and Saturdays. In connection with this change, however, the firm made a noteworthy innovation. Instead of deciding the matter by itself and announcing its conclusion, it printed ballots and requested the members of the staff to vote whether they preferred the earlier closing on Saturdays or uniform luncheon and closing hours throughout the week.[27]

Until 1892 there had been no shortening of Ayer working hours during the winter months. The excuse for early closing from June to September had been the heat of Philadelphia's summer. In October, 1892, however, the employees voted to shorten the luncheon hour on Friday and Saturday, as they had done in the summer, in order to close an hour earlier on Saturday (i.e., at five o'clock) during the winter.[28] This arrangement continued without change, except for the advance of closing time one hour during summers, until 1899.[29]

In 1899 the first advertising of the National Biscuit Company increased the work of N. W. Ayer & Son to the point where the

Ayer management felt unable to shorten the working day during the summer as it had previously done. It therefore addressed the following notice to its employees:[30]

To Our Employees:
re EARLY CLOSING.

We have approached this question this year with great misgiving, for the reason that we have been unable to see how the work now in hand can be promptly done in reduced hours. It must be apparent to every one that we are now unusually loaded for this time of year. The nature of the work is also somewhat peculiar, that is to say, with it we are being placed on trial by new clients whose disposition to give us further business will be affected by the expedition and ability with which we handle the business we now have in hand.

The business feeds us all. To shorten our working hours, therefore, at the expense of slighting or delaying our work would be to injure every one of us — employees and employers alike. (Speaking of injury, let us also be careful that no one is hurt in the halls and stairways in rushes such as have recently followed the closing gong.)

In view of present conditions, we have thought the following the best arrangement for this season — to close at four o'clock Saturdays and five o'clock other days, but to shorten the lunch period to one-half hour every day. This schedule to go in effect Saturday, July 1st, and terminate Saturday, September 2d, 1899.

It must also be kept in mind that vacations are to be taken during this same period. We, therefore, ask every employee to see not only that his or her own work does not fall behind, but also to be watchful and helpful in all the work of the department, working after five o'clock or at other hours whenever the welfare of the business demands it.

This arrangement made a 50-hour week for the summer, whereas the employees had previously had a 48-hour week during the hot months.

In June, 1900, the Ayer firm instituted for the first time in its history the Saturday half-holiday. Although limited to the summer months, it marked a notable advance in the direction of a longer week end.

Thus far, it is evident that the Ayer management was willing to make concessions toward a shorter working day and week only by a rearrangement of the time of work. Save for ten or twelve weeks during the summers, there had been no reduction in the number of hours worked per week. In 1902, however, the Ayer management announced that the closing hour would be put ahead to 5:30 throughout the year, reducing the regular working week from 54 to 51 hours. The reasons given for the change are particularly interesting:[31]

Our idea in doing this (which, on the present pay-roll basis, would cost us over $5,000 per year) is to enable you to get out on the street before the six o'clock trolley rush, and also enable this to be done without a crowd about the elevators. [The firm had moved into new quarters and was using elevators for the first time in its experience.] We would make the lunch period one hour every day instead of four days as heretofore. This will allow ample time to get up and down the elevators at noon without confusion.

We are quite willing to try this new order of things *on one condition, namely, that you will work until 5.30 o'clock, taking after that hour whatever time you may wish to wash up, put on hats and wraps, and leave the building in an orderly manner.*

In 1905 the Ayer employees began to receive a half-day off on May 30. Some years earlier, New Year's Day had been added to the Christmas, Thanksgiving, and Fourth of July holidays. A request for a half-holiday on February 22 was denied, and Labor Day was not yet being celebrated.[32] When the suggestion was made that the firm grant Saturday half-holidays during six months of the year, the attitude of the management seems to have been summed up by J. A. Wood, who, in reply to the assertion that the staff could do as much in five and a half days as six, asked: "If this is true, does it not mean that our present force is eight per cent too large? If that be true should not the number be reduced?" [33] Two years later (April, 1907), however, the firm adopted the Saturday half-holiday for the entire year, thereby reducing the regular working week to $47\frac{1}{2}$ hours.[34]

Further shortening of the working hours came in October, 1912, when the hour of opening was changed from 8:00 to 8:30 and the closing time advanced to 5:00, with Saturday hours running from 8:30 to 1:00 p.m. The change reduced the working week of the Ayer staff from $47\frac{1}{2}$ hours to 42 at a single stroke.[35]

While this reduction was partially offset by the abandonment of premium time, it was by far the greatest step toward shorter hours which N. W. Ayer & Son ever made, and it was granted in a year when the firm's volume of business was shrinking and profits were turning into actual losses. It is significant, too, that the Ayer management had obviously revised its former opinion about hours of work. In announcing the new schedule it expressed the belief:[36]

. . . that a reasonable shortening of our business hours would result in the speeding up of our business machine and not only would we accomplish as much in a shorter period of time, but its accomplishment of necessity would be more spirited. . . . Human beings, engaged in the kind of work in which we are engaged, if not properly and spiritedly employed, wear out sooner, and their work is less valuable than under other conditions.

For more than a decade after the shortening of hours in 1912, no further change was made. In May, 1924, however, the Saturday closing was changed from 1:00 to 12 noon.[37] Three years later (May, 1927) the opening hour was moved from 8:30 to 9:00 a.m., thus reducing the working week to 38 hours, approximately one-third less time than the staff regularly worked between 1869 and 1902.[38] In the summer of 1928 the Ayer firm closed its offices altogether on Saturdays, retaining only a handful of workers to receive incoming messages and handle any emergency requests which might arise. The step was a tentative one, and in connection with it the following communication from the president to the staff may be quoted, not only because it reported the experiment a success but also because its general tone contrasts so strongly with the attitude held by the Ayer management of earlier years:[39]

TO THE MEMBERS OF OUR ORGANIZATION:

Our experiment of Saturday closing during the summer has apparently worked no disadvantage to our clients. This is in no small measure due to the thorough and competent manner in which the members of our organization have executed the work in their charge.

It affords us real satisfaction to extend this Saturday holiday to include Saturday, September first.

We make this announcement thus far in advance in order that provision may be made for all work in hand and that full advantage may be taken of the Labor Day week-end.

Since 1932 the agency has been closed on Saturdays throughout the year. Originally a depression measure, this reduction to the 35-hour week is now permanent.

The hours of work observed by N. W. Ayer & Son should, of course, be compared with those of other business firms. While no general statistics are available on the hours of office workers specifically, the data for all industry show that the average American worked over 58 hours per week in 1890 when Ayer employees worked 54; 54.6 in 1910 when Ayer employees worked 47.5; 53.5 in 1915 compared with 42; 50.4 in 1920 compared with 42; and 49.9 hours in 1925 when the Ayer staff worked only 41. With regard to reduction in working hours, therefore, N. W. Ayer & Son was consistently ahead of the general trend.[40] There is no reason to suppose, however, that the Ayer firm was ahead of the majority of the firms with which it had to deal. In fact, the only existing evidence on this point suggests that until recent years, at any rate, the Ayer agency lagged behind. Thus, in 1905, when Wood recommended to Ayer the granting of a holiday on May 30, he stated:[41]

The opportunity to dispatch work [on May 30] is curtailed by the closing of engravers, electrotypers, our customers, and in fact all with whom we are allied except the newspapers (who never close), and the omission of mail deliveries deprives us of the power to take action on rush work for out-of-town customers.

It must be recognized, on the other hand, that the continual necessity of dealing with newspapers "who never close" gave some justification for keeping the agency open during as much of the day as possible.

No comparison of working hours is fair that ignores the holidays and vacations which employees receive. By 1902 most of the Ayer staff were receiving two weeks' summer vacation with pay.[42] One must consider, further, the amount of time put in outside the regular office hours. No specific data on this point are available, but, according to persons who worked in N. W. Ayer & Son between 1883 and 1910, many of the staff, including comparatively young girls, regularly worked several evenings a week, receiving only supper money as compensation.[43] This extra work was offset in part at least by the premium time earned. When overtime is considered, the improvement in Ayer working hours is even more marked than the office hours indicate, for overtime rapidly diminished after the World War I period until, for the clerical staff at least, it has entirely disappeared except for occasional emergencies.

Early Working Conditions

We know nothing about the atmosphere in which the staff worked during the first fifteen years of the agency's life, but the office rules which were enforced in 1884 give an illuminating glimpse of the working conditions which apparently prevailed, with little change, until about 1900. They reflect a disciplinary attitude of management which was typical of American business during the period.[44] Needless to say, this attitude has long since disappeared from the Ayer agency, but in 1884 Ayer employees worked under the following rules:

BUSINESS RULES
of
AYER & SON'S ADVERTISING AGENCY
PHILADELPHIA.

One. — The offices shall be ready for business occupancy by 7.55 A.M.

Two. — All employees, unless absent from the city, or specially excused by the firm, are expected to be at their respective desks ready for business at 8 A.M., and at 1.30 P.M., sharp. WE APPRECIATE PUNCTUALITY. The sounding of the Gong will be the signal for commencing and stopping work in all Departments.

Three. — One hour, from 12.30 to 1.30 P.M., will be allowed for lunch.

Four. — Employees who, from sickness or any other cause, find it necessary to be absent from business even for a part of a day, are expected to advise the firm at the earliest opportunity, of the occasion for and probable continuance of such absence. Failure to do so will be accepted as indicating a lack of interest.

Five. — During business hours, loud talking, jesting, laughing or smoking will not be allowed, and the employees are particularly requested to avoid conversation about any matters other than those strictly pertaining to the business of the firm.

Six. — Each employee will occupy his or her own desk, which will be supplied with all necessary appliances; and intercourse with any other employee during business hours must be as infrequent and of as short duration as the exigencies of the case will permit. Letters or papers concern those only in whose possession or on whose desk they may be.

Seven. — Our business is divided into EIGHT DISTINCT DEPARTMENTS, each under the charge of a chief clerk, to whom all assistants in that department will look for instructions, and who in turn will account to the firm for all that transpires in the department.

Eight. — It is preferred that so far as practicable all communications between the different departments should be through their respective heads, rather than between their assistants.

Nine. — A bell-boy will be in attendance for the delivery of any messages that may be required in the course of business between the various departments. All such messages not delivered in person must be sent by the bell-boy; and loud calling from one desk or department to another is STRICTLY PROHIBITED. The boy must never be sent outside of the building, unless by one of the firm.

Ten. — The hours of business will be from 8 A.M. to 12.30 P.M., and from 1.30 to 6 P.M., unless otherwise specified; but each day's business MUST BE COMPLETED, so far as practicable, THAT DAY even if to do so requires extra work. Preparations for departure should not begin before the sounding of the Gong. Any person desiring to leave earlier must first obtain permission from the head of the department, or from one of the firm.

Eleven. — All employees are requested to wipe their feet before entering, to cultivate neatness in personal appearance, to keep their desks clean and tidy, externally and internally, and especially to avoid loitering about the halls or entrance. REMEMBER! ours is a business place; we mean business; and we desire all our employees to look and act business.

Twelve. — All salaries will be paid every Saturday afternoon; and the cashier is forbidden to advance any money during the week on salary account, except on presentation of a written order signed by one of the firm.

Thirteen. — The books of account and the newspaper files are the property of the firm, and the only persons having any right of access to either are those to whom their care has been particularly entrusted. Other employees desiring information from either must obtain it from these persons or under their direction. Under no circumstances will any employee be allowed to remove from the office any papers belonging to the files, except it be for business purposes; and then they must be obtained from the chief clerk of the File Department, and to him returned.

Fourteen. — Private communications addressed to employees will be sent to the chief clerk of each department for delivery to the person addressed. Personal correspondence is, however, entirely out of place during business hours, and cannot then be permitted.

Fifteen. — Employees will be called to the office to see visitors who may inquire for them, but such visiting should not be encouraged. Visitors must not be admitted into any department without permission from the firm.

Sixteen. — These regulations are considered a part of the contract with every person in our employ; therefore none may complain of discharge for failure to observe them.

Having always endeavored to render each position in our gift as agreeable as possible to its incumbent, we in return expect from every employee a careful attention to our interests, and a ready compliance with all our requests. We shall therefore anticipate from all such a careful observance of these rules as will make them mutually beneficial. Should they at any time be found unjust or onerous in any particular case, it will afford us pleasure, on satisfactory evidence, to at once remedy such defect.

                                        N. W. Ayer & Son

May 1st, 1884.

The emphatic note of discipline which appears in these rules was quite unfeigned. Like other business men of the time, Ayer mistook the appearance of busyness for efficiency and good management: employees were there to work, and the way to make them earn their salt was to keep them strictly up to the mark.

Like his contemporaries, Ayer expected a complete loyalty which at times seems to have amounted to obsequiousness. The employer offered work and paid wages, and any favors which he might grant his employees were supposed to be regarded as the result of benign generosity and not as a right to which they were entitled in the name of decency or efficiency. In 1881, for example, the Ayer management withdrew the early closing for summer which it had granted for several years, later explaining, "The very evident disinclination on the part of some of our employees to remain a minute more than the prescribed time of closing, no matter how important the work at hand, has led us to hesitate about reducing in any degree the hours of labor." In the following summer, however, the firm did allow the staff to stop work at four on Saturdays and intimated that, if the workers showed a "proper appreciation" of the privilege, closing hours for the other days of the week might be advanced during the summer of 1883.[45]

Older employees agree that the atmosphere of the Ayer agency used to be marked by rush, strain, and pressure — interferences and drains on energy which are normally absent in the Philadelphia offices today. Their recollections are corroborated by a description of the Ayer offices published by an outside observer in 1893:[46]

The office of N. W. Ayer & Son is in the Times building on Chestnut Street. It is a large office and has a great deal of noise about it — far more than is necessary, I think, and of a particularly exasperating kind. Every desk has a knob which is turned to the right and starts an electric bell. These bells go incessantly. At the Bureau of Information which confronts you at the door, the attendant gives a twist on the knob in reply to your question, and immediately a small boy appears to conduct you to the proper department. A dozen other callers arrive in the meanwhile and each case demands also a whir-r-r of the bell. All this time the bookkeepers are whirring for some other bookkeepers, the correspondents are whirring for their stenographers, the checking clerks are whirring for their papers, and the order clerks are whirring for their copy. The upstairs men are whirring for the downstairs men and the downstairs men are whirring for the upstairs men. And the two private offices take a hand in it every few minutes. If the firm claimed to do ten million dollars' worth a minute, and noise was any criterion, I should accept the statement without a question. My shattered nerves didn't recover their wonted calmness till I had spent an hour in a boiler factory. So much for quiet Philadelphia.

Creative work would, of course, be extremely difficult in such an environment, and the increasing importance of the creative side of advertising (planning, writing, and artistic design) is undoubtedly one of the main factors which have brought about a complete change in atmosphere. The increased use of such labor-saving and time-saving devices as the typewriter, the adding machine, and the telephone has undoubtedly improved the working environment. Credit must also be given to specialization of work and employees, improved methods of operation, better personnel, shorter hours, and better management generally. All these have helped to eliminate the need for the old discipline, and to reduce the fatigue and frayed nerves which hampered efficiency in the early years.

The important point is that there was in the Ayer agency, as in American business generally, a change in the working atmosphere. It is strongly evident in the difference in tone and attitude of the "Business Rules" of 1884 and the notice "To Our Employees" of 1899 quoted in the preceding section, on the one hand, and the letter "To Members of Our Organization" of 1928, on the other. We hear a great deal today about the terrific pace of modern business, and we forget that there used to be an exasperating, petty discipline which has now almost disappeared. Much remains to be done in American industrial relations, but there has been a very real advance, and, in terms of human history, it has been relatively swift.

Rewards for Service

The primary reward which members of the Ayer staff receive is, of course, their weekly wages. N. W. Ayer & Son was never noted for paying more than the prevailing wage rates. In the opinion of many employees, indeed, its regular scale of payment until recent years was somewhat under the current rates more often than above them; but there have been additional compensations which must be considered with the regular wages. Although the evidence is very fragmentary, the Ayer employee of recent years has received more remuneration for his work than did his predecessors.

A brief examination of Ayer compensation in the 1870's will provide a basis of appraisal for recent years. George O. Wallace was hired in 1870 as the first employee. He came at the age of twenty, having had several years of experience; he was to occupy a position of responsibility and trust; and he asked $10 a week for his services. Ayer persuaded him to accept $9.62 ($500 a year instead of $520), and increased the amount to $12.50 a year later.[47] Another employee was hired in 1872 at $9.62 a week. In the next year two men were added at $15 a week, one of whom received $20 a week in 1874 as cashier and bookkeeper — the highest amount paid to anyone at the time except the two partners. McKinney came in 1875 at $15 a week, and he was receiving only $23.08 ($1,200 a year) when he was admitted to partnership. The highest amount paid to any employee in 1876 was $25 a week, to an older man who was engaged in soliciting new business. From these and other data of the period, it is evident that an adult worker who possessed business experience was paid from $10 to $15 a week for ordinary work in the Ayer agency, and that the top salary, even for a successful solicitor, was $25. Boys working full time were paid from $5.80 to $8.00 a week.[48]

Further light is thrown on compensation at that time by the salaries received by the partners between 1880 and 1884. In 1880 Ayer allowed himself $100 a week, while Wallace and McKinney received $25 each. In 1881–82 Ayer and Wallace continued at these rates, while McKinney was advanced to $40 a week. In 1883 Ayer increased his own salary to $134.62 a week ($6,900 a year), while the other two partners each received $50 a week. The same amounts were paid in 1884. The three men received profits in addition, but these were mostly left in the business, and their salaries probably may be taken to indicate the highest compensation that an important member of the Ayer organization could possibly expect at the time.[49] Probably this scale of payment was typical of American business at the time.

In view of the general trend of prices and wages during the period from 1873 to 1896, it is not likely that the Ayer scale of wages changed materially until after the upturn in 1897. No information on the point is available, but the fact that a college graduate began to work for N. W. Ayer & Son in 1899 at $12 a week[50] suggests that Ayer wages in 1899 were about the same as those of 1876. Employees received increases in pay from time to time, of course, but these were usually given only when there had been actual advancement in position on the staff involving increased responsibilities and duties. And, at least while J. A. Wood was in charge of the office force, the firm rarely gave a wage increase until an employee had not only shown that he deserved it but had also firmly and repeatedly asked for it. Old employees recall their pleasant surprise when, about 1910, the firm began to give increases before they were requested. Old employees also agree that the Ayer policy of remuneration became more liberal as Wilfred Fry gained in influence with the firm.[51]

The wages paid by N. W. Ayer & Son shortly after World War I contrast strongly with those of the early years. In 1922 and 1923 the wage scale ranged from the $6 or $7 a week paid to messengers through the $90 to $150 a week which many of the representatives, artists, and writers received, to salaries of $12,000 and $15,000 a year paid to a few of the top representatives and copymen. While complete figures unfortunately are not available, data relating to more than half the staff indicate that roughly 18 per cent of the employees were paid from $6 to $10 a week (most of those in this group were messenger boys and girls, often working part-time), 8 per cent from $11 to $15, 18 per cent from $16 to $20, 14 per cent from $21 to $25, with more than 40 per cent receiving $26 or more. That is to say, over 40 per cent of the Ayer employees in 1922 and 1923 were receiving a larger salary than the best-paid employee received in 1876. About 7 per cent (excluding all partners) were receiving $100 or more a week, which contrasts with the $100 weekly salary which Ayer allowed himself forty years earlier.[52] Since 1923, of course, the scale of payment has increased, and after 1936 the financial rewards for working in N. W. Ayer & Son improved substantially, but definite figures are not available.

The wide variation in salaries in recent years is, of course, the result of the wide range of experience and ability which modern agency work involves. A large part of the staff is engaged, as in the 'seventies, in clerical or bookkeeping work which requires accuracy but no great amount of skill or initiative; there is also

a great deal of typing and stenographic work for which no special talent is needed. There is also a relatively large number of
secretarial and supervisory positions which involve a fair amount
of judgment, initiative, and responsibility, and which are therefore paid at a better rate. Beyond these come a smaller group
of positions demanding technical skill and experience — artists,
printers, compositors, layout men, and the like, with correspond-
ingly higher wages. Most highly paid of all are the principal copywriters, plans men, representatives, and general executives, both
because their special abilities are comparatively rare and because
their work has a direct and important bearing on the amount of
business handled by the firm as a whole.[53]

It is, of course, possible for employees to improve their earnings by showing diligence, ability, and a capacity for learning.
Indeed, in advertising circles N. W. Ayer & Son has long been
regarded as a training school for people who want to enter the
field of general advertising; and those who come to the firm without specific agency experience usually regard Ayer training and
experience as a part of their compensation during the first year
or two.[54] The willingness of the Ayer management to reward employees as they become more valuable is well illustrated by the
personnel history from 1920 to 1923. During 1920 there were 290
wage increases for a staff averaging 497 employees. These increases ranged from 5 to 80 per cent, the average, mean, and
modal increases falling between 11 and 20 per cent. In 1921, despite the marked depression which followed the postwar boom, 26
increases were given. In 1922 there were 233 increases for a staff
averaging 483 members. The amount of increase ranged from 4
to 90 per cent, with the typical figure again falling between 11
and 20 per cent. In 1923 the salary increases numbered 360 for a
staff averaging 486. The range for increase was about the same
as before, but the typical figure was closer to 20 per cent than it
had been in 1920 or 1922. It is important to note, too, that the
Ayer management did not hesitate to give two and even three
increases to an employee in a single year if he deserved them.
During the four years under examination, 150 members of the
Ayer staff received 2 wage increases, 69 received 3, 19 received
4, 4 received 5, and 1 employee even obtained 6.[55]

Additional Rewards

In addition to regular salary, N. W. Ayer & Son has conferred other material rewards upon its employees, namely, several types of cash bonuses, inexpensive vacations, and group life insurance.

Cash bonuses were first given in recognition of the length of service for N. W. Ayer & Son, usually as a part of an anniversary celebration. Thus, at the end of the firm's first twenty years, Ayer gave his staff a dinner and presented $50 to each member who had been in his employ for five years, $40 to those of four years' service, and so on down to $5 to those who had been with the firm less than a year; the amount thus given totaled $2,500.[56] The lean profits of the following decade hardly warranted any bonuses; but 1899 and 1900 brought prosperity to the firm, and, at a dinner celebrating McKinney's twenty-fifth anniversary with N. W. Ayer & Son, the partners handed out $3,150 to their employees, the checks varying in amount from $125 to those who had twenty-five years of service to their credit, down to $25 to the ones who had been with the firm for five years.[57]

In 1917 the Ayer management gave out $30,797 in cash to 187 members of its staff as extra compensation for the increased business handled during 1916. On this occasion the bonuses were supposed to be gauged roughly to the relative contribution of each of the recipients to the firm's prosperity during the year and ranged from $25 up to $5,000.[58]

On several occasions before 1917 the Ayer agency had recognized the twenty-fifth, thirtieth, and thirty-fifth service anniversaries of employees by presentations of money. At the close of 1917 the management announced that such recognition would be extended and made uniform, as follows: on his tenth anniversary of service an employee would receive $50; on the fifteenth, $100; on his twentieth, $150; and so on, recognition being given at five-year intervals. In addition the firm announced that, beginning with 1918, those who had completed twenty-five years' service would be given three weeks' vacation instead of two each year.[59] In 1919 the firm instituted the practice of presenting a silver medal to every employee on his fifth service anniversary.[60]

In 1926, while continuing the recognition of service, the firm instituted two plans of profit-sharing for members of the staff.[61] The first, known as the Jarvis A. Wood Beneficial Fund, was open to all employees of sixty days' service or more and was designed to encourage thrift and coöperation in the work of the firm. To participate in its benefits an employee had to deposit not less than 5 nor more than 10 per cent of his weekly salary. In addition to 4 per cent interest on the sums deposited, the firm contributed to the Fund enough money to pay 66⅔ per cent on the total deposit to those whose salaries averaged less than $50 per week for the year, 50 per cent to those whose salaries averaged between $50 and $100 per week, and 33⅓ per cent to those whose salaries averaged more than $100 per week.[62] To encourage members to continue their savings there were restrictions on the amount of money which an employee could withdraw. To enable a member to use his savings in emergency, however, without losing the benefit of the Fund, provision was made to permit borrowing up to 60 per cent of the amount to his credit, with interest at 6 per cent. This arrangement is essentially an amplification of a former plan, the F. W. Ayer Savings Fund, established in 1912, by which the employees could deposit small sums weekly during the year toward a Christmas fund. On these deposits the firm had paid considerably more than the current rate of interest, the amount in 1920, for example, exceeding 9 per cent.[63]

The second of the two profit-sharing plans was called the F. Wayland Ayer Employees' Trust. It was designed to reward members of the staff who performed "outstanding service — service that contributes especially to the profits and prospering of this business." [64] Employees of two years' standing were eligible to participate, but the members of the Trust were selected annually by the partners of the firm after a review of the total accomplishment of each eligible employee during his connection with the firm, the length of his service, and meritorious service performed by him during the year. Points were awarded by the management after considering these three factors, and the total score awarded to each employee determined his share of the money which the firm allocated to the Trust. Each year the partners credited to the Trust an unvarying percentage of total net profits "after deductions for the Jarvis A. Wood Fund and a reasonable return on capital investment." [65] Hence the size of the Trust Fund varied directly with the firm's net earnings. Of the sum appropriated to the Trust, 10 per cent was held for contingencies and the rest was distributed to the employees selected for membership. Members of the Trust were not eligible to participate in the Jarvis A. Wood Fund.

When N. W. Ayer & Son changed from a partnership to a corporation in which employees could own stock, the Employees' Trust was abandoned. It was expected that stock ownership would provide the incentive to extra effort that the Trust had created. The Jarvis A. Wood Fund continued to operate until 1939, although after 1930 it paid only the current rate of interest allowed by savings banks.[66] During the period 1926 to 1932, inclusive, the Fund had an average of 315 members. In the opinion of the Ayer management the Fund served a good purpose, both in encouraging thrift and in stimulating interest in profitable operation.[67]

The Ayer management for many years also supplemented the salaries of its employees by offering inexpensive vacations. In 1906 the firm established Hill Top Camp on F. W. Ayer's farm at Meredith, N. Y., for the use of Ayer employees during the summer months. It maintained the camp and paid the railway fares of employees who used it, while the employees paid $3.50 per week to cover the cost of food and supplies.[68] Originally the scheme was popular, but of course few people care to spend every vacation in the same place, and by 1915 interest in the camp had waned to the point where the firm decided to discontinue it. Ayer subsequently established Meredith Inn in the same beautiful surroundings, and arranged that his employees should receive accommodation in it at low rates. This special privilege continued down to 1940, when the property was sold in connection with the settlement of the Fry estate.[69]

Lastly, N. W. Ayer & Son has given its staff insurance against death from any cause. In November, 1917, the management purchased group insurance for all employees of more than three months' standing — the arrangement provided for the payment of a year's salary (but not to exceed $3,000) in case of death. All the costs of the insurance were borne by the firm, and, being group insurance, it terminates automatically when the employee leaves the organization. That the protection was of value is indicated by the fact that 20 claims were paid before the plan had been in operation six full years.[70]

As indicated in Chapter VIII the present management has instituted a system of bonuses based upon profits and has shown itself to be genuinely interested in advancing employees financially as well as in status and responsibility. It is evident that the material rewards received by Ayer employees have been considerable. Taking the extras into consideration, the rank and file of the staff have probably received better remuneration than they would have received for similar work elsewhere.

OPPORTUNITIES FOR ADVANCEMENT

In addition to the various monetary rewards which the Ayer employees have received, they have been able to look forward to promotion: opportunity for advancement has always existed throughout the Ayer organization, and since 1936 it has been unusually good. Indeed, the chance for development is regarded by both the management and the staff as one of the principal advantages of working in the Ayer organization. Men have risen from errand-boy jobs to department headship, to partnership, and, since incorporation, to presidency. The firm has always promoted from within rather than hired executives from outside, and for over thirty-five years there has been no significant departure from this policy.

The Ayer firm has not found any easy solution for one of the most trying problems connected with promotion: occasionally a man who has risen to an important position does not justify his promotion, or perhaps, after a short period of success, he deteriorates or fails to advance with the rest of the organization. He then becomes not only a handicap to management but also an obstruction in the way of advancement all along the line. This creates a dilemma which every business concern has to face: for the good of the business, such men ought to be dismissed; but such cold-blooded action is a poor recompense for sincere efforts and provides no encouragement to loyalty in the rest of the staff. On the other hand, to retain obsolete executives inevitably discourages initiative and breeds discontent among ambitious younger members of the staff. This result, of course, tends to deprive a firm of the steady succession of talent which it needs.

In the Ayer agency this problem of blocked advancement was plainly evident between 1932 and 1936, partly as a result of the depression. The present management, however, has succeeded in coping with it. A number of older employees were pensioned, others who were obviously in the wrong pew were assisted in finding employment elsewhere, and a considerable number of promising men could be promoted as a result. The situation was handled with a tactful efficiency which was unprecedented in the firm. As a result, those who were displaced took the change with good grace, and the morale of the staff was noticeably improved.[71]

As the Ayer firm has grown, one problem of promotion has emerged which presents special interest and difficulty. The Ayer management, following general business practice, has tended to promote to general executive positions men who distinguished themselves as field representatives, copywriters, plans men or other specialists of the agency business. Sometimes, as a result, men who were essentially expert advertising technicians were placed in positions requiring a high degree of talent for general business administration. Occasionally one of them was able to adapt himself to the new situation, but in many instances the firm deprived itself of a good technician without gaining a capable administrator. In recent years the Ayer firm has begun to appreciate the distinction between an advertising expert and a general business executive, and has endeavored to develop its promising employees in administration as well as technical proficiency. This development is, of course, in harmony with the general tendency of business to exercise more discernment in assigning employees to specific jobs.

In recent years the management has adopted the policy of shortening the period of observation through which new employees must pass. If they show promise, they are quickly placed where they can best develop; if not, they are promptly released. This helps to avoid any accumulation of dead wood in the firm, and it likewise forces the person involved to find himself without delay. The opportunities for development on either the creative or the administrative side of the agency's work, plus the management's sincere desire to advance promising young people as rapidly as possible, have given a fine challenge to the younger employees. The change in managerial attitude since 1936 in this respect can hardly be exaggerated. Previously advancement had been possible but slow, and the firm had shown no great desire to push its staff ahead. To have done so would have meant sharing ownership and profits to a greater degree than Ayer or Fry would have considered proper. Batten and his associates, on the other hand, are acutely aware that the agency is no longer a family business, that it is an institution which will survive and grow only in so far as it develops capable executives. The policy is to restrict ownership to people who are actively engaged in the business, and there is full recognition of the fact that the next succession of management must come from within the ranks. Hence the firm regards the development of capable managerial material as one of its major problems, and it aggressively seeks talented personnel and actively pushes employees up as fast as possible.

Working for N. W. Ayer & Son has thus resumed something of the spirit of adventure which should exist in business and which, for reasons which are not altogether clear, has tended to wane in American industry and commerce during the past decade.

PERSONNEL POLICY IN TIMES OF DEPRESSION

N. W. Ayer & Son has always prized long service and loyalty in its workers, and it has also been reluctant to reduce wages or the size of its staff in times of business adversity. This attitude was summed up by F. W. Ayer in 1912:[72]

We have had a kind of feeling of pride . . . a sense of satisfaction in the consciousness that the help in our place had permanent positions — on good behavior. . . . If business slackened, we did not dispense with their services. Take for instance the time when the N. K. Fairbanks business was taken from us, that dropped probably a fourth right out of our business that year. We didn't let a single person go — we kept them right along, — promoting efficiency, as we thought — and at the same time recognizing the loyalty of these people who, we thought, would respond in kind.

At the same time Ayer was compelled, however, to accompany this review of past policy with an announcement that circumstances made a modification inevitable in 1912. The firm had lost several important accounts, was losing money, and needed to reorganize its staff in order to reduce expenses.[73] Between October, 1912, and October, 1914, the firm gradually diminished the number of employees by approximately 15 per cent. This decrease had no parallel in Ayer history until 1932. On the whole, the Ayer staff had had unusually steady employment. There were no material decreases in the numbers employed as a result of the panics of 1893, 1896, 1907, or 1920.[74]

And, while there are no satisfactory data for the early years, apparently the firm likewise avoided wage and salary cuts in times of stress, with the exception of the depression following 1929. After the panic of 1907 had injured his business, Ayer summoned a conference of departmental heads to consider making a reduction in wages; but, after discussing the matter, he decided that his business, rather than his employees, should bear the brunt of hard times. There were no wage cuts after the crash of 1920, despite the fact that the Ayer business was fairly hard hit.

Nowhere does the Ayer management show its consideration for its employees more strongly than in the trying years after 1929. Other agencies began to cut salaries in 1930, and the typical reduction by rival firms in 1931 was 10 per cent.[75] But, although the Ayer executives voluntarily reduced their salaries in 1931, the rest of the Ayer staff received no reduction until 1932, during which year two cuts were made, totaling from 19 to 23 per cent of the former wages.[76] This was a little less than the reduction typically made by other agencies during the period 1930–32.[77]

In 1933 further retrenchment became necessary, and the Ayer management faced the choice between further adjustments in wages and discharging part of the staff. It compromised by giving each employee one day off per week without pay, with the absences spread through the week in order to permit the agency to operate as usual. This solution aroused discontent among some of the younger members of the staff. They felt that a judicious pruning of dead wood throughout the organization would have reduced

pay roll expense, would have increased efficiency, and, by improving the positions of those who remained with the firm, would
have built up the morale of the staff. To the management and
others, however, such an attitude appeared unduly selfish. It was
clearly undesirable to add to the general unemployment; those
who might be regarded as dead wood had given long, faithful
service and had earned generous treatment; and it was as essential
for the staff's morale to reward loyalty as to encourage ability and
ambition. Since no solution could please everyone, it seemed wise
and fair to distribute the unavoidable hardship among all. The
Ayer management was not unmindful of the fact that its compromise made possible the immediate expansion of an experienced
staff as soon as business improved.[78] Whatever one may think of
the ultimate wisdom of this arrangement, one must admire the
determination of N. W. Ayer & Son to place humanity above
considerations of profit or machine-like efficiency. On the other
hand, the Fry régime had erred in letting so much dead wood accumulate before 1932. The present management is trying very
hard to avoid a repetition of that mistake while maintaining the
basic policy of providing for a stable and continuing organization.
It is clear that the management has always attempted to provide
for its workers the economic security which we as a nation have
come to hold dear.

THE SPIRIT OF THE INSTITUTION

By this time it must be apparent to the reader that, for many
years, paternalism dominated relations between the management
and the employees of N. W. Ayer & Son — not entirely the harsh,
domineering spirit which paternalism too often suggests to the
modern generation, but rather a feeling of kinship and mutual
dependence, a bond of sympathy and joint responsibility between
management and worker which benefited both. Ayer and his
partners felt a genuine personal interest in the welfare of their
employees and earnestly sought to help them advance. In their
opinion, and in the opinion of their time, the relationship involved
complete authority in the management and unquestioning obedi-
ence in the staff, and to some extent this view carried over from
business into private life: management which is on a highly

personal basis can hardly recognize office hours. Such an arrangement was typical of nineteenth-century business; it embodied the constructive aspect of individualism, and it possessed a great deal of solid merit.

One may or may not approve of paternalism in business, but it is not easy to draw the line between paternalistic discipline and benefaction, on the one hand, and intelligent management discharging its proper functions, on the other. Whatever we may think of the methods and ideas which the early Ayer management favored, there can be no question as to its good intentions. Premium time was to encourage punctuality, service bonuses were to foster loyalty, the savings funds and the Employees' Trust were to encourage thrift and attention to the work at hand. Ayer and his associates prized such habits and sought to inculcate them in the employee for his own personal good. Few people will agree on the limits to which a business enterprise can be expected to go in providing for the welfare of its employees and in developing their abilities and opportunities, but N. W. Ayer & Son has always assumed considerable responsibility in these matters. It has given its workers steady employment, encouraged them to work for advancement, and it has improved working conditions and rewards as it has gained in prosperity. It has dealt generously — almost too much so — with employees who have ceased to be useful in the organization.[79] It has taken care of employees who were victims of financial or physical misfortune; and, while it has no regular system of pensions, the firm has provided for workers who have grown old in its service.[80]

All these measures have helped to make the Ayer staff a closely knit and coöperative body. Both present and former employees speak proudly of their connection with N. W. Ayer & Son, and there has long been a strong *esprit de corps* within the staff. It has been particularly evident that the management holds a power over the staff which is based not upon fear but rather upon respect, loyalty, and even affection. And, while no reliable data are available on the turnover of labor, the service records indicate that a large portion of the staff has stayed with the firm year after year. In 1905 about 32 per cent of 225 employees had been with N. W. Ayer & Son five years or more; 19.5

per cent had been on the staff for ten years or more.[81] In 1928, despite a rapid expansion in numbers after World War I, 31 per cent of 666 employees had five years' service or more to their credit, and 13.5 per cent had been with the firm at least ten years; 44 employees had been on the staff between twenty and fifty years.[82]

After World War I there was a definite decline in Ayer paternalism. Among various factors, the growth in numbers and the placing of a large portion of the staff in branch offices did much to diminish the personal bond between the staff and the management. Every Ayer worker still had easy access to the head of the firm, but the relations were inevitably more functional than personal. The change was partly the result of the shifting attitude of employees generally toward their work. A job formerly had been a stepping-stone toward a career in business, to which all other interests and activities were subordinated. Later, a feeling developed that a job was merely a means of livelihood, essential to be sure, but not the dominating interest in life. And along with this feeling there was a growing tendency to introduce a measure of democracy into business enterprises. Workers wanted to be treated as responsible individuals, not as objects of paternal benevolence; and they indicated a growing desire to have a share in determining their conditions of work. Management, on the other hand, was gradually learning to use intelligent leadership and coöperation in place of the personal drive of yesterday's small enterprise.

Whatever the full explanation, the shifting currents of many economic and social forces after World War I brought change to N. W. Ayer & Son. One manifestation of this change was a relatively sudden movement of the Ayer employees to organize themselves for social and recreational activities. In the fall of 1919 a group of employees organized a basketball team which contested successfully with other teams in Philadelphia. In 1920 the House Recreation Committee was appointed; this, with the management's encouragement, organized an Ayer dramatic society, interdepartmental games, a girls' basketball team, and an Ayer baseball team which participated in Philadelphia's industrial leagues. Under the Committee's guidance the employees launched for themselves (with the firm bearing the expenses) a magazine called *The Next Step,* held a summer picnic for the entire staff, organized a tennis tournament and a gun club, and wound up the year with a Christmas celebration which has since become an annual Ayer festivity.[83]

The success and vigor of the outside activities of the Ayer staff is clear evidence that the employees were able to act as a group without suggestion from above. The management lent its support to the movement, it is true, but all the initiative and work came from the employees themselves. Never before had they shown such an autonomous spirit. Out of the formal organization, in which the employees had been continually subservient to the management, there seemed to be developing an informal social unity independent of managerial encouragement. Possibly the unusual burst of collaborative effort among Ayer employees in the social sphere came as a result of the habit of organized effort which people throughout the United States had learned during World War I, a spirit of coöperation which died but slowly as the hour of need passed away. At any rate, it looked for a time as if the old spirit of paternalism was going to be replaced by staff democracy.

The new tendency, however, soon subsided; the pressure of business after 1922, the rapid expansion of the staff after 1923, and a multitude of forces within the Ayer firm and without, all combined to check the budding inclination of the Ayer employees to substitute their own initiative and coöperation for acquiescence in the old paternalism. The social activities continued to some extent in subsequent years, a few of them down to the present day. But, while the staff continued to feel a certain degree of unity, no closely knit social organization — formal or informal — developed out of it. Indeed, the Ayer employees tended to draw together in small groups, determined to some extent by occupational association within the agency.

There has never been any movement among the Ayer employees to organize themselves for collective action in dealing with the management.[84] There has, indeed, been little occasion for such a movement. The management has generally treated its employees well. The staff is essentially an aggregation of white-collar workers, ranging from unskilled clerks to artists and highly trained technicians, who have little basis for spontaneous common action.

Paternalism diminished in the Ayer organization after the death of F. W. Ayer. President Fry continued to regard employees as members of the "Ayer Family" to whom the firm owed rather definite responsibilities; but the swift changes of the 1920's, both inside the agency and out, sped the disintegration of the old bonds and widened the gap between the management and the main body of employees. Some unifying force was needed as a substitute for the old paternalism, some sort of organization of the workers — formal or informal — which would foster a spirit of whole-hearted coöperation with the management. Today it is evident (as it was *not* twenty years ago) that satisfactory working conditions and output can best be maintained by recognizing and working through the natural though somewhat intangible social organizations (i.e., informal groupings) which people always form when thrown together by their daily occupations. Otherwise psychological resistances develop which not only breed discontent but interfere with effective work.[85]

The Ayer management had been dimly conscious of the problem of employee morale, and it had appointed a director of personnel who tried to provide an adequate link between the employees and the top executives. Such a person, however, was necessarily a representative of the management and as such could not fill the need. Considering the limited body of information available at the time about personnel problems, there was probably not much that the Ayer management could have done. Its chief mistake was the one which is still common in American industry: it assumed that the actions of its employees were governed by logic; it took too little account of the sentiments involved; and it made no attempt to test decisions affecting workers by the reactions of the workers themselves. Morale is exceedingly difficult to measure, but fifteen months of rather close association in 1932 and 1933 convinced the writer that it was not what it should have been and that the national economic situation alone did not explain the existing discontent.

Subsequent events have borne out that conviction. When Batten became president in 1936, one of his first concerns was the morale of the staff. He possessed a special advantage in that he had worked and played side by side with many members of the staff during more than twenty years, he had a keen understanding of men, and he knew some of the things that the Ayer employees wanted. Within a short time he succeeded in getting the rank and file to feel that they had a personal share in the Ayer business and that they could and should participate more actively in its management than they had done in the past. At the same time he pointed out that their outside activities might well bear directly upon their jobs. Stating that the management intended "to give everyone an opportunity to capitalize upon his outside interests, activities, and talents," Batten announced that it would "be the policy of the House to encourage activities outside the business." [86]

Unlike the previous Ayer management, however, Batten avoided any paternalism by encouraging the employees to work out their own ideas instead of doing what the management thought they should do. The response was immediate. They formed the Curfew Club to sponsor various types of outside activities — social, athletic, and educational. Within the Club they organized "interest-groups" to study agency work, short-story writing, shorthand and typing, photography, public speaking, dramatics, and such other topics as members wanted to pursue. By the fall of 1938 activities were in full swing and were meeting with an eager response. The management supplied the necessary quarters and equipment, but left the rest to the employees themselves. Here was the unifying force needed to fill the gap left by the old Ayer paternalism, and there is already plenty of evidence that it is going to do more for the Ayer business and for the employees themselves than paternalism at its best.[87] And the activities which began in 1938 did not die out as they had in 1921–1922. World War II inevitably caused some curtailment, but they surged ahead in 1946 and 1947. Perhaps the most striking of these activities has been a series of meetings called "The Other Fellow's Job" in which representatives of the various departments tell about their own specialized work. This has been educational for the younger, less experienced employees, and it has also been very beneficial in enhancing the *esprit de corps* and in giving employees a broader understanding of their own work in relation to the activities of the organization as a whole.

On the whole the Ayer agency has always been an attractive place to work. The staff has long contained an extraordinary number of able and interesting people who like their jobs, enjoy their work, and carry over into their private lives the friendships that develop during office hours. The advances in their working conditions have kept pace with progress in American business at large. The improvements have been tangible (hours, remuneration, and physical surroundings) and intangible, and in recent years the latter aspect has stood out. The working atmosphere used to be somewhat heavy with tradition, moral attitudes, and smug complacency. During the past twelve years the moral attitudes have become less oppressive; during the past ten years the smug complacency has vanished. Tradition remains, but it is now more a living spirit — a challenge and a source of inspiration, rather than a temptation to preserve the *status quo*. The atmosphere today is free and alive. The prevailing spirit is one of contagious enthusiasm, effective coöperation, and pride in the craft of advertising.

CHAPTER XIX

FINANCIAL AND ACCOUNTING HISTORY
OF N. W. AYER & SON

THE history of a business enterprise is never complete until the financial side of its operations has been traced. The growth of a firm in terms of dollars reflects its development in a general way. The ability to earn profits and expand is, of course, a major criterion of business success, though obviously not the only measure. In any economic system — capitalistic, communistic, or otherwise — results must be weighed against costs. This is especially true in our present economic society, for the calculation of income and expense is necessarily a fundamental ingredient of capitalism in general and of private enterprise in particular. Out of such calculations arise the financial policies which affect all other operations.

Since financial results are highly important, the method of reckoning them must also be considered. We must look at the accounting procedure as well as the financial statements — at the means by which results are determined as well as the results themselves. In a large measure, the success of a business enterprise over a considerable period depends upon the maintenance of adequate records of its financial transactions. Such records show where profits are being made, where money is being lost, and how control over operations is maintained. Primarily, the account books of N. W. Ayer & Son are of interest because of the light they throw upon the history of the firm. At the same time, they may well contribute something to the general history of accounting in America, which remains to be written. For the latter purpose they are of especial interest because it is largely within the past three-quarters of a century that the recording of business transactions has evolved from mere bookkeeping to a highly developed and intricate system of accounting, appropriate to the vastly increased scale and complexity of modern business activities.

The financial and accounting history of N. W. Ayer & Son, unfortunately, must remain fragmentary for the present. In part, this necessity is dictated by the loss or destruction of certain essential records, particularly for the period before 1900 — the kind of obstacle which the historian frequently has to face. In part, it is due to the natural reluctance of the Ayer management to reveal detailed information about its financial position and operations. By many business firms, particularly advertising agencies, such data have long been regarded as private and highly confidential. The Ayer agency has never supplied any financial information in response to the inquiries of publishers' associations about credit rating; and, since its incorporation, the firm has given its stockholders (all of whom are employees) only such information as they could glean from hearing the reports read aloud at the annual meetings.

To some extent this policy of secrecy arises from the nature of the firm's ownership. Until 1929 it was a partnership with the majority interest held jointly by Ayer and McKinney, later by Ayer alone, and finally by Fry. To make public the agency's accounts meant giving out a great deal of information about the private fortunes of these men, especially since many of Ayer's outside enterprises were for years recorded on the agency books. With a good deal of justification, most of us hesitate to make such an exposure of private financial status. The incorporation of the Ayer firm in 1929 enlarged the group of owners somewhat, but until 1936 the agency was still to a considerable extent the personal property of a single individual who did not care to reverse a well-founded policy. There is, moreover, a widespread feeling in the agency field that the release of facts about a particular agency's internal operations provides too much material for gossip and misinterpretation by rivals.

In order to facilitate the writing of the present volume, however, the Ayer firm did give free access to all the available records for the years before 1900 and to a substantial part of those for the later period. It also supplied additional information from recent private ledgers to fill some of the gaps in the story. Upon these data and upon numerous conferences with the treasurer and members of the Accounting Department the following sections have been based.

Financial History, 1871–1948

Table 15, which follows, shows the dollar volume handled by N. W. Ayer & Son annually from 1871 through 1930. Figures for later years are not available, but the firm has weathered the economic storms since 1930 with very impressive strength. As indicated in Chapter VIII, the total annual billings dropped between 1936 and 1941, after which they recovered sharply and quickly exceeded the previous peak reached in 1930.

An examination of the profit figures affords much food for reflection. The high rate of profits in the first years of operation is particularly noteworthy when compared with the later results. Expenses were low, risks were fairly high, and the gross margin of profit was not limited (as it later became) to a fixed percentage of the expenditures on behalf of clients. The decline in the rate of profits is to be explained, in part at least, by the adoption of better business methods among publishers and the resulting reduction in commissions allowed to agents, by keen competition among agents, and by the growing expense of operation resulting from copywriting, merchandising, and other services which have been added to the original agency work of placing. General business conditions affected the operating results, especially in the depressed 'nineties. Other factors were the separation from the agency business of the religious newspaper concessions (1882), which accounted for a substantial part of the drop in volume and profits in 1883, and the relative decline of the revenue from trade in printers' supplies and from such ventures as *Ayer & Son's Manual for Advertisers* and the *American Newspaper Directory*. For many years N. W. Ayer & Son, it will be remembered, derived income from the advertising which these two publications contained.[1]

The gross profit from the principal sources of Ayer earnings for 1878, as shown in Table 16, indicates their relative importance.

Similar figures for the period 1880–96 are given in Table 17.

TABLE 15

TOTAL ANNUAL VOLUME AND NET PROFIT, 1871–1930

Year	Volume[a]	Net Profit	% of Gross Vol.	Year	Volume[a]	Net Profit	% of Gross Vol.
1871	$ 30,634	$ 5,980	19.5	1901	$ 2,140,174	$ 101,541	4.7
1872	48,295	8,420	17.4	1902	2,159,802	109,504	5.0
1873	79,910	13,570	16.9	1903	4,107,530	288,844	7.0
1874	108,900	18,931	17.4	1904	2,098,340	15,290[b]	0.7[b]
1875	130,164	19,342	14.9	1905	3,546,374	108,621	3.1
1876	132,712	11,307	8.6	1906	4,281,583	207,611	4.8
1877	195,792	9,722	4.9	1907	4,433,078	149,613	3.4
1878	228,643	17,372	7.6	1908	3,699,252	67,152	1.8
1879	251,763	16,177	6.4	1909	4,267,539	68,525	1.6
1880	366,963	21,466	5.8	1910	5,464,655	100,949	1.8
1881	629,301	47,864	7.6	1911	5,364,641	95,307	1.8
1882	876,346	81,510	9.3	1912	4,508,237	22,127[b]	0.5[b]
1883	530,296	408	0.08	1913	5,141,933	102,727	2.0
1884	917,639	79,910	8.7	1914	4,873,101	100,003	2.1
1885	594,015	3,113	0.5	1915	4,782,558	52,720[bc]	1.1[b]
1886	679,774	32,102	4.7	1916	6,668,110	257,459	3.9
1887	635,795	75,952[b]	11.9[b]	1917	6,760,220	121,877	1.8
1888	1,113,574	33,148	2.9	1918	6,528,146	73,001	1.1
1889	803,864	18,535	2.3	1919	13,734,070	662,413	4.8
1890	1,264,467	55,624	4.4	1920	13,777,435	488,472	3.6
1891	1,208,506	32,739	2.7	1921	11,321,122	157,159	1.4
1892	1,582,772	70,902	4.5	1922	10,881,959	112,732	1.0
1893	1,749,267	74,291	4.3	1923	11,574,077	122,262	1.1
1894	1,555,347	28,373	1.8	1924	13,715,971	358,523	2.6
1895	1,781,909	57,286	3.2	1925	17,074,222	541,580	3.2
1896	1,724,838	7,696	0.4	1926	26,068,807	1,278,808	4.9
1897	1,603,646	7,265	0.5	1927	28,695,622	1,468,431	5.1
1898	1,579,251	3,853	0.2	1928	28,863,670	1,297,352	4.5
1899	2,030,524	58,383	2.9	1929	32,634,877	1,755,145	5.4
1900	1,380,181	7,743[b]	0.6[b]	1930	38,068,614	........[d]	...

[a] The volume figure includes gross receipts from all sources. The net profits were arrived at after deducting all expenses, including salaries to partners and periodic write-offs on account of bad debts and depreciation. Dollar figures are shown to the nearest dollar; percentages to the nearest tenth of one per cent.

[b] Loss.

[c] Beginning in 1915, the volume and profit figures were adjusted to show the total business actually handled for clients within the period instead of the total orders booked. Hence the results for 1915 are not strictly comparable with those of previous years, but the figures thenceforth gave a truer picture of the business for each calendar year.

[d] Profit figures for 1930 and subsequent years not available for publication.

SOURCE: 1871–76, Ledgers 1 to 4; 1876–1930, summary figures supplied by the treasurer of N. W. Ayer & Son.

Complete figures for later years were not available for study, but Table 18 gives both volume and gross profit from the sources of income in 1902, 1905, and 1908.

For the post-World War I period only a limited number of monthly figures were accessible. Of these the data for the month

TABLE 16

SOURCES OF GROSS PROFIT, 1878

Sources	Cost for Year	Gross Profit[a]	Amount
Advertising......................			$51,906.07
Merchandise......................			2,103.36
Ayer & Son's Manual..............			1,844.56
Space concessions:			
Lutheran Observer..............	$3,300	$ 775.43	
Standard and Home Journal.......	3,600	60.26	
Christian Instructor.............	1,500	1,084.56	
Christian Statesman.............	600	849.09	
Reformed Church Messenger......	800	594.48	
Presbyterian Journal............	400	544.16	
		$3,907.98	
National Baptist................	4,500	*350.55*[b]	
Total from space concessions....			3,557.43
Total gross profit for year........			$59,411.42

[a] This gross profit was calculated *after* allowing ordinary agency commission, which is included under Advertising above. For explanation see pages 31–33.
[b] Loss.
SOURCE: General Journal, Apr. 1–Dec. 31, 1878, folios 420, 621–622.

of July in 1920, 1923, and 1926 are given in Table 19. While not strictly comparable, they afford a rough basis for comparison with the data for the period 1902–08.

Only a few figures for the operating results of other agencies are procurable, and those only for very recent years; but such data, while not strictly comparable, throw additional light upon the Ayer profits. In 1925 the billings of 59 members of the American Association of Advertising Agencies totaled $104,831,932 on which the gross profit reported was 14.29 per cent, and the net profit reported was 2.63 per cent.[2] The Ayer net gain for the same period was 3.2 per cent. Members of the A.A.A.A. whose annual volume was $10,000,000 or more showed the following net profits on total volume:[3]

	1928	1929	1930	1931	1932
Range (%)	2.2–4.0	1.7–3.3	1.2–3.0	0.6–2.6	0.6–2.5
Median figure	2.4	2.9	2.0	1.4	1.4

These percentages were calculated *after* an allowance of 6 per cent on invested capital; furthermore, they cover three years for

TABLE 17

PRINCIPAL SOURCES OF GROSS PROFIT, 1880–1896

Year	Advertising	Merchandise	Newspaper Annual	Ayer & Son's Manual
1880	$ 44,241	$ 8,931	$ 8,938	$1,168[a]
1881	61,163	12,750	6,948	744[a]
1882	104,087	14,996	13,550	368[a]
1883	62,891	12,609	18,777	224
1884	112,147	12,534	19,736	713
1885	71,287	11,656	22,133	327
1886	87,557	12,714	19,616	831
1887	74,990	9,606	17,526	1,289
1888	130,449	14,453	14,415	181[a]
1889	92,638	9,372	23,484	27[a]
1890	144,321	8,986	12,301	0
1891	121,041	5,663	18,341	678[a]
1892	171,459	6,283	16,791	0
1893	187,004	7,555	18,772	10[a]
1894	162,244	5,747	17,228	215[a]
1895	189,185	4,178	18,418	0
1896	168,791	4,069	.....[b]	193[a]

[a] Loss.
[b] No information obtainable.
SOURCE: Firm Ledgers 1, 2, 3 (1880–96).

TABLE 18

Business and Revenue, 1902, 1905, 1908

	Advertising	Electro-types	Drawing & Engraving	Newspaper Annual	Merchandise Transfers	Printing Dept.	Total
1902							
Business................	$2,011,543	$29,962	$22,276	$30,900	$33,686	$31,233	$2,159,601
Gross Revenue..........	259,264	4,125	2,109	13,026	6,640	3,207	288,370
Ratio of Revenue to Business..	12.9%	13.8%	9.5%	41.2%	19.7%	10.3%	13.4%
1905							
Business................	$3,325,936	$61,276	$46,483	$32,379	$68,677	$11,622	$3,546,374
Gross Revenue..........	441,811	8,127	5,741	18,038	6,434	.....	480,150
Ratio of Revenue to Business..	13.3%	13.3%	12.4%	51.7%	9.4%	.....	13.5%
1908							
Business................	$3,445,576	$56,938	$55,207	$36,377	$90,864	$14,290	$3,699,252
Gross Revenue..........	442,639	7,231	4,431	19,979	3,980	.....	478,258
Ratio of Revenue to Business..	12.8%	12.7%	8.0%	55.0%	4.4%	.....	12.9%

Source: Summary of operations, 1902–08.

which no Ayer results are accessible. Accordingly, no accurate comparisons can be made, but it is evident from the figures given, as well as from data which cannot be published, that N. W. Ayer & Son's earnings between 1925 and 1929 were somewhat above those of typical rival agencies.

TABLE 19

JULY BUSINESS AND REVENUE, 1920, 1923, 1926

	Advertising	Electrotypes	Drawings and Engravings	Printing	Total Volume[a]
July, 1920					
Business..........	$1,193,756[b]	$14,102	$25,240	$31,904	$1,398,703
Gross Revenue.....	119,833	1,599	3,335	2,204	182,550
Ratio of Revenue to Business........	10.0%	11.3%	13.2%	6.9%	13.1%
July, 1923					
Business..........	$ 660,743	$10,088	$20,989	$19,494	$ 755,791
Gross Revenue.....	90,463	1,334	2,604	1,462	117,878
Ratio of Revenue to Business........	13.7%	13.3%	11.9%	13.3%	15.6%
July, 1926					
Business..........	$2,107,596	$13,970	$43,454	$27,085	$2,024,425
Gross Revenue.....	302,013	1,414	6,209	2,235	313,667
Ratio of Revenue to Business........	14.3%	10.1%	14.3%	8.3%	15.5%

[a] These figures include certain items and adjustments not shown in the columns to the left.
[b] This figure includes $399,604 in fixed-price advertising on which the gross profit was less than 1 per cent, thus bringing the average gross profit for all advertising for the month down to 10 per cent.
SOURCE: Monthly Revenue and Expense Book, 1919–26.

The Ayer management attributes the favorable comparison to the large volume of business done and believes that agencies with the same amount of billings would show about the same results. In recent years the firm has continued to be profitable, but the depression years naturally reduced the rate of earnings. Moreover, since 1929 certain items of expense have so increased as to cut sharply into profits. The expansion of market research and copy testing since 1930, for example, has added to expense, although it has greatly improved the quality of work done.

Turning to the expenses which have been charged against revenue, we have Table 20, which is based upon the classification of expenditures used by the Ayer firm between 1878 and 1896.

One or two features are noteworthy. General expense tended to decrease slightly in relation to total volume. Salaries and wages varied from 3.6 to 7.5 per cent of volume but do not indicate a definite trend except a slight rising tendency in the 'nineties. Traveling expense, expense from correspondence, and the cost of self-advertisement show no well-defined movement except a slight downward tendency after 1889. On the whole, they shed little light on the declining profits for this period. The explanation seems to be found more in the decline of certain types of revenue, as shown above.

In 1900 the classification of expenses was changed, so that later figures are not comparable with those of the period before 1897. Table 21, however, provides a rough basis for comparing expenses in certain years before and after World War I. The data for 1902, 1905, and 1908 are for the entire year. Those for 1920, 1923, and 1926 are for the month of July alone, as the only figures procurable. The amounts for traveling expense should not be compared directly. The increase of the vacation habit has greatly reduced soliciting during the summer months. Moreover, much of the soliciting which was done from Philadelphia in the early years was later done from branch offices. Probably a fair comparison could be made between traveling expense in the early years and traveling plus branch office expense in the later period.

In Table 22 we have income and expenses for a representative year in the period after World War I, just as they were summarized for the Ayer management. The noteworthy fact is that over two-thirds of the total operating expense is salaries and wages.[4]

The most striking feature, perhaps, is the fact that many expenses stood in about the same relation to volume after 1900 and after World War I as they did in the period 1880–96. If any conclusion can be safely drawn, it is that, while the expense

TABLE 20

PRINCIPAL ITEMS OF AYER EXPENSE, 1878–1896 [a]

Year	General Expense [b]	% [c]	Salaries & Wages	% [c]	Traveling Expense	% [c]	Expense Account Correspondence [d]	% [c]	Business Advertising	% [c]	Suspended Accounts	% [c]
1878	$14,294	6.2	$13,468	5.9	$2,450	1.1	$2,737	1.2	$3,334	1.5	$3,520	1.5
1880	15,600	4.3	18,158	4.9	3,250	0.9	3,619	1.0	2,682	0.7	1,521	0.4
1881	20,097	3.2	26,926	4.3	3,706	0.6	4,292	0.7	5,336	0.8	4	..
1882	18,781	2.2	31,824	3.6	3,431	0.4	5,070	0.6	3,008	0.3	0	..
1883	22,715	4.3	37,062	7.1	8,741	1.6	4,708	0.9	2,097	0.4	18,058	3.4
1884	20,508	2.2	42,390	4.6	4,167	0.5	4,593	0.5	1,608	0.2	174	..
1885	20,332	3.4	42,157	7.1	6,653	1.1	3,659	0.6	2,541	0.4	0	..
1886	22,144	3.3	46,074	6.8	6,449	0.9	3,011	0.4	3,179	0.5	5,118	0.8
1887	20,805	3.2	47,905	7.5	6,370	1.0	2,768	0.4	2,082	0.3	16,473	2.6
1888	34,657	3.1	51,999	4.7	6,041	0.5	4,432	0.4	1,784	0.2	1,250	0.1
1889	34,991	4.3	60,139	7.5	6,536	0.8	4,740	0.6	6,765	0.8	6,310	0.8
1890	33,311	2.5	59,693	4.6	10,256	0.8	4,599	0.4	4,778	0.4	2,515	0.2
1891	42,757	3.7	71,532	5.9	12,952	1.1	5,721	0.5	[e]	..	0	..
1892	35,297	2.2	76,041	4.8	11,512	0.7	4,470	0.3	5,409	0.3	2,877	0.2
1893	45,171	2.6	79,814	4.6	11,893	0.7	4,658	0.3	3,927	0.2	29,275	1.7
1894	36,966	2.4	81,173	5.2	13,281	0.9	4,538	0.3	6,096	0.4	9,973	0.6
1895	40,151	2.3	91,784	5.2	11,935	0.7	5,384	0.3	2,833	0.2	10,134	0.6
1896	41,188	2.5	97,033	6.1	14,505	0.8	6,561	0.4	8,284	0.5	14,363	1.1

[a] Data for 1879 too incomplete to be included.
[b] No information has survived to indicate precisely what this item contained. Rent, supplies, depreciation, and miscellaneous expense were undoubtedly included.
[c] This figure was obtained by relating the expense to gross volume for the year.
[d] Apparently this item carried expenditures for postage stamps.
[e] Data for year incomplete.
SOURCE: Firm Ledgers 1, 2, 3.

TABLE 21

AYER EXPENSES AT SELECTED PERIODS, 1902–1926

	1902 Expense	% of Vol.[a]	1905 Expense	% of Vol.	1908 Expense	% of Vol.	July, 1920 Expense	% of Vol.	July, 1923 Expense	% of Vol.	July, 1926 Expense	% of Vol.
Business Getting:												
Executive Expense	$18,750	0.9	$32,843	0.9	$34,066	0.9	$9,063	0.6	$6,813	1.0	$7,863	0.4
Soliciting	27,904	1.4	41,630	1.2	76,648	2.1	14,633	1.0	10,121	1.5	23,786	1.1
Traveling	13,976	0.7	21,012	0.6	26,856	0.7	2,884	0.2	1,542	0.2	128	..
Branch Office		..	9,953	0.3	18,560	0.5	15,859	1.1	26,847	4.1	36,296	1.7
Service:												
Business Dept.	11,862	0.6	17,609	0.5	18,471	0.5	6,114	0.4	3,671	0.5	6,716	0.3
Copy Dept.	26,474	1.3	32,114	0.9	59,214	1.6	26,702[b]	1.9	25,349[b]	3.8	36,419[b]	1.7
Forwarding Dept.	25,685	1.3	22,694	0.6	23,269	0.6	6,087	0.4	5,945	0.9	8,383	0.4
Admin. & Maint.:												
Executive	24,377	1.2	32,842	0.9	34,066	0.9	9,063	0.6	6,813	1.0	7,863	0.4
Registry	11,749	0.6	11,196	0.3	13,229	0.4	4,868	0.3	3,213	0.5	4,579	0.2
Accounting	17,698	0.9	18,866	0.5	20,166	0.5	3,406	0.2	2,950	0.4	1,206	0.06
General Expense:												
Building	14,146	0.7	10,875	0.3	12,649	0.3	2,945	0.2	4,148	0.6	5,223	0.2
Business Adv.	1,740	0.09	1,723	0.05	4,283	0.1	8,990	0.6	11,510	1.7	10,925	0.5
Stationery & Supplies	1,445	0.07	2,501	0.07	2,138	0.06	579	0.04	1,345	0.2	1,508	0.07
Collection & Legal Expense	737	0.04	1,509	0.04	1,875	0.05	51	..	512	0.07	460	0.02

[a] The percentage figures were obtained, as in earlier tables, by relating expense to total volume for the period.
[b] Since the Art Bureau was not separately reported in the earlier years, its expenses have been added to those for the Copy Department.
SOURCE: For early period, summary of operations 1902–08; for postwar period, Monthly Revenue and Expense Book.

TABLE 22

OPERATING FIGURES FOR A REPRESENTATIVE YEAR (1924)

Total Billings for Year [sales]................	$13,715,971.22	100.00%
Cost of Space, Services and Material Purchased for Clients.............................	11,780,383.24	85.89
Income from Billings.......................	$1,935,587.98	14.11%
Interest and Discount......................	13,248.83	.10
Other Income.............................	79,372.79	.58
Total Income before Expenses...............	$2,028,209.60	14.79%
Expenses		
Salaries and Wages........................	$1,131,453.72	8.25%
Rent, Heat and Light......................	83,751.18	.61
Traveling Expenses........................	125,958.61	.92
Telephone and Telegrams...................	21,147.18	.15
Postage..................................	14,160.94	.10
Printing.................................	6,190.38	.05
Office Supplies and Stationery...............	8,216.04	.06
House Advertising.........................	128,084.95	.93
Collection and Legal Expense...............	18,220.20	.13
Subscriptions and Donations................	5,362.18	.04
Branch Office Sundry Expense...............	12,684.30	.09
Insurance................................	14,955.27	.11
Taxes...................................	10,205.70	.07
Bad Debts...............................	4,257.46	.03
Depreciation.............................	50,328.15	.37
General Expense..........................	34,710.71	.25
Total Expenses........................	$1,669,686.97	12.17%
Net Profit for the Year.....................	$ 358,522.63	2.62%

SOURCE: Treasurer of N. W. Ayer & Son, Inc.

ratios are fairly constant over a long period, they vary from year to year because the size of the staff cannot be quickly adjusted to sudden fluctuations in volume, either up or down. This is evident from a comparison of disbursements for salary and wages during the month of July for the years 1919–26, as shown in Table 23.

When these percentages are compared with those for salaries and wages in the period 1880–1896, it is evident that this source of agency expense has increased in the interval. As already indicated, this and certain other items of expense have increased since 1929 as a result of the expansion of radio business and various types of agency research. Moreover, since 1929 various new taxes have had to be paid: that for social security, for example, has added substantially to expense.

TABLE 23

July Salary and Wages Expense, 1919–1926

Year	Volume (Total Billings)	Salary & Wages	% of Volume
1919	$1,354,044	$ 57,520	4.24
1920	1,398,703	86,832	6.22
1921	855,587	85,654	10.01
1922	747,036	68,652	9.18
1923	755,791	72,819	9.64
1924	927,606	78,439	8.46
1925	1,072,891	113,844	10.62
1926	2,024,425	134,153	6.55

Source: Revenue and Expense Sheets, 1919–26. Operating statements by years were not available.

We turn now from current operations to the financial resources and obligations of the firm. According to F. W. Ayer's own statement the initial capital which went into the Ayer firm in 1869 was $250. The first year for which complete figures are available as to assets and liabilities is 1872, at the end of which the bookkeeper made a trial balance in the ledger itself. From this trial balance the following statement of the assets and liabilities of N. W. Ayer & Son can be drawn up.

The Sunday School account was not, properly speaking, a firm account, and it is included here as an example of the way in which, for many years, the Ayer books contained personal as well as advertising accounts. It is evident that the original $250 had grown rapidly during the three years and eight months following the agency's establishment. Furniture and fixtures, apart from the Printing Department, were evidently written off entirely. Further growth is evident from the status of the Ayer firm at the end of 1874, shown in Table 25.

TABLE 24

BALANCE SHEET, DECEMBER 31, 1872

Assets		Liabilities	
Cash...................	$ 2,098.44	Sundry Accounts Payable.	$ 1,448.20
Due from Customers.....	20,144.14	Due to Publications......	15,779.12
Due from Publications [unused space]........	1,125.10	Dauchy & Co. [another agency from which Ayer bought space].........	4,622.54
Printing Dept...........	2,417.82	Bills Payable...........	841.01
F. W. Ayer (Sunday School account)..............	225.88	N. W. Ayer.............	5,137.83
Bills Receivable.........	7,083.76	F. W. Ayer.............	5,266.44
	$33,095.14		$33,095.14

SOURCE: Balance Account, Ledger 1 (1870–73).

From the ledger cash accounts it is clear that, until the 'nineties, the Ayer firm's cash balance frequently ran low, partly at least because it was extending long credits to customers both on current

TABLE 25

BALANCE SHEET, DECEMBER 31, 1874

Assets		Liabilities	
Cash...................	$ 2,428.27	Sundry Accounts Payable.	$23,832.24
Due from Customers.....	40,459.33	Due to *Nat'l Baptist*......	1,333.33
Bills Receivable.........	9,414.08	Due to *Lutheran Observer* .	500.00
Suspended Accounts.....	491.13	Due to Dauchy & Co.....	2,818.89
Stock & Fixtures........	1,860.90	Bills Payable...........	3,000.00
Real Estate............	3,158.77	Net Capital............	26,328.02
	$57,812.48		$57,812.48

SOURCE: Compiled from the accounts in Ledger 2 (1874–75).

accounts and on bills receivable. Thus, the cash balance on Dec. 31, 1873, was down to $90 — doubtless a result of the difficult conditions following the panic of September, 1873. Bills receivable at the time stood at $12,668. The accounts receivable were doubtless five or six times this amount. To some extent, the accounts receivable were offset by accounts payable, and the Ayer firm regularly had bills payable (principally to banks and publishers) outstanding. From the accounts between 1900 and 1925, together with frequent evidence of advances to publishers, it is apparent that advertisers always owed N. W. Ayer & Son from 10 to 35 per cent more than the agency owed to publishers, while bills receivable usually exceeded bills payable and often amounted to three, four, and even five times the bills payable outstanding. This was particularly true in the 'eighties and 'nineties when agencies were expected to help finance the advertising of their customers.[5]

Of the assets and liabilities of the Ayer firm after 1900 by far the two largest items are accounts receivable from clients and accounts payable to publishers. Bills payable rose to a peak of $850,000 in 1917, when the firm was obliged to finance a rapid growth of business while making large purchases of Liberty Bonds. These bills, in contrast with the earlier ones which represented bank loans, were sold in the open market. By 1926, bills payable had dwindled to $50,000 — less than one-fifth the amount of bills receivable outstanding. To conduct its business today, the firm has to maintain a cash balance of $1,000,000 to $2,000,000, depending somewhat upon the season. Occasionally it has had to have much more than the latter figure, especially in financing U. S. Army advertising (see page 185 above).

When the new building was erected, in 1927–29, the Ayer firm financed a large part of the expense by a mortgage of $1,200,000. Despite the lean years after 1930, payments on the principal of the mortgage were made at double the rate mentioned in the terms of the indenture. By April, 1939, the mortgage had been reduced to $500,000.[6] As indicated earlier, the building was subsequently sold, thereby eliminating a heavy fixed investment.

While no detailed information has been released regarding the Ayer working capital, N. W. Ayer & Son has always held the highest credit rating with publishers and with mercantile agencies. It is clear, moreover, that the assets on the agency's books, before Fry's death, did not give an adequate picture of the firm's financial strength. In any case of need Ayer's ample personal fortune was available, together with the support which his banking interests gave. After the incorporation of N. W. Ayer & Son, the personal liability of the partners for obligations of the agency, of course, came to an end. But it was still true that the fortune which Ayer had left to his daughter and son-in-law stood as a bulwark to the firm's very solid financial structure.

Actually the business as such is financially stronger today than at any time in its history. The cash on hand is substantially greater than it ever was in Fry's administration, and the ratio of current assets to current liabilities now is maintained at more than four to one, whereas it was around two to one in the 1920's. The net worth of the business has increased more than 100 per cent over what it was at the time of incorporation, in spite of the fact that the company purchased and retired $4,000,000 worth of its own stock and substantial amounts in dividends and bonuses have been paid out in recent years. The net worth of each share of stock, owing to the increase in net worth and sharp reduction in number of shares outstanding, is now (1948) more than twelve times greater than it was at the time of incorporation in 1929. Unquestionably the period of advertising prosperity since 1941 has been a factor in the firm's current financial strength, but it owes much to conservative management since 1936.

This strong financial position is reflected in Table 26 where we have a recent (1948) consolidated balance sheet for N. W. Ayer & Son, Inc. That balance sheet is startling for the fact that the original investment of $250 has, in eighty years, grown nearly twenty-thousand fold to $4,638,000, all out of earnings reinvested in the business. It is surprising also because it shows a highly liquid position with a current ratio of 4.85. The investments consist mainly of government bonds and are highly liquid, too. The current liabilities involve mainly the amounts due to publishers and broadcasting companies, while the long-term liability refers to the amount still owing to the Fry estate. This could be paid out of cash without embarrassment, but since it is at a low rate of interest, the Ayer management prefers to discharge it in minimum payments and maintain a strong cash position. This is particularly desirable at the present time because the rapidly expanding volume of billings will, if continued, increase the firm's capital requirements.[7]

This admittedly brief and fragmentary review of Ayer financial operations and resources is offered on the ground that a little information is better than none at all. Its purpose is to give some

TABLE 26

Consolidated Statement of N. W. Ayer & Son, Inc., and Subsidiaries
January 1, 1948

Assets		Liabilities	
Current..............	$4,762,340.43	Current..............	$ 977,414.95
Investments..........	1,246,718.70	Long Term Liabilities..	437,069.95
Fixed................	154,821.02	Deferred Credit (Prepaid Advtg.)........	182,499.96
Deferred Charges.....	71,489.37	Capital & Surplus.....	4,638,384.66
	$6,235,369.52		$6,235,369.52

Source: Treasurer of N. W. Ayer & Son, Inc.

indication of the kind of material which a well-rounded history of a firm ought to contain.

Position of N. W. Ayer & Son in the Industry

It is interesting to compare the size of N. W. Ayer & Son's business with that of other prominent agencies. Since all agencies guard very carefully the exact figures concerning their current business, such a comparison cannot be precise; but enough data are available to indicate the Ayer agency's relative position in a general way. Until 1900 the four largest advertising agencies, according to most observers, were N. W. Ayer & Son, Lord & Thomas, of Chicago, J. Walter Thompson, of New York, and George P. Rowell, of New York. In 1882 N. W. Ayer & Son claimed first place in volume of business handled,[8] a claim which apparently Rowell alone was willing to challenge, and in 1894

Rowell himself credited Ayer with having the largest agency in the country.[9] Ayer's priority was also confirmed by the publisher of the *Ohio Farmer* and the *Michigan Farmer* in 1898,[10] though this claim was based upon the publisher's own experience and cannot be taken as conclusive for the industry as a whole.

Rowell's agency declined rapidly in the late 'nineties, and the race for first place then seems to have been between Lord & Thomas, J. Walter Thompson, and N. W. Ayer & Son. In 1906 the Lord & Thomas agency claimed that its annual business was $4,000,000.[11] Evidently it was about the same size as Ayer's. N. W. Ayer & Son had passed the four-million mark as early as 1903; and, while its volume for 1905 had been only $3,546,000, it was above $4,000,000 again in 1906 when the Lord & Thomas claim was made. Even if the latter is accepted at face value (most agencies of the early period were prone to exaggerate their billings), it is evident that the Lord & Thomas agency was no larger than N. W. Ayer & Son.

The next available comparison is the record of business placed by various agencies with the Curtis Publishing Company in 1910 and subsequent years. Between 1910 and 1912 Lord & Thomas ranked first in volume placed with Curtis publications, and Ayer second. In 1913 and 1914 both Lord & Thomas and the George Batten Company ranked ahead of Ayer, but in 1915 Ayer again held second place.[12] This is hardly conclusive evidence, however, for in 1915 Ayer ranked first in the volume of business placed in *Good Housekeeping,* a position which the firm held regularly until 1927, when J. Walter Thompson took the lead and left N. W. Ayer & Son in second place.[13] Ayer placed more business in *System* in 1921 than any other agency,[14] ranked second in Associated Business Publications in 1923 and first in 1924.[15] While the amount of business placed in any one publication or group of publications does not prove the point, the fragments of evidence gathered indicate that N. W. Ayer & Son was still among the largest agencies in the period 1910–24; also, its chief rivals for first place in size were still Lord & Thomas and J. Walter Thompson. Of the agencies doing business in 1930 the best information available indicates that only six had a volume of business exceed-

ing $20,000,000 for the year, the typical agency having annual
billings of between $250,000 and $500,000.[16] N. W. Ayer & Son
was, of course, one of the six.

Since 1930 no reliable information has been available as to the
relative size of agencies. For some years the J. Walter Thompson
agency, which has a substantial amount of foreign business, has
been generally credited with first place, with Young & Rubicam
(an Ayer offshoot) rivaling Ayer for second place, Batten, Barton,
Durstine & Osborn running fourth, and Foote, Cone & Belding
(formerly Lord & Thomas) in fifth place. The exact amount of
billings for each agency is still a closely guarded secret, and the
figures published by *Fortune* and *Advertising Age* are guesses at
best. The Ayer agency has, like many others, repeatedly refused
to divulge current figures because it feels they would be misused
or misrepresented, and it sees no particular benefit to be derived
from disclosure. It has, however, offered to make audited figures
available provided other agencies will do likewise. It is not afraid
of the facts, but it wants to be sure that its own figures, properly
verified, are not compared with inflated or noncomparable data
concerning other agencies. Certainly in this book the Ayer management has gone further than any other agency to make its internal operations a matter of public record.

Some indication of the Ayer firm's importance to the advertising
industry up to 1929 may be gained by comparing the volume
handled by N. W. Ayer & Son with the total advertising done in
the country as revealed by the United States Census reports
(see Table 27). Considering the fact that there were more than
one thousand advertising agencies in the country,[17] it is apparent
that the Ayer firm has been one of the most important factors in
the industry.

Development of the Ayer Accounting System

The purpose of this section is to trace some of the developments of accounting practice and procedure in N. W. Ayer & Son.
It has been prepared for those readers who are especially interested in the details of accounting practice, as well as to round
out the survey of the principal aspects of Ayer development. If

the general reader finds the material somewhat technical, he may, without losing much of the main story, skip to the section on accounting policy which follows.

We can never know exactly what the system of recording was during the early months of N. W. Ayer & Son. There is no ledger covering the first year of business, and all the books of original

TABLE 27

RELATION OF AYER VOLUME TO TOTAL ADVERTISING IN THE
UNITED STATES, 1880–1929

Year	Volume of Advertising in the United States	Ayer Volume in Relation to Total (%)
1880	$ 39,136,306	.94
1890	71,243,361	1.77
1900	95,861,127	1.44
1905	145,517,591	2.44
1909	202,527,925	2.11
1914	255,412,144	1.91
1919	528,299,378	2.41
1921	676,986,710	1.67
1923	793,803,469	1.45
1925	923,272,673	1.85
1927	1,030,221,019	2.76
1929	1,120,238,395	2.91

SOURCE: The total volume for the United States, used here, represents the figures given in the Census of Manufactures for advertising in magazines and periodicals plus, in 1927 and 1929, the volume of broadcast advertising over the National Broadcasting network, as reported in *National Advertising Records*. Until 1927 the amount of advertising broadcast by N. W. Ayer & Son did not constitute an important part of its volume, nor was the broadcast advertising in the country generally large enough to affect the comparison.

entry before 1900 have been destroyed, save a portion of the general journal for 1878. It is possible, however, to determine the general nature of the missing records from the ledgers which remain. The first ledger extant contains a few accounts dating from the fall of 1869 (the first entry in John Wanamaker's account was dated September 27, 1869), but most of the transactions recorded belong to 1870 and 1871. Since many balances are "brought forward from the old Ledger," it is more than likely that only one ledger had been used previously. The surviving record was labeled "Ledger 1," probably for the reason that it was opened about the time that F. W. Ayer turned over this part of his work to a regular bookkeeper and the bookkeeping was put on a more formal basis.

Ledger 1 was a general ledger containing all the accounts of the business. Although the corresponding journal is missing, it is evident from the manner in which entries were indexed that only one journal (referred to as the "Day Book") was used as a book of original entry. All transactions, regardless of size or frequency, were entered in the Day Book, and postings were made in the usual manner directly to the general ledger which contained all the accounts of the business. In addition, there were doubtless memorandum books and records of invoices, contracts, and so forth; but evidence as to their existence is lacking. The usual first special journal, the Cash Book, had not yet appeared in the Ayer system. The various accounts kept in Ledger 1 were:

Assets	*Liabilities and Capital*
Cash	Accounts with Media
Accounts with Customers	Accounts with Supply Houses, etc.
Bills Receivable	Bills Payable
Printing Dept. (mixed)	
	N. W. Ayer
	F. W. Ayer
	F. W. Ayer's Church Account
	Balance (annual)
Expense	*Income*
Expenses	Discount
George O. Wallace	Interest
	Profit and Loss (current)

F. W. Ayer's Church account was not properly an account which belonged on the agency books, as has already been pointed out. The Profit and Loss account was handled in a special way. The ordinary transaction of the agency involved a charge to a customer and a credit to a publication for space bought for advertising. The difference between the amount so charged and credited was applied directly to the Profit and Loss account, thus:[18]

100	Stephen F. Whitman.....................	20.00	
1	National Baptist.......................		15.00
150	Profit & Loss..........................		5.00
	To adv. 1 Column 2 times in N.B.		
	payable in trade		

At the end of the year 1871 the Expense account was closed into
the Profit and Loss account, and the remaining balance distributed to the proprietorship accounts. There is no evidence that a
trial balance was taken. At the end of 1872, however, a balance
account was used showing in detail the balance of each account
in the Ledger.

The list of accounts given above reflects a small business in
which relatively few types of transactions occur and in which
little attempt is made to analyze financial operations. It provided
as much information, however, as was needed by the proprietors,
who were necessarily familiar with all details of the business. The
system made no provision for internal check: all the bookkeeping
work was done by one person, and there was apparently no separate accounting for petty cash.

So simple a system could not long survive in an advertising
agency where the number of transactions involved in dealing with
hundreds of newspapers made it almost physically impossible to
keep the books up to date when postings had to be made individually. The introduction of a cash book in 1875 cut down the
burden of posting considerably by allowing summary postings to
cash at the end of each week, but the first development which
recognized the peculiar needs of the business was that of Debit
and Credit Journals in July, 1877. By that time the number of
publications with which the agency was dealing had grown from
the original eleven in 1869 to over a thousand, and the number
of customers had also increased considerably. The method of
applying profit and loss, described above, became too cumber-
some, and special journals were introduced to reduce labor. An
account was set up in the General Ledger entitled "Advertising."
Charges to customers for space in media were made through the

Debit Book from which individual postings were made to the customers' accounts and the corresponding credits were made *in summary* to the Advertising account. In the same way, credits to publishers for space bought were entered in the Credit Book from which postings were made individually to the publishers' account and the corresponding debits posted in summary to the Advertising account. By this means the profit on space transactions was accumulated in the Advertising account, which in turn was closed into the Profit and Loss account at the end of the accounting period. The introduction of the Advertising account had the added advantage of separating advertising income from income yielded by other sources.

At the same time (1877), accounts with publishers were taken out of the General Ledger and put into a separate record called the "Newspaper Ledger." This first split in the General Ledger came as a result of the increasing number of accounts with publications, which made a single ledger too bulky for convenient handling. The change was probably accompanied by specialization among the bookkeepers; with the introduction of the special journals and the subdivision of the ledger it became possible for several persons to work on the books at the same time. No evidence on this point has survived.

The newspaper ledgers are analogous to the special purchase ledgers of the usual business enterprise, for in them were recorded the purchases of space bought by the agency for its customers. This brings out one phase of the advertising agency business worth noting. Most business concerns make purchases from a few sources and sell to a large number of customers, and in the accounting system of such firms the customer's accounts are normally the first to be segregated in a special ledger. An advertising agency, in contrast, often buys space in over a thousand papers for a single customer. To record the numerous transactions with a host of publications requires a large amount of space, and it was for this reason that the Ayer newspaper accounts were the first to be segregated. It should be noticed, however, that no control account was set up in the General Ledger. Consequently neither ledger could be balanced separately; the new ledger was not regarded as a subsidiary record. This fact and the close supervision by the partners comprised the only internal check to be found in the accounting system.

The subsequent ledger development may be outlined in summary form. In 1880 the General Ledger was again divided into the Personal Ledger and the Firm Ledger. The Personal Ledger contained all accounts with customers, together with those of the firms (apart from publishers) from which the agency made purchases. The Firm Ledger contained principally internal agency accounts, as follows (1880–84):

Partners' Capital Accounts
Partners' Personal Accounts
Bills Payable
Bills Receivable
Cash
Expense (general)
Stamps (after 1881 this was "Expense a/c Correspondence")
Traveling Expense
Salaries & Wages
Advertising (a transfer account)
Business Advertising (expense)
Interest (mixed income and expense)
Furniture & Fixtures
Printing Department (capital account)
Real Estate (several capital accounts)
Merchandise (transactions in printers' supplies and goods accepted
    from customers in lieu of cash)
Stock (stationery & supplies)
Newspaper Annual
Ayer & Son's Manual
Shrinkage[19]
Contingent
Suspended Account
Donations
Several investment and loan accounts
Building (expense)
Due Bills

In 1900 the Firm Ledger was divided into the Private Ledger (with its own Private Journal), which contained the partners' capital and personal accounts, and the General Ledger, which contained the principal current income and expense accounts. As with the Newspaper and the Personal Ledgers, no control accounts were established when the Private and General Ledgers were introduced. Only by taking the totals of all the accounts in all the ledgers could the books be brought into balance. The only subsequent change in the ledgers was the division of the Personal Ledger alphabetically, the transfer of publishers' accounts from bound volumes to a card-index system in 1913, and the addition, in 1917, of a special ledger for the *Newspaper Annual*.

The division of accounts between the Private and the General Ledgers is clearly evident from the following list of accounts contained in each (partially summarized) in 1904:

Private Ledger Accounts, 1904

Partners' Capital Accounts

F. W. Ayer
H. N. McKinney
A. G. Bradford
J. A. Wood

Partners' Personal Accounts

F. W. Ayer
H. N. McKinney
A. G. Bradford
J. A. Wood

Keystone Type Foundry

Keystone Type Foundry — Partnership
      "   "   "   — Investment
      "   "   "   — Bills Receivable
Bills Receivable
Loan Accounts
Interest on borrowed money
Interest & Discount (revenue)
Suspended Accounts
Life Insurance
Loss & Gain
Contingent Account

Shrinkage
Furniture & Fixtures — Times Bldg.
  "   " — Mariner & Merchant
  "   " — Printing Dept.
  "   " — New York Office

Real Estate

Accounts for Individual Pieces of Property
Mortgages
Investments

GENERAL LEDGER ACCOUNTS, 1904

Cash
Cash — New York Office
Stamp Account
Bills Receivable
Advertisers' Preliminary Account
Furniture, Fixtures — New York Office
Fire Insurance (Unearned)
Bills Payable
Sundry Artists & Engravers
Sundry Accounts Payable
Pay Roll General
Pay Roll Office
Income & Expense — on Real Estate Holdings
Personal Accounts with Employees

Service Revenue

Commission Advertising
  "   Increases
  "   Cancellations
  "   Reductions
Fixed Price Advertising
  " " Increases
  " " Cancellations
  " " Reductions
Outdoor Advertising Increases
  "   " Cancellations
  "   " Reductions
Estimate Expense
Outdoor Advertising Expense

Loss and Gain

Newspaper Annual
Suspended Accounts   Current
Electrotypes
Drawing & Engraving
Printing Department Expense
      "   "   Stock
Current Loss & Gain
Blunder Account
Cash Difference
Interest and Discount

Business Obtaining

Soliciting Department
New York Office Expense
Traveling Expense
Executive Expense (Current)
Traveling Expense of Individual Representatives

Business Operating with Advertisers

Business Department
Copy and Design Department

Business Operating with Newspapers

Forwarding Department

Business Administration & Maintenance

Registry & Filing Department
Business Advertising Department
General Accounting
Business Department Accounting
Forwarding Department

General Expenses

Business Advertising
Office Building
Stationery
Sundry Expense & Supplies
Collection & Legal Expense
Calendar
Ayer & Son's Manual [this had ceased to be a source of income]

Donations
Telephone Expense
Keystone Type Foundry Sales Expense
Fire Insurance (Earned)

The subsequent General and Private Ledgers show only very minor changes in the accounts used. It is particularly noteworthy that the classification of expenses in 1926 was essentially the same as that for 1904.

In contrast with the comparatively simple development of the Ayer ledgers, the firm's records of original entry have undergone expansion and specialization to a notable extent. The first change, as we have seen, was the division of the Day Book into the General Journal and the Cash Book in 1875, followed by the Debit and Credit Books in 1877. In 1880 a new special journal, the Merchandise Journal, was introduced for entering all transactions concerning the purchase, sale, or exchange of printers' supplies and other goods handled by the Ayer firm in connection with the buying and selling of space. About 1900, long after the agency had ceased to trade directly in such materials, the Merchandise Journal became the Credit Transfers Journal, used in clearing accounts between N. W. Ayer & Son (which bought space from the publishers) and the Keystone Type Foundry which sold type and other printers' goods to them. It is evident from the ledger posting marks that a Day Book was used after 1880, in addition to the General Journal, but the nature of its entries is not known.

Between 1880 and 1895 N. W. Ayer & Son added a Publishers' Cash Book in order to simplify and segregate the recording of the largest group of disbursements made by the firm. In this journal the debits were posted individually to the publishers' accounts, and the offsetting credits were handled by summary postings, the total of the cash discounts going to the discount account in the Firm (later the General) Ledger, while the total cash credits were transferred to the General Cash Book instead of being credited directly to the ledger cash account. There being no separate cash account in the Private Ledger which was added in 1900, the cash transactions in the Private Journal and Ledger were put through the General Cash Book exactly as were those from the Publishers' Cash Book. By 1901 a Check Register was being kept along with the two cash journals, possibly in order to have in one book a chronological record of disbursements which were going through two separate records of original entry.

By 1900 the agency was also using a Petty Cash Book and a Petty Cash Fund. Previously all payments except those to publishers had been entered, regardless of size, in the General Cash Book. After the Petty Cash Book had been introduced, the small disbursements were entered in it, and the total was posted periodically to the Cash Book, so as to be included in the summary credit to the cash account. Later (1913), when the firm began to use vouchers as a basis for journal entries, the petty disbursements were returned to the General Cash Book and entered in a special column headed "Cash Drawer." As the agency's business grew, the volume of receipts presently made a Customers' Cash Book necessary (1920). This was used much as the Publishers' Cash Book: credits were posted to individual customers' accounts, while the debits were collected and posted in summary, this time directly to the cash accounts.

About 1900 another special journal was introduced for the recording of sundry accounts payable to all creditors except publishers, under the title of "Sundry Accounts Payable Record." This corresponded to the invoice register often used by business concerns, except for the fact that the principal stock in trade of the company, advertising space, was not recorded in it. Debits were distributed to columns headed by various account classifications, with both a personal ledger and a general ledger column for miscellaneous debits. These last two columns were posted in detail and the rest in summary. The total credit was posted to the account headed "Sundry Accounts Payable" which was set up in the Personal Ledger. Space was also provided to show settlement. Since no accounts were kept with many such creditors, this journal served also as a ledger for these accounts. By 1913 the form had been changed slightly by cutting down the number of columns and showing settlement only through the offsetting debit to Accounts Payable in the Cash Book.

The transactions which presented the greatest difficulties in handling were those which were the peculiar function of an advertising agency, the purchase on behalf of a customer of advertising space, drawings, engravings, and electrotypes. The difficulty arose partly from the commission method by which the agency received its compensation. On behalf of any one customer the agency would deal with many publishers, artists, and engravers; on the other hand, it would be dealing with any one publisher or engraver on behalf of many clients. Consequently, it was necessary to break down any transaction of this nature into its separate elements, in order to be able to determine the various discounts allowed and the commission to be collected from any one customer. Something more than the ordinary method of recording a purchase was required to facilitate quick and accurate bookkeeping. The Debit and Credit Books, which were introduced in 1877, reduced the bookkeeping labor considerably; however, they did not provide a convenient means of computing the commissions due from open-contract customers. Further, it was advisable to provide records which would show at a glance the net credits to publishers and the charge to the customer of the net cost of space, plus the agency's commission. To this end, the firm in 1892 combined the Debit and Credit Books into one record, with the debits to customers shown in detail on the left-hand page and containing a column for accumulating the credits for summary postings to the Advertising Account; on the right-hand page the credits to publishers were entered in detail, with a column for accumulating the offsetting debits which were periodically posted to the advertising account. By means of this arrangement a customer who wished to check the amounts billed for space and commissions could audit his charges on the agency's books very easily. This feature began to be important in the 'nineties when a number of clients insisted on verifying the net costs to the agency.

To handle the numerous changes in rates and orders after advertising had been placed with publishers, the Ayer firm had, by 1893, instituted another group of special journals similar to the Debit and Credit record: one for cancellations, one for revisions of the customer's order, and a third for rate increases and reductions by publishers. (None of these journals has survived to indicate their exact form.)

In 1900 the system of entering transactions was changed to the one used up to 1937. In place of the Debit and Credit Book which had been written up by hand, a loose-leaf printed form was devised, called a Debit and Credit Sheet, which could be filled out on a typewriter. (The Ayer firm began to use a number of loose-leaf records at this time.) As soon as a client had approved a schedule of advertising, the Business Department made out a Debit and Credit Sheet for his order. At the top appeared the name of the client, the product advertised, and other essential information; below were itemized the papers in which the advertising was to appear, together with specifications as to the amount of space, position, number of insertions, and other instructions, for each publication. The blank then went to the Forwarding Department (later Media-Contract) where, in the extension spaces provided, clerks entered the gross price for each paper, the amount of the agency and cash discounts, and the net credit to the publishers. For open-contract orders the net prices for all papers were totaled and the Ayer commission added, to arrive at the charge to the client. For fixed-price advertising the charge was the sum of the gross prices.

After the Forwarding Department had issued formal orders to the publications concerned, the "D & C" form was sent to the Accounts Department. There, as soon as the checking records showed that the orders had been fulfilled properly, the debits to customers and credits to publishers were posted in detail. The offsetting credits and debits were summarized on recapitulation sheets and posted in total to one of the following nominal accounts in the General Ledger: Commission Advertising, Fixed-Price Advertising, and (from D & C sheets for outdoor placing) Outdoor Advertising. These accounts were, of course, a breakdown of the one Advertising account set up in 1877. After the postings had been made, the D & C sheets were bound and filed for reference. Similar sheets were used to record cancellations, revisions, and rate changes.

The new arrangement improved accuracy because both customers' and publishers' ledgers were posted from the same original record. It made recording easier because the journal record could be typed and the sheets for each client could be handled separately until bound. Lastly, it facilitated auditing by open-contract clients, for the same sheet or series of sheets showed both the charges to their accounts and the credits to publishers. Moreover, it enabled each client to audit his accounts on the Ayer books without seeing the accounts of other Ayer clients, since separate sheets were used for each client both in the D & C journal and in the ledger.

By 1900 the Ayer agency had also developed special journals for recording the purchases of drawings, engravings, and electrotypes. One of these was the Drawings and Engravings Record, through which credits were made to the firms supplying the materials and debits were made to the Ayer customers. The difficulty was that each engraver's bill contained many small items which had to be allocated to the accounts of many different customers. To these separate charges the agency had to add its commission. In order to simplify work and segregate the income from this source, the following procedure was followed. Upon the receipt of an engraver's or artist's bill, an entry was made in the Drawings and Engravings Record in a section headed "Final Record," crediting the total to the particular firm's account in a column headed "Sundry Artists and Engravers." This was posted to the proper account in the Personal Ledger. The items of the bill were then listed as charges to the individual advertisers concerned in a section headed "First Disposition"; but, instead of their regular accounts being used, preliminary accounts were set up to which the debits were made. These total debits balanced the credit under "Final Record." As soon as enough charges had been collected in the preliminary account of the advertiser to warrant sending a bill (the individual charges were usually small), an entry was made in the Drawings and Engravings Record in a final disposition section: the preliminary account was credited for the total net charges, the Drawings and Engravings account in the General Ledger was credited for the amount of the agency's commission to be added in the bill, and the customer's regular account was debited for the sum of the two credits. The preliminary accounts thus tended to clear, while the ledger Drawings and Engravings account showed the agency's revenue from this source. Any items in the engraver's bill which could not be allocated to a particular customer were charged against the Drawings and Engravings account. There was also a section on the pages of the Drawings and Engravings Record in which the settlement of artists' and engravers' bills was noted from the Cash Book, so that an examination of the Record quickly showed the bills outstanding against the agency on this account at any time.

Charges for electrotypes were entered in a special journal called "Electro Charges," which was similar in effect to the Drawings and Engravings Record but somewhat simpler to operate since no preliminary accounts were used. Another journal contained the first recording of Bills Receivable.

In addition to these special journals and the ledgers already described, the Ayer firm had a number of auxiliary accounting records, used for balancing ledgers and obtaining operating figures. As already noted, neither the General nor the Private Ledger contained control accounts for the other divisions of the ledger records. To overcome the difficulties raised by this arrangement, whenever it was necessary to balance the books the firm used split-up sheets in a Ledger Postings Record, together with a Trial Balance Book. The Ledger Postings Record was a columnar form in which the various ledgers (Private, General, Newspaper, and Personal) were listed across the top of the page, while down the left-hand side were listed the various journals from which postings were made to the ledgers. The total journal postings for each month were then entered in the Ledger Postings Record as debits or credits in the column of the ledger to which they had been posted. By a totaling of the ledger columns the total of monthly postings to each ledger from all sources was obtained. The balance of debits and credits appearing in each ledger at the beginning of the period was then added, the accounts closed out during the period were subtracted, and the results showed the final balance of debits and credits which should appear in each ledger. A column at the extreme right was used for cross-totaling the journal postings and ledger balances, providing a means of showing that the entire system was in balance.

The Trial Balance Book contained sheets for recording the regular monthly trial balance. The accounts appearing in each ledger were listed down the left side of the page, and their monthly balances were entered in the monthly columns headed up across the page. The totals of these columns gave the debit and credit balances appearing in the ledger. These could then be compared with the figures in the Ledger Postings Record. Thus, the Ledger Postings Record and the trial balance sheets took the place of the ledger control accounts which most business firms use.

Monthly statements as to financial condition were obtained from the "Asset & Liability and Revenue & Expense Book." In this record all the real and nominal accounts were listed from the Private and General Ledgers, together with lines for different groups of accounts payable and receivable from the Personal and Newspaper Ledgers. One set of pages was used for the asset and liability accounts and another for the income and expense accounts. In the first two columns, following the titles of the real accounts, the balance of the debit or credit entries for the month was shown; in the second two columns, the balances for the year to date; and in the third pair of columns, the net assets and liabilities. For the section relating to expense and revenue accounts, the headings of the columns were: Business, Revenue, Expenses, Salaries, Loss, and Gain. The loss or gain appearing in the revenue and expense section agreed with the excess of debits and credits appearing in the corresponding asset and liability section. By means of this record it was possible to follow the results of the firm both by months and by years.

To summarize, the accounting records used by N. W. Ayer & Son in 1900 were as follows:

Records of Original Entry

Blotter ⎫
Day Book ⎬ used for petty cash transactions

Private Journal
General Journal
General Cash Book
Publishers' Cash Book
Debit & Credit Records:
    Commission Advertising
    Fixed Price Advertising
    Outdoor Advertising
    Cancellations
    Revisions
    Increases & Reductions

Drawings and Engravings Record
Electro Charges
Sundry Accounts Payable Record
Bills Receivable Journal
Credit Transfers Journal [formerly Merchandise Journal]
Record of Attendance

Ledgers

Private   Personal
General   Newspaper

Auxiliary Records

Ledger Postings Record
Trial Balance Book
Assets & Liabilities and Revenue & Expense Record

As already indicated, there were no important changes in the Ayer accounting records between 1900 and 1936 save the introduction of the vouchers system of making journal entries in 1913. In essentials the records used in 1936 were almost identical, in both form and manner of use, to those of 1900. Even the establishment of branches made no essential change. All the important accounting functions continued to be handled in Philadelphia. The only bookkeeping done in the branch offices (except the ones in foreign countries) was for the petty cash transactions which were reported monthly to headquarters.[20]

In 1937 a number of modifications were introduced, both in the accounting system and in the classification of accounts. The D & C method of summarizing charges for customers was abandoned, and a single-order plan was substituted which made the work of the billing division much more simple and flexible. The D & C sheet had covered the entire approved schedule of a client's advertising, often for a period in excess of a year. Revisions in plans were commonly necessary, and consequently a great deal of time and effort had to be spent in correcting the D & C records and ascertaining the proper charges to clients. Under the new plan the basis of accounting entries was a duplicate of the actual order sent to each publication for one insertion or a short series of insertions. The principle of the D & C record was retained, but the record itself was eliminated and with it the countless corrections which were a part of the old system. Moreover, a great deal of order-copying was eliminated, thereby saving time and expense and removing a source of errors.

About the same time, the general accounts were combined in one ledger with adequate control over the usual customary subsidiary ledgers and records. In addition, a new classification of accounts was installed in order to provide the management with more useful information, as well as to facilitate the preparation of the numerous reports required by federal, State, and other governmental divisions for tax and statistical purposes.

ACCOUNTING POLICY OF N. W. AYER & SON

With the development of appropriate accounting records and technique, the Ayer firm evolved a number of accounting policies which are of interest. One of the most important of these relates to the classification of accounts. At first there was little attempt to segregate different sources of income or expense, the important thing being to earn a profit from the business as a whole. As we have seen, however (pages 31–33), Ayer did keep books in such a way that he could determine whether his advertising concessions in religious papers yielded a profit beyond the usual agency commission. Later accounts were set up in order to show separately the gross revenues from advertising, trade in merchandise, the *Annual*, the *Manual*, and interest. On the cost side, the breakdown (until 1900) was by type of expense (wages, traveling expense, et cetera) and not by department or customer. It is important to note that only certain direct expenses were considered in arriving at the profit from the various sources listed. Such items as salaries and wages, rent, and general overhead were not charged against the *Annual* or the *Manual*, and hence the profits shown for them gave only a limited clue as to net results.

In 1900 the Ayer firm began to classify income as to revenue derived from commission, fixed-price, and outdoor advertising, drawings and engravings, electrotypes, and the *Annual*. It also began to allocate direct expenses among the respective departments of the business, but no attempt was made to apportion the general overhead expenses among the various divisions. To this day, little effort has been made to determine accurately the cost

of maintaining various divisions of agency service. The exceptions
are in those departments where work may be done which is directly chargeable to customers. Thus, in the Printing Department
the standard Typothetae cost system is applied, and printing
charges are determined for each job according to approved modern practice. In most other divisions, as we have seen, the principal expense is wages and salaries, and the management feels that
it would not be feasible to allocate them among individual clients.

One change in the method of calculating revenue (referred to
in footnote c, Table 15) calls for comment. Orders for advertising
are, of course, placed with media owners well in advance of publication. Since such orders are subject to revision or cancellation,
they are not true assets to the agency until the advertising has
appeared. Until 1915, however, the Ayer accounts treated all
revenue on the basis of business booked, rather than on the
amounts actually billed to customers. If in any month an unusually large volume of orders was placed to run in future months,
the revenue for that month would, as a result, be overstated. To
some extent the bookings would average out over the years, each
month getting the benefit of business to be placed in the future;
but the difference between billings and bookings was often large.
In 1915 the system was altered somewhat to show the volume of
advertising actually billed each month, instead of the volume of
orders sent out. Thereafter, the monthly statement contained a
notation of unearned commissions.

Nearly all the direct expenses have been handled on an accrual
basis since 1900 for the purpose of yearly statements, but not
until recently were such items as depreciation, taxes, and interest
accrued on a monthly basis. The practice of taking regular depreciation was slow in developing. No charge at all was made on this
account until the end of 1880, when Furniture and Fixtures were
written down from $4,946.44 to an even $3,000 and 10 per cent
was charged against the printing-office equipment. In the following year Furniture and Fixtures were written down by $666.95 to
$3,300; but no other write-offs were made until in 1887 and 1888
when both the Furniture and Fixtures account and that for the
printing equipment were written down more than 10 per cent each
year to round sums. No charges were made in 1889 or 1890; be-

tween 1891 and 1896 the firm wrote off the Furniture and Fixtures account 10 per cent annually. In the same period the Printing Department account was not handled in this uniform fashion; in 1891, 1893, and 1894 approximately 10 per cent was charged off, but no depreciation was taken in 1892 or 1895, and in 1896 the amount written off was $400 against $10,396.76, or slightly less than 4 per cent. In general, the firm has taken depreciation regularly since the late 'nineties; but, instead of creating a reserve, it has charged the amount written off directly to Profit and Loss and credited it directly to the property accounts. The depreciation so taken during the 1920's was approximately two and one-half times the governmental allowance for income-tax purposes. Since the incorporation of the firm in 1929 the maximum rates allowed by the government have been used by the firm in calculating its operating results.

The method of handling bad debts has been similar to that for depreciation. Losses from bad debts having been small, the Ayer agency has never had a reserve for loss on receivables; but it has used a procedure which gives much the same effect. Beginning in 1874, the firm transferred to an account entitled "Suspended Accounts" all accounts receivable which were judged to be uncollectible. These were reviewed from time to time and a portion written off to profit and loss. Thus, at the end of 1878, accounts to the amount of $3,041.78 were transferred to Suspended Accounts. Of the accounts already so transferred, eleven were written down 50 per cent and six were written off entirely, with a charge to profit and loss of $1,312.87. Any payments received on these items were credited to Suspended Accounts. Apparently the review of doubtful accounts was made annually for many years; but since 1921, at least, the revaluation has been made more frequently. According to the treasurer, the realization on suspended accounts between 1921 and 1932 was at least 5 per cent above the adjusted value, indicating conservative evaluation.

The only reserve carried on the Ayer books is the contingent account which is used for general protection against stringency. It first appeared in 1882 when $25,000 was set aside; the purpose of this reserve was not recorded. Two years later the sum was distributed to the partners' accounts without having been used at all. No further reserves were set up until 1900; since that year there has always been a contingent reserve.

It is clear that the Ayer firm has been conservative in valuing its assets and in determining its profit as a whole. It is equally clear that for the past sixty years the chief emphasis of the Ayer accounting procedure has been upon strict accuracy in recording the various purchases of space and material on behalf of individual clients. The books have been designed to record disbursements in detail; and all entries, for at least the past fifty years, have been checked by two or more persons to increase accuracy.

Since about 1890, moreover, N. W. Ayer & Son has allowed clients to audit their own accounts on the Ayer books, even to the extent of reviewing canceled checks to publishers in order to verify the charges for space. This unusual emphasis upon the strict mathematical accuracy of accounts with clients is, of course, closely related to the open-contract policy. Every business concern strives to avoid errors in charges to customers, but in most transactions it is merely a question of recording the sale price. In the Ayer firm the matter is more complicated and the correctness of charges is much more important. Since N. W. Ayer & Son receives a commission on expenditures for clients, it loses both out-of-pocket expenses and its revenue upon them if any disbursement for space or materials is not assigned to the accounts of individual clients. The Ayer selling price, in short, cannot be determined until the expenditures have been made and recorded. Moreover, the Ayer agency, by its open-contract arrangement, stands in a fiduciary relation to clients; and, if a client should discover any error in the agency's charges, his confidence in the firm is likely to be shaken. He may decide that, if the agency is not to be trusted in accounting for expenditures, it is not to be trusted in other respects. The abandonment of the cost-plus arrangement for commissionable media has made no difference in this respect, for there are still substantial expenditures on the client's behalf for which the agency charges a commission on the net cost (mainly art work, printing, and radio talent). Realizing all this, the Ayer management has placed unusual stress upon correct charges to clients. By so doing it has won an enviable reputation for integrity and honesty.

The concern of the Ayer firm over the accuracy of its billings to clients seems to have diverted its attention away from a close analysis of the cost of its own internal operations. In general, the management has been content with knowing the principal sources of revenue and expense, without analyzing them in much detail. It has attempted to keep expenses down, of course, but it has generally thought of expenses in the aggregate rather than particular items in relation to the revenue they produce. Thus, as already pointed out, most of the indirect and overhead expenses were omitted from the calculation of revenue from the *Newspaper Annual* and the transactions in printers' supplies. More important still, the firm has never calculated the cost of soliciting a prospective client against the probable value of the business in terms of net gain. Nor has the firm ever related all the costs of handling a particular client's business to the revenue derived from it. Undoubtedly the management has kept such considerations in mind, but its judgments about them have been based upon general observation and estimates rather than recorded facts. The chief control over costs, in short, has been the personal supervision of Ayer and the men who succeeded him in the financial management of the firm.

In 1912, at the time of the general reorganization of the staff and of general procedure, an attempt was made to institute some cost accounting: to break down by departments all the disbursements previously classified as general expense, and to record the time spent by the staff in serving particular clients. The attempt failed, however, partly because the management was unable to obtain the genuine coöperation of the staff and partly because the allocation of overhead seemed so arbitrary and caused so much debate that the results were regarded as not worth the trouble involved. This, of course, is a familiar outcome of first efforts at cost accounting. In most lines of business, notwithstanding, the need for continual elimination of unnecessary expense has been so urgent for competitive reasons that repeated attempts to analyze costs have had to be made until a workable system of cost accounting has been attained. Perhaps the most surprising aspect of Ayer accounting development is the fact that no material change was made in the classification of expenses between 1900 and 1936. This failure to press further the analysis of costs is fairly clear evidence that the firm had not kept abreast with the general development of accounting technique, but this was apparently true of competing firms as well.

In the advertising agency business generally there has been little attempt to ascertain the cost of serving individual clients, even in recent years.[21] Some observers have regarded this fact as evidence that agency profits were large enough to make close control over costs unnecessary. It is fairly clear, however, that agencies do not make unusually large net earnings, and a more plausible explanation seems to be that agency executives have been creative advertising men for the most part, rather than business managers per se, and that they have had neither the training nor the inclination to devote much attention to the technical aspects of administration. This was not true of F. W. Ayer, but he belonged to the old school of managers who controlled operations and expenses by personal supervision rather than by the systematic analysis of records. Now that agencies like N. W. Ayer & Son have outgrown such personal control, their cost accounting is beginning to receive serious attention.

In connection with cost control, it is significant that the treasurer of N. W. Ayer & Son began to work out, after 1921, a system of summary expense records in order to establish something closely akin to budgetary control. The Ayer business admittedly does not lend itself to a strict budget of expenditures. Because it is dependent upon a few relatively large accounts for most of its volume, the firm is subject to sudden and drastic fluctuations in volume of business arising from the loss or gain of a client. The policy of having a "balanced" clientèle, evolved since 1940 (offsetting large accounts with medium and small-sized accounts), has helped to minimize the effect of the sudden loss of a client, but a certain degree of fluctuation will continue to be inevitable. Estimates of expense naturally would have to undergo constant revision to bring them into proper alignment with the business handled.

The treasurer's system of control in 1934 was as follows: the monthly figures for the direct operating expenses of all departments of the agency were tabulated on a large sheet. One sheet was used for each year. The various departments of the business were listed down the left side. The columns across were for the months of the year, thus making possible a running comparison of the expense of each department from month to month during the current period and previous years. Any increase in expense called for explanation. Obviously, however, this system assumed that past expenses were justified and were not ordinarily subject to revision. The success of its operation, moreover, depended almost entirely upon the judgment and alertness of the treasurer.

One is bound to conclude, I think, that N. W. Ayer & Son was slow in adapting its accounting system to current needs. Indeed, it is hardly an exaggeration to say that the recording of financial transactions in the Ayer firm hardly advanced beyond the bookkeeping stage until 1936 and that accounting, in the sense of the careful analysis and use of the records for purposes of internal financial control, had been used only to a very limited extent by the Ayer management before that time.

This backwardness has harmed no one but the firm itself, for a closer control over internal costs would not affect the prices paid for media or advertising supplies; and, in view of the competitive situation and the attitude of both agencies and media owners toward any material reduction of prices below the gross rates established by the media owners, it is not likely that N. W. Ayer & Son would have reduced its commission, had it been able to cut down its costs of operation. The most probable result of better cost control would have been larger net profits for the Ayer agency itself.

It is significant that early in 1935 the Ayer management, for the first time in the firm's history, arranged to have its own accounts[22] audited by outside accountants with a view to revising the whole system of financial records and control. The changes instituted during 1937 and 1938 were the outcome of that move and stand as concrete evidence that the management is bringing Ayer accounting up to date.

CHAPTER XX

CONCLUSION

ONE aspect of the history of N. W. Ayer & Son has not yet been touched upon. The critical reader is likely to ask, "But what about the general public to whom most advertising is addressed?" The question is a fair one, but the answer for a number of reasons must be incomplete.

N. W. Ayer & Son has not, as a general rule, had any direct relations with the public at large. Like other agencies it has dealt with the public only indirectly, as the purchasers (actual or potential) of the goods and services which its clients have had to sell.[1] To an advertising agency the consuming public constitutes a market to be studied and divided into homogeneous groups or strata, to be made familiar with names and products, to be appealed to by various means, and to be persuaded to act in certain ways.

Of course, it must be said at once that, while agencies do not deal directly with the public, their activities have important effects upon the daily lives of millions of people. But it is scarcely possible to disentangle the influence of advertising from the myriad other influences at work in modern life. Even if it were possible, we should certainly not be able to isolate the particular effects which could fairly be attributed to the Ayer agency as distinct from those which come from the advertising industry as a whole. Moreover, any adequate discussion of the effects of advertising would by itself fill a large volume, and it would of course lead us a considerable distance from the history of N. W. Ayer & Son. It would also require a great deal more evidence than is to be found in the activities of any single firm.

SOME COMMENTS UPON THE DIRECT EFFECTS
OF ADVERTISING

Any final appraisal of the Ayer agency must, however, take some account of the social consequences of its work, and a few comments, though admittedly incomplete, are necessary. The reader must bear in mind that the discussion shifts here from the Ayer agency alone to the industry as a whole. What is true of the one is not necessarily true of the other. And the reader should note that here and elsewhere the word "advertising" really means *advertisers,* for advertising is a tool, not an independent force.

Some of the consequences follow directly from advertising, while others are indirect results. Let us first consider the former. Advertising provides the consumer with information and influences his purchases. If the information is accurate and useful, the consumer is helped in his daily life. If the influence improves the wisdom of his purchases, he is benefited. But it is precisely over these conditions that the debate about advertising becomes heated. Downright falsity presents no difficulty, but literally true information may be seriously incomplete or may be presented in a misleading way, so that it is really deceptive. And what constitutes useful information or wise buying for the individual consumer depends largely upon his individual situation and personal opinions, rather than upon any definite objective criteria. Every intelligent person can recall instances of advertising which, according to widely accepted standards, misrepresented facts or promoted socially undesirable products or led individual consumers to spend money foolishly. But these are instances of the *abuse* of advertising, not inherent characteristics; no one today can determine, even in a rough approximation, whether or not they are relatively numerous. About the only conclusion that we can reach here is the almost useless one that some advertising harms some people and that, on the other hand, some advertising benefits some people. It is, like much of modern technology, an instrument for good or evil, depending on the motives of the one who uses it.

We know that the direct effect is to transfer money from some pockets into others, but the process has not been carefully analyzed. Economists are only beginning to develop carefully considered theories about the economics of advertising — theories which must be tested for their validity before we can accept them.[2]

We should note also that advertising often plays an active part in economic and social change, since it encourages people to do such things as (for example) to add fruit juices to their daily diet, spend a large portion of their income on motor cars, or place a high value upon college education.[3] I use the word "encourages" advisedly, because no evidence exists to indicate that advertising really creates new demands, although it certainly stimulates an awareness of needs — and of answers to those needs. It seems merely to intensify desires that already exist in people's minds. However that may be, the effect upon our culture is undeniable even though it is difficult to analyze and measure. But here again, whether it is to be regarded as detrimental or beneficial depends upon one's personal attitudes and ideology, plus an evaluation of particular advertising. There is no absolute standard by which we can judge it apart from specific uses, which may be misuses.

My own personal conclusion is that advertising, in spite of obvious abuses, is essential to a free modern industrial society. Certainly it is inevitable in any free competitive economic organization in which specialization and large-scale production have created a wide gap between producer and consumer. Failure to sell what the producer makes means social waste and unemployment. Indeed, advertising of one sort or another is a necessary adjunct of mass production, whether in an individualistic or socialistic or totalitarian régime (although much of it may be eliminated under a dictatorship by rationing commodities among the consumers). The employment of advertising by government agencies in Soviet Russia, Great Britain, and the United States provides noteworthy examples of this.[4]

The amount of economic waste which advertising involves is frequently exaggerated. Most of what actually exists is really inherent in competitive enterprise and must be charged against the many very real gains which we have reaped from the competitive system. It is also true that advertising is usually a more economical method of sales promotion than personal solicitation; hence, to the extent that it has supplanted the personal salesman it has benefited society economically.

There has been a considerable waste in advertising which arises not from competitive situations but rather from such sources as ill-conceived campaigns and ineffective advertisements. But this type of waste has been largely the result of inadequate knowledge and faulty technique. In eliminating these the advertising agency of the better type has been one of the most important influences at work. It must be said, too, that some of the shortcomings of the advertising industry have been caused by the failure of economists to provide an adequate background of theory for advertising practice.

Some of the wastes and abuses might be eliminated by wise governmental control, but our ability to provide the right kind of supervision — the kind which will ensure the best interests of society as a whole — is at least doubtful. Men do not automatically become wise or benevolent on entering government service. By the time we have acquired the knowledge necessary to eliminate such wastes, governmental control will probably be made unnecessary by the actions of private enterprise in search of profit through reduction of expense. Still, recent federal legislation has already helped to eliminate some objectionable practices.

I do not want to be understood as approving all the advertising that we have had in the past, or even a very large portion of it. Beyond any question there has been misrepresentation, downright dishonesty, stupidity, indecency, and the lowest kind of vulgarity in advertising. But these qualities, though prevalent in advertising, are not inherent in it or peculiar to it. They are also to be found in literature, drama, classroom lectures, and even in sermons from the pulpit. To a large extent the objectionable qualities of advertising are the fruit of its cross-fertilization by cheap, superficial psychology and sensational journalism — strains which have found their way, unfortunately, into many other aspects of modern life.

Advertising is what men make it. It is a powerful tool both for private profit and for social control. If we use it wisely, it can be a valuable means to economic and social advance.

The consumer is too often ignorant, misguided, and lazy. Left to his own devices, he will not absorb the output of our modern industrial machine. Advertising is one of the forces which increases his "propensity to consume." [5] Modern business can either prey on his weaknesses or help him to produce and consume in the manner most likely to keep our economic machine running somewhere near peak efficiency. The amount of profit which is to be gained by preying upon the consumer is limited, however, while that to be gained by helping him is almost without bounds.

Advertising is one of the influences leading to the opening of new vistas, the pursuit of new interests, and the material enrichment of our daily life. We may eventually decide that we have overvalued Progress — the kind of advance which brings us creature comforts, automobiles, radios, and physical wealth of all kinds — and that we have too often been vainly striving after gilded baubles or have been making life more glamorous but less secure. We may conclude that modern methods of production are hostile to the best artistic impulses of man and that we have been diverted from the pursuit of more satisfying spiritual values. Up to the present, however, we have prized material wealth, we have striven to satisfy many economic wants, and we have been able to attain those ends only by an elaborate division of labor and large-scale methods of production, thereby making necessary a complex system of distribution. We may well eliminate some of the abuses of advertising, but advertising of a kind we must have or else return to small-scale local manufacture.

To some extent the Ayer firm has been conscious of the direct social effect of its work. Witness its decision to refuse the advertising of alcoholic beverages, patent medicines, and other wares which it regards as objectionable from the public point of view. Moreover, in the copy it has prepared, especially since 1905, the Ayer agency has avoided most of the features which have brought advertising into disrepute. In many respects it is unfortunate that advertisements are not labeled to indicate the agency which is responsible for them. If this were done, the public would see that the work of N. W. Ayer & Son is generally on an exceedingly high level. It is probably true that the Ayer agency has not fully considered the social consequences of its activities; but I should hasten to add that the same statement can be made about engineers, politicians, ministers, university professors, and people who write books. Certainly the history of the firm shows very definite progress in this respect.

Some Indirect Effects of Advertising

An agency's activities for its clients affect the public indirectly as well as directly. Our newspapers, magazines, and radio broadcasts are supported mainly by advertising, and both advertisers and agencies have a certain amount of influence upon their content beyond the actual advertising itself. This influence ordinarily takes the form of censoring any material which might injure the advertiser's business. I have found no indication that N. W. Ayer & Son ever exerted pressure to compel a publisher to include any material in his editorial columns that should not have been there, but on numerous occasions it has urged editors to support or oppose legislative enactments which would affect the interests of clients. Such action is inevitable — indeed necessary — under democratic government. So long as it is not accompanied by intimidation, the frank expression of opinion is highly desirable.

While the Ayer agency has never attempted to force the inclusion of material in publications, it has occasionally sought (with some success) to have news items or editorial opinions suppressed. In the early 1900's, when it was handling the advertising of the Standard Oil Company, the National Biscuit Company, and that of other large-scale enterprises then coming into prominence, the Ayer agency had to contend with the current propaganda[6] against large corporations. Naturally, the agency objected to the hostility which a number of publications openly displayed toward these concerns, *after accepting their advertising*. The attitude of the Ayer firm then and today is well indicated in a statement which H. N. McKinney made to a gathering of publishers:[7]

In the handling of the advertising of the American Tobacco Company we have not infrequently been urged by the business department of the newspapers to give them a certain advertisement, and immediately after the advertisement appeared there was inserted either in the editorial or news items a direct attack upon the product thus advertised. I have no

fault to find with the man who conscientiously opposes the use of tobacco in any form, and I am willing to concede that a man may have
such convictions on the subject that he feels it his duty to give them publicity in the columns of his newspaper, but I contend that if this is the
case, the advertising department of the paper ought to refuse to insert
the advertisement. In other words, it is neither fair nor businesslike to
take a man's money for an advertisement and then use the reading columns of the paper to destroy the value of his investment. I have no defense to make of any wrong, nor would I ask any newspaper to suppress
an article of legitimate news; but, on the other hand, there is nothing to
be gained either in morals or business and much to be lost in both by
unjust, unnecessary and untruthful attacks upon reputable advertisers.

Nowadays, publishers are more careful about biting the hand
that feeds them. Agencies do not often have occasion to protest,
but the absence of protests or direct threats does not mean that
advertising has ceased to influence the content and treatment of
the reading matter. The editors have learned to make precaution-
ary expurgations to forestall criticism. Actually the result is seldom very serious. Minor items of news are toned down or ignored,
and problems which ought to be freely discussed are sometimes
soft-pedaled. But no advertiser, regardless of the extent of his
advertising, can suppress or minimize big news.

The influence of advertisers is not by any means the most important one affecting the contents of our newspapers, magazines,
and radio programs. Pressure groups who do not advertise at all —
religious and political organizations, for example — exert restraint
which at times far exceeds anything the most misguided advertiser ever dreamed of creating. The most active, powerful, and
relentless censor of the Press is the reader, and the voice which
ultimately dominates our radio programs is the average listener.[8]
It is very interesting in this connection that in 1929 the Ayer
agency was not permitted to present a radio lecture for one of its
clients on the sociological aspects of venereal disease. The broadcasting company admitted the importance of the subject and the
need for dealing with it, but dared not stir up a loud protest from
listeners.[9]

We must recognize, too, that advertising revenue saves our
Press from the corruption and political control which have long

existed in certain foreign countries, where newspapers are mainly organs of propaganda. All evidence today indicates that what we have to fear is not commercial influence but political pressure. Advertising helps to support our freedom of public utterance.

It is possible that the Ayer agency has actually helped to lessen outside pressure upon editors from one direction. McKinney often said that his hardest task in dealing with the officials of large corporations around 1900 was to persuade them to buy advertising space instead of editorial opinion. They thought only of a paper's editorial or news influence on the public as it related to them. He urged them to secure public patronage and goodwill through the advertising columns, and he succeeded in bringing some of our largest corporations round to his point of view.[10]

One must remember, of course, that in conducting its daily activities the agency helps to make cheap reading matter and free radio programs available to the public.[11] Many of our periodical publications and broadcasts may not be worth having, and it might be wise, in any case, to support them by other means; but certainly few magazines or newspapers could survive without the revenue which advertising provides.[12] But these matters all involve questions of morals or public policy which cannot be considered here; our present concern is merely to note the consequences of a single advertising agency's activities in the past. As said before, it is practically impossible to isolate for analysis the indirect social effects of advertising placed by any given agency. They belong to the industry as a whole, and specifically to the firms which advertise.

Social Value of the Advertising Agency

On the whole, the most important social effect of an agency's work is its influence upon our economic system. The ultimate purpose of advertising (and the business firms which use it) is to assist in the economical exchange of goods and services. Its chief justification, all things considered, is the possibility of lowering the cost of the things we consume by reducing either manufacturing or marketing costs. Critics have emphasized the expense of advertising and have too often ignored the question as to whether other means could perform the same work as cheaply or effectively. If it had not proved its merits in this respect, *when properly used,* advertising would not occupy the important position it holds today.

The advertising agency must, therefore, be judged primarily by its services to advertising and advertisers. As I have shown in the preceding chapters, N. W. Ayer & Son attained its present position of leadership by diligent attention to the needs of its clients. It has always bought space economically, it has been a leader in improving advertising copy, and it has served clients not only by making their advertising effective but also by improving their merchandising and selling arrangements. Above all, it has done notable work in educating business men as to the proper function of advertising; and it has, together with other agencies, contributed one of the most constructive and money-saving procedures to be added to the general marketing process: the collection and analysis of the facts regarding markets, buying habits, and consumer preferences which precede the advertising campaign.

While these services have been performed primarily for the clients of the agency, they have also benefited the general public. Like other business firms, N. W. Ayer & Son has not considered the consumers' interests in the past as much as might have been desirable, but it has been more careful about them than many of its rivals have been. Further, it is becoming conscious of the fact that the best interests of consumers are closely allied to those of its clients. The application of the basic Ayer policy of serving advertisers means that in the future the agency will have to study the needs and desires of the public more carefully than any agency has ever done in the past. There are many practical difficulties in the application of such a policy, but the Ayer firm has made progress in the right direction, especially since 1940.

Rapid Review

N. W. Ayer & Son began in 1869 as the agent of publishers. After attempting to serve both publishers and advertisers, it cut through the confusion which marked the agency business in general and became the avowed agent of the advertiser, with a system of compensation appropriate to the new relation. To its original function of space-buying, the firm gradually added the preparation of advertising copy, the selection of advertising media, the study of markets, the correlation of advertising with other sales efforts, and even the study of products from the point of view of their appeal to the public. It is evident that the Ayer agency has not stood still. It has been steadily evolving into a business unit having a much wider scope of activities and functions than the agency of 1870 or even 1890. It has clearly tended toward the assumption not only of the entire advertising function but also of important parts of the marketing function as a whole. Since 1939 it has expanded into the broader field of public relations, giving counsel to clients on a scale which far exceeds the scope of marketing as such. How far any advertising agency should go in this direction is an open question, but the tendency in N. W. Ayer & Son has been plain for at least seventy years.

N. W. Ayer & Son opened its doors when the agency business was in swaddling clothes. In the face of bitter competition and periods of general economic adversity it forged ahead to a towering position in American commerce. Through its open contract it helped to bring order out of chaos in the advertising industry. It was a pioneer in market research, in the improvement of advertising copy, and in the analysis of advertising media. It was among the leaders not only in the mastery of advertising technique but also in the development of a professional attitude toward its work. By honest, determined, and intelligent efforts to make advertising effective, it has earned the gratitude and respect of advertisers and media owners alike. If it has chosen to play a lone hand rather than coöperate closely with fellow agencies, it has at least offered them a shining example of efficient service and fair competitive practice.

Over the years the firm has gathered together a staff of skilled workers, won their loyalty, and welded them into an effective organization capable of carrying out the policies of the Ayer management. Through careful administration and conservative policies the business was made to earn ample profits for its owners and, at the same time, to acquire great financial strength. It has proved its ability to withstand both harsh adversity and head-turning prosperity. For sixty years it has been one of the two or three largest advertising agencies in the world, and in the quality of its work it has occupied the same high rank. To advertising men generally the name Ayer has long stood for excellence, stability, and strength.

The old adage, "Nothing succeeds like success," may partly explain the success of N. W. Ayer & Son. Sheer luck, too, is a possible factor to be reckoned with. But the Ayer firm has had no monopoly of these beneficent influences. Although Rowell, Pettengill, and several other prominent agents of the nineteenth century enjoyed the impetus of a good start, their businesses have long since disappeared. Fortune smiled on others with no lasting result. Only a handful of today's agencies were founded before 1890. The Ayer agency survives today, as I have already shown, because F. W. Ayer had a genius for wise organization and management and because successors emerged who could make his firm live on as a continuing institution within the organization which he developed. Courage, intelligence, and, above all, a firm adherence to sound policies — these qualities in the Ayer management have enabled it to adjust the business to changing circumstance and to weather all storms.

The success of N. W. Ayer & Son transcends in significance the realm of business alone. This firm and others like it have helped to build the American nation. Many historians have been content to ignore the tremendous achievements of private enterprise; too many of them have focused their attention upon the blots and shadows which mar the record. They have assailed individualism and attacked the profit system without knowing what they condemned. It is time that we studied the whole record of business carefully in a more dispassionate frame of mind. We have allowed abuses to obscure the fundamental services performed by business. Private enterprise works for profit, to be sure; in the majority of cases, however, this system of reward is consistent with the social point of view which we now emphasize.

We have had a continent to settle, great resources to exploit, cities and factories to build, and trade and industry to develop. These ends were accomplished by individual effort, hard work, and intelligence. There was no other way. Given the actual circumstances — our historical background, the multiplicity of interests and opportunities, the growing complexity of economic life, the irrational nature of man, and other unpredictable elements — we could not possibly have achieved what we wanted in any other way. There were wastes and abuses, of course, because human society progresses but slowly, just as Nature has done in the long course of biological evolution — by the tedious and costly process of repeated experiment and adaptation. It is no reflection upon the ultimate merits of social control that we cannot satisfy our everyday wants by regimentation or fiat. We do not yet know enough; and, until we have learned how to organize and motivate people successfully in government enterprise, we must continue to depend largely upon private business to supply our needs.

Whatever views one may have about the future, it is clear that individual firms like N. W. Ayer & Son have done the bulk of our work in the past. It is clear, too, that a few men have supplied the driving force and brains which enabled them to do so successfully. They need no praise or blame, but from their history we may learn much of lasting worth.

APPENDIX

DISTRIBUTION OF AYER ADVERTISING
BY COMMODITIES

IN ORDER to study Ayer clients from the point of view of the products they sell, we have attempted to break down the agency's dollar volume at different periods in its history into amounts spent on selected commodity groups. Some explanation of the principles governing these analyses is desirable. The tables given in the text are for the general reader who is interested only in rough generalizations. The information which follows is for the student who may wish to examine the data in greater detail.

The nature of the available figures presented certain problems at the outset, owing to the difficulty of relating expenditures to particular products. It was utterly impossible to do this for any year before 1877 because, with few exceptions, no records exist to show what products were advertised. Even in 1877 and 1878 more than a quarter of the Ayer volume came from other agents, with the result that, since only the name of the original agent appears on the Ayer books, neither product nor client can now be identified.

For the early period, moreover, only a fraction of the Ayer business came on the open-contract plan, so that there was no assured continuity of advertisers; therefore, the accounts were more likely to shift from one agency to another. Since this might introduce too much variation in any one year to give an accurate cross section of the business in the early period, it seemed advisable to enlarge the sample by analyzing two years, especially in view of the large number of items which could not be identified.

The reader should note that the percentages for 1877 and 1878 are worked out by using as base the totals of the amounts traced rather than the total of the agency's volume of business. Thus for 1877 the total volume was $195,791.75, but the amounts identified with the advertising of particular products total $131,628.30, and this figure was used as the base. To use the larger total as base would not change the order of importance, but it would alter the relative proportions; and the results would then imply that the unidentified sums fell into entirely different categories, which is not likely.

For the years 1900 and 1901 the difference between the total volume and the amounts traced is so small (less than 1 per cent) that either figure could be used. We chose to calculate the percentages with the total volume as the base (these totals differ from those in Table 15 because the analysis here was on the basis of billings, whereas Table 15 shows, until 1915, the total orders booked).

Having studied the data for two years in the early period and for two years in the middle period of the firm's history, we should have been consistent, perhaps, and taken two consecutive years in the recent period — say 1921 and 1922, or 1929 and 1930. It happened, however, that records had been instituted by the treasurer of the firm in 1921 which greatly simplified the work of analyzing the figures for any one year between 1921 and 1930. This influenced us to change our objective slightly so as to study the changes in commodities advertised in the post-World War I decade. To analyze every one of the ten years was out of the question, so we compromised by taking 1921, 1925, and 1930.

The classification of commodities is only approximate and must be taken with caution. Are chemical fertilizers, for example, to be classified under chemicals or agriculture? What is to be done when a single advertiser advertises — sometimes in the same advertisement — products which fall into two separate categories? To look up every single advertisement and calculate its cost so as to make the division accurate even for 1930 alone would have involved colossal labor and expense. For other years it would have been utterly impossible because of the lack of essential records. It was necessary, therefore, to classify the expenditures for each firm according to its principal business. Thus, notwithstanding the fact that flashlights and batteries are really hardware and anti-freeze solutions might well be regarded as automobile accessories, the National Carbon Company's advertising was all classified as chemicals. The advertising of seed companies which also sell fertilizers was put under seeds and nursery stock. We were compelled to make similar arbitrary decisions in dealing with other products. The following data must, therefore, be regarded as suggestive rather than precise.[1]

Sources used for the computations: for 1877 and 1878, Ledgers 3, 4, and 5; for 1900 and 1901, Personal Ledgers 25, 30, 35, and 40; for 1921, 1925, and 1930, records supplied by the treasurer of N. W. Ayer & Son, Inc. A slight discrepancy may be noted between the totals arrived at here and those given in Table 15 for the years 1921 and 1925. This apparently resulted because adjustments and corrections which were made before arriving at the final volume figure were not made in the records supplied for our analysis. Since the difference was less than 3 per cent and considerable trouble and expense would have been involved in reconciling the two sets of figures, without greatly altering the final outcome, we decided against trying to trace the source of the difference. Accordingly, we related percentages to the amount traced rather than the official volume figures for 1925 and 1930.

1877 AND 1878

Commodity Group	1877 Amount	Per-centage[a]	1878 Amount	Per-centage[a]
Patent medicines and treatment...	$ 20,261.42	15.4	$ 48,222.49	26.0
Books, tracts, etc..............	17,474.55	13.3	14,991.40	8.1
Jewelry and silverware..........	18,743.41	14.2	8,680.96	4.7
Greeting cards and chromos......	5,596.32	4.2	19,056.71	10.3
Dry goods and clothing.........	8,941.51	6.8	14,959.11	8.1
Seeds and nursery stock.........	9,602.28	7.3	11,730.92	6.3
Machinery, hardware, and building materials....................	8,441.72	6.4	7,221.06	3.9
Schools and colleges............	5,480.14	4.2	8,238.50	4.4
Tobacco products..............	1,506.67	1.1	11,971.88	6.5
Pianos and musical instruments...	4,898.26	3.7	6,444.98	3.5
Food and food drinks...........	1,039.05	.8	9,177.46	4.9
Newspapers and periodicals......	8,204.13	6.2	1,116.05	.6
Household furnishings...........	3,193.18	2.4	4,527.96	2.4
Hotels and restaurants..........	1,676.35	1.3	4,768.29	2.6
Patents and war pensions procured	3,257.77	2.5	2,298.30	1.2
Agents wanted.................	2,889.13	2.2	929.45	.5
Houses and real estate..........	1,688.21	1.3	2,017.84	1.1
Sewing machines...............	2,975.26	2.3	665.90	.4
Toilet goods..................	1,617.45	1.2	1,390.00	.7
Railroads and transportation......	990.10	.8	1,322.67	.7
Farm and dairy implements......	280.50	.2	1,482.96	.8
Insurance and financial..........	678.40	.5	1,081.07	.6
Puzzles, tricks, and novelties......	814.73	.6	823.89	.4
Firm notices..................	531.61	.4	922.52	.5
Office equipment and supplies.....	270.00	.2	568.78	.3
Printing and supplies...........	405.65	.3	380.65	.2
Livestock and poultry...........	57.50	.04	502.23	.3
Legal notices.................	113.00	.1	24.75	.01
	$131,628.30	100.00	$185,518.78	100.00

[a] The percentage has been figured with the total amount traced as the base.

1900 AND 1901

Commodity Group	1900 Amount	Per- centage[a]	1901 Amount	Per- centage[a]
Foods and food drinks.......... $	310,978.23	21.59	$ 284,790.69	14.79
Fuel.........................	125,251.78	8.69	216,152.30	11.22
Patent medicines...............	216,104.73	15.01	66,270.52	3.44
Tobacco products..............	31,080.78	2.16	209,713.18	10.89
Newspapers and periodicals.......	88,031.63	6.11	134,510.23	6.98
Schools and colleges............	72,648.86	5.04	117,867.08	6.12
Seeds and nursery stock.........	58,663.59	4.07	89,774.68	4.66
Confectionery and soft drinks.....	69,295.14	4.81	77,824.32	4.04
Farm and dairy implements......	47,869.18	3.32	91,672.18	4.76
Correspondence schools.........	53,853.01	3.74	56,943.49	2.96
Toilet goods...................	45,474.95	3.16	61,141.61	3.17
Carriages.....................	31,504.12	2.19	48,976.52	2.54
Men's wear....................	27,323.51	1.89	52,917.68	2.75
Dry goods and clothing.........	43,299.72	3.00	35,138.22	1.82
Jewelry and silverware..........	17,681.42	1.23	57,409.21	2.98
Women's wear.................	23,578.55	1.64	50,767.84	2.64
Books and tracts...............	20,710.33	1.44	40,390.41	2.10
Paints and hardware............	15,423.19	1.07	32,427.11	1.68
Machinery....................	39,502.86	2.74	7,474.65	.39
Plumbing and heating...........	13,532.58	.94	27,499.40	1.43
Household appliances...........	16,383.62	1.14	19,885.15	1.03
Pianos and musical instruments...	9,918.07	.69	24,659.68	1.28
Metals........................	544.35	.04	22,097.73	1.15
Public utilities, communication and transportation...............	4.45	...	20,832.32	1.08
Textiles......................	9,999.96	.69	10,767.61	.56
Building materials and fences.....	4,974.08	.35	11,325.09	.59
Household furnishings...........	6,109.16	.42	6,826.75	.35
Travel.......................	6,021.70	.42	6,250.44	.32
Banking......................	4,831.55	.34	5,205.24	.27
Office equipment and supplies.....	1,041.82	.07	6,983.15	.36
Automobiles and accessories......	5,456.51	.38	637.00	.03
Agents wanted.................	1,023.60	.07	3,560.43	.19
Livestock and poultry...........	2,030.11	.14	2,310.86	.12
Scientific instruments...........	1,830.76	.13	1,761.80	.09
Houses and real estate..........	2,102.92	.15	1,340.63	.07
Greeting cards and chromos......	1,108.56	.07	1,542.95	.08
Stock foods and tonics..........	439.12	.03	1,750.28	.09
Fertilizers....................	462.30	.03	1,205.55	.06
Printing and engraving..........	1,237.25	.09	64.42	...
Hotels and restaurants..........	592.50	.04	144.21	.007
Patents procured...............	241.40	.02	319.75	.02
Miscellaneous.................	2,506.35	.17	5,578.92	.29
Unidentified..................	10,158.97	.70	11,261.17	.58
	$1,440,827.27	100.00	$1,925,972.45	100.00

[a] Percentages have been calculated with the total volume of billings as the base.

COMMODITIES ADVERTISED BY AYER   591

1921

Commodity Group	Amount	Percentage of Total[a]
Tobacco products	$ 2,493,594.43	22.53
Food and food drinks	1,235,028.94	11.16
Dry goods and clothing	865,704.67	7.82
Correspondence schools	751,626.24	6.79
Newspapers and periodicals	705,987.68	6.38
Schools, colleges, and camps	607,252.87	5.49
Household supplies and equipment	520,323.26	4.70
Office supplies and equipment	488,854.11	4.42
Jewelry and silverware	437,186.59	3.95
Communication and transportation	353,807.83	3.20
Automobiles, tires, and accessories	284,940.39	2.58
Building materials and supplies	266,050.96	2.41
Confectionery and soft drinks	245,241.90	2.22
Gasoline, oil, and fuel	235,370.77	2.13
Seeds and nursery stock	212,049.61	1.92
Drugs and toilet goods	172,905.05	1.56
Musical instruments	142,832.28	1.29
Books and maps	141,623.92	1.28
Paints and hardware	131,966.47	1.19
Real estate	128,917.52	1.16
Metals	104,363.85	.94
Stock foods and tonics	90,242.60	.82
Sporting goods	77,977.57	.70
Insurance and financial	77,653.81	.70
Plumbing and heating	68,555.08	.62
Shoes, trunks, and leather goods	35,251.05	.32
Fertilizers	34,623.26	.31
Chemicals	18,025.87	.16
Livestock	17,808.91	.16
Machinery	16,589.44	.15
Farm Equipment	8,160.18	.07
Unclassified	95,949.50	.87
Associations (included above)	(346,188.43)	(3.13)
Total amount traced	$11,066,466.61	100.00

[a] Percentages have been calculated with the total traced as the base. This total differs from the total of billings for the year by less than 3 per cent.

1925

Commodity Group	Amount	Percentage of Total[a]
Food and food drinks.................	$ 2,404,381.22	14.40
Chemicals..........................	1,549,720.40	9.28
Drugs and toilet goods.................	1,370,627.40	8.21
Dry goods and clothing................	917,136.93	5.49
Tobacco products.....................	855,496.87	5.12
Confectionery and soft drinks...........	792,321.95	4.75
Real estate..........................	772,094.45	4.62
Household supplies and equipment.......	633,119.69	3.79
Automobiles, tires, and accessories.......	576,804.06	3.45
Radios and phonographs................	573,285.69	3.43
Schools, colleges, and camps.............	566,982.07	3.40
Communication and transportation.......	558,148.44	3.34
Office supplies and equipment...........	561,086.30	3.36
Correspondence schools.................	535,637.73	3.21
Insurance and financial.................	533,110.20	3.19
Jewelry and silverware.................	517,411.80	3.10
Gasoline, oil, and fuel.................	516,612.14	3.09
Newspapers and periodicals.............	397,679.39	2.38
Shoes, trunks, and leather goods.........	392,043.45	2.35
Books and maps......................	349,634.22	2.09
Building materials and supplies..........	327,910.80	1.96
Musical instruments...................	290,302.92	1.74
Seeds and nursery stock................	246,512.69	1.48
Stock foods and tonics.................	146,033.72	.87
Machinery...........................	77,670.28	.47
Sporting goods.......................	39,961.18	.24
Paints and hardware...................	32,331.65	.19
Metals..............................	30,443.98	.18
Plumbing and heating..................	23,955.20	.14
Farm equipment......................	14,204.05	.09
Livestock............................	8,295.48	.05
Unclassified.........................	90,192.71	.54
Associations (included above)...........	(345,199.24)	(2.07)
Total amount traced................	$16,701,149.06	100.00

[a] Percentages have been calculated with the total amount traced as the base. This total differs from the total of billings for the year by less than 3 per cent.

1930

Commodity Group	Amount	Percentage of Total Volume
Automobiles, tires, and accessories........	$ 9,686,704.05	25.45
Tobacco products.....................	6,818,462.72	17.91
Food and food drinks..................	5,969,735.37	15.68
Drugs and toilet goods.................	2,410,492.86	6.33
Chemicals...........................	1,679,186.25	4.41
Confectionery and soft drinks............	1,640,485.81	4.31
Communication and transportation.......	1,361,981.95	3.58
Dry goods and clothing.................	1,178,753.79	3.10
Gasoline, oil, and fuel.................	745,604.08	1.96
Household supplies and equipment........	638,502.00	1.68
Office supplies and equipment...........	597,443.12	1.57
Plumbing and heating..................	577,653.46	1.52
Schools, colleges, and camps............	574,476.63	1.51
Jewelry and silverware.................	531,845.39	1.40
Correspondence schools.................	451,097.99	1.18
Machinery and metals..................	379,219.87	.99
Building materials.....................	367,804.02	.96
Musical instruments...................	341,581.41	.90
Stock foods and tonics.................	330,777.40	.87
Newspapers and periodicals.............	286,120.52	.75
Seeds and nursery stock................	246,404.90	.64
Household furnishings..................	223,464.00	.59
Insurance and financial.................	221,435.29	.58
Paints and hardware...................	204,458.36	.54
Shoes, trunks, and leather goods.........	89,848.03	.24
Sporting goods.......................	85,272.40	.22
Farm equipment......................	72,114.95	.19
Real estate..........................	33,485.34	.09
Hotels..............................	31,322.31	.08
Livestock...........................	30,342.04	.08
Books and maps......................	21,272.09	.06
Unclassified.........................	241,267.60	.63
Associations (included above)...........	(1,468,733.52)	(3.85)
Total Volume....................	$38,068,616.00	100.00

NOTES AND REFERENCES

CHAPTER I

1. Until the first edition of the present study appeared (1939) the only treatise dealing specifically with the advertising agency was Floyd Y. Keeler and Albert E. Haase, *The Advertising Agency, Procedure and Practice* (N. Y., 1927), which set forth the organization and operational methods of an agency without presenting any background material. Later a more comprehensive and penetrating book appeared — F. Allen Burt, *American Advertising Agencies* (N. Y., 1940). In addition, of course, there are a few memoirs, such as George P. Rowell's *Forty Years an Advertising Agent* (N. Y., 1906, reprinted 1926), which provide useful raw material.

2. James W. Young, *Advertising Agency Compensation in Relation to the Total Cost of Advertising* (Chicago, 1933), p. 15.

3. U. S. Bureau of the Census, *Census of Business: 1935. Advertising Agencies* (Washington, 1937), p. 4.

4. No reliable figures on agency billings have been published since those for 1935, but with the Printers' Ink index (average of 1935–39 = 100) running well beyond 260 it seems evident that the billion-dollar mark has been passed.

5. Article entitled "Advertising" in the *Encyclopaedia of the Social Sciences* (N. Y., 1930); Young, *op. cit.*, pp. 14–17, 36–38; George B. Hotchkiss, *An Outline of Advertising* (N. Y., 1940), pp. 54–55, 135–136.

6. Henry A. Sampson, *A History of Advertising* (London, 1874), pp. 19–60; D. C. A. Hemet, *Traité pratique de publicité* (Paris, 1912), pp. 1–6; Hotchkiss, *op. cit.*, pp. 6–7.

7. Sampson, *op. cit.*, pp. 50–140; Frank Presbrey, *The History and Development of Advertising* (N. Y., 1929), pp. 35–61, 118–137; article entitled "Newspapers" in *Encyclopaedia Britannica* (14th ed.); Joseph P. Bachem, *Das Eindringen der Reklame in die deutschen politischen Tageszeitungen* (Munich, 1929), pp. 26–27; Hotchkiss, *op. cit.*, pp. 10–32.

8. Ralph M. Hower, "The Wedgwoods — Ten Generations of Potters," *Journal of Economic and Business History*, vol. iv, no. 2 (Feb., 1932), pp. 303–305.

9. Paul-Louis Hervier, "L'Evolution de la publicité," *La Nouvelle Revue* (Aug., 1906), p. 378.

10. James M. Lee, *History of American Journalism* (Boston, 1923), pp. 111–112.

11. R. B. Westerfield, "Middlemen in English Business," in *Transactions of the Connecticut Academy of Arts and Sciences*, vol. xix (May, 1915), pp. 111–455; see also N. S. B. Gras, *An Introduction to Economic History* (N. Y., 1922), pp. 188, 239, 260–269, 305, 312–314; Alfred Marshall, *Principles of Economics* (London, 1920), pp. 293–297.

12. *The Times* (London), *Anniversary Number, 1785–1935*, Jan. 1, 1935, p. xviii.

13. Lee, *op. cit.*, pp. 74–77; George H. Payne, *History of American Journalism in the United States* (N. Y., 1920), pp. 24–32, 68; S. N. D. North, "The Newspaper

and Periodical Press," *Tenth Census of the United States, 1880* (Washington, 1884), pp. 12–13.

14. Various New York and London business directories for the period 1800 to 1830; Presbrey, *op. cit.*, p. 261.

15. Daniel J. Kenny, *The American Newspaper Directory and Record of the Press* (N. Y., 1861), p. 121; North, *op. cit.*, p. 47.

16. *V. B. Palmer's New Yorker* (N. Y.), Dec., 1851; brief history of the advertising agency in an advertisement of N. W. Ayer & Son, 1878; S. M. Pettengill, "Reminiscences of the Advertising Business," *Printers' Ink* (hereafter referred to as *P. I.*), Dec. 24, 1890, pp. 686–690; Rowell, *op. cit.*, pp. 71–74; Presbrey, *op. cit.*, pp. 261–264.

17. Letter dated June 29, 1846, quoted in *V. B. Palmer's Business Men's Almanac, 1855* (Philadelphia), p. 40.

18. Advertisements, 1844 and 1845, in the possession of N. W. Ayer & Son, Inc., Philadelphia. The material in this collection will be referred to henceforth as A. C. Where the evidence is obviously from the Ayer records, however, the location will not be cited.

19. Presbrey, *op. cit.*, pp. 261–264.

20. Advertisement of W. W. Sharpe & Co., Inc. (a New York agency whose founder had worked for Palmer); *The Fourth Estate* (N. Y.), May 30, 1918, p. 15; information obtained from two of Palmer's grandchildren in 1922 by a member of the Ayer firm, memo. A. C.; Burt, *op. cit.*, pp. 244–245, credits Palmer with starting in Philadelphia in 1838 and with opening a New York branch in 1840, but no sources are given.

21. Palmer advertisements, 1844–45, A. C.

22. *Ibid.*, 1845, 1849, 1850; S. R. Niles (Palmer's successor in Boston) to N. W. Ayer & Son, June 3, 1876, A. C.

23. "Death of John Hooper," *P. I.*, Jan. 1, 1890, pp. 203–205; Rowell, *op. cit.*, pp. 140–143.

24. Advertisement in *V. B. Palmer's New Yorker*, Dec., 1851, A. C.

25. Palmer's advertisements dating from 1844 to 1855, A. C.; Pettengill, *loc. cit.*; Rowell, *op. cit.*, pp. 71–74.

26. Rowell, *op. cit.*, pp. 28–32, 237–240. For a brief account of the founding of several early agencies see Burt, *op. cit.*, pp. 244–254.

27. Cf. North, *op. cit.*, pp. 35–36, 88.

28. George P. Rowell, in an advertisement for his agency published in 1878, A. C.; also reprinted in Rowell, *op. cit.*, pp. 237–249.

29. I have been unable to find any straightforward contemporary statement as to why the publishers continued to allow the agent a "commission" after he had ceased to be their actual agent. However, a careful reading of Rowell's memoirs and the reasoning of publishers from 1890 to the present, as expressed from time to time in *P. I.* and as set forth by Young, *op. cit.*, part I, sections ii and iv, will support, I believe, the explanation here set forth.

30. Rowell, *op. cit.*, pp. 63–68.

31. See especially Westerfield, *op. cit.*, pp. 111–455.

32. Rowell, *op. cit.*, p. 67. The early Ayer ledgers show that advertisers still received long credit terms in the 'seventies and 'eighties.

33. Rowell, *op. cit.*, pp. 98–109, 144–145, 189.

34. Advertisements of lists by Pettengill, Rowell, Ayer and others dating from 1869 to 1880, A. C.

35. Cheaper, that is, for the individual concerns that were trying to sell goods. Whether advertising saves money for consumers as a whole is a highly involved and much debated question which cannot be discussed here. For a detailed study of this aspect of advertising see Neil H. Borden, *The Economic Effects of Advertising* (Chicago, 1942).

CHAPTER II

1. Private records of the Ayer family in the possession of Mrs. Wilfred W. Fry, daughter of F. W. Ayer; typescript genealogy, "Family of Ayer" (undated), compiled by George S. Potter, and "John Ayer of Haverhill," anon. (undated), in the New England Historic Genealogical Society; *Vital Records of Lee, Massachusetts, to 1850* (Boston, 1903).

2. F. W. Ayer to William Warner, Monmouth, Illinois, Feb. 2, 1904; F. W. Ayer to Frank R. Morris, Bennington, Vt., June 11, 1904; undated MS, prepared under F. W. Ayer's direction shortly before his death, henceforth referred to as MS A., A. C.

3. *Ibid.*

4. F. W. Ayer's mother died when he was three years old. When he was six, his father married Harriet Post, who soon won the boy's full affection and respect (Ayer family records; interviews with Mrs. Wilfred W. Fry).

5. *Ibid.*

6. MS A., A. C.

7. Stenographic report, speech of F. W. Ayer, Dec. 15, 1916.

8. MS A., A. C.

9. Sten. rep., speech of F. W. Ayer, Dec. 15, 1916.

10. Frank Luther Mott, *A History of American Magazines* (Cambridge, 1938), vol. iii, p. 72.

11. F. W. Ayer in the *Baptist Watchman-Examiner,* July 26, 1917; sten. rep. of F. W. Ayer's remarks in conference with publishers, Jan. 8, 1920; MS A., A. C.

12. *Ibid.*

13. *Ibid.*

14. Contemporary notes on a talk by F. W. Ayer to his employees, Jan. 4, 1897.

15. At least, his secretary of a few years later gained this impression.

16. Circular advertisement of N. W. Ayer & Son, 1877 or 1878; MS A., A. C.

17. Circular advertisement of N. W. Ayer & Son, 1877.

18. This statement is based on the fact that Ayer had the exclusive representation of the papers named in 1870 and 1871, according to an advertisement sent out in 1870 and the entries in Ledger 1. Ledger 1 is not the first ledger of the firm; it follows the first, which has long been lost, and most of its entries date from 1870–71.

19. Allan Nevins, *The Emergence of Modern America, 1865–1878* (N. Y., 1927), pp. 236, 245–248, 412.

20. Presbrey, *Hist. and Devel. of Advg.,* pp. 281–282.

21. The following statement is based on the assumption that the firm operated on the same basis in 1869 as in 1871. From Ledger 1 and other contemporary sources it is reasonably clear that no essential change in the firm's business arrangements took place in this period.

22. Cards, advertisements, and letterheads in Scrapbook A; Ledger 1 (1870–73); F. W. Ayer's Letter-book (1870–73), A. C.

23. Ledger 1, Profit and Loss accounts and *passim.*

24. General Journal, Apr. to Dec., 1878. (This is the only general journal for the period before 1900 that has survived.)

25. Ledgers 1 and 2 (1870–74); Ayer advertisements dating from 1871 to 1876.

26. Ledgers 1, 2, and 3; advertising proposal forms used by Ayer, 1878–84.

27. See above, p. 14.

28. MS A.; *Methodist Home Journal,* Oct. 18, 1873.

29. James D. Morrison, "Mr. F. Wayland Ayer's Place in the Creation and Conservation of Baptist Work in the State and Nation," *F. Wayland Ayer, 1848–1923* (Philadelphia, 1923), pp. 15–17.

30. F. W. Ayer to his uncle, George Post, Nov. 30, 1871.

31. F. W. Ayer, "A Half Century of Advertising," *The Next Step* (a periodical published from time to time by Ayer employees), Aug., 1921.

32. *American Newspaper Annual* (Philadelphia, 1882), p. 7.

33. Firm advertisement, 1870; *Methodist Home Journal,* Oct. 18, 1873. As early as 1876 the story was started that this expansion took place in the fall of 1869, but someone's memory erred. The advertisement cited shows that the agency was still located at 530 Arch Street on June 2, 1870, which is conclusive.

34. Speech of F. W. Ayer, Sept. 25, 1912.

35. Ledger 1.

36. F. W. Ayer to his uncle, George Post, Nov. 30, 1871.

37. The move took place in February, Camden *Democrat,* Mar. 9, 1872.

38. Expense Account, 1872, Ledger 1.

39. Ledgers 1 and 2.

40. *Methodist Home Journal* (Philadelphia), Oct. 18, 1873.

41. F. W. Ayer's Letter-book, Feb. 8, 1873, *et seq.*

42. F. W. Ayer's account, Ledger 2; interviews with Mr. and Mrs. Wilfred W. Fry and officers of the firm.

43. The accounts of F. W. Ayer and George O. Wallace in Ledger 2; firm advertisement in the Philadelphia *Public Ledger,* Oct. 1, 1873.

44. *The Advertiser's Guide,* published by N. W. Ayer & Son, vol. i, no. 3 (Dec., 1876).

45. Firm advertisement, 1877.

46. Printed announcements to publishers dated Oct. 20, 1877, Feb. 20 and June 22, 1878; firm advertisement, 1878; Ledger 4.

47. John E. Joy was a bookkeeper in Palmer's agency until 1858. In 1858 Palmer is supposed to have sold his agency to Joy, Coe & Sharpe, but the Philadelphia directories of the period list Palmer's agency until his death in 1863. Since Palmer's agency was at 441 Chestnut Street and Joy, Coe & Sharpe at 439 Chestnut Street, the two firms may have been connected. In 1863 both were listed at 441 Chestnut. In 1868 the agency appears under the name Coe, Wetherill & Co. See *McElroy's Philadelphia Directory,* 1842 through 1867; *Gopsill's Philadelphia Directory,* 1868 and 1869; and the *Philadelphia City and Business Directory,* 1869 through 1878.

48. The death of H. A. Wetherill was noted in the *American Journalist and Advertisers' Index,* published by Coe, Wetherill & Co., Jan., 1877, p. 3.

49. Account with Coe, Wetherill & Co., Ledger 4.

50. See below, pp. 87–88.

51. Profit and Loss accounts, and those of publishers' and printers' supply houses in Ledgers 2–5, 10, 15, 20, 25, 30, 35, covering transactions from 1872 to 1900.

52. *Ibid.; Ayer & Son's Manual for Advertisers,* Philadelphia, 1874, *et seq.*

53. *The Advertiser's Guide,* vols. i–iii (1876–78); firm advertisement, 1877.

54. Clippings in Scrapbook A; J. W. Young, *Agency Compensation,* pp. 30–31. The issue was still being debated in *P. I.* through the 1890's.

55. Expense accounts, Ledgers 1–4 (1870–79), and Private Ledgers 1–4 (1880–1910).

56. This and the following paragraphs dealing with the advertising handled are based on entries in Ledgers 1–5 (1870–79), together with the contents of Scrapbook B covering the years 1878 and 1879.

57. Nevins, *op. cit.,* pp. 267, 277–278, 319–323.

58. Rowell, *Forty Years an Advg. Agt.,* pp. 366–380 and *passim;* Claude Hopkins, *My Life in Advertising* (N. Y., 1927), pp. 73–95; Mark Sullivan, *Our Times* (N. Y., 1929), vol. ii, pp. 508–516.

59. Nevins, *op. cit.,* p. 172.

60. Ledgers 1–5; *Ayer & Son's Manual for Advertisers; The Advertiser's Guide,* vols. i and ii. Cf. North, "Newspaper and Periodical Press," p. 131.

CHAPTER III

1. For further details see Chapter XIX.

2. J. W. Young, *Agency Compensation,* pp. 26–29.

3. Rowell, *Forty Years an Advg. Agt.,* pp. 237–249.

4. The scrapbooks in the Ayer Collection contain scores of clippings (1871–80) in which editors complained about the selfishness and unfairness of most advertising agencies. Of course, their views must be taken with a large grain of salt.

5. Sten. rep., speech, Dec. 15, 1916.

6. *Ibid.;* Rowell, *op. cit.,* p. 135.

7. Nevins, *Emergence of Modern America,* pp. 188–201.

8. F. W. Ayer, "A Half Century of Advertising," p. 5.

9. This version of the incident is based upon F. W. Ayer's recollections on four different occasions: a talk given to his employees in 1905; another on Dec. 15, 1916; remarks in a business conference with a number of publishers, Jan. 8, 1920; and the article cited in the preceding note, written in 1921. The wording of the conversation differs somewhat in the four accounts, but the essential details are identical.

10. Circular advertisement of George P. Rowell & Co., dated N. Y., Jan. 27, 1875, A. C. The details of the scheme were amplified in a later circular which is reprinted in Rowell, *op. cit.,* pp. 237–249.

11. For many years the tradition in the Ayer agency has been that the open-contract-plus-commission plan originated in the spring of 1873. A careful examination of the ledgers, however, shows conclusively that it was not actually tried until 1876 and was not formulated before 1875 at the earliest. That the germ of the idea came from Rowell's plan is stated explicitly in a letter from H. N. McKinney (an Ayer partner after 1878) to Messrs. A. Schilling & Co., San Francisco, Calif., Feb. 15, 1890.

12. This interview has been reconstructed from the accounts contained in F. W. Ayer's speeches of Dec. 15, 1916, and June 19, 1922. The two narratives differ slightly as to the exact wording of the conversation, but the ideas are the same. Ledger 2 shows that the Dingee & Conard account began in 1874, and that it was handled on the competitive basis until Jan., 1876.

13. Speech of F. W. Ayer, Dec. 15, 1916; Ledgers 2–4; Gen. Jour., Apr. to Oct., 1878. (This is the only part of the General Journal that has survived for the period before 1900.)

14. *Ibid.;* interviews with officers and employees of N. W. Ayer & Son.

15. Ledgers 2–5 (1873–79); Private Ledgers 1–4 (1880–1910); interviews with employees who were connected with the Ayer agency during the period from 1883 down to 1938.

16. No other interpretation of Rowell's many later advertisements seems plausible to the writer; furthermore, Ayer representatives as late as 1900 complained of his underbidding for business.

17. Interviews with former employees of N. W. Ayer & Son.

18. Sten. rep., speech, 1905.

19. For this and the following facts about McKinney's early life I am indebted to his son, William Ayer McKinney. Statements about his character and ability are based upon opinions obtained in interviews with his friends and business associates.

20. So described by Nelson Chesman in *The Men Who Advertise* (N. Y., 1870), p. 12.

21. Various accounts with H. N. McKinney & Co., Ledgers 1–4; Expense account, Ledger 4; interview with W. A. McKinney.

22. *Ibid.*

23. Advertisement, 1877.

24. Gen. Jour., Apr. to Dec., 1878.

25. The realignment was referred to repeatedly in the 1888 and 1889 issues of *P. I.*, though the full implications were clearly not understood. See especially Dec. 1, 1888, p. 245; Dec. 15, 1888, p. 262; Sept. 1, 1889, pp. 70–71; Nov. 1, 1889, pp. 120–121.

26. Rowell, *op. cit.*, pp. 308–315; Young, *op. cit.*, pp. 26–29. Young quotes Rowell as saying that special agents were numerous by 1880. The context (especially pp. 290, 298) shows clearly, however, that Rowell was referring to 1887 or 1888. There is further evidence in Rowell that the special agent was not common until the late 1880's: Richard S. Thain, in a letter quoted by Rowell, pp. 451–452, stated that he was the first special agent in Chicago when he opened his own office there in 1889.

27. Young, *op. cit.*, pp. 26–29.

CHAPTER IV

1. This account of the Nichols-Shepard contract is based upon the stenographic record of the remarks of F. W. Ayer on June 19, 1922, together with the story as McKinney told it to his son, who related it to the writer. Ledger 5 (1878–80) and Scrapbook E (1880–84) show that the first advertisement for the Nichols-Shepard Company was sent out in Jan., 1880.

2. Speech of F. W. Ayer, Sept. 9, 1908; pay rolls, 1908–1920; interviews with employees.

3. Presbrey, *Hist. and Devel. of Advg.*, pp. 307–308.

4. Lee, *Hist. of Amer. Journalism*, p. 226.

5. Folder advertising N. W. Ayer & Son, dated Apr., 1880, A. C.

6. Philadelphia *Evening News*, Mar. 29, 1884; proofs of advertisements in Scrapbook E (1880–84).

7. This opinion was expressed when Ayer hired the first full-time copywriter for his agency, John J. Geisinger (later of the Federal Advertising Agency of New York), according to a statement by Geisinger to the writer. Lord of Lord & Thomas was likewise opposed to the preparation of copy by the agency (J. W. Young, *Agency Compensation*, p. 29).

8. Pay roll list, 1888; interviews with former employees.

9. National Advertising Co., *The National Advertiser* (N. Y., 1887), p. 30.

10. Advertisements of George P. Rowell & Company, in *P. I.*, 1891.

11. Interviews with J. J. Geisinger and other Ayer employees familiar with the period; Charles Austin Bates, "First Person Singular," *Advertising & Selling* (hereafter referred to as *Adv. & Sell.*), Apr. 3, 1929, p. 24.

12. Copy books of N. W. Ayer & Son for the period 1890–1910; interviews with employees; pay rolls, 1900.

13. Advertisements in *P. I.* and various newspapers, 1892, preserved in Scrapbook D.

14. General Ledgers 1–5; Newspaper Ledgers 5 *et seq.;* notes of the monthly meetings of Ayer solicitors, May to Dec., 1896.

15. Sidney A. Sherman, "Advertising in the United States," *American Statistical Association Reports,* New Series, vol. vii, no. 52 (Dec., 1900).

16. Rowell, *Forty Years an Advg. Agent,* pp. 144–145, 445; Presbrey, *op. cit.,* pp. 464–478.

17. Form letter sent out by J. Walter Thompson under date of June 13, 1895, A. C.

18. Ayer announcements dated Aug. and Oct., 1896; notes of the monthly meetings of Ayer solicitors, May to Dec., 1896.

19. F. W. Ayer, "Advertising in America," *One Hundred Years of American Commerce,* Chauncey M. Depew, editor (N. Y., 1895), pp. 76–83; fragments of correspondence between N. W. Ayer & Son and the National Biscuit Co. during 1898; advertising booklets issued by N. W. Ayer & Son in 1899; interviews with employees; *Tide,* Aug., 1931, p. 22.

20. Advertisements of N. W. Ayer & Son, A. C.

21. Bundle of contracts with publishers dating from 1882 to 1895, A. C.

22. John Lee Mahin, "Breaking In," *Advertising Fortnightly,* Nov. 7, 1923, p. 21.

23. See above, pp. 42–43.

24. Advertisement dated Apr., 1880, announcing the forthcoming publication of the *Annual,* A. C.

25. *Ibid.;* Private Ledger 1; Newspaper Ledgers 6 *et seq.,* covering the years after 1880; copies of the *American Newspaper Annual* from 1881 to 1914.

26. Rowell, *op. cit.,* pp. 191, 277–279.

27. Entries in Ledgers 1 (1870–73) *et seq.*

28. Printed form sent out to publishers in 1880 and a number of years thereafter, A. C.

29. Note in Ledger 5, f. 3348 (1880–84).

30. Interviews with employees.

31. Pay rolls, 1880–90, A. C.

32. Personal Ledgers 5, 10, *et seq.,* dating from 1878; Private Ledgers 1–3 (1880–1900); sten. rep., speech of A. G. Bradford, treasurer of N. W. Ayer & Son, Sept. 26, 1912; interviews with former employees. Though the evidence is incomplete, this appears to be one instance of a wholesale house (the Mather Manufacturing Co.) becoming primarily a manufacturing concern (the Keystone Type Foundry).

33. Advertisements of the Religious Press Association, 1880; accounts in Private Ledger No. 1; pamphlet issued by N. W. Ayer & Son in 1887 in reply to criticisms of its relations with the Religious Press Association.

34. Sten. rep., speech of F. W. Ayer, Sept. 16, 1912; printed notice, "Business Rules," May 1, 1884.

35. Interviews with former employees.
36. Announcement sent out in 1909, A. C.; *American Newspaper Annual and Directory,* 1909.
37. Interviews with publishers in New York and Boston.
38. *Annual and Directory,* 1914; memo. left by J. A. Wood regarding the profits of the *Annual and Directory,* 1910–1920.
39. Title page of 1947 edition.
40. Private Ledger 1 (1880–84).
41. Minutes of the Keystone Type Foundry, pp. 43, 69.
42. Statement by A. G. Bradford, Sept. 26, 1912.
43. Minutes of the Keystone Type Foundry, *passim.* The Ayer agency was not the only one to engage in this business nor was it the last. Nelson Chesman & Co., of St. Louis, was trading type and ink for space in 1890 (see advertisement in *P. I.,* Jan. 29, 1890, p. 311), and the Dauchy agency was still offering direct exchanges in 1916 (*American Press,* 1916, no. 36, p. 1).
44. Minutes of the Keystone Type Foundry, *passim;* memo. of J. A. Wood, who was vice-president of the Keystone Type Foundry. The stock was held by the Ayer firm until Harry A. Batten became president (1936). Between 1937 and 1941 the firm sold practically all holdings of this type in order to make its assets more liquid. See Chapter VIII below.
45. J. W. Young, *op. cit.,* pp. 23–33.
46. Quoted from a clipping from an unidentified Philadelphia newspaper describing a banquet of the Ayer staff, dated May 12, 1887, Scrapbook B.
47. Advertisement on the cover of the *Farm Implement News,* May, 1886.
48. "Our Creed," a folder advertising N. W. Ayer & Son, 1887.
49. Edward W. Bok, *A Man from Maine* (N. Y., 1923), pp. 113–116; Curtis advertisement in *P. I.,* July 9, 1890, p. 34. An examination of old files of the *Ladies' Home Journal* shows that through 1890 the publication contained patent medicine advertising and other types of copy now considered objectionable by most newspapers and magazines.
50. Personal Ledgers 1–5, 10, 15, 20, 25, 30, 35, 40, 45, 50, 55 and 60, containing accounts with customers from 1870 to 1912.
51. Interviews with Ayer employees.
52. Notes on monthly meeting of solicitors, June 22, 1896.
53. Personal Ledgers 35 and 40.
54. Summary statement of volume and profits supplied by the head bookkeeper of N. W. Ayer & Son.
55. Analysis of accounts, 1877–78 (see below, p. 210); Rowell, *op. cit., passim.*
56. *Ibid.,* pp. 366–405; "George P. Rowell between Two Fires," *The Fourth Estate,* July, 1895; "Mr. Pettingill's Appeal," *P. I.,* Apr. 27, 1904, p. 45.
57. Analysis of accounts, 1900–01.
58. Sten. rep., speech of F. W. Ayer, Sept. 9, 1908.
59. Analysis of accounts, 1900–01.
60. Sten. rep., speech of F. W. Ayer, Sept. 9, 1908.
61. Form letter of solicitation, Sept. 6, 1902, Scrapbook J (1900–06), p. 44.
62. H. U. Faulkner, *The Quest for Social Justice* (N. Y., 1932), pp. 236–237; Sullivan, *Our Times,* pp. 511–531.
63. Copy Book 48-A, A. C.
64. Ayer may have been influenced somewhat by the policy of rival agencies. John Lee Mahin, a prominent agent at the time, asserted as early as 1901 that his

agency "declines all kinds of liquor and 'fake' patent medicines, and other objectionable advertising" (Mahin to the National Correspondence Institute, Washington, D. C., June 22, 1901, A. C.). Whether Mahin carried out this policy or not, I do not know.

65. Personal Ledgers 5, 10, 15, 20, covering the period from 1880 to about 1890.

66. Ledgers 25, 30, 35.

67. Customers' Ledgers 30, 35, 40 and 50.

68. Interviews with men who were employees of N. W. Ayer & Son and of the National Biscuit Co. at the time; correspondence between the two firms, 1898 to 1900 in file #6035 of the National Biscuit Co., New York City, made accessible through the courtesy of Roy E. Tomlinson, president; "National Biscuit," an interview with A. W. Green (then president of the National Biscuit Co.), *P. I.,* Apr. 18, 1906, pp. 3–12.

69. "Concerning Staples" and other advertising booklets issued by N. W. Ayer & Son in 1900.

70. Personal Ledgers 35, 40, 45, and 50; copy books for the period 1900–10.

71. Summary figures supplied by N. W. Ayer & Son.

72. Advertising circulars, 1882, 1885, A. C.

73. *Ibid.,* Feb. 4, 1891.

74. *Ibid.,* Feb. 28, 1894.

75. Interview with Miss Adeline Engles, who was the agency's first stenographer.

76. Advertisements in the A. C.: memo. of Jarvis A. Wood based on the statement of H. N. McKinney, who devised the motto.

77. Interviews with former employees.

78. *Ibid.;* the minutes of the meetings held by the Ayer solicitors in 1896 and 1897 repeatedly refer to delay and confusion.

79. Firm announcement, undated, but issued only a day or two after Wallace's death; interviews with former employees.

80. *Ibid.;* letters of McKinney to Ayer in the period from 1904 to 1909.

81. W. A. Law, president of the First National Bank of Philadelphia, to J. A. Wood, Aug. 3, 1921.

82. Interviews with Mrs. Wilfred W. Fry and with former employees.

83. *Ibid.;* Ledger 15, showing the opening of a new account for Ayer & McKinney on June 1, 1889; records of the American Jersey Cattle Club; and interview with R. M. Gow of that organization. The story of Ayer's favorite hobby is told in considerable detail in *The Jerseys of Meridale,* by Harold G. Gulliver (Philadelphia, 1924).

84. Firm announcement, Jan. 1, 1898.

85. Interviews with officers and employees, past and present, of N. W. Ayer & Son.

86. *Ibid.;* interviews with publishers in Boston, New York, and Philadelphia who had had business dealings with N. W. Ayer & Son through Bradford.

87. Pay rolls, 1899–1900; interviews with employees.

88. Advertisement inserted in eight Philadelphia papers on Nov. 6, 1895.

89. The building was owned by the Girard Estate and took its name from the clause in Girard's will in which he described himself: "I, Stephen Girard, of the City of Philadelphia, Mariner and Merchant."

90. Advertisements, Jay Cooke & Co., in the Philadelphia *Inquirer,* Jan., 1861; announcement card of Jay Cooke & Co., 1861, on file in Baker Library, Harvard University; material gathered by Jarvis A. Wood in the A. C.

91. Firm announcements, 1903, 1905, 1910, 1911. The Ayer firm had had some previous experience with representatives in cities other than Philadelphia. In 1878 and 1879 J. E. Coe had maintained an office in Boston and was evidently Ayer's representative there, since Ayer regularly contributed to his office expense (Ledger 5 and General Journal for 1878). In 1883 Ayer experimented by having one of his employees work out of Chicago (Private Ledger 1); he had established a representative with desk space in Chicago in 1908, evidently paving the way for the establishment of a branch (General Ledger 1).

92. Notes of monthly meeting of solicitors, May 25, 1896, A. C.

CHAPTER V

1. Summary volume statistics supplied by the head bookkeeper of N. W. Ayer & Son.

2. This and the related paragraphs which follow are based upon interviews with officers and employees of N. W. Ayer & Son, with a number of advertisers and publishers who were in close business relations with the agency, and with men in the general field of advertising who were in a position to observe N. W. Ayer & Son from the outside.

3. Sten. rep., meetings of the Ayer staff, Sept. 25–29, 1912.

4. F. W. Ayer had married Rhandeena Gilman in 1875. They had two daughters, Alice Biddle Ayer, who married Hardin H. Wheat and died in 1904, and Anna Gilman Ayer, who married Wilfred W. Fry and died in 1944.

5. Memos. left by J. A. Wood, dated 1917–18; pay rolls, 1917–18.

6. F. W. Ayer, "A Half Century of Advertising," p. 17.

7. Notice sent to clients, Sept., 1918.

8. J. W. Young, *Advg. Agency Compensation,* pp. 37–38.

9. Summary figures supplied by the head bookkeeper of N. W. Ayer & Son, Inc.

10. *Ibid.*

11. Sten. rep., speeches of the fiftieth anniversary celebration, A. C.; interviews with publishers.

12. McKinney to Ayer, Aug. 21, 1908, A. C.

13. This and the preceding paragraph about McKinney's character and contribution to the Ayer agency have been based upon interviews with his son, William Ayer McKinney, business associates, and clients of N. W. Ayer & Son whom he had known. The quotation from Earl D. Babst is taken from *Editor & Publisher,* May 4, 1918.

McKinney was one of the closest friends of Victor Lawson, famous publisher of the Chicago *Daily News.* See Charles H. Dennis, *Victor Lawson, His Time and His Work* (Chicago, 1935).

14. Interviews with publishers and Bradford's associates in N. W. Ayer & Son.

15. Ayer's published articles were apparently confined to the following: "Advertising in America," in *One Hundred Years of American Commerce,* Chauncey M. Depew, editor (N. Y., 1895); a discussion of agency compensation in a letter sent to publishers, Mar. 18, 1921, printed in *Editor & Publisher,* Mar. 26, 1921; and "A Half Century of Advertising" in *The Next Step,* Aug., 1921.

16. Sten. rep., speech, 1905, A. C.

17. Sten. rep., conference with a group of publishers, Jan. 8, 1920, A. C.

18. Sten. rep., memorial services held in Camden, N. J., shortly after Ayer's death, A. C. (Apr. 14, 1923).

19. Dr. Clarence A. Barbour, president of Rochester Theological Seminary, in *F. Wayland Ayer, 1848–1923* (Camden, 1923), p. 11.

20. This statement is based upon scores of case records collected by the Harvard University Graduate School of Business Administration, particularly those used in studies of business policy, which reveal a surprising failure on the part of some of the most important American business concerns to define the problems.

21. *Dairylike Majesty Imp. 198188* (Meredith, N. Y., 1929), p. 7.

22. Gulliver, *Jerseys of Meridale,* pp. 6–12; interviews with employees of Ayer and McKinney; interview with R. M. Gow, treasurer of the American Jersey Cattle Club.

23. Sten. rep. of the fiftieth anniversary celebration, Apr. 4, 1919.

24. Sten. rep. of memorial service referred to above, note 18.

25. Gulliver, *op. cit., passim;* interview with R. M. Gow.

26. In addition to the activities mentioned in the text, Ayer was, at the time of his death, president of the Camden & Suburban Railway, vice-president of the Camden Horse Railway, director of the First National Bank of Philadelphia, and director of the Camden Fire Insurance Association; he had also served nine years as a director and three years as vice-president of the American Jersey Cattle Club, besides heading important committees; he had taken part in national politics and had been a Republican elector for New Jersey in the presidential campaign of 1916.

27. The above paragraphs relating to F. W. Ayer are based upon Ayer's few recorded speeches; obituaries in the New York *Times,* Mar. 6, 1923, p. 21, col. 3, and the *Delaware Express* of Delhi, New York, Mar. 9, 1923; *F. Wayland Ayer, 1848–1923* (Camden, N. J., 1923); and interviews with people who knew Ayer personally. These interviews included, among others, Mr. and Mrs. Wilfred W. Fry, officers and members of the staff of N. W. Ayer & Son, Inc., and the following:

In the publishing field — Paul Bloch, publisher of the Pittsburgh *Post-Gazette* and other papers; Philip Collins, general manager, Curtis Publishing Company; James C. Dayton, former publisher of the New York *Journal;* Joseph Gannon, of the advertising department of the New York *Times* and formerly with N. W. Ayer & Son; Fred Healey, vice-president and advertising director, Curtis Publishing Company; Frederick Kendall, editor of *Advertising & Selling,* former managing editor of *Printers' Ink;* Lee Maxwell, president, Crowell Publishing Company; A. H. Marchant, advertising manager, Boston *Post;* Adolph Ochs, publisher, New York *Times;* Charles C. Parlin, manager, commercial research, Curtis Publishing Company; William F. Rodgers, advertising manager, Boston *Transcript;* Ellery Sedgwick, editor of the *Atlantic Monthly;* Charles Henry Taylor, manager and treasurer, Boston *Globe,* former president of American Newspaper Publishers' Association.

From the advertising industry — Ernest Elmo Calkins, president, Calkins & Holden until 1931; Joseph J. Geisinger, vice-president, Federal Advertising Agency, formerly with N. W. Ayer & Son; Albert E. Haase, counsel for Association of National Advertisers, former associate editor of *Printers' Ink* and *Printers' Ink Monthly;* William H. Johns, president, Batten, Barton, Durstine & Osborn; James O. O'Shaugnessy, former executive secretary, American Advertising Agencies Association, subsequently an officer of Outdoor Advertising Corporation; Frank Presbrey, founder of the Frank Presbrey Advertising Agency.

Among Ayer clients — Earl D. Babst, chairman of the board of directors, American Sugar Refining Co., former general counsel for National Biscuit Co. and its first vice-president; Charles William Colby, director, Remington Rand; Friedrich Reidermeister, treasurer and director, Steinway & Sons; Ralph E. Weeks, president, International Correspondence Schools.

Others — James C. Colgate, of James B. Colgate & Co.; R. M. Gow, treasurer, American Jersey Cattle Club; Dr. John R. Mott, international secretary, Y.M.C.A., chairman of Institute of Social and Religious Research; and a number of persons in Philadelphia and New York who happened to have had some slight contact with F. W. Ayer and could, therefore, give an impression of his personality.

CHAPTER VI

1. Interviews with publishers, clients, men in the advertising industry, and employees of N. W. Ayer & Son.

2. Firm announcement, 1918; interviews with W. M. Armistead and other Ayer executives.

3. Firm announcement, Jan., 1920; interviews with Kessler, Mathes, and Fry.

4. Firm announcement, Jan., 1923; interviews with Thornley and other Ayer executives.

5. Alfred N. Whitehead, *Adventures in Ideas* (N. Y., 1933), p. 7.

6. Address delivered at the tenth annual meeting of the American Association of Advertising Agencies, Washington, D. C., Oct. 27, 1926, reprinted in *Papers of the American Association of Advertising Agencies, 1927* (N. Y., 1927), pp. 3–14.

7. *U. S. Census of Manufactures,* 1931, p. 526; *ibid.,* 1921, p. 753.

8. See data given below, Chapter XIX.

9. See below, Chapter XVIII.   10. Pay roll sheets, 1924.

11. Minutes of firm meeting, Oct. 29, 1920.

12. A detailed description of the building, written by the architect, Ralph B. Bencker, and accompanied by many photographs, is contained in *The Architectural Forum,* Oct., 1929, pp. 432–471.

13. Philadelphia *Public Ledger,* Oct. 13, 1927, and Apr. 2, 1929; Philadelphia *Inquirer,* Feb. 5, 1928; *Editor & Publisher,* Apr. 6, 1929; speeches and records in the A. C.

14. Minutes of Representatives' Conference, N. Y., Dec. 2 and 9, 1922, June 2, 1923; Publicity Bureau Memo. to Pittsburgh office, Oct. 25, 1923; interviews with Ayer employees concerned with these programs; interview with the late George McClelland, formerly of the American Telephone and Telegraph Co.'s broadcasting division, later vice-president of the National Broadcasting Co.; William Peck Banning, *Commercial Broadcasting Pioneer* (Cambridge, 1946), pp. 153–154.

A number of books on radio have stated that advertising was broadcast for the first time in the summer of 1923 — e.g., Herman S. Hettinger, *A Decade of Radio Advertising* (Chicago, 1933), p. 107. But Ayer records show that the agency arranged commercial broadcasts in 1922, and this date is confirmed by the National Broadcasting Co. itself. The very first sponsored broadcast was a talk on real estate for the Queensboro Corporation over WEAF on Aug. 28, 1922, 10 minutes for $100. (See advertisement in the fiftieth anniversary number of *P. I.,* July 28, 1938, inserted between pp. 192 and 193; also Banning, *op. cit.,* p. 90.) But it was apparently arranged directly between the sponsor and the station.

15. The writer is indebted to George McClelland for verifying from records of the National Broadcasting Co. dates establishing the priority of the Eveready Hour.

16. Interviews with Ayer employees; pamphlet, *About the Eveready Hour,* published by the National Carbon Co. (N. Y., 1928).

17. Broadcasts over interconnecting stations were made successfully by both wire and short-wave channels in the fall of 1923, but they were essentially experimental and were not sponsored by advertisers. *Recommendations for Regulation of Radio Adopted by the Third National Radio Conference* (Department of Commerce, Washington, 1924), p. 33.

18. This discussion of the emergence of broadcast networks has been based on an interview with the late George McClelland; interviews with Ayer employees; Publicity Bureau correspondence files, 1927; Merlin H. Aylesworth, "The National Magazine of the Air," *The Radio Industry* (Chicago, 1923), pp. 228–234; Frank A. Arnold, *Broadcast Advertising* (N. Y., 1930), pp. 8–12; Hettinger, *op. cit.*, chap. vi; historical material in advertisement of the National Broadcasting Co. cited above, note 14; Banning, *op. cit.*, chaps. vi, x, xi, xv and xvii. Banning's statement (p. 261) that the Eveready Hour was launched on Oct. 6, 1924, is in error except in so far as it refers to a particular combination of stations.

19. Under the leadership of the U. S. Department of Commerce, the industry forbade direct advertising over radio as early as 1922, and this attitude continued for a number of years. *Proceedings of the Fourth National Radio Conference and Recommendations for the Regulation of Radio,* 1925 (Department of Commerce, Washington, 1926), p. 18; "New Wings for Words," *P. I.,* fiftieth anniversary number, July 28, 1938, pp. 372–379. See also Banning, *op. cit.*, pp. 118–120, 259–260.

The Ayer views on the use of radio in its developmental stage are indicated by the fact that the agency's broadcasting activities were handled by its Publicity Bureau until 1928. That agencies generally first regarded radio as a medium for goodwill rather than direct advertising is indicated by Herman S. Hettinger and Walter J. Neff, *Practical Radio Advertising* (N. Y., 1938), p. 21. One of the earliest writers on broadcasting asserted, "Ordinary and extensive advertising by radio is either futile or wasteful." Hiram L. Jome, *Economics of the Radio Industry* (Chicago, 1925), p. 284.

20. Since 1930 a number of books have appeared which deal with the problems, techniques, and utility of radio advertising. To date the best three of these seem to me to be Hettinger and Neff, cited in the preceding note; *The Advertising Agency Looks at Radio,* Neville O'Neill, editor (N. Y., 1932); and Warren B. Dygert, *Radio as an Advertising Medium* (N. Y., 1939). Two other books, dealing with some of the broader social and cultural implications of radio broadcasting (including advertising), are well worth some attention: Columbia University Bureau of Applied Social Sciences, *The People Look at Radio* (Chapel Hill, 1946), and Charles A. Siepmann, *Radio's Second Chance* (Boston, 1946).

21. The data published on this point by *Media Records* and such advertising periodicals as *P. I.* and *Adv. & Sell.* do not give conclusive proof because the depression caused a reduction in the use of periodical advertising just when radio advertising was beginning to increase rapidly. Allowing for this, however, I believe the statement to be substantially correct. See also Neil H. Borden, Malcolm D. Taylor and Howard T. Hovde, *National Advertising in Newspapers* (Cambridge, 1946), pp. 33–37.

22. Correspondence of the Ayer Publicity Bureau, 1922–28.

23. Interviews with Ayer employees; pay rolls, 1922–30.

24. That other investigators have encountered the same difficulty is indicated by Hettinger, *A Decade of Radio Advertising,* p. vii.

25. Publicity Bureau correspondence, 1923–28; pamphlet, *About the Eveready Hour;* interviews with members of the Ayer radio division and the late George

McClelland; pamphlet, *Giants in the Air* (N. W. Ayer & Son, 1937); Banning, *op. cit.*, pp. 153–154, 261.

26. Philadelphia *Public Ledger*, Apr. 30, 1929.

27. Statement of the firm of Evans, Bayard & Frick who drew up the agreement. The trust agreement itself contained the statement that it was the intention of the five partners "to secure to themselves as fully as may be the continuance of the policies and leadership upon which the continued success of the business depends." Since the combined interests of the five men still constituted a clear majority after more than 100,000 shares had been sold to other officers and employees, it is evident that the agreement could have had no other object than enabling Fry to control the firm by controlling the votes of all five men.

28. Interviews with the president and treasurer of N. W. Ayer & Son, Inc.; voting trust agreement dated May 1, 1929; letter to members of the Ayer staff explaining the plan for granting broader ownership of stock, dated May 17, 1929.

29. *Adv. & Sell.*, Oct. 2, 1929; *Advertising News* (London), Nov. 1, 1929.

30. Correspondence with the Ford Motor Co., 1930.

31. Inter-office correspondence, July 8, 1919.

32. J. A. Wood to E. N. Vose, editor of *Dun's International Review*, Dec. 9, 1924, A. C.

33. California Prune Growers' Association and Ford Motor Co. correspondence, Business Department files, 1927; interviews with members of the Ayer staff.

34. Squibb and Ford correspondence, 1928; Ford and Steinway correspondence, 1929; interviews with Ayer executives.

35. Ford correspondence, 1929–30; interviews with Ayer executives; interviews with members of three important firms in New York representing South American newspapers.

36. Representative's report, Nov. 16, 1931; Ford correspondence, 1931.

37. The general story of the Ayer expansion as related here is based upon a study of all the correspondence and reports relating to it in the Ayer files, covering the years 1929 to 1932, inclusive; many conversations with Boaz Long and other executives; and, for an outside point of view, interviews with publishers' representatives referred to in note 35. These interviews, for obvious reasons, were confidential and names must be withheld.

38. *Standard Trade and Securities. Basic Statistics*, vol. 88, no. 9 (Apr. 29, 1938), p. D–50.

CHAPTER VII

1. As explained in the Author's Preface, the intensive research for this volume covered the period prior to 1933. The present chapter is a sketch, designed to bring the general history of the firm up through 1936. Since it has not been based upon a thorough study of all the possible source material, this chapter must be regarded as tentative and somewhat incomplete for the period after 1933.

2. *Standard Trade and Securities, Basic Statistics*, vol. 88, no. 9 (Apr. 29, 1938), pp. D–50 and D–51.

3. For a brief account of the rise of this institution see M. M. Zimmerman, "Super-Market, Miracle of Modern Merchandising," *P. I.*, Dec. 15, 1938.

4. See Burford Lorimer, "Advertising Adopts the Comic Strip Technique," *Adv. & Sell.*, Apr. 1, 1931; James S. Tyler, "Comics," *ibid.*, Apr., 1938.

5. The lengths to which testimonial users went is indicated by the fact that in 1930 Mrs. Franklin D. Roosevelt was reported to have received $1,000 for endors-

ing furniture, and attempts were made (apparently without success) to obtain an endorsement from Mrs. Calvin Coolidge. (Boston *Evening Transcript,* Sept. 28, 1933, p. 1.) See also "The Inside of the Testimonial Racket," *Adv. & Sell.,* Jan. 7, 1931.

6. This strong statement is based not only upon a reasonably close familiarity with the advertisements which have appeared in this country since 1800, but also upon opinions of advertising men as expressed in such trade papers as *Adv. & Sell., P. I.,* and *Tide,* especially in 1931, 1932, and 1933. Among the worst offenders were certain manufacturers of cigarettes, soap, sanitary napkins, alleged disinfectants and deodorants, and yeast.

7. These generalizations are based upon many discussions with executives of various business firms, agencies, and publishing companies between 1932 and 1934, plus a perusal of numerous speeches and articles on the subject in advertising journals and elsewhere covering the years 1931–38. It is impossible to cite here all the facts and opinions expressed, but I am confident that anyone who merely examines the titles listed under "advertising" for this period in *The Readers' Guide to Periodical Literature* and *Bulletin of the Public Affairs Information Service* will agree that my statements are reasonably accurate.

See, in particular, Charles Austin Bates, "Rebates and Recognitions," *Adv. & Sell.,* Jan. 21, 1931; Weston Hill, "Re: Bates and Rebates," *ibid.,* Feb. 18, 1931; John Benson, "The Agency in the Depression," *ibid.,* Apr. 28, 1932; "Union Carbide Demands Agency Commission," *ibid.,* Jan. 6, 1932, and the subsequent notice of retraction, *ibid.,* Feb. 3, 1932, p. 40; H. A. Batten, "An Advertising Man Looks at Advertising," *Atlantic Monthly,* July, 1932; "Advertising Needs Cleaning from Within," *P. I.,* Apr. 5, 1934; A. M. Miller, "Where There's So Much Smoke . . . ," *Adv. & Sell.,* Aug. 2, 1934. For direct testimony that one of the leading cigarette accounts (Lucky Strike) was handled by the Lord & Thomas agency in 1930 at the reduced rate of 12.75 per cent of the net cost, see "How Hill Advertises Is at Last Revealed," *P. I.,* Nov. 17, 1938.

8. John Allen Murphy, "The Turnover in Advertising Accounts," *Adv. & Sell.,* Mar. 16, 1932; Frank E. Fehlman, "The High Turn-Over of Agency Accounts," *ibid.,* Apr. 12, 1934.

9. "How Has the Depression Affected Agency-Client Relations?" *P. I.,* Nov. 5, 1931; interviews with executives and employees of N. W. Ayer & Son.

10. "How the Depression Has Affected Advertising Agency Overhead," *P. I.,* Nov. 12, 1931; H. S. Gardner, "Mergers in Advertising," *Adv. & Sell.,* Apr. 28, 1932.

11. For a summary of advances made during the depression, see Cy Norton, "Advertising Marches On," *P. I.,* Dec. 3, 1936.

12. The chief fruits of this controversy were J. W. Young's *Advertising Agency Compensation;* a mimeographed criticism of it by Albert Haase, "An Analysis of a Report Called Advertising Agency Compensation" (Association of National Advertisers, Inc., 1933); a detailed study by Albert Haase, *Advertising Agency Compensation* (N. Y., 1934); and finally criticisms of the latter: "An Advertising Agent Looks at the Haase Report," *Adv. & Sell.,* Nov. 22, 1934; "Magazine Men Would Retain Present Agency Plan," *P. I.,* Dec. 13, 1934; and *Analysis and Criticism of a Study Entitled Advertising Agency Compensation . . . ,* published by the American Association of Advertising Agencies (N. Y., 1935).

13. By Stuart Chase (N. Y., 1925).

14. By Stuart Chase and F. J. Schlink (N. Y., 1927).

15. By Arthur Kallet and F. J. Schlink (N. Y., 1933).

16. By M. C. Phillips (N. Y., 1934).

17. For information on the first effects of the Commission's new powers, see "F. T. C. Copy Standards," *P. I.,* Sept. 15, 1938.

18. Estimate of the Consumers' Counsel Division of the Department of Agriculture, cited by Hazel Kyrk in the *Journal of Political Economy,* Dec., 1938, p. 906.

19. Advertisements, cover page, *P. I.,* Oct. 20, Nov. 24, and Dec. 22, 1932.

20. *Ibid.,* Mar. 22, 1934, and July 1, 1937.

21. Interviews with Ayer executives; pamphlet, N. W. Ayer & Son, Inc., *Outdoor Advertising* (Philadelphia, 1931); Hugh E. Agnew, *Outdoor Advertising* (N. Y., 1938), chap. ii.

22. For a brief account of the use of motion pictures as an advertising medium, see Hugh E. Agnew and Warren B. Dygert, *Advertising Media* (N. Y., 1938), pp. 426–431. See also L. B. Sizer, "Movies for Selling," *Industrial Marketing,* Nov., 1937.

23. H. A. Batten, "An Advertising Man Looks at Advertising," *Atlantic Monthly,* July, 1932; "Wanted: A Pillory," *Adv. & Sell.,* Aug. 4, 1932; "Vulgar Advertising: A Blot on the Face of Civilized Business," *P. I. Monthly,* Aug., 1932; a speech, "Advertising and Hard Times: A Challenge to American Business," before the Association of National Advertisers, Atlantic City, Nov. 16, 1932; "Our Advertising Buccaneers," *Adv. & Sell.,* Nov. 24, 1932; "False Faces, Notes on the Current Advertising Hallowe'en," *P. I. Monthly,* Dec., 1932; "If Advertising Should Be Discredited," *Dry Goods Economist,* Mar., 1933.

24. Interviews with Ayer executives; Crossley, Inc., *Co-operative Analysis of Broadcasting* (privately issued, 1931); "N. W. Ayer Seeks Lowdown on Radio Coverage," *Adv. & Sell.,* Dec. 23, 1931.

25. Interviews with officers and employees of N. W. Ayer & Son. Since the writer was in Philadelphia studying the Ayer agency from June, 1932, to September, 1933, its history during that eventful period is based on personal knowledge to a large extent.

26. Those who find the emblem lacking in distinction should, in fairness to the designer, bear in mind that Coiner had to prepare it literally overnight without any advance notice.

27. The writer was in Philadelphia during the first three months of the NRA and learned at first hand about the services rendered by N. W. Ayer & Son. The above account is based upon personal knowledge, interviews with members of the Ayer staff, and correspondence between the Ayer firm and the National Recovery Administration, especially R. D. Smith to Wilfred W. Fry, Aug. 17, 1933.

28. Wilfred W. Fry to P. D. Saylor of Canada Dry Ginger Ale, Inc., July 28, 1933.

29. Statement released on Aug. 25, 1933; reprinted in *Editor & Publisher,* Aug. 26, 1933, and in other newspapers at about the same time.

30. Canada Dry copy, 1928–32; Dole Pineapple Juice advertisements, 1933 and 1934; Clicquot Club Ginger Ale advertisement, 1934; French Line advertisements, 1933 and 1934.

31. The two vice-presidents were Mathes and William B. Okie, later principals of J. M. Mathes, Inc. Information concerning their resignation is based upon interviews with Wilfred Fry and other officers of N. W. Ayer & Son, together with a number of persons not now connected with the firm, including several who joined the new agency. See also *Tide,* Jan., 1934, p. 18.

32. It is hopeless to attempt a complete compilation, but a few examples may be cited here: At least two agencies split off from the firm of Charles Austin Bates of New York in 1901–03 (*P. I.,* Aug. 19, 1903, pp. 21–23); four agencies sprang up from the ruins of Pettengill & Company in 1904 (*Publisher's Guide,* May, 1904, p. 9); much more recently a new agency grew out of the Campbell-Ewald Company of Detroit (*Tide,* Mar., 1934, p. 70). For other examples see the news section of almost any advertising trade publication.

33. *P. I.,* Oct. 9, 1919, p. 110.

34. Young & Rubicam to R. P. Robinson of the Ayer staff, June 6, 1923. For a recent account of the founding of Young & Rubicam see John Orr Young, "Adventures in Advertising," *P. I.,* vol 222, no. 10 (Mar. 5, 1948), pp. 27–30. See also Walter Lowen, "The Genealogy of Advertising Agencies," *Adv. & Sell.,* Mar., 1944, pp. 28, 119–120.

35. For this appraisal of Fry the author accepts full responsibility. It is based on personal acquaintance and observation over a period of two years, plus many interviews with members of the Ayer organization at all levels.

36. Theodore E. Steinway, "Wilfred W. Fry," *P. I.,* July 30, 1936.

37. Issue of July 28, 1936, p. 18. Wilfred Washington Fry was born at Mt. Vision, New York, the son of a minister. He spent his boyhood in Otsego and Delaware counties, New York, and attended Mt. Hermon School, Mt. Hermon, Massachusetts, 1892–96. For thirteen years he was engaged in Y.M.C.A. work, after which (1909) he joined N. W. Ayer & Son. At the time of his death he was president of N. W. Ayer & Son, Inc.; of N. W. Ayer & Son of Canada; of the Religious Press Association, Philadelphia; of Meridale Dairies, Inc., of New York City, Camden, New Jersey, and Atlantic City; governing director of N. W. Ayer & Son, Ltd., of London, England; and master of Meridale Farms. He was also president of the Camden & Suburban Railway, the Camden Horse Railroad Co., and the West Jersey Traction Co. He was a director of the First National Bank of Philadelphia, the Great American Insurance Co., the American Alliance Insurance Co., the Great American Indemnity Co., the Associated Re-insurance Co., and the Rochester-American Insurance Co. — all of New York; and the County Fire Insurance Co. and the Fidelity-Philadelphia Co., of Philadelphia.

He had served as president of the Camden Y.M.C.A., 1923–35; was made chairman of the International Committee of Y.M.C.A.'s in 1932; in 1935 he had been elected president of the Board of Trustees of Jefferson Medical College and Hospital of Philadelphia. He was president of the board of trustees of Northfield Schools, East Northfield, Massachusetts, a trustee of Crozer Theological Seminary, Brown University, and Colgate University, a member of the board of managers of Franklin Institute and also of the American Gild of Organists. In 1927 he had been given an LL.D. degree by Colgate University with the following citation: "Able organizer and administrator, capable and inspiring leader, man of fine intelligence and strong character, he has not been content to reserve those powers for his own personal advantage, but has felt the obligation to use them for the service of his fellow men." See *Adv. & Sell.,* July 30, 1936, pp. 30–32; New York *Times,* July 28, 1936, p. 19; *P. I.,* July 30, 1936, pp. 30–32.

38. See New York *Times,* Oct. 20, p. 45; Oct. 21, p. 50; Nov. 25, p. 14; Dec. 11, p. 9; Dec. 17, p. 51 — all for the year 1936. See also *Time,* Nov. 2, 1936, pp. 55–56.

39. The facts here presented are based upon the sten. rep. of the hearings on *George H. Thornley v. N. W. Ayer & Son, Inc., Anna Ayer Fry and Adam Kessler, Jr., Executors, et al.,* Common Pleas, no. 3, Philadelphia, Sept. Term, 1936, no.

1848, in equity. It is also based upon excerpts from the minutes of meetings of directors, stockholders, and trustees of N. W. Ayer & Son, Inc., together with interviews with Batten, Jordan, Lauck, and Thornley, and legal counsel from both sides.

CHAPTER VIII

1. This chapter is based on firsthand observation and many interviews with executives and subordinate employees at intervals during the period 1938–39 and in 1947. It must be regarded as tentative because it is not based on a careful analysis of written records. As to the main outlines of the story and the over-all impression, however, the author feels confident. Anyone who knew the Ayer organization intimately in the period before 1940 and returned to it in 1947 could not fail to note the striking changes for the better. It must be said, too, that the significant developments in recent Ayer history are less a matter of specific, documented events than of intangible but nonetheless definite and important changes in attitude.

2. For many years Batten has been one of a small group of men who have actively guided the Community Chest of Greater Philadelphia. For some time, too, he has been a director and member of the executive committee of the Philadelphia Symphony Orchestra, a director of the Pennsylvania Working Home for Blind Men, and a director of the First National Bank of Philadelphia.

3. This paragraph is based largely on personal observation and many conversations with the staff during 1932–33. Top management at that time dismissed such conclusions as inaccurate and misleading. Events since 1936 have, however, confirmed their essential soundness.

4. Interview, December, 1947.

5. New York *Times,* Jan. 23, 1939, p. 20.

6. For obvious reasons it has not been possible to obtain a release of documentary evidence on this episode, but the writer has satisfied himself as to the substantial accuracy of the story.

7. Harry A. Batten, "This, or Silence," *P. I.,* Nov. 14, 1941.

8. This brief discussion of the Creative Production Board is based on interviews with executives and an examination of many sets of minutes. The minutes reflect remarkably frank and penetrating discussions, while the testimony of all executives reveals extraordinary agreement as to the impact of the meetings on the staff. But it is the way in which the mechanism has been used, rather than the mechanism itself, which has yielded such impressive results.

9. "Policy Memorandum," June 13, 1944, p. 30.

CHAPTER IX

1. All the material in this chapter is based primarily upon records of N. W. Ayer & Son, Inc., especially the personal ledgers, correspondence since 1925, and bound volumes of advertising copy prepared by the agency. Since these records are not available for public inspection and since the citation of specific documents would sometimes reveal identities which must remain anonymous, at least for the present, I shall not usually make detailed citations of authority. The reader will, of course, bear in mind that the mention of a firm as an Ayer client does not necessarily mean that the relation exists at the present time. Some firms change their advertising agency every year or two.

2. Specifically, concerns with headquarters in England, France, Switzerland, Brazil, Argentina, and Japan.

3. Statement made in circular letters sent out in 1904 by N. W. Ayer & Son.

4. Cf. Bachem, *Das Eindringen der Reklame;* Presbrey, *Hist. and Devel. of Advg.,* pp. 35–73.

5. For an extended treatment of some of these issues see Borden, *Econ. Effects of Advg.*

6. Cf. Presbrey, *op. cit.,* pp. 522–530; J. W. Young, *Agency Compensation,* pp. 28–38.

7. F. W. Ayer to J. A. Marsh, Cleveland, Ohio.

8. Advertisement of N. W. Ayer & Son, 1893.

9. Sten. rep., speech of H. N. McKinney, Jan. 5, 1905.

10. Based on stenographic notes, meeting of Ayer solicitors, Jan. 5, 1905, and interviews with former employees of N. W. Ayer & Son. This incident is also related in an article, "Henry N. McKinney, a Great Advertising Man," in *P. I.,* May 9, 1918.

11. The following paragraphs on N. W. Ayer & Son's own advertising are based upon material preserved in the Ayer scrapbooks, together with an examination of the files of *P. I.*

12. As late as 1921, N. W. Ayer & Son received a check for a subscription to *P. I.* (forwarding letter to Printers' Ink Publishing Co., Oct. 5, 1921).

13. The text of the advertisements used in this series before 1929 was published in book form as a series of essays — N. W. Ayer & Son, *In Behalf of Advertising* (Philadelphia, 1929).

14. Advertising circular, 1896.

15. *P. I.,* Aug. 11, 1910.

16. *Ibid.,* July 14, 1910.

CHAPTER X

1. It must be remembered that most publishers had two prices for their space. The upper was the "gross" rate at which they would sell directly to advertisers. The lower was the "net" rate at which they sold to agents. The difference between the two was referred to as the agent's "commission," but was really a trade discount.

2. Minutes of solicitors' meetings, 1896 and 1897; reports of solicitors, 1901; sten. notes, meeting of Ayer employees, 1905; interviews with officers and employees.

3. Contracts in operation between 1891 and 1930, A. C. No contracts for earlier years have been preserved, but from other evidence it is reasonably certain that their terms were much the same.

4. Sten. notes, remarks of F. W. Ayer, Jan., 1905.

5. Sten. rep., meeting of Ayer staff, Sept. 26, 1912.

6. Sten. rep., speech of F. W. Ayer, Dec. 15, 1916. Unfortunately the incident was not dated.

7. Canceled contracts, 1891–1933; minutes of solicitors' meetings, 1896–97; reports of solicitors, 1901.

8. Quoted from the contract form used between 1901 and 1910.

9. For a few years after 1876, as I have noted in Chapter III, the Ayer management charged several different rates experimentally before deciding on 15 per cent, and it has continued the Dingee & Conard contract at 12½ per cent down to the present. Between 1899 and 1906 the firm charged only 10 per cent on outdoor advertising and on the printed pamphlets and other material which it prepared for clients.

Since 1906 the agency has made the preparation of booklets, catalogues, etc., a matter of separate estimates and agreements. And, owing to the conditions imposed by the national organization of the owners of outdoor advertising media (now Outdoor Advertising, Inc.) the Ayer commission plan has not applied to outdoor advertising since 1906. Instead the agency charges the rates set by the outdoor media owners and takes its compensation from the discount which they grant to advertising agencies.

10. Contract form, 1933. While this was the standard form, the terms varied slightly in particular cases, as when the agency did not handle all forms of a client's advertising or handled it for only part of the client's line of products.

11. That the problems of compensation for television were bothering others is evident from *Time,* vol. lii, no. 22 (Nov. 29, 1948), pp. 88–90.

12. This assertion represents my own general conclusions after talking to advertising men, clients, and publishers and after examining many documents and articles on the subject. It is obviously impossible to make a statistical study of all the contracts made by all the agencies in the industry covering any extended period of time.

13. This generalization refers to the principal media which general agencies handle for advertisers. The percentage varies somewhat according to the type of media. The statement, of course, does not apply to media which do not allow commissions or discounts to agencies, but there is clear evidence that the handling of even these non-discount media is affected by the traditional method of compensation: a great many agencies that take as their remuneration the discount allowed by publishers handle the non-discount media without charge. See J. W. Young, *Agency Compensation,* p. 72; Haase, *Advertising Agency Compensation,* tables vi and vii, pp. 40–41.

14. See, for example, J. W. Young, *op. cit.,* p. 27, and an able study far removed from it in space, time, and method, Victor Mataja, *Die Reklame* (Munich, 1920), pp. 187–217.

15. A draft of the agency code was published in *P. I.,* Aug. 31, 1933, pp. 25–28.

For a detailed discussion of the commission plan, see especially William J. Reilly, *Effects of the Advertising Agency Commission System* (N. Y., 1931), and the studies by Young and Haase to which reference has already been made (see note 12, Chapter VII). See also Hotchkiss, *Outline of Advg.,* pp. 590–592; Melvin T. Copeland, *Principles of Merchandising* (Chicago, 1924), p. 286; H. K. Nixon, *Principles of Advertising* (N. Y., 1937), pp. 19–20; C. H. Sandage, *Advertising Theory and Practice* (Chicago, 1936), pp. 514–518.

16. J. W. Young, *op. cit.,* p. 36.

17. Form letter to clients, Sept., 1918.

18. *P. I.,* Sept. 19, 1918, p. 77; J. W. Young, *op. cit.,* p. 38.

19. The one point on which most agencies agree, even insist, is that agency service cannot be standardized. Cf. J. W. Young, *op. cit.,* pp. 122–124.

20. Haase, *op. cit.,* p. 67.

CHAPTER XI

1. This chapter has been based primarily on material in the Ayer files relating to advertising plans. Most of the available documentary evidence belongs to the period between 1917 and 1933, the earlier records having been destroyed; but enough information has been gleaned from various sources to provide a reasonably accurate sketch of the methods used in earlier years.

2. See M. T. Copeland, "The Managerial Factor in Marketing," in *Facts and Factors in Economic History* (Cambridge, 1932), pp. 596–619.

3. Advertisement of N. W. Ayer & Son in *Harper's Magazine*, Jan., 1893, p. 52.
4. Cf. Hotchkiss, *Outline of Advg.*, pp. 138–142.
5. Cf. *ibid.*, pp. 148–173.
6. Cf. Lyman Chalkley, Jr., "Agency Tactics Hinder Market Research Development," *Adv. & Sell.*, Jan. 4, 1934.
7. Haase, *Advertising Agency Compensation*, stresses this issue as one which faces all agencies, and he produces, especially in chaps. iii and vi, considerable evidence to support a widely held view that the traditional method of compensation has been hampering the agency's normal evolution.
8. This statement is based upon comments made by many clients in letters to N. W. Ayer & Son, and also upon personal interviews which the writer has had with more than thirty men who have had a chance to compare objectively the work of the Ayer agency with that of its leading competitors.
9. For a good general discussion of advertising plans, their objectives, the selection of media, and other features, see Hotchkiss, *op. cit.*, pp. 86–110, 339–395, 427–448.
10. Sten. rep. of remarks to Ayer staff, Jan. 5, 1905.
11. Letter to N. W. Ayer & Son from a client, dated Dec. 11, 1929.

CHAPTER XII

1. This chapter is based upon correspondence, files of advertising copy, and other records belonging to N. W. Ayer & Son, together with many interviews with clients, employees, and publishers, mainly for the period before 1935. So much of it represents summaries and generalizations from a great many accounts that individual citations can seldom be given.
2. Cf. Hotchkiss, *Outline of Advg.*, pp. 273–341.
3. Cf. J. W. Young, *Agency Compensation*, pp. 52–65.
4. H. N. McKinney to Edward D. Adams, Sept. 28, 1893, referring to article in *P. I.*, June 28, 1893, pp. 755–761; Ayer space-buyers' computations dated Sept. 29, 1893.
5. An excellent example of the substantial savings attained by the Ayer agency in this way is set forth in detail in the case of *N. W. Ayer & Son* v. *United States Rubber Co.*, 282 Pa. 404, 128 A. 103.
6. Based upon interviews with publishers and their representatives in New York, Boston, and Philadelphia. One prominent New York publisher went so far as to describe the Ayer Media Department as "head and shoulders above the rest," and went on to support this assertion by examples of its efficiency and the citation of important rival agencies who regard the choice of media and purchase of space as routine clerical jobs. In such agencies sales pressure and favoritism soon become factors in the purchase of space.
7. This section is based upon information contained in *The Science of Advertising*, published by N. W. Ayer & Son in 1874; printed requests for checking copies, dated 1876–81; a description of the Ayer checking service in a pamphlet — *To Philadelphia Business Men*, published in 1878; another description in *For Value Received*, 1930; correspondence with publishers and clients; interviews with employees; and personal observation of the checking during 1932 and 1933.
8. Neil H. Borden and Osgood S. Lovekin, *A Test of the Consumer Jury Method of Ranking Advertisements* (Harvard Business Research Studies, no. 11, Boston, 1935).
9. For a discussion of the nature and technique of modern public relations work, see Bronson Batchelor, *Profitable Public Relations* (N. Y., 1938). It is worth

noting that, out of nine advertisements reproduced by that author in the appendix to illustrate effective public relations copy, three were prepared by the Ayer agency.

10. Advertisements in *P. I.,* July 2, 1936, and subsequent issues.

11. Address, "Public Relations," by H. A. Batten, before the Association of National Advertisers, Hot Springs, Va., Apr. 28, 1937.

12. The Steinway account first appeared in Ledger 35, June, 1900.

13. This account of the work of N. W. Ayer & Son for Steinway & Sons is based upon records in possession of N. W. Ayer & Son, together with an interview with F. Reidermeister, treasurer of Steinway & Sons, Inc.

14. This account of the Hills Bros. advertising has been based upon correspondence and other records in the files of N. W. Ayer & Son.

15. This story has been based upon correspondence between the Ford Motor Company and N. W. Ayer & Son, together with data supplied by the Media Department.

CHAPTER XIII

1. Except where otherwise indicated, the material for this chapter is drawn entirely from the copy books, A. C.

2. Lee, *Hist. of Amer. Journalism,* pp. 279, 311; Presbrey, *Hist. and Devel. of Advg.,* pp. 232–245. The feeling that the use of display was unfair persisted long after the rule against it began to be abandoned. See letter from H. F. Gunnison of the Brooklyn (N. Y.) *Daily Eagle* in *P. I.,* Mar. 26, 1890, p. 534.

3. Presbrey, *op. cit.,* pp. 244–252.

4. Cf. *ibid.,* pp. 256–258.

5. Advertisements in *P. I.,* Mar. 11 and Nov. 18, 1891, and Oct. 20, 1894.

6. Cf. Presbrey, *op. cit.,* pp. 382–387. For a brief discussion of the various processes of reproducing illustrations, see Carl H. Greer, *Advertising and Its Mechanical Reproduction* (N. Y., 1931), pp. 177–264.

7. *P. I.,* Dec. 15, 1888, pp. 259–260.

8. Presbrey, *op. cit.,* pp. 356–359.

9. For a discussion of types of appeals and advertising strategy, see Copeland, *Principles of Merchandising,* chaps. vi and ix.

10. Presbrey, *op. cit.,* pp. 386, 473.

11. "A New Departure," *Art in Advertising,* Apr., 1895.

12. Depew, *One Hundred Years of Amer. Commerce,* p. 81.

13. The earlier attitude of artists is well revealed in an advertisement of the Pictorial League, which produced illustrations for advertisers, in *P. I.,* Nov. 12, 1890, p. 505. The offer to submit illustrative material ended with the admonition, "Be sure to state the nature of your business."

14. Deane Uptegrove, "The Four Million Picks Its Pictures," *Adv. & Sell.,* June 6, 1935.

15. Of the agencies which received more than one award for advertising copy during the seven years Batten, Barton, Durstine & Osborn received nine, Gardner Advertising Co. four, Calkins & Holden three, Blackman Co. and Young & Rubicam two each. It should be noted that the first-named submitted material every year except one in which one of its officers served on the committee of judges. This was not true of the other agencies.

16. Much of the literature about copy testing is to be found in the current advertising periodicals. A good discussion of the methods developed up to 1934 is to be found in L. E. Firth, *Testing Advertisements* (N. Y., 1934).

CHAPTER XIV

1. See above, pp. 156–157.

2. Personal Ledgers 25, 30, 35, 40, and 45.

3. Notes of a meeting of the Ayer soliciting staff, Dec. 1, 1905. Earlier in the same year McKinney urged the same view: "Don't let us settle down to the thought that we cannot successfully handle more than one customer in the same line of business. . . . In cases when that would not be good business policy, [let us] decide that we cannot do it; but let us consider them exceptions to the general rule that we can and will handle different concerns in the same line of business." (Remarks to Ayer employees, Jan. 5, 1905.)

4. Inter-departmental memo. dated Feb. 14, 1923.

5. Apparently both occasions were the result of the desire of the junior executives to get new business without sacrificing existing accounts. That the senior executives may not have been aware of the situation does not, however, relieve them from blame. It is their responsibility to know which accounts are being accepted.

6. Letter from a branch office to headquarters, dated Feb. 15, 1930.

7. Letter to the author, dated Dec. 30, 1947.

8. H. N. McKinney to Franklin Mills Co., Lockport, N. Y., Dec. 24, 1895.

9. Some observers believe that lavish entertainment for business-getting purposes declined during the depression years (*P. I.,* July 14, 1938, p. 6).

10. Several clients, when interviewed, made particular mention of the fact that Ayer representatives did not resort to lavish entertainment in their efforts to gain business.

11. As early as 1896, the Ayer staff complained of this handicap. Minutes of the monthly meetings of solicitors, 1896, A. C.

12. See, e.g., Hopkins, *My Life in Advg.,* pp. 86–95, 151–156, 193–197; and Rowell, *Forty Years an Advg. Agt.,* pp. 366–380, 402.

13. Private Ledgers 1, 2, and 3; Personal Ledgers 10, 15, 20, 25, 30, 35, and 40; interviews with officers of N. W. Ayer & Son, Inc.

14. Individual Ayer officers have sometimes made substantial investments in firms which were Ayer clients. Several of them, for example, held considerable amounts of stock in Canada Dry during the 1920's. Such investments seem invariably to have been made because the officers concerned believed the clients were likely to develop profitable concerns, but in some instances they might be open to the objections usually raised against direct ownership by the agency. For a discussion of the issues involved, see "How Many Agencies Own Interests in Their Clients?" *Adv. & Sell.,* Mar. 18, 1931.

15. Program for solicitors' meeting, Mar. 31, 1906, A. C.

16. It is noteworthy, in this connection, that the majority of members of the Association of National Advertisers continue to agree to the traditional method in spite of the strong and well-founded attacks which the Association has made upon that method. The explanation lies partly in the normal human inertia of such members and partly in the combined resistance of the American Association of Advertising Agencies and of many publishers to any efforts towards a change in the system of compensation.

17. *Ayer* v. *Devlin* (179 Mich. 81, 146 N. W. 257) involved the question of liability for advertising which the client contended was placed out of position. The decision was that the client was liable, since he had not discontinued the advertising upon receiving full information as to the position in which his adver-

tisements would be placed. The amount of money involved was relatively small, and the interpretation of the Ayer contract itself was not an issue.

18. In the Court of Common Pleas, no. 4, of Philadelphia, *N. W. Ayer & Son* v. *United States Rubber Company*, 282 Pa. 404, 128 A. 103. A thirty-page report on the trial and verdict was published in *P. I.*, Apr. 26, 1923.

19. Letter from one Ayer executive to another, dated Mar. 28, 1927.

20. Letter dated Aug. 25, 1926.

21. For obvious reasons I do not cite the date and other details which might make possible the identification of the advertiser.

22. See, in this connection, Mabel Taylor Gragg and Neil H. Borden, *Merchandise Testing as a Guide to Consumer Buying* (Harvard Business Research Studies, no. 22, 1938).

23. Letter dated Oct. 27, 1926.

24. N. W. Ayer & Son to Phillips & Clark Stove Co., Geneva, N. Y., June 30, 1903.

25. Inter-office memo., dated Apr. 24, 1929.

26. Inter-office memo., dated Jan. 23, 1930.

27. For further information on this subject, see vol. 11 of the Harvard Business Reports, *Coöperative Advertising by Trade Associations,* with introduction and commentaries by Neil H. Borden.

28. Letter to the head of an association, dated July 27, 1923.

29. *Ibid.*

30. Communication dated Oct. 29, 1926.

31. Letter to a client, dated May 21, 1926.

32. Inter-office correspondence, letter dated Jan. 1, 1926.

33. Memo. of the Public Relations Department, Apr. 13, 1929.

34. In its early days, however, the Ayer firm did occasionally exert its influence for or against legislation which affected clients. In 1886, for example, N. W. Ayer & Son joined with John Wanamaker in a successful fight against an increase in the rate of postage on fourth-class matter (printed notices sent out by the two firms in 1886, and a form letter sent out by John Wanamaker, dated June 1, 1888). In 1897 the Ayer agency sent out letters urging florists and seed growers to protest against the free distribution of seeds by Congressmen (form letter, dated Dec. 27, 1897). Such activities are somewhat rare in Ayer history.

35. Sten. rep., remarks to Ayer employees, Jan. 5, 1905.

36. Letter to client, dated Mar. 5, 1930.

37. Inter-office memo., dated June 24, 1926.

38. Report of a solicitor, dated Jan. 1, 1901.

39. Inter-departmental memo., Sept. 22, 1930.

40. See, for example, John Allen Murphy, "The Turnover in Advertising Accounts," in *Adv. & Sell.*, Mar. 16, 1932, pp. 17–18, 70–71.

41. This section is based mainly upon a careful examination of all the canceled contracts in the Ayer files up to Dec. 31, 1932, together with all the information about the loss of accounts which could be gleaned from the correspondence files, and interviews with Ayer officers, employees, and with a limited number of publishers, clients, and advertising men outside the Ayer firm.

42. No accurate data are available on the average life of accounts in other agencies, but a number of experienced agency men have estimated that the typical account stays with one agency for three and a half years. See Frank Finney, "Concerning the 'Long Life' of Accounts," *Adv. & Sell.*, May 10, 1934.

CHAPTER XV

1. See above, Chapter II, esp. pp. 30–35.
2. F. W. Ayer to N. W. Ayer, July 11, 1872.
3. Advertisement of N. W. Ayer & Son, 1876.
4. This sketch of the middle period of agency development, which briefly reviews some of the material given in Chapters II and III, is based on the sources cited therein.
5. MS A., A. C.
6. This part of the statement was true, but it did not give the whole truth, for some of the stock of the Religious Press Association was held then, as in 1933, in the name of the agency and entered in its ledger as an asset. The amount held, however, was always relatively small.
7. Booklet published by N. W. Ayer & Son, 1887, A. C.
8. Old space contracts, 1882–95, A. C.
9. *Ibid.*, blank form dated Mar. 9, 1897, A. C.
10. Orange Bulletin Co., Cincinnati, to N. W. Ayer & Son, Feb. 3, 1886.
11. S. D. Coleman, St. Louis, to N. W. Ayer & Son, Sept. 17, 1886.
12. *Our Silent Partner*, Waterville, Me., Nov. 1, 1894.
13. F. W. Ayer to E. W. Thomas, Philadelphia, Nov. 7, 1871.
14. Advertising proposal, 1876.
15. *Ibid.*, Mar. 25, 1876, A. C.
16. Due-bill forms, A. C.
17. Gen. Jour., 1878; advertising proposals 1878–84, A. C. Cf. Robert Frothingham, "Early Advertising Solicitations," *Adv. & Sell.*, Oct. 13, 1932, pp. 30–32.
18. Advertising proposal, Nov., 1875; account with *Sat. Eve. Post* in General Ledger, 1875.
19. See above, pp. 42–43.
20. Advertising proposals, 1881.
21. Wm. Stahl, Quincy, Ill., to Axtell, Bush & Co., Pittsburgh, Pa., Jan. 13, 1896. Copy in A. C.
22. Correspondence between N. W. Ayer & Son, Axtell, Bush & Co., and others, and advertisements of the *National Stockman & Farmer,* Feb., 1892, to Nov., 1898; letters in *P. I.,* Nov. 13, 1895, p. 21, and Jan. 22, 1896, p. 28.
23. Sten. rep., remarks of Cyrus H. K. Curtis at memorial service for F. Wayland Ayer, Apr. 14, 1923. Cf. Bok, *A Man from Maine,* pp. 107–116. The date of the first Curtis advertising to be handled by Ayer was 1885, according to the Ayer ledgers.
24. Rowell, *Forty Years an Advg. Agt.,* pp. 308–315; J. W. Young, *Agency Compensation,* p. 27.
25. Lee, *Hist. of Amer. Journalism,* pp. 352–353.
26. Young, *op. cit.,* pp. 4–12; Albert H. Kent, "National Representation of a Group of Daily Newspapers," *Careers in Advertising,* edited by Alden James (N. Y., 1932), pp. 335–337.
27. Excepting, of course, the comparatively few direct advertisers who have succeeded in continuing special arrangements made in the 'seventies and 'eighties; excepting, too, advertisers who have *sub rosa* agreements with publishers or agents for less than card rates.
28. This and the preceding paragraph embody conclusions set forth in Young, *op. cit.,* pp. 26–33, but they are based primarily on articles and exchanges of

opinion in *P. I.,* during 1889, 1890, and 1891; see especially A. H. Siegfried, "The Special Agency System," April 15, 1891, pp. 503–505.

29. *P. I.,* June 15, 1889, p. 620, and Feb. 26, 1890, pp. 395–398. See also the report of a meeting of the Inter-State Association of Dailies in *P. I.,* May 14, 1890, pp. 778–779.

30. Young, *op. cit.,* p. 32.

31. Data supplied to N. W. Ayer & Son by Caswell & Moore of Phoenixville, Pa., Mar. 5, 1897.

32. Young, *op. cit.,* pp. 32–35.

33. *Ibid.,* pp. 37–38, 97–100.

34. *Ibid.,* pp. 5–12. Standards of recognition for the radio industry were announced in "Radio Audit Bureau Studied," *P. I.,* Sept. 27, 1934.

35. Canceled contracts, 1898–1900, and accompanying correspondence.

36. Canceled contracts, 1901–13.

37. Memoranda of the Ayer Outdoor Advertising Department, 1900, 1905, 1910; interviews with the former head of the Department; *Tide,* Aug., 1931, p. 22. *Tide* puts the number of licensed representatives at 5 in 1910, 30 in 1913, but otherwise agrees with the facts recorded in Ayer papers.

A brief historical sketch of outdoor advertising developments in the United States is to be found in Hugh E. Agnew, *Outdoor Advertising* (N. Y., 1938); the study does not go deeply into the question of compensation.

38. See especially *Chas. A. Ramsey Co.* v. *Associated Bill Posters of U. S. and Canada et al.,* 260 U. S. 501 (1922).

39. Minutes of the meeting of Ayer partners, Oct. 29, 1920; *Tide,* Aug., 1931, p. 22; interviews with Ayer executives, several rival agents, and one officer of Outdoor Advertising, Inc.

40. F. W. Ayer to the Transcript Company, Portland, Me., Jan. 1, 1898.

41. F. W. Ayer to J. A. Wood, Dec. 3, 1898.

42. This sentence suggests that Ayer favored payment by publishers. Probably the implication is the result of hasty and careless composition. Ayer thought publishers should allow a discount to agents, but he plainly favored payment by the advertiser.

43. *P. I.,* Mar. 27, 1901, pp. 3, 5.

44. Sten. rep., speech to Ayer staff, Jan., 1905.

45. Letter to publishers, Mar. 18, 1921.

46. As indicated in Chapter III, the correct date was 1876 instead of 1873.

47. Young, *op. cit.,* p. 161.

48. It is worth noting that the commission system of compensating advertising agents is still used in Great Britain. Its merits and demerits are briefly stated in a recent and important study, P E P, *Report on the British Press* (London, 1938), pp. 77–78.

49. Rowell, *op. cit., passim;* Presbrey, *op. cit.,* pp. 544–552.

50. Depew, *One Hundred Years,* p. 79; see also above, pp. 82–83.

51. Frank Munsey, "Advertising in Some of Its Phases," an address to the Sphinx Club of New York, printed in *Munsey's Magazine,* Dec., 1898, pp. 476–486.

52. Announcement to publishers dated Apr. 1, 1910; *Annual* for 1910.

53. Prospectus of Audit Bureau of Circulations, 1914, A. C.; *American Newspaper Annual and Directory,* 1915.

See also Audit Bureau of Circulations, *Scientific Space Selection* (Chicago, 1937).

54. Data derived from *N. W. Ayer & Son's Directory of Newspapers and Pe-*

riodicals (the title was changed from *American Newspaper Annual and Directory* in 1930) for 1939 and 1948 by members of the Ayer Directory Department.

55. Outdoor coverage is now analyzed by Traffic Audit Bureau, Inc. For a description of the origin and methods of this organization, see Agnew, *op. cit.* See also Traffic Audit Bureau, *Standard Circulation Values of Outdoor Advertising* (N. Y., 1938).

The first extensive analysis of radio station coverage was undertaken in 1930–31 by Crossley, Inc. Sponsored by advertisers and agencies, it was continued and results were given to subscribers under the heading *The Co-operative Analysis of Broadcasting.* Other independent surveys are now being provided by Daniel Starch, Inc., and L. M. Clark, Inc., both of New York City. A number of other organizations make special analyses for clients, and, of course, a considerable amount of information is collected and made available by various broadcasting units.

56. Sten. rep., conference of Ayer employees, Jan. 5, 1905. The same attitude was expressed a little less baldly in a letter to Balmer dated Mar. 18, 1905.

57. Sten. rep., "Our Attitude toward the Publishers and Their Representatives," talk before the Ayer staff, Sept. 26, 1912.

58. N. W. Ayer & Son to Iowa publishers, July 15, 1921; files of the Ayer Forwarding Department, 1921–23.

59. N. W. Ayer & Son to the advertising manager of a well-known national magazine, dated Mar. 27, 1930.

60. Copy of letter in A. C. dated 1889.

61. Letter dated Dec. 1, 1928. Names deleted for obvious reasons.

62. It is noteworthy, however, that the Ayer firm has long forbidden members of its staff to accept from publishers any gift or favor having monetary value. (Notice to employees, June 1, 1900, referring to established rules in this matter.) In recent years the management has found it necessary to warn employees against accepting lavish entertainment from media owners or their representatives.

63. Summary prepared by N. W. Ayer & Son, dated Jan. 26, 1926.

64. Business Department correspondence, 1926–32.

65. Frank L. Swigert (now deceased) to the Illinois Press Association, Urbana, Ill., Nov. 11, 1932.

66. Advertising proposals, 1876–1900, A. C. See also Rowell, *op. cit.,* p. 321.

67. Advertising proposal dated May, 1880, A. C.

68. Advertisements and proposals, 1876–1900.

69. Letter to publishers, dated July 5, 1899.

70. "An Ayerogram," 1908.

71. S. W. Corman before the Southern Newspaper Publishers' Association, June 14, 1915.

72. *Ibid.*

73. Correspondence about publicity in Ayer files, 1919–20.

74. Correspondence of Publicity Bureau, 1922–30.

75. Form letter sent out by N. W. Ayer & Son in 1925 and used, with unimportant variations in wording, since 1923.

76. May 23, 1925, p. 22.

77. Correspondence of the Publicity Bureau, 1920–30; interviews with publishers in Boston, New York, and Philadelphia.

78. *Wilmer Atkinson, An Autobiography* (Philadelphia, 1920), pp. 179–180, 183–194.

79. Advertisements, proposals, and a few letters from publishers, 1874–84, A. C.

80. Report of the fourth annual convention of the A.N.P.A., *P. I.*, Feb. 20, 1890, pp. 395–398.
81. Edward W. Bok, *The Americanization of Edward Bok* (N. Y., 1924), pp. 340–351.
82. Presbrey, *op. cit.*, pp. 531–540.
83. Booklet issued by the Curtis Publishing Co., Philadelphia, undated but received by N. W. Ayer & Son on Oct. 6, 1910. A later version appears in E. E. Calkins, *The Business of Advertising* (N. Y., 1915), pp. 338–340.
84. Memo. on copy censorship, 1912; correspondence with clients and publishers, 1920–32.
85. Letter to publishers sent out at various times during 1920.
86. For a good discussion of the censorship of advertising by the British Press, see P E P, *op. cit.*, pp. 181–184.
87. Correspondence with publishers, 1920–32; interviews with officers and employees of N. W. Ayer & Son.
88. Speech of S. W. Corman, cited in note 71.
89. Address of F. L. Swigert, cited in note 65.
90. Minutes of meeting of Ayer partners, Oct. 19, 1920; interviews with Ayer executives.
91. Sten. rep., conference with members of the Ayer staff, June 19, 1922.
92. Interviews with Ayer executives; memo. of the treasurer of N. W. Ayer & Son.
93. In the Ayer files there are printed forms, dating from 1876, which were sent out to publishers regarding missed insertions.
94. Correspondence files of the Media Contract Department, 1919–22.
95. This and the preceding paragraphs of the present section are based upon records in the Ayer files dating from 1876 to 1932, the testimony of Ayer employees of long experience, and interviews with publishers.
96. Quoted in *The Fourth Estate*, July 2, 1921, p. 12.
97. This statement was made to the writer in 1932 by the late Adolph Ochs of the New York *Times*. Similar sentiments are contained in letters and clippings in the Ayer files dating from 1872 to the present.

CHAPTER XVI

1. Ledgers 1–15, covering the years 1871–85.
2. *Ibid.;* Gen. Jour., Apr. to Dec., 1878.
3. Printed proposal, dated Feb. 23, 1876, A. C.
4. Copy of a letter written "nearly a year ago" enclosed with a letter dated Jan. 22, 1889, from N. W. Ayer & Son to a European agency.
5. Invitation dated Mar. 17, 1888, A. C.
6. Speech to Ayer employees, June 19, 1922.
7. *P. I.*, May 1, 1889, p. 499.
8. N. W. Ayer & Son to J. L. Mahin, July 9, 1901.
9. N. W. Ayer & Son, *Forty Years of Advertising* (Philadelphia, 1909), pp. 25–30.
10. *American Advertising Agents' Association, Report, Third Annual Meeting* (N. Y., 1903), *passim.*
11. A. L. Thomas to F. W. Ayer, Apr. 27, 1904.
12. F. W. Ayer to A. L. Thomas, May 11, 1904. A death in Ayer's family accounts for the delay in answering.
13. A. L. Thomas to F. W. Ayer, May 14, 1904.

14. F. W. Ayer to A. L. Thomas, May 18, 1904.

15. Memo. dated May 17, 1904.

16. Memo. dated May 16, 1904.

17. Memo. dated May 17, 1904. Names deleted for obvious reasons.

18. A. L. Thomas to F. W. Ayer, May 23, 1904.

19. U. K. Pettingill, a Boston agent, failed in Apr., 1904, owing about $1,000,000 (*Newspaperdom*, Apr. 7, 1904, pp. 1–2). He is not to be confused with S. M. Pettengill, a pioneer agent who had died some years earlier.

20. F. W. Ayer to A. L. Thomas, May 31, 1904.

21. *Editor & Publisher*, June 16, 1917, pp. 3–4.

22. See, e.g., *The Ethical Problems of Modern Advertising*, Vawter Lectures, Northwestern University (N. Y., 1931); Presbrey, *Hist. and Devel. of Advg.*, pp. 546–548; J. W. Young, *Agency Compensation*, pp. 3–4.

23. Presbrey, *op. cit.*, pp. 545–546.

24. *Agency Association Progress in the United States.* Address by Newcomb Cleveland in London, July 15, 1924, published by the American Association of Advertising Agencies (N. Y., 1924), *passim*.

25. J. W. Young, *op. cit.*, p. 38.

26. *The Ethical Problems of Modern Advertising*, pp. 64–65.

27. Business Department correspondence, 1926.

28. J. A. Wood to an Ayer client, Jan. 19, 1925.

29. Wilfred W. Fry to various organizations, June 30, 1933.

30. This and the following paragraphs dealing with the attempt to devise an NRA code for agencies are based upon interviews with executives of N. W. Ayer & Son and information published in trade journals, notably *Adv. & Sell.*, Aug. 31, 1933, pp. 25, 44, 46; *P. I.*, Aug. 31, 1933, pp. 25–28, Oct. 19, 1933, pp. 84–85, Oct. 26, 1933, p. 32, Aug. 9, 1934, pp. 22, 24–25; *Tide*, July, 1933, p. 26, Sept., 1933, pp. 10–12, Oct., 1933, pp. 56–60, Aug., 1934, p. 26, Sept., 1934, p. 66.

31. Quoted in *Adv. & Sell.*, Aug. 31, 1933, p. 44.

32. *Loc. cit.*

33. This statement was not made officially, but it was widely circulated in advertising circles at the time the first draft was published and apparently came from the committee. See *P. I.*, Aug. 31, 1933, pp. 25–28; *Tide*, Oct., 1933, pp. 58–60.

34. This statement is based upon conversations with four representatives from important rival agencies, made in 1932–34.

CHAPTER XVII

1. Advertising pamphlet, *To Philadelphia Business Men*, published by N. W. Ayer & Son in 1877, describing the work of the agency and the arrangement of the business in the quarters which the firm entered in 1876.

2. Ledger 5 (1878–79); Private Ledger 1 (1880–84); pay roll lists, 1880; Ayer advertisements, 1880–82; interview with W. J. Clark, formerly head bookkeeper of N. W. Ayer & Son (1878–98).

3. Attendance records and pay roll lists, 1882–1900.

4. *Ibid.*

5. See above, pp. 77–80.

6. Pay roll lists, 1892–1900; interviews with former employees of N. W. Ayer & Son.

7. Minutes of the monthly meetings of Ayer solicitors, 1896, report of committee presented Jan. 4, 1897.

8. This and the following paragraphs dealing with the reorganization of 1900

are based upon the Ayer pay roll lists for 1900, together with interviews with former employees.

9. Interviews with men who were employed in the preparation of Ayer copy from 1892 onward.

10. *Ibid.;* pay roll lists, 1898–1914. The reorganization of the Copy Department, which was worked out in 1912, took effect in Jan., 1913.

11. Pay roll lists, 1916–17; interviews with members of the Ayer staff.

12. "Of Interest to Advertisers," *National Printer-Journalist,* Sept., 1894, pp. 434–435.

13. Sten. rep., speech of F. W. Ayer to staff, Sept. 9, 1908.

14. Interviews with members of the Ayer staff; pay roll lists, 1914–20.

15. Interviews with members of the Ayer organization; correspondence of the Publicity Bureau, 1922–29; pay roll lists, 1920–30.

16. Interviews, Business Department correspondence, 1925–30; pay roll lists, 1920–30.

17. "What About Radio?" a manual prepared by N. W. Ayer & Son for its own staff members, 1931.

18. Pay roll lists, 1914–20.

19. Pay roll lists, 1912–30.

20. For the explanation of this, see above, pp. 406–407.

21. Pay roll lists, 1912–26.

22. This entire section owes much to Professor M. T. Copeland's "The Managerial Factor in Marketing," pp. 596–619; also to his course in Business Policy at the Harvard Graduate School of Business Administration.

23. In recent years there has been an attempt to distinguish between management and administration, between the control of the process of executing policies and the formulation of those policies. See the article on "Management" in the *Encyclopaedia of the Social Sciences,* vol. x (N. Y., 1933). But in the Ayer firm the two functions have always been inextricably blended, and they cannot be treated separately.

24. Summary of F. W. Ayer's remarks to solicitors, Jan. 4, 1897.

25. *Ibid.*

26. Remarks of F. W. Ayer to employees on June 19, 1922, quoted from sten. rep. of a speech by Wilfred W. Fry on Sept. 19, 1923, A. C.

27. See Copeland, "The Managerial Factor," p. 603; Harry R. Tosdal, *Principles of Personal Selling* (N. Y., 1925), pp. 42–46, 352–373.

28. Interviews with Theodore F. Miner, who was an Ayer employee 1883–99 and died in 1932; Eugene Greiner, who worked for N. W. Ayer & Son from 1882 until his death in 1933; Miss Adeline Engles, who has been with the firm since 1886; and several others whose service dates from the late 'eighties.

29. Letter from Theodore F. Miner to a member of the Ayer staff, May 24, 1926.

30. The first general meeting was held on Dec. 28, 1892. Notes on the discussion, A. C.

31. Memo. on conference, June 22, 1896.

32. *Ibid.,* Oct. 5, 1896.

33. A. C.

34. Letter to solicitors, Mar. 8, 1898.

35. Minutes of a meeting of Ayer solicitors, Dec. 1, 1905.

36. Pay roll lists, 1905; interviews with Ayer employees.

37. Interviews with officers and representatives of N. W. Ayer & Son during 1932, 1933, 1934, and 1947; interviews with former employees.

38. Interview with Miss Adeline Engles; pay roll lists, 1880–90.

39. Various letters and memoranda in the Ayer files relating to this period.

40. Announcement dated June 30, 1903. From the Ayer expense accounts it is evident that no extensive use of the telephone was made until the firm moved into new quarters late in 1902.

41. Among the Ayer papers are a number of solicitors' reports for 1900 and 1901, summarizing soliciting experience and prospects in particular districts and lines of business.

42. See below, Chapter XIX.

43. Memo., "Three Committees," dated Apr. 24, 1905.

44. Notes on remarks by F. W. Ayer before a conference of employees, Apr. 25, 1907.

45. Announcement of appointment of a general manager, dated Mar. 21, 1911. Other aspects of this change were dealt with above, pp. 103–107.

46. Sten. rep., speech to Ayer staff, Sept. 25, 1912.

47. See in this connection James A. Bowie, *Education for Business* (Oxford, 1930), especially chaps. i–iii.

48. Sten. rep., conference of Ayer staff, Sept. 25, 1912.

49. *Ibid.,* Sept. 28, 1912.

50. See Kenneth Groesbeck, "How the Advertising Agency Works," *Careers in Advertising,* pp. 77–83.

51. In 1922 and 1923, for example, six members of the Editorial and Art bureaus and one from the Plans Department regularly met with the representative concerned in order to formulate a policy with regard to the advertising of each of the various clients. Copy Department memo., 1923.

52. Minutes of firm meetings in 1920, 1923, 1924. Since the minutes of such meetings were not systematically recorded or preserved, the evidence is necessarily fragmentary.

53. *Ibid.,* Oct. 29, 1923.

54. Interviews with officers of N. W. Ayer & Son, Inc.

55. Wilfred W. Fry to members of the Ayer staff, July 29, 1929.

56. Organization charts, 1932, 1938.

CHAPTER XVIII

1. F. W. Ayer to George Post, July 28, 1873.

2. This attitude was expressed by Ayer in a letter to M. A. Stille, Oct. 14, 1872, and appears indirectly in many other sources.

3. Interviews with the vice-president in charge of personnel, as well as with other members of the Ayer staff.

4. Expense account, Ledgers 3 and 4; interviews with former employees; pay rolls, 1880–1900.

5. Interview with Joseph W. Gannon, later of the New York *Times,* who was the first to be hired as a result of the new policy.

6. Letters and memoranda by J. A. Wood, dating from 1900 to 1903.

7. Clippings and memoranda by J. A. Wood, 1919 and 1920; résumé of the experience of the principal Ayer representatives, dated June 27, 1923; letter inviting a man to join the Ayer staff, Jan. 14, 1924.

8. Letter to a prospective client, Mar. 27, 1922.

9. Expense account, Ledgers 1–5 (1870–79).

10. Recollections of Frank J. Post, an Ayer employee from 1876 to 1880, in letters to F. W. Ayer, Apr. 27, May 3, and May 9, 1903.

11. Pay roll lists, 1880–1932.

12. Cf. Joseph A. Hill, *Women in Gainful Occupations, 1870–1920*. Census Monograph no. ix (Washington, 1929); *Census of Business: 1935. Advertising Agencies*, p. 9.

13. Pay roll lists, 1880–1932; interviews with officers and employees of N. W. Ayer & Son.

14. Ledgers 1–5; pay roll lists, 1880–1932; interviews with employees.

15. Pay roll lists; interviews with officers and employees.

16. Pay roll list, Sept., 1938.

17. The statements in this paragraph are based upon a few references to the working day in F. W. Ayer's letters, 1871–73, together with inferences drawn from later innovations cited below.

18. Printed notices, May 30, 1885, June 12, 1886, and similar announcements in later years.

19. Printed notice, Sept. 1, 1886.

20. Printed announcements, dated Feb., 1882, and subsequently, to 1890.

21. Printed notice, Sept. 30, 1890.

22. Printed pamphlet addressed to employees, Feb., 1896.

23. Printed notice, Feb., 1895. Seven complaints about dishonesty of reporting time of arrival were made in 1896 and 1897 (notices dated Sept. 7, 1896, and Feb. 6, 1897).

24. Printed notice to employees, Feb. 6, 1897; recommendation of the office committee, May 31, 1905; memo. of J. A. Wood to F. W. Ayer, June 6, 1905.

25. *Ibid.;* occasional reports on the working of the premium time, 1905–12.

26. Printed notice, May 31, 1888.

27. Printed ballot, June 16, 1892, with J. A. Wood's notation as to the vote in favor of the four o'clock closing.

28. Printed ballot, Oct. 1, 1892.

29. Printed notices, June 18, 1894; Sept. 2, 1895; June 12, 1896; June 17, 1898.

30. *Ibid.,* June 30, 1899.

31. *Ibid.,* Nov. 3, 1902.

32. J. A. Wood to F. W. Ayer, May 15 and June 6, 1905; report of the office committee, May 31, 1906.

33. J. A. Wood to F. W. Ayer, June 6, 1905.

34. Letters of appreciation from employees, dated Apr. 27 to May 1, 1907.

35. Notice to employees, dated Oct. 12, 1912, instituting the new hours on Oct. 16.

36. Sten. rep., conference of Ayer employees, Sept. 28, 1912.

37. Memo. of J. A. Wood dated May 3, 1924.

38. The records of the Personnel Office show that the change was instituted on May 2, 1927.

39. Wilfred W. Fry to the Ayer organization, Aug. 24, 1928.

40. Paul H. Douglas, *Real Wages in the United States, 1890–1926* (N. Y., 1930), pp. 112–117, 209–210.

41. This view was explicitly stated in Wood's memo. of June 6, 1905, and was implied in earlier documents concerning office hours.

42. Printed announcement regarding vacations, Apr. 18, 1902.

43. Interviews with former employees; printed notice regarding overtime, Dec. 11, 1903.

44. Printed notices dated May 1, 1884, Sept. 30, 1890, and Nov. 3, 1902; interviews with employees.

45. Printed notice to employees, dated Mar. 16, 1882.

46. *Art in Advertising,* Sept., 1893.

47. Expense account, Ledger 1, 1871–72; F. W. Ayer, "A Half Century of Advertising," in *The Next Step,* Aug., 1921, p. 31.

48. Expense accounts, Ledgers 1–5 (1871–79).

49. Private Ledger 1 (1880–84).

50. Interview with Joseph Gannon.

51. Interviews with Ayer employees.

52. Information obtained from the recommendations for increase in salary, 1922–23.

53. *Ibid.;* interviews with officers of the firm.

54. Interviews with members of the Ayer staff, former Ayer employees, and employees of rival agencies.

55. Based on analysis of the recommendations for increase in salary, 1920–23.

56. *National Baptist,* Feb. 9, 1889.

57. Memo. and clippings preserved in J. A. Wood's papers relating to a dinner for the Ayer staff, held on Dec. 26, 1900.

58. Remarks of F. W. Ayer to employees, Feb. 2, 1916; list of employees and their bonuses, Jan. 2, 1917.

59. Printed notice dated Dec. 31, 1917. In 1919 the bonuses thus paid totaled $1,950; in 1922 the total was $3,750; in 1928 the total was $12,950. Memo. regarding service recognition.

60. Notice dated Sept. 8, 1919.

61. Printed booklet, dated Mar. 1, 1926, describing the plans.

62. For example, an employee receiving $50 per week deposited 10 per cent, or $260 a year. Interest earned was $5.20. The Fund paid him 66 2/3 per cent of $260.00, or $173.33, making his total credit at the end of the year $438.53. If no withdrawal was made, at the end of the second year the employee received 4 per cent on the $438.53 and on the new deposits, plus 66 2/3 per cent on the new deposits.

63. *The Next Step,* Dec., 1920.

64. *Two Plans of Profit Sharing,* 1926, p. 17.

65. *Ibid.,* p. 18.

66. Letter to members of the Fund, Jan. 20, 1932.

67. Interview with the treasurer of N. W. Ayer & Son, who serves as manager of the Jarvis A. Wood Fund. Membership in the Fund stood at 291 in June, 1926, rose to 399 in June, 1931, and fell to 187 in Dec., 1932.

68. Memo. regarding Hill Top Camp expenses, 1907–14.

69. Notice to employees dated Mar. 12, 1915; interviews with officers and employees of N. W. Ayer & Son.

70. Aetna Life Insurance Co. to Keystone Type Foundry, Feb. 11, 1918; memo. regarding the cost of the benefits and cost of the insurance, 1919–23.

71. This conclusion is based on conversations with a number of staff members, including the president, several departmental heads, and a few of considerably lower rank. The change in morale between 1934 and 1948 is unmistakable. Perhaps the most impressive evidence on this point is the testimony of men who have returned to Ayer after a number of years in the Services during World War II. Some were doubtful about coming back, but friends persuaded them that opportunities in the firm and the working atmosphere there were fundamentally improved. Every one of those to whom the writer talked (they were purposely selected from different

levels and different departments and were simply asked to talk about their impressions upon returning rather than being questioned on specific points) testified as to the improvement they found; more important still, they were able to cite concrete instances of the changes to which they referred. Their sincerity and enthusiasm were unmistakable.

72. Sten. rep., speech to Ayer employees, Sept. 25, 1912. Ayer exaggerated the effect of the Fairbanks cancellation. The ledger accounts show that the billings did not exceed 15% of the total.

73. *Ibid.; Newspaperdom*, Nov. 23, 1911, p. 12; operating results for 1912.

74. Pay roll lists, 1880–1932.

75. J. W. Young, *Agency Compensation*, p. 145.

76. In February, 1932, those who had been earning between $10 and $25 per week received a 5 per cent cut. Those earning more were given a 10 per cent cut. In May, 1932, a further cut of 15 per cent was applied to all except those earning less than $10 a week. Data supplied by the vice-president in charge of personnel.

77. J. W. Young, *op. cit.*, p. 145.

78. Interviews with officers and employees during a period of several months after the decision to spread the available work among the current employees.

79. One employee, for example, was discovered to have defrauded the firm of unknown thousands of dollars through a series of bogus orders for materials. The Ayer management not only refused to prosecute, but recommended the man to another firm, at least as a skillful worker.

80. Memo. on personnel by J. A. Wood extending, with gaps, from 1896 to 1925; interviews with officers and employees.

81. Memo. on length of service of employees, Mar. 9, 1905.

82. *Ibid.*, July 1, 1928.

83. *The Next Step*, Aug., Sept., Dec., 1920, and Feb., Aug., Nov., Dec., 1921; annual invitations to the Ayer Christmas celebration, 1921–33.

84. The Printing Department presents something of an exception to this statement. In 1921 printers of Philadelphia struck for shorter hours and a substantial number of Ayer employees joined the walkout. Although the Ayer management claimed to have an open shop in its Printing Department, a number of employees alleged in 1921 that they found it necessary to join the printers' union in order to avoid unfair discrimination by their superiors in the Ayer Printing Department. The same complaint was made to the writer in 1933 and 1934.

85. I have in mind particularly the general evidence which is brought together in Elton Mayo's *The Human Problems of an Industrial Civilization* (N. Y., 1933), and T. N. Whitehead's *Leadership in a Free Society* (London, 1936), together with the tentative reports on studies in the Western Electric Co.: F. J. Roethlisberger and W. J. Dickson, *Management and the Worker* (Cambridge, 1939); F. J. Roethlisberger, *Management and Morale* (Cambridge, 1941); also Elton Mayo's *The Social Problems of an Industrial Civilization* (Boston, 1945).

86. "To the Members of Our Organization," Sept. 1, 1938; interviews with officers and employees.

87. *Ibid.;* "First Activities of the Curfew Club," Oct., 1938.

CHAPTER XIX

1. See above, pp. 42–43.

2. *Papers of the A.A.A.A.*, p. 38.

3. J. W. Young, *Agency Compensation*, p. 137.

4. This is similar to average figures for the industry for 1935. See *Census of Business, 1935. Advertising Agencies* (Washington, 1937), pp. 3 and 6.

5. Cf. J. W. Young, *op. cit.,* p. 31.

6. Information from the Trial Balance Sheets, 1903–26, supplemented by statements of the treasurer.

7. A recent article in *Fortune,* "J. Walter Thompson Company" (Nov., 1947), provides some basis for comparison. That agency is reputedly the largest in the world in terms of billings, but its capital and surplus are apparently smaller than Ayer's and its current ratio is only 1.23, a figure which the Ayer management would regard as dangerously low.

8. Advertising circular.

9. See *P. I.* cover page, Feb. 4, 1891, and an editorial in the issue of Feb. 28, 1894.

10. Lawrence Publishing Co. to N. W. Ayer & Son, May 24, 1898, citing volume of business received between May 15, 1897, and May 15, 1898.

11. Advertisement in the *Atlanta Journal* (Georgia), Aug. 30, 1906, p. 4.

12. Data supplied by Divisions of Detail, Curtis Publishing Co., Apr. 18, 1933.

13. Data supplied by the business manager of *Good Housekeeping,* Apr. 18, 1933.

14. *System* to N. W. Ayer & Son, Jan. 4, 1922.

15. Pamphlet published by Associated Business Publications, 1925.

16. J. W. Young, *op. cit.,* p. 15.

17. *Census of Business: 1935. Advertising Agencies,* p. 3.

18. This journal entry has been reconstructed from the three accounts concerned in the ledger, using the form of the Gen. Jour. (Day Book) in 1878.

19. The meaning of this account is evident from the journal explanation of a debit to Profit and Loss (Dec. 31, 1878) of $1,124.39, and a credit to Shrinkage: "The above sum transferred to Shrinkage Acct. which together with the sum all ready to credit of that acct. equals 20% of the amount due by Newspapers at this date — and represents the estimated shrinkage in value of said indebtedness owing to its being, for the most part, payable in advertising."

20. For several years between 1920 and 1929 the New York and Chicago offices were really subsidiary partnerships with self-contained accounting systems, but this fact brought no important change in the Philadelphia accounting.

21. Cf. J. W. Young, *op. cit.,* pp. 124–143, especially p. 136; *Advertising Age,* Dec. 1, 1934, pp. 1, 28; Stanwood A. Morrill, "Agency Cost Accounting Plan," *P. I.,* Apr. 25, 1935, pp. 25–27.

22. Its internal accounts, that is, as distinct from those with clients which are frequently audited by outside accountants, as has already been indicated.

CHAPTER XX

1. Two minor exceptions to this statement may be noted. Many of the advertisements which the firm has published to advertise its own services and to promote the general cause of advertising reach the general public. Secondly, representatives of the Ayer agency frequently interview consumers, in person or by mail, in the course of the consumer surveys which are now a regular part of the firm's work.

2. Until recently there has been no adequate formal consideration of the economic aspects of advertising by competent economic theorists, partly because a good many economists have been emotionally prejudiced against the subject, and partly because advertising is an exceedingly slippery subject for analysis, having the additional difficulty that reliable data about it have only recently begun to be

available for study. The following references will be found useful: Alfred Marshall, *Industry and Trade* (London, 1923), pp. 305–307; articles by Fred E. Clark, George B. Hotchkiss, and W. D. Moriarty, with accompanying discussion, in *American Economic Review*, supplement, Mar., 1925, pp. 5–41; Collis A. Stocking, "Modern Advertising and Economic Theory," *ibid.*, Mar., 1931, pp. 43–55; "Advertising and Economic Theory; a Criticism," *ibid.*, Dec., 1931, pp. 685–690; and D. Braithwaite and S. Dobbs, *The Distribution of Consumable Goods* (London, 1932), chap. vii. A significant technical contribution to the theoretical aspects is to be found in Edward Chamberlin, *The Theory of Monopolistic Competition* (Cambridge, 1938), chaps. vi and vii. A well-balanced but less technical discussion than those above is contained in Hotchkiss, *An Outline of Advertising*, already cited, pp. 62–85.

For the general reader, who wishes to avoid the technical theory while getting some idea of the effects of advertising, a critical and fairly balanced discussion is to be found in Margaret G. Reid, *Consumers and the Market* (N. Y., 1938), chaps. xix, xx, xxi.

The following two books, in spite of their prejudiced and carping approach, contain much sound material and provide a good antidote for the extravagant claims which are too often made on behalf of advertising: Stuart Chase and F. J. Schlink, *Your Money's Worth*, cited above, and F. J. Schlink and Arthur Kallet, *100,000,000 Guinea Pigs* (N. Y., 1933).

The Economic Effects of Advertising, by my colleague, Professor Neil H. Borden, and previously cited, is the outstanding study at present.

3. Some evidence on the influence of advertising upon American culture is presented in Robert T. and Helen M. Lynd, *Middletown* (N. Y., 1932), pp. 81–84, 153–167, 491. In appraising advertising one must bear in mind that it is only one of many forces at work and that it is in turn a resultant of the total situation.

4. See A. S. J. Baster, *Advertising Reconsidered* (London, 1935), pp. 8–9; also Lucien Zacharoff, "The Soviet's Unique Advertising Problem," *Adv. & Sell.*, Jan. 28, 1937; and Beatrice Miller, "Advertising in Moscow," *P. I. Monthly*, June, 1938.

5. For the implications of this, see J. M. Keynes, *The General Theory of Employment, Interest, and Money* (London, 1936), bk. iii.

6. Of course, not all the criticisms of big business can be regarded as propaganda. Some of them were accurate and necessary. The line between legitimate discussion and education, on the one hand, and misleading information and argument, on the other, is not easy to draw. But much of the writing against the "trusts" was unquestionably scurrilous abuse by self-seeking persons, and, instead of being helpful, it really befogged the issue and hampered the achievement of a wise solution.

7. Excerpt from an address before the Ohio Editorial Association, Jan. 27, 1904, printed in a pamphlet entitled *Relation of the Newspaper to the Advertising Agency in the Development of New Business* (Philadelphia, 1904).

8. Cf. Gerald W. Johnson, "Freedom of the Newspaper Press," *The Annals of the American Academy of Political and Social Science*, vol. 200 (Nov., 1938), pp. 60–75. For an incisive discussion of the similar problem in Great Britain, see P E P, *Report on the British Press*, pp. 181–184.

9. Ayer correspondence files, Jan., 1929 (identities withheld by the author).

10. Address before the American Newspaper Publishers' Association, N. Y., Feb. 19, 1904; interviews with some of McKinney's associates.

11. For this aspect of the influence of advertising in America, see A. M. Schlesinger, *The Rise of the City, 1878–1898* (N. Y., 1933), pp. 183–201; Faulkner, *The*

Quest for Social Justice, 1898–1914, cited above, pp. 248–258; Preston W. Slosson, *The Great Crusade and After, 1914–1928* (N. Y., 1931), pp. 345–371.

12. In 1911 a newspaper, *The Day Book,* was founded in Chicago, to be supported exclusively by subscriptions. It did not prosper and was finally suspended during World War I when the high cost of paper made continuation impossible without an increase in its already high price. The newspaper was not popular with women because it lacked department-store advertising (Lee, *Hist. of Amer. Journalism,* pp. 408–409).

The more recent history of *P. M.* is equally illuminating, though its financial difficulties stemmed not only from its policy with regard to advertising but also from its editorial policy as a whole. One must recognize, of course, that the public would be willing to pay the full cost of at least a few newspapers and magazines rather than go without, if those which are subsidized by advertising were not available.

APPENDIX

1. Students who are interested in going further in this investigation for recent American advertising should consult the statistics published by *Media Records* and *Advertising & Selling* from time to time. Some data for 1922 and 1927 are included in Professor M. T. Copeland's article, "Marketing," in *Recent Economic Changes* (N. Y., 1929), pp. 414–419.

INDEX

Abuses, 13–19, 92–93, 129–130, 138, 147–149, 354–356, 393–394, 455–457, 576–578.
See also Ethics; Unfair practices; Waste in advertising
Accounting, 175, 462–466, 482, 533–574; policy, 568–574.
See also Auditing; Cost accounting; Financial history of firm
Accounting Department, 462, 469–470, 473, 563.
See also Bookkeeping Department
Accounts,
competing, 339–344, 383;
refusal and resignation of, 90–93, 185, 219, 245, 339–344, 362, 382–383, 579;
size of, 181–183, 207-208, 235, 339, 352, 355;
split, 344–346;
turnover of, 149, 383–384, 587
Additions, *see* Expansion
Administration, 30–48, 123–125, 139–145, 152–172.
See also Control; Management; Partners; Policy
Advertisements,
cost of, 15, 274–275, 281, 306, 353, 386–387, 390–392, 411–412, 431–434;
early, 44–48, 77–80, 295–302;
examples of, 226–228, 296–297, 299–301, 304, 306–310, 312, 314–320, 322–325, 328–334, 438–439.
See also Copy
Advertisers,
relations with media, 8–10
Advertiser's Guide, 42, 82, 396
Advertising,
abuses, 13–19, 92–93, 129–130, 138, 147–149, 354–356, 393–394, 455–457, 576–578;
and general culture, xxx, 6–7, 45–49,

92–93, 125–130, 215–216, 315–317, 575–583;
appeals, 126, 129, 153, 264–265, 295–335, 337, 429–430;
appropriations, 207–208;
background of, 6–7;
coöperative, 206, 215, 352, 363–365, 592–593;
cost of, 15, 274–275, 281, 306, 353, 386–387, 390–392, 431–434;
definition of, 183;
distribution of, by commodities, 210, 213–214, 587–593;
early, 6–7, 44–48, 77–80, 295–302;
economic aspects, 575–583;
effects of, 576–582;
foreign, 140–145, 152–153;
functions of, 3–7, 19, 112, 124–125, 130, 133–134, 229–230;
government control, 9, 155–156, 191, 246, 426;
history of, 3–19;
institutional, 95, 261, 272, 304, 311, 323;
postwar, 109, 125–130, 209, 215, 430;
results of, 281–283, 292, 575–586, 597 n. 35;
waste in, xxx, 74, 270, 577–578.
See also Social value of advertising; *specific commodities*
Advertising Age, 551
Advertising Agencies,
and World War I, 107–109;
and World War II, 183–186;
as representatives of newspapers, 13;
as special agents, 14, 53–54, 69–71, 401–405, 414–417, 514, 600 n. 26;
censorship by, 366, 425–431, 580–582, 607 n. 19;
compensation of, 13–15, 51–52, 57, 61, 108–109, 231–247, 351, 354, 386, 393–399, 402, 406–412, 432–434, 443, 450–451, 457;

Felt and Tarrant Comptometers, 205, 321, 323

Fences,
advertising of, 590

Ferris Brothers Co., 297, 301, 376

Ferry (D. M.) & Co., 129, 205, 296, 303

Fertilizers,
advertising of, 590–591

Fiftieth anniversary, 109–110

Finance, 154, 172, 533–574.
See also Accounting; Capitalization; Cost; Expenses; Stock, ownership of

Financial advertising, 589–593

Financial capitalism, xxix

Financial history of firm, 192–195, 533–574.
See also Accounting; Capitalization; Expenses; Finance; Risk-taking; Stock, ownership of

First National Bank of Philadelphia, F. W. Ayer's connection with, 115

Fixed-price basis, 231–233, 235

Food, groceries, and food drinks,
advertising of, 94–95, 129, 209–215, 274, 287, 299–300, 305–306, 334, 340, 589–593.
See also Beverages; Coffee

Foote, Cone & Belding, Inc., 326–327, 331–332, 551

Ford Motor Co., 129, 141–143, 145, 261, 293–294, 314, 317, 322

Foreign advertising, 140–145, 152–153

Foreign Affairs, 267

Foreign offices, 140–145, 152–153, 187

Fortune, 226, 551

Forwarding Department, 461–462, 465, 469, 563

Founding,
of firm, 20–49

French Line, 272, 318–320

Freshman, E. N., 443

Frey, Charles Daniel, 324

Fry, Mrs. Wilfred W., 107, 163–165

Fry, Wilfred W., 107, 124, 139–140, 158–169, 171, 179, 194–195, 200, 470, 492–495, 517, 530, 534, 548, 611 n. 37

Fuel and lubricants,
advertising of, 590.

See also Gasoline

Fuller & Smith & Ross, 331–332

Functions,
of advertising agencies, 3–6, 18–19, 34–35, 47–48, 56–58, 69–102, 112, 125, 130–134, 137, 229–230, 244, 271–294, 385–389.
See also Service

Gardner Advertising Co., 616 n. 15

Gasoline,
advertising of, 129, 191, 206–207, 287, 309, 591–593.
See also Standard Oil Co.

Geisinger, John J., 600 n. 7

General Electric Co., 185

General *vs.* special agents, 401–405, 414–417.
See also Representatives, special

Geographical problems, 349–350

Girard Estate, 101, 603 n. 89

Glassware, 376

Glucose Sugar Refining Co., 93

Godey's Lady's Magazine, 391

Goetz Silk Manufacturing Co., 307

Gold Dust, 93

Golden anniversary, 109–110

Good Housekeeping, 332, 550

Goodyear Tire & Rubber Co., 191

Government,
advertising by, 155, 185–186, 191, 322, 330, 610 n. 26

Government regulation, 9, 155–156, 191, 246, 426.
See also NRA

Grant (B. H.) Research Associates, 332

Great Britain,
agency compensation in, 620 n. 48

Greeting cards and chromos,

Groceries, *see* Food, groceries, and food drinks
advertising of, 589–590

Haase, Albert,
report by, 247

Hamilton Manufacturing Co., 87

Hanes Underwear, 129

Hardware,
advertising of, 95, 222–223, 589–593

Harper's, 226

Harriman, E. H., 114